TENNESSEE LAWMAN

History of the Men and Women Behind the Badge

Eddie M. Ashmore

Turner®
PUBLISHING COMPANY
Nashville, Tennessee • Paducah Kentucky

Preface and Acknowledgments

This chronicle was compiled out of genuine respect for the men and women behind the badge, individuals who put their life on the line daily for the rest of us. Dedicated law enforcement officers in the State of Tennessee stand between the citizens of the Volunteer State and the anarchy that would reign were it not for their commitment to duty and service.

History is more than dates and events; it is the story of individual sacrifice and dedication to duty. Biographical insights into the lives of officers are the heart of this recounting of Tennessee's law enforcement history. Space prohibits telling the story of every Tennessee law officer and those told here are representative of many others.

It has been said, "Police work is 99% boredom punctuated by 1% of sheer terror." Those moments of sheer terror too frequently result in the death of a law enforcement officer. Many of those stories are told lest we forget their sacrifice. The memory of those killed in the line of duty must be a living reminder of the heroic deeds of those who choose this work. Each tragic incident that takes the life of an officer in the line of duty leaves in its wake pain and emptiness in the lives of family members, friends and colleagues of the fallen officer.

The terrorist attacks of September 11, 2001, reminded us that average men and women are thrust into crises and respond heroically. As throngs of humanity ran from scenes of destruction and peril, fire and police personnel raced into danger. Many did not return. That same selflessness and sense of duty plays out everyday on the streets and roadways of Tennessee. When the alarm sounds they run to the trouble while the rest of us flee.

But not all police work is sheer terror, it includes routine mental and physical exertion and it includes tedium. Telling the story of the normal day's work is important to understanding the law enforcement officer's job. The best accounts of day to day duty are in the words of the lawmen themselves.

Use of the term "lawman" in the title and throughout is not intended to diminish the contribution of female officers. The word is used because it is immediately recognizable and association with stories of historical peace officers. Although women doing traditional police work is a relatively recent phenomenon, today female officers stand side by side with their male counterparts in every facet of police work. The leadership women have demonstrated in law enforcement is illustrated by those holding command ranks in agencies across the state. Their dedication to duty is confirmed by the sacrifice of female officers who have fallen while wearing the badge.

The statewide story of Tennessee law enforcement has not been told before. However, a number of agencies have published histories in yearbooks and souvenir programs in the late nineteenth and twentieth centuries. The work of dedicated researchers that developed these histories was used extensively in the writing of this volume.

The most extensive historical research and writing on any law enforcement agency in the state was done by Joseph E. Walk on the Memphis Police Department. In addition to historical data published in MPD yearbooks Mr. Walk has produced a number of research documents on various aspects of the Memphis police force. His most passionate effort has been researching line of duty deaths in Memphis and Shelby County.

Lon Eilders developed an especially good history of the Chattanooga Police Department in the late seventies. The two main history researchers and writers of the Tennessee Department of Safety were Fred W. Schott Jr. and Leland D. Chaffin. Researchers and writers on the Knoxville Police Department history were Rick

Ferguson and Ida Webb. Byron Grizzle developed a timeline of historical events of the Davidson County Sheriff's Office. Mary Buck of the Clarksville Police Department researched and wrote a history the force. This list is not intended to be exhaustive and debt is owed to all who have contributed significant work to the history of Tennessee law enforcement.

Chris Cosgriff and his work with the Officer Down Memorial Page on the Internet provided an important component of the research. Extensive use was made of this web site and its very important contribution to the history of law enforcement and the sacrifice of those who have served in its ranks.

Other secondary sources included narratives, chronicles and general histories of law enforcement in the cities, counties and state of Tennessee. *Flyin' Bullets and The Resplendent Badge*, the biography of Sevier County Sheriff Ray C. Noland elegantly told by his daughter Ersa Rhea Smith with the help of his grandsons C. Robin Smith and Chris A. Smith, provided particularly helpful insights into the life and work of a county lawman.

A number of collectors and historians of law enforcement insignia and memorabilia have shared information and experience important to the insignia section. Tennessee collector Paul Margulies has generously shared images and knowledge. John Connors provided important information on state law enforcement in Tennessee that he gleaned over many years of research. Police collectors and historians who have been instructive include James C. Casey, Larry Croom, Steve Curry, Vic R. Elliott, Clarence Gibson, Chip Greiner, Donald Hawkins, William Herald, Thomas Herring, David S. Hume, George Jackson Jr., Roderick Janich, Ed Lanati, Alan Levy, Ken Lucas, Pat Lynch, John McKinney, James B. McMillian, Bob Murray, Steve Nibarger, Stan Oda, Pat Olvey, Mark Pyne, Larry and Debbie Vertrees and Fred Yorsch.

The majority of this volume is the product of original research from primary sources, both written and oral. Official documents and reports, as well as newspaper accounts were the main written sources. Some sources are quoted at length to give a flavor of the language used by those originally reporting events and presenting ideas. Departments and agencies have provided both documents and photographs. The original sources of photographs have been acknowledged where they are known.

Research assistance was provided by Jack Wood and Robert Taylor of the Jackson-Madison County Library, Kenneth Fieth of the Metropolitan Nashville and Davidson County Archives, John Dougan of the Memphis and Shelby County Archives, Marylin Bell Hughes and others of the Tennessee State Library and Archives, Debbie Morris of the Jackson Sun, Tammye Droked of the Tennessee Supreme Court Law Library in Jackson, Tracey Howerton of the Nashville Public Library. Numerous others assisted as well.

The author's deepest debt is to the individual law enforcement officers who shared experiences, insights and oral tradition. Those involved in the incident served as unique primary sources for activities and observations. Many of these individuals, listed in the bibliography, have also provided photographs and other materials.

Deep and personal appreciation is also expressed to Dr. Jean Moore Ashmore, wife of the author, for her abiding patience throughout this writing project. Her proof reading and suggestions have also enhanced the final product.

Dedicated to the Men and Women
Who Serve Behind the Badge

and Especially to
the Fallen Officers of
Tennessee Law Enforcement
Who Made the Supreme Sacrifice
in the Line of Duty

All profits from the sale of
TENNESSEE LAWMAN
will be donated to the Tennessee chapters of
Concerns Of Police Survivors (COPS)

Introduction

The rule of law is basic and essential to civilization and the enforcement of those rules of society determines whether that society is one of order or chaos. The community bestows upon a select few of its members the responsibility and the authority to provide that enforcement and to ensure order and safety. The rich history of Tennessee law enforcement demonstrates the commitment of the men and women in agencies across the state to providing their fellow citizens an environment of safety and stability in which to live and work.

Throughout most of history the law enforcement function was provided by members of the community at large or military personnel who either executed punishment for crime on the spot or took offenders to civil or religious authorities for pronouncement of judgment. Rudimentary police forces existed in many early cultures. In ancient Mesopotamia, Nubian slaves were put to work guarding the marketplace. Their stature, dress and skin color made them a visible presence and ideal for crime control. Among the public safety functions organized in Rome by Augustus Caesar was the Roman "vigiles." This nighttime watch force composed of freedmen was authorized both to fight fires and deal with lawbreakers.

American colonists, in what would become the United States, brought the system of law enforcement from their native land. The system had its beginnings in medieval England. The old-English system included a "shire-reeve" who was the representative of the Crown in each shire. This position transferred to America as the county sheriff. In the English countryside the parish constable was the primary law enforcement officer and as town and cities grew, constables, who served during the day, were augmented at night by "the watch," a group assigned to guard the gates and to patrol the streets. The constable and night watch transferred to America as well. Boston formed a night watch in 1635 and Dutch settlers in New Amsterdam (now New York City) established the Burgher Guard, a paid group of night patrolmen, in 1658. The watches were loosely organized and principally made up of unpaid volunteers. Similar organizations were formed as towns and cities grew throughout the land before and after the Revolutionary War.

The origins of the modern professional police force are found in the reforms implemented by Sir Robert Peel in 1829 in London. The Metropolitan Police of London was founded on the fundamental concepts still central to policing: crime prevention, crime detection and public cooperation. The backbone of the force was the "Peelers" or "Bobbies" who patrolled London's streets as a visible presence to deter criminal activity. The force was trained, paid a salary and wore a uniform.

The metropolitan system of policing soon came to America. The first paid professional police force in the United States was formed in New York City in 1845. The same style uniform found in London was adopted with the addition of an eight-point brass star worn as a breast badge. Other major cities formed similar forces. Individual policemen often resisted wearing a uniform in the period prior to the Civil War. The wearing of uniforms during the war changed the attitude among police officers.

The Metropolitan Police came to Tennessee, nominally at least, in the reconstruction period following the Civil War when Tennessee's Governor William Gannaway Brownlow created the Metropolitan Police District of the County of Shelby to police the Memphis area. The force had statewide powers and metropolitan forces were formed in Nashville and Chattanooga as well. These groups wore federal army style uniforms and had little support from the general populous. They were known as "Brownlow's Band."

The history of law enforcement in Tennessee was consistent with that in the rest of the nation. Before county and town governments were organized, pioneers posted watches in the fort-like compounds at night to alert the group to any hostile threat. When county governments were established, the sheriff was among the first officials selected. Some sheriffs were appointed by North Carolina officials even before Tennessee was a state.

As counties developed, constables were selected to provide law enforcement at the local level. The law officer in newly formed towns was the town constable. A night watch was also appointed to maintain peace and order between sunset and sunrise.

Early Tennessee lawmen enforced criminal and civil law, serving papers of the county and town court, collecting taxes and arresting law breakers. They also took on many other responsibilities necessary to the community including health, sanitation and public works.

In addition to other duties, sheriffs had the responsibility for punishment of felons. Punishment was corporal and public, as in medieval Europe and ancient Rome. Beatings of up to 39 lashes, branding and cutting off ears were punishment for lesser felonies. Murderers and other major felons were hanged. These punishments were carried out in the public square or on other public grounds and were witnessed by the whole community. This was the consequence for criminal behavior until 1831 when the Tennessee State Penitentiary House was built. The county sheriff continued to execute murderers by hanging until 1909.

By the middle of the nineteenth century, night police replaced the night watch and the title "Marshal" was being adopted for the chief law enforcement officer in towns and cities. For the most part, however, law enforcement remained a part-time force of citizen lawmen whose qualifications were character and physical prowess.

Traditional law enforcement was virtually suspended in Tennessee during the years of Civil War. In the decades following the war lawlessness was rampant throughout the state. Reestablishing law and order was further challenged by economic and social upheaval. Law and order resembled that in the "wild west." The bravery and grit of many lawmen were tested by desperados resorting to gunplay.

A national scourge grew out of these conditions. Mobs resorted to lynching to resolve what they considered outrageous offenses. Tennessee was afflicted as other states, north and south, by people who took the law into their own hands to execute individuals without trial. Some of those killed were criminals, others were guilty only of racial or social actions unacceptable to the majority population. Dedicated lawmen condemned lynching and many put themselves in harm's way to protect prisoners and to preserve the rule of law.

Many more black people were lynched than white and most lynchings were led by predominately white mobs. From time to time a group of black citizens formed a lynch mob. The *Jackson Whig and Tribune* of July 26, 1873, reported the lynching of a white man in southwest Madison County by a group of fifteen black men because he had "violated the person of an old negro woman in the neighborhood." The only persons brought to court as a result of the lynching were the sons of the white landowner on whose property the lynching occurred. The young white men were accused of being "accessories before the fact in the killing," but were found not guilty.

Lynching became an accepted practice by many. After the ambush and murder of federal revenue agents in 1892, one newspaper ran the headline, "After the Assassins -- If Caught, Judge Lynch Will Try Them" and wrote that the bootleggers who committed the brutal murders "would never be tried, but lynched forthwith." "Judge Lynch" was a common reference in newspapers. The crime of lynching continued well into the twentieth century.

At the dawn of the twentieth century police forces were staffed with full-time career officers. The nature and breadth of law enforcement changed significantly in the first decades of the new century. Technology drove much of the transformation, especially the appearance of the automobile. The improvement of the highway system to accommodate automobiles brought about the creation of the Tennessee Highway Patrol. Traffic enforcement added greatly to the work of local police force as well. The most common mode of transportation for traffic officers prior to the second world war was the motorcycle.

The acquisition of police cars and the expansion of their use in the thirties altered the nature of patrol work for city police department. Foot patrolmen walking beats began to disappear. Radio technology dramatically improved police communication and added to the effectiveness of police officers in vehicles.

Scientific investigation methods such as the use of fingerprints and the development of identification bureaus had a major impact on law enforcement. The growing complexities of law enforcement led to a growing number of lawmen that were trained in the new methods and technologies of police work. The FBI initiated training programs for local law enforcement and FBI special agents led training sessions across Tennessee as the prospects of a second world war grew.

In the years of prosperity that followed World War II, law enforcement began to experience changes that reshaped the nature and character of police work and police officers. Generally speaking, law enforcement is a reflection of the society as a whole and the dynamics that affected the social order between the 1950s and the 1970s shook policing agencies nationwide. The status quo of police work became untenable and agencies had to adapt to a new environment.

Law enforcement in the middle of the twentieth century was a more mature version of policing that developed in the thirties. Law enforcement officers were predominately male and white. Lawmen were also typically rough and tumble, quickly responding to antagonism or resistance with force.

Political influence and sporadic incidents of corruption affected police work less than in the days when power brokers like Edward Hull "Boss" Crump routinely used state and local police to do their political bidding. Although even Boss Crump, who served as Memphis Commissioner of Fire and Police early in his political career, understood that significant graft and corruption and the failure to curb crime was bad politics.

The energy and industry that the nation developed to fight and win a world war was redirected to enhance life here at home. Domestic growth led to prosperity greater than the country had ever known. With the prosperity came a greater expectation on the part of the citizens of the country. An outcry arose among those not in the mainstream for the rights of equal access to the promises and benefits of the new prosperity.

Law enforcement was at the middle of the social upheaval that accompanied the change that took place from the 1950s through the 1970s. Law enforcement agencies were themselves changed as a part of the process. Black officers were hired by some departments for the first time and other departments increased the number of black officers. Female officers no longer served only as matrons, but began to work in traditional law enforcement roles as patrol officers and detectives.

Another important dynamic affecting law enforcement was the growing importance of education and training. Physical prowess, once the most important attribute for lawmen, was now tempered by the need to grasp the new technology crucial to police work, to recognize recent laws regarding police conduct, and to understand the behavior of the people they confronted on duty.

The era of the professional law enforcement officer dawned, driven by ever more sophisticated technology and public expectation that officers would use the least amount of force possible. The opening of the Tennessee Law Enforcement Training Academy in 1966 was one of the most important advancements in law enforcement in the state. The education level of state and local policing was also enhanced by the growing number of officers entering law enforcement with degrees and the increase in criminal justice programs at colleges and university.

With all the changes and developments through the years the heart of police work is still the local police officer on the street. New tools and approaches cannot replace alertness and dedication to duty. That was true of the night watchman at a frontier compound, the city marshal facing down a desperado or today's highly trained patrol officer.

Another constant for these public servants who wear a badge is that they put their lives on the line each day. The stresses on the modern law enforcement officer makes that more true than ever. Former Memphis Director of Police Services Walter E. Crews noted that life expectancy in the United States is over 77 years, but that life expectancy of an American police officer is only 57 years. Yet, for some individuals, it's the only job they've ever wanted to do.

The occupation brings satisfaction and sorrow. A number of officers expressed sentiments similar to Captain Linuel L. Allen of the Tennessee Highway Patrol, "It's a satisfying job if you like helping people and working with people. You're going to see some things you don't want to see. You're going to see kids killed. You're going to see their little bodies torn up. And you're going to take it home with you; if you're human you're going to take it home with you. You're going to shed tears for those families. Don't misunderstand, you're going to get to where you can handle the job, but it's going to hurt. There's going to be some long days and long nights. Sooner or later you're going to lose some of your friends." The death of a friend and colleague on the job is certainly among the most sorrowful moments in policing.

Those officers lost in the line of duty represent another constant of police work through the years, the willingness of the men and women in law enforcement to stand between their fellow citizens and dangers. The sacrifice of those who die in the line of duty is the ultimate symbol of society's debt to the men and women who wear the badge.

Early Statewide Law Enforcement

Law enforcement was a local concern in the few settlements that existed when President George Washington signed the 1796 act making Tennessee the sixteenth state. Law breakers were arrested, judged, and punished in the community in which they committed their crime. Citizen lawmen, including elected sheriffs in some areas, enforced civil and criminal laws.

Local authority and responsibility for enforcing the law was part of the tradition of self reliance that grew to symbolize the American character. This sense of local authority often created conflict as state and federal law enforcement officers expanded their duty into the domain of local lawmen. Even the use of militia troops to quell serious threats to the community was a local matter, because early militia forces were formed from units in each community.

As soon as governmental entities were formed in the territory, even before Tennessee was a state, sheriffs were charged with enforcing the law. The North Carolina Legislature established a "district county westward of Cumberland Mountain" called "Davidson County" in April 1783 and Sheriff Daniel Williams was appointed Davidson County's first law officer. Sheriff Williams' duties were much the same as sheriffs today.

Sheriff Williams and other early sheriffs could hardly keep the peace county-wide. Early settlers who moved into the western territories of the North Carolina were true frontiersmen and had to rely on themselves in all matters, including protection against threats to life and property. Threats came from the occasional brigand but more frequently from Native American warriors.

Tennessee pioneer Abram Mason, who eventually settled Mason's Grove in Madison County, made the six-month trip from Virginia down the Ohio and Cumberland rivers to Davidson County in 1790. They killed buffalo, elk and other game for food until they ran out of gun powder. Nineteen families initially set out in a large keel bottomed boat, dodging Indians and rapids. Nine families completed the trip in dugout canoes.

Settlements were mainly small stockade type forts established by prosperous settlers. A few larger compounds included a military presence. A string of forts existed from Knoxville to Nashville in the late eighteenth century. Traveling from Knoxville, the fort at Campbell's Station, seven miles to the southwest, was next stockade and the southernmost settlement in eastern Tennessee. Westward was a fort and settlement at Blackburn's, west of the Cumberland Mountains, then Fort Blount on the Cumberland river, a fort at Bledsoe's Lick and finally the French Lick fort at what became Nashville.

Andrew Jackson in military uniform a few years after he was pressed into duty as a lawman to arrest a rough frontiersman.

Mason's trip was only a year before Major General Arthur St. Clair lost nearly 700 soldiers and settlers north of where Cincinnati now stands. Indians also took dozens of women and children captive, a practice in many Native American cultures. The settlers found similar hostility in the area of Fort Nashborough. Mason reported, "The Indians were killing, and stealing horses all around us." He told of a number of killings and of women being abducted and carried back to the Indian nation. General James Robertson and his son were wounded in one raid.

After a 1793 Cherokee raid in which a young man was killed, neighbors in the settlement followed the raiding party to the Tennessee River, killing a number of the group and bringing prisoners back to the fort. They also brought back the scalp and hat of one of the women settlers who had been killed. When raids were frequent, Mason's family and others stayed at area forts. Mason served as one of the guards posted as a lookout.

> The Indians were still troublesome, and father was drafted to guard the outside forts. I went and served his tour. I hadn't to go but a mile and a half, we were so near the outside. I had to go to William Cash's Fort and set at the back of a field and watch while the others worked. My orders were, if I saw any Indians, to fire at them and run to the fort; but none came while I was there.

William Cash was a brother-in-law to General Robertson. In the spring of 1794, the Indians were still "troublesome" and his family "forted" at Philip Shute's fort a half mile farther from their home. They went home in the day and worked; at night they went back to the fort.

For many decades, law enforcement remained a part-time enterprise of citizen-lawmen. Even constitutional law enforcement officers, the sheriff and the constable, had other occupations. Although the sheriff may have been paid a stipend for the performance of routine duties, these early officers were compensated for their service mostly from the fees and fines they collected or for special one-time duties.

An example of the ad-hoc nature of law enforcement that often marked the frontier days of the state is recorded in the book, *Dropped Stitches in Tennessee History*. The incident involved one of Tennessee's most famous citizens, Andrew Jackson, around the turn of the nineteenth century.

Russell Bean was a fearless and fearsome frontiersman with a hard reputation. He was charged with assault and battery and had threatened to kill the first man who approached his house. When the case came to court in Jonesboro, Judge Andrew Jackson was on the bench. The sheriff told the judge that Bean sat on his front porch with pistols in his lap and that officers had not been able to arrest him. Jackson said, "Summon every man in the court house, and bring Bean in here dead or alive." The sheriff responded to Jackson, "Then I summon your honor first."

Jackson left the bench saying, "By the Eternal, I'll bring him!" He walked to Bean's house outside of town, pistol in hand, along with a crowd following at a safe distance. As Special Deputy Sheriff Andy Jackson neared Bean's place and came within shooting distance, Bean rose and called out, "I'll surrender to you, Mr. Devil!" and laid down his arms. Jackson delivered him to the courtroom, tried and heavily fined him.

As towns grew early in the nineteenth century, municipal law enforcement developed and took on the form of a nightwatch system. By the middle of the century, larger cities had full-time personnel and an organized police function headed by a Town Constable, City Marshal, or Chief of Police.

At the outbreak of the Civil War martial law was imposed in much of the state as federal troops occupied larger towns and cities in Tennessee. In other locations what law enforcement existed was at the discretion of local citizens and usually without benefit of due process.

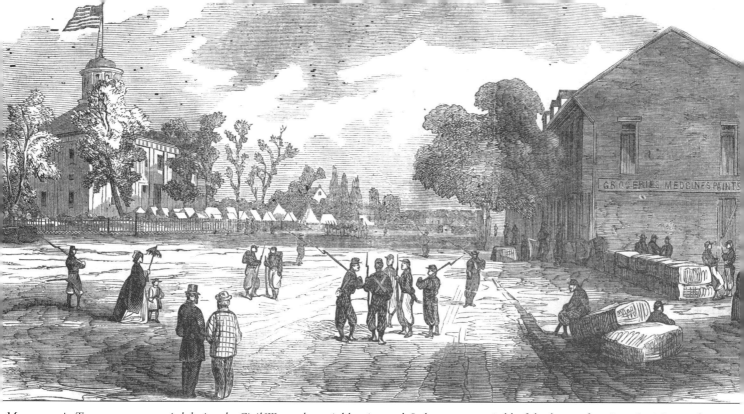

Many areas in Tennessee were occupied during the Civil War and martial law imposed. Jackson was occupied by federal troops from June 6, 1862, until June 6, 1863. This illustration published in the October 11, 1862, issue of Harper's Weekly showed an encampment in the courthouse square with cotton bales used for fortification.

In locations where federal or confederate troops occupied, normal policing for the protection of life and property of the citizenry did not exist. Federal authorities articulated intentions that the military would protect persons and property in occupied areas. The realities of war, however, meant occupation forces spent much energy suppressing citizens suspected of guerrilla tactics against the occupiers. In addition, the need to feed and equip troops resulted in extensive pillaging and confiscation of food and goods belonging to local residents.

The exigencies of war could cloak illegal acts to the point that robbery, rape or murder was prevented only by the character of individual soldiers. Jackson, Tennessee, diarist Robert Cartmell wrote that what little order existed during the town's occupation was a result of restraint exerted by Yankee army officers and if the privates were left alone they would have hanged the citizens.

The report of one incident bore this out. Andrew Taylor, a resident of Madison County, told the story of a roving Union soldier coming to the family home to steal. The bushwhacker started up the stairs to the second floor where the family had taken refuge. Taylor told him not to come up, but the soldier paid no attention and continued up the stairway. Taylor shot and killed the man. Taylor then put the dead soldier over the back of his horse and took him into Jackson. He

brought the body to the Commander of the occupying federal force and told him what had happened. The Commander told Taylor that he did exactly right and to go on home.

The most infamous acts of murder and other violations on the citizens of Tennessee during the war were perpetrated by "home-grown Yankees," and the most notorious of these was Fielding Hurst. Lieutenant Colonel Fielding Hurst of the 6th Tennessee Union Cavalry was a native of McNairy County in West Tennessee. His command left a wake of burnings and murder.

Hurst's actions against the civilian population as well as Confederate war prisoners were so egregious that southern forces denounced him and his band as outlaws and not entitled to be treated as prisoners of war. Northern commanders were unable to control him. Hurst stole and destroyed property, killed noncombatants and routinely killed captured Southern soldiers, often mutilating their bodies.

On one occasion, Hurst and his men robbed a Jackson businesswoman of $5,139.25. She reported the action to federal officials who ordered Hurst to return the money. Hurst rode back into to Jackson and extorted money to repay the woman from residents of Jackson under threat of burning the town. The townspeople gave him the money and he burned the town anyway. In another incident, Hurst captured

Confederate Captain Wharton and a portion of his men. They were killed and their heads used as mile markers along the road from Purdy to Lexington.

When the Civil War ended law enforcement was returned to local authority. Only men who signed a loyalty oath were allowed to vote, so county and city officers were elected who would cooperate with the federal loyalists elected to run the state.

Tennessee's first experience with a state police force was during the reconstruction period. The state legislature established a police force, the Metropolitan Police, to replace existing police in the largest cities of the state. It was not a state police force of the style that exists today, but the police officers of the force had authority statewide and were under the control of state officials.

Parson William Gannaway Brownlow was selected governor of Tennessee after the war and formed the Metropolitan Police. Brownlow wanted a police force under his control primarily for two reasons, to suppress the turmoil and lawlessness that characterized the post-war period and to assure control of the ballot box.

The metropolitan police concept was the innovative form of municipal law enforcement prominent in the period. Created by Robert Peel in London, the system had been implemented in New York, Chicago, Cincinnati and St. Louis. Brownlow followed the example of the Governor of New York who had enacted the metropolitan system under state authority for the purpose of taking control of the corrupt New York City Police Department from city officials.

The act to establish the Metropolitan Police District in Tennessee was passed on May 14, 1866. The act focused on Memphis and Shelby County but was extended to include Nashville and Chattanooga. Section 1 of the act defined the primary district.

Be it enacted by the General Assembly of the State of Tennessee, That the County of Shelby is hereby constituted, for the purpose of police government and police discipline, a District, which shall be known and called the Metropolitan Police District of the State of Tennessee.

The act vested authority for the control of the force in three commissioners appointed by the governor and defined the structure of the force to include captains, sergeants and patrolmen. The superintending commissioner functioned as the chief of police. The Board of Mayor and Aldermen of the city of Memphis was assigned responsibility to pay all expenses of the

Parson William Gannaway Brownlow was elected governor of Tennessee during reconstruction. Brownlow established the Metropolitan Police that took over law enforcement in Memphis, Nashville, and Chattanooga. The force had statewide authority.

force including accommodation for a station house and personnel costs. Salaries were set in the act at $3,000 per year for the superintending commissioner, $2,500 for the other two commissioners, $1,600 for the captains, $1,400 for sergeants, and $1,200 a year for patrolmen.

In addition to the standard duties of keeping the public peace and enforcing criminal, sanitation and other laws, members of the force had the power to arrest without warrant and without regard to where in the state they might be. Section 20 of the act spelled out their statewide authority.

The members of the Police force of said Metropolitan Police district, shall possess in every part of the State of Tennessee, all the common law and statutory powers of constables, except for service of civil process; and every warrant for search or arrest issued by any magistrate of this State, may be executed in any part thereof by any member of the police force of the said Metropolitan Police District.

The act abolished the existing police force in Memphis and abolished the office of City Recorder, who presided on the city court. It gave the power of justice of the peace to the commissioners of the Metropolitan Police District for hearing cases related to city ordinances.

The reason for the creation of the Metropolitan Police was complex. In part, the nature of the post war era encouraged the breach of civil and criminal law. Those who had been community leaders prior to the war were stripped of power, removing any remnants of local stability and services. In addition, most of the population, white and black, was repressed during Reconstruction. These factors added to the general upheaval and exacerbated instability in the social and economic conditions. Individual and collective lawlessness flourished.

Brownlow addressed the state legislature about the lawless conditions in the state's capital. He was speaking of Nashville but the same could be said about law and order across the state of Tennessee, and, for that matter, the entire South and much of the nation.

The reputation being acquired by Nashville, the Capital of your state, and the great commercial emporium of Middle Tennessee, is humiliating to every friend of law and order. Murders, robberies, and burglaries are the order of the day. No man is safe, day or night within a circuit around Nashville, whose radius is eight or ten miles.

Municipalities across the state were trying to rebuild their police function with few resources and many other needs. This was a slow process given the fact that so many men who had previously served as policemen had been killed or disabled in the war and most others were trying to eke out a living for their families.

Law enforcement was weak while economic and social conditions provided a permissive environment for lawbreakers. Plus, much of the effort of lawmen was directed at maintaining control over the recently freed black population.

Many felt the main reason behind the creation of the Metropolitan Police was the governor's desire to enforce the franchise law. One of the most repressive steps taken after the war was to withhold the right to vote from those who had been loyal to the Confederacy. Brownlow urged state leaders "to guard the ballot-box faithfully and effectually against the approach of treason, no matter in what character it may come."

For a number of years after the war, Election Day became an occasion for violent confrontation. As a result, special police were appointed to exert control and sometimes state authorities called out the State Guard to ensure the peace and "to guard the ballot box." Nashville's *Republican Banner* expressed the thoughts of many in a commentary that ran as the bill that created the Metropolitan Police was being debated in the state legislature.

We have a suspicion—perhaps it amounts to more than a suspicion—that a military force in obedience to the will of the Governor is thought to be necessary to carry out the Franchise law, and this is the secret of the Metropolitan Police Bill.

Rioting in Memphis that involved members of the local police force may have been the precipitating factor for passage of the Metropolitan Police Act. The bill languished in the legislature for a number of months, but was revived with the onset of the rioting, and the bill passed less than two weeks following the riots.

The Metropolitan Police were in many respects more of a military force than a police force. They wore military style uniforms and drilled in the fashion of soldiers.

Brownlow used the Tennessee State Guards in locations across the state where no force of Metropolitan Police existed. As the elections of 1867 approached, 1,700 of Brownlow's State Guard were sent to conservative counties. The Governor said the force was needed to take action against the "rebellious conduct of the people," because "The indications are that we are to have disturbances at different points prompted by bad rebellious men."

Conflict frequently arose between the local population and the state guards. One such incident occurred in Jackson not long after the State Guards arrived in 1867. One night between 10 and 11 o'clock, a drunken party of the militia had an encounter with Captain J. T. McCutchen and they ordered him home from town. He joined with other ex-Confederate soldiers and they were discussing what should be done with the militia when a shot rang out. Captain March exclaimed, "They've shot someone!" The militia had, indeed, shot Major Thomas H. Hartmus. A battle ensued that lasted only a few minutes before the State Guards fled.

The event almost erupted into full-scale conflict, but level-heads prevailed. The next morning, a delegation of prominent citizens went to the militia camp and demanded the assailants be turned over to civil authority. Militia officers reported that those involved had left the camp. Several squads of volunteers were organized to pursue them, but the culprits had vanished. After this event the militia kept to their camp at night.

The Metropolitan Police and State Guards became known as "Brownlow's Band" to most white Tennesseans and were looked upon as thugs. The Ku Klux Klan came into being in reaction to carpetbaggers and other elements of Reconstruction that were odious to white southerners. Intimidation by Brownlow's Band incited activity by the "Kukluxers." The lawless actions of both Brownlow's Band and the Klan escalated in response to each other, and innocent citizens, black and white, suffered as a result. Law enforcement for decades afterwards would be impacted because of the mindset created by events of the reconstruction period.

The metropolitans were probably the most successful in furthering the causes of law enforcement in Nashville. Although the force was not accepted by the population during the period they replaced the existing Nashville police officers, they did establish a reputation for good law enforcement during their brief tenure.

Brownlow was elected to the U. S. Senate in 1869 and the repressive measures of reconstruction began to wane under his replacement, Governor Dewitt Senter. The Metropolitan Police Act was repealed on November 5, 1869, and control of the police forces of Memphis, Nashville and Chattanooga reverted to the elected officials in those cities.

The State of Tennessee also hired a few lawmen to capture escaped convicts and arrest horse thieves, problems that plagued the state immediately after the war. These individuals ranged the state on horseback chasing desperados. One such lawman was James M. Davis, a young veteran of the Confederate army. Davis later joined federal law enforcement and died in the line of duty as a deputy collector of the Alcohol Tax Unit of the Bureau of Internal Revenue.

Lawlessness remained rampant in the last quarter of the nineteenth century. For the most part county and city officers enforced the law without state involvement. The most serious breach of the peace was the Coal Creek Wars in 1891 and 1892. The Anderson County uprising of miners eventually resulted in deployment of the entire Tennessee State Militia.

The conflict grew out of the use of prisoner labor in private industry, a program enacted by the state legislature in 1865. The convict lease system resulted from the post-war circumstances of rampant lawlessness and economic hard times. The system devolved from the widespread practice of allowing prisoners to work off their fine on street gangs and other public projects that began prior to the war and was extensively used after the war. The practice continued in the form of chain-gangs through much of the twentieth century.

Revenue from private industry for prisoner labor was seen as a quick way to generate dollars for the depleted state treasury following the war and was commonly employed in southern states. The lease of convict laborers to private industry such as coal mines, plantations and railroads created a threat to the livelihood of those free workers who were displaced. Conflict between free workers and the state convict lease system was inevitable.

The first uprising of miners came at Briceville in January 1871 when free miners of the Tennessee Coal and Iron Company struck for higher wages and an end to the use of convict laborers. A major revolt began in July 1891 when 300 free miners surrounded the stockade holding convicts near Coal Creek. They marched the 40 prisoners and their guards to railroad boxcars and shipped them to Knoxville.

Governor John "Buck" Buchanan came to Coal Creek and met leaders of the miners. No agreement was made and the governor left three companies of the state militia to maintain order. When prisoners were again sent to work in the mine the free miners again loaded prisoners, guards and militia on a train and sent them to Knoxville. Reinforcements were also disarmed and sent packing and the stockade burned.

In 1892, the Governor, with the support of the legislature, sent in a large contingent of the Tennessee National Guard armed with Gatling guns and heavy artillery. Fort Anderson was built on Militia Hill in the Wye Community by prison labor. Several battles with the free miners followed. At one time the guardsmen were faced by 1700 miners. Over 500 miners were arrested and 27 killed before the free miners surrendered in October 1892.

The Coal Creek Wars focused public attention on the convict labor system and sentiment largely favored the free miners. Governor Peter Turney took office in 1893 and the general assembly voted to build a new state penitentiary and end convict leasing when existing contracts expired in 1896.

Although the major conflict was over, skirmishes continued. On the night of April 19, 1893, a mob of about a hundred miners attacked the convict stockade at Tracy City. Deputy Warden D. W. Schriver was in command of the stockade when pickets ran inside at 11:00 p.m. announcing the attack. Miners and guards opened fire. Guard S. A. Walden was defending a port hole when a load of buckshot hit him in the abdomen and legs and he soon died. The body of one of the miners was found the next morning. When word

Company C, First Regiment, Tennessee National Guard was part of the militia contingent sent by Governor John "Buck" Buchanan to put down the miners rebellion in 1891 and 1892. The photograph was taken in August 1892, a few weeks prior to the end of the conflict that became known as the Coal Creek Wars. Troops were again sent to the area the following year after an assault on the convict stockade in Tracy City.

reached Nashville of the attack, Governor Turney sent a special train with 125 militiamen to maintain order.

In the early twentieth century, two major law enforcement issues drew the attention of leadership at the state level. One issue was an extension of the battle law enforcement was already waging against illegal whiskey production. Since the Whiskey Rebellion soon after the founding of the nation, federal, state and local lawmen worked to enforce laws that required distillers to pay taxes on their product. Tennessee had more than its share of moonshiners because many distillers of revolutionary times fled to the frontier and the Appalachian mountain ranges to escape paying the whiskey excise tax.

By the early 1900s, the nation was moving toward completely prohibiting the production and sale of whiskey and the focus of law enforcement shifted. Tennessee enacted laws to prohibit the manufacture and sale of intoxicating liquors in 1909, a decade before national prohibition. Enforcement of these laws varied from location to location. Although pressure

from temperance organization led to stricter enforcement, the city of Memphis under Mayor Edward H. "Boss" Crump continued to resist closing establishments that violated prohibition and nuisance laws. The situation was exacerbated when Memphis saloons opened on election day in 1914, despite numerous injunctions.

Governor Ben Hooper appointed a special counsel in 1914 to urge enforcement and to prosecute cases under these laws. Early in January 1915 the Governor appointed two Memphis attorneys as special counsels for Memphis and Shelby County charged to "press the enforcement of the nuisance law against saloons and gambling dens in Memphis." Governor Hooper also established a Board of Narcotics Control in 1914. The board consisted of the State Health Officer and the Pure Food Inspector and was charged with enforcing laws on habit-forming drugs.

Governor Thomas Rye took office in 1915 and took action to directly affect politicians who refused to abide by state legislation. Governor Rye promoted the Ouster

Law that led to Mayor Crump being removed from office for not enforcing prohibition laws. Control of alcoholic beverages continued to be an issue and many officers across the state died in the line of duty in enforcing liquor laws, but overt resistance of any consequence to the enforcement of the laws ended.

The other major law enforcement issue in the early 1900s was more bloody and openly destructive. A number of regional outbreaks of criminal activity occurred in the first decades of the twentieth century. The "Night-Rider" phenomena were a series of uprisings that set farmer and fishermen in a bloody battle against rich and powerful business interests. Men and some women dressed in masks and robes similar to those worn by the Ku Klux Klan rose up to fight against those that they believed were robbing them of their livelihood. Murder and the destruction of property marked these violent outbreaks.

The first and longest lasting series of the major night-rider episodes was the Tobacco War or Black Patch War. The uprising took place over a number of years between 1904 and 1908, and approximately one thousand individuals participated. The conflict grew out of a tobacco buying monopoly by the American Tobacco Company. The company set prices so low that many farmers took up arms rather than accept what they considered a pittance of the true value of their crops. The assaults of the night-riders on the company and the farmers who sold tobacco to the company took place primarily in Kentucky.

In Tennessee the problem was limited mainly to Montgomery and Robertson Counties and was not on as large a scale as it was in Kentucky. Governor John Isaac Cox essentially ignored the uprising. His successor, Governor Malcolm R. Patterson, offered a reward for information on the capture and conviction of the outlaw farmers. He also threatened to call out the state militia, but never did so.

The most dramatic night-rider activity in Tennessee happened as a result of fishermen being denied use of Reelfoot Lake for commercial fishing. Many individuals around the lake made their living from fishing and selling their catch. The property that included most of the lake belonged to a non-resident and the land was purchased by a group incorporated as the West Tennessee Land Company. The company claimed exclusive fishing rights to the lake for commercial purposes and demanded that fishermen pay a royalty on their catch. Soon after this demand, the fish docks were burned, other property was destroyed and individuals who cooperated with the land company were assaulted.

The seminal event in the episode took place on the night of October 19, 1908. Judge R. Zach Taylor, called Colonel Taylor, and Captain Quentin Rankin, both of Trenton, had traveled to Walnut Log on legal business unrelated to the land company. They were, however, the attorneys who had incorporated the land company and threats had been made against them in the past.

During the night, about sixty masked men rode up to the hotel and abducted Taylor and Rankin. The next morning Rankin's body was found at the edge of the lake about six hundred yards from the hotel. A noose was tied around his neck on a ten foot length of rope. The left side of his body near the hip was riddled with small pellets from a shotgun. He had also been shot in the arms and the back of his head had been blown off at close range. Rankin's teeth had been knocked in by a blow with a club. Everyone assumed that Taylor too had been killed.

Sheriff Eastwood of Obion County led a posse of armed men from Union City in search of the night-riders. Sheriff Haines of Lake County joined the search with a posse from Tiptonville. Governor Patterson called up three Nashville companies of the state militia, 114 men, under the command of Colonel W. C. Tatum, assisted by Major R. F. Martin and U.S. Army Captain Charles B. Rogan. Two Memphis companies were ordered to the scene as well. The Governor also offered a $10,000 reward for the arrest and conviction of Rankin's killers.

Colonel Taylor, who had escaped death, came walking into Tiptonville on Wednesday. He related what had happened the night he and Rankin were taken from the hotel.

Monday night Captain Rankin and I went to Reelfoot Lake in response to a letter from a Mr. Carpenter, of Union City, who wanted to lease some timber land. On our arrival at the lake we went to the log house, or Ward Hotel, and early after supper retired. Some time during the night we were aroused by someone knocking at our door, and on opening the door a mob of masked men was found standing in the hall. We were ordered to dress, and as the leader of the mob said he wanted to talk to us, we put on our clothes and accompanied the men to the banks of the lake, some distance from the hotel.

The leader of the mob talked with us, telling us we were associating too much with Judge Harris [principal in the land company] and were taking entirely too much interest in the lake. He said that the course of Harris and the West Tennessee Land Company in prohibiting free fishing was causing the starvation of women and children, and that something had to be done.

I never dreamed that the mob intended us any harm, but just then they threw a rope around Captain Rankin's neck and swung him to a limb. He protested and said, "Gentlemen, do not kill me," and the reply of the mob was a volley of fifty shots.

This was the first evidence of any intention to harm us, and when the firing began, I jumped into a bayou and made for a sunken log. Behind this I hid and the mob fired several hundred shots into the log. They evidently believed I was dead, for I heard one of them say, "He's dead and let him go," and with that he rode away.

I remained in the water until the mob was well out of hearing and went to an island in the lake, where I remained all day Tuesday. At night I started out and walked all night, coming up to a house at 6 o'clock this morning.

Eventually, over fifty of the night-riders of Reelfoot lake were either tried or turned state's witnesses against their neighbors. Most of the physical evidence was destroyed. Five masks and two robes worn by the night-riders were discovered by militiamen in a tin bucket on Nick's Towhead, an island in Reelfoot Lake.

Another series of night-riding incidents occurred during 1909 in Humphreys County in connection with the peanut-growing industry. Governor Patterson again used the militia as a state force and sent in thirty national guardsmen to quell the criminal outbreak. Similar incidents continued.

State authorities seemed helpless to stop the killing and destruction of marauding bands that overwhelmed local law enforcement. The gangs faded into the background when troops showed up. The need for a force of state law enforcement officers gained support among the states legislators. The result was the creation of the Tennessee State Rangers, an emergency force to ferret out organized lawlessness is the state.

The group was modeled after the Texas Rangers created nearly a century earlier. Exploits of the Texas Rangers were prominent in the newspapers in 1914 because of their role in the cross-border raids of Mexican rebels under Pancho Villa.

The State Rangers were created as a small force to be deployed by the governor to protect persons and property from violence of organized forces. The legislation was enacted as Chapter 74 of the public acts of 1915, signed into law on May 4.

Section 1. *Be it enacted by the General Assembly of the State of Tennessee,* That there be hereby created a State Constabulary, to be designated and known as the State Rangers, to consist of ten members who shall be appointed by the Governor and who shall hold office for the term of ten years, subject to removal by him for sufficient cause.

Section 2. *Be it further enacted,* That when acts of violence occur in any county of the State whereby the rights of persons or property are violated or jeopardized by organized forces, or by any considerable number of persons acting in conjunction or singly, and which may be brought to the attention of the Governor, he shall, in his discretion, direct the State Rangers to police such County, or any part thereof, so disturbed, to suppress such acts of violence and to arrest all persons engaged or aiding and abetting therein.

Section 5. *Be it further enacted,* That each of the regular members of the State Rangers . . . shall have authority to summon and swear in the posse comitatus when necessary to meet any emergency . . .

The State Rangers had the same powers conferred on sheriffs. The bill was amendment to exclude counties with a population of 190,000 and over as designated in the 1910 federal census. The only such county was Shelby County, so the Rangers did not have jurisdiction in Memphis and surrounds. The State Rangers were attached to the Adjutant General's office and were paid $3 per day when on duty. Special rangers appointed by the governor and posse members earned $2 per day.

Within a short time the State Rangers were used in several emergencies primarily in a detective capacity. In June 1915 the governor ordered rangers into Stewart County where a band of night-riders were burning property and intimidating people. A few individuals were killed. A grand jury was convened on June 2 in Dover to hear charges and three state rangers were sworn in to round up the accused. Tennessee State Rangers A. C. Turner of Stewart County, Thomas Tansill of Williamson County and Alexander C. Stafford of Montgomery County were the first three to serve under the act. The rangers elected Thomas Tansill as chief ranger. E. A. Tucker, William Smith

Tennsssee State Ranger Alexander C. Stafford was one of the first three state rangers sworn in on June 2, 1915, following appointment by Governor Thomas Rye. The state rangers were ordered to bring to justice the night-riders who had terrorized Stewart county since the previous fall. Stafford was a former Clarksville chief of police and served six years as sheriff of Montgomery County.

and E. J. Frazier of Stewart County and Otto Robinson, Clay Stacker, Cave Johnson, B. L. Perkins, Jim Moss and Hugh Parchman of Montgomery County were sworn in as deputy rangers.

The rangers were experienced lawmen. Alexander Stafford was first elected as a constable in 1876 and served as chief of the Clarksville Police Department from 1888 to 1895. He remained with the force until 1900 and then served six years as sheriff of Montgomery County. State Ranger A. C. Turner served as sheriff of Stewart County from 1886 to 1892 and again from 1902 to 1908.

The judge who swore them in referred to them as "the highest peace officers in the state." He encouraged them to make arrests as peacefully as possible but confirmed that "they had the right to use such force as was necessary to repel an assault or to make an arrest."

Six days after they were sworn in, one of the

rangers and two deputies drove three prisoners to the county jail in Clarksville. Four days later another three prisoners were deposited behind bars. Patrols and arrests continued until the night-riding stopped. The rangers gathered evidence for the Attorney General to use in prosecution under the Ku Klux Klan statute. Rangers stayed in the county until January 1916.

Another ranger was sent to Sequatchie County to investigate a Ku Klux Klan group. He worked undercover for a time and gathered evidence for prosecution. He then gathered a posse and arrested a number of suspects, sending eleven to the Hamilton County Jail at Chattanooga where they were questioned. The ranger and his deputies were on duty for less than a month and ended the marauding.

World events soon created a wider concern for a statewide police force. Fears of a radical uprising led to the creation of the Tennessee State Police. The proposed state force embroiled Governor Albert Houston Roberts in the biggest controversy of the 1919 session of the Tennessee legislature.

The Russian Revolution led to the "Red Scare" in the United States and elsewhere in the world. Many, including Governor Roberts, feared that domestic radicals posed the threat of an outbreak of violence. Following the National Guard Act of 1916, calling up the state guard required approval of the state legislature. Roberts feared the delay caused by getting legislative approval would endanger the state and submitted a bill to create a state police force that he could quickly use to quell mob violence or a radical insurgency.

His opposition saw the proposal as a strike-breaking measure, but they were not in the majority. The *Nashville Banner* expounded the predominant view, "as the law now stands the governor is absolutely without power to summon out a military force, even though the capitol building were being torn to the ground by anarchists."

The act establishing the Tennessee State Police (TSP) was passed March 29, 1919. The force was appointed by the Governor and directly under his command. The officers were organized by congressional districts and were to be called into service when needed to meet an emergency.

Be it enacted by the General Assembly of the State of Tennessee, That there be, and is hereby created a State Police Force, to be designated "Tennessee State Police," consisting of not more that 600 regular officers, of the following numbers and grades: Ten District officers, one of whom shall be assigned by the Governor to each of the congressional districts of the State; one County officer for each of the 96 counties of the State, and 494 sectional officers, to be appointed from the several counties as the Governor may in his discretion, think proper; and such special officers as may be necessary to be appointed to meet an emergency; *Provided*, that the number of special officers appointed, in any grade, shall not exceed 20 per centum of the total number of regular officers authorized by this Act for that Grade.

The principal duty of the state police was to maintain law and order during incidents of unrest in the state, specifically "to suppress all affrays, riots, routs, unlawful assemblies, or other acts of actual or threatened violence to persons or property in this State." TSP officers were appointed by the governor to 6-year terms. The governor could designate direction and command of state police officers to any department of state government, including the District Attorneys General. Officers were sworn according to an oath of office specified in the bill.

I do solemnly swear that I will well and faithfully perform the duties of the office of district (county or sectional) officer, Tennessee State Police, to the best of my ability, for the term appointed.

And I do solemnly swear that I will bear true faith and allegiance to the State of Tennessee, and that I will serve the State of Tennessee honestly and faithfully against all her enemies, whomsoever, and that I will obey the orders of the Governor and of the officers placed over me, according to law.

State police officers were appointed to specific sections of each county, but their authority was not limited to that locale. They had the authority to respond to an emergency in any part of the state with the full authority of their office. Their authority, however, did not exceed that of the sheriff "as the principal conservator of the peace of his county," but was intended to supplement his protection of persons and property.

The TSP was not intended to be a full-time standing law enforcement agency. Officers were called to duty from time to time to meet specific emergencies, and therefore they were not salaried but were compensated only during the period of their duty. Regular officers and special officers were paid by the day, $3.00

for district officers, $2.50 for county officers, and $2.00 for sectional officers.

Numerous applications and recommendations for state policemen were sent to Nashville. In a July 10, 1919, response to one such letter, Governor Roberts explained that "the State Police Bill is now in effect. We have so far appointed only members of the national guard to the State Police force." He also wrote that the officers were employed "only in case of riot and insurrection."

Governor Roberts said in his January 4, 1921, legislative message that the paramount duty of the Chief Executive of the state was "to see that the laws are properly enforced." He said the State Police Bill was one of the most important pieces of legislation in recent years, and refuted the bill's naysayers.

I believe the people may safely trust any man who may be elected Governor of Tennessee to exercise the powers conferred by this statute in such manner as to protect and safeguard the rights of the people without infringing upon the right of any.

Governor Roberts' political opponents used the creation of the State Police against him in the next election. The Nashville Banner's political cartoonist pictured the governor in a policeman's hat looking in the grass for "Imaginary Reds" while real problems in his administration were being ignored.

The Tennessee State Police in this early form was issued a small shield-cut-out-star consistent with badges worn in the period. The TSP never functioned to put down radical uprisings. Almost a decade later, however, a small group of Tennessee State Police officers was hired to perform duty as a patrol force on the highways of the state.

When the Highway Department was created in 1919, the only section of the act that referred to law enforcement related to the notification of the county clerk when vehicle ownership was transferred. The act specifies that, "it shall be the duty of all peace officers of the State of Tennessee to arrest and prosecute violators." This reference was to city and county law officers, not a state police system.

The advent of the automobile changed the dynamics of traffic on the roads of Tennessee. The first real road in the state was constructed in 1795, connecting Knoxville and Nashville. The *Knoxville Gazette* reported on July 1 of that year, "The new wagon road to Nashville won't be thoroughly completed until October 1st, but a wagon of ton weight has actually passed over it." The greatest danger of traveling that early roadway was attack by hostile Indians.

The first law regulating the use of "highways" was contained in the Public Acts of 1837-38 and required that "Every driver or person having charge of a vehicle shall give half the road when meeting another vehicle by turning to the right so as not to interfere with passing." Although much progress was made in roadways and traffic laws since those days, an explosive era of increased vehicular traffic was about to occur.

Governor Austin Peay took office in 1923 and began a major road and bridge construction initiative. To accomplish this and other goals he had for the state, Governor Peay reorganized the executive branch of state government, including the Highway Department. His efforts brought about an enormous expansion of Tennessee's roadway system.

Traffic safety was a growing concern for the state. Not only was the network of highways extended to new areas, but roadbed improvements and paving meant automobiles could travel at faster rates. The advances in convenience and serviceability of these new thoroughfares brought an unwelcome consequence. Traffic accidents and fatalities soared. With no drivers training or license requirement, anyone could take a car onto the state roadways. Drunken drivers were commonplace. Automobiles were not equipped with any safety devices. In addition, overloaded trucks created highway maintenance problems and added to the danger.

Traffic enforcement was the duty of city and county law officers. The state Chamber of Commerce was concerned because local constables or other "minor officials" were creating public relations problems because of how they treated out of state visitors who were stopped for traffic violations. In June 1926, a push began, encouraged by the U. S. Department of Commerce, to enact Uniform Traffic Laws in the state. The need was also recognized for a state level enforcement arm to see that traffic regulations were obeyed.

State Highway Commissioner C. N. Bass carried the administration's message in a December 1926 speech calling for the 1927 legislature to enact a strict traffic code and establish a state police force. The suggestion was that the force be funded from a "nominal driver's license fee." He also noted that the highway "department, acting under the authority of the Reorganization act, now has three policemen on this work and the presence of one of these men on a section of road tends to immediately promote orderly driving." The act which reorganized the highway department contained no specific language regarding hiring policemen, but did contain references that empowered the commissioner to hire personnel required to accomplish provisions of the act.

Governor Peay, in his January 6, 1927, legislative message, placed a range of law enforcement issues before the legislature for action.

> I recommend to your consideration some provisions for the better enforcement of our traffic and temperance laws. Travel on the highways is becoming more dangerous. I recommend that the Department of Highways be permitted to employ a few guards to protect the traveling public on our highways and see to the enforcement of our traffic laws and that they be invested with police powers to arrest reckless, drunken and incompetent drivers. These guards should be compensated from the fines and be under the control of the department to insure decent treatment of the public and to prevent them from becoming overzealous or oppressive. Local officers in the various counties are engaged with their ordinary duties and devote little or no attention to the regulation of travel and traffic on the highways of the state. Some provision of the same kind should be enacted for the better enforcement of our temperance laws. The liquor situation is not being handled satisfactorily. The small fees which our enforcement officers now

receive, are wholly inadequate. In fact, the work of a sleuth is now being imposed on our sheriffs and their deputies without compensation. They get a small fee for arrest and perhaps as a witness. To apprehend violators, often they must lay in hiding for hours or days in remote and inaccessible places during all kinds of weather. The remedy, in my judgment, is to compensate these officers with a substantial portion of the fines which are assessed and collected in liquor cases. This done, we will see a quick and substantial improvement in the enforcement of these laws.

Although Governor Peay referred to the law officers as "guards" rather than policemen, the newspaper reports referred to the governor's proposal as "a state police system." Strong opposition greeted both Peay's recommendation for state law enforcement and his funding proposal. A drivers license law would not be enacted for a decade.

Another funding concern of Governor Peay was the significant amounts of revenue from automobile licenses that were not being paid to the state. This funding source was important to the highway construction program. When the legislature failed to act on either a uniform traffic code or a state traffic police, Governor Peay used the existing State Police legislation to put a force in service to enforce license tag laws and laws requiring transfers of cars and licenses. The State Police were placed under Commissioner Williams of the Department of Finance and Taxation. After Peay's death later that year, Governor Henry Hollis Horton continued implementation of statewide police force.

The state force was headquartered at 105 Memorial Building in Nashville and consisted of only a dozen or so officers at any one time. They primarily enforced laws that generated revenue for the state, such as license and title fees. When they enforced traffic laws they did so as proxy for local authorities and the fines collected went to the counties where they were collected.

James J. Lester was the first TSP officer hired. John W. "Johnny" Burgess was among the early men hired and named chief of the force. Before joining the TSP, Burgess served four years as a motorcycle officer with the Nashville Police Department and two years in the same capacity with the Davidson County force.

State policemen commissioned on June 6, 1927, were Doug Sloan, Delbert R. Jenkins, Fort H. Wilkerson, John Norwood, Jerry Cottar Jr., William Ewing, and R. Willard Jett. Commissions were issued by the Adjutant General.

Employed in 1928 were Wallace P. McCleash, Lewis Simpkins, Jimmy Burgess, and Robert Malone. Others on the force included Earl Robertson, Tom Webb, Ernest Shumake, and Amos Bracey.

State policemen's uniforms were initially tan gabardine and later changed to police blue. Officers purchased their own uniforms, except for a coat and cap provided by the state. They wore riding boots and Sam Brown belts with holster in the cross draw position.

The state provided insignia, a cap badge, a breast badge and uniform patches. The breast badge of patrolmen was an eagle-top, pinched shield and the hat badge was an eagle-top medallion with crossed batons. Sergeants wore an eagle-top teardrop breast badge and an eagle-top medallion on the cap. The shoulder patch of the TSP was a stock winged-wheel patch with a custom rocker mounted over it identifying the agency. It was worn on both arms midway between the shoulder and elbow.

State policemen rode motorcycles almost exclusively as they moved about the state. Until the late 1930s motorcycles were the most common mode of transportation for traffic officers.

The force was not well received by the public. Local resentment to outside authority aimed at collecting revenues from taxes or fees caused much of the problem. Collection of liquor and tobacco taxes by "revenuers" had created conflict for decades. The collection of state automobile license and title fees was resented as well. Local citizens also charged state policemen with being heavy handed in the performance of their duty.

In November 1927, Tennessee Supreme Court Justice Colin P. McKinney said, "The Highway Police Department is in poor favor with the public. I have talked to people in the three Grand Divisions of the State, and the general impression prevails that many unnecessary arrests are being made in order to procure fees and justify the creation of this department." He suggested that the State Police confine their activities to arresting reckless drivers and those driving while intoxicated. Commissioner Williams stated that in his opinion that his department was justified only by its enforcement of the revenue laws, and pointed out that traffic enforcement was the responsibility of local officers.

Local courts were not supportive of the force's activity. State policemen led by Sergeant D. R. Jenkins arrested 17 people in Knoxville on the charge of "failing to notify the state highway department through

Motorcycle patrolmen of the State Police trained in Shelby Park in 1927 on whatever equipment was available, including bicycles for novice motorcycle riders.

the county court clerk of their purchase of an automobile, the title of which became changed and vested in them, and thus transfer the registration of said automobile as required by law." The charges were not prosecuted and a newspaper headline read, "State Speed Cops Cases Dismissed."

Although local authorities sometimes asked that state policemen be sent into their county to enforce revenue collections, newspapers warned citizens of their pending arrival, as in a notice from an East Tennessee daily.

Merchants who have not purchased their 1928 license plates better be careful, for the next thirty days the state traffic policemen have arrived.

F. H. Wilkerson and R. W. Jett reached Johnson City Saturday afternoon and are making their headquarters at the Windsor Hotel for the next month. The state officers are making this trip to Johnson City for several purposes in addition to the checking of delinquent auto licenses purchasers. Ad Valorem, Merchants and special privilege license will also be checked in detail and all merchants are requested to place their licenses in prominent places in their stores where they can be found without difficulty.

"We will visit all merchants in Washington and Carter Counties the next thirty days and all who have not purchased proper licenses will have to

do so, or be subject to fine," stated Wilkerson. "Of course we will give a great amount of our attention to the 1928 license plates and speeders on the highways and these violators will also be cited," added the officer.

Wilkerson and Jett will ride motorcycles part of the time and will also use an automobile, so motorists will have much difficulty in keeping an eye on the state cops.

The actions of the State Police was also being challenged legally, especially traffic enforcement. In responding to an attorney's letter in January 1928, Commissioner Williams explained the administration's rationale for the group.

The officers who are generally known as "State Police" are in reality revenue officers whose duty it is to collect State revenue and that the enforcement of the traffic laws is merely incidental to their prime purpose. The speed laws, of course, should be enforced by the local authorities for there is not special legislation making it incumbent upon the state to apprehend violators of these laws.

Of course our officers desire to help the local authorities enforce any laws and since they use motorcycles they are often times called upon to apprehend violators of the speed laws. The salaries of these officers approximates one hundred and fifty dollars each.

The State Police was successful in enforcing revenue collections. Within the first six months of creating the standing force, collection of automobile license fees increased by more than $200,000. Fines collected in their first year, 1927, amounted to $35,093.45 and ranged from only $60 collected in January to over $6,000 in the months of June and October. Operating costs in 1927 were $32,069.27, $19,265 for salaries, $9,604.27 in traveling expenses and $3,000 for motor equipment. State policemen earned $150 a month and the monthly payroll for the 13 man force at yearend was $1,975.

Chief Johnny Burgess continued as head of the State Police in 1928. The force of state policemen consisted of Sergeant Delbert R. Jenkins, James T. "Jimmy" Burgess, R. Willard Jett and Fort H. Wilkerson in the Knoxville area, Robert J. Malone in Memphis, Sergeant Tom C. Webb in Chattanooga, Wallace P. McCleash and Amos Bracey in Jackson, and in the Nashville area, W. D. Sloan, John Norwood, T. Jerry Cottar Jr. and Earl T. Robertson.

Chief Burgess expressed his concerns over the limited size of the force and believed the state needed at least three times the number of officers. Commissioner Williams told one local official that he might have to reduce the force unless the legislature appropriated money to maintain it, explaining, "It is true, of course, that some revenue can be secured that otherwise would not be collected and that a considerable amount of money can be brought in from fines; but these fines, as collections in other misdemeanor cases, revert to the counties and thus do not aid the State in the expense incident to police work."

After a special request from White County, Fred Black was commissioned as a State Policeman in September 1928. He was placed on the force with the understanding that the county would pay all of his expenses including his salary. The county reached an agreement with Black that he would receive all the fines that he collected as his pay.

As 1929 began Policeman Wallace McCleash was transferred from Jackson to Knoxville and Sergeant Tom Webb was moved from Chattanooga. When asked not to transfer McCleash, the commissioner explained that the department had a policy to move State Police officers from time to time because of the size of the force. It was probably more than coincidence that both of the men had complaints made against them, even though investigations showed the complaints were unsubstantiated.

TSP officers became involved in law enforcement activities beyond traffic patrol and the collection of fees and taxes. When Sheriff Tom F. Brown was shot and killed by his predecessor in that office in April 1928, a state policeman joined the posse. The *Nashville Tennessean* of

Tennessee State Policeman R. Willard Jett wore the standard uniform of the state police force and the breast badge of his rank.

April 11 reported the involvement of this unnamed officer in the hunt for the fugitive killer.

POSSE WAITING AT HOME
OF SLAYER OF SHERIFF
State Policeman Joins Cumberland Hunt

The state policeman said to be en route to Crossville to join the hunt of G. W. Walker, passed through Rockwood this afternoon. The

Four members of the Tennessee State Police who served during the late twenties. As identified on the original picture, they were Sergeant D. R. Jenkins, F. H. Wilkenson, R. W. Jett, and J. T. Burgess. The motorcycles were Harley Davidsons and the only marking is a sign atop the front fender that read "State Police." Sergeant Jenkins is wearing an eagle-top teardrop style badge, and the policemen are wearing eagle-top pinched shields. The sergeant is also wearing a different style hat badge. The shoulder patch is an winged wheel with "Traffic, Police" over which was a rocker panel with the words "State of Tenn." and was worn between the shoulder and elbow. Revolvers are worn in a cross-draw style on a Sam Brown belt.

posse was reported this afternoon as being back of Hollman mountain.

The role of the Tennessee National Guard in major civil disturbances continued to be vital. The guard was called in to quell disorder in May 1929 in Johnson City and Elizabethton. A strike at the American Cigar Box Manufacturing Company in Johnson City led to conflict. The most serious lawlessness resulted from the strike at two Elizabethton textile plants producing rayon including violence and treats of dynamiting and killing by members of the labor union at the American Bemberg and American Glanstoff plants.

The TSP remained too small to solve the problems faced by the state. The need for a uniform state code and an enforcement agency was more and more apparent. The highways of the state were growing evermore dangerous as the General Assembly convened in January 1929. State finances were also in a poor condition, with the state facing a multi-million-dollar deficit. Governor Henry Hollis Horton in his January 14, 1929, legislative message stressed the need for expanded traffic laws, their enforcement and a way to pay for the patrol force.

The increasing use of motor vehicles and the construction of modern roadways have necessitated in the interest and protection of those who must use the roads a stricter regulation of traffic than now exists. Although the automobile has been of great service to the present generation it has, when unregulated, many sins to answer for, and its use has been seized upon by law-violators to facilitate their operations. Daily we are confronted with news accounts of loss of life and other accidents which might have been prevented by the observation of reasonable prudence. There seems to be a certain portion of the population to whom gasoline is an intoxicant, and a number of persons from whom reason flees when they are behind a steering wheel. The lives and property of the more prudent should not be threatened by the reckless and it is apparent that this recklessness cannot be curbed by mere moral suasion. "The automobile is an instrument of power which by some will be selfishly used until by the attrition of conflict a *modus vivendi* is established that adapts it to its proper place in the scheme of things." I believe that a driver's license should be issued to competent operators and that without such license no citizen should be allowed to drive a car in this State. This license should be subject to revocation for certain offenses against the safety and the morals of the public. A conviction for the violation of the laws prohibiting the sale and transportation of intoxicating liquor should serve to revoke the operators license. The bootlegger and the rum runner deprived of the use of the automobile would be far less potent public enemies. The

Members of the Tennessee State Police in December 1928 at Centennial Park in Nashville. The five uniformed officers on the right were sergeants, distinguishable by chevrons and the badge styles they wore.

Department of Finance and Taxation should be entrusted with the duty of issuing such licenses. The protection thereof should be used for patrolling the highways and the excess above such cost converted into the State treasury of the general highway fund.

Political wrangling marked the opening of the General Assembly's regular session, but after much discussion, a major revision to Tennessee's traffic laws passed the legislature and Governor Horton signed the act into law.

Providing for an enforcement agency did not make it through the legislature in the regular session of 1929. The existing force of state policemen were charged with enforcement of the new traffic laws. Enforcement began in a relaxed manner, with more warning being given than arrests made. However, Chief Johnny Burgess informed drivers that was about to change. The *Nashville Tennessean* reported his comments on May 4, 1929.

CHIEF BURGESS ORDERS TRAFFIC LAW ENFORCED
Final Warning Is Issued to Automobilists.

Chief J. W. Burgess of the state police issued final warning Saturday against violators of the new state traffic laws, announcing that the drive against the violations of these laws would be put on in earnest starting Sunday.

Hundreds of motorists have been arrested or warned against insufficient lighting of head-lights and tail-lights for the past week and enforcement of the "Stop" law at arterial highways is being put into effect.

The major violations are against the stops at highways designated by the yellow state arterial signs, stops at railroad grade crossings, and improper lights.

Passing on curves and brows of hills is likewise prohibited and will be rigidly enforced by the state officers. Davidson county in particular will be patrolled by the state police Sunday in the start of the campaign and motorists are warning against violations of these newly instituted laws.

The relationships between the TSP and many citizens of the state grew even more strained. The *Nashville Tennessean* described the general perception of the force as being "obnoxious, bullying and disgraceful to the state." Their role as "revenue agents" had worked against the standing force since its creation. The expanded role of enforcing the traffic laws increased public sentiment against them.

One Nashville motorist arrested by a state policeman and subsequently rearrested by a county deputy was convicted of reckless driving. He brought action challenging the legality of the state police. His attorney filed an injunction against paying State Police officers a monthly salary of $150, because the 1919 law provided that they be paid only $2.50 or $3.00 per day. Beginning July 15, 1929, patrolmen worked without pay until the courts could rule on the injunction.

A reporter asked Chief Johnny Burgess, who had been taking flying lessons in August 1929, why he was learning to fly an airplane. His answer showed both a sense of humor and a vision for the future.

"Our police have been accused of hiding out and lying in ambush to catch law-breaking motorists," said Mr. Burgess humorously, when asked about his flying. "Now, I'm expecting to have somebody accuse me of flying over them trying to catch a violator. I've ridden motorcycles and automobiles, and I don't want to be left behind now. Airplanes and air transportation are going to be big factors in everyday life in a short while now, and it's not unreasonable to believe that before long one or two of the state department will have to purchase planes in order to keep up with the times."

Questions concerning the legality of the state police have been raised many times, and at the present an injunction has restrained the state Comptroller from paying the regular salaries to the officers on the state force. "We're up in the air most of the time anyway, so why not get up there sure enough," was Johnny's laconic summary of aviation related to his regular work.

The ruling of the court granting the injunction to stop payment of salaries to members of the Tennessee State Police came on August 15, 1929. The state police ceased to exist and the force of 20 patrolmen was disbanded. Chief Burgess had no comment other than to explain "that the chief duties of his force had been the enforcement of the license laws of the state, with stress on the new 1929 traffic laws during the last few months during the lull in license law violations. He added that the state police sought only persons who drove recklessly to endanger the lives of other motorists in violation of the 1929 traffic laws fostered by the Nashville Automobile club."

An appeal was made to the Tennessee Supreme Court, but the decision of the lower court was upheld. The future of statewide law enforcement was now clearly in the hands of the General Assembly. The need for continued state enforcement of the license laws and the new traffic laws was clear as well and most other states had created state police or highway patrol agencies.

Former state policemen were transferred to other state jobs, some with the Motor Vehicle Bureau and others with the Highway Department. It would be another decade before the Tennessee State Police Act was repealed in 1939 when the Department of Safety was created, but the agency did not function after 1929.

Tennessee Highway Patrol
Department of Safety

During the last months of 1929, with the Tennessee State Police no longer patrolling the state's highways, traffic enforcement was again solely in the hands of local authorities. The already dangerous situation for travelers worsened.

The labor strikes at the American Glanzstoff and Bemberg rayon plants in Elizabethton that year gave further evidence that the state needed a force of officers to deal with civil and labor disturbances. The governor dispatched 800 National Guardsmen to restore order to the city.

Legislators reconvened in a special session in December 1929. The mood was less political and more businesslike. The U.S. stock market had crashed, the nation was in the grips of an economic depression, and Tennessee was in dire financial condition. Among the other legislation introduced in the extraordinary session, Governor Henry Horton submitted a bill to create a state highway patrol. He made the case for a traffic enforcement patrol in his December 2, 1929, legislative message.

> I would invite your attention to the situation that now exists upon the highways of our state to the very great jeopardy of human life and property. A uniform traffic law similar to the one enacted in our sister states, was placed upon our statute books. However, no provision was made for the adequate enforcement of the law. Since the decision of the courts holding that no authority existed in law for the employment of a state patrol force, I am informed that fatal accidents upon our highways have increased by more than one hundred percent (100%). It must be obvious therefore that some means for patrolling the highways, for enforcing the laws, and for the protection of human life, must be provided. It is our imperative duty to do this without delay. I, therefore, earnestly recommend that authority be given for the employment of traffic or patrol officers on the highways vested with authority to enforce the traffic regulations and laws and also to aid in the collection of the license fees and taxes due the State from the owners of motor vehicles and other delinquent privilege taxpayers.

Legislation was supported by such groups as the Nashville Automobile Club, because of the increasing danger and confusion on roadways. Opposition to the proposed legislation was based on what most considered the "fee grabbing" activities of the State Police and their overbearing manner in dealing with the public.

The concerns of those who opposed a state police force were tempered by the recent appointment of Charles M. McCabe as Commissioner of Finance and

Taxation. McCabe, born in Nashville in 1869, brought a mixture of public and private service to the position. He had served as city treasurer of Nashville from 1899 to 1904, assistant postmaster in Memphis in 1913, postmaster of Nashville from 1920 to 1924. McCabe held important positions in business between those stints as a public servant, and was president of a Nashville manufacturing company before his appointment as Commissioner of Finance and Taxation on September 11, 1929. McCabe was respected for his integrity and competence.

Legislation was enacted to establish a statewide agency to patrol the highways of Tennessee on December 13, 1929. The body of officers was organized under the control of the Department of Finance and Taxation and according to the geographic divisions of the state Highway Department.

Be it enacted by the General Assembly of the State of Tennessee, That there is hereby created a police force to be known and designated as "The Tennessee Highway Patrol," which shall consist of one Chief, one Assistant Chief for each Field Division according to the present or any future organization of the State Highway Department, and not more than one member to each fifty miles of highway on the State Highway System.

John L. Sullivan, a decorated veteran of World War I, was the first to be selected as a Tennessee Highway Patrolman.

The Act specified that the primary duty of the Tennessee Highway Patrol (THP) was the enforcement of the laws related to Tennessee's roadways. The Act stated that the patrol was "to enforce all laws, and all rules and regulations of the Department of Highways and Public Works of the State of Tennessee regulating traffic on and use of said highways." Secondarily, the force was to assist the Commissioner of Finance and Taxation and the county court clerks in the state "in the collection of all taxes and revenue going to the State, and in the enforcement of all laws relating to same." The THP had all the necessary police powers to perform their duty including the right to make arrests and the right to serve criminal warrants and subpoenas. The right to arrest, however, was limited to state revenue and road laws.

Personnel and other expenses of the patrol were to be paid from the Motor Vehicle Fund of the state, but were not to exceed 5% of the fund each year, approximately $180,000 at the time. Patrolmen were required to wear uniforms while they were on duty, the uniform to be designated by the commissioner. Officers had to be at least 21 years of age and were sworn in by taking an oath specified in the Act.

I do solemnly swear that I will support the Constitution of Tennessee, and will well and faithfully perform the duties imposed upon me as a member of "The Tennessee Highway Patrol" to the best of my ability; and that I will serve the State of Tennessee honestly and faithfully, and will obey the orders of the officers and officials placed over me according to law.

The *Nashville Tennessean* provided insight into the debate on the floor of the State Senate in an article published following the Senate's approval and before the Bill was signed into law.

Uniformed Highway Patrolmen working on a straight salary, and designed for the protection and not the prosecution of law-abiding motorists, were authorized by the State Senate Tuesday by a vote of 23 to 4. The minor opposition exhibited was directed at the now defunct State Police whose actions were characterized as obnoxious, bullying and disgraceful to the state, and expressions were given that only confidence in Commissioner Charles M. McCabe's supervision of the newly created force caused the approval of a State Highway Patrol such as was authorized by the senate.

The original members of the Tennessee Highway Patrol posed on the steps of the state capitol building in Nashville on March 12, 1930, the first day as a uniformed force. From left to right in the front row were Johnny Burgess, instructor; Toll E. Fowler, assistant chief, Memphis division; J. O. Davis, chief; Charles McCabe, commissioner of finance and taxation; Governor Henry H. Horton; R. H. Baker, state highway commissioner; Servis Evrard, assistant chief, Knoxville division; and Joe B. Williams, assistant chief, Nashville division. In the second and third rows were twelve district sergeants, Homer Cook, Benton McMillin, Robert Cravens, Charles Hash, Marion C. Holt, Marshall Wood, Jo B. Morton, John L. Sullivan, Ambrose Hash, Clyde Odil, Hallie Hamm and James English along with 30 patrolmen.

Without the services of the officers to enforce either the state traffic laws or the license laws for almost six months, the state will probably be ready within the next few weeks to start a well uniformed and well organized Highway Patrol to functioning, officials indicated, as a result of the strong sentiment for the protection of lives and property shown both in the Senate and House.

Several hundred applications for positions with the new state law enforcement agency were received in the first few days after the Bill was signed into law. Excerpts from another newspaper article quoted Commissioner McCabe regarding his expectation of members of the Patrol.

"It is not my intention to annoy motorists, but to help them," he said today. "For the first few weeks the patrolmen will merely instruct motorists, calling attention to minor violations, and not making arrests."

"Patrolmen will be selected with extreme care," the Commissioner said. "It is my purpose," he declared, "to recommend only men who have clean records and who not only will clean up the highways, but will popularize the State Patrol. Any man who falls short of expectations will not stay long."

The command structure consisted of the chief, an assistant chief for each of the three divisions and a sergeant to supervise each of the twelve districts. Chief J. O. Davis was selected as the Commander of the Patrol. The three assistant chiefs selected to command the divisions were Assistant Chief Joe Boyd Williams in the Middle Division headquartered at Nashville, Assistant Chief Toll Fowler in the Western Division at Memphis and Assistant Chief Servis L. Evrard in the Eastern Division at Knoxville.

Chief Davis informed applicants that the most dangerous hour for accidents was between 4:00 p.m. and 5:00 p.m. The most traveled hours were from 1:00 p.m. to 10:00 p.m. each day and those were the hours patrolmen would be required to work. Patrolmen were to patrol singly during daylight hours, but would patrol in pairs after nightfall.

The selection of 55 patrolmen from 3,250 applicants took place in January and February 1930. The average age of the group was 28 years, the average height of 5' 11" and with the equivalent of a high school education. Sergeant John L. Sullivan, a decorated veteran of World War I, was the first patrolman selected. A number of former state policemen were hired.

Fifty-five motorcycles and five cars were purchased in January 1930. The Chief of the Patrol and the Division assistant chiefs had cars assigned to them. The

Individuals responsible for bringing the Tennessee Highway Patrol to the state's roadways. From left to right were Patrolman Jerry Carter, Sergeant Homer Cook, Governor Henry Horton, Commission of Finance and Taxation Charles McCabe, and Chief J. O. Davis.

remainder of the men, sergeants and patrolmen, rode Harley-Davidson motorcycles. To the basic factory model motorcycles, the state added red lights, a B&M friction siren, a first aid kit and a carbon tetrachloride fire extinguisher.

The motorcycles had no special paint job, but were marked in the same fashion as the State Police motor-cycles, with a sign mounted atop the front fender that read "Tenn. Highway Patrol." As these first units were replaced, new motorcycles received custom paint jobs with the name of the agency painted on the sides of the gas tank. A motorcycle repair shop was established behind the state highway garage on Charlotte Avenue and staffed by two mechanics.

The uniform consisted of forest green riding trousers, full-length jacket, and soft-edged service cap with a brown leather bill. Winter uniforms were made of wool and summer of gabardine. The blouse, or shirt, worn with the uniform was white. The force was not required to wear the jacket in the summer of 1930 and it was decided that a tan shirt was a better color for the uniform than white. Shirts, ties and shoes were furnished by the patrolmen. Standard ties were worn with the jacket, but patrolmen wore bow ties in the summer. Neckwear regulations were generally relaxed; a patrolman could wear red ties, bow ties, mufflers or pretty much what the individual patrolman wanted to wear. Patrolmen spent so much of their time on duty that most had few civilian clothes and wore the uniform even on their time off. They were often on the road away from home for days at a time and lived out of their saddlebag.

Uniforms and equipment issued to patrolmen con-sisted of two pair of pants, one blouse jacket, one leather-billed cap, one Sam Brown Belt, a gun, a breast and a cap badge and a set of leather puttees. Puttees were soon replaced by brown leather riding boots. Pistols were .38 caliber with a four-inch barrel. Holsters were military style with a flap to cover the weapon and were worn for cross draw. Specially made swivel holsters were introduced within a couple of years. These were worn by the Patrol for many years.

The first breast badge of the Tennessee Highway Patrol was a stock eagle-top circle with the state seal in the center. The first hat or cap badge was the same style as had been worn by the State Police, an eagle-top medallion with crossed batons on either side of the state seal and a number panel below.

The number assigned to a patrolman appeared both on the breast badge and the cap badge. The same number also was stamped on the patrolman's sidearm and painted on the "motor" assigned to him. Patrolmen frequently referred to the motorcycle abbre-viated as the "motor." The number identified the patrolman and his essential equipment.

The design of the arm patch was a modified state seal with "Highway" at the top and "Patrol" at the bot-tom of the circle around the seal. The first patches were made of felt and worn on the left sleeve of the jacket approximately half way between the shoulder and the elbow. Initially, no patch was worn on the shirt.

Many of the new law officers had never ridden motorcycles. Johnny Burgess, formerly Chief of the State Police, served as the instructor for the initial training of the Patrol. He took the new men to Shelby Park in Nashville for motorcycle training. It was said that trainees at least learned to "aim" their motorcy-cles, if not to ride them. A number of times, men and cycles had to be fished out of the park lake, as well as hedges and ditches. The method of teaching the men to ride was said to be quite simple, place the man on the motorcycle, put the cycle on the rear wheel stand, start the motorcycle, rev it up and push the cycle off the stand. At that point it was every man for himself.

New patrolmen spent one month in training before beginning patrol duty on the highway. Training, other than operation of a motorcycle, included traffic laws, tax and revenue laws, court procedures and first aid. During training, the new patrolmen stayed at the Noel Hotel at Fourth and Church in downtown Nashville.

The workday was from 7:00 a.m. to 5:00 p.m. on Monday, Tuesday, Thursday and Friday, and from 1:00

Patrolmen and motorcycles undergo final inspection in Nashville's Memorial Square on March 12, 1930, prior to receiving assignments to patrol districts across the state. The first motorcycles had no markings other that a small sign atop the front fender that read "Tenn. Highway Patrol."

p.m. to 10:00 p.m. on Wednesday, Saturday and Sunday. The pay was $150 per month with an allowance of 50 cents per day for one meal.

Even before the new patrolmen went to work, impersonators took advantage of the public anticipation of their arrival. Two drunken taxi drivers were arrested for pulling a car over on the Murfreesboro Pike. When the incident was reported to Assistant Chief Joe Boyd Williams by Constable George Greer, he started an investigation. The two were arrested by Davidson County Motorcycle Officer H. G. Lokey and placed in jail. It was conjectured that other such cases had occurred but had not been officially reported.

A banquet was held at the Noel Hotel on the eve of the Patrol departing Nashville to take their assignments. Governor Henry Horton cautioned the men against the excesses of previous state police forces, "The eyes of Tennessee are upon you. You are going to make for yourselves and for your state a reputation. You go not as lords, but as servants of the people. You are chosen for what you are and the eyes of Tennessee are focused on you. The stranger in Tennessee must

receive every courtesy from your hand." Chief Davis reinforced the governor's caution, and reminded them, "You are primarily out to save lives."

The Tennessee Highway Patrol took to the highways of Tennessee on March 11, 1930. The *Nashville Banner* reported the charge given them by the chief and the commissioner.

> Members of the State Highway Patrol starting out on their assignment Tuesday were instructed by Chief J. O. Davis and Commissioner Charles McCabe of the Department of Finance and Taxation to watch for drunken drivers and keep the highways safe for motor traffic. They were designated as "Messengers of Good Will" by Commissioner McCabe, who also praised them for their deportment during their weeks of preliminary training.

Patrolmen disbursed from Nashville into 12 districts across the state, divided among 3 divisions. The 12 districts were established to be commanded by a sergeant. The sergeant was responsible for practically everything in his district. He was in charge of the men,

Patrolman John T. "Speedy" Mullen at Sky Harbor Airport on Murfreesboro Road in Nashville. The Harley Davidson motorcycle is one of the first with the THP custom paint job. The sign on the front fender was the only identification on the initial motorcycles purchased for the Patrol.

assigning them to roadways, determining their patrol route and schedule and specifying their duty. He was responsible for all the equipment, assuring sufficient tires and other routine supplies were maintained for motorcycles and automobiles.

The Chattanooga District was under Sergeant Robert S. Cravens of Chattanooga and had eight men to patrol the counties of Bledsoe, Bradley, Hamilton, Marion, McMinn, Polk, Rhea and Sequatchie. The Clarksville District was under Sergeant James English from Franklin and had four men to patrol the counties of Cheatam, Dickson, Houston, Humphrey, Montgomery, Robertson and Stewart. Clarksville patrolmen were Clyde T. May, George O. Pace and Ruben Payne. The Cookeville District was under

Sergeant Benton McMillin from Livingston and had four men to patrol the counties of Clay, Cumberland, DeKalb, Fentress, Jackson, Overton, Pickett, Putnam, Smith, Van Buren and White. Cookeville patrolmen were E. A. Farley, Sidney Outlaw and Hugh Blake.

The Jackson-Selmer District was under Sergeant Hallie Hamm from Selmer and had ten men to patrol the counties of Benton, Carroll, Chester, Decatur, Gibson, Hardeman, Hardin, Haywood, Henderson, Madison and McNairy. The Johnson City District was under Sergeant Joseph R. Morton of Bristol and had four men to patrol the counties of Carter, Hawkins, Johnson, Sullivan, Unicoi and Washington. The Knoxville District was under Sergeant John R. Norton from Centerville and had eight men to patrol the counties of Anderson, Blount, Campbell, Knox, Monroe, Morgan, Roane and Scott.

The Lawrenceburg District was under Sergeant Clyde Odil from Columbia and had four men to patrol the counties of Giles, Hardin, Hickman, Lawrence, Lewis, Perry and Wayne. Lawrenceburg patrolmen were Carl D. Hickman, Lee Loveless and Jerry Holt Jr. The Memphis District was under Sergeant Charles Monroe Hash from Springfield and had eight men to patrol the counties of Crockett, Fayette, Lauderdale, Shelby and Tipton. Memphis patrolmen included E. D. Petty and Clifford West. The Morristown District was under Sergeant Ambrose Hash from McMinnville and had four men to patrol the counties of Claiborne, Cook, Grainger, Greene, Jefferson, Sevier and Union.

The Nashville District was under Sergeant Homer Cook from Lewisburg and had eight men to patrol the counties of Davidson, Macon, Maury, Rutherford, Sumner, Trousdale, Williamson and Wilson. Nashville patrolmen included M. W. Williams, John Mullins, George O. Griffin, W. W. Hargis and T. J. Cottar. The Troy District was under Sergeant Marshall Wood from Dyersburg and had four men to patrol the counties of Dyer, Gibson, Henry, Obion and Weakley. The Tullahoma District was under Sergeant Marion C. Holt of Lynchburg and had 4 men to patrol the counties of Bedford, Cannon, Coffee, Franklin, Grundy, Lincoln, Marshall and Warren. Tullahoma patrolmen were N. G. Solomon, George H. Layman and F. L. Lynch.

The first offices for the new patrol were set up at the division garages of the state highway department. Over the next few years, the THP began to construct small structures in various parts of the state to provide basic district office facilities. The narrow stone buildings faced a major highway.

It was not long before a fourth division was formed. Sergeant Robert S. Cravens became the head of the Chattanooga Division. At that time the divisions were numbered. Knoxville became the First Division, Chattanooga the Second Division, Nashville the Third Division and Memphis the Fourth Division.

The Patrol immediately began a campaign to improve safety on the state's highways. An agreement was made with automobile service stations across the state to provide free safety inspections from April 14 through May 10. Governor Horton issued a proclamation declaring the period the "Save-a-Life" campaign, and urging drivers to take advantage of the free inspection of brakes, horn, lights, steering mechanism, windshield wipers and mirrors.

Less than a month following the celebratory banquet in the Noel Hotel and only days before the initiation of the "Save-a-Life" campaign, tragedy struck the young force. The date was April 3, 1930, a Thursday. Memphis District Sergeant Charles Monroe Hash was returning to Memphis with Patrolman E. D. Petty around 11:30 p.m. after a full day on patrol. Hash had stopped a car with faulty lights to warn the driver. Petty was about two blocks ahead of Hash and doing about 50 miles an hour on the Bristol Highway (Summer Avenue). Hash was traveling about 75 mile per hour in order to catch up.

A car had stopped in the oncoming lane waiting for another vehicle to pass before the driver turned onto Graham Avenue. As the driver began his turn, he saw Hash's motorcycle coming toward him and he stopped. Hash struck the car's left front wheel.

Sergeant Hash was thrown ten feet from the point of impact. His left leg was severed below the knee and broken above the knee. Along with internal injuries and multiple contusions, his left wrist was broken and his skull was fractured. Hash was rushed to Methodist Hospital on Union. His left leg was amputated at the hip, and initially he was expected to live. However, at 1:40 a.m. on Friday of the following week, April 11, 1930, Sergeant Charles M. Hash died of his injuries.

Hash was a native of Springfield, Tennessee, 31 years old and single. He served twelve years in the Navy before beginning his career in law enforcement. Patrolman Clifford West took his place as sergeant of Memphis District.

The incident marked the first death in the line of duty for the THP. Assistant Chief Toll Fowler warned his men that they would be suspended if they drove over 40 mph while on routine duty. Despite efforts to encourage safety, motorcycle patrol was dangerous. Hash was the first of 12 patrolmen to die as a result of a motorcycle accident in the Highway Patrol's initial thirteen years. Motorcycles became affectionately know as "Death on Wheels" to the men of the Patrol who rode them daily. In the history of the Tennessee Highway Patrol more officers were killed in the line of duty as a result of motorcycle accidents than from any other cause.

Reception of the Highway Patrol across the state was mixed. Even when the patrolmen were welcomed into a community, guidelines and expectations often accompanied the greeting. In his welcoming speech to the new patrolmen, Hohenwald Mayor Tom Petway stated, "Three words express the sentiments of Lewis County, help, aid, assist."

Knoxville District patrolmen stood with 1934 Ford patrol car #5. Patrolmen were in the standard uniform for patrol duty on motorcycles. Standing from left to right were Patrolman Roy Purky, an unidentified patrolman, Patrolman James Seehorn and Sergeant Niles Pace. Sergeant Pace is wearing a different badge style.

Relationships between the state agency and local agencies continued to be strained, in part due to the reputation of the State Police and in part due to general resentment of outside law enforcement. Many local lawmen saw the Patrol as outsiders who came to meddle in local affairs and usurp local authority. One local officer was quoted as saying, "They're sending people down here from Nashville to arrest my people and I ain't going to put up with it."

One patrolman reported going to a Middle Tennessee county at the request of authorities to slow down traffic. Eight or ten motorists were cited. The next day in court an attorney for one of the motorists asked the patrolman how fast his client was going. The officer answered, "60 miles per hour." After a few other questions the attorney asked, "And how fast did you have to go to catch my client?" The patrolman said, "Around eighty." The lawyer turned to the judge, "Give me a warrant for this officer's arrest." During the recess that followed, the patrolman was called to the phone. It was THP headquarters in Nashville. The lawman later reported how the episode ended, "They told me to get out of there and come back to Nashville. I did. They dropped the charges against me and I dropped the charges against his client. I guess you could say we compromised."

The Patrol was given special duty to protect revenues collected at the state's eight toll bridges. As the depression worsened, toll operators were being robbed with increasing frequency, plus some toll collectors were misappropriating fees. The THP was assigned to apprehend the guilty parties.

Patrolmen tried to provide nominal coverage in all counties of the state, even though there were more counties than patrolmen. In many counties they spent long hours on bad roads. Sometimes men left the district office and did not return for three or four weeks. In many small towns there was no hotel and they had to stay in boarding houses.

On one occasion, the citizens of Copperhill refused to purchase license plates. A contingent of patrolmen was dispatched to the town to collect the revenue. After finding no room at either of the two boarding houses in town, they asked a police officer of the town where they might stay. He told them that no one in town would board them for fear that somebody angered at having to purchase a license plate might blow up the boarding house. The patrolmen found a place to stay in Ducktown.

Patrolmen also spent a great amount of time checking privilege licenses of businesses. The impact of the

Increasing traffic on Tennessee's highway system kept the new patrol busy. Soon a similar accident took the life of THP Assistant Chief Edward Kennedy of the Knoxville Division.

nationwide depression on Tennessee made these revenues of great importance. Often the officers performed these tasks in civilian clothes in order to get inside the business. Patrolmen in plain clothes, license inspectors and other state revenue inspectors carried a smaller badge to identify themselves as members of the THP.

Authority was not given to the Patrol to carry weapons in the 1929 legislation and sometimes officers were arrested by local lawmen for carrying a sidearm. After one such incident where a patrolman was arrested in West Tennessee on a weapons charge, the 1931 state legislature enacted TCA-4-707 authorizing THP personnel to carry weapons.

It is lawful for Tennessee highway patrol officers employed by the Tennessee Highway Patrol to wear or carry a pistol at such times as they are in uniform and on active duty, in like manner as the city or metropolitan police officers.

Chief J. O. Davis remained in command of the Patrol in 1931. Benton McMillin was named as one of the assistant chiefs. Increasingly, highway patrolmen were asked to enforce laws not directly related to their primary duty. When the legislature passed a bill making it illegal to destroy or remove plants on public lands and on orders from Commissioner McCabe, Chief Davis to instruct members of the THP to protect trees, shrubs, vines, flowers, moss and turf along the states highways from vandals.

The practice of moving patrol officers from place to place became a routine part of the management of the THP, especially to discipline officers. Local leaders often asked reconsideration when a patrolman in their area received orders to move. Commissioner McCabe in a May 5, 1931, letter responding to one such request, explained the reason for the policy, "We have learned from experience that the State Highway Patrol renders more efficient service when its members are

moved occasionally than when they work in the same place over a long period of time." Those most likely to be moved were men who were the target of complaints.

Albert Williams was appointed Commissioner of the Department of Finance and Taxation in 1932 and Joe Boyd Williams was appointed Chief of the Patrol. The two remained in the positions for only one year. The Highway Patrol was often more affected by political changes and actions at the state level, than local politics. Many patrolmen fell to the political axe in the 1932 when the election brought a new administration to power. The force was reduced to 36, about half of its original strength.

A number of factors likely contributed to the reduction in force. Members of the Patrol may have been politically aligned with the incumbents, or may have antagonized local officials who were aligned with the new administration. Budget cuts due to the economy played a role as well.

Three assistant chiefs under Chief Joe Boyd Williams were Homer Cook in Nashville, Servis L. Evrard in Knoxville and Hallie Hamm in Memphis. Monthly pay for the chief was $333.33, $250 for assistant chiefs, $165 for sergeants, $150 for patrolmen and $125 for newly hired patrolmen.

Commissioner Dancy Fort was appointed to head the Department of Finance and Taxation in 1933 by Governor Hill McAlistar. Dancy Fort was born in Adams, Robertson County, in 1870. He graduated from Cumberland University with a law degree in 1891 and practiced law in state and federal court. Fort served as State Senator from Robertson and Montgomery counties from 1907 to 1911. After his term as Commissioner, he served as judge of the Ninth District. Benton McMillin was selected to serve as Chief of the THP. Both men served until 1937. James English was named Chief of the Nashville Division.

The depressed economy had an additional impact on patrolmen in 1933. Salaries of patrolmen were cut from $150 to $100 per month. Sergeants' salaries dropped to $125. The pay scale remained depressed for a decade. The per diem for a meal was reduced to 35 cents and if a patrolman claimed the full amount for every day, Memphis Assistant Chief Hallie Hamm would ask, "What, did you have onions on all those hamburgers?"

Fifty-one persons worked for the Tennessee Highway Patrol in 1933. By category they were Chief Benton McMillin; two assistant chiefs, James English and Hallie Hamm; five sergeants, M. S. Anderson, John T. Davis, Tyler Green, Stirling B. Odom and B. M. Wood; one desk sergeant, Tyler Berry; 31 patrol-

Accessories for the winter uniforms of patrolmen while riding motorcycles including a leather headcover and goggles. Patrolmen wore heavy leather gloves with large cuffs. Some patrolmen wore the mitten-style gloves produced for Harley-Davidson, shown on the right.

men, J. B. Albright, Scott Alexander, William Carter, Clovis Lee Cole, W. J. Evins, W. E. Foote, James T. Gill, T. M. Godwin, George O. Griffin, W. C. Hale, James R. Harrison, Carl Hickman, M. L. Hogan, Stanley Jackson, R. W. Jett, Homer F. Johnson, E. C. Johnston, Trabue Lewis, Lee Loveless, Clyde T. May, Fred Mayo, Hobson Mayo, Clyde Odil, George Pace, James T. Phelps, S. C. Rhodes, H. E. Ruffin, Joe S. Shipp, Hugh Slate, C. P. Smith and Shobe Smith; three privilege tax inspectors, F. L. Lynch, Sidney Outlaw and J. A. Scandlyn; two mechanics, Walter R. Jones and D. H. Walp; and six stenographers, Mrs. Estelle Bailey, Ruth Crain, Louise Ellis, Alexia Marshall, Inez Shipp and Mrs. H. G. Trythall.

Assistant Chief James "Jim" English was in charge of the Third or Nashville Division and Assistant Chief Hallie Hamm commanded the Memphis Division. The other two divisions were temporarily under the command of sergeants. The Fourth Division (Memphis) covered the western end of the state from the Mississippi state line to the Kentucky state line and from the Mississippi River to the Tennessee River. The division consisted of Assistant Chief Hallie Hamm, Sergeant B. Marshall Wood, four patrolmen in Memphis, two in Jackson, one in Selmer, one in Dyersburg, one in Union City, and one in Paris.

Assistant Chief R. A. McMillan, a Knoxville attorney and lieutenant colonel in the Army Reserve, took command of the THP First Division (Knoxville) on May 1, 1933. McMillan developed either physical or emotional problems and went "mysteriously missing" from his post in July. Patrol Chief Benton McMillin went to Knoxville and put Sergeant John T. Davis in temporary command.

Edward Eugene Kennedy, a friend of McMillan's, was made assistant chief of the division in 1932. Kennedy was an active proponent of automobile safety, establishing several branches of the Knoxville Safety Council.

The danger that patrolmen faced was evidenced by those who were not on this list two years later. Three THP members lost their lives in the line of duty within a single year from mid-1933 to mid-1934. On the last day of July 1933, mechanic Walter Ray Jones, 34, was killed in Nashville on a motorcycle. Patrolman Lee Glenn Loveless, 25, died on February 3, 1934, from injuries suffered in a motorcycle accident on Highway

Patrolman Willie West "Bill" Harmon and his motorcycle were outfitted for winter patrol duty. Harmon joined the Patrol in 1936.

24 in Smith County a week earlier. Three months later, May 2, Sergeant Clovis Lee Cole died from injuries received in a motorcycle crash at court square in Union City on April 29.

Equipment was at a premium during the early years of the THP. Carlton V. French joined the Patrol the day before Loveless' fatal accident. Nashville Division Assistant Chief Jim English told French, "We've got an old raggedy motorcycle. That's all we have left out there for you to ride." Unit number 29 was about worn out and French asked, "What about number 13 motorcycle?" Number 13 was the unit on which Loveless died. English told him he could have the unit as soon as it was repaired.

Patrolman H. Trabue "Trib" Lewis near Waverly in 1934 on motorcycle #17.

Sergeant John Davis on patrol in 1934. Davis later became assistant chief of the Knoxville division. Emergency equipment on motorcycles included a red light on the left side of the handle bars, a white light on the right and a friction siren.

Patrolman French was assigned to the Memphis Division on March 1, 1934, and joined patrolmen Homer Johnson, H. S. Crow and one other in the Memphis District under Sergeant Clifford West. Assistant Chief Hallie Hamm commanded the division, and Alexia Marshall was his secretary. The division had a small space in the Traffic Bureau of the Memphis Police Department. Assistant Chief Hamm followed Toll Fowler, the first commander of the division. Hamm was followed by Marshall Wood, Jim Galloway, and Clifford West as assistant chief of the division during the 1930s. Clifford West was sometimes headstrong and was transferred a couple of times, to Knoxville and to Chattanooga, before being appointed assistant chief in Memphis.

French rode unit number 29 for a few weeks until number 13 was repaired, getting a new front fender and crash bar. When French left Memphis to exchange motorcycles the temperature was 22 degrees. The thermometer read 18 when he reached Nashville and patrolmen at headquarters had to help him off the motorcycle. Number 13 became French's badge, pistol and motorcycle number for the next ten years, and he got sergeant's badge 13 on his promotion.

The Tennessee Highway Patrol lost one of its chiefs on August 22, 1934 from injuries suffered in an automobile accident the day before. Knoxville Division Assistant Chief Ed Kennedy's car was involved in a head-on crash on Highway 70 at the top of Cumberland Mountain near Crab Orchard in Roane County. The chief died at 8:00 a.m. the following day.

Assistant Chief Kennedy was a passenger in his own car at the time of the wreck. He seldom drove his own car because he did not consider himself a good driver. Kennedy was reported to have survived five other fatal car crashes, one of which occurred in 1909 and was the first fatal automobile accident in the city of Knoxville. Assistant Chief Kennedy was 52 and the highest-ranking officer of the Patrol killed in the line of duty.

Three months later, the Tennessee Highway Patrol lost the first officer to gunfire. Patrolman Lindsley D. Smith was shot to death in Tullahoma. A call was received at the police station at one o'clock Sunday afternoon, December 2, 1934, that a drunken man was beating his wife. Tullahoma Patrolman Ernest C. Armstrong drove to the residence. The subject came out of his house with a .45 caliber automatic pistol and shot Armstrong in the left chest, the bullet pushing his badge into his flesh. A second shot entered his body under the right arm and a third lodged in his spinal

Patrolman Carlton V. French on motor #29, the first motorcycle he rode when he joined the Tennessee Highway Patrol in 1934. French had just finished tightening everything up on the unit, note the tool kit on the sidewalk behind the cycle, and was about to ride it from Memphis to Nashville and exchange it for motorcycle unit # 13. Photo was in mid-March, 1934, in front of French's house.

Patrolman Clifford West, Patrolman Rudy Jehl and Patrolman Carlton French, three of the Memphis men from left to right, circa 1935 on Union Avenue.

The Tennessee Highway Patrol gathered circa 1936 at the Parthenon in Nashville. Commissioner of Taxation and Finance Dancy Fort stood in the front row in an overcoat. Those from left to right in the front row were Assistant Chief Clyde May of the Chattanooga Division, Assistant Chief James English of the Nashville Division, Fort, Chief of the Patrol Benton McMillin, Assistant Chief John T. Davis of the Knoxville Division, and Assistant Chief Marshall Wood of the Memphis Division.

cord, paralyzing the officer. Armstrong was able to get off one shot before he fell to the street. He hit his shooter in the arm.

Tennessee Highway Patrolman Smith and THP Sergeant W. C. Hale were at City Hall when the alarm came in of the shooting. Smith sped to the scene on his motorcycle. Sergeant Hale and Charles Holt, assistant city waterworks superintendent and Tullahoma Fire Chief, took Holt's truck to the scene.

The officers learned that the drunken gunman had hidden at a nearby church. They found him in the crawl space beneath the building. Holt fired his shotgun, striking the gunman. The drunk scrambled from under the church firing his .45. Holt was shot and fell dead about fifty feet away as he ran for cover. Highway Patrolman Smith came around the church he was shot through the left arm and both lungs. Highway Patrol Sergeant Hale next exchanged shots with the man. Hale hit the gunman in the stomach and in the head, killing him instantly.

Tullahoma Patrolman Armstrong and Highway Patrolman Smith were rushed to hospitals in Nashville. Highway Patrol Sergeant Clyde Odil was injured in a collision with an automobile as he and Highway

Patrolman F. L. Lynch were speeding down Gallatin Road to meet Smith's ambulance and escort it to Protestant Hospital.

Patrolman Lindsley D. Smith died of gunshot wounds on December 17, 1934, becoming the third lawman killed in the incident. Officer Armstrong died the week before. Smith was 38 years old and had been assigned to duty in the district only a short time earlier.

Traffic patrol on a motorcycle continued to be the most dangerous duty. Patrolman Landon Earl Hicks was killed in a Roane County accident, three miles outside of Kingston, on June 17, 1936. Patrolman Paul Summers died after his motorcycle struck a car on Franklin Road as he returned to Nashville around midnight on August 8, 1936. Many patrolmen were also seriously injured aboard motorcycles during these years. Patrolman Bill Pearson was en route from the Lawrenceburg office to assume duties in Knoxville when a car pulled into his path. He sustained a broken ankle and head injuries.

The majority of patrolmen were involved in some type of motorcycle mishap. As long as serious injury was avoided, officers often found a humorous side to the incident. Patrolman Carlton French was chasing a carload of drunks when two bird dogs ran over the shoulder of the road and into his path. French swung his motorcycle and missed the first, but not the second. "I hit him and went sliding down the highway. It tore the Sam Brown belt in two and tore my britches off me just like you'd take a pair of scissors and cut them off," he recalled. "I bought an old sweater and cut the sleeves out. I pulled it down like a skirt and came on into Memphis." In addition to losing a pair of britches, French broke his collarbone in the accident.

The Tennessee Highway Patrol grew in success and recognition through the mid-1930s. Not only was it becoming a continuous presence on the highways of Tennessee, it performed many ceremonial duties in the state including escorting the kings and queens of the Memphis Cotton Carnival. It also played a significant role in representing Tennessee in the parade at the annual National Convention of the American Legion.

The tradition of appearing in the American Legion parade began in 1933 when 16 patrolmen rode motorcycles to Chicago. They left at 3:00 a.m. from Nashville and arrived that evening at 7:00 p.m. It took the unit two days to get to Miami the next year. They appeared in the convention parade every year until World War II and resumed in 1948, returning to Miami. Sergeant H. Trabue "Trib" Lewis was in charge of the unit following the war. The motorcycles were shipped by train or truck to parade sites. The units often arrived strewn on the floor of the transport when they arrived. Trib Lewis got communication technician

Memphis District Sergeant Charles Monroe Hash, left, was returning to Memphis on April 3, 1930, when a car pulled into the path of his motorcycle. Sergeant Hash died on April 11, the first THP officer killed in the line of duty. East Tennessee Assistant Chief Edward Kennedy, right, was killed as a result of injuries suffered in a head on collision near the top of Cumberland Mountain near Crab Orchard on August 22, 1934.

James Beal to build transport stands for the motorcycles.

The Highway Patrol, Motor Vehicle and Mileage Tax Unit grew to 114 personnel by 1936. Supervisors were Chief Benton McMillin; four assistant chiefs, John T. Davis (Knoxville), James English (Nashville), Clyde May (Chattanooga) and Marshall Wood (Memphis); one chief inspector, Wade Hampton; 14 sergeants, G. W. Griffin, W. C. Hale, R. Willard Jett, S. F. Johnson, S. B. Odom, Clyde Odil, George Pace, Niles Y. Pace, Albert Pearson, Sidney B. Outlaw, J. A. Scandlyn, Hugh Slate, C. F. Webb and Clifford West; and one desk sergeant, H. A. Ormes.

Additional law enforcement personnel were 47 patrolmen, M. S. Anderson, Jim H. Albright, Scott Alexander, H. K. Carrier, C. C. Connor, H. S. Crow, S. W. Crowe, Gordon Dickson, V. W. Dowland, A. H. Duggins, Ross Dyer, W. E. Foote, Carlton V. French, James T. Gill, James R. Harrison, Raymond C. Hennessee, Carl Hickman, L. E. Hicks, M. L. Hogan, W. G. Holden, Rudy E. Jehl, Homer F. Johnson, Trabue Lewis, Earl Lucas, F. L. Lynch, Fred Mayo, Hobson Mayo, John M. McKenzie, J. N. McMackin, Robert Mitchell, John L. Nolen, Wiseman Parkhurst, James Phelps, Robert Robinson, H. E. Ruffin, Hollis Simmons, C. P. Smith, Shobe Smith, Jesse Speegle, Paul Summers, Ed Cole Taylor, Melton Taylor, Charles

Tennessee continued to upgrade highway signage to enhance traffic safety. Chester Hamby, left, posed with road sign that warns of a dangerous curve ahead, and Assistant Chief Clifford West, right, showed off a new speed limit sign.

Thompson, Paul Thompson, Charles Wayland Jr., Charles W. Ward and William Winfrey; and 15 license inspectors, Doc Allen, John Bond Jr., A. J. Brandon Jr., Frances Hudson, Delbert Kennedy, Solon Maddux, Chester Mathis, Harry Miller, Paul Monasco, Roy Oakley, Albert Rhodes, John Shea, Lee Taylor, Wade Thompson and Connie Wilkinson.

Support personnel were one mechanic, H. D. Walp; one secretary to the chief, Amy Light; one mileage tax clerk, Ed Malone; one license clerk, Ollie

Two THP officers involved in the first line of duty death resulting from a shooting. Patrolman Lindsley Smith, left, was shot to death in Tullahoma in December 1934 as he and other lawmen tried to arrest a wife-beater. Sergeant W. C. Hale, on the right, shot and killed Smith's assailant who had also killed two other officers. (Nashville Banner photo)

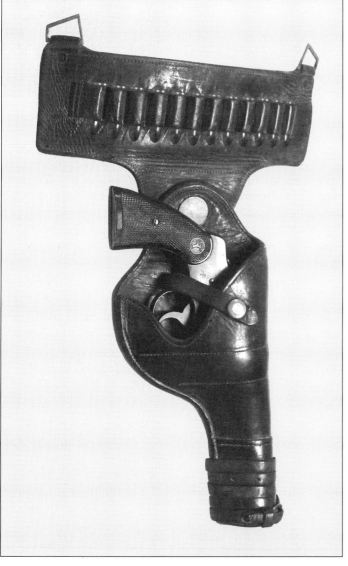

Patrolmen were issued Colt .38 caliber, 4" barrel Police Model revolvers. Perfection Brand swivel holsters were made especially for and marked "Tennessee Highway Patrol" by Charles T. Hulan of Wartrace, Tennessee. Twelve round of ammunition were carried in loops at the top of the holster, which also included brass attachment for the Sam Brown belt. The bottom of the holster was equipped with a tie-down strap, but patrolmen often wrapped the strap around the base of the holster. The pistol pictured here is No. 129, carried by Chester Hamby, who also wore badge No. 129.

Dillingham; eight clerks, John Bostick, Mattie Lou Cooper, Martha Earthman, Elizabeth Epperson, Mrs. C. M. Hamilton, Mrs. Turner Johnson, Mrs. Pearl Kirkpatrick and Inez Shipp; fourteen stenographers, Lilly Hugh Anderson, Dean Buie, Ruth Crain, Elizabeth Dorris, Mrs. Ross Dunn, Loretta Hughes, Georgianna Hunley, Virginia Lowe, Alexia Marshall, Ruth Rundle, Mrs. H. G. Tyrthall, Wylene Wilcox, Mrs. Thelma Wilson and Mrs. William Wilson; one ditto machine operator, Albert Wilson; one multigraph operator, L. A. Willoughby, one assistant multigraph operator, L. P. Seigentaler; and two porters, Judge Buford and Harry Mills.

Willie West "Bill" Harmon, the first highway patrolman hired from Sequatchie County, and Patrolman Patton, the first hired from Bledsoe County, joined the Patrol in 1936. As other patrolmen, they worked all over the state. Patrolman Bill Harmon was assigned to the Chattanooga District, but worked mostly in Middle Tennessee in the Clarksville and Manchester areas.

The Department of Administration was created in 1937. Commissioner Wallace Edwards headed the department by appointment of Governor Gordon W. Browning. The 65-member THP was moved from the

Department of Finance and Taxation to the Department of Administration. Wallace Edwards was born in Cottage Grove, Henry County, Tennessee in 1897. He served during World War I in the Headquarters Company of the 114th Field Artillery. After the war he served as trustee of Henry County and for three and a half years as secretary to Governor Henry Horton.

Chief Joe Boyd Williams again headed the Patrol for the next two years. The work of the Patrol was significantly expanded during the year as was its personnel. The number of uniformed men in the THP at the start of 1937 was 110. By the end of the year, the Patrol had nearly 200 employees. New patrolmen worked six months without a day off. After that they got two days off a month, but days off could not include Saturday, Sunday or a holiday.

A redistribution of patrolmen was ordered as a part of the restructuring. Patrolman Carl Hickman was reassigned to Athens as part of the transfers ordered. Patrolmen Hickman and W. A. Winfrey were made partners on motorcycles duty. They were traveling north on Lee Highway outside of Chattanooga on the afternoon of September 15, 1937, when a school bus made a left turn crossing their path. Patrolman Winfrey swerved to the right, sideswiped the bus, and managed to keep his balance, suffering only minor injuries to his left hand. Patrolman Hickman was killed instantly when he struck the bus and was thrown 20 to 30 feet.

Three of the new patrolmen added in 1937 were Chester Lee Hamby, Cecil W. Strader and Lewis R. Boone. Strader went on the Patrol straight out of high school. Hamby was 22 years old and the first patrol-man appointed from Roane County. Boone was 23 and from Erin. They were typical of the young men joining the THP. Hamby told his friends, "I had hardly been out of Roane County, then I joined the Highway Patrol. They sent me to Memphis and gave me a gun and a motorcycle. Boy, was that a rude awakening." Patrolman Carlton French served as Hamby's training officer.

The Highway Patrol adopted a new breast badge for patrolmen and sergeants. An eagle-top pinched shield in silver tone was worn by patrolmen and in gold tone by sergeants. Supervisors above the rank of sergeant continued to wear an eagle-top sunburst style badge that had been adopted a few years earlier. The hat badge remained the same.

The THP was involved with all aspects of public safety including assisting natural disaster victims. The Patrol did extensive emergency duty during the 1937 flood. In Memphis, patrolmen were assigned for a time to the Memphis Police Department to escort and assist refuges from up river that landed along Riverside Drive. Refuges were bused to flood shelters at Central High School and the Fairgrounds.

Patrolman Carlton French was assigned to assist flood victims in Dyersburg and hauled refugees by automobile from the Finley schoolhouse to the Methodist church on high ground. Before the job was finished, the exhaust pipe had to be removed to keep the engine from drowning out.

French boarded a Coast Guard cutter in Finley to help victims along the Mississippi River. The cutter came upon a barn with floodwaters covering part of the roof. They heard a radio playing inside. One of the Coast Guard men jumped off the boat, knocked a hole

Members of the Highway Patrol and other law enforcement officers gathered to honor Patrolman Earl Hicks. Hicks was killed in a Knox County accident on Monday, June 1, 1936, while on patrol. Motorcycle duty was dangerous and claimed the lives of many patrolmen in the early years of the force.

In 1938 Patrolmen Gordon "Pop" Dickson, left, and Chester Lee Hamby rode the "70 Beat," Highway 70 between Memphis and East Tennessee. They patrolled the highways until nightfall, staying in a town along the route and continuing patrol the next day. They learned chasing a speeder down a gravel road was dangerous for a motorcycle officer.

in the roof and saw a man laying on the hay listening to a radio. The sailor said, "Come on boy, get out of there, this thing is fixing to float away." The radio listener replied, "No, I'm alright, go on about your business, but ain't them folks up in Louisville having a hell of a time?"

Two patrolmen were killed in the line of duty and a number of others injured in fall 1938, all while patrolling on motorcycles. A patrolman was injured on the Asheland Highway on his way to Knoxville to help direct traffic at the American Legion Air Show on September 24. Sergeant W. G. Holden was injured in a crash at the show.

Patrolman Lewis R. Boone, one of the 1937 recruits, was thrown from his sidecar equipped motorcycle and killed on October 18, 1938, near Pigeon Forge. He had been riding a standard two-wheeler and received the new motorcycle earlier that day. Shortly before 8:00 p.m. the sidecar struck a ditch and the motor was thrown into a rock bluff.

Another young officer, Patrolman Charles J. Gearhiser, 24, who was seriously injured the previous June in a collision with a car in downtown Dyersburg, was killed on the outskirts of town on November 12, 1938. He and Patrolman Clarence Turner were patrolling the Dyersburg-Jackson Highway. As they topped the crest of a hill, Patrolman Gearhiser pulled his motor to the right to avoid an oncoming truck and struck Turner's motorcycle. Turner was thrown clear and treated for a cut on the back of his head. Gearhiser bounded into the side of the truck and fell to the highway. The patrolman was pinned to his motorcycle as it slid 75 feet along the highway. As so many others killed in motorcycle crashes, Patrolman Gearhiser died of head injuries.

Highway patrolmen adjusted their life style to motorcycle duty. A patrolmen often left his home station on a motorcycle, patrolled until nightfall and spent the night in a town on the route. The next day he continued patrol. If he stopped someone, he left his motorcycle and drove the man's car to the nearest justice of the peace's office. After the hearing, the patrolman had to get back to his motorcycle the best way he could. With no radio, if the district headquarters needed to reach the patrolman, they would call a grocery or other store along the route. The patrolmen stopped at selected stores to check for messages.

Patrolman Chester Hamby rode the "70 Beat," traveling U.S. Highway 70 from Memphis into East Tennessee. The duty provided Hamby a good opportunity to visit his home and wife in Harriman, located on U.S. 70. Patrolman Hamby frequently rode with Patrolman Gordon "Pop" Dickson. Patrolman Mitchell Moody, stationed at Rockford, rode a "beat" that took him up Asheland Highway to Dandridge, across to Rutledge, and back down Rutledge Pike.

Hamby quickly learned the difficulties of chasing a car on a motorcycle. Often when he got after a speeder, the driver headed for a gravel road. The chase was over at that point, because it was almost impossible to maneuver a motorcycle at high speed on gravel.

Patrolmen had to keep their guard up all the time. One night Patrolman Hamby arrested a drunk driver. He parked his motorcycle and got into the automobile. The man's female companion was sitting in the front seat of the car while Hamby drove it to a justice of peace. The woman was wearing high-heel shoes. Hamby noticed her cross her leg and begin fumbling with her shoes. The next thing he knew, she had hit him in the head with one of her high-heel shoes.

Local officials often called on the Highway Patrol for hazardous duty. In one case, a man in Haletown on the Tennessee River near Jasper killed his entire family and barricaded himself in the house. Sheriff's personnel and other local lawmen refused to go in and called on the Patrol. Highway Patrolman Bill Harmon went into the house, pulled the killer out and put him in jail.

Patrolmen weighed trucks with portable scales to be certain they did not exceed the weight limit for commercial vehicles.

Less hazardous duties included checking privilege licenses and collecting mileage tax on out of state trucks. Such duties were particularly unpopular in the years of the Great Depression, but the revenue was crucial to the state. Trucks frequently hauled loads that exceeded the maximum weight limit. To prove the excess weight a patrolman had to weigh the truck with a portable hand scale. The situation was usually only a nuisance for the trucker, because the compensation from his excess load more than covered the fine.

Operation of the hand scales required that the patrolman position the scales and have the truck drive up on the scales. He then flipped two levers to get the weight reading. This was repeated two more times, because the combined readings on all three axles were required to determine the weight of the truck.

The Patrol was assigned a new duty when the legislature passed the Tennessee Driver License Law in 1937, making Tennessee the 32nd state to require a driver's license. The THP was charged with administering the drivers license program. The Safety Education unit was also organized in 1937 to encourage driver safety.

The driver license law provided a six-month grace period during which motorists could acquire a license by mail at a cost of 50 cents per year without having to take a test. Over half a million licenses were issued before testing began. A driver manual was available in January 1938 and the first tests were administered on April 18 at a number of locations.

Passenger buses were big business in the 1930s and a bus was required to have a Tennessee license if it passed through the state. Sometimes a bus company interpreted the law loosely. Patrolman Carlton French rode 61 Highway from Memphis to the Mississippi

Patrolman Willie West "Bill" Harmon, left, and Assistant Chief C. F. "Dick" Webb in front of the Second Division THP office in Chattanooga in 1938. Harmon had the largest number of traffic convictions in the division for the year.

state line. He often stopped for a cold drink just across the state line at a country store. While there one day, a Greyhound Lines bus from Mississippi stopped and soon one from Tennessee pulled in. In front of the patrolman, the two bus drivers switched their license tags.

When French got back to headquarters, he told Assistant Chief Clifford West, "I'm fixing to stir up a hornet's nest," and explained what he had seen. The following day he rode back to the state line and again observed the exchange of license tags. He followed the northbound bus until it was well in the state of Tennessee, then he stopped the bus and gave the driver a ticket. In court the bus company was fined and the next day the company purchased $20,000 worth of Tennessee license tags.

The Chattanooga Division, under Assistant Chief C. F. "Dick" Webb, led the patrol in traffic arrest convictions in 1938 with 1,376, collecting $13,900 in

fines. Patrolman W. W. "Bill" Harmon had the largest number of convictions and Patrolman Earl A. Lucas produced the largest amount of fines. Other statistics for the division that year included 457,800 miles traveled, 19,119 warnings issued, 24,951 drivers licenses checked and road information given to 6,833 motorists.

The Accident Records Bureau was established on January 1, 1938, to receive and maintain accident reports. The bureau resulted from a 1937 law requiring motorists to report all accidents to state officials.

Sergeant E. C. McGlynnan and Patrolman Matthew "Matt" Pratt headed the Accident Prevention Bureau established in 1939 and worked with each district to promote safety. One method used was development of maps for each county on which traffic danger spots were marked for the benefit of patrolmen and the public. Sergeant Jimmy Phelps worked with Pratt on maps for Madison County and other counties in the Jackson District.

The year 1939 was the most significant year in the history of the Tennessee Highway Patrol since its creation a decade earlier. The Public Acts of 1939 distributed the responsibilities of the Department of Administration among a number of newly created departments. As a part of this legislation, the Department of Safety was created. Newly elected Governor Prentice Cooper appointed G. Hilton Butler as director of the Department of Safety at an annual salary of $4,200.

The department was divided into three divisions, the Highway Patrol Division, the Driver's License Division and the Safety Education Division. Director Butler had direct command of the Highway Patrol Division and served as Chief of the Patrol Division as well as director of the department. The rank of Lieutenant was created in January 1939 to assist in day to day operations of the Patrol Division and R. Willard Jett was promoted as the first holder of the rank. The Driver's License Division was under Supervisor and Chief Clerk Howell MacPherson and Safety Consultant George Morelock was responsible for the Safety Education Division.

Governor Cooper fired patrolmen across the state and hired back those he wanted to keep, plus he hired new officers. Greg L. O'Rear was one of the first new patrolmen to join the Department of Safety. O'Rear began his law enforcement career on May 1, 1939, at the salary of $120 a month for a 12-hour workday and two days off a month. Before his career ended he served multiple times as Commander of the Patrol and Commissioner of the Department of Safety.

A supervisor flanked by two patrolmen in 1936 stand in front of the recently constructed Rockwood office. The patrolman standing on the far right was Mitchell Moody.

Prentice Cooper was campaigning for Governor in Lawrenceburg in 1938 and saw O'Rear in the crowd. O'Rear was working in the Salant shirt factory at the time and playing semi-pro baseball and basketball. He had gained notoriety locally by scoring 100 points in a basketball game. Cooper told the 6' 8" and 245-pound O'Rear to come see him after the election. It was said that the Governor asked, "O'Rear, can you ride a motorcycle?," and O'Rear answered, "I think so, Governor, but if I can't, I can tote it under my arm."

The following spring O'Rear went to see the Governor and joined the 65-member force. After 30 days of training at the YMCA in Nashville and a brief assignment in Nashville area, he was sent to Lawrence County. He was the only patrolman in the area and his office was a filing cabinet in a corner of the Lawrenceburg City Hall. O'Rear patrolled west to Jackson, east to Winchester, north to Nashville and south to the Alabama state line. His abilities brought rapid promotions to Corporal in 1942 and to Sergeant in 1944. He recalled the life of a patrolman during his early career with a *Nashville Tennessean* reporter.

We had mostly rock dirt roads back then. I had to cover them in every kind of weather on an 80 Harley Davidson. It didn't make any difference if the temperature was down to zero. The motorcycle had a windshield on it. That kept some of the cold off. The only time you didn't ride was when there was too much ice on the road.

You would be riding down the road and a fellow at a country store would flag you down and tell you to call the office. We didn't have radios then. There would be a wreck somewhere.

You were out there by yourself. Several times, a car I would be chasing would force me off the road. A motorcycle can't fight a car. I was lucky. I never got hurt that way.

The only time I ever had a spill was in front of Vanderbilt hospital. This driver . . . drove out in front of me. I left the motorcycle. I slid for about 50 feet. I would slide for a while on my belly. That would get too hot and I would slide on my back for a while. It messed up my uniform and it didn't do my hide any good, but I wasn't hurt too badly.

If you arrested a drunk driver, you locked your motorcycle on the spot. You drove his car to the jail and hitchhiked back.

Patrolman Greg O'Rear stood by his motor soon after joining the Tennessee Highway Patrol. When O'Rear was hired, he was asked by the governor if he could ride a motorcycle. O'Rear responded, "I think so, Governor, but if I can't, I can tote it under my arm."

Motorcycle Patrolman Chester Lee Hamby in April 1939, on his 25th birthday, a few days before he was paralyzed in an accident as he was on his way to the Peabody Hotel to escort Governor Prentice Cooper.

I worked a lot with sheriff's officers, helping them raid stills and joints that were selling liquor. We raided a few slot machine places, too.

The Patrol continued to build expertise in both traffic and other law enforcement. Willard Jett had attended the FBI National Academy in Washington, D.C., while he was a sergeant in 1938, becoming the first Tennessee Highway Patrol officer to take advantage to the federal training. James English soon attended the school as well, giving the Patrol two graduates of the FBI National Academy.

Three Patrol officers attended the National Institute for Traffic Safety at the University of Michigan in

August 1939. George Morelock, safety consultant of the Safety Education Division studied safety organization and public education. Patrolman Matt Pratt studied accident investigation. Sergeant Edmund McGlynnan, head of the Accident Reporting Bureau, studied accident reports and records.

The FBI began providing training at the state and local levels. Sergeants James T. Phelps, Sam Johnston, and James T. Gill and Patrolmen Lawrence A. "Blackie" Mayfield, Mitchell Moody, T. D. Seymour, Matt Pratt, Robert Bibb, Clyde Keeson and Bill Williams attended a two-week FBI School at the University of Tennessee in January 1940.

Fourteen Patrol officers representing districts across the state attended the two-week National Institute for Traffic Safety Training at the University of Tennessee in August 1940. The group was led by Sergeant Claude Briley and included Sergeants E. C. McGlynnan and Stirling Odom and Patrolmen Matt Pratt, O. B. Garner, Virgil Orr, Lawrence "Blackie" Mayfield, George Clanton, Rudy Jehl, David Glass, Robert Routt, Cecil W. Strader, Ted Fowlkes and Carl Hill.

Danger continued to be a part of wearing the badge and often when least expected. A gun battle broke out in Jackson about 11 o'clock on a March night in 1939. Jackson District Patrolman LaVerne H. Maxwell had finished his tour and was on his way to the Neely Hotel for the night when a drunk staggered across Royal Street and fell directly in the path of his patrol car. Maxwell dodged the man, but stopped to check on him.

As Maxwell approached, the drunk got up, pulled a .32 caliber revolver and began firing. Patrolman Maxwell pulled his .38 and returned fire. The drunk emptied his pistol, missing Maxwell. Maxwell hit the drunk in the right shoulder, the right arm and the right leg. The drunk lived to face charges despite the three bullet wounds.

Danger from reckless drivers was usually unexpected as well. Patrolman Chester Hamby was one of the motorcycle officers acting as personal escort to Governor Prentice Cooper during the 1939 Memphis Cotton Carnival. On the morning of April 15, 1939, Hamby was scheduled to escort Governor Cooper and Governors for two adjoining states to the Mississippi state line for a trip to Jackson, Mississippi.

Hamby was en route to the Peabody Hotel when a car pulled out in front of his motorcycle at the corner of Union Avenue and Watkins Street. He was thrown fifteen feet over and beyond the car. The accident ended Hamby's career with the Patrol. His spine was broken and he remained paralyzed from the waist down for the rest of his life.

Hamby had been reinstated to the THP only a few days before the accident occurred. He was one of the patrolmen fired when Cooper's administration came into office and then rehired. After his recuperation, Hamby was elected a Justice of the Peace in Roane County in 1942 and continued in that role until his death in 1961. He kept in touch with his friends on the patrol and frequently saw a number of them when they brought lawbreakers to be tried before him as JP.

Highway patrolmen were about to face new dangers. As a part of the Act creating the Department of

Safety, the Patrol was assigned enforcement duty for the Local Option Liquor Law, the Livestock Control and Regulation of Livestock Diseases Act, the Forest Fire Fighting Law, the Aeronautics Board of Public Utilities and regulation of advertising signs on highway right-of-ways.

The axe became the primary weapon for a new enforcement effort launched in 1939. Governor Prentice Cooper was determined to curb the flaunting of state and county liquor and gaming laws across Tennessee by roadhouses and other establishments. Department of Safety Director G. Hilton Butler was reluctant to undertake the night raiding activity desired by the Governor.

Their disagreement came to a head in the summer of 1939. Governor Cooper and Director Butler met with West Tennessee Division Assistant Chief Clifford West and Senior Patrolman Carlton French in a Humboldt hotel during the Strawberry Festival. Cooper laid out a plan for the Memphis patrolmen to begin liquor raids.

As they wrote down the places Cooper wanted them to raid Butler said, "They're not going to do that. I'm Chief of the Highway Patrol and they're not going to raid." Cooper turned and said, "Butler, I'm the Governor. They're going to raid, and if you don't like it, you can quit." Butler did quit, effective August 1939, saying, "I ain't no policeman." Butler remained on the Governor's staff as an administrative assistant.

Major Tom E. Morris was appointed to succeed Butler as Director of the Department of Safety and served as functional Chief of the Patrol. Morris, a highway maintenance engineer in Chattanooga, was from Springfield and had a noteworthy military career. He enlisted in the Marine Corps and served from 1912 to 1916 and was a First Lieutenant in the Cavalry of the American Expeditionary Force from 1917 to 1919. Morris held positions with the Tennessee Department of Highways and Public Works from 1920 to 1939. He also served as the Chairman of the State Drivers License Law Committee in 1936. Morris had served continuously in the Officer Reserve Corps of the U.S. Army from 1923.

Director of Safety Morris' first appointment when he assumed the post in August 1939 was the promotion of Lieutenant R. Willard Jett to the rank of Inspector. Inspector Jett, a member of the Highway Patrol since its inception in 1929, was made Sergeant during the Browning administration and Lieutenant the previous January. The rank of Inspector was essentially the second in command of the uniform patrol.

A contingent of Tennessee Highway Patrol participated in September 1939 American Legion convention parade in Chicago. Governor Prentice Cooper was being honored by the Legion. Carlton French was at the right end of the second row of motorcycle patrolmen.

Director Morris continued to wear his military uniform with the THP badge over the left breast. Morris had no reluctance about raiding and under his leadership the Patrol began making raids on illegal operations of all sorts and the axe began to swing. "We tore up nightclubs, broke up whiskey stills, and everything else," Patrolman French remembered.

Governor Cooper confirmed reports in August 1939, that he had authorized a secret squad to train for nightspot raiding duty. The "flying squadron" was under the direction of an unnamed former FBI agent and men in the unit were to be separated from their regular duties. Eventually raiding squads were developed within divisions across the state.

During the first 10 days of September 1939, the Patrol raided 80 places equally divided between the three grand divisions of the state. Morris reported that some persons tried to "tip off" nightclub operators.

At one place where patrolmen were breaking up slot machines, the telephone rang while the men were conducting the raid. The person on the other end of the line was warning the proprietor that patrolmen were to make a visit to the place. "Listen," said the proprietor as he took down the transmitter and turned it toward the noise, "the law is already here."

On the first weekend of October 1939, 36 roadhouses were raided in east and west divisions of the state. Later in the month, Middle Tennessee Chief Lynn Bomar, with Patrolmen Bill Williams, Bill Pearson and

Highway Patrol Division Four, the Memphis Division, in 1939 in front of the Doughboy at Overton Park. First Row from left were Sergeant Jimmy T. Phelps, Bill Chester from Jackson, Bill Evans, George Clanton, Carlton French, Jim Abernathy, Jim Routt and Sergeant Freddy Mayo. Second Row from left to right were Dave Glass, Carl Caldwell, Bill Brent from Jackson, Jim Albright from Somerville, Assistant Chief Clifford West, Clarence Turner from Dyersburg, Rudy Jehl, T. Fletcher and B. G. Graves from Dyersburg.

Robert Routt, raided the Nightingale on Franklin Road and confiscated six one-armed bandit slot machines, two "race horse" machines and made five arrests. The group then proceeded to the Owl Club, Riverview Camp, The Oaks and Teenie's Place where they had similar success.

From the time raids began in August 1939, through the end of the year, the Patrol's night raiding squads made 450 raids and confiscated between $60,000 and $80,000 worth of equipment, liquor and gambling money. They made 400 arrests.

The raiding intensified in 1940. The combined forces of the Nashville Police Department and the Highway Patrol made a series of raids on bootleg establishments in the city of Nashville on a Saturday night in February 1940. Chief of Police John Griffin and Highway Patrol Inspector Willard Jett led the raiders. At a house near the State Capitol, they confiscated 150 gallons of moonshine whiskey, 26 barrels of mash and a 1,500 gallon steam still.

Raiding parties were sometimes resisted with gunfire. In February 1940, West Tennessee Chief Clifford J. West was fired on by a bootlegger in an early morning raid on a roadhouse near Jackson. The bullet barely missed West's head. He returned fire and the bootlegger surrendered.

Members of the Memphis Division raided three gambling parlors in downtown Jackson in August 1940. Twenty-nine individuals were arrested, including a state representative and the superintendent of schools. One of the gambling establishments was on the third floor of the Robertson Building across an intersection from the Madison County Courthouse. Patrolman Carlton French recounted how they gained entry.

> There was a fellow downstairs at the door, and he wouldn't let you in unless you knew somebody. We sent Jim Albright in, looking like he was about half drunk. When Jim got in the door he grabbed that fellow and put his arm around his

neck and said don't say anything. About six or eight of us ran upstairs and tore that thing up.

Many times patrolmen went out raiding on Friday night and got back home on Sunday. The most dangerous raids were on stills, where guns frequently came into play. In some Patrol offices the raids became a competition, if one patrolmen found a slot machine, others would not rest until they got one too.

The Highway Patrol withstood legal challenges to its authority to make enforcement raids. The Tennessee Supreme Court eventually ruled on the matter in June 1940, stating that the 1939 Act gave the Patrol authority by implication, since patrolmen were qualified as lawful officers.

The Patrol also began a new effort to fight drunk driving that resulted from bootleg operations. Sergeant Sam Johnson announced the arrest of 25 roadhouse patrons for public drunkenness as the result of a new strategy used by highway patrolmen in the Nashville District. Johnson had his patrolmen routinely "visit" night spots on Saturday evening and keep an eye out for drunk drivers.

THP officers kept an eye on suspicious drivers of all types. On the night of January 3, 1940, Patrolmen Matt Pratt and J. A. Hailey arrested a man and his wife who were both ex-convicts and wanted for several robberies and federal narcotic law violations. The pair had eluded officers in four states. They were captured about 20 miles north of Nashville. Among items confiscated when they were arrested were $1,000 worth of stolen drugs and a .45 caliber automatic pistol. Patrolman Hailey described the capture.

We had orders for the pickup of the couple. Pratt and I were cruising on Highway 112 when a car passed us as we topped a hill. We thought that it might be the couple we wanted but the car was a Pontiac instead of a Chevrolet. We decided that we could hold them anyway for passing on a hill so we crowded the car over to the side of the road.

He answered the description and there was a woman with him, so we brought them in. The woman had the gun; when we asked for it, the man looked at his wife and said, "Let them have it." She reached for the gun, which was stuck in the top of her skirt, but I stopped her and took the gun myself.

More routine highway enforcement included monitoring the lawful weight limits of trucks. The limit

Patrolman Greg O'Rear was assigned to the Lawrenceburg office as the lone highway patrolman in the area and became a familiar sight on the roadways of south-central Tennessee.

was increased to 20,000 on April 1, 1939. The legal weight for trucks was 18,000 pounds at the beginning of 1939 and during the first three months of the year 728 trucks, were cited for violation of the limit.

A number of high-profile personnel changes occurred during 1939 and 1940. Clyde Odil was appointed Chief of the driver's license division in July 1939. He had served as examiner in the Hohenwald district for several months.

An original member of the patrol, James English, who had served for a time as Nashville Division Assistant Chief, was promoted from the rank of Sergeant-Instructor to Lieutenant-Instructor in November 1939. English was in command of training and chief of the driver's license division.

Lieutenant English was promoted to chief clerk in November 1940 upon the death of Chief Clerk Howell MacPherson. Sergeant Hurley E. Riddick was promoted to Lieutenant in English's place, but not with the responsibility of Instructor.

Assistant Chief Lynn Bomar of the Middle Tennessee or Nashville Division was transferred to Knoxville in December 1939, to succeed Assistant Chief Niles Y. Pace of the East Tennessee or Knoxville Division. Pace took over the Nashville Division. The transfers were to be temporary and were done in line with Morris' policy of acquainting division heads with conditions in all sections of the state.

Two senior men left the Highway Patrol in March 1940. East Tennessee or Knoxville Division Assistant

Memphis District Highway Patrol officers were about to make a raid. Left to right were Smith, the radioman, McDougal, Assistant Chief Cliff West, Joe Sheridan, Jim Albright, Carlton French, Stuart Dean, T. Taylor and Wimpy Robertson, the dispatcher.

Chief Lynn Bomar resigned to become director of safety for the city of Knoxville. Sergeant E. C. Taylor was promoted to fill the position. Assistant Chief Taylor, 33, joined the Patrol in 1933.

Also in March 1940, Inspector Willard Jett resigned to join the Nashville Police Department at the rank of Sergeant and as Chief of the department's motorcycle unit and director of training. Jett had requested release from the Patrol the previous November 1939 to join the Nashville force, but Governor Cooper denied his request "after he was advised by Major Tom E. Morris that he could not dispense with Jett's service without damage to the Highway Patrol setup."

A series of command changes took place in December 1940, as a result of the demotion of Middle Tennessee or Nashville Division Assistant Chief Niles Y. Pace. Pace was reduced to the rank of Sergeant and sent to Johnson City. East Tennessee Assistant Chief Ed Cole Taylor was transferred to Nashville as assistant

Chief of Middle Tennessee and Sergeant Sam Johnson was promoted to East Tennessee Assistant Chief.

Governor Prentice Cooper wanted THP officers to be mindful for their duty and public image. The job of a member of the Patrol could be jeopardized not only by misconduct, but by the appearance of misconduct. Governor Cooper fired Patrolman Bill Winfrey and another patrolman when he saw the two at the Strawberry Festival in Humboldt and thought they were idling and flirting with a pretty girl. The two had been assigned to catch a man who was selling marijuana at the event. Assistant Chief Clifford West went to Nashville the next day to talk Cooper out of the firings.

Patrolman Blackie Mayfield and another patrolman were fired when Cooper saw them eating in a restaurant with a beer sign in a small town east of Nashville. The Governor did not want officers to have the appearance of drinking on duty by being anywhere beer was served. Their Assistant Chief was able to get them back on the Patrol as well.

44

Patrolman Carlton French, left, and Sergeant Jimmy Phelps displayed gambling paraphernalia confiscated in the raid on the gaming establishment in the Robertson Building across the street from the Madison County Courthouse in Jackson. The photograph was made at the State Highway Garage in Jackson.

Political influence heavily impacted the Patrol. Decisions as basic as hiring and firing patrolmen were often made based on politics. Going against the wishes of a powerful politician could create problems for a patrolman and no one had more political power statewide than Edward Hull "Boss" Crump. On one occasion Roxie Rice, Mr. Ed Crump's right hand man, called the Memphis office of the Highway Patrol and requested a man.

When the patrolman arrived, Rice gave him some papers and told him to take the documents to an attorney and political leader in Fayette County. The patrolman said, "I'm no messenger boy," turned and left the office. The patrolman soon found himself reassigned to the opposite end of the state. He later commented wryly to former Memphis colleagues, "That's good looking country up there around Jellico."

Although politics continued to affect members of the THP, the stability of their employment was enhanced on August 30, 1941, when Governor Prentice Cooper issued an Executive Order giving Civil Service status to members of the Patrol. This provided a new level of assurance for patrolmen that their jobs would not be subject to termination at the political whim of a new state administration. The first Civil Service tests, which included written examinations and interviews, were given in July 1942 at Nashville, Memphis and Knoxville.

The strength of the Highway Patrol in 1940 was 70 patrolmen and 23 drivers license examiners. Director Morris pressed the legislature for more men saying, "We need at least 150 patrolmen." Morris

decided to add the rank of Corporal to provide an additional level of structure within the force and to give recognition to senior patrolmen. Patrolmen who were at a higher grade of pay were promoted to corporal.

The number of patrolmen was increased in 1941 and training of the Patrol was enhanced. Two classes of recruits were added to the force at mid-year. A school was established in June 1941, at Clarksville to provide 30 days of training for new patrolmen. Seventeen applicants were in the first class and fourteen in the second. This increased the strength of the Patrol to 100 men. Most of the new men filled positions of patrolmen who had volunteered for military service.

First line Patrol Supervisors were given additional training in a broad spectrum of law enforcement issues as the likelihood of world war grew. Lieutenant James English attended a 10-day FBI school in Washington on sabotage and espionage. Safety Director Tom Morris required sergeants to hold a week-long school to include topics related to wartime concerns. The session began on Sunday, November 2, 1941, in the State Office Building and covered tactics, motor vehicle law, public relations, fingerprinting, evidence, firearms, accident investigation, civilian defense, communications, criminal law, search and seizure, federal statutes, administrative records, national defense investigations and driver licenses.

The need for new and different equipment was a concern for the Director Morris. The Patrol had 95 motorcycles and Morris began replacing motorcycles with cars. New vehicles received in July 1941, were 40 Harley-Davidson motorcycles and 13 Chevrolet sedans. This brought the number of patrol cars to 57 plus automobiles used by the driver's license division. Automobiles were preferred for patrol principally because they were safer for patrolmen than motorcycles. Cars were better able to patrol roadways during bad weather as well.

The THP uniform underwent changes as the Patrol moved to automobiles. Riding britches and leather boots were not necessary to safely operate a patrol car. Patrolmen began to move to straight-legged pants and low quarter shoes. The scarcity of leather during the war years and the resulting high cost of boots encouraged the change. The change took time because the Patrol continued to use motorcycles and pants were too expensive to be discarded before they were worn out.

Governor Prentice Cooper directed the Patrol to create a communications division in 1939 and Morris initiated plans for a radio system. Five or six cars in the Nashville area were equipped with radios using the Nashville and Davidson County radio system. Radios provided one-way communication from the headquarters transmitter to receivers installed in patrol cars.

Preliminary efforts in the use of radio equipment had been promising. The Patrol did field tests of radio communication in 1935 over the 1KW experimental station W4XAJ. The WSM facilities were used after the Nashville station went off the air at dark. The transmission was received as far away as Toronto, Canada.

The Nashville District of the Patrol shared a radio system with the Davidson County Sheriff's Office following Sheriff Ivey Young's installation of the system in 1937. The THP agreed to furnish dispatchers as its contribution to the enterprise.

Percy E. Griffith, a Vice President of the Braid Electric Company in Nashville, installed the sheriff's system. Governor Cooper hired Griffith in 1940 at $1 for the year as a full member of the Department of

The uniform of highway patrolmen circa 1940 included riding pants and boots with an optional heavy leather coat. Patrolmen from left to right were Carlton French, Carl Caldwell and Jim Albright.

Patrolman Bill Harmon was transferred to an automobile in the early forties after his hand and wrist were injured in a motorcycle accident in Rhea County. He continued to wear his riding britches while driving the 1940 Ford patrol car.

Safety. Griffith's assignment was to create a radio communications system for the Tennessee Highway Patrol and to run the communications operation. Griffith was soon given the rank of lientenant and served as Head of Communications for the department until his retirement in 1970.

Two cars were equipped to test two-way radio communication and were assigned to the "Maneuver Division." With the U. S. Army beginning extensive maneuvers in Middle Tennessee in 1941, the THP provided support and the two cars were stationed in the temporary Maneuver Division, headquartered in Lebanon, Tennessee. The transmission range for the units was approximately 12 miles.

Work proceeded on the THP radio system. Prison labor was used to clear the land, construct towers and buildings and string wires for the radio equipment. Nashville station WBVM came on line September 19, 1941; Memphis WDBW on February 26, 1942; Chattanooga WJBV on August 4, 1942; and the last of the four stations, Knoxville WKVT, on December 18, 1942, completing the radio communication system.

World War II was in full swing when the communication system was completed and parts were in short supply. R. R. Turner, the first engineer, often used relays and other parts from confiscated slot machines to keep the radio system going. Also, the military had placed a freeze on permits for high frequency FM broadcast bands that permitted longer range communication.

The Patrol got a low frequency AM band designated for police that allowed two-way communication, but the transmission signal was weak and patrolmen could not communicate car to car. The AM car radios had 35 watt transmitters that broadcast at 1126 megacycles. The four base stations broadcast at one-kilowatt on 1618 megacycles. Many standard citizen AM radio receivers could monitor THP car radio transmissions.

The network provided communication with 98 radio equipped cars. Communication with cars was frequently hampered by the terrain and the weak signal from the car transmitter. Radio operators put calls out three times in a ten minute period and hoped the patrolman was close to his radio and the signal was not blocked by a hill. Patrolmen did not want to miss any excitement and stayed close to their radios. The technology was still new and the equipment was unreliable. Dispatcher "Speedy" Cunningham said technicians spent most of their time making repairs.

The Nashville station only had three dispatchers, a Sergeant and two civilians. If a dispatcher was out, a patrolman had to fill in and patrol officers went to great lengths to get out of radio duty. Dispatchers got the opportunity to see what patrol was like as well. The shortage of men meant that dispatchers, following radio duty, often rode a tour in a patrol unit.

Early communication personnel wore a small eagle-top sunburst breast badge with a hand holding bolts of lightning in the center. They wore the same hat badge as other members of the Patrol with "Radio" stamped in the rank panel.

The THP provided constant support to U. S. Army maneuvers in 1941. Thirty-five patrolmen were assigned to escort and generally assist the movement of soldiers and equipment. This was the beginning of the Patrol's support of the military throughout the war years.

When Pearl Harbor was attacked on December 7, 1941, the military ordered the Tennessee Highway Patrol to immediately ground all aircraft and place a guard on them around the clock. Guard posts at airports were manned for three days. Patrolmen were also posted on all bridges for two weeks while civilian guards were hired.

Roadways were frequently shut down to accommodate army exercises. Patrolman Bill Harmon and his partner worked in the Tullahoma area and closed down a state road several times a day for specific periods while the army shot across the road during artillery and tank practice.

The THP patrolled roads in the maneuver area twenty-four hours a day. Patrolmen worked twelve-

Patrolman with a 1941 Pontiac Straight-8 Fastback. Patrolmen assigned to patrol cars continued to wear riding pants used by motorcycle riders, since they might need to patrol on either vehicle. Also, pants were too expensive to replace until they were worn out.

hour shifts. Increased traffic, military and civilian, meant the highways needed to be patrolled around the clock. Many factories ran on a twenty-four hour schedule producing war materiel. The era of a single shift each day for the Tennessee Highway Patrol was abandoned, never to return.

Robert Lynn Bomar was appointed Director of the Department of Safety on August 14, 1942, when Major Tom Morris resigned to rejoin the Army. Director Lynn Bomar was a native of Bell Buckle in Bedford County and a towering figure. He was a former Vanderbilt University All-American football player and played two years of professional football with the New York Giants. After a number of years in business, Bomar began a law enforcement career as a deputy US Marshal from 1934 to 1939. He served as Division Assistant Chief of the THP from March 1939 to February 1940. Bomar served as director of public safety for the city of Knoxville from 1940 to 1941 and rejoined the Patrol in January 1942. Director Bomar was named to the War Traffic Advisory Committee.

Other personnel changes included the appointment of J. J. Dolan as supervisor and attorney of the Drivers License Division. Lieutenant Hurley Riddick was made Head of the Safety Education Division.

In one of his first acts, on October 7, 1942, Director Bomar declared all highways in Tennessee to be "congested areas," allowing him to impose a 35 mph speed limit statewide. Before the year was out, gas rationing was implemented and the THP became responsible for enforcing the regulation.

The war continued to create significant turnover in THP personnel. Most of the able young men of the Patrol joined the military. Director Bomar called for men to fill the vacancies. He relaxed recruiting standards to men "who are over 38 years old and who have dependents, without lowering the physical requirement."

The salary for a patrolman in 1942 was $1,524 per year or $127 per month. First-class patrolmen earned between $1,680 and $1,800 based on longevity. Other salaries were Corporal $1,800-$1,980, Sergeant and Staff Sergeant $2,040-$2,160 and Lieutenant and Staff Lieutenant $2,220-$2,364. Veterans returning from wartime service received priority in consideration for positions on the Patrol.

The "oldest profession" flourished with so many servicemen in the state. The 1943 legislature enacted prostitution laws and a law designed to control the problem of venereal disease. The THP was empowered to enforce the laws.

The Patrol performed one duty that few knew about, escorting submarines and other military vessels through the state's waterways. Groups of five to twelve submarines on their way from Wisconsin and Illinois shipbuilders to New Orleans were escorted by the Navy and Coast Guard down the Mississippi River. The first sub made the trek in January 1943. When the flotilla reached the Tennessee line, a Navy tug contact-ed the THP headquarters in Memphis by radio. Patrolmen then closed all bridges and ferry crossings on the river until the convoy passed. If patrol units were not available, the convoy stopped mid-river until units were in position.

Similar duty was performed on other rivers in the state. One patrolman recalled waiting on the Cumberland River bridge at Ashland City one Sunday from 8:00 a.m. until 5:00 p.m. for a sub-chaser on its way to the Ohio River from the builder, the Nashville Bridge Company.

By June 1943, forty-two highway patrolmen were assigned to assist the military. The Second Army established a permanent presence in Middle Tennessee. The Highway Patrol's temporary Maneuver Division in Lebanon was under Sergeant James T. "Jim" Gill. Gill gained a reputation for close coordination with the armored divisions in the area. Frequently, he would tell the patrolmen in his command, "Boys, we're going to be busy tonight, the tanks are going to run." The frequency of such phrases gained him the nickname "Tank."

One THP member had the "honor" of getting chewed out by General George S. Patton. The patrolman was leading a column of tanks under Patton's command. As they went through Sparta under black-out conditions, the column somehow got lost. The general berated the patrolman as only Patton could. Once they got on the proper route and reached their destination, Patton called the patrolman over and apologized.

Highway patrolmen put their life on the line working in the Maneuver Division. Patrolman William Howard James was killed Monday, September 14, 1942, in Murfreesboro while he was directing a military convoy. He was unable to make a turn and his motorcycle crashed into a telephone pole. James, age 24, was one of the extra patrolmen that had been recently assigned to support Army maneuvers.

Regular patrol duty remained dangerous as well. Patrolman William Hinkle Crutcher was patrolling State Highway 112 north of Bordeaux late in the afternoon two years later. The 27-year-old Marine Corps veteran was in pursuit of a vehicle when he swerved to avoid a car crossing his lane. The motorcycle got into loose gravel on the shoulder of the road and Crutcher lost control. He plunged down an embankment and struck a guy wire. Patrolman Crutcher died three days later on August 3, 1944, without regaining consciousness. He had been a member of the force for nine months.

In February 1943, the entire Patrol was given a $2 per month increase in pay. When Carlton French was

Patrolman James Seehorn in 1943. The motorcycle had a front-end shroud as protection against the weather. The red emergency light to the left of the headlight and siren were forward of the cover.

Over 100 members of the Patrol met with Governor Prentice Cooper and Safety Director Lynn Bomar on March 3, 1944. They were photographed in front of the War Memorial in Nashville. The command of the patrol was standing in the front row at the lower right side of the photo. From left to right were Nashville Division Assistant Chief Bill O'Lee, Knoxville Division Assistant Chief George Burdette, Memphis Division Assistant Chief James T. Phelps, Chattanooga Division Assistant Chief C. F. "Dick" Webb, Director of the Department of Safety and Chief of the Highway Patrol Lynn Bomar, and outgoing Memphis Division Assistant Chief Clifford J. West.

promoted in 1944, Sergeant's pay was $185 a month. Increased pay was a bright spot in an otherwise difficult time. Patrol units got plenty of use and patrolmen plenty of overtime. They worked their regular shift and kept on working until the job at hand was completed. Although the hours were long and the duty difficult during the war years, one new recruit, who later headed the THP, recalled the excitement of getting his commission and the joy of finally getting his first assignment on the roadways of Tennessee.

Patrolmen took pride in their duty and held themselves to a high standard. An example of that took place in Jackson in 1943. Tennessee Highway Patrol Sergeant Bill Winfrey turned himself in to city officials for violating the parking line ordinance and paid the fine of $1.

Even the most dedicated patrolman needed basic equipment to do his job. The war compounded procurement problems for the THP. Vehicles of the force were severely stressed by the additional duty and replacements were rare. Automobile assembly lines were converted to the production of military vehicles during the war years and acquiring rolling stock for the Patrol was nearly impossible. The department located nine Ford six-cylinder cars at a dealership in

Long Island, New York, in 1943. Patrolmen were sent north to drive the cars back. The units had flat-head six-cylinder engines that did 65 mph wide open and used more gasoline than eight-cylinder engines. Seven more Fords were found in Philadelphia. As soon as they arrived, they were painted cream and black and placed in duty. These were the last new patrol units acquired until after the end of the war.

Wartime rationing made it difficult to get basic supplies necessary to patrol the highways. Gas, tires, engine parts and other essentials were rationed and virtually unavailable to all but the military. Trabue Lewis was appointed maintenance officer in 1943 and served in that capacity until his retirement. He spent much of his time before the Rationing Board requesting items necessary for the Patrol to function.

Tennessee Highway Patrol personnel provided security for Presidents and other dignitaries when they visited the state. Patrolmen escorted President Franklin D. Roosevelt a number of times including to the dedication of Warm Spring, Georgia, to the funeral of Speaker Joseph Byrns in Nashville and to Chickamauga Dam in Chattanooga. Patrolmen drove Mrs. Roosevelt from Memphis to an event at Shiloh Park. The Patrol continued to provide security for

Patrolman A. C. Jared with one of the THP's well worn wartime patrol cars in 1945.

Training increased and expanded into many new areas during World War II. Instruction in the use of gas masks was given in 1945 to Chattanooga Chief Dick Webb on the left, Inspector James Gill from headquarters in Nashville in the center and Memphis Chief Jimmy Phelps on the right.

every president since. On July 16, 1947, two members of the Patrol went to Washington, D.C., to serve in an Honor Guard for President Harry S. Truman.

The Patrol escorted celebrities as well. Actors Bud Abbott and Lou Costello came through Memphis on a war bond tour. They rode on motorcycles with patrolmen to the Penal Farm, then into Crump Stadium and, after they finished their speeches, back to the Peabody Hotel. Bud Abbot rode with Carlton French and Patrolman Elbert Kennon carried Lou Costello. The celebrities rode on the motorcycle seat and the patrolmen sat forward on the tank.

Patrolman Bill Harmon's motorcycle duty was ended following an escort incident in Rhea County. Harmon wrecked his motorcycle avoiding a child that ran out in front of President Roosevelt's procession at the Dayton Strawberry Festival. The accident seriously injured Harmon's hand and wrist. After he recovered, he was assigned duty in a 1940 Ford patrol car.

Not long after he began duty in a patrol car, Patrolman Bill Harmon stopped a drunk and loaded him in the back seat. "Loaded" was the term used by patrolmen when they made an arrest and put the prisoner in the patrol car. As they drove to the jail the old man kept fumbling around and saying, "I'm going to kill you." Harmon ignored the threat. At the jail, the jailer went out to get the prisoner and found a pistol in the floor board. Had the drunk been able to get to his weapon, Harmon might well have been killed.

The Patrol continued to face the same crimes and many of the same issues it had in its first decade, but it had established itself as a force to be reckoned with across the state. Conflict with local law enforcement remained a part of the challenge for the THP. Assistant Chief George Burdette, of the Knoxville District, received a tip about a bootleg operation in October 1943. He got a search warrant and drove in an unmarked car with five patrolmen to a motel on

Highway Patrol School held at Smyrna Army Air Base September 1-12, 1946.

Training of the 1946 recruits of the Patrol was done under the watchful eye and with the participation of, from left to right, Lieutenant Clydell Castleman, Inspector Jim Gill, FBI Special Agent in Charge D. F. Hoffstedder, and Commissioner of Safety Lynn Bomar.

Tennessee Highway Patrolmen gathered in Columbia preparing to make a sweep of the Mink Slide district. Rioting and the shooting of local lawmen in February 1946 brought patrolmen from Nashville, Memphis, Knoxville, and Chattanooga. Nashville Assistant Chief J. J. Jackson sat on the wall at the far left, Knoxville Assistant Chief George Burdette was the sixth form the left on the wall, and Patrolman Blackie Mayfield stood at the far right, hands in pockets.

Highway 25 West. They confiscated 32 cases of liquor, but the bootlegger, a cousin of the sheriff, was not on the premises. Burdette sent one of the patrolman back to Campbell to pick up the Highway Patrol unit.

As the patrol unit returned, Burdette and his men saw that the bootlegger had a gun stuck in the patrolman's back that was driving the vehicle. A shoot out erupted and one of the patrolmen shot the bootlegger. The bootlegger had gotten out of jail just that week after being convicted of murdering a man with an axe. The cousin-sheriff arrived and arrested all the patrolmen on a charge of murder.

On the day of the hearing, Director of Safety, Lynn Bomar, entered the courtroom. He was followed by a line of Tennessee Highway Patrolmen armed with automatic weapons, who stood along the wall on one side of the courtroom. The opposite wall of the courtroom filled with sheriff's deputies similarly armed. Bomar announced that he was taking his men out. District Attorney General Howard Baker Sr. called on all of his skills of diplomacy and knowledge of the law. He worked out a suitable compromise. Bomar left the

courtroom with his men and no one learned which patrolman fired the shot that killed the bootlegger.

Tennessee Highway Patrolmen and State Guardsmen confiscated weapons during racial rioting in the Mink Slide district of Columbia, Tennessee, on February 26, 1946. All weapons were held until settlement of the unrest.

A double killing in 1944 required a major commitment of THP personnel. The wife and daughter of the superintendent of the Pikeville Training School were brutally murdered by a house-boy inmate at the school. They refused to let him have the keys to their car and he killed them with an axe. The sheriff caught the killer and returned him to Pikeville. He was shot and killed by a mob and rioting broke out. The Highway Patrol was called in and stayed at the school for several days to prevent further violence.

Law enforcement jobs related to the war effort and jobs that resulted from the improved national economy after the war were opportunities for patrolmen. Bill Harmon who was making $125 a month as a Tennessee Highway Patrolman joined the U. S. Border Patrol at $300 per month and moved to Brownsville, Texas. Harmon returned to Tennessee later as Chief of Police for Nuclear Security at Oak Ridge for the Manhattan Project's nuclear propulsion aircraft research.

Carlton French left the Patrol in 1945 when the Legislature turned down the pension plan for the Highway Patrol. Ed Reeve left at the same time. French briefly served as a Memphis Police Officer and then became a Special Agent for the Illinois Central Railroad, where he remained for thirty years until he retired.

The head of the Department of Safety was elevated to cabinet level on July 1, 1945, and given the title Commissioner. Lynn Bomar became the department's first Commissioner and served in the role until January 1949. Bomar continued to hold the position of Chief of the Patrol in addition to Commissioner of the Department of Safety. J. J. Dolan continued as Supervisor of the Drivers License Division. Lieutenant Clydell Castleman headed the Safety Education Division until 1947 when Lieutenant Nolen Puckett took over safety education responsibilities. Castleman, a former pitcher for the New York Giants, graduated from the FBI National Academy in July 1945.

Bomar headed the Patrol at the time of one the state's most dramatic incidents of racial conflict. The incident in Columbia started with a dispute over the repair of a radio between a black ex-Navy man and a white repairman on Monday, February 25, 1946. The repairman was pushed through a plate glass window, and ended up in the hospital. The injured repairman was well respected and the brother of a war hero, who had become a member of the Tennessee Highway Patrol. Talk of lynching among the white population and a growing crowd of armed black citizens brought the town to the brink of rioting.

Highway Patrolmen provided security during the CIO strike at Henry I. Siegel & Co. in Dickson, Tennessee, February 1947. Left to right in the photograph on the front fenders were Assistant Chief J. J. Jackson and an unidentified sergeant, and atop the cargo were an unidentified patrolman and Patrolman Elmer Craig, later to serve as chief of the Patrol. All were armed with automatic weapons.

Sheriff J. J. Underwood arrested the leaders of the crowd of about thirty whites. At the same time, Columbia Chief of Police J. W. Griffin with Will Wilsford and two other uniformed policemen walked into Mink Slide, the section of town where the black population was concentrated. House lights were turned off and around 200 armed men had gathered. The law officers were met with shotgun fire when they passed through the lighted intersection into Mink Slide a little after 8:00 p.m. All were hit, one seriously. They retreated without unholstering their weapons. The sheriff called the Governor who called Commissioner Bomar to send in the Highway Patrol and Acting Adjutant General Hilton Butler to send in the Tennessee State Guard.

The State Guard was created to provide military protection against sabotage and riots within the state while the National Guard responded to international conflicts. The State Guard was created in 1941 and only existed for five years. Its members were teenagers and men ineligible for the draft, many of whom were World War I veterans.

Tennessee Highway Patrol Sergeant Greg O'Rear was first on the scene. Nashville Division Assistant Chief Johnny Joe "J. J." Jackson and Sergeant Dave White arrived in Columbia within an hour. An initial contingent of state forces, 67 patrolman and 59 state

The first Emergency Mobile Unit or "Disaster Van" of the Communication Division of the Department of Safety was built in 1947 to facilitate communications during man-made or natural disasters in the state. Standing in front of the van from left to right were Charlie Bacigalupo, L. B. Dillard, James Beal, and Lieutenant Percy Griffith, individuals key to the implementation and operation of the unit.

guardsmen, joined city and county forces during the night. Patrolmen spread their patrol cars out as they drove the roadway into Columbia so that the line of headlights would be longer and it would appear that the number of lawmen was greater than it actually was. Commissioner Bomar soon arrived and took command, setting up temporary headquarters in the sheriff's office.

Random shots were fired throughout the night. Around 3:00 a.m. THP Assistant Chief Jackson, armed with a sawed-off shotgun, and Sergeant White, armed with a .30 caliber army carbine, led a raid and arrested fourteen leaders of the armed black group. They were charged with attempted murder.

By morning, nearly 100 Highway Patrolmen and over 200-armed State Guardsmen had arrived and martial law was declared. About 400 members of the State Guard were deployed before the incident was over. At 6:07 a.m. Commissioner Bomar led a three-pronged systematic sweep of Mink Slide. The Force collected all firearms, which were held until the unrest ended. Sporadic gunfire greeted the Force. Highway

Patrolman Ray "Slick" Austin was hit by shots fired from atop a barbershop. Heavy fire was returned by state and local forces. Many were arrested and taken to jail without any fatalities. Three leaders of the rioters were arrested by Sergeant E. B. Nolen, Sergeant Don Kelley and Corporal W. A. Griffin.

The sheriff's office and jail was a two story residence that had been converted to serve as jail, sheriff's office and residence for the sheriff's family. By Thursday morning, over 100 prisoners were crowded into the two jail cells. With lawmen using the facility for a headquarters and prosecutors interviewing prisoners, the building was cramped and some rooms were serving multiple purposes.

The room that served as the sheriff's office was one of the most heavily used rooms. A bed had been moved in for quick naps. The cache of weapons confiscated from Mink Slide was unloaded and stored in the room as well. Two deputies and a newspaper reporter were in the room on Thursday afternoon, February 25, tending to business. The hall outside the office was crowded with highway patrolmen and other law officers. The lawmen had surrendered their weapons before entering the detention area.

After questioning, three prisoners were taken to the sheriff's office to await bail. Two were among the group that fired on the four Columbia police officers the previous Monday night. Cartridges were either brought into the room or were found in a jacket hanging on the wall. While sheriff's deputies were distracted by other duties, two of the prisoners managed to load two rifles stacked in the room. The reporter was the first to notice, but the two had fired by then. One shot grazed a deputy.

The unarmed law officers outside reacted. As the sheriff ran toward the gunfire, THP Assistant Chief J. J. Jackson grabbed Underwood's pistol. Other weapons were passed to those nearest the door. Jackson, Sergeant Dave White, Sergeant Fred Cole Waldrop, Patrolman C. A. Cartwright and Corporal Billy Griffin, son of Columbia's Chief of Police, shot the two armed prisoners. Both died in transport to a Nashville hospital. The third prisoner stood in a corner with his hands in the air and was not injured.

The national media covered the Mink Slide incident and events that followed. The racial aspect of the conflict was highly publicized in the court cases that grew out of the affair.

The Highway Patrol was called on to restore order and maintain peace at a number of labor and civil disorders. A strike at the Vultee Aircraft Plant in

The first FM radios for patrolmen were installed in the Kingsport District in 1948. From left to right were Patrolman C. W. Walker of Johnson City, radio technician James Beal in the trunk installing the radio equipment, Patrolman Roy Purky of Greeneville and chief radio engineer Lieutenant Percy Griffith. (Photo from the Kingsport News)

Nashville at the end of the war was one such instance.

The Department of Safety recognized the need for better communications to coordinate personnel and activities during serious emergencies. In 1947, an Emergency Mobile Unit commonly referred to as the Disaster Van was constructed by the Patrol. It was the second such unit in the nation. The first was built in the aftermath of a disaster in Texas City, Texas, that killed hundreds and did hundreds of millions dollars in property damage.

The lack of a mobile command and communication center had hampered response to the emergency in Texas City. Tennessee needed the mobile unit for use at strikes and civil disturbances occurring in the state as well as for disasters. The bed of the truck that served as the THP Disaster Van was constructed of 1/4" steel plate and the body had gun ports on all sides. The vehicle was equipped with a mobile radio transmitter.

The communications staff in the late forties consisted of Lieutenant Percy Griffith and three technicians, James Beal, L. B. Dillard and Charlie Bacigalupo. The unit had a car and a pickup to provide service statewide.

The communication system needed to be upgraded. Some supervisors had FM radio units and could talk car to car. The rest of the Patrol had AM radios with their limitations. Weak transmission meant that a patrolman far from the district office or surrounded by mountains was out of radio contact with headquarters. He either had to go to a high elevation to transmit or call headquarters by telephone, often a long distance call. Wrecker services or others often called for a patrolman who could not communicate by radio. And AM radios did not allow car to car communications.

The AM radios took a second or so to "wind up" before transmitting and each one had a distinctive hum or noise to it. An experienced communications operator like Speedy Cunningham could identify the caller when he heard the transmitter break.

The department began installing FM radios in patrol cars in 1948. They were bulky two-piece units with two channels. F1 channel was used for communication between the station and patrol cars and F2 for car-to-car. The first FM units were installed in the Kingsport District soon after the District Office was built, because of the reception problems being experienced by patrolmen in the mountainous area. AM receivers were not removed from vehicles and for several years and when radio traffic became heavy the dispatcher would tell patrolmen to turn on the AM receiver. Public broadcast AM radios were strictly forbidden in patrol cars.

Patrolmen who were military veterans and members of the VFW served as a color guard for parades and public events.

Four channel radios were installed in the sixties, and federal grants during the seventies funded the installation of modern consoles across the state. The first console was installed in Memphis in 1972 and the next at Jackson in a small concrete building on State Street across from the state garage. It took about five years to install the consoles across the state. At the same time, eight channel radios were placed in cars and mobile repeaters were installed to increase the transmission range.

The enforcement efforts of the Patrol remained strong. Inspector Jim Gill led another group of gambling and liquor raiders that included Assistant Chief William E. Crawford, Sergeants Trabue Lewis and Elmer Craig, Corporals A. T. "Big'un" Ellis and John Hancock and Patrolmen J. R. Proctor, Raymond Donnell and William Albert Homes. One of the most dramatic of their raids was at the swank Ridgetop Inn on Springfield Highway. They pulled up to the night spot and casino that straddled the Davidson-Robertson county line about 10:30 p.m. and began their work. Before leaving with seized contraband, they took axes to dice and roulette tables, other gambling equipment and illegal liquor.

The Patrol went through major organizational changes during the second administration of Governor Gordon W. Browning. Commissioner Sam K. Neal took the helm at the Department of Safety in January 1949. Former Commissioner Lynn Bomar left public service until 1956 when he became warden of the Tennessee State Penitentiary, where he served until his death in 1964. Commissioner Neal was a Cookeville native with a background in newspaper publishing. He served during the war in the Office of War Information with the US Navy.

The position of Chief was re-established to place

an experienced law enforcement professional between the Commissioner and the uniformed ranks the THP. Chief W. T. "Fuzz" Shelton was appointed to command the Patrol. Shelton was a tank sergeant in Patton's Third Army during World War II and commanded a constabulary battalion stationed in Berlin. He came to the Patrol from Oak Ridge where he served as Assistant Chief of the Atomic Energy Commission security patrol. Shelton served as chief through September 1952.

A number of other command changes were made soon after the administration change. Supervisor J. J. Dolan remained as Head of the Drivers' License Division. Lieutenant Leslie Jett was put in charge of the Safety Education Division. William E. Crawford, a former inspector with the Memphis Police Department, was named Assistant Chief of the West Tennessee or Memphis Division, headquartered at Front and Exchange. Existing division Assistant Chief James Phelps was demoted and reassigned to Nashville, but he resigned instead. A number of patrolmen were dismissed "for the good of the service" in the realignment. The firings were considered a political move and most patrolmen were quickly hired by other agencies, including five by the Shelby County Sheriff's Office.

In May 1949, serious charges of misconduct and racketeering were made against division Assistant Chief Crawford and other THP officers in the division for protecting bootleggers and slot machine operators. Commissioner Neal made several trips to West Tennessee and interviewed both Patrol personnel and county officials. A few patrolmen were dismissed as a

A group of patrolmen with friends in 1949. Patrolman Leslie Jett, left, a member of the THP color guard, wore a VFW cap. The two officers on the right were Sergeant Harlson and Patrolman Glen Kemp. They wore the white background shoulder patch made as the first patch worn on shirts.

Sergeant Elmer Craig and the new 1949 Ford patrol car assigned to him when he took command of the new Highway Patrol station near Springfield. He also supervised the offices at Waverly and Clarksville. The new Ford had a red emergency light installed at the center of the grill. Sergeant Craig wore the white background shoulder patch, the first patch worn on shirts.

result of his investigation, but none as a result of the charges that were made.

At the end of June, it was determined that the charges against division Assistant Chief W. E. Crawford were unfounded. Evidence and affidavits showed that two individuals had met at the Hotel Claridge in Memphis during the Cotton Carnival and conspired to smear the new division Assistant Chief. Crawford and others were cleared. During the two months of the investigation, the Patrol made a number of raids to assure the public that the state agency enforced the law.

Commissioner Neal's policy continued to focus on the Patrol's safety work on the highways. He wanted to expand the number of patrolman and patrol cars on the highways of Tennessee. Effective July 1, 1949, the Commissioner completely reorganized the enforcement division of the Patrol. Neal said the purpose of the reorganization was "to place the patrolmen on the road a maximum number of hours during the day and to carryout selective enforcement."

Eight geographic divisions were established across the state and a captain was placed in command of each. The rank of Division or Assistant Chief was abandoned. The captain was assisted by a lieutenant and most divisions included an officer responsible for safety education and three men for communication. Patrolmen were assigned to towns throughout the division.

Larger offices within the division were under the command of a Sergeant or Corporal and included a drivers license section. Local offices were the training grounds for THP leadership. Sergeant Elmer Craig was assigned to supervise the new Springfield station on Greenbrier Pike on July 23, 1949. Craig also supervised the offices at Waverly and Clarksville. Other officers at the Clarksville station were Corporal John Hancock, J. J. Hammett, H. N. Loveless, and Corporal A. A. Carroll. Two patrolmen were assigned at stations in smaller towns to cover the area.

Chief Fuzz Shelton gave the divisions a name representative of that part of the state. The First or "Smoky Mountain" Division was headquartered in Knoxville and commanded by Captain George Burdette and Lieutenant Mitchell Moody. The division had a total of 35 officers stationed in eight communities.

The Second or "Valley" Division headquartered in Chattanooga at the National Guard Armory on Holtzclaw Avenue was commanded by Captain C. F. "Dick" Webb and Lieutenant Printest Dainy Garland with 34 officers in seven locations. Webb resigned in September 1950, amid a flurry of accusations from men who served in his command.

The Third or "Blue Grass" Division headquartered in Nashville was under Captain J. J. "Bullet" Jackson and Lieutenant Lawrence A. "Blackie" Mayfield with 38 officers in seven cities and towns. The Fourth or "River" Division in Memphis, with Captain W. E. Crawford and Lieutenant David Glass in command had 39 officers in seven locations.

The Fifth or "Holston" Division in Kingsport was

Sergeant Henry Heer, left, and Patrolman Arthur M. Lashlee in 1949.

Patrolman Leon Miller soon after he joined the Highway Patrol in 1949.

The class of 1949 attended Recruit School at Smyrna Air Base from July 5 through July 23. It was the most complete and comprehensive training school ever held for rookie patrolmen. Greg L. O'Rear had been promoted to Lieutenant on June 1, 1947, and placed in charge of training. A Lieutenant's monthly gross pay was $245, which after taxes and retirement deductions made net pay $210.90 a month.

The first week of training focused heavily on the legal and procedural topics including criminal law, technique of arrest and gathering and preserving evidence, all taught by FBI Special Agent Glenn Trusty. FBI Special Agent W. E. Hopton taught case preparation and interrogation of suspects and witnesses. J. J. Dolan of the THP taught laws of arrest and Attorney General Paul F. Bumpus taught courts and court procedures. Courses in traffic and other safety issues were taught by THP personnel and experts from other agencies.

commanded by Captain John T. Davis and Lieutenant Frank Williamson and had 33 officers in nine communities. The Sixth or "Cumberland" Division was headquartered in Cookeville and commanded by Captain Joe Sanford and Lieutenant Carl Hill with 16 officers in five locations.

The Seventh or "Davy Crockett" Division at Lawrenceburg was under Captain Greg L. O'Rear and Lieutenant Henry Heer and had 21 men in seven towns. The Eighth or "Cotton" Division was headquartered at Huntingdon and commanded by Captain Robert Fletcher and Lieutenant LaVerne H. Maxwell with 24 men at six locations.

The headquarters of the division, or later the district, was where the captain maintained his office. The captain's office and headquarters of the Eighth Division moved from Huntingdon to Jackson temporarily in 1956 and permanently in 1968.

By the late forties, the Patrol had developed a standard curriculum for rookie patrolmen. The force numbered 168 and 76 recruits were added on July 4, 1949, bringing the total sworn personnel to 231. The class of recruits was the largest in the history of the Patrol to that date. Among the recruits were 22-year-old Leon Miller who served most of his years at the Rockwood office before joining the TBI in 1968, Dusty Hale who transferred to the TBI in the spring of 1957 and Robert D. "Bob" Thomas who spent most of his career in Nashville and retired as a lieutenant in 1977.

Patrolman Lawrence A. "Blackie" Mayfield joined the Highway Patrol in the thirties and followed J. J. Jackson as captain in command of the Nashville District. Mayfield was known as a free-spirit and here was shown testing an alternate mode of transportation.

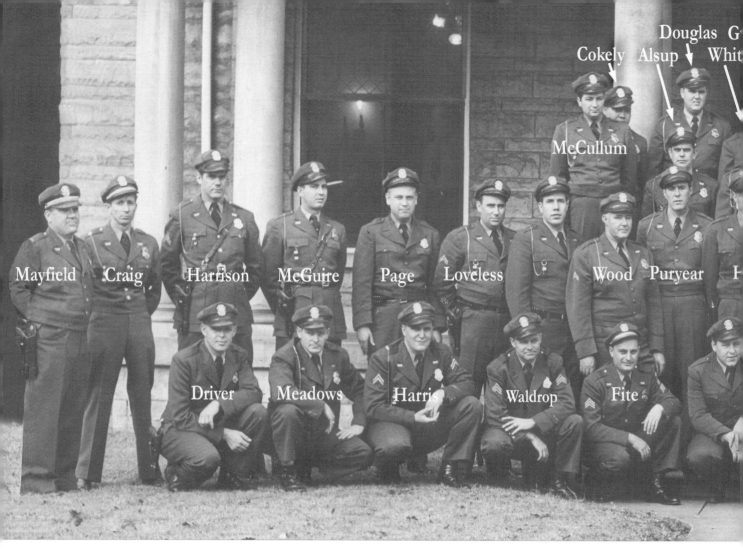

Cokely Alsup Douglas G Whit

McCullum

Mayfield Craig Harrison McGuire Page Loveless Wood Puryear H

Driver Meadows Harris Waldrop Fite

Nashville or "Bluegrass" Division officers met on West End Avenue around 1950. On the left half of the photograph, kneeling from left to right were R. S. Driver, James Meadows, Corporal Gene Harris, Sergeant Fred Cole Waldrop, Sergeant T. G. Fite, and an unidentified patrolman. Standing from left to right in the second row were Lieutenant Lawrence A. "Blackie" Mayfield (second in command of the division), Sergeant Elmer V. Craig, Corporal Collie Harrison, William C. "Mickey" McGuire, Fenton Page, Corporal Loveless, unidentified, Corporal Lee Wood, Bill Puryear, and Leonard Hill. Standing on the porch from left to right were patrolmen McCullum, Roy Cokely, Hubert Alsup, Charles O. Douglas, White, and Bill Gunter.

The second week of training concentrated on the use of weapons such as the .45 caliber submachine gun, 12 gauge shotgun, .38 caliber revolver, gas guns and grenades. A significant portion of the time was spent on the firing range and was conducted by FBI Special Agents Glenn Trusty and Frank Alden. Trusty also taught Judo and other self defense tactics. THP Chief Fuzz Shelton gave report writing lessons with instruction on all report forms used by the Patrol. Those who passed the written examination were graduated in a ceremony featuring Governor Gordon Browning.

Conducting the school was Greg O'Rear's last duty as training officer. O'Rear was promoted to Captain and when the school was over he took up his command of the 11-county Seventh Division in Lawrenceburg.

The rookie class of patrolmen that graduated

worked a ten-hour day and got four days off a month. Patrolmen were expected to make a certain amount of arrests each day, not because of a quota system, but based on the assumption that if you put in a day's work, you would ticket a certain number of drivers violating the law. The patrol drove mostly Chevrolets, but began switching to 1949 Fords.

The rookie patrolmen were spread among the new divisions. Leon Miller and one other patrolman were stationed at Kingsport under the command of Captain John T. Davis. Davis, a strong and respected leader, was an original member of the Highway Patrol.

Miller went to Kingsport on a Wednesday and that Saturday night, just after midnight, he was hit head on by a car hauling a load of liquor. Miller was driving a new 1949 Ford. The bootlegger that hit him was the real-life character that inspired the movie "Thunder Road."

On the left of the photograph, kneeling from left to right were Thomas W. Moore, Hatcher, Vallie Haynes, Otto Murphy, O. B. Garner, James J. "Brudder" Schuller, and Delbert McCormick. Standing from left to right in the second row were "Coolie" Graves, Corporal Sam Ross, Ed Johnson, Corporal Harold Cross, Tommy Hayes, J. W. McCrary, Charles Graham, Corporal Wyatt Hailey, Sadie Payne, and Captain J. J. "Bullet" Jackson (division commander). Standing on the porch from left to right were Sergeant Arthur M. Lashlee, Ed Hatfield, unidentified, Paul Taylor, J. C. "Dimp" Jamison, Truman Clark, Patrick, Woods, Lum Edwards, Corporal Walter Toon, and Ray Austin.

With most counties in the state dry, traffic in illegal liquor was constant. Bonded whiskey was transported in packages wrapped in brown paper, called "lugs." Lugs were marked according to brand, for example Seagram's VO was marked "VO." Each lug contained a number of bottles, for example 3 fifths or 8 pints, and were loaded in the trunk or in place of the back seat and covered with a blanket. A load might be 60 or 65 cases.

White whiskey or moonshine was usually contained in Mason jars. Drivers would transport bonded whiskey from cities and moonshine from rural areas. Patrolmen often knew what they were hauling based on the direction they were driving. The drivers were good, knew the back roads and were a challenge for patrolmen to catch.

The Patrol had an unwritten rule for survival as a patrolman. New patrolmen had to demonstrate the ability to control the situation when making an arrest. If a fight developed, the highway patrolman was expected to prevail. Miller recalled, "They sent you to a station and if you had to arrest somebody and you got whipped, they'd transfer you to another station. If you got whipped again, they let you go."

Miller, a former Carson Newman football player, was never "whipped" and when he was transferred it was to his home in Rockwood. The Rockwood office was housed in one of the early THP stations built around 1936. The three officers assigned there during the early fifties were Sergeant Cecil W. Strader and Patrolmen Ed Walker and Leon Miller. Walker and Miller later transferred to the TBI.

Not only did individuals move between duty stations, but stations moved from town to town and from

Lieutenant Leslie Jett took movie footage for a Highway Patrol produced safety film in 1950.

A group of safety officers in the late forties with motion picture cameras for use in presentations of school groups and others. Patrolmen from left to right were Price Sain, W. E. Harrison, Leslie E. Jett, Glen Kemp, and Lieutenant Hagan. The civilian photographer was James Dorris.

time to time new offices were created. In August 1950, the station in Sparta was moved to Smithville and two patrolmen were assigned to a new station at Tullahoma in September 1950.

Although most patrolmen were occasionally transferred, Thomas J. Cantwell spent virtually his entire career with the Patrol at the Sevierville station. When he joined on July 1, 1951, the Sevier County substation was in Gatlinburg. Cantwell and a corporal set up the Sevierville station. Patrolman Fred Ellis became Cantwell's partner in 1954. The Gatlinburg station was later closed. Eddie Oury also joined the Patrol in 1951, following service in the Navy. Oury was the son of a professional wrestler and grew up in East Tennessee. He spent most of his THP career in Scott and Cocke counties.

THP communications head, R. R. Turner, tests teletype communicates with law enforcement at Fort Monmouth, New Jersey, in 1951. The system was the forerunner of the NCIC.

Patrolmen were often transferred as a disciplinary measure or because they fell out of favor politically. One patrolman was assigned to another duty station. When he reached the new assignment he was met at the bus terminal and told to report to another location. The officer was sent all over the state before he was allowed to settle into a new assignment. Political disfavor could also get a patrolman fired.

Reassignments of patrolmen and relocation of offices usually related to increased traffic congestion or other safety issues. The soaring rate of traffic deaths on Tennessee's highways was the ever present concern of the Highway Patrol. Enforcement and driver education were the primary tools in reducing death on the roadways of the state.

Safety Commissioner Sam K. Neal was determined to slow speeding drivers, one of the major causes of fatalities on the roadways. The authority to establish speed limits was vested in the state legislature. Neal, however, as Commissioner of Safety, had the authority to determine what speed constituted reckless driving. He determined that speed to be 70 MPH during the day and 60 MPH at night. This defacto speed limit became effective August 30, 1950. At the same time, the Commissioner instructed the Patrol to crack down on very slow drivers who also created reckless conditions.

The Safety Education Division made a number of movies to dramatize the dangers of speeding and reckless driving, which were used to promote driver safety to clubs and schools. Lieutenant Leslie Jett, Director of the Division, shot film and oversaw the production of the movies. Jett was the brother of former Inspector R. Willard Jett and joined the patrol in the late forties

The Highway Patrol built good working relationships with local law enforcement by establishing a substantial presence across the state with capable officers. Lawmen from left to right in this circa 1950 photograph were Highway Patrolman Bobby H. Fyke, Highway Patrolman Thad Felts, Johnson County Sheriff K. B. Maddron, and Mountain City Chief of Police Metter. Sheriff Maddron served several terms as sheriff, the first beginning in 1926.

after World War II where he served four years as a Flying Tiger in China, Burma and India.

The expanding department took over the Clover Bottom Farm near Donelson and spent $16,000 to convert the space to offices. The Third or Nashville Division of the Patrol moved to Clover Bottom in April 1950, from the State Office Building where the Department of Safety was headquartered. Other central offices, except for the administrative offices and the drivers license division, soon followed. Vacated space at the State Office Building was converted into space for a Highway Patrol school including reopening the firing range in the basement that had been taken over for storage.

Sergeant Fred Waldrop was in charge of the THP armory. He maintained weapons needed for major crime related incidents and riot control including submachine guns, shotguns, rifles and teargas guns. The armory was located in the basement of the State Office Building near the firing range.

Specialized weapons were frequently carried in potentially dangerous encounters. During the Enka Plant strike and labor riots in Morristown, Sergeant Tommy Sams, Patrolman Leon Miller and four other patrolmen spent almost three months at the site of the dispute. Frequent flare ups led to serious personal injuries and property being blown up and burned. When an incident became violent, Sergeant Sams called headquarters and 50 cars with 2 men each were dispatched to restore peace. When the large force left, problems started again. On one occasion strikers set fire to an automobile and the Patrol officers responded to see if anyone was injured. They were quickly surrounded by a mob of strikers. The patrolmen had only pistols but Sams carried a Thompson submachine gun.

A burley union organizer from New York walked up to the Sergeant and told him the strikers were going to shove the weapon up his rear end. Sergeant Tommy Sams pulled back the bolt on the Thompson, cocking the automatic weapon and pointed it directly at the union man. Sergeant Sams said, "Yeah, but it will be empty when you do." The confrontation ended.

Heroic actions of Patrol officers reminded citizens of the danger inherent in law enforcement. Corporal Dennis O. Trotter and Patrolman Brownlee Reagan of the Knoxville division put their lives on the line on May 6, 1950. They responded to reports of a car being driven recklessly near Lenoir City. They saw the car, a Yellow Cab, as it sideswiped another car and forced it off the road. They tried to stop the cab and it sped away.

Corporal Trotter pulled along side the taxi. The driver swerved, trying to ram the patrol car. One of the occupants tried to break out the back glass in an attempt to fire on the patrol car. Patrolman Reagan leaned out the car window and fired five shots. Two hit the fender and bumper, the other three shots flattened two of the cab's tires. When the car stopped, the officers arrested two occupants and found the body of the taxi driver in the front seat with a bullet in his head.

Knoxville Division Captain George Burdette questioned the arrested subjects. Initially the two denied

Charles W. Danner became a Tennessee Highway Patrol on July 2, 1951. He was stationed at Rogersville and Mountain City before moving to the governor's residence in 1953 at the rank of corporal. Danner was named troop commander in 1967.

Patrolman Tom Moore stood by a 1951 Ford patrol car. Following more than a decade on the Patrol, Moore was transferred to the TBI where he served for many years.

knowing anything. Then one said, "Give me a cigarette and I'll tell the whole story." The two killers had drunk beer all afternoon, getting up the nerve to rob a tavern. They shot the taxi driver for his car. Trotter and Reagan arrested them before they could dispose of the body or do the robbery.

Patrolman Reagan, a Gatlinburg native, had been on the Patrol for only a month. Knoxville Captain Burdette praised him, "That was his first taste of real action and he showed that he could fire a gun, making all the shots count."

Commissioner Neal made the first presentation of the Department of Safety's new commendation ribbon to Corporal Trotter and Patrolman Reagan the following November. The citations were awarded as a special commendation for outstanding performance of duty. The ribbon was gold and black and was to be worn by an officer on his blouse at all times.

Sergeant Dan Morris and Patrolman L. E. Morris of the Eighth Division were given plaques by the Tennessee Safety Council for their actions in November 1949. They saved the life of a 10-year-old Jackson girl who was overcome by carbon monoxide fumes in the back seat of a car.

The two highway patrolmen administered artificial respiration and rushed the girl to the hospital. Attending physicians said the girl would have died without their quick actions.

The officers of the Highway Patrol assisted citizens of Tennessee in ways unrelated to their work as lawmen. On Christmas Eve 1950, the men of the Nashville Division distributed 550 baskets of food to families in need. Each basket contained 25 different food items and weighed nearly one hundred pounds. The project was financed by a charity girls basketball game organized by Captain J. J. Jackson. Other similar projects were done throughout the Patrol.

A number of uniform changes were made in the late forties. Eisenhower or "Ike" jackets were issued in April 1949 as a part of the regulation uniform. The new jackets were first distributed in the Memphis Division, then in Nashville and afterwards in Knoxville, Chattanooga and Kingsport. Sam Brown belts were not worn with the Ike jackets, but continued to be worn with the old-style blouse on dress occasions.

Although shoulder patches were worn on uniform coats or jackets from the founding of the Patrol, the first patches were worn on uniform shirts in 1948 and 1949. The earliest shirt patches came about when a group of patrolmen ordered the patches and wore them on the left shoulder. The patches were the same as coat patches except with a white background. In 1951 official issue patches were purchased by the department and became standard on uniform shirts. Summer shirts were poplin with regular plastic buttons. Metal buttons with the state seal were used on the wool gabardine winter shirts.

Cookeville District patrolmen raided the residence of a Sparta bootlegger in 1952. Lugs of bonded whiskey were found behind a hidden panel. From left to right were patrolmen Tom Fugitt, Norman "Jeep" Farley, Robert H. Beadle, an unidentified patrolman, and White County Sheriff Bill Hobbs.

A class of 59 new patrolmen took a six-week training course at Montgomery Bell state park in the summer of 1950. The class was made up of 39 men who had less than one year's experience in the THP and 20 new recruits who were added to perform new civil defense duties. The new patrolmen brought the number in the agency to 280.

The school was much like a military boot camp including beans as a staple at meal time. Reveille was

Patrolman T. J. Cantwell with one of the many carloads of white whiskey he confiscated in Sevier County.

The Highway Patrol frequently worked with county officers to raid moonshine stills. Assisting the Rutherford County sheriff and his deputy in the early 1950s were from left to right Patrolman Leonard Hill, Patrolman Wyatt Hailey, and Corporal John D. Sanford.

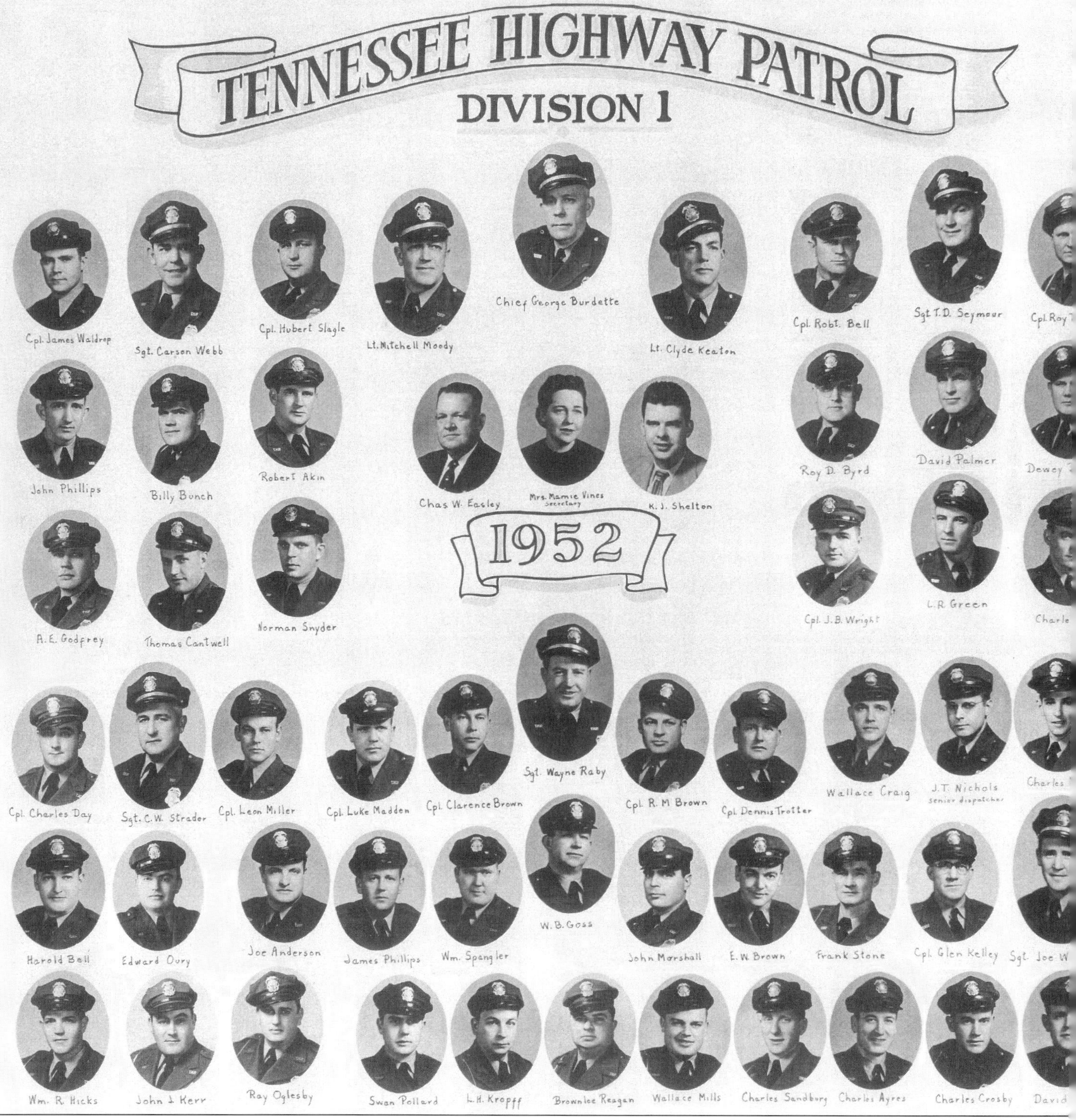

TENNESSEE HIGHWAY PATROL
DIVISION 1

Cpl. James Waldrop

Sgt. Carson Webb

Cpl. Hubert Slagle

Lt. Mitchell Moody

Chief George Burdette

Lt. Clyde Keaton

Cpl. Robt. Bell

Sgt. T.D. Seymour

Cpl. Roy

John Phillips

Billy Bunch

Robert Akin

Chas. W. Easley

Mrs. Mamie Vines
Secretary

K. J. Shelton

Roy D. Byrd

David Palmer

Dewey

A. E. Godfrey

Thomas Cantwell

Norman Snyder

Cpl. J. B. Wright

L. R. Green

Charle

1952

Cpl. Charles Day

Sgt. C. W. Strader

Cpl. Leon Miller

Cpl. Luke Madden

Cpl. Clarence Brown

Sgt. Wayne Raby

Cpl. R. M. Brown

Cpl. Dennis Trotter

Wallace Craig

J. T. Nichols
Senior dispatcher

Charles

Harold Bell

Edward Oury

Joe Anderson

James Phillips

Wm. Spangler

W. B. Goss

John Marshall

E. W. Brown

Frank Stone

Cpl. Glen Kelley

Sgt. Joe W

Wm. R. Hicks

John J Kerr

Ray Oglesby

Swan Pollard

L. H. Kropff

Brownlee Reagan

Wallace Mills

Charles Sandborg

Charles Ayres

Charles Crosby

David

Composite photograph of Division One of the Tennessee Highway Patrol in 1952. The division was headquartered in Knoxville and commanded by Division Captain George Burdette. The various district offices in the division were headed by the sergeants spread throughout the photograph and staffed by those patrolmen and corporals nearest the sergeants.

blown at 7:00 a.m. each day and classes began at 8:00 a.m. Classes lasted until 5:00 p.m. with an hour break for lunch at noon. The men bunked three to a cabin and were in bed by dark, because cabins had no electricity for lights. Trainees stayed in camp except for weekend leave from 5:00 p.m. Saturday until 8:00 a.m. Monday. Beyond the basic training schools, each division had special training programs for all patrolmen.

Administering the increasing number of motor vehicle laws and maintaining related records was an expanding responsibility for the Patrol. In 1949 the legislature split the Tennessee Highway Patrol into the Division of Motor Vehicles and the Division of State

Corporal Lloyd Wayne Tubbs confiscated a batch of moonshine in Madison County in 1954.

Sergeant Cecil W. Strader and Corporal Leon Miller with a car trunk load of illegal whiskey captured in Roane County in the fifties. The bottles of bonded alcohol are wrapped in brown paper, and were called "lugs." Each "lug" contained a number of bottles with the brand noted on the wrapping.

Highway Patrol. The Financial Responsibility Division was also created in 1949. Roy M. Bates served as the first director of the Financial Responsibility Division. During the first year of the division, July 1, 1949, through June 30, 1950, 536 automobile licenses were revoked. Of those, 160 were restored after owners paid damages ordered by the courts.

The legislature created the Motor Vehicle Title Division effective March 1, 1951, and motor vehicle laws were significantly revised. At the same time the Division of Motor Vehicles was moved from the THP and placed directly under the Commissioner of the Department of Safety. The new title division was headed by Wirt Courtney and was to be housed at Clover Bottom. Courtney worked out of his home in Franklin, Tennessee, organizing the title division while office space was being prepared.

The title records function began as the Unsatisfied Judgment Law passed in 1937 at the same time as the Drivers License Law. The Unsatisfied Judgment Law provided that the drivers license be revoked for anyone who could not pay the judgment against him for a traffic accident. The law was revised in 1949 as the Financial Responsibility Law and was broadened in 1951, when the Financial Responsibility Division was assigned to the Department of Safety and David Alexander was placed in charge. Approximately 1,500 licenses were revoked in 1951.

The Patrol became increasingly involved in assisting local agencies with criminal cases. One such case

was the murder of a Humboldt truck driver in the summer of 1950. The body was dumped in Kentucky Lake near Camden, but the murder proved to have been committed in a tourist court cabin in Jackson. THP Captain Robert H. Fletcher, Corporal Bill Chester and other member of the Patrol arrested two for murder and two others for aiding and abetting murder.

Patrolman Paul Summers, left, died on his motorcycle in Nashville on August 8, 1936. Staff Sergeant Fred Cole Waldrop, right, was killed in a automobile accident on Saturday, April 1, 1950, in Goodlettsville.

The legislature created the Tennessee Bureau of Criminal Identification (TBI) on March 14, 1951, to provide a specialized investigative unit to assist local authorities. Formation of the bureau resulted from a botched murder investigation by untrained deputies in Greene County in December 1950. The state was urged to provide professional criminal investigators to handle such crimes. Six THP officers became the first agents of the new unit. Joe Boyd Williams, one of the original division assistant chiefs of the Patrol, was selected director of the TBI.

Commissioner Neal acted to standardize practices and performance throughout the THP and issued the Tennessee Patrolman's Manual. The 156-page handbook was designed as a practical help for personnel in the field, giving examples of incidents a patrolman might encounter and citing Tennessee law related to the performance of their duty in the situation.

Commissioner Neal was well respected by patrolmen and often stopped and talked with them when he was out on the road. When the budget was tight and a patrolman's uniform pants or shirt appeared worn, Neal authorized a replacement from supply. Before Neal departed, he would tap the patrolman on the shoulder and say, "I want to tell you one thing. I'm all the politics you ever need on the Highway Patrol."

Highway Patrol raided and broke up the swank Ridgetop Inn on the Springfield Highway, one of the most notorious gambling nightspots in the state. From left to right were Inspector Jim Gill, Patrolman J. R. Proctor, two clerks of the casino, Sergeant Trabue Lewis, Corporal John Hancock and Sergeant Elmer Craig. (Nashville Banner photo)

The salary of patrolmen in the early fifties was at three levels, starting patrolmen were paid $245 per month, after six months pay was increased to $260 and to $275 after one year. Top pay for a corporal was $290 per month. In addition to federal taxes, 7% was deducted from pay for retirement. A health insurance plan was offered by 1954 and the premium was also deducted.

The department purchased Pontiacs for sergeants, lieutenants and captains around 1950. As the vehicles were replaced with newer cars, the Pontiacs were assigned to patrolmen. Marking on the doors of patrol cars and elsewhere were painted by hand by Otto Werrbach in Nashville. Hand painted markings were discontinued in 1958 when the department began to use decals.

Electrical systems on the Pontiacs were six volt and they did not have heavy duty alternators as the Fords did. Unless the motor was running three or four radio calls would drain the battery. Patrolmen were mostly in flat-head V-8 engine Fords with a few 6-cylinder Plymouths in the Memphis area. The first overhead valve engines cars acquired by the department were 1954 Fords.

The only emergency lights on cars were red covers to the spotlight. Some patrolmen added red emergency dome lights to their patrol units by finding an individual or business to donate the light. The department began furnishing standard red emergency dome lights in 1954.

The Department of Safety continued to expand functions and organizational units. In 1951, R. .R. Turner of the Communication Division initiated the first inter-agency radio teletype contact with officials in Ft. Monmouth, New Jersey. This began the sharing of information among law enforcement departments

Governor Clement ordered a Highway Patrol crackdown on nightclubs with illegal liquor and gambling operations in November 1953. Here patrolmen raided a gambling operation in Davidson County.

in distant locales. The system grew to include several other states and was the forerunner of the National Crime Information Center (NCIC).

When Governor Frank G. Clement took office in January 1953 the state had serious financial problems. Highway Patrol cars were not in good condition and if it cost over $25 to fix a patrol car, the unit was parked.

Clement appointed G. Hilton Butler to serve as commissioner of the Department of Safety. Butler had been the first head of the newly formed department in

1939. In May Butler was recalled by the Army to be its state director of public safety and he resigned. James English was named acting commissioner of Safety.

The Patrol lost two supervisors in the line of duty in the early fifties. Staff Sergeant Fred Cole Waldrop, one of the best known and most respected officers on the Patrol, died on March 9, 1950, as the result of an accident near Goodlettsville the previous day.

Corporal A. T. Ellis was driving the vehicle as he and Staff Sergeant Waldrop were speeding with red

District heads met in Memphis in 1953. Those seated on the left side of the table from foreground to the back were Captain Percy Griffith, Communications; Captain Greg O'Rear, Lawrenceburg District; Captain C. F. "Dick" Webb, Chattanooga District; Lieutenant Henry Heer, Lawrenceburg District; Lieutenant Robert Fletcher, Safety Education, Lawrenceburg District; Inspector J. J. Jackson, Nashville; Lieutenant Fred Scott, Memphis District; Lieutenant Laverne Maxwell, Jackson District; Lieutenant Dainy Garland, Chattanooga District; and John Cherry, Memphis District. Captain Sam Johnson, Jackson District, sat at the end of the table. Standing at the end of the table from left to right were Commissioner G. Hilton Butler, Captain Trabue Lewis from Nashville and Administrative Assistant Matthew Pratt. Seated on the right side of the table from the back and forward were Lieutenant Mitchell Moody, Knoxville District; Lieutenant T. G. Fite, Nashville District; Captain Jimmy Phelps, Drivers License; Captain Ted Fowlkes, Nashville District; Captain Frank Williamson, Kingsport District; Captain Joe Sanford, Cookeville District; and Captain George Burdette, Knoxville District.

lights and siren to join a manhunt. Ellis swerved to avoid a collision with a automobile and Waldrop was thrown from the car, striking his head on the pavement. Staff Sergeant Waldrop was treated at the hospital and sent home. He remained fully conscience until he died of a blood clot at 1:40 a.m.

Waldrop joined the Patrol in 1941 and was promoted to sergeant in 1944. Among his crime fighting exploits, the Giles County native single-handedly captured the two Clarksville "target" slayers in 1947 and with Captain J. J. Jackson he captured an FBI public enemy who had killed one policeman and shot another.

Sergeant Oliver Devard Williamson was stationed at Brownsville on March 21, 1952, when a series of tornadoes swept through West Tennessee. He was dispatched to Dyersberg to help organize rescue efforts after a tornado killed several people and did extensive property damage. Patrolmen Joe Johnston and Tommy Hill were dispatched from Covington to assist there. As Sergeant Williamson approached Dyersberg on RoEllen Highway around 9:00 p.m., another black funnel touched down and threw the patrol car 300 yards. The shattering impact of the vehicle killed the sergeant.

The Disaster Van was totaled in an accident en route to Lexington, Tennessee, to assist local officials following a 1952 tornado. The Disaster Van was later replaced by a second generation mobile communications center contained in a specially adapted 1956 GMC bus. This Mobile Disaster Radio Unit bus was later replaced by a mobile command and communication facility in a semi-trailer.

At least one member of the Patrol had a personal mobile center. Lieutenant Blackie Mayfield, who had an independent nature, fell out of favor with the new administration and was transferred to a new duty station. Thirty days later he was transferred again. After three months of this, Mayfield drove a small mobile home to Commissioner Butler's office and reported, "I've got my house in order and I'm ready to go anywhere you send me, just let me know when." His transfers stopped.

Routine duty was eye opening for some young patrolmen. They saw a different side of life than they had known. Patrolman Roy B. Cheatam, born in Alamo, Crocket County, began his law enforcement career in 1952 stationed in Selmer. Cheatam was issued uniforms that were ordered for Sergeant Williamson who was killed in the tornado. Cheatam was a church goer and unexposed to the honkytonks he worked on weekends.

Patrolman Cheatam and others went out on Friday and worked until they saw the sun come up on Saturday morning. They slept a little while and went back out to work all of Saturday night until Sunday morning. Cheatam recalled, "The people in those dance halls were just crazy." During the day things were slow and experienced officers shared insights

President Harry Truman attended the Ramp Festival in East Tennessee at Newport in 1955. The THP was escorting the motorcade when a newsman was knocked off a bridge into the creek. Sergeant Arthur M. Lashlee went to the man's aid along with another individual. The president came down to check on the fallen newsman. To the left of Truman was Patrolman Mickey McGuire, and to the right were Captain J. J. Jackson and Governor Frank Clement. The photograph appeared in the May 1955 issue of Life Magazine.

A group of Kingsport District officers in 1954. Kneeling from left to right were Sergeant Grover Cox, Lieutenant Carson S. Webb, Captain Frank Williamson, Patrolmen Paul Crabtree, and Patrolman Harold Flemings. Standing from left to right were Lieutenant Thomas Doug Seymour, unidentified, Patrolmen H. E. "Chub" Wollerver, Patrolman Don Meredith and Patrolman Clarence D. Hamby.

about duty on the Patrol. Once a week a roving crew came to Selmer and other small towns for half a day to

Corporal Lloyd Wayne Tubbs worked this wreck in the Jackson District in 1954. Dealing with injury and loss of life on Tennessee highways was one of the most difficult duties of Patrol officers. Unfortunately it was one of the most frequent duties as well.

give drivers tests and issue licenses. Patrolmen assisted the crew.

William W. Luttrell was appointed commissioner of the Department of Safety in July 1953 and served until May 1956. Luttrell, a native of Knoxville, served 38 months in the European Theater during World War II, including 26 months as a prisoner of war after he was captured in North Africa. Luttrell was elected to two terms as commissioner of finance for Knox County prior to his appointment to state government.

Other members of the command structure included Major Matthew Pratt as Executive Officer, Inspector Robert E. Bibb as head of the Highway Patrol Division, Everette D. LaFon as director of the Drivers License Division, Lieutenant Joe H. Patterson as safety consultant of the Safety Education Division, and Leslie C. Brown as director of the Financial Responsibility Division. Administrative units were the

Troopers gather for a meeting in Memphis in 1954. Most wore the new western-style hats, but a few still wore leather-bill caps.

Communications Section headed by Captain P. E. Griffith as radio engineer, the Finance Section under Budget Officer Wanda Tindall, the Maintenance Section headed by Captain Trabue Lewis, the Supply Section under Staff Sergeant Robert Z. Mayo, the Central Records Section directed by Staff Sergeant E. C. McGlynnan and the Personnel and Training Section commanded by Captain Henry M. Heer.

Captain Trabue Lewis came on the Patrol in the early thirties and rode a motorcycle in Humphries and Dickson counties east of the Tennessee River. In the early days patrolmen wore brown boots, and until the day Lewis retired in the late sixties, he wore brown boots. J. J. Jackson and a number of other from "the old school" also retired in the sixties.

Governor Clement launched an offensive against law breakers on two fronts in November 1953. First,

Radar units added to the Patrol's ability to catch speeders and lower the death toll on Tennessee's highways. The first units were put into service in March 1954. Members of the THP in East Tennessee checking out this new unit were from left to right, Lieutenant T. G. Fite, Patrolman C. T. Ayres and Captain George Burdette of the Knoxville District.

Patrolman Jim Chitwood works radar in 1955. On the right Chitwood monitors the radar for passing speeders. On the left he writes a citation for a driver pulled over after exceeding the posted speed limit.

70

he ordered a Highway Patrol crackdown on nightclubs with illegal liquor and gambling operations. Captain J. J. Jackson of the Nashville Division led axe-wielding raiders into some of the most notorious night spots in the state including the 400 Club near Cleveland and the Roost Club in downtown Tullahoma. Similar raids began across the state.

Captain J. J. Jackson had just returned to duty after a number of months off with a bout of tuberculosis. During his absence Blackie Mayfield was made temporary captain, T. G. Fite acting lieutenant and Arthur M. "Gap" Lashlee acting sergeant.

On the second front, the governor committed $100,000 from his emergency safety fund to launch a campaign to curb traffic fatalities. The combination of two lane roads, heavy traffic and cars with limited safety equipment led to an enormous amount of accidents and many deaths. The money went to hire 16 additional patrolmen, to purchase more patrol cars and to acquire new equipment for catching reckless drivers. A major change for patrolmen was the elimination of the two-man car. In order to cover more territory, only one patrolman was assigned to each patrol car.

New sub-stations were opened including one at Portland, Sumner County, in May 1953. Patrolman Thomas D. Moore who joined the Highway Patrol in July 1952 was transferred from Gallatin as the first man stationed at the new office. Moore was given Walter Toon's patrol car when Toon was transferred to the TBI. Moore stayed in Portland until 1954 when he took the promotional exam for corporal. Corporal Moore moved back to the Sixth Division in Smithville where he stayed until he made sergeant June 1, 1964. He then moved to Sixth Division headquarters at Cookeville and supervised four outlying counties.

Clarksville Highway Patrol officers at the office on Madison in 1954. The front row from left to right included Sergeant Gene Harris, Lieutenant Elmer V. Craig, and Corporal Ben Bradshaw, The second row from left to right were patrolmen Lester Winningham, Bobby H. Fyke, Tommy Hayes and Eddie Joe Williams. They wore the "Ike" jackets and the newly issued western style hats.

Equipment further evolved in the fifties. New technology provided sophisticated enforcement tools from red roof-lights on rolling stock to aircraft. The first Air Police Patrol plane went into service in 1953. The single-engine fixed-wing aircraft turned out to be a short lived experiment.

Major Matt Pratt ordered five radar units, the first radar equipment for the THP. The use of radar had proven successful in Memphis, Chattanooga and Oak Ridge. The radar units were delivered in April 1954 and three more were ordered. They were distributed to areas of the state with the most traffic. Since no statewide speed limit existed, radar was used to stop drivers who exceed the reckless limit set statewide or speed limits set in congested zones. Statewide speed limits were established by the legislature in 1955. The day time speed limit was 65 mph and the night time limit was 55 mph for cars and 50 mph for trucks.

Radar units were augmented by 24 electric speed timers in 1955. New "get tough" tactics were employed to catch speeders and other reckless drivers. Selective enforcement was done in statistically dangerous locations and time periods. Saturation enforcement used large numbers of patrolmen to focus on the most dangerous highway sections. Parking marked cars at conspicuous spots for psychological effect was used in the "visibility operation" of the campaign.

Patrolman Eddie Joe Williams cited a driver on July 12, 1955, for traveling 43 mph in a 30 mph zone on Gallatin Road at Ardee Avenue in Nashville. It was a routine stop that called for the violator to pay a $10

Members of the Kingsport District were training in automatic weapons at the firing range in 1954. The corporal is firing a .45 caliber Reising submachine gun.

Corporal Leon Miller with his 1955 Ford patrol car.

fine and court costs. However, the driver appealed the conviction and the case went to the Tennessee Supreme Court as a legal challenge to the use of radar in the state. The court upheld the conviction in a May 3, 1957, decision and established radar as a reliable and lawful means of traffic speed enforcement.

Sergeant Bob Thomas was over radar operation in the Nashville Division in the early sixties. There was only one unit for the thirteen counties in the division and Thomas moved from county to county. Sometimes Thomas worked with a patrolman and radar unit from another division and set up the two units about two miles apart to test the reaction of drivers caught by radar. Occasionally a driver learned the hard way and got two tickets. Highway fatalities decreased in the state following the deployment of radar units.

Personnel changed in top posts of the Patrol in late summer 1954. Captain J. J. Jackson was promoted to inspector. Inspector Jackson, 6' 5" and 210 pounds, joined the THP as a patrolman on July 5, 1939, and demonstrated strong leadership. Jackson was elected president of the Tennessee Law Enforcement Officers Association in 1962.

Jackson replaced Robert E. Bibb, who became the director of the Bureau of Records and Statistics, assuming control of the data of the patrol and its 350 employees. Bibb had been with the Patrol since April 15, 1935, and had replaced Paul Lilly as inspector only a year earlier.

Captain Henry Heer, personnel and training officer, was promoted to major and executive officer of Safety. He replaced Matthew Pratt who resigned to enter private industry. Henry Heer was a graduate of

the FBI National Academy and had been promoted to captain the year before. Lieutenant Mayo Wix was promoted to captain and replaced Heer and Lieutenant M. E. Kinchum succeeded Wix as lieutenant of the Third Division.

Uniform and insignia changes took place in the mid-fifties. The forest green cap with brown bill that had been worn since the creation of the Patrol was replaced by a wide-brimmed Stetson-styled felt campaign hat. The change was made to distinguish state officers from county patrolmen. The hats were purchased at the cost of $13.83 each and were issued in November of 1953. They were first issued in the Nashville area and then to divisions across the state. For over a year the hats were worn without insignia.

The basic working rank of the Highway Patrol was changed from Patrolman to Trooper in late 1955. The rank of corporal was abolished. Those holding the rank of corporal became troopers but retained corporal's pay. Trooper pay was raised to $310 a month.

A new badge style, an eagle-top sunburst, was adopted at the same time as insignia for troopers and sergeants. The eagle-top sunburst had been worn by supervisors above sergeants since the early thirties. A miniature of the breast badge was used as a hat badge on the western style hat. Numbers on the new badges were issued on a seniority basis. Men who had been on the longest got the lowest numbers.

A new shirt style was introduced in 1957 that featured forest green pocket flaps and shoulder epaulet

Trooper Bobby Fyke inspects the contents of confiscated lugs of whiskey in 1955. The load was destined for Knoxville and confiscated on U.S. 31W northbound.

straps. Collars were sometimes worn open in the summertime. Shoulder patches began to be worn on both sleeves. The new style shirt continued as part of the uniform into the twenty-first century.

Sergeant A. M. Lashlee wore the uniform and newly adopted badge style in 1955. The uniform included the "Ike" jacket and Stetson style hat. The badge was the same style worn by supervisors above sergeant since the mid-thirties, but it was new to sergeants and the style also worn by troopers, the new basic rank of the Patrol. A miniature of the badge was worn as the hat badge.

A converted bus and auxiliary vehicles served as the Mobile Disaster Radio Unit in the late fifties.

G. Hilton Butler returned as commissioner of Safety on April 16, 1956. He named W. E. "Bud" Hopton, director of the Tennessee Bureau of Criminal Identification, as deputy commissioner. Hopton continued in role until the left the department in 1971. Greg O'Rear was named head of the uniformed Patrol. The title of the chief uniformed officer of the Patrol was changed from Chief to Troop Commander. Greg O'Rear was the first to hold the title, although the title Chief continued to be used, the troop commander being the chief of the Patrol.

Two men played key roles in the leadership of the Department of Safety and the Highway Patrol in the fifties and sixties. The service of Major G. Hilton Butler and Greg L. O'Rear spanned five decades. Butler first served as director of the department in January 1939 and O'Rear completed his final stint as commissioner in January 1971.

G. Hilton Butler and Greg O'Rear served together in the top positions of leadership twice under appointment by Governor Frank G. Clement. Butler was appointed commissioner of the Department of Safety. O'Rear was named troop commander of the Highway Patrol.

Physically, the two were quite a contrast. Butler was short and O'Rear was 6' 8" tall, but any reference to "Mutt and Jeff" infuriated the two. Commissioner Butler would sit on his leg in the patrol car so he could see better and look taller. He had a fear of flying and his driver Mickey McGuire was frequently called at 2:00 or 3:00 in the morning when the commissioner had a meeting in a distant part of the state.

Butler served as state Revenue Department commissioner, director of Selective Service during World War II and twice as adjutant general of the Tennessee National Guard. He was awarded the Legion of Merit for service in

The Murfreesboro Post in 1957 stood in front of one of the building constructed for the Patrol in the thirties. From left to right, kneeling in front were Patrolman J. C. Ledbetter, Lieutenant John D. Sanford, and Patrolman Bill Blackburn. Standing were Patrolman Charles Armstrong, Patrolman Bill L. Jones soon after he joined the Patrol, and Sergeant Bill Puryear.

commander from 1963 to 1965. O'Rear served two terms as commissioner of the Department of Safety, from January 1959 to August 1963 and from August 1965 to January 1971. O'Rear was the first career THP officer to become commissioner of Safety. He was age 45 at the time. After he retired from Safety in 1971, Greg O'Rear continued his service to the state as sergeant at arms for the House of Representatives.

Commissioner Butler and Troop Commander O'Rear made a number of personnel changes in 1956. Inspector J. J. Jackson was promoted to senior inspector. Henry M. Heer was promoted to major and given the post of executive officer. Captain Mayo Wix took Heer's place as head of the Personnel and Training Section. Captain James T. Phelps was made director of the Drivers License Division. Lieutenant Joe H. Patterson took over safety education and Edmond C. McGlynnan was put in charge of the Accident Records Bureau. Sergeants Arthur M. Lashlee and William C. "Mickey" McGuire were promoted to lieutenant.

The Captain Noah A. Robinson of the Eighth Division moved his office from Huntingdon to Jackson in 1956, a temporary move. During the time when the Eighth Division office was in Huntingdon, troopers in Madison County worked out of the THP radio station on State Street in Jackson.

Division commanders were Captain George Burdette in Knoxville, Captain C. F. "Dick" Webb in

World War II. Among Butler's accomplishment was the publication of a textbook, *The Tennessean and His Government,* for use at the American Legion's Boys State. Besides serving as the Department of Safety's first director, he served three additional terms as its commissioner, January to May 1953, May 1956 to January 1959 and January 1963 to August 1965. He completed his service to the department in 1968 after serving two years as the first director of the Tennessee Law Enforcement Training Academy.

Greg O'Rear became a patrolman on the Tennessee Highway Patrol in 1939 and quickly moved through the ranks. He was promoted to corporal in 1942, to sergeant in 1944 and to lieutenant in 1947. In 1949 O'Rear was made captain of the Lawrenceburg Division. He first became troop commander or chief of all uniformed personnel of the THP in 1956, serving until 1959. He served an additional term as troop

Troopers Doug Pearce, left, and Melvin Holland hold bonded whiskey confiscated in a Jackson raid in February 1956.

The Lawrenceburg office in 1955 included seated from left to right R. A. Webb, Bobby Wright, Captain Greg O'Rear, Wilton McNutt and Hayes Cathy. Standing from left to right were Irving Dorning, C. B. "Cornbread" Martin, James M. "Bud" Abbott, Bob Green and John Sloan.

Chattanooga, Captain C. B. "Ted" Fowlkes in Nashville, Captain Stuart M. Dean in Memphis, Captain Frank "Bowser" Williamson in Kingsport, Captain Joe Sanford in Cookeville, Captain M. L. Hamilton in Lawrenceburg and Captain Noah A. Robinson in Jackson.

Executive Officer Major Henry Heer announced a change in uniform policy that added to trooper comfort. For the first time, personnel were allowed to go open-collared and wear no tie during the hot summer months.

The Volunteer Survivorship Contribution Fund was created by the ranks of the Patrol as a way for members of the Patrol to support those left behind as a result of a death in the line of duty. Each member of the THP contributed $10 when an officer gave his life in the line of duty and the money was presented to the survivor to defray expenses. The agency had approximately 400 sworn officers. The family of Trooper Oscar Morris, who was struck and killed by a hit and run driver in Lebanon in April 1956, was the first recipient of the fund. The $10 Club, as it was known, collected $3,990 from the 399 members of the Patrol.

A changing society meant the Patrol was increasingly called on to help maintain law and order. On

Labor Day weekend 1956 riots broke out in Clinton, Tennessee, over court-ordered desegregation. Fifty patrol cars with 100 heavily armed troopers pulled into the public square and deployed. The disturbance was quickly ended.

The fifties were dangerous on the highways of Tennessee and the nation. The Patrol lost two of its own to automobile accidents in the fifties. Trooper Oscar Newton Morris was struck and killed by a drunk driver while giving directions to another driver on Highway 70 near Lebanon on May 9, 1956. The drunk driver fled the scene. After checking on Trooper Morris, a college student to whom the trooper was giving a ride got behind the wheel of the patrol car and chased the suspect. The student was able to stop the suspect and held him until officers arrived.

Trooper Raymond Hendon was killed near Smyrna on June 3, 1957, while he transported blood to a needy recipient. As a result of the incident, the Patrol began a no-escort policy.

Lieutenant William Edmund Smith unexpectedly died of a heart attack at his home shortly after midnight on January 29, 1959, at age 43. Smith joined the Patrol in 1940 and was assigned to Columbia. He moved to Memphis in 1947 and was promoted to lieu-

miles. The operation was supported by a fixed-wing airplane, a helicopter, wreckers and ambulances. Just a few hours before the roadblock began a two car accident killed one and injured 8, reminding everyone of the importance of the event.

Individually as well as collectively, the Tennessee Highway Patrol excelled. A personal achievement by Trooper Roy Hedge set a record in the calendar year 1956. While patrolling Marion County Hedge made 1,286 arrests and each case resulted in a conviction. This was the first time a THP officer achieved a 100% conviction rate for an entire calendar year.

In March 1957 the Tennessee Highway Patrol became the first agency in the nation to use helicopters in police work. Sergeant Truman Clark and Trooper Bob Seamon left for the Texas Bell Helicopter factory in March 1957. After their completion of pilot school at the facility, the first Bell 47 helicopter was delivered to the THP and put into service on March 22, 1957. A second helicopter arrived in July 1957. The following year the Patrol acquired the first military surplus helicopter. Truman Clark was the first THP chief pilot and later held the rank of captain.

The Patrol wasted no time in demonstrating the value of the helicopter in law enforcement. "Operation Whirlybird" was initiated on April 18, 1957, in Roane County near Rockwood. A triple roadblock was set up in the area near the intersection of highways US 70 and U.S. 27. Under the direction of the helicopter, 25 violators were arrested in a three-hour period and 3,258 cars were

The THP used massive roadblocks in the late fifties to catch illegal drivers and establish a safety presence on Tennessee highways. Newly acquired Patrol helicopters were used as a platform for aerial photograph.

tenant in 1957. Sergeant Leon Harris was promoted and took over lieutenant duties in Memphis.

Commissioner Butler was committed to bringing down the death toll on the highways of the state. The Patrol began to employ massive roadblocks in the spring of 1956 in an effort to apprehend drunk and unlicensed drivers and to establish a safety presence. "Longitudinal roadblocks" were set over long stretches of highways for visibility, "speed blocks" involved mass use of radar units in conjunction with regular patrol units and "drunknets" utilized late night roadblocks to catch drunk drivers.

On October 2, 1956, a 180 mile long roadblock called "Operation Long Line" was set up. One hundred troopers were used to establish the presence along US Highway 41, one trooper was stationed every two

The Patrol began use of helicopters in 1957. Two Bell 47 helicopters were purchased initially. The fleet was soon expanded with military surplus aircraft. Inspecting one of the new helicopters were from left to right Jackson District Lieutenant LaVerne Maxwell, pilot Lieutenant Bob Seamon in the chopper, head of the aviation unit Captain Truman Clark and Jackson District Captain Noah Robinson.

The largest officers on the Patrol in 1957 from left to right were Joe Patterson, James M. Abbott, J. J. Jackson, Clyde Hullander, Bobby H. Fyke and Greg O'Rear. Some or all of the group traveled with the good will tour to cities across the state promoting traffic safety.

checked. In August, large numbers were painted on the top of patrol cars so they could be identified from the air.

Because of their novelty, helicopters were used initially for public relations. Law enforcement and safety uses for the aircraft quickly expanded including search and rescue missions. The first helicopters did not have heaters and an early wintertime search and rescue mission had to be suspended because the weather was so cold that pilots were unable to handle the controls. Heaters were installed and contributed to the success of a cold weather mission in the early spring of 1960. Helicopter pilot Lieutenant W. T. Sircy and other THP flyers flew supplies into rural mountain families stranded by a 42-inch snowfall.

The Patrol used a variety of strategies to catch dangerous drivers. Nighttime roadblocks were initiated. The visible presence of patrol cars changed driving habits only temporarily and radar "traps" or "nets" were introduced to augment roadblocks. Unmarked cars were created by sanding Patrol emblems from the sides of patrol cars and removing emergency dome lights. The THP focused on all issues that impacted highway safety including vehicles with burned out or damaged lights and drivers that were driving too slowly.

Former President Harry Truman stopped for a cold drink at a country store while he was campaigning for John F. Kennedy in Tennessee in the late fifties. Those with the president from left to right were Joe Henry (in military uniform), Don McSween (in front seat passing the cola), Robert Clement (father of the governor, standing behind McSween), Truman, Governor Frank G. Clement, THP Lieutenant Harold Cross and THP Inspector J. J. Jackson (in suit).

some years earlier when two patrolmen stopped to checkout a "Goodtime" house at 12th and Charlotte in Nashville. When the alarm was raised inside the house that the police were coming, comments were made by some that they didn't care about the police. Someone in the house said, "You better care, that's them yellow jackets." Butler decided that "Yellow Jackets" was the right name for the unit.

The Yellow Jackets wore a special uniform that consisted of black pants with a yellow leg stripe, a yellow shirt with black pocket flaps and epaulet, a black tie or ascot, black leather motorcycle boots and a yellow leather jacket with black trim for winter wear. Their patch was the same as other troopers except that it had a black background with yellow letters and trim. Motorcycles ridden by this elite unit were yellow and had the picture of a yellow jacket painted on the lower portion of the windscreen. The Yellow Jackets were highly visible and effective.

Members of the Yellow Jackets were all volunteers. They were under the command of Lieutenant Elmer V. Craig and over the period of its existence included Sergeant Charles Graham, Sergeant J. W. McCrary, Trooper Oval Page, Lieutenant John E. Hancock, Trooper Richard Pope, Trooper William Harper, Trooper Charles Armstrong and Trooper Charles T. Wakefield. The unit lasted for less than a year, but made an impact across the state. The use of the Yellow Jacket image on the motorcycle windshield and the designation were discontinued after Greg O'Rear became commission of Safety, but use of the colorful motorcycles and uniforms were used until they wore out.

Such innovations helped the Patrol deal with traffic enforcement challenges that grew as the highways

Inspector Mickey McGuire patrols a snowy country lane beside woodland pond in the winter of 1959.

improved. Tennessee embarked on a surge of highway construction in the late 1950s that was more extensive than any since Governor Austin Peay undertook his highway building program in the 1920s. The first portion of the system of interstate highways was opened on December 19, 1958. It was a 1.8 mile section of I-65 in Giles County running from the Alabama state line to U.S. 31. From this small beginning, over 1,000 miles of interstate highways were constructed to crisscross Tennessee.

Patrol cars got a new look in April 1958. The cream and black color scheme continued. Markings consisted of applied decals with the designation "Tennessee State Trooper" in reflective paint along the top of the front fender and door on each side and on the trunk. A state seal was applied on the front doors. The new paint scheme made patrol cars more visible,

Helicopters were used to draw the public to the statewide safety tours of the late fifties and early sixties.

Former President Harry Truman flew into Jackson in 1959 campaigning for John F. Kennedy. From the left were Jackson Police Department (JPD) Traffic Lieutenant Carl Lee Johnsey, THP Captain Noah Robinson, Governor George Blanton, Truman, THP Lieutenant Joe Burton Williams and JPD Traffic Officer D. L. Murphy.

especially at night.

The western-style campaign hat was dropped from the uniform in March 1959 and the Patrol readopted the eight-point service cap. The crossed baton cap badge style was readopted as well, except "Trooper" now appeared in the number panel for troopers. The designation "Highway Patrol" remained on the shoulder patch until it was changed to "State Trooper" in the late sixties.

Troopers were issued summer uniforms for the first time in decades in the summer of 1960. Previously, the uniform change from winter to summer consisted of discarding the uniform jacket. The color and style of the new lighter weight uniforms were the same as those worn in the winter, tan shirts with green trim and green trousers.

A knee-length, double-breasted overcoat that flared out at the bottom was provided for winter wear. The coat was popular with many because it was warm in the cold winter months. For other it was unpopular and called the "Turkey Gobbler" because of the bottom fan. The coat could be dangerous, because when the coat was buttoned the trooper had to draw his sidearm through a slit in the pocket. It difficult to get to the weapon and the revolver was prone to become tangled in the coat. The coats were quickly modified to solve the problem. A wind-breaker style jacket was provided as a uniform option in 1965.

The legislature authorized a major increase of personnel in 1956. New troopers were added over the following two years. A salary increase was authorized for current personnel as well, to be effective July 1, 1957. The first 43 new troopers were trained by August 1957 and four were assigned to Kingsport, six to Cookeville, six to Knoxville, ten to Nashville, five to Chattanooga,

four to Lawrenceburg, five to Memphis and three to Jackson. In September 1957, 70 new troopers graduated from the training school at Sewart Air Force Base in Smyrna after three weeks of intensive training. Ten air policemen graduated at the same time.

Trooper Bill L. "Billy" Jones was one of the new Highway Patrol officers added in 1957. After training, Jones was stationed in Lebanon for three months before he was moved to Murfreesboro. Seven years later he was promoted to sergeant in Franklin with responsibility for supervising troopers in Williamson and Rutherford counties.

Fred Schott Jr. was among the 1958 class of recruits that also trained at Sewart Air Force Base. The class graduation picture was taken on the War Memorial Auditorium steps near the capitol. Governor Clement invited the new troopers to the governor's residence for lunch. They were entertained by Johnny Bragg and his quartet. Bragg was a prisoner at the state penitentiary and had written the song "Just Walkin' in the Rain."

Fred Schott served as chaplain of the Patrol beginning in 1958. In addition to his full-time road work as a trooper, he provided religious services that ranged from offering prayers in public and private gatherings to conducting funerals for troopers.

Greg L. O'Rear served as commissioner of the Department of Safety during the first term of Governor Buford Ellington from 1959 to 1963. C. F. "Dick" Webb was appointed troop commander of the

Members of the Knoxville District prepare for the Fourth of July weekend in 1960. Captain George Burdette stood behind the first car surrounded by his troopers. The Patrol got a new look in 1958, including a redesign of patrol cars, new uniforms for troopers and the re-adoption of the uniform cap.

THP officers meet with members of the Kentucky State Police to review plans for a roadblock in the early sixties at the Tennessee-Kentucky border near Fort Campbell. From left to right were Inspector J. J. Jackson, Captain Arthur Lashlee, Trooper Ed Beckman, two KSP officers, Lieutenant Elmer Craig, Trooper Jim Cassidy, Major Henry Heer and another KSP officer.

Patrol. Other senior commanders were Senior Inspector J. J. Jackson and Inspector William C. "Mickey" McGuire. Major Henry M. Heer remained executive officer. Lieutenant Elmer Craig later held the position. Section leaders continued in their position, and Ronnie Bledsoe was named Public Relations and Information Officer.

Commanding officers frequently participated in enforcement duties. Inspector Mickey McGuire came face to face with a gun wielding parolee from an Ohio corrections facility on January 25, 1960. The man wrecked a stolen car, fired at two lawmen and fled into the woods off Woodmont Boulevard near Franklin Road as McGuire drove up. Inspector McGuire found him hiding in the brush. The felon taunted McGuire to get closer and then fired at the officer. The bullet just missed. McGuire lunged at the criminal and wrestled the gun away.

The Third or Nashville District was under the command of Captain James T. "Jim" Gill. Elmer Craig, M. E. Kinchum and A. M. Lashlee were lieutenants.

The district moved into a new headquarters building on Murfreesboro Road in 1958. Other district commanders included Captain George Burdette in Knoxville. Captain P. D. Garland headed the Chattanooga District until Captain Jewel Weese took command in June 1968 after Garland's retirement. Captain Stuart M. Dean was in command in Memphis, Captain Frank Williamson in Kingsport, Captain Joe Sanford in Cookeville, Captain M. L. Hamilton in Lawrenceburg and Captain Noah A. Robinson in Jackson.

A number of new district headquarters building were built in the sixties. The Fourth or Memphis District moved from Poplar and Yates into its new headquarters on Summer Avenue (Highway 70) at Elmore Road in April 1960. The Kingsport District headquarters was completed on Brooks Circle in October 1962 and named the "Frank K. Williamson Building" for the longtime district captain. Knoxville's headquarters was moved to a new building at Kingston Pike and Buckingham Road in May 1966. The

Trooper John McCord working radar in December 1961 soon after he joined the Patrol.

and Wall. McCord decided early in life that he wanted to be a member of the Patrol. His father became a Highway Patrolman in 1943 when he returned from service in the Navy. Henry Heer went on the Patrol at the same time and the two became close friends. After the senior McCord left the force, Heer would frequently visit in his THP vehicle. Young John McCord made up his mind to be a Tennessee Highway Patrolman.

McCord was assigned to Williamson County in 1962. He worked four days and three nights including all weekend nights. Troopers got five days off a month, but not all at one time. Budget restraints once again meant that patrol cars with serious problems might sit on the side of the road for weeks at a time. The problem was exacerbated because most patrol cars were old and many roads were not paved.

Cooperation between troopers, police departments and sheriff's offices was extensive and the Patrol handled much more than traffic and wrecks. A sheriff might have only two or three regular deputies and a few part-time deputies. Deputies typically worked days and after they went home, any crime that occurred was given to the Highway Patrol. If a bad murder was committed the sheriff came out, otherwise troopers handle all types of crimes.

The sergeant, in addition to working patrol with troopers, was in charge of all Patrol activities in the

Cookeville District headquarters was moved from highway 70 to a new building on Bunker Hill Road in May 1967. The Eight District moved into a new building near I-40 on Country Club Lane in Jackson in February 1968, permanently relocating the headquarters office from Huntingdon.

Trooper John McCord began duty with the Patrol on August 7, 1961, working in Nashville and living in the barracks with Troopers Ed Beckman, Mark Milton

Members of the Kingsport District in the sixties wearing the overcoats called "Turkey Gobblers" by many officers. The coats were warm, providing winter comfort. Some officers didn't like the coats because revolvers had to be drawn through the side pockets, but the coats were quickly modified to solve the problem.

The two best shots from each district were candidates for the THP pistol team and gathered in November 1963 at the Hambone Range of the Tennessee State Prison. Seated from left to right were Captain Mayo Wix (Training Officer), Trooper Charles Peacock (District 7), Trooper A. C. Davis (District 2), TBI Agent Walter Bearden (District 1), Trooper Guy Piercey (District 8), Lieutenant James Meadows (District 3), Trooper Tom D. Moore (District 6) and an unidentified trooper (District 5). Standing from left to right were Trooper Raymond Shetters (District 2), Trooper John R. Dunaway (District 4), Commissioner Greg O'Rear, Trooper William Greene (District 1), Trooper Sterling Trent (District 5), Trooper Frank Evetts (District 6), Trooper C. B. Martin (District 7), Trooper Milton Frederick (District 3), Trooper John Etheridge (District 8) and Sergeant Tom W. Moore (District 4).

county. He supervised the three or four troopers, managed reports and resolved problems. Serious problems were passed on to the lieutenant and the most serious to the district captain. Some counties did not have a sergeant and the sergeant in a nearby county was called when needed.

Confrontations while making arrests was a matter troopers had to deal with on their own. Troopers rode by themselves and patrol cars had no prisoner screen between the front and back seats. Lucion R. English joined the Highway Patrol in June 1962 and was stationed in Memphis until 1865 when he was transferred to Somerville in Fayette County. English recalled that a lawbreaker was not arrested unless the trooper was man enough to put him in the car and get him to jail. It was routine with the many ruffians breaking the law on the highways that a trooper had to "whip'em" to get them in the car.

The Patrol took on a number of new safety and enforcement initiatives. Safety efforts were extended to the sky in September 1959. Troopers were authorized to check aircraft and pilots and report any unsafe operation of aircraft.

The Financial Responsibility Law was strengthened in 1959 resulting in large numbers of license revocations. Patrolmen went out and served warrants on individuals with revoked licenses. Commissioner

O'Rear requested additional men and cars in 1961 to deal with additional license revocation matters. The courts declared the law unconstitutional in the seventies and new law was enacted to provide for a hearing before a drivers license could be revoked.

Troopers began riding school buses in the fall of 1959 to better ensure the safety of traveling school children. Walkie-talkies were used to report motorist who failed to stop during loading and unloading of buses or broke other laws affecting school safety

In December 1961 the THP received its first unmarked patrol cars. The only unmarked units at the time were radar cars. The media was told only that the number of cars was "substantial." Troopers in unmarked cars wore uniforms and when a car was pulled over at night, the trooper switched on the interior dome light so he could be recognized as a law officer. The cars had portable emergency dome lights for use while working accidents.

Troopers also initiated activities for fellowship and to help their community. Troopers in the Chattanooga area formed Lodge 16 of the Fraternal Order of Police in January 1960. They united to combat juvenile delinquency and help those in need including delivering food baskets to the needy families at Christmas.

When Governor Frank Clement took office for his second term in 1963, G. Hilton Butler was again

The Highway Patrol added a six-man Water Safety unit in 1963. The unit was under the command of Lieutenant Charles Graham and had three boats that worked public water area across the state.

appointed commissioner of Safety. Greg O'Rear moved to the position of troop commander. Headquarters personnel were mostly continued. Captain C. B. "Ted" Fowlkes was place in charge of the newly created Arrest Records Section. A number of changes were made at the district command level. Captain M. L. Hamilton took over in Knoxville, Captain Melvin H. Hutsell in Chattanooga, Captain Arthur M. Lashlee in Nashville, Captain Odell Huddleston in Cookeville and Captain Laten Mullins in Lawrenceburg.

Boat safety legislation was passed by the General Assembly and the Patrol was assigned enforcement responsibility. A six-man Water Safety unit formed in 1963 that included Lieutenant Charles Graham, Sergeant Connie D. Smiley and Trooper Jeffery Kirby. The unit was equipped with three boats, one worked in Middle Tennessee, another in West Tennessee and the third in East Tennessee. These troopers worked across the state apprehending violators, promoting water safety, and recovering bodies in water-related fatalities. The unit wore white uniforms and a special blue shoulder patch. Two years later the water safety program was transferred to the Game and Fish Department.

New troopers continued to be hired and sworn in prior to receiving formal training. Training session were usually scheduled within a few months after a large group of troopers entered service. One group of new troopers including Troopers John W. Horton and Glenn Wallace had a swearing in ceremony that almost didn't happen. The new class was told to be at THP headquarters in the Cordell Hull Building on January 1, 1964, to be sworn in by the governor. There was snow on the ground as they drove to Nashville to find no one in the office because New Year's Day was a holiday.

When the governor or anyone else had shown up by the afternoon, someone called the Governor's Mansion. The governor knew nothing of the ceremony but told the group to come to the mansion. Horton and Wallace were with the Eighth District and rode to the governor's residence with Captain Noah Robinson and Lieutenant Tom Brooks. Governor Frank G. Clement met them at the back door and called every one by name. They sat down at a long table and were fed before the swearing in ceremony. After the event the new troopers went back to their home district and began work.

The state legislature provided for the creation of a state-wide police training academy in 1963 and Tennessee Law Enforcement Training Academy opened in 1966. The school was modeled after the FBI National Police Training Academy and facilities were built in Donelson. The training academy was an independent agency and trained not only state law enforcement officers but officers from municipal police department and county sheriff's offices across the state.

G. Hilton Butler, who was serving as commissioner of Safety at the time, was named first director of the training academy on August 3, 1965. He served in the capacity for two years. Butler's assistant was Charles Grigsby who had served 15 years as an FBI special agent with the Nashville office.

Charlie Grigsby took over as director of the academy when Butler left and served as director for eight years. Grigsby turned the academy into a nationally recognized police training school. He was a hard nosed disciplinarian and insisted officers in the school go by the rules, reminding them that, "A mistake here can cost an officer his life later." The academy trained 6,000 Tennessee law officers in its first ten years.

Improved communication brought another important law enforcement advance. Interstate communications were still primitive. To check the registration of a California vehicle, a trooper radioed headquarters

The Patrol formed a riot squad in the early sixties. The unit trained at Smyrna Army Air Base, and here were practicing the wedge formation used for breaking up unruly crowds.

*The Clarksville office in the early sixties was staffed by, from left to right in the front row, James "Catfish" Leath, Eddie Cantrell, Lieuten[a]
Hancock, Dick Pope, and Bob "Rapid Robert" Riggs; and from left to right in the back row, Sergeant James Dycus, Charles Armstrong, B[...]
Fyke and James Wahl.*

where a 3' x 5' card was filled out. Nashville then passed the message on to Memphis and they radioed Forrest City, Arkansas, and the message was thus relayed from point to point. A California registration check took from three to five days.

A modern teletype system, the National Law Enforcement Teletype System (NLETS), was implemented in 1964. Trooper Larry Hitchcock was sent to Atlanta, Georgia, to train on the system. Hitchcock joined the Department of Safety as a civilian radio operator in 1960 when he returned from the military and transferred to uniform in 1963. Hitchcock had used teletype equipment in the Navy. NLETS revolutionized communication between states. Requests from states adjacent to Tennessee were returned within an hour.

Highway Patrol Troop Commander Greg O'Rear was once again name to the post of Commissioner of the Department of Safety in August 1965 when Butler was appointed to head the academy. Major Elmer V. Craig who was named executive officer of the Patrol earlier in the year was promoted to troop commander on August 3, 1965.

Troop Commander Craig was clean cut with a military bearing and was a graduate of the Northwestern Traffic Institute. He served a brief time with the Marine Corps in 1945, but soon returned from California with an honorable discharged due to his asthma. He joined the Highway Patrol in 1946, was promoted to Corporal on May 11, 1948, and to Sergeant two months later on July 15, 1948. During his time as a lieutenant in the late fifties, he commanded the Yellow Jackets motorcycle unit.

Elmer Craig began his law enforcement career in the early forties as a motorcycle officer with the

Inglewood-Madison Fire and Police Department, private subscription fire and police department. Wh[...] Craig served as a traffic officer at the element[...] school in morning and afternoons, he met a youngs[...] by the name of Fred Schott, who was captain of t[...] school safety patrol. The two served together on t[...] Patrol and both had a distinguished career.

Command of the Kingsport District changed September 1965 when Captain Thomas Doug[...] Seymour, a 28-year-veteran of the Patrol, took over[...] head of the district. Lieutenant James E. Meadows h[...] served as acting captain of the district following Fra[...] Williamson's promotion to inspector for E[...] Tennessee on April 1.

The Highway Patrol responded to a number [...] riots and strikes in the early sixties. In August 19[...] troopers were called out to the state penitentiary [...] resolve a hostage situation. An Army tank was used [...] put down the riot. Two rebellious inmates were a[...] thwarted in an earlier hostage taking. In the summ[...] of 1964 the Patrol helped to put down a riot at Brus[...] Mountain Prison when inmates rebelled at bei[...] forced to work in the facility's coal mine.

Troop Commander O'Rear faced a personally d[...] ficult duty shortly before becoming commissioner. T[...] Patrol was ordered by Governor Frank Clement [...] restore order to the Murray Ohio bicycle plant [...] Lawrenceburg in April 1965. The strike had creat[...] instability throughout Lawrence County. Troop[...] went in and arrested a number of the leaders. The s[...] uation escalated and 100 troopers were ordered [...] quell the disturbance and arrested 100 more striker[...]

The situation became personal for Greg O'Rear [...] Tuesday, April 20. His brother, who was also a giant[...]

President John F. Kennedy visited Nashville in 1963 before his fateful trip to Dallas. The Tennessee Highway Patrol provided security. Standing behind the president's car was Commissioner Greg O'Rear, Sergeant Hoyt Sanford and Lieutenant John Hancock. Inspector J. J. Jackson stood in the background over Hancock's shoulder.

the first black troopers. Johnson was processed first and since Tennessee was the first southern state to hire black troopers, Johnson held the distinction of being the first black trooper in Tennessee and in the South. Johnson was assigned to the Memphis office and worked mainly in Shelby County, although he worked some in Nashville and sporadically in Dyersburg.

For new Trooper Claude Johnson it was the realization of a childhood dream. Beginning in the 6th grade on career days he said, "I want to be a state trooper." Lieutenant Jerry W. Scott gave Trooper Johnson an orientation to the Patrol when he began work. Johnson recalled that his fellow troopers quickly became his second family. Trooper Johnson also worked with the TBI and federal agencies from time to time. Being a black trooper gave him an advantage while working undercover because no one suspected him of being a law officer. Johnson transferred to the TBI as a narcotics agent in 1972.

Trooper Hall was assigned to the Nashville District and began road duty in Williamson County under the tutelage of Trooper John D. McCord. Trooper Grady began work in the Drivers License Division.

Experienced members of the Patrol were glad to share knowledge gained through the years with young troopers. Captain Printest Dainy Garland saw many changes in his 30 years on the Patrol. Dainy Garland commanded the Chattanooga District during two periods, 1960 to 1963 and 1967 to 1968. Officers received a hash mark every two years at the time. Garland joined the Patrol in 1937 and had hash marks all the way up his arm. The veteran officer counseled

a man, was a striking welder and among the strike leaders. Commander O'Rear said to the other lawmen, "Okay, boys, you stay here and I'll do the first one." He proceeded to arrest his brother. Troopers then began arresting other strikers and "loading them." Some strikers greased their bodies and lay in the road so troopers could not pick them up. The THP foiled the ploy by bringing in a two-ton truck and sliding the strikers into the back of the vehicle.

An important step in diversity came to the Highway Patrol on October 1, 1965, when Claude Isaiah Johnson, James Hall and John Grady became

Officers stationed at the Rockwood Station in the early 1960s were, from left to right, Trooper Roy Mynatt, Trooper Raymond Cox, Lieutenant Cecil Strader, Sergeant Leon Miller, Trooper Bill Elliot and Trooper Roy Johnson. The station was among those built in the late 1930s.

Commissioner G. Hilton Butler moved his office to a newly opened section of I-40 in 1964 to symbolize the presence of the Highway Patrol on the interstate. Butler was seated at the table wearing pith helmet. Captain A. M. Lashlee, commander of the Nashville District, was seated with him and Captain Harold Cross stood behind them. Trooper Pete Hatcher was seated on the motorcycle on the left and Trooper Ed Beckman was on the motorcycle on the right. Helicopter pilot Lieutenant W. T. Sircy stood beside his aircraft.

new troopers about the dangers of working alone in remote areas and transporting prisoners with no prisoner screen between the front and back seats. Garland cautioned them to recognize they were not invincible and warned, "Don't get into any situation out here on the side of the road that you can't get out of by yourself."

Larry Wallace became a trooper in 1967 under the command of Captain Garland and was initially assigned to Hamilton County. He was transferred to Polk County and partnered with Waymon Deverell. Deverell was a veteran of the Patrol, quiet in manner and steady in his duty.

Buford Ellington began his second term as governor in 1967. Greg O'Rear was reappointed to the post of commissioner of Safety. O'Rear drove a black Pontiac. The commissioner's license tag number was 2; tag number 1 was reserved for the governor. W. E. "Bud" Hopton, director of the TBI, continued as

deputy commissioner. Governor Ellington appointed Claude A. Armour to the post of Special Assistant to Governor on Law and Order.

The Department of Safety was reorganized and divided into divisions. Charles W. Danner was named head of the Highway Patrol Division and its 500 troopers. Troop Commander Danner became a patrolman with the Tennessee Highway Patrol on July 2, 1951. He was stationed at Rogersville and Mountain City before moving to the governor's residence in 1953 at the rank of corporal. He worked revocations during that time as well. Danner made sergeant in 1955, lieutenant in 1958, and staff lieutenant as the governor's aide in charge of security. He was serving as safety lieutenant in the Knoxville District when he was named troop commander.

The position of Assistant Troop Commander was added in 1967. Assistant Troop Commander Stuart M. Dean was responsible for West Tennessee and Assistant

The swearing in ceremony that almost did not happen, but finally took place on New Year's Day 1964 at the governor's mansion. The four men in suits in front of the new class of troopers were from left to right Governor Frank G. Clement, Commissioner of the Department of Safety G. Hilton Butler, TBI Director and Deputy Commissioner Bud Hopton and Highway Patrol Troop Commander Greg O'Rear. Highway Patrol commanders and supervisors accompanying the new troopers stood in the background.

Troop Commander M. Lewis Hamilton had charge of East Tennessee.

Inspectors J. J. Jackson and William C. "Mickey" McGuire continued and Assistant Inspectors Noah A. Robinson and Frank Williamson were appointed. Captain Delbert McCormick was named maintenance supervisor. District commanders were Captain W. E. Raby in Knoxville, Captain P. D. Garland in Chattanooga succeeding Lewis Hamilton, Captain A. M. Lashlee in Nashville, Captain Neverett L. "Nev" Huffman in Memphis succeeding Stuart Dean, Captain Douglas Seymour in Kingsport, Captain Odell Huddleston in Cookeville, Captain Laten Mullins in Lawrenceburg and newly-promoted Captain Richard Dawson in Huntingdon (soon moved to Jackson) replacing the late Tom K. Brooks. Captain Clarence D. Hamby replaced Douglas Seymour as commander in Kingsport in August 1968. Captain Charles Butler took command of the Lawrenceburg District in October 1969.

Troopers worked 9-hour shifts. The Jackson District had a 72-man force and 39 cars. Cookeville had a force of 57 troopers. About 70 troopers were assigned to the Chattanooga District.

The Drivers Control Division included Captain Leslie C. Brown as director of the Financial Responsibility Section, Captain E. V. Craig as chief of

the Drivers License Examination Section, Larry M. Ellis as director of the Drivers License Issuance Section and T. G. Fite as director of the Accident Records Section. Bud Hopton remained director of the TBI, also considered a division. The Safety Education Division was headed by Captain Joe H. Patterson.

Technological advances continued to improve the working environment for the Patrol. One enhancement in particular was welcomed by troopers who spent much of their day in a patrol unit. The first rolling stock of the Patrol with four doors, automatic transmissions, power brakes, commercial AM radios and air conditioning was purchased in 1967. The 150 Fords were purchased not long after 100 Fords were purchased without the features. Governor Ellington had committed that if he won the election, troopers would get air conditioned cars. In 1966 the Patrol had two cars with air conditioning, one for the commissioner and one for VIPs. Over the next eight years all cars were air conditioned.

The numbering scheme on license tags on THP vehicles went through a change in the sixties. During the first decade of the Patrol, the agency used the same style tags as the public at large. During the 1940s and 1950s Patrol vehicle tags were marked "THP" with a number. In the 1960s "THP" continued to appear with a three digit

Commissioner O'Rear welcomes the Highway Patrol's first black troopers in October 1965. Standing behind the commissioner from left to right were Trooper John Grady who was assigned to the drivers license division, Trooper Claude Isaiah Johnson who was assigned to the Memphis District and Trooper James Hall who was assigned to the Nashville District.

Tennessee Highway Patrol members serving in the Tennessee National Guard's 30th Armored Division were visited by Governor Frank G. Clement in 1965 during exercises in Ft. Stewart Georgia. Those in the front row from left to right were Roy Todd, Harold Smith, Guy Piercey, Governor Clement, T. T. English, Gary Pinner and unidentified; in the second row were Bill Henry, Homer Smith, Tommy Morris, Billy Moore, Joseph Muschler, unidentified and James Dyer; the third row were unidentified, Thomas Moore, Mason Black, Mark Melton, Jerry Kemp and unidentified; and the forth row were Jack Frazier, Bill Barrett, Eddie Cantrell, John McCord and unidentified. Bill Barrett later went to the Kentucky State Police and was killed in the line of duty in Bowling Green.

number. The first digit of the number was the district number, Knoxville 1, Memphis 4, Jackson 8, and so forth. The last two numbers were the car number.

The introduction of blue emergency dome lights also occurred in 1967. The change grew out of complaints received by Sergeant Bob Thomas while he served as a hearing officer in the Driver Improvement Program. All emergency vehicles including ambulances and wreckers had red lights. Drivers complained they were pulled over by vehicles that were not police vehicles. Sergeant Thomas drafted a bill to change lights on police vehicles, and only police vehicles, to blue.

State Senator Lowell Thomas, former Madison County Sheriff, and State Representative Rob Robertson sponsored the bill in the legislature. Bar lights were introduced to display the new blue emergency lights. In 1978 the act was amended to permit

municipal law enforcement to use one blue and one

Trooper Roy Mynatt, left, was killed in a fiery car crash while chasing a speeder near Rockwood in February 1968. Trooper Eugene Brakebill died in October 1966 of a heart attack that followed a pursuit.

red light on their vehicles to distinguish the police departments from the state troopers.

The Patrol got new and more versatile electronic radar devices in 1969. The early seventies brought greater mobility to radar units, compact two-way radios and improvements to a wide range of equipment used by the THP.

Changes taking place in society were as dramatic as those in technology. The 1960s and 1970s were marked nationwide by upheaval in socio-economic and racial relations. The Department of Safety and especially the Tennessee Highway Patrol were routinely called out to help restore peace and order when public disturbances erupted.

The Patrol changed its policy regarding the simultaneous service of family members. Johnny Craig joined the Highway Patrol on February 4, 1968. Craig was the son of Elmer V. Craig and for the first time two family members were allowed to serve on the Patrol at the same time. Johnny Craig began his service in the THP with eight years in communication. He later provided security at the governor's residence during Governor Blanton's term. Craig then went to the Nashville office and worked in administration until his final assignment of six years with CID prior to his retirement in 1995.

The Civil Rights Movement was under way and cities across the state were faced with racial confrontation growing out of marches and sit-ins. The situation that caused the most serious breech of peace in the state combined labor and racial issues. The 1968 strike of garbage and sanitation workers in Memphis gained wide support among civil rights leaders including Dr. Martin Luther King Jr. who joined demonstrations in Memphis.

When violence erupted in the city in late March, 250 riot squad trained troopers were ordered into Memphis on Thursday, March 28, 1968, to assist local authorities in restoring order. Troopers from the Kingsport and Knoxville districts loaded on a C130 transport and flew to Nashville where they were joined by troopers from Lawrenceburg, Cookeville and Nashville. The Patrol developed riot squads earlier in the decade and each division had either one or two units of 10 or 12 men each. They trained from time to time, but logistics for the troops had to be organized on site when they were called out to an incident.

In the Memphis deployment, troopers worked 12-hour shifts out of the command post at the Memphis Police Department's Armour Center. Eight troopers and four city and county officers formed three-car tactical response units. These

Troopers Fred Hillis, left, and Thomas J. Cantwell worked Sevier County. Cantwell spent practically his entire career with the Highway Patrol at the same post.

units responded to disturbance calls for the following week. The organization of these units became a prototype for other cities across the country that soon face similar outbreaks.

The situation cooled by Wednesday, April 3, and most THP units were released to return to their regular duty stations. The following night, April 4, 1968, Dr. King was standing on the balcony of the Lorraine Motel in downtown Memphis when a shot rang out and an assassin's bullet killed the civil rights leader. Violence exploded in Memphis, across the state and throughout the nation with an intensity not experienced before or since.

Troop Commander Charles Danner was at the governor's residence reporting to Governor Ellington when the call came from Claude A. Armour, special assistant to governor on law and order, that Dr. King had been shot and killed.

The THP was ordered back into Memphis. Arkansas and Mississippi highway patrol officers responded with assistance. Four car tact units were formed with one Arkansas State Police, one Mississippi Highway Patrol, one Tennessee Highway Patrol, and one Memphis Police Department car. They kept people off the streets, and were able to limit riots. Special agents of the TBI including J. Hugh Bauer and Jack Blackwell were quickly on the scene to assist in the investigation and TBI Director Bud Hopton flew in from Nashville.

THP riot units were also ordered into Nashville. On Friday night, April 5, rioting erupted on the campus of Tennessee State University in Nashville including numerous exchanges of gunfire. Police shot out street lights that made the visible to snipers and searched a dormitory, looking for those firing at law

Greg O'Rear in 1968 during his final term as commissioner of safety. Standing behind him were Troop Commander Charles Danner, District Three commander Captain Arthur Lashlee and Lieutenant John Hancock.

officers. On the following Sunday, law enforcement officials returned to the campus when arsonists burned ROTC housing.

Other incidents occurred in the years that followed. Jackson police and Madison County deputies were called to quell a riot at Lane College on Saturday evening, March 22, 1969. The college had been the site of disorders for three weeks and the science building was burned two days earlier. Tennessee Bureau of Criminal Identification Special Agent Jack Blackwell was one of the first state law enforcement officers on the scene. Local officials called the THP for help. Troopers began to move toward Jackson from counties around the state and assembled at the fairgrounds

Rebellious students and instigators roamed the campus and the tension was palpable. At 6:00 p.m., Madison County Sheriff Guy announced he had warrants to serve on several individuals. As officers moved into the crowd to make arrests, the crowd blocked the lawmen.

At about that time, sirens were heard and fifty Highway Patrol cars moved up Lane Avenue. The cruisers stopped and two or more riot squad troopers exited each car. The 125 troopers pulled down the face shields on their riot helmets. Each man carried a two-handed baton. The state lawmen marched four abreast to where the rioters stood. The THP commander gave the crowd three minutes to move inside. When time was up, the column of troopers marched forward and swung their batons. Troopers then took two steps to

the side and four other troopers filled the gaps. The phalanx of troopers, now eight abreast, stepped forward and swung their batons a second time. The crowd moved inside or left the scene.

Sixty-nine were arrested including a woman from Chicago who called herself "Sister Soul." She was one of the instigators of the riots and destruction and threatened to kill the president of the college. TBI Special Agent Blackwell learned she had relatives in Haywood County and found out where she was staying. Sister Soul was arrested at the Illinois Central train station.

A curfew was imposed and order was gradually restored. The Jackson police maintained a presence on the campus for two weeks. Troopers moved out after about a week. The Patrol was called to similar duty during civil disturbances in Chattanooga in summer 1971.

Riots and civil disturbances were difficult duty for the Patrol, but the most dangerous duty remained patrolling the highways. Trooper Roy Alfred Mynatt was working near the temporary terminus of Interstate 40 outside Harriman on February 11, 1968.

Troopers Mynatt and Sergeant Leon Miller ate supper at the county jail. Mynatt said he was going to quit smoking and gave his cigarette lighter to Miller as proof. When they left, Miller headed to Rockwood and Mynatt toward Harriman. It was a cold Sunday evening. Mynatt stopped to fill up with gas and then pulled up beside Troopers Roy Johnson and Glenn Brummitt who were watching the stop sign at a dangerous intersection. They said they were going to drive a while and Mynatt decided to stay at the location and watch the stop sign.

Troopers Johnson and Brummitt were headed into Rockwood on highway 61 when a car pulled in behind

District 8 Troopers Glenn Wallace, left, and Melvin Holland with their Plymouth Fury patrol car in the sixties.

them. Then they saw Mynatt running fast toward them. As Mynatt passed them and pulled in the front their cruiser, his wheels got just off the pavement and he lost control of his patrol car. The vehicle turned three flips, landed upside down and hit a car coming from the other direction. The patrol unit, with a full tank of gas, exploded. Trooper Mynatt was killed either by the collision or by the fire.

His fellow troopers and Sergeant Miller, who arrived soon after the collision, tried to put the fire out with extinguishers. It was futile and they watched helplessly as flames rose from the wreck. Mynatt never made a sound and his body was burned beyond recognition. They conjectured that Mynatt was chasing the car that pulled in behind Johnson and Brummitt. Mynatt was known as a driver with great skill, but he was unable to regain control because of his speed and the uneven surface.

More THP troopers were killed in the line of duty during the 1960s than in any decade since the 1930s. A number of other troopers were seriously injured.

Five officers died in automobile accidents. Trooper Edward C. Jowers was killed in Memphis on August 3, 1962. Trooper Joseph Emanuel Dillard died in Medina on September 15, 1964. Trooper William Gordon Barnes was killed in a two-car collision on January 22, 1966, a mile east of Waynesboro as he made a U-turn while working chase with a radar car. Trooper Michael Theodore Dafferner was killed six miles north of Knoxville on the night of April 6, 1966, when his car left state highway 33 and plunged down an embankment. Trooper C. B. Martin died near Sparta on May 4, 1969.

Colonel Charles Danner and Commissioner Claude Armour appointed majors in 1971 as part of the command structure. Division majors were responsible for two districts. Majors were from left to right Clarence Hamby, Chattanooga and Lawrenceburg districts; Robert "Bob" Seamon, executive officer to the colonel; Neverett L. "Nev" Huffman, Nashville and Cookeville districts and later procurement officer; John Fields, drivers control; Harry P. Montgomery, Knoxville and Kingsport districts; and Arthur M. Lashlee, Memphis and Jackson districts.

Trooper Robert Green was seriously injured in an accident on Highway 11W near Morristown in 1967 when a tractor trailer he was about to pass pulled into his lane. Trooper Walter Russell was struck by a car and critically injured as he was preparing to do a spot check of traffic on Highway 27 in Roane County in September 1967.

Lieutenant Samuel W. Gibbs was shot and killed in the line of duty on August 11, 1966, in Shelbyville by a jail escapee. In pursuit of two prisoners who escaped from the Bedford County jail, THP Lieutenant Gibbs and Shelbyville Police Department Sergeant Johnny Wheeler went to the home of a relative of one of the escapees. They found the two inmates in a bedroom closet. As the lawmen attempted to handcuff the two, one of the prisoners knocked Lieutenant Gibbs' .38 caliber service revolver to the floor, retrieved it and shot Gibbs in the abdomen and Sergeant Wheeler in the hip. Wheeler survived his wound but Patrol Lieutenant Sam Gibbs died at 9:00 that evening.

Sergeant Gene Bollinger was shot in the arm in November 1965 when he and Trooper John Collins pulled into a truck stop where two men were struggling over a shotgun. Bollinger survived the 24 pellets that ripped into his arm.

On a lonely country road near Knoxville, Trooper Ross Haynes pulled over a black and white 1956 Pontiac for an invalid license plate decal. Two men exited the car. One of them pulled a pistol and shot Trooper Haynes four

Trooper John Chandler stands ready for motorcycle pursuit at a road-block in 1971 on Murfreesboro Road, Nashville.

THP Command in April 1971 included from left to right in the front row Commissioner of Safety Claude A. Armour, Captain Guy Nicholson, Captain Jerry Simmons, Major Harry P. Montgomery, Captain Tony Hansberry, Major Neverett L. "Nev" Huffman, and Colonel Charles W. Danner. The second row from left to right included Captain Jewel E. Weese, Captain Charles B. Butler, Captain Truman Clark, Captain James R. Dodson, Major Arthur M. Lashlee, Captain John B. Edwards, Major Clarence Hamby, and Captain Mayo Wix. From left to right in the back row were Lieutenant Colonel Richard M. Dawson, Captain Joe H. Patterson, Major John Fields, Major Robert "Bob" Seamon, Captain Clifton Shipley, and Captain John W. Lumpkin.

times. Haynes returned fire before he collapsed. Trooper Haynes survived his wounds.

Two troopers died in the line of duty of heart attacks. Trooper Kenneth Rice Moore died while on patrol on Rutledge Pike on the afternoon of February 2, 1964. Trooper Eugene Brakebill suffered a fatal heart attack after chasing a suspect in Greene County and died on October 9, 1966.

Twenty-six-year-old rookie Trooper Dennis Frizzell was seriously injured in a two-car accident on Murfreesboro Road on March 6, 1970. Frizzell, driving an unmarked car, was chasing a car he believed to have been involved in the shooting of Metro Nashville Police Officer Joe Thomas McEwen earlier in the evening.

Claude A. Armour was appointed commissioner of the Department of Safety in 1971 when Governor Winfield C. Dunn took office and began a period of dramatic change for state law enforcement. Armour began his law enforcement career as a patrolman in the Memphis Police Department in 1941. He served with the Navy in the South Pacific and was wounded in action. He returned to the MPD and worked his way through the ranks to the position of chief of the

Memphis force. Armour was the first person to rise from the police ranks to the position of commissioner of fire and police and served longer in the position than any other individual in the city's history. Commissioner Armour named former Memphis Chief of Police James C. MacDonald as deputy commissioner in November 1973. Commander Danner had previously functioned in the role.

Commander Charles W. Danner continued as top uniformed officer in the Patrol. Danner had a radio

Department of Safety executive meeting with Memphis command included from left to right Colonel Charles Danner, Captain Roy Cheatam, Captain Milton Frederick, Sergeant Ron Hill and Commissioner of Safety Claude Armour.

The original THP Tactical Squad was formed in 1972. Members of the original squad were from left to right Sergeant John D. McCord, Jerry Webb, Wayne L. Britt, Paul Tackett, Billy H. Ford, David Ray, Roger Farmer, John W. Horton, Russell Wheeler Jr. and Lieutenant Joe E. West along with Colonel Charles Danner and Commissioner Claude Armour on the far right.

and tall antenna set up at his house near Mt. Juliet so he could listen in to traffic reports and other communication across the state. Richard M. Dawson was appointed lieutenant colonel and Captain Tony Hansberry took command of communications for the department. Headquarters offices of the Patrol were moved to the Andrew Jackson Building.

Commissioner Armour and Colonel Danner made a number of changes in the Department of Safety and the Highway Patrol. One of the most dramatic actions involved the transfer of 95 supervising officers in the Patrol, most of which involved promotion of the officer. One cold snowy February morning, Armour called all the captains in and informed them of their new duty assignment.

Sergeant Roy B. Cheatam was in the Memphis office when Captain Nev Huffman called. The captain congratulated Cheatam, "You've been promoted to lieutenant," then he said, "and you've been transferred to Nashville effective Monday morning." Huffman then asked the new lieutenant to give him phone numbers from the recipe box containing 3' x 5' cards with names, addresses and phone numbers of District Four personnel.

Patrol officers waved to each other as they passed on the way to new assignments that Monday morning. Cheatam and Huffman stayed together in a room they rented in Nashville for about six months until public school were out and their families moved to join them. Four captain were promoted to major as commanders of Patrol divisions of two districts each. Major

Clarence Hamby was placed in command of Chattanooga and Lawrenceburg districts, Major Neverett L. "Nev" Huffman in command of Nashville and Cookeville districts, Major Harry Montgomery in command of Knoxville and Kingsport districts and Major Arthur M. Lashlee in command of Memphis and Jackson districts.

The transfers facilitated promotions since it was easier to supervise personnel with whom new commanders had not worked as peers. The moves were also made in part to rectify complacency among some in the Patrol. The action had an impact on the morale of

Tactical Squad commanders Sergeant John McCord, left, and Lieutenant Joe West show equipment to Knoxville Captain John B. Edwards in 1972. Three other members of the squad observed from the background.

Trooper Billy H. Ford, one of the first members of the TACT Squad, demonstrated use of baton in riot condition.

"bird" colonels in the Army. Previously the troop commander wore four stars as epaulet brass. The THP supply acquired the new insignia from Ft. Campbell.

Other uniform changes included a change in leather goods. The new three-inch belt, cross-draw holster, cartridge and handcuff cases were coated with Pattina-Tiara, a high gloss finish. A one-inch black stripe was also added to trouser legs.

Uniforms were also changed late in 1971 for female driver license examiners. Members of the section wore uniforms similar to those of troopers. The new style uniform consisted of a forest green jacket and skirt and a brimmed cap of the style worn by female members of military, also in green. The breast badge adopted for examiners was a small eagle-top teardrop style.

some long-time officers who were transferred. For others the promotion was opportune. Lieutenant Billy Jones was promoted from sergeant, transferred to Cookeville and given command of 16 counties.

Troopers took on a new appearance early in 1971. The uniform cap used through the years was permanently retired. Uniform headgear became a forest green campaign or "Smokey Bear" hat, in felt for winter and straw for summer. The hats were purchased from the Stratton Company in Winchester.

Many supervisors like the old service caps because of the "scrambled eggs" on the bill, but many despised the caps, referring to them as "taxi driver" or "bus driver" caps. It was a practical problem for some men. When Greg O'Rear was commissioner, he had a rule that the cap was to be worn all the time, even while in the car, under penalty of three days off without pay. Trooper Sturgeon was 6'9" and had to break down the front part of his cap and let the cap badge lay on the bill so he could sit in the car.

Hat badges changed with the new wide-brimmed campaign or peak hats. The hat badge for troopers once again became the miniature breast badge that had been worn with the western style hat. Hat badges and epaulet brass for supervisory ranks were fashioned after military insignia, chevrons for sergeants, a single bar for lieutenants, a double bar for captains, a brass leaf for majors and a silver leaf of lieutenant colonel. The rank title for the commanding officer of the Patrol became Colonel rather than Chief or Troop Commander and his hat badge was the eagle worn by

Trooper Billie Jo Meeks and Sergeant Wayne Britt exit the Jackson District office. Trooper Meeks became the first female enforcement officer on the Patrol on July 17, 1973. (Jackson Sun photo)

Trooper Roger Farmer, one of the first members of the TACT Squad, demonstrated the fire power available to the Tactical Squad. The station wagon was one of the original vehicles assigned to the unit.

Armour made several organizational changes to the THP. The Planning and Research Division was organized in August 1971. Roy B. Cheatam, who was serving as administrative lieutenant for the Third District, was originally given a 90-day temporary assignment to redo the general orders of the Patrol. The first task was developing a five-day work week schedule and a man-power allocation formula for use in all 95 counties. Both were completed by the end of the year. The five-day work week began on October 1, 1971.

Roy Cheatam was made the first captain of Planning and Research, which consisted of him, a secretary and a young trooper who was a recent graduate of the Northwestern police school. The general orders were completed in 1972. A small book had been put out years before, but was not used. New general orders were similar to military order manual systems. Information was shared among other agencies through the National Police Officers Planning Association for state troopers and state police organizations.

Captain Cheatam also commanded supply and set up a new system to manage uniforms and weapons. Planning and Research developed procedures for gathering evidence in drunk driver cases so offenders could be prosecuted for vehicular homicide.

An Employee Credit Union for the Department of Safety was chartered on January 1, 1972. The benefits to employees were quickly recognized. An asset pool from savings accounts quickly grew and loans were available to individuals for various purposes.

Command of the THP in 1974. From left to right in the front row were Governor Winfield Dunn, Commissioner of Safety Claude A. Armour, Lieutenant Colonel Richard M. Dawson, Division Four Major Arthur M. Lashlee, Colonel Charles W. Danner, and Deputy Commissioner of Safety James C. MacDonald. The second row was from left to right Division One Major Harry P. Montgomery, District 8 Captain Jerry Simmons, Division Two Major Clarence Hamby, Division Three Major Jewel E. Weese, Staff Services Major Neverett L. "Nev" Huffman and Executive Officer Major Robert "Bob" Seamon. In the back row from left to right were District 5 Captain Guy Nicholson, District 4 Captain Glen C. Haun, District 3 Captain Charles B. Butler, District 1 Captain John B. Edwards, District 2 Captain Clifton Shipley and District 6 Captain James R. Dodson. District 7 Captain John W. Lumpkin was not available for the photograph.

Governor Winfield Dunn congratulated troopers receiving the Governor's Merit Award in 1972. From left to right were Lester Gooding, Leon Standford, Dunn, Joseph Muschler and Robert Harris.

thought, if you can't beat them, join them." Linuel Allen's interview was successful and he did "join them."

Patrol personnel became more diverse in the mid-seventies. Ida C. Nicks had been hired in July 1965 as the first female safety consultant, but Trooper Billie Jo Meeks became the first female enforcement officer in the THP on July 17, 1973. Trooper Meeks was assigned to the Jackson District. Others female officers soon followed. Trooper Terri C. Seabrook became the first black female trooper in January 1977 and was assigned to the Knoxville District. Robbie L. Hancock was the first female trooper assigned to the Governor's Security Force.

Captain Mayo Wix who was in charge of trooper training at the academy in 1974 recalled the changes in training since he joined the Patrol in 1948. "Back then," Wix said, "they would give a man a uniform, hand him the keys to a patrol car and put him to work. He got his training on the job for the most part."

By the mid-seventies an applicant had to meet specific standards, was put through a vigorous screening before being hired and given a full-time training course of at least eight weeks. Starting pay for a trooper was $620 per month as compared to $290 in 1948. Steve Browder of McNairy County, a member of the March 1974 recruit class, expressed the sentiments of most trainees who were asked why they wanted to be a trooper, "Because I think they are the most respected law enforcement officers in Tennessee and I wanted to be one of the best." From the academy Browder was

assigned to Gibson County with training officer Sergeant Kelly Shearin.

Personnel benefits were improved during the 1970s. The Fourth of July 1974 marked the first time in the history of the Tennessee Highway Patrol that members received compensation for working on a holiday. The legislature passed a law in 1974 that members of the Patrol retiring after 25 years of service were to be presented with the service revolver they had carried, along with an identification card. The most significant salary benefit of the decade, longevity pay, was enacted in 1977 and became effective on New Year's Day 1978. Members of the Patrol were paid an extra $5 a month for each year of service. This financial recognition for longevity compensated veteran officers for their loyalty to the Patrol.

For a brief period in 1974 and 1975, troopers got help from the U.S. Congress in controlling the speed of drivers. Due to a worldwide oil shortage, the speed limit on highways nationwide was set at 55 mph. Traffic fatalities were dramatically lowered during the period of the lower speeds.

The Highway Patrol Retired Troopers Association was formed on April 6, 1977, to provide an opportunity for retired officers to keep in touch and become involved in mutual interests. Charter members of the organization were John Hugh Bauer of Memphis, Norman E. Farley of Lafayette, T. G. Fite of Nashville, Milton D. Frederick of Nashville, Percy E. Griffith of Nashville, Glen C. Haun of Knoxville, H. Trabue

Troopers Glenn McCarthy, left, and Linuel Allen review a silhouette target on the firing range with Trooper Kelly Shearin, right, in 1975. Shearin was a long time member of the Highway Patrol's pistol team and firing range instructor. (Jackson Sun photo)

"Trib" Lewis of Nashville, Alton P. Sain of Nashville, Fred V. Scott of Memphis, Robert D. Thomas of Nashville, Walter G. Toon of Nashville, Dennis O. Trotter of Clinton, Joseph L. Williams of Jackson and Mayo Wix of Nashville. Membership and funds grew and in 1991 the group donated over 30% of its funds to the prevention of child abuse.

A uniform change in May 1976 made working troopers more comfortable. Short sleeved shirts with open collars became the standard uniform in the warm months of May to October. Another policy change that brought significant improvement in working conditions was the one-man-one-car allocation of rolling stock. Rather than drawing a car from the pool, each trooper was personally assigned a patrol unit. Everyone benefited from the change. Troopers had full-time use of the vehicle and the Patrol benefited from the increased visibility of troopers, faster call-out response time and lower maintenance costs on the units. A generic license plate for all state vehicles was adopted in the mid-seventies. It was green in color and marked "Gov't Serv."

Troopers continued to be transferred for disciplinary purposes. Men kidded about the threat with the comment that "if you did something wrong you'd go to Mountain City." One trooper loved the Mountain City assignment. As winter approached each year, he called the district office and say, "It snowed last night, I'll see you in the spring."

Governor Leonard Ray Blanton took office in 1975 and appointed Joel Plummer commissioner of

Tactic Squad members toured the state to show the unit's capabilities. Uniformed officers with one of the unit's 1972 Plymouth station wagons were from left to right Troopers Roger Farmer and Wayne Britt and Lieutenant Joe West.

the Department of Safety. Plummer was a veteran of the Korean conflict and began his law enforcement career with the Montgomery County Sheriff's Patrol in 1955. He joined the THP in 1960 and was stationed in Columbia and later in Clarksville. He was elected Sheriff of Montgomery County in 1966 and served three terms as sheriff before being elected county trustee.

Commission Plummer named Colonel Richard M. Dawson to head the Patrol. Dawson had served as lieutenant colonel under Colonel Danner. Dawson served with the U.S. Army Military Police in Europe from 1950 to 1954 and joined the Tennessee Highway Patrol in December 1956. He was the 1962-63 class valedictorian at the Northwestern University Traffic Institute in Evanston, Illinois, from which Plummer also graduated. Dawson became assistant troop commander of West Tennessee in July 1970, before becoming second in command of the Patrol in 1971.

Lieutenant Colonel Arthur M. "Father" Lashlee was appointed to serve as second in command of the Patrol under Dawson until his retirement in 1978. Lashlee began his 30-year career with the Patrol in April 1948. He progressed quickly through the ranks to corporal in 1950, sergeant in 1953, lieutenant in 1956, captain in 1963 and major in 1971.

Major Joe H. Patterson took command of Training and Safety Education after his promotion from captain and took the post of lieutenant colonel upon Lashlee's retirement. Billy Jones was promoted to captain and took over the Training Division in 1978 assisted by Lieutenant Ron Edwards.

Trooper John Allen and his canine partner Gator looked on as Sergeant Roger Farmer examines the Tact Squad's Pepper Fog unit in December 1976. (Jackson Sun photo)

The uniformed patrol remained divided into four divisions. The First Division included the Knoxville and Kingsport districts, the Second Division was Chattanooga and Lawrenceburg, the Third Division was Nashville and Cookeville, and the Fourth Division was Memphis and Jackson. Major Glen Haun was promoted from captain and replaced Lashlee as commander of the Fourth Division.

The hot summer of 1975 and a steady diet of pork chops triggered a riot at the Tennessee State Penitentiary in Nashville. Prison officials called for the assistance of the Highway Patrol and the Nashville police to put down the rebellion that became known as the Pork Chop Riot. A show of force and the use of Nashville's dog squad effectively restored order to the prison. Troopers remained at the prison for a period to maintain control.

Safety Commissioner Joel Plummer was impressed with effectiveness of the dog squad of the Nashville police. Plummer recognized the potential of a dog unit and supported a proposal by Trooper John B. Allen Sr. for creation of K-9 teams for the Tact Squad.

A K-9 Unit was added to the Tactical Squad in November 1976. Tact Squad member Trooper John Allen trained with Gator, the first four-legged member of the Patrol, and formed the THP's first K-9 team. The Metropolitan Nashville Police Department provided the training for the 20-month-old German

Shepherd. Trooper Bill Spangler and Bear soon formed a second team. The teams were used in criminal apprehension, searches for children and elderly citizens, crowd control, explosives detection and other tasks for which canines were uniquely adapted.

The THP continued to build resources for a wide range of law enforcement duties. The patrol took delivery of a new high-tech communications semi-trailer in August 1975. The large trailer contained two dispatch stations with the ability to communicate on all THP and emergency frequencies. The unit included sleeping facility for three, a bathroom and shower, cooking facilities and a "war room." It could be powered from an electrical drop, but was capable of being fully self-powered by two 15 kilowatt generators. The first assignment of the unit was the Tennessee State Fair in September 1975.

The Tact Squad expanded its equipment by purchasing bomb disposal equipment from a federal grant received in June 1976. The equipment included a one-ton van with bomb disposal trailer, portable x-ray, bomb sled, cryogenic devices and related items. Its greatest use was to dispose of abandoned dynamite, which was usually old and unstable.

Two Hueys, Bell UH-1B helicopters, were added to the Aviation Section in 1976. They were military surplus and acquired with the assistance of the state office of Civil Defense. The choppers were used for

Jackson District trophy-winning pistol team in 1975 included from left to right Linuel L. Allen (future captain of the district), Glenn H. McCarthy, Kelly Shearin, Staff Sergeant John W. Horton and John "Short Stroke" McCadams. Behind them from left to right were Captain Guy T. Piercey, Colonel Richard Dawson (former captain of the district), Lieutenant Colonel Arthur Lashlee and Sergeant Ron Edwards.

many and varied purposes by the Patrol. One was out-fitted with passenger seats and nice interior. The other was the "work horse" of the Tact Squad and fitted with a donut ring in the center for repelling. The Hueys were also used for search and rescue, medical transport and VIP transport as well. Sergeant Mike Dover was the primary pilot for the Tact Squad and served as pilot to Commissioner Plummer.

Lieutenant Ralph S. Swift took command of the Tactical Squad on September 1, 1977, upon his promoted from sergeant. Swift, a native of Cookeville, joined the Patrol in 1972.

A program to assist motorists who became stranded on one of Tennessee's interstate highways was inaugurated on December 5, 1977. The Assistance to Interstate Drivers (AID) program was the result of legislation recommended by Commissioner Joel Plummer and funded from an increase in the drivers license fee.

Captain Fred Schott Jr. and Lieutenant Charlie Graham of Safety Education implemented the program. One hundred men were hired and 100 new 1978 Plymouth patrol units equipped with a wide range of tools. The first group of 39 new troopers graduated from the academy in September.

Equipment included a K-bar-T tool (similar to a giant can opener), a twenty-pound fire extinguisher, Fix-a-Flat, an air compressor that worked off the cigarette lighter to air up a tire, along with two or three

Motor Vehicle Enforcement officers checked vehicle registration during this September 1976 road block. At the time Motor Vehicle Enforcement was a division of the Department of Revenue. In 1983 the force was transferred to the Department of Safety. (Jackson Sun photo)

different sized crowbars and pry bars for extrication. Troopers were trained in the essentials of assisting motorists. The program especially targeted visitors to the state, who numbered approximately 45 million annually.

The day before the program was to be launched, Schott and Graham were eight cars short. The dealer explained the cars were at the Kentucky-Tennessee line. The hauler was over-loaded and over-length for existing Tennessee regulations. Schott told headquarters by radio, "Get a car up there and tell him not to stop for anything or anybody until he gets those cars here." When the cars rolled in, radios, blue lights, decals and road assistance equipment were quickly installed.

All 100 new AID units were lined up the next day in front of the Air National Guard hangar at Berry Field in Nashville. Commissioner Plummer and Governor Blanton made remarks, the governor gave each trooper a key to a car and the troopers left in a convoy with blue lights flashing. At Donaldson Pike and I-40 they split up, half of the units went east and the others west. Over the CB radios in the cars, troopers heard truckers chattering, "I don't know what's goin' on, but it must be something terrible bad, there's smokies all over."

One of the first incidents of a wild-trucker chase in the nation took place along I-40 on August 16, 1977. Trooper Linuel Allen was joined by a number of other troopers as they chased the tractor-trailer to Henderson County and back to Madison county. Jackson police and Madison County deputies joined

Commissioner of Safety Joel Plummer greets the Patrol's first K-9 teams circa 1978. From left to right were Sergeant John B. Allen Sr. with Gator (the first K-9 Unit in the Patrol), Plummer and Trooper Bill Spangler with Bear (the second K-9 Unit).

Governor Ray Blanton signed the 1977 bill creating the Assist Interstate Drivers (AID) program. Standing behind the governor were, from left to right, Captain James Chandler, Captain Billy Parker, Major Joe H. Patterson, Representative Shelby Rhinehart (house sponsor of the bill), Lieutenant Colonel Arthur M. Lashlee, Captain Jesse Roberts, Commissioner of Safety Joel Plummer, Major Harry Montgomery and Colonel Richard M. Dawson.

the chase. The trucker crashed into around 20 vehicles, wrecked three police cars and tried to run over Allen several times. The driver had a drug or fatigue related psychosis. When he was finally stopped at the 79 exit after a 50 mile chase, he came out of the cab fighting and it took five officers to subdue him.

The Highway Patrol tried to be ready for irrational or premeditated actions on executive protection details. The Patrol provided executive security to high profile leaders of state government including the Speaker of the House, Speaker of the Senate and Governor. Security details were provided for visits to the state by the president or other dignitaries.

Steve Browder replaced Jim Caraway in 1977 as executive protection for the Speaker of the House Ned McWherter. Browder served as his security detail and driver. He received executive security training from the Secret Service and State Department.

The Patrol supported local law enforcement during the Memphis Police Department strike in the summer 1978. State officers worked 12-hour shifts for the duration of the strike. Troopers were instructed not to write traffic tickets on city streets so they didn't have to travel back to Memphis and spend time in city court.

Violence had been threaten by strikers and when all the lights went out in Memphis one night, troopers were concerned. Troopers Linuel Allen and Jimmie Van Leach kept their shotguns handy that night, as did other troopers. The black-out incident turned out to be someone throwing a wrong switch at the power plant.

The Assist Interstate Drivers (AID) program was launched in December 1977 by Captain Fred Schott Jr. and Lieutenant Charlie Graham of Safety Education. The trunk of each patrol car assigned to the duty was equipment with items necessary to lend aid drivers with an emergency. (Jackson Sun photo)

Command officers of the Patrol met in December 1981 to discuss arrangements for the World's Fair in Knoxville. Seated around the table from left to right were Ron Edwards, W. C. Amacher, Lieutenant Colonel Jerry Kemp, Paul Tackett, Clifton Shipley, Jerry Beaty, Major Jesse Roberts, Earl Hullett and Phillip Edwards. Standing at the rear from left to right were Commissioner of Safety Gene Roberts, Colonel Billy L. Jones, Larry Hitchcock, Milton Frederick, Joe Blankenship, Roy Cheatam and Joel Parham. All held the rank of captain except as noted.

The THP had outgrown its operational facilities in Nashville. Additional space was needed to expand and consolidate services. Facilities specifically designed to the requirements of technology used by the Patrol were also needed. The Multi-Purpose Center was built behind the Third Division Headquarters in Nashville in two construction phases. The first phase of the complex housed vehicle maintenance, radio repair, TCIC and the Supply Section.

Sergeant Frank Steinmetz demonstrated the importance of wearing a seat belt during a automobile accident. The Convincer was used in the eighties to simulate a 5 mph collision. (Jackson Sun photo)

A helicopter hangar and repair area was a part of phase one as well. Aviation was under the command of Lieutenant Colonel Joe Patterson and he was the prime mover in getting the aviation facility built. Sergeant Mike Dover flew Patterson to Jackson Mississippi where the Mississippi Highway Patrol had a state of the art facility. Patterson got the information needed, pushed it through the approval process and when pilots were getting the building ready for occupancy, Patterson pulled off his gear and helped them paint. Dover said, "The building should be called the Joe Patterson building."

The second phase of construction included a Drivers License Station, Safety Education and Training offices and space for the Driver Control Hearing Office. The Center was completed in 1979. Major Charles W. Danner took command of Driver Control in 1979 after serving as liaison officer between the Patrol and the Highway Department. Danner remained in the position until his retirement in January 1983.

Governor Lamar Alexander was chief executive of the state from 1979 to 1987. During his two terms as governor three individuals served as commissioner of the Department of Safety. Gene Davis Brian Roberts was appointed commissioner in January 1979. Roberts had been a reporter and editor with the Chattanooga Times, an FBI special agent, and vice-mayor and commissioner of fire and police of Chattanooga.

Colonel Bill L. "Billy" Jones headed the Highway Patrol and served as deputy commissioner of the Department of Safety, the first colonel to officially serve in that role. Lieutenant Colonel Joe Patterson served from 1978 to 1983. Commissioner Roberts resigned in January 1983 to run for mayor of Chattanooga. Gus A. Wood III replaced him as commissioner and served from February 1983 to March 1985. Billy Jones was named commissioner of Safety in March 1985 and served until January 1987. Colonel Paul Johnson commanded the Patrol from March 1985 to January 1987 and Lieutenant Colonel Jerry Kemp served from 1983 to 1987.

Lieutenant Mike Dover became chief pilot of the Aviation Division in 1979 after Captain W. T. Sircy became fleet manager. Dover was promoted to captain in January 2003 and took command of the Support Services Division until his retirement in June 2004. Former Tact Squad member and K-9 officer John Allen became a pilot in 1982 and flew until his retirement in 2005.

Lieutenant Dover made a number of important enhancements to the aviation unit. He acquired fire

retardant Nomex flight suits for pilots. The first suits were black with a gold stripe down the sides and sleeves, but the color was soon changed to brown. Pilots also got leather flight jackets similar to World War II bomber jackets. When pilots patrolled the road they changed into regular uniforms.

The rank of Warrant Officer was established as the rank for pilots. Pilots had held the rank of sergeant and the chief pilot, the rank of lieutenant. Warrant officer was an interim rank between sergeant and lieutenant and provided a higher pay scale for pilots. The breast badge was designated "Warrant" in the rank panel. Dover's badge as chief warrant officer was numbered "1" and the rank panel designated "Chief Pilot." The rank was abandoned in June 1979 and pilots reverted to sergeants and Dover to lieutenant, but their pay was not reduced.

The Patrol's aviation unit and tactical squad worked around the clock on May 4, 1979, to rescue flood victims in the Mill Creek area of Nashville and other area of Davidson, Wilson and Rutherford counties. Trooper Denny King was the only member of the Tact Squad trained to repel from a helicopter who could get to the airfield that morning. The Huey outfitted with a donut ring for the Tact Squad was down for radio repair, so Warrant Officer Mike Dover prepared the VIP appointed Huey. Aviation Mechanic Jim

Patrol commanders gathered at Christmas in 1983 were from left to right J. W. Sisson, Phillip Edwards, Bob McDonald, John McCord, Joe Blankenship, Larry Hitchock, Gene Bollinger, Jerry Scott, Jerry Kemp, Gerald Allen, Paul Johnson, Paul Tackett, Joel Parham, Buddy Amacher, Jerry Beaty, Commissioner Gus Woods and Colonel Billy L. Jones.

Governor's presentation of awards to top achievers in the Tennessee Highway Patrol. Seated from left to right were Rickey Leonard, Randy Pack, Lester Waugh, Tennessee Governor Ned Ray McWherter, Patricia Maines (later Riggs), Jim Webb, Roger Nelson and Joe Agee. Standing from left to right were Lieutenant Colonel Steve Browder, Colonel Larry Wallace, Commissioner Robert Lawson of the Department of Safety and CID Director Jimmie Van Leach.

Stewart flew as the crew chief. Regular crew chief Trooper James Piercey Jr. was able to get in later in the day.

They flew over the flooded three county area rescuing stranding individuals and saving the lives as several that were about to be swept away in the deluge. King used the door handle as a donut ring to secure repelling equipment and Dover called on flying skills honed over his career. In the 24-hour period they rescued 78 individuals who were in eminent danger. Mike Dover said it was very gratifying, "We plucked people out of the devil's hand." Among awards given for the service, Trooper King received a citation for bravery recognizing the lives that he saved at the risk of his own life.

Lieutenant Dover and his pilots also had important law enforcement functions, especially in drug enforcement. In a single month, October 1979, helicopter pilots spotted over $12,000,000 worth of marijuana crops, which were then destroyed.

The Underwater Search and Recovery Unit was organized in January 1979 as a part of the Tactical Squad. Two innovative and successful traffic safety programs were introduced in 1979 as well, the Selective Traffic Enforcement Program (STEP) and Operation CARE (Combined Accident Reduction Effort).

Captain Larry D. Hitchcock became commander of communications in 1981, the third to hold the post. Hitchcock was well experienced in communications where he made sergeant in 1967 and lieutenant in 1973. He was responsible for deployment and operation of the Patrol's first modern command post in a large tractor-trailer from its activation was in 1975.

A major commanded each division, East, West and Middle Tennessee. The three were Major Paul Tackett, Major Joe Blankenship and Major Fred Schott. The divisions were used as a structure for specialized matters such as the riot squads. The division structure was abandoned about 1980 and the eight districts again became the primary organizational structure of the uniform patrol. The majors were reassigned. Schott was placed over financial responsibility, Blankenship over the fleet and Tacket over internal affairs. Fifth District headquarters moved from Kingsport to Fall Branch in 1983.

John McCord was promoted to captain in December 1983 and went to Nashville to command District Three. He continued the practice of working nights and weekends, which was good for motivating officers in the field. They never knew when he was touring the district.

The Tennessee Highway Patrol celebrated its fiftieth anniversary in 1979 with a luncheon and reception at the Hyatt Regency in Nashville. The Fiftieth Anniversary Committee produced a commemorative weapon as a memento of the occasion. The specially designed blue Smith & Wesson, Model 19, 4" barrel revolver was decorated with an image of the State Trooper patch and gold-filled lettering.

In 1980 the Tennessee Bureau of Investigation, formerly the Tennessee Bureau of Criminal Identification, was reorganized and made independent of the Department of Safety. New TBI Director Arzo Carson guided the Bureau through the process of becoming autonomous.

THP officers continued to be involved in investigative work even after the move of the TBI. One such case was likely responsible for the line of duty death of Sergeant Paul L. Mooneyham Sr. Mooneyham suffered a fatal heart attack on April 4, 1981, during the investigation of the murder of Sullivan County Sheriff's Sergeant Arthur Lane. The heart attack was attributed to the stress and long hours of the investigation. Mooneyham was a 22-year veteran of the THP.

All of the Patrol's expertise, from traffic control to dignitary security, was needed in 1982 when the World's Fair came to Knoxville. Twenty troopers from each district were assignment to the duty and stayed in the abandoned mental hospital for the duration of the fair. Troopers used wards including the seclusion room for sleeping space.

Senior pilot Lieutenant Mike Dover was assigned to 24-7 duty at the university hospital flying medivac missions. Patients were flown to the trauma center when ground transport was slowed due to Knoxville traffic. His efforts proved the value of medivac helicopters for the state of Tennessee and soon after the University of Tennessee, the University in Chattanooga and Vanderbilt University initiated airvac programs.

"Out Squads" of the Tact Squad were organized in East Tennessee and West Tennessee during the World's Fair. Sergeant Linuel Allen supervised the West Tennessee squad. The out squads were dissolved in 1987 due to training issues and the difficulty of maintaining proficiency of the squads given the other duties assigned to its members.

The Criminal Investigations Division (CID) was created in 1983 as a part of consolidation initiative by Governor Alexander. The Motor Vehicle Investigations Section of the Department of Revenue was transferred to the Department of Safety. The section was formed in 1979 to combat vehicle thefts and was originally staffed by six commissioned officers and two support personnel. Investigators such as George Crab developed great skills in the investigation of automobile related crimes. The section worked closely with the TBI as well as federal and local agencies.

As a division of the THP, the CID continued its auto theft work. It also took over internal affairs investigations of the Patrol and soon became involved a wide scope of investigative work. As the division grew it was divided into three districts, west, middle and east with a supervisor over each.

Another state enforcement group was transferred to the Department of Safety effective February 15, 1983. The Motor Vehicle Enforcement Division was transferred from the Department of Revenue.

Responsibility for commercial vehicle size and weight limits originated with the Patrol when it was created in 1929. The motor vehicle enforcement function stayed with the Patrol when the THP was moved to the Department of Administration and when the Department of Safety was created. In 1954, however, enforcement of weight and registration laws moved back to the Department of Finance and Taxation and was called the Field Service Division. The name of the unit was changed to the Motor Vehicle Enforcement Division in 1959 when the department's name was changed to The Department of Revenue.

When the Motor Vehicle Enforcement Division was merged into the Department of Safety in 1983, it retained its basic function of enforcing laws related to commercial vehicles, but became involved in other law enforcement duties as well. The division was organized around the four scales located on interstate highways.

Major Maggie Mae entered service in 1987 as the Patrol's first drug dog. Trooper Lee Chaffin was Maggie Mae's handler. The two worked together for nine years.

The first of these scales became operational in 1965 on I-40/I-70 west of Knoxville. Division I operated the Knox County scales, Division II the Coffee County scales, Division III the Robertson County scales and Division IV the Haywood County scales.

The Tennessee Law Enforcement Training Academy also became a part of the Department of Safety in 1983. The academy was renamed the Jerry F. Agee Tennessee Law Enforcement Training Academy in honor of the late popular, law enforcement oriented state senator. The curriculum of the academy met the requirements of the Peace Officer Standards and Training (POST) Act passed by the general assembly in 1981.

Herman L. Yeatman, former correction commissioner, served as director of the academy from April 1976 until October 1984. He was followed by brief tenures by Phillip Davidson and Robert N. Green before Roger Farley, a former TBI special agent, became director and served through September 1991. Fred Phillips took over as director of the academy on October 1, 1991.

The Tennessee Law Enforcement Training Academy marked the 20th anniversary of its first graduation by graduating a class of 33 trainees in December 1987. Governor Ned Ray McWherter gave the graduation address upon completion of the 12-week, 600-hour curriculum school.

Promotions in rank brought both new responsibly and a fresh learning curve. Perhaps no change was as

The Tact Team in 1992. Standing from left to right in the front were Trooper Lee Chaffin, Lieutenant Don Green (on point) and Sergeant Tommy Hale. Standing from left to right in the back row were troopers Michael "Bucky" Morgan, George Dittfurth, Terry Petty, Phil Hardin and Jim Grant.

dramatic as the move from trooper to sergeant. New sergeants usually had better support when taking on the new duty than Linuel Allen got on his promoted to sergeant in 1980. The two long-time Jackson District sergeants Orvin W. Gates and Ben Joyner both went on vacation for two weeks.

Assuming division responsibility was also demanding. Major Fred Schott Jr. was assigned command of Driver Control in 1983. The division included financial responsibility, driver license issuance, computer services, data entry and accident records.

The National Governors' Association held its 76th annual meeting in Nashville in July 1984. Lieutenant Dickie Pope was in charge of the overall security for the event. Sergeant Denny Wade King was in charge of the personal security of each of the governors. Major Fred Schott was responsible for security and transportation logistics of the nation's governors arriving by air.

Denny King was promoted to lieutenant in 1985 and placed in command of Governor Alexander's secu-

Highway Patrolmen gathered on the steps of the Carroll County Courthouse in the nineties. From left to right were Trooper Marty Pollock, Lieutenant Robert Melton, Trooper Paul "Nat" Moore, Sergeant Lester Waugh and Trooper Bobby Fuller.

Original members of the Wolf Pack. Kneeling from left to right in the front row were Scott Dickson, Randy Nauman, Michael Pipkin, David Brown and Randy Maynard. Standing were Eric Weingeroff, Reaker Bass, Randy Pack, Gerald Hardin, Mark Norrod, Sergeant George Dittfurth, Sergeant Lonnie Ashburn and CID Director Jimmie Van Leach.

rity detail. King began with the Patrol in 1974 and after briefly patrolling in Green County he was stationed in the Kingsport District. In 1978 he was assigned to the Tact Squad. King's first duty at the governor's residence was in November 1979 where he was promoted to sergeant in 1981.

Troopers were provided a range of new equipment in 1985. Protective vests, nightsticks, waterproof winter boots, fur caps and lightweight jackets with zip out lining for fall and spring were provided all members of the Patrol. The Smith & Wesson .357 magnum revolver was adopted as the standard sidearm.

The Tactical Squad was an eight-man team in 1985 when Trooper Lee Chaffin joined the unit. The group was a "go to" squad, responding to emergency incidents, as well as providing VIP security and special assignments requiring advance work. Members cross trained as counter-snipers, bomb technicians and hazardous materials technicians. Chaffin became a paramedic.

The squad worked out of Chevrolet vans supplied and configured so that they could be lived in for a week. An army cot was placed in the aisle in the back and mosquito netting hung over the back door. Handling and stopping were difficult because the van was loaded down with equipment. Two four-wheel drive Broncos were acquired in 1988.

Changes in Tactical Squad equipment since the unit's creation were dramatic. The Pepper Fogger was replace by gas dispersion canisters with pre-mixed chemicals. Commercially made disrupter stands for explosives replaced handmade plywood and pipe disrupters.

Counter-snipers moved from modified Remington .308 rifles to military Remington 700P .308 sniper rifles. Automatic weaponry, initially the post-Vietnam M16A2 rifle, was replaced by the Uzi firing 1200 rounds a minute and then by the Navy version of the MP5, improving fire power and accuracy. The MP5 selector switch allowed single shot, three round burst or fully automatic firing. Accessories included laser sight, muzzle flashlight and silencer. In the nineties the name of the unit was changed from the Tact Squad to Special Operations.

Original members of the Wolf Pack. Kneeling from left to right in the front row were Phillip Perkins, Sam McCoy, Danny Talley, Jim Tate and Brian Harmon. Standing were Commissioner Robert Lawson, Sergeant Linuel Allen, Sergeant Ray Fletcher, Johnny McDonald, Greg Roberts, Robert Nicholson, Richard Austin and Micah Whitten.

The Tactical Squad was responsible for the security plan of the inauguration of Governor Ned Ray McWherter in 1987. The governor named Robert Lawson commissioner of the Department of Safety. Lawson had previously been sheriff of Bradley County. He served as commissioner until November 1994.

Larry Wallace was selected colonel of the Highway Patrol and deputy commissioner of Safety. He served in the position until 1992 when he was appointed director of the Tennessee Bureau of Investigation. Wallace, a native of Athens, Tennessee, began his law enforcement career as a member of the Athens Police Department. He joined the Patrol in 1967 and became a TBI criminal investigator in 1973. Following two terms as sheriff of McMinn County, Wallace returned to the TBI in 1980.

Wallace also served as administrator of the Criminal Investigation Division. He revised the methods and operations of the division, and initiated a program that involved the judiciary in the review of Vehicular Homicide procedures.

Stephen Ross Browder, a native of Selmer, was appointed lieutenant colonel of the Patrol in June 1987. After tours of duty with the U.S. Army in Vietnam where he earned the Purple Heart. Browder joined the Highway Patrol in 1974 and was stationed in the Jackson District. He was promoted to sergeant in 1979 and to lieutenant in 1986.

Browder was in charge of security for Governor-elect Ned McWherter and organized security at the governor's residence before moving to the post of lieutenant colonel. He retained executive security oversight as part of his responsibility. Following his retirement in 1995, Browder went to work for the TVA in executive security.

Major John D. McCord served as executive officer of the Highway Patrol with responsibilities including the Aviation Division, the Tactical Squad, and the Governor's Marijuana Eradication Task Force. McCord was a native of Williamson County and joined the Patrol on August 4, 1961. He was initially assigned to Davidson County and a year later to

MVE Officer Michael L. Rector, left, was found dead on his front lawn in May 1990 after participating in an undercover operation. Trooper Douglas W. Tripp, right, was shot and killed during a traffic stop in Claiborne County in May 1991.

Williamson County. McCord was promoted to sergeant in 1970, to lieutenant in 1976 and on December 1, 1983, to captain in command of the Nashville District. Captain Larry Hitchcock transferred to headquarters in 1988 as support to McCord. McCord and Hitchcock continued in these roles until their retirement in January 1995.

Colonel Standefur headed Motor Vehicle Enforcement. Eddie Stephen Cole retired from the TBI and joined the Department of Safety to head Internal Affairs. He was initially placed in the Major slot of Motor Vehicle Enforcement, but his job title was later changed. He investigated complaints against troopers, drivers license examiners, commercial vehicle officers, drivers registration officials and academy personnel. Cole kept the position until he retired in 2000. Tom Hunton joined the Department of Safety in February 1988 at the rank of major and took over as director of the Motor Vehicle Enforcement Division.

The Department of Safety moved its offices to Foster Avenue on February 13, 1987. The complex included old residence halls and other facilities of the Tennessee Preparatory School. Major Fred Schott managed the reconstruction and renovation of the complex. The central building was connected to other buildings by enclosed walkways on two levels. The facility included not only executive offices but centers for operational functions.

Major Schott retired from activity duty in the Patrol in 1987. He continued to be active with Patrol's chaplains program, which provided counseling for post-traumatic stress disorder, peer counseling for traumatic events such as shootings and similar support for members of the Patrol. The benefits of counseling for trooper was increasingly recognized. Colonel Jerry W. Scott later required everyone who was involved in

a traumatic event to participate in counseling. It was important for everyone to do, because the officer needed counseling more than he thought and if everyone got counseling, it removed the stigma that exists in some peoples minds. Thanks to one generous gift the chaplains program spent approximately a quarter of a million dollars on equipment for the Highway Patrol such as radios, Nextel mobile telephones for supervisors, and over $100,000 for chemical suits.

A Drug-Free Tennessee was on of the programs initiated by Governor McWherter in 1987. One of the first actions related to the program was the addition of the Patrol's first drug dog in 1987. Major Maggie Mae and her handler Trooper Leland D. "Lee" Chaffin quickly demonstrated proficiency in drug seizures. The two worked together for nine years. Chaffin remembered, "She was a great dog. She really made me look good."

On their first search, just out of school, they worked a house suspected of containing drugs. Maggie Mae found little stashes in pictures on the wall and similar locations, then she hit on the bathtub. The tub was sealed against the wall and Chaffin could not figure out how they hid drugs behind the tub. Three pounds of drugs were found when troopers tore the bathtub out. Drugs had been placed there through a trapdoor in the external wall.

Major Maggie Mae not only had a nose for narcotics, but a sixth sense for danger. Once after searching a housing complex, a crowd of residents began to converging on Trooper Chaffin. Maggie sensed aggression and began to walk in circles around Chaffin. The encroachment stopped. In another situation, Chaffin's attention was focused on a number of suspects and he did not know an individual was sneaking up behind

Trooper George Van Holcomb, left, was struck and killed by a tractor-trailer in January 1992 while working an accident in Decatur County. Sergeant James D. Perry, right, died of a heart attack during a foot pursuit in October 1999.

Pilots Lieutenant Dennis Kent and Sergeant John B. Allen Sr. flew this THP Bell UH-B1 "Huey" patrolling the 1996 Olympic Games whitewater event on the Ocoee River in Polk County, Tennessee.

him. Maggie Mae, at the troopers side also eyeing the suspects, suddenly turned and attacked the man behind Chaffin.

Using funds from federal grants, the activities of the small CID force was expanded to include drug enforcement. Illegal drug traffic and other criminal activity had increased at rest stops along Tennessee interstate highways. The CID created an Undercover Narcotics Unit in 1988 to work drugs crimes and to clean up other problems in the rest areas.

Jimmie Van Leach was chosen as director of CID in October 1988. Leach joined the Highway Patrol in 1977 and transferred to the TBI shortly before it

moved out of Safety. He was currently the Special Agent in Charge of the Eastern Division of the TBI.

The focus of CID drug investigations moved from more populated areas to counties with limited local enforcement resources. In the early nineties the CID had maximum personnel of 18 and averaged about 2,000 drug cases a year, seizing approximately one million in cash and one half million in other assets.

The division also worked property crimes. They received a tip from an informant in 1989 that a stolen semi-trailer was parked at the North 40 Truck Stop on I-40. CID set up observation across the highway to catch the thief in possession of the stolen goods. About two weeks into the stakeout a big rig pulled into the truck stop and briefly blocked investigators view of the trailer. During that time the thief hooked up the trailer and left.

Investigator Steve Russell, who joined the Patrol in 1983, had only recently transferred to CID and as the "new guy" took the brunt of the blame from his fellow officers for letting the trailer get away. He was determine to find the thief and the stolen property. One Sunday morning Russell got a call from an informant at the truck stop saying the truck came back and had just left on I-40 headed for Memphis. Russell jumped in his car and headed for I-40. As luck would have it, when Russell pulled off the ramp at mile marker 87 he was directly behind the truck. After a few miles

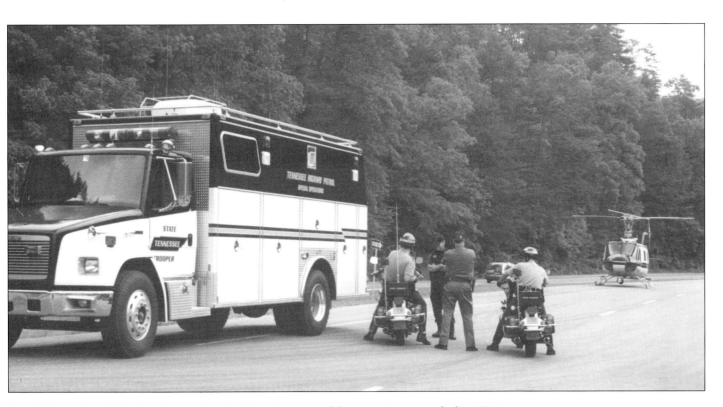

Special Operations of the Patrol was equipped with various state of the art equipment in the late 1990s.

Investigator Russell stopped the truck, capturing the trailer load of stolen tires and the thief.

In 1993 Investigator Russell headed the investigation of an auto theft ring in Big Sandy. Russell and Investigator Danny Sullivan from East Tennessee working under cover shut down the gang that was bringing in cars from several states. Russell continued to exhibit initiative and tenaciousness and was promoted to sergeant in 1996 and was transferred to Weakley County. Three years later he was promoted to lieutenant.

In the late eighties the CID, in connection with federal law enforcement, made a major case against a Knoxville felon who was one of the biggest car thieves in the southeastern United States. It was discovered that Michael Lloyd Rector, a young officer with the Motor Vehicle Enforcement Division, was related to the head of the car-theft ring and had worked for him before joining law enforcement.

Rector offered to go undercover in the stolen car operation and was key to developing evidence in the case. On May 31, 1990, following the investigation, Officer Rector's body was found on his front lawn by his wife. He had been shot at close range with a 9mm semi-automatic pistol. The murder was never prosecuted, but the ring-leader of the car theft operation was prosecuted under the federal RICO statute, forfeited his property and was sent to a federal prison.

Requests from county officials for the CID to investigate murders and other crimes increased. For a period the unit responded to these requests, but due to the overlap with the mission of the TBI, the CID abandoned general investigations and returned to doing mostly auto theft, odometer fraud, drivers license fraud and internal affairs investigations.

Among other operational and equipment initiatives the Patrol began tests in the late eighties to determine the best semi-automatic service weapon available. Initially the department selected a 9mm Smith & Wesson pistol in 1988. The change to .40 caliber as the standard service weapon was soon made to improve stopping power. Green leather jackets were provided to troopers for wear during the cold months in 1990. A few years later they were replaced by lined nylon jackets. A gold-tone license plate with the state seal and black numbers was adopted for Highway Patrol vehicles in the nineties.

The THP lost a number of officers in the line of duty in the late eighties and early nineties. Trooper Samuel F. Holcomb Jr. was killed on March 27, 1988, when he was struck by a vehicle on I-40 in Dickson County. Holcomb

Trooper Bobby J. Maples, left, died in November 1999 of a heart attack he suffered while assisting a motorist. Trooper John G. Mann, right, was in a foot pursuit in Davidson County in January 2001 when he was struck and killed by a vehicle. Trooper Mann was awarded the Medal of Valor posthumously.

stopped a suspicious vehicle and as he was exiting his patrol car he was struck from behind by a driver who had been blinded by the early morning sunlight.

Trooper Douglas Tripp was shot multiple times and killed while he sat in his patrol car on May 19, 1991. The gunman told authorities that he shot the trooper because he didn't deserve a speeding ticket. Tripp was 42 years old.

Trooper George Van Dorse Holcomb of the Jackson District was struck and killed by a tractor-trailer while working a DUI-related accident in Decatur County on January 26, 1992. TBI agent Chris Carpenter reported that Holcomb saw the tractor trailer was out of control, unable to stop and headed for the crowded accident scene. Holcomb ran toward the crowd warning people to move. At the last moment he ran off the side of the roadway. Fatefully, the rig was headed in the same direction. The semi struck the wrecker and smashed into Trooper Holcomb, crushing his body against the side of a small ravine.

Trooper Bobby L. Lindsey Jr. survived a near fatal shooting when a bullet barely missed his heart. Lindsey responded to a call on a DWI driver and spotted the car pulled over at the intersection of Highway 412 and I-40 at the 79 exit. As Lindsey approached the car he saw the rear window on the drivers side lower. Lindsey thought the driver was lowering the window by mistake, when the driver fired out the back window, striking Lindsey in the chest.

The shooter then drove onto I-40 heading west, but pulled to the side of the road near mile marker 78. He got out of the car, leaving it in gear, walked into the ditch and shot himself through the head.

When the call of Lindsey's shooting went out and the shooter's car was found, troopers grabbed equipment and rushed to the scene. The group was waiting for trailing dogs before setting off the manhunt when the body of the gunman was discovered.

A number of changes occurred in commercial vehicles enforcement the late eighties and early nineties following federal and state legislation. For the Patrol it brought new requirements for the Driver License Division and the Motor Vehicle Enforcement Division. Driver license classifications changed to Class A, B and C for commercial drivers, Class D for regular operators plus other classes. In January 1991 the Motor Vehicle Enforcement Division was restructured as the Commercial Vehicle Division, 54 officers were transferred to the Highway Patrol for training as troopers and the remaining 50 officers assigned to weight stations.

Newly designed patrol cars were introduced in 1991, the first major redesign of markings in over thirty years. Lieutenant Jerry Simmons of Memphis was the longest serving member of the THP at the time

Trooper Stacy Day-Henegar with 50 pounds of marijuana, cash, pistol, and other items confiscated in an arrest made while on patrol in the Knoxville area in January 2003.

and the only one on the Patrol who had witnessed the previous redesign in 1958.

The color scheme remained black and cream, with black hood, roof, and truck lid and cream front and rear side panels and doors. Black and gold stripes ran the length of the car and the front doors contained the outline of the state. The new design won the international police car design award from Law and Order magazine.

The first automobiles with the new markings were high-performance V-8, 1991 Chevrolet Caprices with automatic transmissions and overdrive. The new design on the streamlined, fast-backed vehicles gave a sportier look to the patrol units. The first 171 new patrol cars were delivered in August 1991 and the remainder of the 640 units were put into service over the next three years.

Commissioner Lawson gave another assignment to the Criminal Investigations Division in 1992. The "Wolf Pack" was created to look for traveling criminals at the same time that the officers were enforcing traffic laws. The Wolf Pack Unit was dedicated to criminal interdiction and assigned to the CID. Four sergeants were selected to supervise, Sergeant George Dittfurth, a 20-year veteran from Haywood County stationed in Nashville, Linuel Allen from the Jackson District, Ray Fletcher from Knoxville, and Lonnie Ashburn from Manchester.

Each of the sergeants commanded a team of six to eight troopers. Each team worked as a separate unit. Three of the teams focused on drug interdiction and Allen's team worked criminal interdiction. On a single night in Memphis, working with the Shelby County Sheriff's Office, approximately 100 people were jailed on various charges. A 685 pound load of marijuana was captured in Henderson County, the largest cache of the drug taken in the state at that time, along with a great deal of cash and a major drug dealer. Sergeant Johnny Craig was responsible for disposition of seized contraband from CID, the Wolf Pack, and other THP units after court cases and other legal processes were completed. Confiscated goods were auctioned or otherwise sold. The revenue went to the Department of Safety or local sheriff's offices.

District captains felt the pinch of having their best officers assigned to work for CID. The Wolf Pack was placed under the command of Major John McCord, commander of the field division of the Patrol.

Colonel Larry Wallace was appointed director of the TBI in September 1992. The position of colonel of the Patrol remained vacant for the balance of Governor McWherter's term. The work of the colonel was taken over by Major John McCord until his retirement in January 1995. Captain Larry Hitchcock took on the duties of executive officer. Lieutenant Colonel Steve Browder continued to manage communications, support services, and administrative functions. Commissioner Lawson brought Fred Phillips from the academy to be deputy commissioner.

Richard Dawson was appointed commissioner of the Department of Safety in November 1994 when Robert Lawson resigned. Dawson served until January 1995.

The recruit class of 1994 was the first in five years. The 14-week school had 46 trainees. It was a diverse class with eleven women, four of whom were black, and ten black men. The class brought the number of commissioned troopers on the Tennessee Highway Patrol to 684.

When the state administration changed in January 1995, Governor Don Sundquist appointed Mike Greene commissioner of the Department of Safety. Colonel Jerry W. Scott was named to head the Highway Patrol. Captain Jim Holtsford served for a time as Executive Officer.

Lieutenant Denny King took charge of security for Governor Sundquist. King continued efforts to upgrade security at the governor's residence. In the early 1980s outside security at the residence was limited to a fence, a mirror and one camera that fogged up when it rained. King served in the security unit through three administrations during which motion detectors, trips and other devices were installed around the fence along with numerous cameras in and around the house.

King remained at the governor's residence after promotion to captain in 1996 and to lieutenant colonel in 2000. King also served as president of the National Governors' Security Association for three years from 1999 to 2002. The organization was responsible for coordinating security details of the nation's governors during the semi-annual governors' conferences and for special events including large numbers of governors.

The officers of the Motor Carrier Enforcement Division of the Public Service Commission merged into the Commercial Vehicle Enforcement Division on July 1, 1996. The units were combined to eliminate the duplication of enforcement responsibilities and improved efficiency. Personnel transferred to the Department of Safety numbered 130.

The THP created its own training academy, the Tennessee Department of Safety Training Center, in a remodeled facility at Clover Bottom in 1997. The center provided recruits 24 weeks of law enforcement instruction and preparation. The center was established because of the expanding demands on the Tennessee Law Enforcement Training Academy for training officers of the sheriff and police departments across the state.

The Department of Safety demonstrated full compliance with of the Commission on Accreditation for Law Enforcement Agencies (CALEA) and was accredited by the commission on November 21, 1999. The fact that the department achieved this goal in a single year was testimony to the professionalism and effectiveness that already existed.

The Critical Incident Response Team (CIRT) was created in April 2001 to assist the department and other agencies in the investigation and/or reconstruction of motor vehicle traffic crashes. Unit members also investigated all criminal homicides worked by the Highway Patrol.

During the years surrounding the start of a new millennium several Tennessee Highway Patrol officers lost their lives in the line of duty. Two died of heart failure. Sergeant James David Perry, a 23-year veteran, suffered a fatal heart attack while searching for a suspect who assaulted an officer in Ardmore on October 3, 1999. Trooper Bobby J. Maples was with the THP for 14 years when he suffered a fatal heart attack while assisting a broken down motorist on November 5, 1999.

Two troopers died as a result of motor vehicle assault. Trooper Lynn McCarthy Ross was killed on July 26, 2000, when his patrol car was struck by a commercial vehicle as he was worked a construction zone on I-40 near Jackson. Ross' vehicle was at the rear of the work-zone with emergency lights flashing when a tractor-trailer struck it from behind. The patrol car was flipped and engulfed in flames with Trooper Ross inside. Ross was a trooper for five years.

Trooper John Gregory Mann was killed when he was struck by a vehicle on January 1, 2001, as he chased a suspected carjacker on foot. Mann was in a vehicle pursuit when the suspect crashed into a retaining wall on I-24 near Nashville. Trooper Mann was able to catch the suspect on foot and was in the process of arresting him when another driver struck both men. The trooper was killed instantly and the suspect was critically injured. The subject who struck Trooper Mann fled the scene. Trooper Mann, a 16-year veteran, was awarded the Medal of Valor posthumously.

Trooper John Robert Davis, a 12-year veteran, was killed in a single vehicle accident on March 17, 2001. He was leaving the scene of an accident when his cruiser went out of control and went into a creek.

Seventy new troopers graduated from the Tennessee Department of Safety Training Center in commencement ceremonies on April 23, 2004. Trooper Cadet Class 404 ceremony participants included, from left to right in the front row, training center director Captain J. R. Perry, Colonel Lynn Pitts, Commissioner of Safety Fred Phillips, Deputy Commissioner of Safety Tom Moore and Major Lee Chaffin.

Denny W. King was appointed commissioner of the Department of Safety in January 2002 upon Commissioner Green's resignation. Commissioner King served until September 30, 2002, when he resigned to accept appointment as the U.S. Marshal of the Middle District of Tennessee by President George W. Bush. Highway Patrol Colonel Jerry W. Scott was named commissioner of Safety beginning in October 2002 and Lieutenant Colonel Mark V. Fagan was promoted to colonel.

Lieutenant Danny Wilson was promoted to captain in January 2002 and took command of the Third District. Captain Wilson was the first African American to hold the rank of captian and command a patrol district.

In January 2003, Fred Phillips was appointed commissioner of Safety by Governor Phil Bredesen. Phillips had nearly forty years of law enforcement experience. The Jonesborough native served as a patrolman for the Johnson City Police Department beginning in 1964 and served three years as a special agent for the TBI starting in 1972. Phillips returned to the Johnson City police force and spent most of the 1980s as chief of police. He was director of the Tennessee Law Enforcement Training Academy from 1991 until his appointment as deputy commissioner of the Department of Safety in 1992, where he served until 1994.

Phillips was elected sheriff of Washington County in September 1994 and honored as "Sheriff of the Year" in 1999. Sheriff Phillips was in his third term when appointed commissioner of Safety.

Charles Thomas "Tom" Moore was named deputy commissioner in 2003 to support the commissioner in day-to-day operations management including the Driver License and Title and Registration divisions. Moore, a Cookeville native, became a trooper in September 1975 following in the footsteps of his father Thomas D. Moore who served with both the THP and the TBI.

Deputy Commissioner Moore had most recently served as commander of the Department's CIRT unit. He previously conducted special Programs in the Training Division and served as the Executive Assistant to former Commissioner Robert Lawson.

Colonel Lynn Pitts took on command of the Patrol. The native of Henderson and a 28-year veteran began as a trooper in 1974 in Bedford County. Prior to his promotion to colonel, Pitts was in charge of five Patrol divisions including planning and research, accident records, driver improvement and federal grants. Major Leland "Lee" Chaffin was named Administrative Assistant to Colonel.

Districts commanders were Captain Charles D. Laxton in Knoxville, Captain Lucious Howard in Chattanooga, Captain Danny Wilson in Nashville, Captain Joe Nunn in Memphis, Captain Glenn Cantwell

Trooper John Robert Davis, left, was killed in a single vehicle accident on March 17, 2001. Trooper Todd M. Larkins, right, was struck and killed by a tractor-trailer while conducting a traffic stop on July 8, 2005.

in Fall Branch, Captain John Eldridge in Cookeville, Captain Jimmy Brown in Lawrenceburg and Captain Linuel Allen in Jackson. Districts were also staffed with an administrative lieutenant and a lieutenant responsible for safety education.

Administrative lieutenants served as acting captain in the absences of the district commander and managed the communications operation, supervising the radio room and other non-sworn personnel. He maintained district records and the district headquarters facility, procured supplies, approved vehicle assignment and issued uniforms, weapons and other equipment to troopers. The administrative lieutenant was also responsible for the evidence vault with the assistance of a sergeant.

In the Jackson District, Lieutenant Curtis Mansfield served as administrative lieutenant and was supported by Sergeant Glenn Taylor. Lieutenant Mansfield joined the Patrol in November 1988 after earning a B.S. in criminal justice and began patrolling the roads in Decatur County. Other administrative lieutenants were Larry French in Knoxville, Danny B. Hall in Chattanooga, Ron Bilbrey in Nashville, Zane Smith in Memphis, William Tate in Fall Branch, Victor Donoho in Cookeville and Steven Hazard in Lawrenceburg.

The eight patrol districts are structured the same and are governed by the same rules, but each has individual characteristics or a "personality." Each district is organized into troops of four to six per district and designated Troop A, Troop B, and so forth. Each troop consists of one to four counties.

Larry W. Rucker was appointed Lieutenant Colonel of the Patrol on May 26, 2004. A native of Morristown, he began his career with the THP in 1973 and spent 20 years as a bomb technician with THP's Bomb Squad. He

was captain over Internal Affairs before being named lieutenant colonel.

Other command personnel included Title and Registration Division Director Paula Shaw, Driver License Division Director Larry Large, Financial Responsibility Division Director Kenneth Birdwell and Captain J. R. Perry, head of Tennessee Department of Safety Training Center. Danny Wright was appointed director of the CID in May 2003.

The Commercial Vehicle Enforcement Division was merged into the Highway Patrol on July 1, 2004, and uniformed personnel of the THP grew to 900. New districts were formed within the Patrol structure with responsibility for managing operation at weight stations across the state, each under the command of a captain. Districts 10 through 14 for the scales in Greene, Knox, Coffee, Robertson and Haywood counties. Commercial Vehicle Enforcement officers became troopers after they received additional training.

The Capitol Police was also absorbed into the Highway Patrol and became part of Administrative District 9 as Capitol Security. Training for officers of the Capitol Police was augmented and all except two became troopers.

The Criminal Investigation Division was transferred from the Department of Safety to the Tennessee Bureau of Investigation on October 6, 2005. The decision was intended to consolidated all criminal investigation under the TBI.

The dangers of traffic patrol came shockingly into focus again on Friday, July 8, 2005. Trooper Todd M. Larkins, 31 years old with five years on the Patrol, was struck and killed by a tractor-trailer while conducting a traffic stop. Trooper Larkins pulled a vehicle over on Interstate 40 in Dickson County. Moments after he exited his marked patrol car, the semi veered off the roadway and into the emergency lane striking Larkins and killing him instantly.

A major reorganization of the Highway Patrol and the Department of Safety began in December 6, 2005. THP Colonel Lynn Pitts retired and Lieutenant Colonel Larry Rucker took interim command. Commissioner of the Department of Safety Fred Phillips resigned and Deputy Commissioner Tom Moore retired. Governor Bredesen swore in Commissioner of Transportation Gerald F. Nicely as commissioner of Safety while a search for new leadership was conducted.

Colonel Mike Walker, a 28-year veteran, took command of Patrol on March 1, 2006. Colonel Walker previously headed the Professional Standards Division and was highly respected by his colleagues. Walker was a

Command of the Tennessee Highway Patrol named in March 2006 were Colonel Mike Walker, seated front, Lieutenant Colonel Albert Strawther, standing right, and Major Tracy Trott. All were veteran members of the Patrol. Colonel Walker previously headed the Professional Standards Division, Lieutenant Colonel Strawther was head of the Safety Education Division and Major Trott commanded troops in five counties of the Fall Branch District.

native of Dunlap and began his law enforcement career as a policeman in Signal Mountain in 1976. He joined the Patrol in 1977 and worked through the ranks. He served as director of the Driver's License Division from 1989 to 1991 and coordinated security for the THP at the Ocoee Olympic site during the 1996 Olympics.

Albert Strawther was promoted from captain to lieutenant colonel at the same time. Lieutenant Colonel Strawther, also a 28-year veteran of the Patrol, was from Lebanon and was serving as head of the Safety Education Division. Strawther previously served in the Training Division, in the Executive Security unit and as Director of the Capitol Police.

Greta Dajani was given responsibility for the Driver License Issuance Division. A week later, veteran THP Lieutenant Tracy Trott was promoted to major in the colonel's office. Major Trott relocated from the Fall Branch District where he commanded troops in five counties.

Significant changes in the structure and policies of the Department of Safety and Highway Patrol were made, including a revision of hiring and promotion practices to eliminate political influence. Four new captains were promoted to district commanders, including the first female captian in the history of the Patrol. Captain Cheryl Sanders took cammand of the Chattanooga District, Captain Raymond Fletcher the Knoxville District, Captain Thomas Smith the Memphis District and Captain Richard Dean Hurley the Fall Branch District. All had over 20 years with the THP.

A history of valiant service is the core of the Tennessee Department of Safety. Today the Tennessee Highway Patrol consists of nearly 1,000 uniformed personnel responsible for safety on more than 87,000 miles of state and federal highways across Tennessee.

An indication of the excellence of the Tennessee Highway Patrol is the recognition of the International Association of Police Chiefs (IACP) in 2005. The THP was awarded two First Place State Police/Highway Patrol Awards, recognizing the Patrol as one of the best in the nation for both its Traffic Safety Enforcement Program and its Commercial Vehicle Enforcement Program.

The Tennessee Highway Patrol celebrated its 75th anniversary in 2005. In those seventy-five years since a group of youngsters learned to balance themselves on two-wheeled patrol units, the Tennessee Highway Patrol and other divisions of the Department of Safety have grown into a modern organization of law enforcement professionals. Those first patrolmen would have little understanding of the technology and resources available to today's trooper, but they share a commitment to duty.

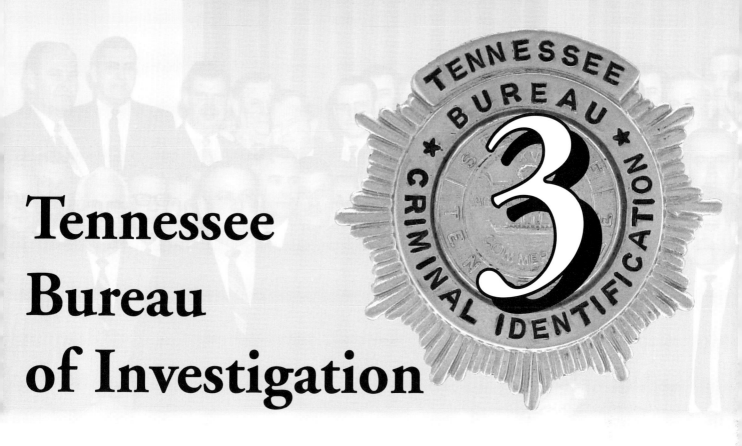

Tennessee Bureau of Investigation

The Tennessee Bureau of Investigation was created in 1951 within the Department of Safety. The agency was first named the Tennessee Bureau of Criminal Identification, but was called the "TBI" even in the earliest days. It was easier for agents in the field to say "TBI" rather than having to explain the name. The letters soon came to represent the Bureau's motto, "Truth, Bravery, Integrity."

Several attempts had been made to set up a state investigative agency. The Tennessee Highway Patrol was not authorized to investigate criminal activity and many considered it important to create an investigative unit within the Highway Patrol. Department of Safety Commissioner Sam K. Neal and Brigadier General Sam T. Wallace, Tennessee's adjutant general, discussed creating a state bureau of investigation in December 1950 because of international tension and hostilities. The two believed that an investigative unit was important to combat sabotage and subversive activities.

The need for a statewide criminal investigation force had become front-page news as the result of a highly publicized murder in Greene County in December 1950. A Gap Creek sawmill operator was shot through the window as he lay in bed. Untrained and inexperienced deputy sheriffs allowed the public to trample the murder scene, destroying footprints and tire marks that may have led to solving the crime. The

publisher of the *Greeneville Sun*, John M. Jones Sr., and the Tennessee Press Association called for the creation of a statewide agency to assist local law enforcement in the investigation of major crimes.

A bill was introduced to create the Tennessee Bureau of Criminal Identification headed by a director and divided into two divisions, one for field investigations and one for scientific analysis of evidence. Chapter 173 of the Public Acts of 1951 was passed on March 14, 1951, and signed by Governor Gordon Browning the following day.

Section 1. *Be it enacted by the General Assembly of the State of Tennessee*, That there is hereby created in the Department of Safety a Bureau of Criminal Identification, which shall be in charge of a Director thereof. Such Director shall be appointed by the Commissioner of Safety with the approval of the governor and shall be a person of experience and ability in the detection of crime.

Sec. 2. *Be it further enacted*, That the Field Division shall consist of not less than six persons who shall be experienced in the detection of crime and in criminal work generally . . . . At least two of such Field Investigators shall be normally detail to service in each Grand Division of the State . . . The Commissioner upon the request of

John M. Jones Sr., publisher of the Greeneville Sun, led the campaign to create the Tennessee Bureau of Criminal Identification, and is often referred to as "the father of the TBI."

the District Attorney General of a Circuit may assign such field investigators to aid such District Attorney General in the investigation of any crime committed in his judicial circuit, but only when said District Attorney General requests such aid . . . . such field investigators . . . shall have the same powers with reference to the execution of criminal process, making arrests, and the like, as does the Sheriff of the county . . .

Sec. 3. *Be it further enacted*, "That the Laboratory Division shall consist of experts in the scientific detection of crime . . . .. ballistics expert, toxicologist, expert in the detection of human blood stains and fingerprint experts and such other persons of expert knowledge in the detection of crime as may be found feasible. It shall be the duty of the Laboratory Division to keep a complete record of such fingerprints as may be obtained by them through exchange with the Federal Bureau of Investigation, with similar Bureaus in other States and from fingerprints obtained in this State. Each peace officer of this State, upon fingerprinting any person arrested, shall furnish a copy of such fingerprint to the Laboratory Division of the Bureau. Likewise,

such fingerprints as are now on file at the State Penitentiary shall be transferred therefrom to the Bureau . . .

The Bureau became the "plainclothes" division of the Department of Safety. Joe Boyd Williams was named the first director of the TBI. Although he had extensive background in law enforcement, Williams was not trained or experienced in scientific investigation. He served as director of the Bureau from 1951 to 1953. Miss Nell Geary served as secretary to the director.

Director Williams, a veteran of the Marine Corps, began his law enforcement career in Los Angeles in 1920. He was one of the original commanders of the Tennessee Highway Patrol (THP) following its organization in 1929. He was the first assistant chief in command of the Middle or Nashville Division of the THP and was the second chief of the patrol, serving in that role under two administrations. He later served as criminal investigator for the Davidson County district attorney general.

Williams served in Army Air Corps Intelligence during World War II. He assisted in the prosecution of war crimes in Tokyo and organized the 75,000-man Japanese police force. He had returned to Tennessee in March 1951.

The investigative staff consisted of six agents, titled Field Investigators. William E. "Bill" Coleman Jr., a Tennessee Highway Patrol corporal assigned to Nashville, was the first individual asked by Bureau Director Joe Boyd Williams and Commissioner of Safety Sam Neal to serve as one of the two agents assigned to Middle Tennessee.

Alfred Thomas "A. T." or "Big'un" Ellis, a Highway Patrol sergeant who had been on the Patrol since 1947, joined with Coleman to cover the 38 counties of Middle Tennessee. A. T. Ellis weighed 14 pounds at birth and carried the nickname "Big'un" all of his life.

Highway Patrolman Kenneth W. Shelton and former chief of the Springfield Police Department, Charles Easley, were the agents for East Tennessee and worked out of Athens. Roger Kennon, an FBI special agent in the Memphis field office, and Robert Ezell, of the Shelby County Sheriff's Department, worked out of Memphis and covered West Tennessee.

The Bureau was assigned two offices in the Cotton States Building in downtown Nashville, one long room and a side room, both small. The only things in the offices were three small desks. Agents had no guns, no badges and no cars. For the first three months the field agents helped the director set up a filing system.

Joe Boyd Williams, former chief of the Highway Patrol, was named the first director of the TBI. He served as director from 1951 to 1953.

The TBI began operation on July 1, 1951. Williams gave the status of the identification bureau at the time in an interview with *Finger Print and Identification Magazine*.

It is divided into two services, the field division and the laboratory division. At the present time we have only put into effect the field division. The laboratory set-up has been delayed due to not having the necessary space available at this time to set up a laboratory, and at the present time no equipment has been purchased and no technicians have been employed.

Although a lab was not immediately set up, fingerprint technicians were hired. The fingerprint identification specialists were Judson Gann, who came from the Davidson County Sheriff's Department, and Ambrose R. Moss, who was hired from the FBI Identification Division to establish a fingerprint and records unit for the TBI. Their title was Crime Technician and they worked out of the Nashville Office. Later Gann did polygraph work and Moss worked narcotics.

The first day in the office Ambrose Moss borrowed a legal pad from the Labor Department located across the hall and made a list of equipment they needed including fingerprint equipment and cameras.

Director Williams asked Governor Browning for $5,000 to buy chairs and equipment.

The Bureau had little equipment. Field agents eventually got badges, guns and notepads. They furnished their own pens. The badge was a small gold-tone sunburst and the sidearm was a .38 caliber revolver.

By October 1951 the Bureau was assigned four cars, Pontiacs. The director had a car and the two agents in each division shared a car. Bill Coleman and A. T. Ellis shared one of the Pontiacs. Ellis lived in Madison and Coleman lived in Nashville, so they took turns picking each other up.

The cars were equipped with a THP radio, but the coverage was very spotty. Sometimes an agent had to drive to the top of a hill in order to get a signal. Field agents mostly depended on the telephone for contact and built relationships with the sheriffs and police departments in their territory.

The TBI's first request from a district attorney general to work a case came in July 1951, a Clay County murder committed that April. A man had been tied to a tree in the Pea Ridge section about 15 miles north of Celina, gagged and shot in the back. Coleman and Ellis set up an office in the Clay County Courthouse and conducted the investigation. The case was solved and a Missouri man arrested.

Bill Coleman recalled early investigations, "We really had no training and winged it the best way we could. But the director was determined he was going to make something of the Bureau and he sent everybody the first few years to the FBI academy. I went through that training in 1952."

One of the first orders of business for the crime technicians was to assemble fingerprint records. Moss developed the design for the fingerprint card and had them printed at the state printing office. He and Gann drove across the state and visited every police and sheriff's department. They gave supplies to each agency and did the best they could to persuade them to fingerprint those arrested and send the cards to TBI headquarters. Often they were met with resistance or concerns such as, "Well, who's going to pay the postage?" But cards soon began coming in to Nashville. The Bureau started collecting fingerprints in May 1952 and within a year slightly under 4,000 sets of prints were received from across the state.

The Bureau began to add agents. Walter Toon joined the TBI as a field agent in 1953. Toon transferred from the Highway Patrol where he served as a sergeant stationed in Gallatin. The THP would remain the primary source for agents during the first three decades of the Bureau's history.

Ambrose Moss was promoted to Field Investigator early in 1953 and Judson Gann and William Kelly "Bill" Whitehurst took charge of the fingerprints. Moss was soon assigned to narcotics investigations. For seven years Moss was the only agent doing drug work and then Wade Ingram was hired from the Board of Pharmacy. The small narcotics unit worked the entire state.

Moss had neither laboratory nor anyone to do drug analysis. The commissioner and assistant commissioner of the Department of Health were personal friends of Moss and he requested their help. Bill Darby and another chemist in the health department lab on the top floor of the Cordell Hull Building did drug analysis and testified in court as to their findings. This work was done at no expense to the Bureau.

Covering the entire state was a challenge for field investigators. Members of the Bureau might leave on Sunday night to be in court in Memphis on Monday morning and then travel to Chattanooga. They might not get back home until Friday evening. This was in the years before interstate highways.

The TBI's start has been characterized as "slow and rocky." Key appointments and promotions were political. The agency became ineffective and morale was poor. Director Joe Boyd Williams left the Bureau in 1953 after Governor Frank Clement took office.

James English was appointed Investigator-in-Charge as temporary head of the Bureau during 1954. English was a former assistant chief of the Highway Patrol and briefly served as acting commissioner of the Department of Safety in 1953. James E. "Jimmy" Thompson, outgoing Shelby County sheriff, took over in the fall of 1954 and briefly served as head of the TBI. A. T. Ellis was given the title Senior Agent and handled much of the day to day oversight of the Bureau.

At one point the original members of the TBI went before Governor Frank Clement. The governor turned in his chair trying to decide if he was going to fire everyone and do away with the Bureau or let the agency continue. He looked at them, thanked them for attending and sent them back their office. They were unsure for some time as to their future.

Despite the tenuous beginnings of the Bureau, encouragement from the Tennessee Press Association persuaded Governor Clement to reorganize the TBI rather than abolish it. The agency needed strong and experienced leadership.

Special Agent Winfred E. "Bud" Hopton, senior resident agent of the FBI's Nashville field office for the preceding 11 years, had an impressive investigative and administrative background and was well thought of by state law enforcement personnel. A. T. Ellis and Bill Coleman went to Governor Clement and asked him to consider hiring Hopton to serve as director of the Bureau.

Clement was a former FBI agent and personal friend of FBI Director J. Edgar Hoover. Hoover allowed Hopton to retire early from the FBI after 27 years in federal law enforcement. Hopton was named to head the TBI and assumed the job on July 1, 1955. He served until 1971, garnering the longest tenure in the position in the history of the agency and establishing a solid reputation for the Bureau.

Hopton graduated from Washington University Law School in St. Louis during the depression years. Wiley Rutledge, dean of the school and future justice of the U.S. Supreme Court, recommended Hopton apply to the FBI and gave him the advise, "Always shoot straight, and I mean that literally and figuratively."

Hopton's accomplishments as a field agent with the federal bureau were notable. Soon after he graduation from the FBI academy in 1934, he was one of two FBI agents who apprehended Charles "Pretty Boy" Floyd. The gangster had killed a number of lawmen and was considered Public Enemy No. 1.

Floyd was spotted in Ohio and as Hopton and his partner approached, Floyd darted from a corncrib and sprinted across an open field toward a wooded area. He fired at the two FBI agents with a .45 caliber auto-

Agents William Kelly "Bill" Whitehurst, wearing hat, and Ambrose Moss in the field with an evidence collection kit open. The ability to perform a scientific investigation at the scene of a crimes was the reason the TBI was created.

Early members of the TBI gethered in 1972. Left to right were Bud Hopton (Director from 1955 to 1971), Ambrose Moss (one of the first crime technician), William E. Coleman Jr. (one of the first criminal investigators), Walter Toon, and A. T. Ellis (another of the first criminal investigators).

matic pistol, but they had Thompson submachine guns and Floyd was mortally wounded. Hopton took off his new trench coat and wrapped Floyd in it. Floyd died at the scene.

Other gangsters of the thirties were pursued and apprehended by Bud Hopton. He was one of the G-Men that tracked down the Barker-Karpis gang, one of the most violent and prolific criminal groups of the period. He said Alvin Karpis was the most cold-blooded of the killers of the era. Hopton was also involved in a shootout with two members of the Irish O'Malley gang at a roadhouse near Kansas City.

During World War II Hopton was an administrative assistant to Director Hoover. He was in charge the night when a report came into FBI headquarters that Nazi saboteurs were landed by submarines on beaches at Long Island and near Jacksonville, Florida. One of the targets of the saboteurs was the aluminum plant at Alcoa, Tennessee.

When Hopton was appointed director of the Tennessee Bureau of Criminal Identification, he announced that his goal was for the TBI to serve Tennessee in the manner the FBI had served the nation. Members of the Bureau found Bud Hopton to be a quiet and deliberate man. He did not talk much and was true to his word. Hopton had a lean face with a long nose and blue eyes. When he was thinking, he had the habit of running his fingers along the length of his nose. In his personal life Hopton was a sportsman

and a great bird hunter. Agents called him either "Mr. Hopton," or "Mr. Bud" in more relaxed moments.

The TBI moved to the Cordell Hull Building in 1955. Hopton installed a record system similar to the FBI's. He initiated a comprehensive training program grounded in scientific crime detection and informed personnel that henceforth all appointments and promotions were to be on a merit basis only. He later commented on the situation at the Bureau during these years.

The TBI really struggled in its first years. We also had to convince the legislature to pass acts giving us any authority. We were just made up of a committed little group of agents and technicians who labored to bring the TBI out of the depths.

Hopton was strict as director of the agency. Agents were required to wear suits and ties and project a professional image. Flashy or "loud" sports coats were prohibited and he expected men to have topcoats. He initially required agents to wear hats, but the requirement was dropped in the early sixties. Hopton specified that agents conceal their weapons, eliminating wearing holsters suspended from their belt. He began keeping performance records and agents who did not meet his standards were dismissed.

The Bureau acquired service weapons for field agents. The .38 caliber Colt Special revolvers were

Director Bud Hopton, standing at left, looked on as Crime Technician Judson Gann demonstrated the polygraph machine on Crime Technician Archie Hamm, seated at right.

from the district attorney-general, to make investigations in connection with violations of the Tennessee Narcotic Laws, any matter pertaining to fugitives from justice, and investigations pertaining to the employees or prospective employees of the Department of Safety.

Director Hopton looked for men who had established a good reputation as effective investigators and individuals with good technical skills. Ethridge C. "Dusty" Hale joined the TBI in the spring of 1957. Hale had been a member of the Highway Patrol since 1949. Earl York, a nephew of WW I hero Sergeant Alvin York, joined the Bureau in 1957. York joined the Highway Patrol in 1939; he retired from the TBI in 1965.

Robert C. "Bob" Goodwin was hired in June 1957 for one month. Hopton had enough money in his budget for one month's pay prior to the new fiscal year, so he hired Goodwin for the month at a salary of $420. Goodwin's permanent employment with the Bureau began on July 1, 1957, with a $25 per month increase in pay. He had been an Army CID investigator and polygraph operator and was discharged the previous fall.

Shortly after he joined the TBI Goodwin spent a month with the ballistics squad of the New York City Police Department. The NYPD had one of the few firearms and ballistics training programs. Goodwin established the TBI firearms laboratory in 1958, the first in the state of Tennessee. The lab was only about six feet wide and consisted of a couple of filing cabinets, microscopes and little else.

In September 1957 Hopton brought two individuals to the Bureau who had grown up together in

marked "TBI" with a control number. Hopton gave handgun "TBI #1" to Governor Frank Clement. Clement later gave the sidearm to a member of his Highway Patrol security detail.

Director Hopton insisted that agents keep a daily log of their activities. He said, "It's not for me, but in case somebody comes and makes a complaint against you, I can go to your daily log and tell them exactly what you did every hour of that day." This was one of many insights Hopton brought from his experience with the FBI. He also didn't like agents to seek publicity.

The TBI was expanded so those agents could be assigned throughout the state. Even with additional agents, the Bureau was still small and a single agent had to work several counties. A. T. Ellis retained the title Senior Agent and served as second in command to the director.

The TBI was given original jurisdiction in narcotics cases by an act of the legislature passed in March 1957. This extended the Bureau's ability to investigate violations of the state's narcotic laws. The act also specified the TBI's authority in the areas of fugitives and internal affairs issues.

Investigators of the Bureau of Criminal Identification are authorized, without a request

Senior Agents Big'un Ellis, left, was a Highway Patrol sergeant when the TBI was formed and he transferred to the new investigative unit of the Department of Safety (Nashville Banner photo). Agent William Warren Jones, right, a trained FBI fingerprint expert joined the TBI after he served as the first identification officer of the Jackson Police Department.

Ramer, Tennessee. Both went to the FBI Fingerprint Division in Washington, D.C., in 1947. They were William Warren Jones and Archibald Burgess "Archie" Hamm.

Warren Jones, after serving two years with the FBI, went to the police department in Jackson, Tennessee, in 1950 as the JPD's first records and identification officer. Jones established a reputation for thoroughness and tenacity. He was tight-lipped about cases and was usually dressed in well-used clothes. One former TBI agent called him the "Columbo" of the TBI. Warren Jones was the only TBI agent west of the Tennessee River for many years.

Archie Hamm was an FBI fingerprint examiner when Hopton hired him to command the TBI's Identification Unit with responsibility for collecting fingerprints and criminal records. He got access to an old vault to serve as an evidence room. The room filled quickly as more and more fingerprints came in from agencies across the state. The state penitentiary sent seven large cardboard filing boxes containing about 8,000 sets of fingerprints that had been accumulated by the state prison system since 1924. There was not sufficient time or staff to organize the fingerprints and they were placed on the floor of the makeshift evidence room.

When Hamm arrived at the Bureau, two employees worked in the Fingerprint and Records Unit. Hamm began to organize records and evidence and in subsequent years he hired additional crime technicians who were formerly employed and trained by the FBI Identification Division. Hamm's title was changed from Crime Technician to Criminal Investigator, with no increase in pay. Primary duties of the unit were to classify and manually search fingerprint cards received from law enforcement agencies throughout the state to determine additional arrest information or wanted notices and to conduct criminal record checks for law enforcement agencies, District Attorneys General and courts.

The unit assisted in the processing of crime scenes for all types of physical evidence. Evidence was properly labeled, preserved and examined at TBI headquarters or forwarded to the FBI crime lab for examination. Law enforcement agencies and TBI field investigators submitted latent prints or items from crime scenes for the unit to obtain latent fingerprints. Latent prints were obtained by using carbon powder, iodine fuming and photography. Latent prints were compared with inked fingerprints on file and the unit prepared detailed written reports of its findings.

Field investigators, also called criminal investigators, often worked out of Nashville in the early days of the Bureau. Although some investigated primarily in West, Middle and East Tennessee, generally agents went where they were needed. The scheduling of field activity was often determined by limited resources. Automobiles were in short supply and when an agent came in from the field with a car, Hopton would make an assignment to another agent to go out.

Major cases affected assignments as well. Occasionally a big case required additional manpower and Hopton would send several people into an area to assist the assigned agent in working the case. Most cases were investigated by a single TBI agent assisted by local lawmen.

Agent John Cribbs, stationed in Dyersburg, was assigned to the case of a headless body fished out of a West Tennessee river in 1957. He took fingerprints and the body was identified as that of a Memphis truck driver. The man's wife, a 28-year-old blonde, was brought to the Dyer County Jail for questioning and denied any involvement.

During the interview Cribbs noted that the woman was obsessed with the cleanliness of her house. Finally he told her that he and other officers were going to search her house for the remaining parts of the dismembered body. Cribbs stood and said, "We'll take that house apart piece by piece if we have to." Anxiety twisted the woman's face and soon she confessed.

Agent Walter Bearden was 28 years old and had been with the Bureau for only six months in June 1958

Robert Fortner, left, reviewed evidence identifying the killer of the driver of Yellow Cab #5, and Archie Hamm verified it. This process enabled either of the two to testify in court.

when he traveled from Knoxville to investigate a murder near Rockwood. The body of a woman was found beside a lonely dirt road. The body had no identification and was not from the area. In a paper sack near the body Bearden found a new dress with a part of a store tag still attached.

Bearden was able to trace the sale of the dress to West Virginia. When he called the state police barracks near where the dress was sold, the trooper said that the woman's husband was standing there reporting her missing. Further investigation revealed that the man had a brother in Crab Orchard, Tennessee, near Rockwood. When questioned, the brother said the husband visited the previous weekend.

The West Virginia man acknowledged he had a brother in Tennessee, but said he had not seen him in three years. Agent Bearden asked West Virginia authorities to hold him. Bearden left to drive the dead woman's husband back to Tennessee. After they crossed the state line Bearden told him about his brother's statement. The killer broke down and confessed to the murder of his wife.

Beginning on July 1, 1958, Director Hopton assigned criminal investigators to specific territories across the state. Each agent was assigned responsibility for investigations in multiple counties. Territories ranged from four to eight counties. Bob Goodwin was assigned to five counties in Middle Tennessee including Wilson County. He continued to do polygraph work along with Judson Gann and did firearms examinations as well.

Even after agents were assigned specific territories, they sometimes worked in other counties. Although Goodwin's assigned territory was in Middle Tennessee, he traveled to West Tennessee to work a budget shortage at Ft. Pillow Prison. The assignment took two or three months to complete. He was later assigned to work a strike at the Goodform Hanger Company that also took a number of months. Bill Coleman worked the coal mine strikes in East Tennessee for about five months.

One of Coleman's most memorable cases was the murder of a restaurant owner near Columbia, Tennessee. The victim was found dead, wrapped in a carpet and floating in the Tennessee River. A tugboat operator spotted the body in the water. Robbery was suspected since it was thought that he carried a lot of money. The murderer turned out to be a one-armed cab driver whose girlfriend became the key witness.

Agents performed whatever duty the director gave them. Goodwin recalled, "When Hopton would call, I would go." Investigators also worked whatever hours were required to get the job done. Sometimes an agent

started a case and worked two or three days straight with little or no sleep and there was no overtime or compensatory time off.

Two cases in the fifties were considered by Director Hopton to be turning points in the perception of the TBI among the citizens of Tennessee. The first of these was a rape case in Belle Meade that became known as the "Phantom Rape Case." A number of similar rapes had plagued the area. Police made an arrest, but the man insisted that he was innocent. The TBI was called in and within a few weeks had solved the case and identified the real rapist from latent fingerprints. Hopton stated, "Nothing pleases the public more than when an innocent man is proven so."

A second watershed case for the TBI was the investigation of Hamilton County Criminal Court Judge Raulston Schoolfield. Statewide exposure resulting from his impeachment before the legislature established the integrity and credibility of the Bureau in the eyes of the citizens of Tennessee.

Judge Schoolfield ran Chattanooga and to a large degree the surrounding county. He fixed cases and "took care" of things. Some things he did for money and some as favors for his friends. His illicit activities

Fingerprint magnifier used by Archie Hamm when all fingerprint identification was done manually. The device was retired to the Bureau museum housed in the Nashville headquarters.

Archie Hamm, left, reviewed fingerprint evidence on a plastic container with TBI Director W. E. "Bud" Hopton. Hopton said of Hamm, "there is no better fingerprint specialist anywhere."

became so widespread and blatant that the public called on the TBI to investigate.

Criminal Investigators William Whitehurst, Walter Toon, Walter Bearden and Ambrose Moss worked with Director Hopton on the case. Retired Memphis Police Department Inspector William J. Raney, a nationally recognized criminal investigator, also briefly joined the Bureau and participated in the investigation. Jack Norman Sr. and John Jay Hooker Jr. were the attorneys for the state. Evidence developed by field agents of the Bureau was collected and assembled by Mr. Norman and Director Hopton. Two file cabinets full of information were gathered on the case.

The Tennessee State Senate found him guilty on three counts: for accepting a car that was paid for in part by attorneys and defendants in his court, for using his power as judge for personal purposes and for gross personal misconduct. Judge Schoolfield was impeached by the State House in 1958 on 24 charges and removed from office in 1961.

The case affirmed to the public at large and to the new members of the agency who had come from the FBI, that the TBI approached law enforcement with integrity and was not a political group. A high point for Hopton and the rest of the Bureau came when a Nashville newspaper columnist declared the TBI "one of the best law enforcement agencies in the United States."

Ten years after the agency was created it not only benefited from an enhanced reputation, but the workload had expanded significantly. In the first ten months of 1961 the Bureau conducted 355 full field investigations and gave technical assistance on 845 other cases. This was more than in the entire previous year and time and a half the year before that. The work was done by nineteen investigators, two narcotics agents and four crime technicians. Director Hopton told interviewers, "We'll have to expand."

The Bureau was not able to solve every case. One particularly brutal incident troubled agents throughout their career. Archie Hamm worked the crime scene of a brother and sister who were murdered in Marion County, Tennessee, in 1962. The two were bound, gagged and tortured. They were burned with cigarettes, beaten, stabbed and scalded. A fingerprint was found on an object believed to have been left by one of the perpetrators. This latent print was never identified despite an exhaustive manual search of all fingerprints on file at the Bureau. Archie Hamm and other fingerprint examiners kept the print on their desk for years and compared it to each new print that came in.

A few years later two fingerprints from a whiskey bottle led to the identification of the killer of a Nashville taxi driver. On January 11, 1965, the driver of Yellow Cab #5 picked up a fare in Nashville who asked to be driven to adjoining Cheatham County. There the cab driver was shot to death by the passenger and robbed of $14. Sheriff Les Binkley and District Attorney General W. B. Lockert requested assistance from the TBI. The cab had frost and ice on it and Sheriff Binkley had it towed and stored in a garage. Archie Hamm and Robert Fortner were assigned to process the cab for evidence.

Agent Bob Goodwin set up the TBI's first firearms laboratory. Goodwin trained with the NYPD in one of the few firearms and ballistics training programs.

Under the watchful eye of local citizens playing checkers around a potbelly stove, Hamm and Fortner lifted latent fingerprints from various areas of the cab including a whiskey bottle found in the glove compartment. Fortner compared prints from the whiskey bottle to the TBI's hard copy fingerprint files and matched them to a nineteen-year-old man. Hamm verified the positive identification. Within 48 hours of the slaying the murderer was arrested. He confessed on January 22, 1965. The killer was convicted in Cheatham County and sentenced to 99 years in prison.

Warren Jones, assigned to West Tennessee, worked a number of cases involving McNairy County Sheriff Buford Pusser. One incident was the 1967 ambush of Pusser and his wife Pauline, in which she was killed. Jones developed a number of good suspects in Corinth, Mississippi, but was never able to gather sufficient evidence to prosecute. He worked with THP troopers in the 1970 auto accident in which Pusser died. The steering suspension was cut from the car for examination to see if the car had been tampered with. Doug Woodlee at TBI headquarters packaged the suspension and sent it to the FBI. The FBI report showed the damage was a result of a high-speed impact.

Once Warren Jones was asked about Pusser and his portrayal in the movie "Walking Tall." Jones said, "You know how Hollywood is. There's a few facts, but 60% or 70% of it was Hollywood."

Competitive examinations were given to individuals who wanted to join the TBI. Director Hopton preferred to hire individuals with some college and a law enforcement background. He often picked highway patrolmen with three years of college who had been working a while. One such applicant was Thomas D. Moore, who was appointed to the TBI in November 1, 1965.

The first question Hopton asked Moore was, "Can you type?" Moore told him, "It's been a while." The first piece of equipment Moore received was a new portable typewriter. He kept the typewriter until his retirement 20 years later.

Agents took field notes while investigating. They then either wrote reports longhand, typed them, or if they were covered up, they could call and ask for permission to go to Nashville and dictate for a day or two. Headquarters and some agents had disk recorders that recorded on small red acetate disks. If left for too long in a hot car, the disks would melt. Later the Bureau moved to newer technology, transcribers that used more durable belts as recording media.

Director Hopton used a worn ESSO road map to point out to new agents the counties in their territo-

ries. Moore was stationed in Cookeville and split the territory previously assigned to Dusty Hale. Moore worked seven counties including Putnam, White, DeKalb, Cumberland and Morgan. He jointly worked Scott County with Hale, who lived in Livingstone. Agents frequently worked outside of their assigned territory and soon after he arrived, Moore worked cases with Frank Evetts in Lebanon, Donn Clark in Carthage and later Preston Huckeby in East Tennessee.

James D. "Jim" Waldrop went to work with the Bureau in January 1966 and was assigned to Greeneville. He had been a member of the Department of Safety since 1947 and was at the rank of lieutenant in the Highway Patrol at the time he joined the Bureau. Waldrop was a B-24 gunner during World War II and was shot down. Members of the resistance were able to get him out of enemy territory. He was called up in the National Guard at the rank of Major during the Cuban missile crisis. Waldrop became chief of security with TVA when he retired from the TBI.

The Bureau consisted of twenty agents in January 1966. Senior Agent A. T. Ellis remained second in command to Director Hopton. Three agents were assigned to narcotics investigation at the time including Ambrose Moss, head of the unit, who worked Middle Tennessee. Wade Ingram worked East Tennessee. Robert Fortner and sometimes J. Hugh Bauer, covered West Tennessee. All three were graduates of the Federal Bureau of Narcotics School. Robert Goodwin continued as the agency's ballistics expert. Three agents were qualified lie detector or polygraph technicians including Goodwin and John Marcum, stationed in Maryville. Polygraph

Agent Bob Goodwin, right, demonstrates polygraph machine on Crime Technician Stephen Cole.

operators were trained at Texas A&M and were some of the first in Tennessee.

To qualify to be a TBI agent a man had to have a college degree with at least one year of investigative work, or have a minimum of five years of law enforcement investigative experience plus eight weeks or more of training at the FBI academy or similar school. Eleven of the agents were graduates of the FBI academy and seven were former FBI agents or technicians.

Criminal investigators worked 18 to 20 cases at once and averaged working 75 hours of overtime a month, without pay. About one third of the force was in court on any day. During 1965 the Bureau conducted over 400 full investigations and closed over 480 cases including some from the previous year. It assisted in over 1000 other cases. The TBI had a 92% conviction rate. Agent's pay ranged from $530 to $650 per month, depending on experience and assignment. The annual budget for the agency was $328,000.

Bud Hopton called field agents in for an annual conference every year soon after the first of the year. Agents spent the night in Nashville and had a critique session the next day with Hopton. Hopton went over the agent's cases, discussed their case load, talked about how many cases they had solved and generally discussed the strengths and weaknesses of their work. He corrected a few people. He didn't brag on anybody much. Agents respected him as a good boss and a good man.

Both Director Hopton and Senior Agent Ellis used a personal touch in working with field agents. If they had a communication, they called. Criminal investigators responded with a sense of urgency. Hopton laughed when he told a story on himself about one mix-up he created.

Agent Ed Walker worked the Chattanooga/Jasper area and Jim Waldrop worked in East Tennessee. Hopton asked his secretary to get Waldrop on the phone. She misunderstood and got Walker on the phone instead. Director Hopton told Walker he wanted him to go to a certain town in East Tennessee to do some interviews, a job that would take several days. Walker didn't question the assignment even though it was out of his territory.

Sometime later in the week Hopton got in touch with Walker and told him to go to Chattanooga from Jasper on an assignment. Walker told Hopton it would be the next day before he could get there from up in East Tennessee. Hopton asked, "What are you doing up there?" Walker replied, "You sent me here Mr. Hopton," and recounted the earlier call.

Director Hopton's leadership and innovations led to increases in the number and rate of solutions of

Crime Technician Steve Cole, foreground, organized the backlog of fingerprint records under the supervision of Archie Hamm, head of the identification section.

crimes investigated by the agency. This in turn enhanced the prestige and acceptance of the TBI by the public and local law enforcement. Success began to overwhelm the Bureau. Former agent Jack Blackwell recalled, "Back then a sheriff couldn't investigate a Coke machine break-in without calling the TBI."

Most local jurisdictions had neither the scientific equipment nor the expertise to do proper investigations and called the TBI frequently. Madison County Sheriff Lowell Thomas said, "I call them in on an average of twice a month. When it comes to dusting a cash register for fingerprints, we're just not equipped for it. The TBI is." Brownsville Chief of Police Darrell Bull gave a similar report, "I call on them often, for break-ins mostly and safecrackings." Unfortunately many times when the Bureau was called in, the crime scene had been trampled and evidence compromised.

The reputation of the Bureau was growing with lawbreakers as well. District Attorney General Baxter Key Jr. of Carthage praised the three agents with whom he worked, Bob Goodwin, Dusty Hale and Tom

Moss   Keesling   Miller   Blackwell   Earl   Williams   Watson   Wald

Winningham   Walker   Helton   Shelton   Fortner   Russell   Chapman   Senior Ag Ellis

Annual conference of the TBI held in the Cordell Hull Building in January 1969: from left to right were Lester Winningham (worked the Winchester area), John Edward Walker (Chattanooga area), Joe Helton (Bradley, Polk and Meigs counties), Kenneth W. Shelton Sr. (Manchester area), unidentified (face mostly hidden), Ambrose R. Moss Sr. (head of narcotics unit, one of first two crime technicians in TBI), James Fox "Jim" Keesling (Lawrenceburg area, then Kingsport area, later with Kingsport police), Robert Wayne "Bob" Fortner (narcotics, firearms, and Assistant Director under Robert Goodwin), William M. Russell (Knoxville area), Leon W. Miller (Rockwood area), Thomas J. "Jack" Blackwell (Somerville area, first supervisor of West Tennessee), William Chapman (Greeneville area), Andrew R. Earl (Columbia area), Billy Joe Williams (identification and organized crime), Steve O. Watson (forehead visible, Knoxville area, Deputy Director under Arzo Carson), Senior Agent Alfred Thomas "Big'un" Ellis (one of first six criminal investigators in TBI), James D. Waldrop (Assistant Director under William Sheets),

Moore. Key said, "When they get in on a case from the beginning, by the time we go to court the defendant is usually ready to plead guilty."

One comment about their impact on the criminal element came directly from the leader of a narcotics gang. Two agents had gone undercover in Knox County. After the investigators had established a rapport with the gang, the head of the criminal enterprise commented, "What you've got to look out for is these damn TBI agents." The gangster was right. He and the other drug dealers in the group were convicted and sent to prison.

James F. "Jim" Keesling began as a field agent with the TBI on January 1, 1968. Director Hopton offered him a job a year earlier after he worked a murder case with TBI agent while he was chief of detectives with the Bristol Police Department. Keesling identified two suspects and Archie Hamm matched fingerprints on a liquor bottle and a glass to one of the two. Hopton called Keesling again in the fall of 1967 after the death of TBI Agent Claude McAfee.

Agent Keesling served his first two years out of Lawrenceburg where McAfee had been stationed. Keesling worked 15 or 18 hours a day on around 100 cases per year in a five county area. Two notable cases he worked were the rape of a ten-year-old girl by her uncle in Hohenwald and a murder in which a man killed his wife and four children.

After two years Jim Keesling returned to East Tennessee as Director Hopton had committed when Keesling was hired. Working out of Kingsport, he continued to cover a number of counties. Not long after he moved, he worked the case of a sadistic killer who brutally raped and murdered a 12-year-old girl. It was the most vicious case of his career.

The General Assembly authorized the hiring of ten additional agents in 1968. One of the men Hopton called was Thomas J. "Jack" Blackwell, the chief of police in Somerville, Tennessee. Blackwell began his career in law enforcement as chief deputy sheriff of Fayette County from 1960 to 1965 and then served as chief of police of Somerville from 1965 to 1968. TBI agents in West Tennessee at the time included Warren

On the right side of the photograph, from left to right, were John A. Marcum (LaFollette area), Eddie Stephen "Young'un" Cole (identification, narcotics, then Cleveland area), George H. Haynes (Nashville area), Director Winfred Earl "Bud" Hopton, Franklin Evetts (Lebanon area), Ethridge C. "Dusty" Hale (Cookeville and Livingston area), Donn M. Clark (Cookeville, Carthage and Huntington area), Douglas D. "Doug" Woodlee (identification, narcotics, records, statistics), Walter Toon (Nashville and Dickson area, later chief of police in Hendersonville), Jack Charlton (West Tennessee area), William Kelly Whitehurst (Nashville and Clarksville area), Archibald Burgess "Archie" Hamm Sr. (identification, Executive Officer under Arzo Carson), Bailey Edward Ashburn (Cookeville Carthage and Greenville area), William Warren Jones (Jackson area), Mizell Preston Huckeby (McMinnville area, first supervisor of East Tennessee), Thomas D. "Tom" Moore (Cookeville area), Robert C. Goodwin Sr. (firearms examiner and polygraph operator, later Director), John C. Sloan (Savannah area), Harold Thomas "Tom" Whitlatch (identification, Lawrenceburg area, organized crime), Wade H. Ingram (narcotics in East Tennessee).

Jones and John Hugh Bauer. Bauer was an attorney and the only agent in the Bureau at the time that had a college degree.

Hopton got to know Blackwell during a period of civil unrest in Fayette County in the mid-sixties. At that time Blackwell was instrumental in forming an Auxiliary Police Department in Somerville. He agreed to join the TBI only after Hopton agreed not to move him out of West Tennessee. Blackwell recalled that the employment process was not complicated.

> I remember they didn't even have my badge ready. Mr. Hopton had my commission card. He didn't have a weapon for me. He said, "You have a pistol?" I said, "Yeah, I've got a pistol." I was assigned to Fayette, Hardeman, and Haywood counties, but I ended up working everything in West Tennessee.

The first badge carried by TBI agents was small, gold-tone sunburst style with the state seal in the cen-

ter. Later blue enamel was added to the ring around the state seal.

Leon W. Miller and Preston Huckeby were also among the ten agents hired by Bud Hopton in 1968. Miller had retired from the Tennessee Highway Patrol with twenty years of service. He spent most of those years in Rockwood, Tennessee. When he joined the TBI he worked the eastern part of the state. Huckeby began in March 1968, also transferring from the THP. He worked Warren, Cannon and Van Buren counties.

Steve O. Watson became a TBI field agent on January 1, 1969, at the age of 27, making him the youngest agent in the Bureau. Watson served four years as an FBI fingerprint technician before serving with the Army Security Agency and then as a member of the Army CID. The Sevier County native was assigned to the Knoxville area.

Watson was transported to Nashville by Agent Bill Russell on January 2 at the director's instruction. At headquarters Hopton told Watson to go out and meet the district attorneys general, tell them he was available to do investigations and start investigating. And,

Retirement party for Dusty Hale in Carthage, December 1969. From left to right were Robert Fortner, Ambrose Moss, Judson Gann, Douglas Woodlee, A. T. Ellis, Thomas Moore, H. Thomas Whitlatch, Billy Joe Williams, Bailey Ed Ashburn, Baxter Key (district attorney general), and Ethridge C. "Dusty" Hale.

Hopton said, "If you don't hear from us, you're doing all right." Archie Hamm took Watson down stairs and showed him the fingerprint kit. He was issued a .38 special handgun, a holster and six bullets. Senior Agent Big'un Ellis had a 1967 Plymouth with a big engine and about 30,000 miles on it. He issued the car to Watson. His fellow agents in East Tennessee were seriously upset because it was a better car than any of them had.

Douglas D. Woodlee joined the Bureau on October 1, 1968, as crime technicians. Eddie Stephen "Young'un" Cole joined the TBI soon after. Both were fingerprint examiners with the FBI and served on the "fingerprint squad" that printed new FBI agents, a prized assignment. Woodlee's first assignment was to organize the contents of the seven cardboard bankers boxes of fingerprints that filled the floor of the old vault that served as an evidence room.

It took Woodlee, Billy Joe Williams and Steve Cole over a year, pushing themselves, to get the 8,000 prints from the state prison system organized so that they could be used. They first sorted by name to identify duplicates. Because the records included inmates back to 1924 they found many duplicates, people who had been put in prison 3 or 4 times. These were recorded on index cards, listing their different prison numbers. They found one felon with 14 different prison numbers.

The quality of fingerprints received at TBI headquarters varied considerably based on the ability and knowledge of deputies taking the prints. Doug Woodlee traveled throughout the state providing training to thousands of law enforcement officers on methods for obtaining legible inked fingerprints.

The structure of the Bureau remained simple. Hopton was the director and for administrative purposes he was also deputy commissioner of the Department of Safety. The TBI did not have administrative support personnel and relied on the Department of Safety for general administrative functions such as finances and personnel. Senior Agent A. T. Ellis assisted Hopton in management of the Bureau.

All agents reported directly to headquarters in Nashville. Certain administrative functions were provided by senior agents in the field, such as receiving time sheets from other agents and forwarding them to headquarters. Warren Jones served as "timekeeper" for West Tennessee. Timekeepers were assigned in other divisions of the state to collect time sheets that all agents prepared twice a month. Warren Jones remained timekeeper until Jack Blackwell took command in West Tennessee.

TBI agents who were not hired directly from the FBI received training at the FBI National Academy as well as classes at the Tennessee Law Enforcement Training Academy after it opened in 1966. Agents typically did not attend the intensive FBI training course immediately. Doug Woodlee graduated from the 100th Session of the FBI National Academy and Jack Blackwell from the 103rd Session, both in 1975. Blackwell was a member of 13th class of the Tennessee academy, attending soon after it opened and was selected president of his class.

Many agents around the state worked out of their homes. Sheriffs and chiefs of police in some areas provided office space for TBI agents. Field offices were also located in district Highway Patrol facilities.

Agents operated independently and without procedures and technology in common use today. If a warrant was to be served, the agent often took along a deputy sheriff, but agents had no backup or tactical unit support if a confrontation developed.

Electronic equipment was very basic and sometimes problematic. On one occasion Jack Blackwell worked undercover in Lake County and took two murder contracts in one day from would be killers-by-proxy. He borrowed a car from a hoodlum in Missouri in case anyone checked on the vehicle and put a reel-to-reel tape recorder under the front seat to gather evidence.

The man who thought he was hiring Blackwell to commit murder was still in the car when the tape ran out. As the end of the tape hit against the recorder mechanism, it made a "swiiit, swiiit, swiiit" sound. The man said, "What is that?" Blackwell told him it was something about the car and turned up the radio. When the man complained that the radio was too loud, Blackwell told him, "I like it loud. Leave it alone." The agent took a deep breath once the man was out of the car.

The first murder case worked by Blackwell after he joined the TBI was in Lauderdale County. The truck belonging to the operator of a nightclub called the Bluff View Inn was found shot up and stuck in a mud hole. The large amount of money the man was known to carry was gone. Leads in the case were few.

Blackwell worked with Deputy Sheriff Lewis Gitchem, a man with strong investigative skills who later became sheriff. They found the man's body dumped in the Forked Deer River near where it flowed into the Mississippi River. Based on motorcycle tire tracks found at the scene, they identified a suspect.

When Blackwell learned the man had the tires changed on his motorcycle and then lied to investigators about it, he knew he had the killer. Blackwell developed evidence to indict the murderer, but before he could be tried he escaped jail. The killer was found in Michigan three years later and brought back for trial.

Agents had all the work they could handle and more. Sometimes Blackwell worked three and four murder cases a week in various counties of West Tennessee. He often worked 110 hours a week and in the final nine months of 1968 he worked nearly 40 criminal cases and assisted in 250 others.

Preston Huckeby found that technology was a persuasive crime-solving tool, even before it was used. He worked a case in Cannon County in which a man claimed his wife had driven away with another man.

Huckeby asked him for his wife's drivers license so he could get her description. When the man produced the license Huckeby knew he was lying, because the woman would not have left without her purse.

Agent Huckeby took his suspect to Nashville for a polygraph test. Agent Bob Goodwin, the polygraph operator, took the man into his office and stayed for almost an hour. When Goodwin returned Huckeby asked how the man did on the polygraph. Goodwin told him that he never administered the test. The man had confessed and agreed to tell where the body was located.

Undercover work was an important tool for the TBI, but combined long hours and the danger of being exposed. A quick wit and fast talk was sometimes all that saved an agent. Ed Ashburn introduced Steve Cole to undercover work in 1971. Just as the operation was about to end, the two were identified as TBI agents.

Agent Ashburn had gone undercover to breakup a car theft ring working in the Chattanooga area. The operation began with TBI Agent Ed Walker and THP Major Clarence Hamby taking Ashburn to the Marion County jail and roughing him up as they put him in a cell. This established Ashburn's reputation as a buyer of stolen cars.

Steve Cole, a crime technician at the time, came into the operation to surreptitiously photograph car thieves who brought stolen cars to Ashburn's hotel. The room was also bugged to record evidence. Cole mostly sat around and let his hair and beard grow until Ashburn asked Walter Bearden to let Cole go into the field. Cole was issued a pistol stamped "TBI

Among the TBI agents gathered in December 1970 were from left to right Tom Moore, Larry O'Rear, Dusty Hale, Director Bud Hopton, Frank Evetts, and Preston Huckeby.

Director William L. Sheets, left, was congratulated by Governor Winfield Dunn, following his appointment as head of the TBI in 1972.

No. 8" on the butt plate, a poor weapon for working undercover.

Sufficient evidence was gathered to issue 68 arrest warrants and they were about to "bust out," the term used by agents when they ended an operation and made arrests. Law enforcement resources gathered in Chattanooga included TBI agents, Highway Patrol members, local police and a school bus to transport prisoners.

On their way to the help in the operation, two troopers stopped to eat at the Red Hot Truck Stop and mentioned to two women who worked there about the roundup. When Ashburn and Cole met the car thieves to invite them to the "party" where they would be arrested, the criminals knew the two were TBI agents and knew about the planned roundup.

Ashburn managed to talk their way out of the situation and ended up buying two more stolen vehicles from the gang that night. The plan for the arrests was adjusted and over the next two days more than 30 were arrested.

Archie Hamm worked to bring new technology to the Criminal Records Unit. He installed the first Ninhydrin Development System in the state in 1969. The technology was used to develop latent fingerprints on paper and other porous objects. Hamm and Jim Gossett of the Metro Nashville Police Department went to the U. S. Postal Service Crime Lab in Cincinnati for a demonstration of the system. The TBI acquired the equipment and Metro soon did as well.

The development system, chemicals and fume hood with a powerful fan to remove chemical fumes were set up in the basement of the Cordell Hull Building. A yellowish powdered chemical solution and acetone revealed fingerprints on paper objects. The fingerprints appeared red or purplish red and were photographed before they faded. The system was an important new tool for evidence gathering.

Overall, laboratory resources remained meager. Toxicology work for Middle and East Tennessee was done in small labs by Bill Darby in Nashville, Raymond Siler in Chattanooga and Gerald Smith in Knoxville.

During the decade of the sixties the TBI established a solid record of accomplishment statewide. Between 1960 and 1970 the Bureau worked 17,755 major cases and established a conviction rate of 93%. The number of cases grew each year, from 1,205 in 1960 to 2,548 in 1969. Most cases were homicide, armed robbery, aggravated assault, rape, burglary, grand larceny, or narcotics. The TBI assisted in cases of kidnapping, extortion, bribery, forgery and auto theft rings. Many agencies relied on the TBI for criminal identification. In 1969 alone, 40,110 fingerprint checks were processed.

Under the leadership of Archie Hamm the professionalism of TBI laboratory and identification section became widely recognized. Hamm established rapport with national agencies including the FBI, Secret Service and postal inspectors. He also developed close working relationships with state agencies such as the Alcohol Beverage Commission and local sheriffs and police departments.

The Bureau moved to the Andrew Jackson Building in 1970. The offices occupied a quarter of the 12th floor where the Tennessee Highway Patrol was also located. The criminal history records of the Bureau were maintained on 3" x 5" index cards and moved with other files of the agency.

The need was growing to automate records at the Department of Safety including those of the TBI. William Carothers "Bill" Thompson, a high school teacher and coach with data processing experience, joined the TBI on April 15, 1971, as a Systems Analyst III. He was assigned to automate drivers license records of the Department of Safety, criminal histories at TBI and other records. All records were to be maintained on the Department of Safety's IBM 360 mainframe.

Assistant Supervisor Doug Woodlee of the Criminal Records Unit had existing index card records keypunched for loading on Safety's mainframe to be copied to magnetic tape. Completion of systems automation of TBI records was slow and completed when TBI separated from the Department of Safety.

Thompson also worked to upgrade communication systems of the Department of Safety. The department had a radio system with 4 channels, one of which was used by the governor. The only other communications device was a punch-tape teletype system used to communicate within the state and with agencies outside Tennessee. Fifteen

The original Narcotics Section on January 15, 1972. From left to right were Senior Agent Alfred Thomas "Big'un" Ellis, Narcotics Unit Supervisor Ambrose R. Moss, Douglas D. Woodlee, Jerry London, Paul Neblett (later Sheriff of Montgomery County-Clarksville), Ray Presnell, Fred Phillips (later Sheriff of Washington County and Commissioner of the Department of Safety), William E. Coleman III, Gary "Boom Boom" Melton, Commissioner Claude Armour of the Department of Safety, Eddie Stephen "Young'un" Cole, Wade Ingram, Richard Zseltvay, Billy Joe Williams, Robert Cameron, Roy N. "Ricochet Rabbit" Bordes, William E. Vest, William E. Coleman Jr., and Walter Bearden.

IBM 2740 teletype terminals were installed in 1965 to expand communications capabilities across the state. The governor sent out the first message. Soon 150 of the terminals were installed statewide.

Director Bud Hopton retired effective the end of 1971 and Walter Bearden was appointed acting director. For the second time in the history of the TBI everyone thought they might get fired when Bearden went to Governor Winfield Dunn and tried to get the TBI moved out of the Department of Safety.

On May 1, 1972, Governor Dunn appointed William L. "Billy" Sheets to head the Bureau. Director Sheets was a native of Ashland City in Cheatham County and had served with the FBI for 30 years, most recently as the senior resident agent of the Nashville office. He spent a number of years in private business beginning in 1966 and in January 1972 was named assistant director of the Tennessee Law Enforcement Planning Agency. The Bureau settled down and things went well for the TBI during the Dunn years. Sheets served as director of the TBI until February 1, 1975.

The Bureau was restructured soon after Sheets took command. James D. "Boogerman" Waldrop, stationed in Greeneville as a field investigator, was named second in charge with the title Assistant Director following the retirement of Senior Agent A. T. Ellis on July 1, 1972. Waldrop was a native of Blaine, Grainger County, Tennessee. He began his law enforcement career as a Tennessee highway patrolman in 1947.

Director Sheets assigned Agent Bill Thompson responsibility for writing grants to fund new initiatives

of the Bureau. The federal Omnibus Crime Control and Safe Streets Act had been passed 1968 and significant federal dollars were available. Thompson later became a TBI field agent and was assigned a territory in Middle Tennessee.

The structure of the Bureau was still simple. The only supervisors were the director and assistant director. All agents reported to Assistant Director Jim Waldrop. The assistant director also provided executive management when the director was out for meeting, or otherwise not available. Waldrop oversaw the activities of the agents and reviewed daily reports that came in from the field. A new agent's manual was compiled in 1972 with the assistance of Allen McNicol.

The Tennessee Highway Patrol remained the primary source of new agents for the Bureau. A transfer within the Department of Safety to the TBI was a major promotion for troopers. The pay for an agent was the same as that of a captain on the Patrol. Plus, a TBI field agent got his own vehicle, wore a suit rather than a uniform, worked on his own schedule and his supervisor was in Nashville.

When hiring, Waldrop asked prospective agents, "Do you have to have supervision?" Then he explained that he was the only supervisor for all the agents in the state, "I get up early and come to the office and call people and find out what's going on and they report to me. I give advice and I assign cases, but you're not going to see me, because I'm the only one in the entire state." He told the applicant what he expected, "I want to know if I can trust you to get up every day and go to work and work as if you had supervisors all around you. Self-start, do the right thing, be honest about it, and get the job done."

Commissioner of Safety Claude Armour appointed section managers with the title Senior Agent. Senior Agent Archie Hamm was responsible for the fingerprint and identification section. Senior Agent Ambrose Moss was in command of the narcotics section. Senior Agent Bob Goodwin supervised the firearms and polygraph section. Goodwin began at this time to teach firearms examination and ballistics to Bob Fortner and Lanny Wilder.

The Bureau had 42 agents statewide in 1972 including one photographer, two in the ballistics section, crime technicians and drug agents. Equipment taken to crime scenes by crime technicians of the Laboratory Division consisted of a box camera, a fingerprint kit and a bag of powder for making plaster casts. Office facilities were limited. Often six technicians worked off one worn metal desk.

As the result of a federal grant written by Bill Thompson, the Bureau received funds in 1972 that allowed Ambrose Moss to expand the Narcotics Division. Roy N. "Ricochet Rabbit" Bordes had been recently added to the unit and served as Moss' assistant. Doug Woodlee and Steve Cole were transferred to the unit. William E. Coleman III, Robert Cameron, Jerry London, Gary "Boom Boom" Melton, Paul Neblett, Fred Phillips and Richard Zseltvay were hired. The new narcotics agents were sent to DEA headquarters in Washington for training.

The hiring of Bill Coleman III marked the first instance of a father and son on the Bureau. His father Bill Coleman Jr., who retired in 1974, was one of the first agents of the TBI. A second father and son duo included another of the first agents of the Bureau, Kenneth Shelton. His son David Shelton became an agent as well.

In November 1972 Jim Morgan, Richard Leigh Grinalds and Claude Isaiah Johnson joined the division. They were the first replacements to the original narcotics group. Agent Claude Johnson transferred from the Highway Patrol and became the first black agent in the Bureau. Johnson worked undercover all over the state. He recalled his good relationships with the field agents, who became his family away from home.

A second grant received in 1973 enabled the agency to further enhance and strengthen the drug unit. David Blackwell, Travis Brasfield, Bob Denny, R. Maxey Gilleland and Charles Lee were among those hired at that time. David Blackwell began on August 16, 1973, and was first assigned to Knoxville. After a

year he moved to Cookeville. John Mehr and Tony Bowers became narcotics officers on November 15, 1975.

The Narcotics Division investigated narcotics and dangerous drug cases. Other criminal investigations were initiated upon request from the office of the district attorney general, but the investigation of crimes related to narcotics and drugs was the responsibility of the TBI by state statute.

The Narcotics Division concentrated its efforts to make cases against drug suppliers, using street peddlers to get to suppliers. Agents often depended on others for leads. Ambrose Moss and his agents had been after one Nashville supplier for a number of months, when a nosy neighbor reported the dealer, leading to the confiscation of 4.5 million amphetamine pills.

The first experience for new narcotics agents was often uncomfortable. Undercover agent Steve Cole made his first drug buy on January 14, 1972, soon after he was assigned to Lawrenceburg. It was a date he would not forget. Tom Whitlatch was the TBI criminal investigator in the area. An informant made a contact for Cole and he was instructed to place a coin in the palm of the dealer and the dealer would sell Cole dope.

When it came time to make the buy, the informant was not around. Whitlatch told Cole to go by himself. Cole's first reaction was, "You're crazy. I haven't ever bought any dope before." After persuasion and coercion, Whitlatch and THP Captain John Lumpkin watched from across a highway as Cole approached the dealer's house. Cole put the coin in the man's palm, trying to control his own trembling hand. He said, "A lid of pot," when the man asked what he wanted. It was all the drug terminology Cole knew.

Cole eyed the man with the long gun standing behind the dealer. The dealer said, "All I've got is a brick." Not knowing what the dealer was talking about, Cole asked how much it cost. His hands were visibly shaking as he counted out $125 for the marijuana.

Agent Claude Johnson's first cases were in the Clinton area where he made cases against a number of dealers. He worked with District Attorney General Arzo Carson after his first "bust out." General Carson brought the first case against a defendant who had sold Agent Johnson two marijuana cigarettes. Johnson had bought heroin, cocaine, marijuana, angel dust and other dangerous drugs from other defendants and did not understand why Carson didn't try the larger cases.

It became apparent, however, when General Carson won convictions on both counts with a sentence of two years and the maximum fine for each. Johnson remembered, "All the others came in begging to plead on their cases." The strategy allowed Agent Johnson to quickly return to investigations rather than spending weeks in court and becoming widely recognized as a TBI agent, destroying his ability to work undercover.

Agents often supplied their own equipment for field work. They bought recorders and whatever else was required to do the job. Field reports were recorded on Dictaphones and belts forwarded to headquarters where they were transcribed on manual typewriters.

Automobiles were usually passed from one agent to another and were often worn out when received. On one occasion the Department of Safety made a fleet purchase of Plymouths including six Grand Furys with half vinyl roofs. The fleet manager assigned the fancy top vehicles to TBI narcotics agents, thinking the car would help the agents "fit in." The cars had black-wall tires marked "Police Pursuit Radials." The unmarked police units were less than desirable for typical undercover work. After pressure from agents, the cars were replaced. Agents still had to modify the replacement vehicles to make them usable for undercover purposes. Later agents frequently used seized vehicles.

Undercover drug work was dangerous and there was no backup. When agents went undercover, they were on their own. They told their supervisor what area they were in and if they didn't show up in a day or two someone came looking for them. When possible agents tried to work together and help each other cover their territory. If agents were able to partner up, at least they had someone to rely on. But as John Mehr recalled, "Sometimes it was a one man deal and you couldn't do much about it."

Narcotics agents working undercover were kidnapped, shot at and beaten up. David Blackwell was kidnapped and when the kidnappers found his TBI credentials they decided to kill him. While one drug dealer was at a phone booth making a call and the other was distracted, Agent Blackwell floored the accelerator, dislodging the kidnapper from the car and made his escape.

An agent had to become skilled at talking his way out of a tight and potentially deadly spot. Steve Cole found himself in such a situation while working drugs undercover in East Tennessee. Assistant Director James Waldrop assigned Cole to Greeneville and he began making drug cases throughout the area.

After working a long evening buying drugs from Greeneville to Kingsport, Cole was arrested by local police along with a group of drug dealers outside of a Johnson City beer joint. After being booked and strip searched, Cole called agent Fred Phillips who made arrangements for him to make bond. Cole clipped the newspaper article recounting the arrests and kept it in his wallet. The event and clipping may have later played a part in saving his life.

Sheriff Willie Wilson and TBI agent Ed Ashburn asked Cole to investigate a night club between Greeneville and Newport, an area with some particularly tough characters. Ashburn got him a car for the assignment.

When Cole walked into the beer joint he was called over by two drug dealers he knew. He sat with them and they began asking him questions. Cole thought it strange but did not realize they might be on to him. Cole said he wanted to buy drugs. The dealers drove down a country road, across a cow pasture and back to the edge of the woods to an isolated cabin. Cole followed. Inside, a dealer rolled a marijuana cigarette and took out a bottle of Boone's Farm Strawberry Hill wine. They put on a 78 RPM record and drank and smoked until the record finished.

One dealer walked to the front door while the other went to the bedroom and returned with a shotgun. He pointed the gun at Cole. They began cursing Cole and telling him he was a TBI agent. Cole's only weapon was a .25 caliber automatic and it was across the room in his jacket. He denied he was a TBI agent. They said they knew the car he was driving was loaned to an undercover agent by the local TBI agent, because one of their buddies overheard the transaction. They searched Cole and found his fake identification and the newspaper clipping recounting his arrest.

Cole, praying the whole time, believing he was going to be killed, knew TBI had no idea where he was and feared he might never be found. After more words the drug dealer put the shotgun down. Cole got his coat and went out the door. The drug dealers followed and more words passed before Cole got in his car and drove away.

Some dangers to undercover narcotics agents were more subtle. Drug agents were assigned to work with the lowest elements of society doing the dirtiest jobs in law enforcement. They worked in circumstances that routinely exposed them to the use of alcohol and worse. Drinking was a common thing for early undercover drug agents and some developed alcoholism.

For many narcotics agents their days working undercover prepared them for successful careers as field agents and as supervisory personnel. Other agents worked narcotics their entire career. Undercover work provided a unique perspective on crime, as John Mehr explained.

> As a drug agent you go out and you're looking for the crime. As a field agent you're called in after the crime has been discovered. Drug agents get a lot of experience because they actually see how the crime unfolds. It gives you a sense of how life works and insight into how to work other cases.

From time to time agents were gratified by the reaction of a drug dealer they brought to court. On two occasions Ambrose Moss was contacted by ex-convicts who expressed appreciation for his work and thanked him for saving their lives and getting their families back. Steve Cole had a similar experience when a college student thanked Cole for saving his life following a sentence of 5 to 15 years for selling heroin.

In the field reactions were less congenial. Agent Claude Johnson worked in the narcotics unit and during his time with the Bureau worked 93 of the 95 counties in the state. Drug problems were growing in East Tennessee when he began with the TBI. Johnson and other agents trained and worked with the drug unit of the Knoxville Police Department. In one undercover operation Johnson went to a pool hall to make a marijuana buy. He sat next to the juke box waiting for the dealer to finish a game. Suddenly he noticed everyone in the all white crowd had picked up a pool stick. He looked to the bar tender for help. The barman, twirling a .45 caliber pistol, remarked he was going to kill someone tonight. Agent Johnson told

the drug dealer he would meet him down the road and quickly left.

Backup agents sometimes meant the difference in life and death. In the mid-seventies agents Leigh Grinalds and Rodney Williams made a buy of PCP from a drug dealer in a secluded spot outside of Murfreesboro. After the dealer saw the agent's money, he went into a woods and brought out the drugs. When Agent Williams put a .44 magnum revolver to the dealers ear and made the arrest, Agent Grinalds saw the dealer repeatedly look toward the woods. Grinalds knew they had trouble.

Agent Grinalds walked to the edge of the woods with his .380 caliber Walther PPK and saw a blue shirt about 30 yards away. He ordered the man out. The man walked toward Grinalds with a shotgun at forearms. The agent yelled repeatedly for him to drop the gun. The next thing Grinalds knew TBI Agent Bill Thompson, one the backup officers, was standing beside him yelling, "Come out from behind that tree." Grinalds turned his head and saw a second gunman behind a tree about ten feet away and the barrel of a shotgun leveled at him. Not only did he thank Thompson for saving his life, the next day he bought a .45 caliber automatic pistol.

Danger was not unique to narcotics agents, field agents also faced deadly encounters. Preston Huckeby wore a reminder of the dangers of law enforcement. He was the first agent through the door at a Chattanooga gambling raid in 1972. A bullet ripped through Huckeby's face and left a dimple in his cheek as a memento of the incident. Director Sheets nicknamed him "Dimples."

Director Sheets also expanded the field investigative force and added lab staff. The Tennessee Highway Patrol and the FBI remained the primary training grounds for TBI agents. William "Bill" Holt, a former MP in the Air Force, was transferred from the THP to the TBI as a criminal investigator in 1972. James Lollar also joined the Bureau in 1972. Jim Taylor, Ray Presnell and Richard Wright joined the TBI as crime technicians in February 1972.

John Carney Jr. went to work January 3, 1973, as a field agent. At 21 years old, he was the youngest agent ever hired and he was one of the first agents hired with a college degree. He earned a law degree while with the TBI. Agent George Haynes helped Carney through processing, taking him to Director Sheets for swearing in and to Archie Hamm for fingerprinting.

Walter Toon had just retired and Carney was assigned Toon's car, a blue Ford with a law enforce-

On the left, TBI Special Agents Leon Miller, in the foreground, and Joe Helton, in the background, escort a murderer to jail. The two agents gathered sufficient circumstantial evidence to convict him of killing a young man and dumping his body in a pond beside a country lane. On the right, Steve Cole's mug shot after his arrest in Johnson City on drug charges while working undercover. The incident helped save his life in a later confrontation with drug dealers.

ment racing package. Hamm took him to pick up the car and showed him how to turn on the radio. Carney spent a week with George Haynes before attending the basic police investigative school at the Law Enforcement Academy. Jim Taylor and Richard Wright were in the class as well. Two week after completing the session Carney returned to the academy for a three week criminal investigation school.

Carney was assigned to the territory Walter Toon formerly had, Cheatham, Dickson and Humphreys counties. Jack Charlton later took back over Stewart, Houston and Humphreys counties; and Carney worked Cheatham and Dickson until his promotion in 1980.

Alvin Daniel and Larry D. Wallace transferred from the THP in August 1973. Wallace began his career in law enforcement in 1964 as a member of the Athens, Tennessee, Police Department. Daniel began with the THP in August 1967. THP Sergeant Lucion R. English joined the Bureau in 1973 as well. English joined the Highway Patrol in June 1962 and was stationed at Somerville in Fayette County.

As a TBI Field Agent, English was assigned Haywood, Lauderdale, Tipton, Gibson and Crockett counties. He moved to Brownsville and although he like others had "cubbyholes here and there in sheriff's offices," he worked mostly out of his house and out of the trunk of his car. After gathering fingerprints using the kit issued to agents and other evidence at the crime scene, all evidence was taken to Nashville where it was often packaged and sent to the FBI in Washington. English was one of about eleven agents for all of West Tennessee. He was soon sent to Texas A&M for training as a polygraph examiner.

On occasion crimes were not solved from physical evidence. Leon Miller and Chattanooga TBI Agent Joe Helton were assigned to a case in Philadelphia, Tennessee, in which the body of a teenager was found in a roadside pond. The young man had gone up the lane to a county house to visit a girl. On his way back, the killer put him in the rear seat of a car and beat the teen to death. Two boys were fishing in the pond the next day and found the young man's body. Not finding sufficient physical evidence to link the man to the killing, Miller and Helton developed circumstantial evidence to convict the murderer.

Miller cleared several unsolved cases when he interviewed a serial killer in Lenoir City. The man killed three people one night and wounded a fourth, a woman who he shot in the head. During questioning the killer confessed to three other killings.

The reputation of the TBI was such that they were usually called in on high profile and politically sensi-

Bud Hopton, left, director from 1955 to 1971; William Sheets, center, director from 1972 to 1975; and A. T. Ellis, senior agent under Hopton.

tive investigations. The case of a noted writer in Humboldt shooting and killing a young man parked on the author's property became highly publicized. Individuals trying to get the writer off planted evidence in the car, making it appear the victim was up to something illegal. A lab technician from the medical examiners office presented the bogus evidence at a news conference and identified himself as a member of the TBI. The district attorney asked for Jack Blackwell to investigate. TBI agents Blackwell and Warren Jones exposed the sham and put the prosecution back on track.

The integrity and impartiality was crucial to the Bureau maintaining its reputation. The TBI worked to end illegal activity by common criminals and when fraternal organizations and clubs whose members were the pillars of the community entertained themselves on slot machines and served illegal whiskey, the TBI raided their private clubs as well.

A number of high-profile murder cases were worked by the Bureau. One involved the killing of a Nashville cab driver by a television news cameraman and a Metro Nashville police officer in 1970. Criminal Investigator George Haynes worked the case for the TBI. The killing grew out of an incident in which a Metro Nashville policeman had stopped a taxi and the cab driver shot him. The cameraman, who was the officer's brother, and another Nashville policeman killed the taxi driver in revenge. Archie Hamm and Doug Woodlee processed the television news cruiser in the basement of the television station and catalogued approximately 220 items of evidence.

In another case the part-owner of a large Nashville automobile dealership was shot and killed by his partner. Bob Goodwin, the TBI's firearms examiner, spent much time and effort connecting a gun that was found to the murder. He then flew with the gun to the FBI headquarters in Washington to verify his findings.

Commissioner of the Department of Safety Joel Plummer, right, congratulated TBI Director Robert C. "Bob" Goodwin on his first day as head of the Bureau, February 26, 1975.

promoted through the ranks to become director. Goodwin joined the agency in 1957 and was Senior Agent in charge of the firearms and polygraph section. In addition to other training Goodwin completed sessions at Indiana State University and the Southern Police Institute in Louisville, Kentucky.

Following Goodwin's appointment the Bureau was restructured. Outside of the Nashville area TBI offices were located in district offices of the Highway Patrol or in sheriff's offices. Goodwin established TBI districts across the state for the first time and assigned supervisors with the title Inspector to manage activities in the geographic divisions.

Inspector Joe C. Hannah was in charge of the area around Chattanooga. Hannah had a knack for solving crimes. He wrote a number of papers on murder investigations and was a guest instructor at the Southern Police Institute.

Inspector Jack Blackwell supervised West Tennessee, which initially included the counties west of Davidson County. The territory was later changed to include the 21 counties west of the Tennessee River.

Inspector Mizell Preston Huckeby was assigned a portion of Middle Tennessee. He worked out of McMinnville and was in charge of 22 counties.

Inspector Walter Bearden was in charge of the East Tennessee counties around Knoxville. Three years later when Bearden retired, Preston Huckeby headed all of eastern Tennessee, which included counties east of Davidson County except Wilson County. Archie Hamm and Ambrose Moss were also given the

Inspector title as unit managers.

Bob Fortner became assistant director under Goodwin. Bureau headquarters moved from downtown Nashville to the Browning Scott Building. The Narcotics Division moved first, along with the Law Enforcement Planning Agency.

The Bureau made changes to its insignia in 1975. The small sunburst badge with a blue enamel ring around state seal was enhanced. Agent Jim Taylor designed a new badge using a stock eagle-top sunburst with a full-color state seal. Taylor also designed a seal for the TBI and new credentials with the state outline and the seal in gold on the printed identification cards.

On one occasion a batch of badges that arrived with incorrect wording. They read "Tennessee Bureau of Criminal Investigation" rather than "Identification." The error reflected that the Bureau was drifting to the use of the term "investigation" even though it was not yet part of the agencies title. The badges were issued, mainly to members of the narcotics unit.

The Tennessee Crime Laboratory was created in July 1975 as the result of a federal grant written by Bill Thompson and Jim Lollar. Crime technicians moved from cramped quarters to a newly constructed facility next to the Tennessee Law Enforcement Training Academy in Donelson. Assistant Director for Forensic Services William J. Darby III served as director of the crime lab that provided statewide services in firearms and tool mark identification, latent fingerprint and physical markings, trace evidence, motor vehicle examination, photography, blood alcohol determination, drug identification, toxicology, serology, hair and fiber identification and volatile accelerant analysis.

Crime technicians James R. "Jim" Baker and Larry E. Hall were transferred from the Criminal Records Unit to staff the Latent Fingerprint Unit of the new lab in October and Hall became supervisor. Early in 1976 Oakley W. McKinney was promoted and transferred to the unit. He was followed by Tony L. Bobo, Hoyt Eugene "Gene" Phillips, Robert McFadden and Don Hampton. Hall, McFadden, McKinney and Phillips continued with the unit and in 1980 were titled Special Agent-Forensic Scientists. Searching the fingerprint records remained a manual operation and latent prints were not compared unless a suspect was identified.

Donna Pence was commissioned as the first female agent of the TBI on August 1, 1976. Ms. Pence began her career in law enforcement as a security officer at Vanderbilt University. After less than a year in that role she became the first female patrol officer in the

TBI Agent William Russell, left, THP Sergeant Sterling Trent, center, and TBI Agent Bill Thompson worked the security detail for President Gerald Ford in a 1975 visit to Tennessee not long after an assassination attempt. Security had to check every culvert between the airport and Knoxville for potential threats.

Metropolitan Nashville Park Police where she served for two years.

With the TBI Pence began as an undercover investigator and for a period was the only female undercover narcotics agent with the Bureau. She and three other agents were almost killed when their small plane crashed during an operation. She also had to talk her way out of a few tight spots. On one drug buy she borrowed a car from a fellow TBI agent. A badge case hidden above the visor was accidentally left in the vehicle. Pence made the buy and was attempting to get information from the dealer when the badge fell out. She talked her way out of the situation by convincing the drug dealer that even though her boyfriend was a cop, she was a drug user.

Pence became a special agent in the Criminal Investigation unit following the birth of her first child. During her twenty-five years with the Bureau she served in a number of supervisory positions including Special Agent in Charge of the Drug Enforcement Unit, Special Agent in Charge for Staff and Career Development, Training and Recruitment Coordinator and Special Agent with the Medicaid Fraud Investigation Unit.

The Organized Crime Division was established in 1977 to investigate groups organized for illegal activity. Ambrose Moss headed the division, which was ini-

tially staffed only by Moss and his secretary. He set out to investigate gambling, prostitution, loan-sharking, labor racketeering and other illegal enterprises. Four agents were assigned to the organized crime unit, Jim Taylor, Bob Denny, Rodney Williams and Steve Cole. They went to Miami to an organized crime school sponsored by the Dade County Sheriff's Department.

Senior Agent Bill Coleman was assigned to the organized crime unit after the Intelligence Division, which he commanded, was discontinued. Soon others including Bill Thompson, who wrote the grant for its funding, were assigned to the unit. Thompson, Ross Haynes and John Mehr were trained by the FBI and served as experts on poker machines, a growing problem in the state.

The Criminal Justice Data and Communications System Division was developed to provide a database of criminals and criminal activity for use by agencies throughout the state. The division also provided direct access to the National Crime Information Center (NCIC) and maintained communications with agencies nationally and internationally. One section of the division maintained crime statistics for operational and research purposes.

Agents were assigned to a wide variety of duties. Agent Claude Johnson, in addition to his work in narcotics, worked on the security detail for two governors and for twenty years was chief of security of the Legislative Black Caucus. His duty with the Black Caucus began when the caucus was created and continued until Johnson's retirement. Agent Johnson was named Inspector of Urban Affairs in 1978, later titled Assistant Agent in Charge and was stationed in Memphis.

Jimmie Van Leach joined the TBI as a criminal investigator in August 1978. Leach began his law enforcement career in campus security before joining the Sharon Police Department. He then served for two years as a trooper with the Highway Patrol before transferring to the TBI. Leach was assigned to Hardeman County on the day that Delphus Hicks was sworn in as sheriff of the county. Sheriff Hicks was the first black sheriff elected in the history of Tennessee. He provided Leach office space in the chief deputy's office at the jail. Later Leach had a small office in the Fayette County Sheriff's Department as well, along with Inspector Jack Blackwell.

Inspector Blackwell and most of the TBI agents in West Tennessee gathered in Greenfield on Saturday night of Labor Day weekend in 1979 following the kidnapping of an 8-year-old girl. Alvin Daniel was the case agent. Other agents who gathered to work the case were Jimmie

Leach, Tommy Lewis, Warren Jones, Floyd Mangrum, Lucion English, Ancel McDuffee, Bob Yoakum and John Carpenter. It was obvious to Blackwell when they drove past the humble home of the girl's family that the case was not kidnapping for ransom and that the girl was most likely already dead. The girl's body was soon found on the bank of a ditch on Bean Switch Road. She had been raped and murdered.

A composite picture of the suspect based on a description of the girl's brother was aired in the media. A woman in Obion County recognized the likeness and named a man with a record for attempted rape in Florida. Blackwell and Leach interviewed the suspect's wife, who told them he was about to leave the state. The young girl's killer was picked up in Huntingdon trying to board a bus to Georgia. Black shoe polish he had used to dye his hair was running down the back of his neck.

Agents found evidence on the man's body that linked him to the rape and sodomy of the girl. The killer broke down and confessed to the crime. Over 20 years later the rapist-murderer was put to death in Tennessee's first execution in four decades.

Crimes against children were the most compelling cases agents worked and frequently the most difficult emotionally. In October 1976 agents Steve Cole and Tony Bowers were called to go to the morgue at Bradley County Hospital in Cleveland. They met detectives of the sheriff's office and forensic pathologist Fenton Scruggs. After removing the body of a four-year-old girl from the cooler, the lawmen began to examine the bruised and torn remains.

They started uncovering her at the feet. She had been held up by her ankles and the bottoms of her feet had been beaten with a tire-knocker used by truckers to test tires on big rigs. They followed the bruises and torn skin up her body as it was uncovered and were all shaken by the time they reached the child's neck. When Cole uncovered the little girl's face the hardened officers broke down and cried. In addition to other torture the child had been fed hot sauce until the inside of her mouth was raw.

The four-year-old girl had been tortured and killed by her mother and stepfather, who were convicted of the crime. The case resulted in the Department of Human Resources revising its regulations and procedures. The child had been removed from the home because of abuse and officials of the state agency had returned her shortly before she was killed. The system was revamped so that a similar fate would not befall another child.

Jim Taylor was named interim inspector of Middle Tennessee when Inspector Joe Hannah took leave due to illness in late 1979. Taylor served in the capacity for eighteen months. He also took command of the Organized Crime Division when Tom Whitlatch retired. Taylor led the largest gambling raid in the history of the state in August 1979. The Knoxville operation included raids on VFWs, Moose Lodges, Knights of Columbus and any group known to be violating the law, netting numerous pieces of gambling equipment and many arrests. An even larger raiding operation was done in Nashville in August 1980.

Larry Wallace returned to the TBI in 1980. Wallace had taken leave from the Department of Safety in the mid-seventies and was twice elected sheriff of McMinn County. He was named Tennessee Sheriff of the Year by the Tennessee Sheriff's Association in 1979. Wallace was the first person added to the Bureau after it separated from the Department of Safety following the end of the Blanton administration.

Much of the traditional work of the TBI continued as normal during the administration of Governor Ray Blanton. However, the Bureau was under political pressure when investigating corruption within the administration. The period was difficult for many field agents.

Allegations of wrong doings within the administration grew and in 1977 TBI Criminal Investigators Charles Lee and Larry O'Rear were assigned to investigate. Lee was a relatively new agent, having joined the Bureau in 1974, with strong analytical abilities. O'Rear, son of former Commissioner of Safety Greg O'Rear, joined the Bureau in August 1970 as only the second agent with a college degree. He had served as a

Cooperation between county officers and the TBI led to confiscation of a large quantity of cash from a drug operation. Left to right were Hardeman County Sheriff's Chief Investigator George Bynum, Hardeman County Sheriff Delphus Hicks, TBI Agent Jimmie Leach, and Hardeman County Deputy Sheriff David Howell.

Slot machines confiscated in August 1980 Nashville gambling raid. TBI members involved with the raid included from left to right undercover agents Danny Hall, Roger Farley, and Larry Wallace, raid coordinator Jim Taylor, and Assistant Director Bob Fortner.

dispatcher for the Highway Patrol for 10 months in 1968 while completing his masters degree.

The two were under constant pressure and their investigation under constant scrutiny from the administration. Eventually they were required to report their moves in advance. On one occasion Lee went to East Tennessee to do an interview and told TBI agent Steve Watson, "You may not want to go with me on this interview, because I'm hot as a firecracker." A number of field agents survived due to the support of strong district attorneys general with whom they worked.

Both Lee and O'Rear resigned from the Bureau shortly before the end of the Blanton term. Charles Lee later became a district attorney general and a circuit court judge. Larry O'Rear became Director of Safety for the city of Cookeville. He returned to the TBI in November 1984 and remained until his retirement on November 1, 2004.

Other TBI agents investigated a number of cases involving members of the Blanton administration. Agent Steve Cole was approached by a person who had evidence of officials selling pardons and he referred her to the FBI. Jack Blackwell investigated payroll irregularities at Ft. Pillow Penal Farm leading to the indictment of a top administration official for having individuals paid who never worked at the facility. Jim Taylor and Ray Presnell investigated incidents of political payoffs. Jim Keesling also made a number of arrests related to activities of the administration.

Governor Blanton left office prior to the end of his term and Lamar Alexander was sworn in early. John Carney and Bill Holt were assigned to work with the Inspector General, an office formed by Governor Alexander and his transition team attorney Fred Dalton Thompson, future U.S. senator.

The FBI asked Carney to select a few TBI agents to guard the State Capitol offices of the administration while the FBI gathered evidence. Carney called Bill

Command of the Tennessee Bureau of Investigation expressed appreciation to Gene Roberts, commissioner of Safety, for his cooperation through the process of the TBI becoming independent from Safety. They presented Roberts a framed copy of the TBI seal when he left the Department of Safety in January 1983. From left to right were Deputy Director Steve Watson, Special Agent in Charge of Special Investigations John Carney, Director Arzo Carson, Commissioner of the Department of Safety Gene Roberts, Assistant Director Jim Keesling, Assistant Director for Finance Bob Pearce and Special Agent in Charge of the Narcotics Division Maxey Gilleland.

Holt, Doug Woodlee, Richard Wright and Thomas Carmouche and asked them if they wanted to step out on a limb. They agreed and six agents of the TBI assisted the FBI. Carney found commutation papers in the capitol office of Governor Blanton's attorney. Evidence was gathered against Governor Blanton and his administration on several corruption charges including selling pardons. A number of administration officials served prison terms.

TBI Director Robert Goodwin, who was dealing with health issues, retired on April 17, 1979. THP Colonel Richard M. Dawson provided oversight of the Bureau for a brief period, although he was not active in the day to day operations.

Arzo Carson was appointed director of the TBI by Governor Lamar Alexander in May 1979. Carson had established a reputation as an aggressive district attorney general who showed integrity and independence. He was willing to take on any and all law breakers including public officials.

Carson began his law career while in the U. S. Navy in World War II. He was about to ship out as an admiral's aide when the Japanese surrendered and was assigned instead to the Judge Advocate General's office processing men out of the service.

After his military service Carson earned an undergraduate degree in philosophy and business administration from the University of Tennessee. He then earned a law degree and built a successful law practice in East Tennessee. Carson spent nearly 20 years in the public sector as a district attorney general before his appointment as head to the TBI. For the next ten years he was a dynamic leader and an articulate spokesman for the Bureau.

Director Carson's initial charge was to reconstitute the TBI as an agency separate and independent from the Department of Safety. Independence was essential to isolate the Bureau from political influence and to insure confidentiality of investigations.

Carson was concerned that the agency have not only structural independence, but functional independence as well. He defined the TBI as a separate and distinct department of government and insulated the director from political influence. The governor would not solely determine the director and the term of the director would be six years so as not to coincide with the gubernatorial term.

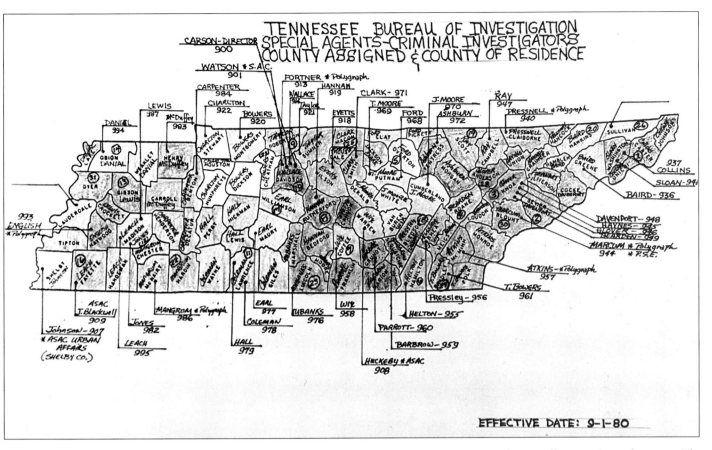

Map showing the assignment of investigators of the independent Tennessee Bureau of Investigation across the state effective in September 1980. The number designated the radio number which was also the agent's car number. The map was prepared by John Carney Jr.

Key to the integrity and internal independence of the agency for Carson was to fuse the Bureau's substantive work with the court trial process. Agents were given subpoena power and authorized to administer the oath and take a sworn statement. The bill further allowed the TBI to take evidence from an investigation directly to a grand jury if a district attorney general declined to prosecute a case that in the judgment of the TBI should be prosecuted.

Legislation to create the Bureau as a separate entity of government was passed and signed by Governor Alexander on March 27, 1980. The independent agency was named the Tennessee Bureau of Investigation.

There is created the Tennessee Bureau of Investigation, which shall be a separate department of state government. A director shall be appointed to administer such department. The director shall be a person of experience and ability in the detection of crime and shall be appointed to a fixed term of office by the Governor from a list of three nominees submitted to him by a nominating commission . . . The bureau shall be

divided into two divisions, the criminal investigation division and the forensic services division . . .

Governor Alexander was careful not to infringe on the independence of the TBI and told people, "Arzo Carson runs the TBI." From a practical stand point the TBI was primarily answerable to the judicial system.

Director Carson emphasized to TBI personnel the importance of conducting investigations so that cases were easy for district attorneys to prosecute. He also stressed the sobering impact on the individual being interviewed of the agent's new subpoena power and power to take a sworn statement. Carson encouraged agents to take along polygraph equipment and an operator to heighten the effect of the interview.

A reorganization plan for the new TBI was developed and Director Carson announced it would take effect on September 1, 1980. While the agency continued to be separated into two general divisions, Carson established five units or functional divisions, criminal investigations, criminal records, forensic services, administrative services and special services. Total personnel numbered 161, which included 45 field agents, 11 narcotics agents and 15 specialized investigation agents.

The title of field agents was changed from Criminal Investigator to Special Agent—Criminal Investigator. Carson provided agents with tape recorders and other equipment needed to perform their duties and instructed them to build a file, which included a brief statement of the circumstance followed with sworn statements of interviewees. He established a five day rule, whereby each agent was to dictate a tape of his activities and send it to Nashville within five days. Tapes were transcribed and reviewed by supervisors. Feedback was then provided to agents.

Special Agent in Charge (SAC) and Assistant Special Agent in Charge (ASAC) were adopted to designate command positions and replace the title Inspector. Special Agent in Charge Steve O. Watson headed the Criminal Investigations Division, the principal investigative unit. Watson joined the Bureau in 1969 and established an exemplary record as an agent in East Tennessee. Carson had worked with Watson and was confident Watson could manage the investigative function of the agency. Watson served as second in command of the TBI as well.

Carson created the administrative position of Executive Officer. Archie Hamm served in the position until his retirement. Duties of the executive officer were to conduct research technology and other needs of the Bureau and to track proposed legislation affecting the TBI.

One concern of the restructuring was a greater focus on white-collar crime and public corruption. The Special Services Division was created to investigate activities including conspiracy, fraud and embezzlement. It replaced the organized crime unit. Special Agent in Charge James F. Keesling, a veteran agent from Kingsport with a strong analytical abilities, headed the division. Carson said he chose Keesling "because he can take an isolated fact and give it relevance in a suspected concealed criminal activity."

Keesling managed two units. A 15-member Special Investigations unit, headed by ASAC John Carney Jr., was formed as a part of the division to assist district attorneys general with prosecution of white-collar crimes. The division also included an 11-member narcotics unit headed by Ambrose Moss.

One notable case of white-collar crime investigated by the new division involved the selling of coal futures to investors in several states. A gang defrauded numerous people in the commodities market scheme. TBI agents including Claude Johnson apprehended the swindlers, confiscating houses, boats, cars and other assets.

The largest embezzlement of public funds in Tennessee was thwarted by the TBI in Washington County. The road supervisor, the county judge and principles of a construction supply company conspired to inflate invoices for dynamite and drill bits so that, for example, 1000 drill bits were paid for when only 100 were delivered. Agent Steve Watson exposed the embezzlement of nearly $250,000.

ASAC Jack Blackwell continued his supervisory role over West Tennessee, which included all counties west of Nashville. He worked out of his home in Somerville. ASAC Preston Huckeby supervised East Tennessee, the counties east of Nashville from McMinnville. Claude Isaiah Johnson, stationed in Memphis, was named ASAC of Urban Affairs.

Field operations remained fractured into small districts across the state, most served by a single agent. In order to manage and control the 68 field agents, better coordination was needed at the division level. Carson insisted that agents maintain confidentiality and demonstrate integrity. These were traits especially important when agents came together to work a major case. Agents who "talked out of school" or who lacked good conduct were released from the Bureau.

Within a year of Carson becoming director it was possible to move 50 agents or more to any part of the state for a poker machine or gambling raid without anyone knowing until the operation was completed. Steve Watson knew what was going on statewide because Jack Blackwell was on top of activities in West Tennessee and Preston Huckeby in East Tennessee.

Tennessee Bureau of Investigation Director Arzo Carson, left, presents West Tennessee Special Agent in Charge Thomas J. "Jack" Blackwell with the new custom badge of the Bureau after it became an independent state agency.

The Criminal Records Unit and the Identification Unit was combined as the Records and Identification Unit and commanded by SAC Douglas D. Woodlee, who had been Assistant Supervisor of the Identification Unit under Archie Hamm. Woodlee joined the agency on October 1, 1968, as a crime technician, worked in narcotics and as an investigator, and served in supervisory roles beginning in 1972.

The Bureau acquired its first crime scene vehicle in 1979. The secondhand green panel van was in poor condition. It had front seats and a straight bench seat in back. The gas gauge didn't work, which Larry Hall found out the hard way when the van ran out of gas on an isolated stretch of Tennessee 412 one dark night near Dyersburg.

A new white GMC Astro was acquired to work crime scenes. Occasionally the van proved too small. Larry Hall worked a double homicide near Kentucky Lake in which an elderly couple was killed by three escapees from Eddyville State Prison in Kentucky. The Astro was too small to hold all the evidence.

SAC William J. Darby III, head of the Forensic Services Division, had directed the crime lab since its creation in 1975. The Administrative Services Division was managed by SAC Robert G. Pearce, previously the chief of fiscal services for the Department of Safety. Pearce joined the TBI to handle its basic administrative functions.

Some former supervisory personnel returned to the field. Assistant Director Bob Fortner returned to the field as a criminal investigator and polygraph examiner working primarily in Middle and West Tennessee. Inspector Joe Hannah of Nashville, the previous number three person in the agency, and Inspector Walter Bearden of Knoxville returned to the field as criminal investigators.

Narcotics Agent Richard Maxey Gilleland was named SAC of the Narcotics Division in 1981. Maxey Gilleland was a Viet Nam veteran with a teaching degree. As a sergeant with the 7th Marines in 1969 Gilleland and his platoon became engaged in hand to hand combat killing a dozen hostile soldiers. Gilleland crossed the rice paddy six times under heavy enemy fire leading wounded marines to safety. Gilleland was awarded the Navy Cross, the second highest award for extraordinary heroism, as a result of "his courage, bold initiative, and unwavering devotion to duty."

Ambrose Moss had retired as head of narcotics in September 1980 after nearly 30 years of service to the Bureau. Taylor Bettis, the operations officer, commanded the unit briefly until Gilleland took charge.

New insignia was created for the newly independent Bureau. A custom, full-color, eagle-top shield badge was designed in a collaborative effort. Director Carson wanted the date March 27, 1980, the creation date of the independent agency, on the badge. Tom Carmouche suggested "TBI" be enclosed in a state shaped panel. Steve Watson, Jack Blackwell and others also took part in the design process and John Carney pulled the ideas together into a drawing of the badge. All badges were marked "Special Agent" except for one badge marked "Director."

The new seal was designed at the same time by Helen Zachary of Clarksville, an acquaintance of John Carney. The seal was modeled after the FBI seal with elements of the previous TBI seal. Ms. Zachary's original hand painted seal was hung in the director's office at headquarters. John Carney identified a passage from a federal court case, which was adopted as the motto of the TBI, "That guilt shall not escape nor innocence suffer."

Director Carson made bold moves to increase pay for TBI personnel. He requested an initial raise of 14.1% for employees of the Bureau and a $2,500 across-the-board raise for agents the following year. He explained the increases were based on inequities in current pay levels and the excessive hours worked by agents for which overtime could not be paid. The director hired capable college graduates regardless of their major, increasing the intellectual diversity of the Bureau. Young graduates were often hired as interns and many became agents.

Director Carson finalized the reorganization with a revision to the titles of the Bureau's executives. Steve Watson was given the title Deputy Director, appropriate to his position of second in command. He continued responsibility for the Criminal Investigations Division. William Darby was titled Assistant Director for Forensic Services, James F. Keesling was made Assistant Director for Criminal Intelligence and Organized Crime and Robert Pearce made Assistant Director for Administrative Services. The title of Jack Blackwell and Preston Huckeby became Special Agent in Charge for West Tennessee and East Tennessee respectively.

Larry Wallace took over as executive officer in 1983, becoming the second to fill the position after Archie Hamm's retirement. Hamm retired in September 1982 after 25 years of service to the Bureau. One of Wallace's assignments was to do investigations for the Tennessee Court of the Judiciary, a panel of judges at different levels across the state that reviewed allegations of misconduct against the judiciary. He also worked on specialized assignments of the

The West Tennessee TBI agents conference in 1982. Left to right were Assistant Director Jim Keesling, Special Agent in Charge of Special Investigations John Carney, Ancel McDuffee, Assistant Special Agent in Charge of West Tennessee Thomas J. "Jack" Blackwell, Alvin Daniel, Tony Bowers, Director Arzo Carson, William Warren Jones, John Carpenter, Jimmie Van Leach, Tommy Lewis, Lucion English, John Mehr, Deputy Director Steve Watson, and Assistant Director for Finance Bob Pearce.

director. After a year Wallace was given the position Special Agent in Charge of Middle Tennessee and became responsible for 27 counties.

The remaining TBI offices located in downtown Nashville at the Andrew Jackson Building were moved out to the Browning Scott Building in 1982 and in 1984 the headquarters of the TBI moved to the Tennessee Preparatory School campus on Foster Avenue. Cooper Hall, formerly a boys' dormitory, was converted to offices for the agency. A couple of years later the Menzler Nix Building was converted to house the new Information Systems Division (ISD). Roger Pelham was placed in charge of the ISD and began projects to automate the criminal history records and to implement TBI's AFIS. Pelham was assisted in the automation projects by Dennis Daniels, Kenneth W. Owen, David Bolme and Candace Wilkerson.

Operationally the Bureau focused principally on investigations of public corruption, major narcotics cases and white-collar crimes. Agents were kept busy with a spate of criminal activity among the sheriffs in the state. Investigations under Assistant Director Jim Keesling and SAC John Carney Jr. led to the conviction of 18 sheriffs and a number of other officials during the 1980s, mainly involving illegal drugs.

A case involving the misuse of steroids at Vanderbilt University received national attention. Articles in *Sports Illustrated* magazine highlighted the work of the TBI.

The use of gambling equipment, especially video poker machines, was prolific in the state and the object of several multiple-agent operations. By 1984, about 200 video poker and similar machines had been seized over a two year period.

The TBI initiated an operation in the early eighties that became one of the few instances of law enforcement action in environmental law. The federal Surface Mining and Reclamation Act of 1977 required that strip mining operators restore lands after mining them. In 1980 Tennessee legislators made failure to follow the guidelines a felony in the state.

Wildcat miners in the mountains of upper East Tennessee ran clandestine mining operations rather than obeying the law. They secretly scraped away top soil, loosened the layer of coal with dynamite and used heavy equipment to remove the coal before the operation was discovered. The wildcatters also intimidated Department of Conservation mining inspectors making it impossible for them to do their job.

An early environmental law enforcement initiative began when Director Carson told the state legislature that the TBI would stop illegal strip mining in Tennessee. He assigned the task to Special Agent Bill Thompson, standing on the ground at the far left wearing a TBI cap. Special agents Bob Fortner, in a short-sleeved white shirt standing to the right of Thompson, and Ed Brock, fourth from the left atop the confiscated earthmover. The other officers are mine inspectors of the Tennessee Department of Conservation.

When the situation was referred to the TBI, Director Carson promised the legislature that he would stop the wildcat mining. Carson assigned the enforcement duty to Agent Bill Thompson. Thompson worked with mining inspectors to form a task force and moved into the mountains to arrest wildcat miners.

Thompson and members of his task force were frequently fired on by the mountain people who were wildcatting. The task force made many arrests and seized equipment worth approximately $30 million. Within a couple of years they essentially put the wildcat miners out of business.

The TBI had original jurisdiction in the pursuit of fugitives and worked a number of high profile cases. One of the most intense involved a deadly duo that overpowered guards and shot their way out of Fort Pillow State Prison in February 1984. They led law enforcement officers in six states on a 29-day manhunt.

The two escapees, one convicted of murdering his wife and daughter in Knoxville and the other a habitual criminal, made their way to Brownsville where they shot at a policeman, killed a local businessman and kidnapped his wife. They forced her to drive them east until they were provided another car 40 miles east of Knoxville where they released the woman. The two drove through North Carolina, Virginia, West Virginia, Ohio and Kentucky.

The TBI developed an intelligence analysis including former acquaintances and life style profiles of the two fugitives. Information provided by the Bureau led to the arrest of a relative in Cleveland, Ohio, and nearly led to their capture in Louisville, Kentucky.

In North Carolina they shot a trooper four times when he stopped the Cadillac they had stolen. A truck driver saw the two speeding away and called authorities. The manhunt intensified and one of the fugitives was cornered in a house of an elderly couple. The woman was so frightened that she had a heart attack and died. The fugitive killer was shot to death in a gun battle with lawmen as he tried to flee. The second fugitive was captured soon after and returned to Tennessee by TBI agents.

A notable 1983 fugitive case involved a female Knoxville attorney who assisted her client's escape from the penitentiary. The felon was undergoing psychological testing after he and other inmates killed two in a racially motivated incident at Brushy Mountain prison. She held a gun on guards while the prisoner bound them and then the pair fled the state.

They were apprehended in Florida after 139 days and returned to Tennessee by special agents of the TBI. Their escapades included daily gambling jaunts to the dog track. The incident generated national news coverage including an article in Rolling Stones magazine. Deputy Director Steve Watson told a New York Times reporter, "Lawyers don't usually help their clients escape the law in quite this way."

The Bureau established relationships with federal law enforcement agencies and took part in numerous cross-jurisdictional investigations. TBI Director Carson met frequently with the special agent in charge of the FBI in Tennessee and officials of U.S. Customs, the Secret Service and other federal agencies. When appropriate, TBI agents were sworn as Deputy U.S. Marshals, giving them federal authority.

The Bureau also took advantage of federal training programs. The TBI had more FBI National Academy graduates in the 1980s than any other agency in the state. Sometimes as many as 3 or 4 TBI agents were sent to the FBI academy at one time. Academy attendance built good rapport with the FBI and graduates tended to rise quickly in responsibility and rank.

One cooperative venture in March 1981 propelled the TBI into the national media. The seizure of 614 pounds of 99.7% pure cocaine in Sevier County resulted from a call by U.S. Customs. Customs and the Texas Department of Safety were tracking the transponder on an airplane operating out of Sevierville. The airplane flew over the Gulf of Mexico to South America, probably they thought, to pick up a load of drugs. On the way back to the United States the transponder was intermittent and they lost contact with the airplane.

The U.S. Customs office in New Orleans phoned TBI Special Agent Bob Denny in Knoxville. Denny and Special Agent David Davenport drove to the airport in Sevierville in the middle of the night and found that the twin-engine Beachcraft Queen Aire had landed. They boarded the plane and found the plastic wrapped cocaine packed in boxes. The two pilots were not found. Denny called Deputy Director Steve Watson, who happened to be in Knoxville, and said, "You need to come to Sevierville. I've got an airplane on the ground, and it has 614 pounds of pure coke on it." Watson asked, "Are you sure?"

The cache was the largest inland seizure of cocaine ever made in the United States to that date. The street value was estimated at $200 million. The decision was made to store the cocaine at the TBI laboratory in Nashville. Watson called Director Carson and told him what they had. Carson said, "Are you sure?" The cocaine was flown to Nashville. When they landed, Carson and other TBI officials were waiting along with representatives of the news media.

Just over a year later, in July 1982, the seizure was dwarfed when the TBI and the DEA, assisted by the THP and the Cleveland Police Department, captured 1,250 pounds of cocaine. The two-pronged dragnet that followed a six month investigation also netted $450,000 in cash, five vehicles, a machine gun and other weapons and the arrest of nine in Cleveland and Loudon. The near-pure cocaine contained in 26 South American-made duffel bags was valued at $400 million. The confiscated drug shipment was produced by infamous Columbian drug lord Pablo Escobar and was the largest inland seizure of cocaine ever made in the United States.

In another joint operation the TBI and the FBI worked a major case in Chattanooga. For the first time, TBI agents worked a wiretap case with the federal agency. Steve Watson remembered his amazement, "We had 10 or 15 agents in Chattanooga sitting on an FBI wiretap." The case netted about $850,000 for the TBI, its share of forfeiture funds. The money was used to update computer operations at the TBI, establishing the Tennessee Information Enforcement System (TIES). Confiscated assets and forfeitures were key to upgrading many resources at the Bureau.

TIES was the result of a three year project of Director Arzo Carson to design a unified system of information management that would facilitate the intelligence function of the bureau. TIES integrated data elements of various automated information systems available to and maintained by the TBI, giving groups inside the Bureau as well as outside agencies information needed to enforce the law and investigate crime.

Gambling and vice operations remained a frequent target of the TBI. Cocke County in East Tennessee was a dry county, but establishments openly sold alcoholic beverages and made practically every other vice available to their patrons. Diane's Lounge was one such place with a well stocked bar and plenty of working girls eager to satisfy customers. Illegal activity in the county was so wide-open that cases were quickly made by undercover TBI agents John Carpenter and Jimmie Leach.

The easiest undercover operation for Carpenter and Leach in East Tennessee concerned a number of gambling places operating in Knoxville. The first few days were non-productive because they were not able

A joint TBI and DEA operation in July 1982 resulted in the confiscation of 1,250 pounds of near pure cocaine valued at $400 million, $450,000 in cash, various other assets, and nine arrests. Individuals central to the operation posed with captured drugs and weapons. Kneeling in front from left to right were TBI special agents David Shelton and Jim Bowers. Standing from left to right were DEA agent Everett Newnam, an unidentified DEA agent, DEA Nashville Special Agent in Charge Bernard Redd, TBI Special Agent Lance Saylor, DEA agent Mona Polan, and TBI Special Agent Howard "Butch" Morris. Bernie Redd later served a TBI Special Agent in Charge of Narcotics.

to get into a single place. One morning as they were having breakfast at a restaurant on Kingston Pike they overheard two men sitting at a nearby table talking about gambling.

Both agents pulled napkins from the dispenser on their table and wrote down what the two men were saying. Details of the entire gambling system in the city of Knoxville were laid out for the TBI agents including how one gambling den was warned about a raid that the TBI had made a year earlier.

Special Agent Bill Thompson and fifteen other TBI agents from Middle and East Tennessee led a raid in January 1983 following an investigation by Steve Cole. They arrested 85 spectators at the cock fights taking place at the Rocky Top Game Club in Cleveland.

Tennessee was a major site for cock fighting in the eighties and hosted the national cock fighting championship. Special Agent Thompson found out that the championship event was held on the weekend closest to the 4th of July each year.

A group of 600 to 700 from all over the United States gathered for the event in Del Rio, Tennessee, in 1987. Several men robbed the gathering and the cock fighters quickly identified the bandits. Once a week or so afterwards a body came floating down the river into Newport. The sheriff told Thompson that something had to be done about the cock fights. The TBI raided the cock fighting championship the next year and arrested over 400 people, the largest misdemeanor arrest in the state of Tennessee.

TBI Agent Jimmie Van Leach, left, and Jackson-Madison County Metro Narcotics Investigator Dennis Mays confiscate 200 pounds of marijuana and arrest the dealer in a motel in Jackson. This December 1984 seizure was the largest quantity of marijuna not in transit ever taken in Madison County.

Local law enforcement continued to ask the TBI for help investigating major crimes. One Haywood County murder investigation in the early eighties took an eerie turn. The body of a girl was found in the Hatchie Wildlife Refuge. She had been stabbed 27 times. Four or five agents were working long hours on the case. A few days into the investigation special agents Jimmie Leach and Tommy Lewis were sitting at the jail after a long day when an aunt of the victim entered and told them she had a dream.

In the woman's dream her niece's killer was chasing her through tall weeds with a knife. They asked her who it was but she said she had not seen his face. Leach and Lewis told her to come back if she had the dream again and saw the killer's face. They didn't expect to see the woman again. One evening soon after, however, she returned and told them she had the dream again and she named the man who was chasing her.

The agents had prioritized the suspects in the case and the man she named was near the bottom of the list. He was only on the list because he knew the victim. On the same day, the man was in court on a DUI charge and unsolicited told the court bailiff, "I want you to know I didn't have anything to do with killing that girl." Brownsville Policeman Johnny Blackburn brought the man to the jail to be interviewed by Leach and Lewis. About 2 o'clock the following morning the man named by the dreamer confessed to killing the girl.

TBI agents were central to solving a cold case in Jackson in 1983. The brutalized body of a 17-year-old Henderson girl was found on May 23, 1981, by a woman walking her dog along U.S. 45 Bypass. The girl was last seen celebrating her high school graduation at the Hat and Cane Club, a night spot in South Jackson.

The district attorney general called the TBI about six months after the murder and the case was assigned to Special Agent Jimmie Leach. After months of interviews and following leads the case remained unsolved. While Leach was at the FBI National Academy in 1983, he described the case to Roy Hazelwood, a renowned profiler of serial killers. Hazelwood gave Leach more than a dozen characteristics of an individual likely to commit such a crime, all of which were later found to be consistent with the killer.

A break in the case came when Huntsville, Alabama, Investigator Al Duffey contacted Madison County Sheriff's Investigator Dennis Mays of the Jackson-Madison County Metro Narcotics Unit about another case. Duffey mentioned a murder suspect they had in jail. As the two talked, Mays recognized the similarities between the Alabama crime and the unsolved case in Jackson.

TBI agents Jimmie Leach and Tommy Lewis traveled to the Huntsville jail for a number of interviews without getting a confession to the Jackson murder. They were on their way down for another interview when the suspect told a deputy sheriff that he wanted to talk with Leach and Alabama Investigator Duffey. The inmate confessed to killing five women including the girl in Jackson.

An agent's memory and a witness with grit led to the capture of another murderer. The killer robbed a store owner and shot him seven times as the merchant sat in his pickup in Jamestown, Fentress County. The victim's sister, a tough 98-pound mountain woman, witnessed the incident and went out into the cold night, tackling the gunman and pulling off his mask.

As she wrestled with the killer in the parking lot, her daughter drove up and ran into the man with her jeep. The bandit dropped his gun, a 59A Smith & Wesson. The daughter got to the gun and handed it to her mother. The killer drew a .38 caliber revolver from his waistband and the two shot it out. He shot the woman through her abdomen and fired a second bullet that grazed her head.

TBI Special Agent Bill Thompson was assigned to the case. The Fentress County woman told Thompson, "When you find him, he'll be shot. I got off two rounds. I know I hit him the first time, but the second time I may have missed him 'cause I was a passin' out." The gun that the killer dropped was traced to the man who sold it. When he described the buyer of the gun, Thompson recognized the description as a man he had put in the penitentiary for another murder.

When the ex-convict was captured, he did have a bullet wound. The victim's sister made a positive identification of her brother's killer.

A number of specialists were commissioned as special agents with the TBI during the eighties. Dr. William Bass, founder of the internationally known "body farm" research facility at the University of Tennessee, was commissioned as Special Agent—Consultant Forensic Anthropologist. Dr. Cleland Blake of Morristown was commissioned as Special Agent—Pathologist. Dr. Leon Reuhland in Middle Tennessee was commissioned Special Agent—Medical Consultant.

Other individuals who were selected as consultants were Dr. A. G. Kasselberg of Vanderbilt on DNA Analysis, Dr. Albert Berry of Tennessee State University on Organizational Planning and Development, Dr. Murray K. Marks of the University of Tennessee-Knoxville on Forensic Anthropology, Dr. Pat Nation on Behavioral Sciences and Profiling, Dr. Bob G. Rouse on Criminal Psychology, Julius Edward Meriwether on Social and Cultural Diversity, Steve D. Canter on Aviation and Larry Vannover on fitness. These individuals added important scientific expertise to the Bureau.

TBI agent Steve Cole relied on the expertise of the consultants when he worked a particularly difficult assignment following the 1983 explosion of a fireworks factory in Polk County at Webb's Bait Farm. Investigation of the incident involved local, state and federal authorities. The ATF took primary responsibility for the investigation. TBI Special Agent Steve Cole, forensic pathologist Dr. Cleland Blake and state forensic anthropologist Dr. William Bass were given the responsibility of identifying the remains of the victims.

Eleven people were killed in the blast. A refrigerated trailer was set up as a temporary morgue. Once the team completed their identification process, family members had to review the remains to confirm the identification. The only identifying mark on one victim was a tattoo on his torso.

The Narcotics Division of the TBI became the central unit of the Governor's Task Force on Marijuana Eradication (GTFME) created by executive order of Governor Lamar Alexander in 1983. The objectives of the task force were to seek out and eradicate marijuana crops and to arrest and prosecute individuals for illegal acts related to marijuana. The four state agencies providing personnel and equipment were the TBI, which administered the grant used for initial funding of the task force, the THP, the Tennessee Alcoholic Beverage Commission and the Tennessee National Guard. A number of local and federal agencies assisted.

Creation of the task force was the idea of TBI Director Arzo Carson and Narcotics SAC Maxey Gilleland headed the interagency unit during the initial years of its existence. The officers in the unit called themselves the "Pot Busters." The work of the task force involved spotting marijuana plants by helicopter or otherwise locating crops, moving in on the ground and destroying plants. The work was hot and dirty for the "ground-pounders." It was also dangerous because fields were often booby trapped.

Helicopter pilots of the Tennessee Highway Patrol were key to the programs success. Pilots like Mike Dover, Tom Ketron and John McAdams became expert at recognizing the unique green of marijuana plants. Lieutenant Dover, nicknamed "Eagle Eye," gained an exceptional reputation as a spotter. A former Cobra pilot in Vietnam, he spotted marijuana patches in gardens, corn fields, woodland clearings, even in interstate medians. Dover spotted over a billion dollars of marijuana during one summer alone. The spotters job had its own dangers. Pilots were shot at and their helicopters hit a number of times.

Processed marijuana was a target of the Bureau as well. The largest cache of marijuana taken in the history of Madison County was captured in 1984 by TBI Special Agent Jimmie Leach and Jackson-Madison County Metro Narcotics Investigator Dennis Mays. The 200 pound haul of the illegal drug was confiscated at a motel on North Highland in Jackson.

The two law officers had arranged to make a buy on earlier occasions, but each time the deal fell through. When they set up the meeting this time they did not notify their supervisors for fear that it would fall through again, so they had no backup. Leach and Mays entered the room with their snitch. When they drew weapons to make the arrest, the dealer lunged at Mays. The attack had little effect. Mays knocked the dealer backward over a bed and handcuffed him. Dennis Mays joined the TBI in 1986.

Undercover drug investigations often took months to complete and increased the likelihood of agents being exposed as law officers. Retribution for being discovered sometimes varied based on the preference of criminals in various sections of the state. Leach said, "In Hardin and McNairy counties they either blow you up or burn you down. In Hardeman and Fayette counties they cut you or shoot you."

Three narcotics agents rented a cabin in Hardin County and worked a number of months during 1986 to make a case on a large cocaine dealer. The dealer was cautious and lifted his shirt every time they met to show he was not wearing a wire or recording device. The undercover agents were expected to do the same.

Over time they bought small quantities of cocaine that tested over 90% pure. They learned the drug was coming into Georgia straight off the boat from Columbia. A major purchase, half a kilo of cocaine, was finally arranged. The field test kit issued for use by the TBI agents indicated the substance was not cocaine. Special Agent Leach recalled, "I knew in my gut it was cocaine and for some reason the test kit was wrong. We went through with the deal."

Leach had the package of cocaine at the TBI crime lab in Nashville the next morning when it opened and was told it was the purest cocaine that ever came through the lab. When the agents went to arrest the dealer he had fled. The night after the first federal grand jury subpoenas were handed out, the cabin rented by the TBI agents was burned to the ground. DEA later arrested the drug dealer in Muscle Shoals, Alabama.

TBI undercover work to foil contract murders gained significance after new legislation increased the penalty for the crime. Contract killing cases often contained an element of the absurd. In one case a Manchester man gave Agent Jim Lollar an IOU to kill his wife.

Madison County Sheriff David Woolfork often said the strangest thing he had ever seen in court was the man who wanted his nephews murdered and fed to the hogs. He referred to a case worked by Special Agent Jimmie Leach when authorities learned a man wanted two relatives killed.

Leach drove to the Old Hickory Mall parking lot one Saturday morning in the parking lot in a Corvette posing as a hit-man. Leach flashed a .45 caliber automatic as the man explained in detail why he wanted his nephews killed and later their wives. After the deal was struck the man asked, "Would a hog eat a body?"

Leach asked what he was talking about and he said he was wondering how to get rid of the bodies. Leach told him to get out of the car. Across the parking lot, the car with the two observing TBI agents was rocking because they were laughing so hard.

TBI personnel in 1985 included 44 field agents doing criminal investigations, 22 narcotics agents, 10 agents with the Special Investigative Unit and 8 Medicaid fraud investigators. Training included 16 weeks of basic training at TBI headquarters in Nashville, 12 weeks of drug enforcement training, four months at the FBI National Academy in Washington and periodic courses in special topics. Agent's pay ranged from $1,345 to $2,384 per month. The annual budget for the Bureau was $8 million.

Criminal investigators remained divided into geographic divisions. The drug unit was a single organizational structure with all agents reporting directly to Nashville. In September 1985 a regional unit of the Narcotics Division was established and John R. Mehr was assigned to the newly created position of Drug Coordinator for West Tennessee. This was the first supervisory position outside of Nashville for the Narcotics Division. Mehr was responsible for eight people including himself, working narcotics in rural West Tennessee and headquartered in Jackson.

The organizational structure of the Narcotics Division was distinct from that of the Criminal Investigation Division. The head of the Narcotics Division was SAC Maxey Gilleland. The drug coordinator position was similar to an ASAC of the narcotics unit.

Mehr joined the TBI in 1975 and was stationed in Nashville, Tullahoma/Manchester, Murfreesboro, Jackson and Dyersburg. He worked the territory for the five years prior to taking the coordinator position.

Narcotics Division SAC Maxey Gilleland decided to return to the field at the end of 1985 and relinquish management responsibilities. Gilleland was the only TBI agent to spend his entire career as a member of the narcotics unit. In the late eighties and nineties Gilleland worked drug cases and most of the solicitation-for-murder cases handled by the TBI.

Bernard "Bernie" Redd joined the TBI early in 1986 to become SAC of the Narcotics Division. Redd was DEA SAC for the Nashville area and a 24-year veteran of the DEA and its predecessor, the Bureau of Narcotics and Dangerous Drugs. SAC Redd headed the TBI Narcotics Division until his retirement in 1992.

SAC Redd changed the philosophy and focus of the narcotics unit. The unit was originally created to assist local agencies with narcotics problems. Many local agencies did not have the personnel or training to combat drugs. The focus of TBI narcotics agencies was arresting drug dealers at the street level.

Redd redirected the focus of the division to major suppliers rather than street dealers. Cooperating more fully with federal and other state agencies, TBI went after the smugglers and higher volume dealers. Working with federal agencies meant the TBI could work wire taps using federal Title 3 authority. The federal partnership also meant that TBI agents did not have to stop at the state line when pursuing narcotics cases. TBI formed ties with the DEA, the FBI, Customs and others. Agents didn't make as many cases, but the cases they made had a greater impact and yielded larger seizures. They began cutting drugs off at the source.

SAC Claude Johnson served as Field Coordinator in 1986 when he was promoted to assistant director upon the retirement of Jim Keesling. As field coordinator, Johnson was stationed in Nashville and worked with agents on problem cases or cases with a racial component. Johnson retired in 1990 as one of only seven agents who retired with a 100% conviction rate.

Assistant Director James F. Keesling retired from TBI in August 1986. He became chief of police for Kingsport and remained in the role for 13 years, developing a well recognized and accredited department. Three other longtime members of the Bureau retired in 1986, Frank Evetts, John Marcum and Bob York.

Deputy Director Steve O. Watson retired on October 2, 1987, after 20 years of service to the Bureau and soon after he received his law degree from the Nashville School of Law in 1987. He took a position with the Inspector General's Office of the Tennessee Valley Authority. John Carney Jr. was promoted to deputy director. Bill Holt assumed the role of SAC of Special Investigations, replacing Carney. Holt had been with the unit since its creation.

A major new tool for criminal identification was acquired in 1986, Tennessee's own Automated Fingerprint Identification System (AFIS). Doug Woodlee and Archie Hamm began work in 1979 to get AFIS for the TBI. AFIS utilized computer technology and allowed crime technicians to search digitized fingerprint records statewide and nationwide in minutes. This was impossible by searching card records manually. Through the early eighties Hamm, Woodlee and Roger Pelham, Director of TBI's newly created Information Systems Division, traveled out-of-state to evaluate systems, but could not obtain funding.

Woodlee organized a multi-agency meeting to unite efforts for funding of AFIS prior to the 1985 legislative session. Law enforcement officials and representatives of the District Attorneys General Conference met at the Tennessee Law Enforcement Training Academy for a strategy session.

Although a budget surplus existed that year, 275 amendments were pending for use of the funds. Woodlee presented the need for and benefits of AFIS to the West Tennessee Democratic Caucus in Representative Ned Ray McWherter's office. Woodlee and Chief Phil Keith of the Knoxville Police Department met with several prominent legislators during the budget hearings in 1985. Representative Shelby Rhinehart was instrumental in securing an appropriation of $1.5 million to purchase AFIS to be installed at TBI headquarters.

The system was installed in 1986 and Woodlee managed the system from its installation until 1998. It grew into a statewide system as 80 law enforcement agencies implemented AFIS technology over the next decade and a half. Sheriff's departments also implemented "live-scan" fingerprinting equipment, which allowed them to submit fingerprints electronically.

In the years that followed, Woodlee continued to press for full compliance by local agencies with state fingerprinting laws. Stan Sellers and others in the Shelby County Sheriff's Office secured legislative sponsorship and the Metro Nashville Police Department was able to secure help with the Middle Tennessee legislative delegation. Tennessee law was amended to require fingerprints of arrested juveniles be taken and submitted to the TBI and to strengthen existing fingerprint laws. The number of fingerprints received by TBI skyrocketed in the years following these changes of the law, greatly expanding the state's database.

TBI crime technicians also took time to volunteer in community service programs. Frank Barker, Stan Jaworski, Mike Leach, Lindel Payton, Bruce Pletcher and SAC Doug Woodlee participated in a program with Nissan to fingerprint children. Approximately 500 children from age 2 months to 16 years were fingerprinted in a single day.

Agent David Blackwell transferred to Nashville in 1986 to develop an expanded electronic surveillance program for the Bureau. Blackwell developed expertise with surveillance equipment while assigned to the Tricities area. Beginning in late 1977 the Bureau began developing better methods of backup for undercover agents. Narcotics Operations Officer Taylor Bettis bought a series of electronic devices, transmitters and receivers, using federal grant money. The Intell-Kit allowed undercover agents to record and transmit and became widely used.

More and more of Blackwell's time was devoted to educating himself and assisting agents in the use of

TBI leadership under Director Arzo Carson in 1988 were from left to right SAC of Special Investigations Division Bill Holt, SAC of Narcotics Division Bernie Redd, Director Arzo Carson, SAC of West Tennessee Jack Blackwell, SAC of Middle Tennessee Jim Taylor, SAC of East Tennessee Bill Thompson, Deputy Director John Carney.

surveillance devices. Outside agencies, local and federal, sought out his guidance as well. Even though the Bureau had limited equipment, agents increasingly used non-conventional investigative techniques.

When Blackwell moved to Nashville in 1986 he remained with narcotics initially, but later became a part of the Special Services unit under John Carney. The Bureau invested in additional and more sophisticated equipment, buying over $500,000 worth between 1987 and 1989. Capabilities acquired included audio-tape enhancement, full technical counter-measures to check offices for bugs and telephones for taps, video surveillance equipment with microwave transmitters and night vision equipment. A number of court presentation systems were acquired as well.

Jim Taylor was promoted to Special Agent in Charge and Director of the Medicaid Fraud Division in 1986 and remained in the position for six years. The Bureau wanted to improve the Medicaid fraud investigation record of the state, because Tennessee ranked last among the fifty states in convictions for Medicaid fraud.

By the early nineties the efforts of Jim Taylor and his investigators paid off and Tennessee reversed its ranking. The state became first in Medicaid fraud convictions, indictments, amount of money recovered and lowest cost per conviction. The efforts brought additional recognition to the Bureau throughout the law enforcement community when Taylor published an article on Medicaid fraud in the October 1992 *FBI Law Enforcement Bulletin*.

Jimmie Van Leach was appointed special agent in charge of East Tennessee by Director Carson in March 1988. Leach replaced SAC Preston Huckeby who retired after 30 years with the TBI.

During the eighties and nineties the TBI progressively focused on organized criminal activity, political corruption and high profile cases. Gary Azbill worked undercover in 1989 as a member of the Banditos biker club in Memphis. A task force involving agents of the TBI and the U.S. Customs Service gathered evidence on the illegal activities of a noted nightclub owner. During the investigation the president of the club married in a large biker wedding that brought motorcycle gangs from around the country.

In the late eighties the Bureau was in the midst of a multi-year multi-agency investigation of a major official corruptions case code named "Rocky Top." The operation was a probe into allegations of corruption in state-regulated bingos and raffles. It was primarily a federal investigation under the FBI, but it was initiated by the TBI in 1984. Assistant Director James Keesling met with an informant in Lewis County one morning about 3:00, who told Keesling about the bribery of state officials to get gambling legislation passed. Roger Farley led the TBI's efforts in the operation.

The TBI continued to work with the FBI until the investigation was completed in 1992. Indictments led

TBI leadership under Director John Carney in 1990 were from left to right SAC of East Tennessee Bill Thompson, SAC of Records and Identification Unit Doug Woodlee, Jeff Long, Richard Wright, SAC of Narcotics Unit Bernie Redd, SAC of Southeast Tennessee Bill Barbrow, SAC of West Tennessee Jack Blackwell, Bob Denny, and SAC of Middlme Tennessee Jim Taylor.

to a former bingo regulator and lobbyist pleading guilty to attempted bribery of a legislator and dozens of people arrested in raids of illegal gambling operations throughout the state. A top state official and a state representative committed suicide as a result of the criminal activity.

The agency continued to provide services to local law enforcement in the way of laboratory analysis, investigative coordination of wide-spread criminal activity and, to a lesser extent, assisting in more complicated routine criminal cases.

The Bureau had grown and changed in many ways over the past decade. The number of agents had expanded significantly including many with specialized investigative and forensic skills. The days of agents having an office in the sheriff's department were gone. A number of well equipped TBI offices were spread across the state. In general the Bureau had become more sophisticated and better able to investigate criminal activity.

John Carney Jr. was named director of the TBI in 1990 following the retirement of Arzo Carson. Carney was the only director to serve as an agent, assistant special agent in charge, special agent in charge, deputy director and director. Carney served until 1992.

Among other personnel changes, John Mehr was named SAC for West Tennessee in 1991 by Director Carney. His appointment followed the retirement of Jack Blackwell after 22 years with the TBI. Bill Thompson retired in 1991 after serving a stint as SAC of Middle Tennessee and then as SAC of East Tennessee after Leach left the TBI in 1988. Carney appointed Bill Barbrow as SAC of Southeast Tennessee, the Chattanooga area. Special Agent Lucion English left the Bureau in March 1988 and was appointed chief of police in Brownsville where he served for six years.

Jack Blackwell was mayor of Somerville in 1992 when he was chosen to serve as the chairman of the nominating commission to select candidates for a new director of the TBI. In May the commission announced six finalists for the position, current Director John Carney Jr., retired Secret Service official H. Edward Creamer, Department of Safety CID Director Jimmie Van Leach, Gibson County Sheriff Joe Shepard, Alcoa Chief of Police William R. Thomas and Tennessee Highway Patrol Colonel Larry D. Wallace. Three names were presented to Governor Ned McWherter in July: Carney, Wallace and former TBI agent Roger Farley.

Larry Wallace was appointed director of the 233-person agency by Governor McWherter in September 1992. In addition to his experience with the TBI, the Department of Safety and as McMinn County sheriff, the 47-year-old Wallace had a strong educational background in criminal justice. He saw the need to expand Bureau personnel and facilities.

Wallace named Jim Taylor to the post of SAC of Middle Tennessee, largest of the districts, encompassing 42 counties. The name of the Criminal Records Unit was changed to the Records and Identification Unit.

Jim Taylor also served as acting deputy director with responsibility for the Criminal Investigation Division. A short time later, in 1993, the Narcotics Division was transferred to Taylor as well. About ten months later responsibility for managing the narcotics function was transferred to the SACs of the four geographic divisions.

SAC Taylor stressed the importance of clearing murder cases and cleared all that came to the Bureau during his watch as head of the Middle District. He also implemented a systematic review of the 36 unsolved murder cases, worked with agents to reinvestigate these cases and resolved them as well. The only murder case left on the shelf was a man who killed two teenage girls and was in prison on another charge.

In light of the TBI focus on high profile and political cases, many local agencies felt the need for greater support in general criminal investigations, especially street-level drug enforcement. Wallace made a commitment to place new emphasis on investigative assistance to local law enforcement agencies.

Wallace pointed out the overlap between the Criminal Investigation Division of the Department of Safety and the TBI. After CID began doing drug investigations, district attorneys general called on them to investigate murders and robberies as well. TBI and CID were being called on to investigate similar crimes, which created duplication of administrative and support functions. The matter was resolved when the responsibilities of the two agencies were redefined, assigning most investigative work to the TBI. Many investigators were transferred from the Department of Safety CID to the TBI.

Governor Don Sundquist issued an executive order in 1996 moving the remaining officers in the drug unit of CID to the TBI. Gary Azbill, Danny Wilson, Aaron Chism, Robert Burnett from Knoxville, Mike Hannon from Newport, Dwaine Johnson and Charles Roundtree were the last transferred.

On a cold January morning in 1994 Middle Tennessee SAC Jim Taylor received a call from the district attorney general in Clarksville. Four employees of a Taco Bell were murdered during a robbery. Taylor responded with a contingent of TBI agents that would number 14 before the case was solved. A single fingerprint was found on the inside of the push up ceiling where the killer had stored his weapons.

All four of the victims had been killed execution style by a single 9 mm pistol shot to the head. A shotgun slug was found as well. An FBI profiler confirmed Taylor's conclusion that one gunman was responsible for all of the murders.

A list of 12 to 15 suspects was developed from current and former employees. A Ft. Campbell soldier who worked part-time at the restaurant emerged as the prime suspect. Investigators found that the soldier had bought a 9 mm handgun and had asked a friend if a shotgun would blow the lock off a safe. It was reported that he had fired the 9 mm through the floor of his duplex. Slugs retrieved from under the floor matched bullets from the four victims.

While the killer was being sought for questioning he slit his wrists and was placed in the army hospital's mental ward. After Taylor met with the commanding general of the base, the suspect was released to state authorities. Within 72 hours of committing the Taco Bell murders the killer was in custody.

In 1994 the TBI became one of the few law enforcement agencies in the country accredited by both the Commission on Accreditation of Law Enforcement Agencies (CALEA) and the American Society of Crime Laboratory Directors (ASCLD). The Bureau was one of only three state criminal investigative agencies in the nation accredited by the CALEA when the certificate was granted on November 19. Laboratory facilities of the Forensic Services Division were accredited by ASCLD in December.

SAC Jim Taylor was assigned responsibility for the Governor's Task Force on Marijuana Eradication in 1994. The eleven-year-old program ranked number 16 in the country. The task force was organized into three teams, Middle Tennessee, West Tennessee and East Tennessee. Two helicopters were assigned to each team and the National Guard furnished a number of "ground-pounders" to assist in cutting and destroying the dope.

"Operation No-Grow" was carried out in 1995 over a large number of counties in Tennessee and Kentucky. The task force worked like a military operation and was one of the largest and most successful operations in marijuana eradication. During the five years from 1993 to 1997 the task force destroyed 3,232,161 marijuana plants in 11,230 plots found in every county throughout the state. Arrests numbered 4,696 and seizures were valued at $6,431,174. Agents found 166 booby traps in the course of their work. This level of enforcement resulted in Tennessee leading the nation in marijuana eradication.

The Appalachia High-Intensity Drug Trafficking Area (HIDTA) was established in April 1998 by the

The Operating Committee of the Governors Task Force on Marijuana Eradication in 1995 reviewed plans for "Operation No Grow." From left to right were TBI ASAC Richard Wright; Lieutenant Bob Eckerman, representative of the Tennessee Highway Patrol; Jimmy Higdon, Chief of Alcoholic Beverage Commission and vice chairman of operating committee; TBI SAC Jim Taylor, coordinator of task force and chairman of operating committee; and Colonel Mike Waggoner, representative of the Tennessee National Guard.

U.S. Office of National Drug Control Policy. Areas within Tennessee, Kentucky and West Virginia were designated as particularly vulnerable to certain types of illegal drug activity. The federally funded program coordinated drug control efforts by local, state and federal law enforcement. HIDTA enhanced the TBI's ability to fight marijuana and other illegal drugs.

Special Agent Alvin Daniel died on February 21, 1995, while still a member of the Bureau. Daniel was well respected and worked a series of high-profile murder cases during his last years. He was the lead agent in the 1991 slaying of a Benton County mussel shell buyer and his fiancee, as well as the July 1993 dismemberment murder of a 19-year-old Good Samaritan in Carroll County. He had worked mostly Obion, Benton, Carroll and Henry counties. Director

Wallace commented, "He was one of the finest criminal investigator in the state of Tennessee."

The danger faced by undercover narcotics agents was realized in January 1999 when the TBI came close to losing its first agent in the line of duty. Maxey Gilleland was working a crack cocaine case when a drug buy went bad and he faced four drug dealers intent on robbing him. While Gilleland wrestled the gun from the first culprit, a second gunman shot him in the back of the head. The shooter stood over him and fired a second bullet into his head. The agent was left on the floor to die.

Agent Gilleland survived the assault, although he lost the sight in one eye and underwent twelve reconstructive surgeries in twelve months. A year later, in January 2000, Gilleland returned to work at the

Bureau in a civilian capacity as executive aide to the director. After six months he qualified to go back to the field. Maxey Gilleland served again in the narcotics unit for three months before taking retirement.

An special agent joined the Bureau on January 2, 1998, who had wanted to be a TBI agent since the age of six. For Marjorie J. Quin it was not a childhood fancy. She was the grand daughter of former Director Bud Hopton and grew up with stories of the FBI and TBI. Quin spent six years with the Cobb County Police Department in Georgia before joining the TBI. After working in the Narcotics Division, she was chosen for the new Technical Services unit formed in 2005 by Director Gwen.

The TBI Intelligence Division was reactivated in 1988 using funds from a federal grant designated for investigation of subversive groups and street gangs. The unit established sections in the geographic divisions of the TBI and evaluated intelligence gathered by other agencies. Special Agent Larry O'Rear of the Cookeville office was one of those assigned to the division. The unit expanded its activity to fugitive location, the sex offender registry and assisting the Secret Service with security for presidential and vice presidential visits. Security duty was frequent when Al Gore Sr. was ill in the late nineties, the vice president visited his father every couple of weeks.

Director Larry Wallace's six-year term ended in 1998. His name along with others was presented to Governor Don Sundquist and Wallace was reappointed to a second six-year term on June 2, 1998. Wallace reestablished the Narcotics Division as a separate unit from the Criminal Investigation Division. Other adjustments were necessary

when the TBI was charged with implementing the new federal law requiring instant check for firearms purchases. This added significantly to the existing background checks done on childcare providers, security guards and others done by the Bureau.

David Bolme, Director of the Information Systems Division, together with Tim Beck and David Jennings developed the Tennessee Instant Check System (TICS). Staff was expanded to implement the system and Doug Woodlee transferred from the Records and Identification Unit to manage TICS.

The system began operation on November 1, 1998. By March 2004, 1,185,708 transactions were processed involving 1,293,515 firearms. The process identified over 1000 wanted individuals and more than 1200 stolen firearms were recovered. The system showed that about 6% of people wanting to purchase handguns had a criminal history.

The TBI moved into a new consolidated headquarters building in Nashville in July 2000 and the grand opening of a consolidated facility in Memphis was held in December 2001. These facilities included new criminal investigation technologies and dynamic communications capabilities with agencies nationwide. The Bureau created an internal uniformed unit to provide security for the facility. Personnel of the unit were issued TBI badges designated with the rank Officer.

The Drug Investigation Division spent much of its resources in the early years of the new millennium dealing with the exploding use and manufacture of methamphetamine. Meth replaced crack cocaine as the fastest growing drug problem. The makeshift labs that turned a variety of household products into meth posed an additional danger to agents. Tennessee became the state with the second largest number of meth labs destroyed in 2005.

Larry Wallace retired as director of the TBI on November 30, 2003, at age 58. During his tenure the number of agents doubled and laboratory and office facilities dramatically improved. By state law, Deputy Director David Jennings, a 50-year-old native of Kingsport and head of the Criminal Investigation Division, became acting director.

Mark Gwyn was appointed to a six year term as director of the Bureau in June 2004 by Governor Bredesen. At the time of his appointment the 41-year-old, 16-year-TBI-veteran was serving as assistant director in charge of the Forensic Services Division. Gwyn was a native of McMinnville and held a Bachelor of Science degree from Middle Tennessee State University. He also completed the FBI National

TBI Director Larry Wallace, left, served as head of the agency from 1992 until his retirement in 2003. Director Mark Gwyn, right, began a six year term in June 2004.

Academy and the Tennessee Government Executive Institute.

Director Gwyn began his law enforcement career in 1985 as a patrolman for the McMinnville Police Department. He was appointed a TBI Special Agent in 1988 assigned to headquarters. In 1992 he was assigned to the field territory covering the 31st Judicial District of Warren and Van Buren Counties. He was promoted to executive officer of the TBI in 1996 and served in that capacity until appointment as assistant director in 2001.

TBI continued to focus on public corruption. The Bureau participated with the Memphis Field Office of the FBI in an undercover sting operation code named "Tennessee Waltz." Indictments were handed down in May 2005 charging six members of the Tennessee state legislature and other public officials with corruption. They were primarily charged with taking bribes to influence state contracts.

Recognizing the growing impact of computer crime, Director Gwyn created Technical Services as a unit to specialize in all types of technology investigation. The unit began with four of five agents involved in electronic surveillance, Internet investigations, evidence recovery, computer forensics, and other related issues.

The investigative strength of the Bureau was enhanced on October 6, 2005, when the Criminal Investigation Division of the Department of Safety was transferred to the TBI. The move consolidated all criminal investigation under the TBI and added personnel positions to the Bureau.

Today the 400-plus-member Bureau provides up-to-date investigative, forensic science and crime information services and support to the criminal justice system throughout the state. The TBI is organized in five divisions. The Criminal Investigation Division investigates crime and criminal activity and responds to emergency situations. The Drug Investigation Division enforces Tennessee's drug control laws.

The Forensic Services Division analyzes biological, chemical and physical evidence in laboratory facilities in Nashville, Knoxville and Memphis. The Information Systems Division processes, maintains and accesses a number of criminal databases and reports statewide crime statistics. The Administrative Services Division provides administrative and technical support to all areas of the Bureau. Regional offices of the TBI are maintained in Chattanooga, Knoxville, Jackson, Johnson City, Memphis and Nashville.

Technology and training have provided significant advances in criminal investigation and identification since the creation of the Tennessee Bureau of Criminal Investigation. Today's TBI has kept pace with the new capabilities available to criminal investigation.

Computer imaging and searching using AFIS technology has replaced the manual system of ink fingerprints on card stock. The need for speed is understood by comparing the quantity of data handled by the Bureau today. In May 1952 fewer than 4000 sets of fingerprints existed statewide. Today the number received each year is close to 400,000.

Technology has changed crime scene investigation. Collecting fingerprints by spreading black powder has given way to the Crime Scope Imager. Laser scanning, digital imaging, DNA analysis and many other technologies have provided valuable new tools to the investigator.

The Tennessee Bureau of Investigation has established itself as one of the most effective criminal investigation agencies in the nation. Its rich history speaks to the consistent and professional manner in which agents of the Bureau fight criminal activity in drug infested alleys and halls of power across the state.

Other State Law Enforcement

Correctional officers were the first state law enforcement personnel in Tennessee. The origin of the department goes back to the founding of the first State Penitentiary House built just outside of Nashville in 1831.

Punishment for crime prior to the state prison consisted of standing in the public pillory, 39 lashes administered at the court square whipping post or other corporal punishment, which included branding and cropping off ears. Murder typically resulted in a public hanging. All punishment in the early years of the state was administered publicly by county sheriffs.

As Tennessee became more settled, the propriety of public beatings and mutilations came more and more in question. Also, the public grew more skeptical that corporal punishment was curbing crime. For the hardened criminal, the pain of a lashing was short lived and the felon quickly returned to his criminal activity. Petitions were sent to the governor and editorials appeared in newspapers across the state calling for a penitentiary to be built so that criminals could be confined.

An act "to provide for building a public jail and penitentiary house in this State" passed the state legislature in 1829. The first guards were hired and the first thirteen prisoners were put into the Tennessee State Penitentiary House in 1831. The facility was located just south of 7th Avenue and Broadway in Nashville. The prison contained two hundred cells, a warden's dwelling, a storehouse, a hospital and other structures. It housed both men and women.

With the opening of the state prison new felony penalties were established. Public hanging continued to be the punishment for first degree murder and it continued to be carried out by the sheriff in the county where the crime was committed. Second degree murder was punished by confinement in the State Penitentiary House for a period of 10 to 21 years, vol-

Front entrance to the Tennessee State Penitentiary House, the state's first prison opened in 1831. Walls were 4' thick and 33' high.

untary manslaughter from 2 to 10 years and involuntary manslaughter from 1 to 5 years. Rape, carnal knowledge of a female child under ten years of age and other sex crimes could be punished by prison terms up to 21 years.

The early nineteenth century historical context of the prison's opening affected some punishments. Arson and other crimes involving the setting of fires carried prison terms up to 21 years because of the devastating effects of fire in towns built almost exclusively of wood. Especially since towns had very little fire fighting equipment.

No standard currency existed for the nation at the time and paper money was produced by many individual banks. Prison terms for over twenty offences related to counterfeiting and passing fictitious money were included in the new code, many carrying a term of up to 15 years in prison.

Prison terms were also set for cutting or disabling the tongue; malicious biting or cutting off the nose, ear, lip, where the person would be maimed or disfigured; fighting a duel, or challenging to fight, or accepting a challenge; posting as a coward for refusing to fight; and dealing at Faro, thimble, and "grand mothers' tricks."

The first prisoner incarcerated in the Tennessee's new penitentiary was a 21-year-old tailor from Madison County who was convicted of malicious stabbing and assault and battery. He entered the prison on January 21, 1831, and served two years. The walls were four feet thick and 33 feet high. Cells were 7.5 feet in length and the 78 prisoners that quickly populated the facility were not allowed to speak to one another or have contact with the "outside" world.

In the 1850s guards traveled to the center of the city to oversee inmates who were employed to build

Early prisoner work detail. Inmates are dressed in traditional prison stripes. (Tennessee Department of Corrections photo.)

Brushy Mountain Prison in 1908.

Tennessee's State Capitol. About 3:00 a.m. on March 29, 1855, one of the prisoners set a fire in one of the prison shops. The fire destroyed a major part of the penitentiary. Prisoners were turned out of their cells to help fight the fire. Some inmates were even taken outside the walls to work the fire engine. No prisoner escaped, but one convict suffocated to death. A new complex was built and the Tennessee State Penitentiary moved to Church Street in 1858.

When Union Troops occupied Nashville in 1863, the penitentiary was taken over and used as a military prison, and soldiers were used as guards. State prisoners were moved to Brushy Mountain and many of the existing guards made the transition as well.

After the war a convict lease system was adopted to allow state prisoners to work for private employers. Inmates were leased to the Tennessee Coal, Iron and Railroad Company in 1870 and guards traveled to the worksite along with the prisoners. The legislature approved state inmates working coal mines and farm lands owned by the state at Brushy Mountain in 1873.

S. A. Walden, a guard at a stockade near Tracy City that housed convicts being leased to mine coal, was shot and killed on the night of April 19, 1893, by a mob of free miners. The convict leasing system was abolished in 1893, but the Brushy Mountain facility continued to be productive using convict labor.

A number of new facilities were constructed during the 1890s. A separate wing was built for female inmates inside the Nashville penitentiary. The Brushy Mountain Prison was built at Petros in Morgan County in 1895. The Tennessee State Penitentiary was moved to new location in Cockrill Bend in 1898 and in 1900 a new building for female inmates opened within the walls of prison. The expansion of facilities resulted in an increased number of guards and better working conditions for existing guards.

Correctional Officer Tommy Simpson with blood hound and Warden Willard Norvell, warden of Fort Pillow State Penal Farm from 1967 to 1973.

At the turn of the century a number of operational changes were made within the prison system. One method that had been used to punish inmates was to suspend them by their thumbs. The practice was outlawed by the legislature in 1904.

State incarceration began for juvenile offenders committing serious crimes. In 1908 one 10-year old boy and one 11-year old boy were committed to the state prison, each to serve 2-3 years. The increasing in such cases led to the opening of the Tennessee Reformatory for Boys in Jordonia outside Nashville in 1911 and the founding of the State Reformatory for Girls in Tullahoma in 1915.

Escapes were always a concern for the prison guard staff. Seventeen prisoners blew out the end of one wing of the prison in 1902. One inmate was killed; two escaped and were never recaptured. A group of prisoners commandeered a switch engine in 1907 and drove it through a prison gate. Seventeen prisoners, including four murderers, escaped in 1926 by sawing out a window. Inmates staged a mass escape in 1938.

Responsibility for the execution of prisoners was transferred from county sheriffs to the state prison system in 1909. The method of execution the death

penalty was changed from hanging to electrocution in 1913 and the first man was electrocuted in 1916. Prisoner execution created new duties for the guard staff that required special capabilities.

Guards responsible for prisoners on death-row and those who participated in the execution process were busy in the first half of the twentieth century. Well over a hundred electrocutions were carried out, 47 during the 1930s alone. Multiple executions were often carried out on the same day, the most was four on March 1, 1922.

Death-row duty was dangerous. Guard J. L. Simms was killed in the line of duty at the Tennessee State Penitentiary on Friday, March 12, 1937, by a death-row inmate in an escape attempt. Simms and another guard were delivering food to death-row inmates. Cell doors were secured by a chain and would only open 12 inches. A prisoner who was to be executed the following week for a double murder asked Guard Simms to place a stool inside the cell. When Simms removed the chain and bent down to put the stool in the cell, the inmate stabbed him in the neck with a 3-inch knife.

The inmate ran out of the cell and knocked down the other guard. The guard got up and shot the murderer twice in the head and killed him. Guard J. L. Simms was 50 years old and had been a prison guard for three years. Before that, he was a patrolman with the Nashville Police Department.

Only one prisoner has been executed in Tennessee on a federal warrant. He killed IRS Alcohol Tax Unit Agent William Milton Pugh during a moonshine arrest and was electrocuted on August 14, 1943.

The state opened a medium security farming facility in West Tennessee in 1938 to ease overcrowding in the Nashville penitentiary and Brushy Mountain. Fort Pillow State Penal Farm was founded near Henning in Lauderdale County to house first time offenders. Otis Preston Caldwell was the first warden at the facility and served for 10 years. Caldwell joined the Memphis police in 1925 and held the rank of inspector when he left the force. The name of the facility was later changed to the Cold Creek Correctional Facility. The Shelby County Penal Farm had been opened in 1928 as a minimum security facility.

The name of the state department responsible for prisons was changed in 1955. The Department of Institutions became the Department of Correction. The title Guard was changed to Correctional Officer. Over the next few decades, the level of violence within prisons was reduced. The use of the strap for disciplining prisoners was outlawed. Segregation of black

Fort Pillow State Penal Farm riot control training class in December 1972. Participants sitting in the front row from left to right were Joel Sutton, Monroe Johnson and Samuel Nason. Standing were J. O. Worlds, Roy Blankenship, Tommy Pipkin, Pete Turnage, Bud Harrison, Lex Sanders, unidentified, Kenny Hayes, Hugh Richards and Billy Howell.

and white prisoners ended. Inmates were provided opportunities for training and education.

Also beginning in the 1960s and 1970s technology and training improved the ability of correctional staff to monitor and control prison inmates. Women were hired to work inside the prisons as correctional officers. However, growing populations in the system and more violent offenders created an increasingly dangerous environment for correctional officers.

The 1970s and 1980s were tumultuous for the Department of Correction, and made the working environment for corrections officers by difficult and dangerous. An inmate revolt over living conditions, known as the "Pork Chop" Riot, broke out at the Tennessee State Penitentiary in 1975. Other law enforcement agencies were called in to assist correctional personnel in putting down the riot.

In 1976 a "sit-down" strike by inmates at Brushy Mountain required a temporary lock-down at the prison. A number of less extensive incidents occurred, some involving hostage taking.

Warden Michael Dutton was in charge of the Tennessee State Penitentiary in the summer of 1985 when overcrowding provoked violence and rioting at the facility. Warden Dutton was familiar with inmate uprisings. He had joined the penitentiary staff in 1973 and experienced the rioting two years earlier.

About 7:00 a.m. on July 3, 1985, prisoners setoff a riot that resulted in major property destruction and the taking of several hostages. Warden Dutton initiated negotiations with inmates. The Department of Corrections was able to resolve the confrontation and by 6:00 or 7:00 that evening, Warden Dutton and his staff persuaded prisoners to return to their cells.

The Tennessee Correction Academy opened in Tullahoma in 1984. The facility built as the State Reformatory for Girls was converted to house the academy. The academy served as the Department's primary training and staff development center.

Correctional Officer Ronald W. Moore was attacked and killed at the Turney Center Industrial

Prison and Farm on August 29, 1981. An inmate stabbed Officer Moore 17 times with a "shank."

Two Turney Correction Center supervisors were killed in a helicopter crash on July 2, 1984, as they searched for three escapees. Associate Warden James F. McPeters and Associate Warden Donald G. Gammons were in a military helicopter from Ft. Rucker, Alabama, when the aircraft struck a power line killing all on board.

Superintendent Michael Dutton was named head of the Correction Academy in late 1995. Dutton, in addition to his service as warden of the Tennessee State Penitentiary, also served the Department as deputy commissioner, warden of Riverbend Maximum Security Institution and Tennessee State Penitentiary, transition director for New Prison Construction and other positions. Dutton managed the academy for more than a decade.

The method of execution in Tennessee was changed to lethal injection on January 1, 1999, and "Old Sparky," the state's electric chair, was retired. The same year, the position of Security Threat Group Coordinator was created in an effort to stem gang activity in the state prison system.

Securing desperate prisoners of the state continued to be a dangerous occupation. Correctional Officer Frederick Gayle Hyatt was strangled and beaten to death when five inmates attempted an escape from the Middle Tennessee Correctional Complex on November 8, 2003. His body was found in the common area about 11:50 p.m. The captive felons stran-

Tennessee State Penitentiary Guard J. L. Simms, left, was killed on Friday, March 12, 1937, when a death-row inmate stabbed him in the neck with a 3-inch knife during an escape attempt. Correctional Officer Wayne "Cotton'" Morgan, right, was killed by three shotgun blasts fired by the wife of a Brushy Mountain inmate outside the Roane County Courthouse in Kingston on August 9, 2005, when she helped the convict escape after a court appearance.

gled Officer Hyatt with a cord from a laundry bag and beat him with his flashlight and a sock filled with canned food. Their escape attempt failed. Fifty-nine-year-old Fred Hyatt was an 11 year correction veteran.

Correctional Officer Wayne "Cotton'" Morgan and other correctional officers escorted two inmates of the Brushy Mountain Correctional Complex to the Roane County Courthouse in Kingston on Tuesday, August 9, 2005, to a court appearance. The wife of one of the prisoners pulled up in an SUV and opened fire with a shotgun, striking Officer Morgan three times. He died of his wounds a short time later.

Today, well trained officers of the Tennessee Department of Correction guard the most dangerous element of society in 15 penal institutions across the state. Those original guards of the early nineteenth century would be amazed by the electronic locks and cameras of today's technology. But the duty now as then requires a special dedication and commitment. These men and women protecting the citizens of Tennessee by assuring that those who have been sent to prison remain behind bars.

Revenue agents of the State of Tennessee were appointed and charged with enforcement of tax laws soon after the state began collecting taxes as a source of state revenue. Investigations and raids on illegal liquor operations were the most dangerous duty for revenue agents.

Three separate tax-collecting agencies existed when state government was reorganized in 1923. They

Correctional Officer received inmate control training at the Tennessee Correction Academy in Tullahoma. The Academy continues to provide the most current training in order to insure the safety of correction personnel and inmates.

were combined into the Department of Finance and Taxation. When the Highway Patrol was created in 1929, it was made a part of the Department of Finance and Taxation. Part of the Patrol's activity was enforcement of the tax laws. Other tax inspectors also carried Highway Patrol badges.

Enforcing the tobacco tax law was a significant duty of inspectors. Agents looked for tobacco being sold without state tobacco tax stamps or with counterfeit stamps. West Tennessee finance department enforcement Chief D. R. Henley, Field Supervisor R. Emmett Swann and Inspectors Richard Jack Bowers, George W. Williams and T. C. Ozment were active in the 1930s and 1940s. They made several arrests in a case of selling counterfeit tobacco stamps in Paris, Tennessee, in 1935. The crime carried a penalty of one to ten years in the state penitentiary.

Inspectors also noted other tax violations during their inspections, such as an unlicensed jukebox. Business owners who neglected to pay privilege tax on music machines were fined. Tax inspectors continued to work with Highway Patrol officers on raids and other tax related activity even after the Patrol was no longer a part of the Department of Finance.

The General Assembly gave the Department of Finance and Taxation broader powers to control liquor in the state in 1949 and authorized 15 additional special agents. One of those agents was killed in the line of duty on January 28, 1951, as the result of what appeared to be a misunderstanding.

Special Investigator Donald Elzie Gresham of the Alcohol Tax Division was shot to death by a taxi driver around 6:00 p.m. at the Gipsy Tea Room, a nightclub on Highway 70 just east of Jackson. Gresham was investigating a liquor violation in Madison County and had just met with an informant. His killer was not a subject of his investigation.

Gresham was seated at the bar when his pistol slipped out of its holster and fell to the floor. A taxi driver picked up the weapon and handed it back to Gresham. In the exchange the pistol fired and a bullet struck the cabbie in his right wrist. The cab driver stepped back and yelled, "You shot me!" With that he pulled his own gun and fired into the agent three times, striking him in the chest and stomach. Thirty-six-year-old Gresham was rushed to the hospital but died ten minutes after arriving.

The Department of Finance and Taxation was renamed the Department of Revenue in 1959. Revenue Commissioner G. Hilton Butler formed a squad of undercover agents in November 1961 to police the liquor industry. The unit policed legal

Special Investigator Donald Elzie Gresham, left, of the Alcohol Tax Division of the Department of Finance and Taxation was shot to death on January 28, 1951. His killing was the result of a misunderstanding unrelated to his investigative work. Department of Finance and Taxation Inspector Richard Jack Bowers, right, enforced tax laws in West Tennessee in the 1930s and 1940s, and later served as chief of police for Jackson.

liquor outlets for violations of the Fair Trade Liquor Law and sales of whiskey for resale.

The Alcoholic Beverage Commission was created in 1963 and given the legal responsibility to license, regulate and inspect all wholesale and retail liquor dealers in Tennessee. Inspectors also monitored establishments with on-premise consumption, issues employee permits and enforces all state liquor laws and regulations including the control of illegal manufacture, transportation and sale of alcoholic beverages. Suppressing marijuana cultivation was also assigned to the commission.

Today, the Alcoholic Beverage Commission continues to enforce laws related to the alcoholic beverages. Two groups in the Department of Revenue enforces other tax laws. Agents of the Tax Enforcement Division manages and tracks delinquent taxpayer accounts for collection and agents of the Special Investigations Division detects, investigates and seeks prosecution of tax-related fraud.

Wildlife conservation and related law enforcement in the state was assigned to Tennessee Wildlife Resources Agency in 1974. The history of wildlife protection by Tennessee began in 1870 with an act to protect fisheries. The exploitation of game and market hunting of quail were forbidden in most counties in the late 1880s.

The general assembly declared all game animals and fish the property of the state in 1903 and named Joseph Acklen the first state game warden. Two years later the Game, Fish and Forestry Department was established and the first hunting license fees were set in 1907, although payment was optional. The agency was reorganized in 1915 and the Department of Game and Fish created.

The number of game wardens grew and their duty expanded with new legislation related to wildlife conservation. The enforcement of game and fish laws often required a firm hand with independent minded outdoorsmen who had traditionally hunted and fished without interference. Confrontations were usually with armed men in wilderness areas. Assaults on Tennessee game wardens became a frequent occurrence.

The Department of Conservation was created in 1937 and Game and Fish became a part of the new department until the Tennessee Game and Fish Commission was established in 1949.

This independent commission resulted from the efforts of the Tennessee Federation of Sportsmen, later named the Tennessee Conservation League. The group wanted Game and Fish to be free of political control and to end the practice of hiring game wardens based on patronage.

The Tennessee Wildlife Resources Agency (TWRA), with oversight by the Tennessee Wildlife Resources Commission, was created in April 1974. The agency set up a central office in Nashville and four regional offices, Jackson, Nashville, Crossville and Talbott.

Today, TWRA has over 500 law enforcement professionals trained in wildlife management. They enforce hunting, fishing and boating laws and manage wildlife areas. TWRA officers complete a two-week training course at the Tennessee Law Enforcement Academy. The school is designed to meet the special needs of TWRA officers. Firearms and self-defense training is vital because a higher percentage of wildlife officers are assaulted than any type of law enforcement professionals.

Other Tennessee state departments, commissions and agencies have law enforcement functions. The Department of Commerce and Insurance has responsibility for oversight of businesses that are licensed by the state including private investigation and security companies.

The Fire Marshal's Office of the commerce department investigates suspicious fires. Fire Marshal investigators looked into many arsons intended to defraud insurance companies. They also investigated fires set to destroy evidence and cover-up other crimes.

In March 1992 a cabin in Hardeman County near Boliver was found burned to the ground and bodies were discovered in the debris. Hardeman County Sheriff Delphus Hicks called in the Fire Marshal's Office and the TBI to assist in the investigation. The Fire Marshal's Office Bomb and Arson Section assigned Special Agents David Randel "Randy" Lipford, James Robertson and Everett Cook to process evidence, which required sifting through ashes and other residue of the cabin. They confirmed six bodies and evidence of gambling, robbery and arson. One of the victims was the son-in-law of the State Fire Marshal Robert Frost.

Investigations by the various law enforcement agencies revealed that the cabin had been used as a clubhouse for high-stakes gambling. On the night of March 30 two participants in a poker game robbed the other six and burned the cabin using gun powder as an accelerant. One of the gamblers was killed by a shotgun blast to the head and the others died in the fire. It was the largest mass murder in Tennessee in decades.

On another assignment Special Agent Randy Lipford of the Fire Marshal's Office worked with FBI Special Agent Gary Boutwell. They jointly investigated the fires that destroyed African-American churches

Investigators from left to right Assistant U.S. Attorney Steve Parker, TBI Special Agent John Simmons and Special Agent Randy Lipford of Bomb and Arson Section of the Fire Marshal's Office examine clothing and other evidence of the Hardeman County mass murder retrieved from a creek by THP divers. The investigators had sifted through ashes and debris of the cabin where the killings were committed.

in Tennessee during the spate of church burnings across the region in the 1990s.

District Attorneys General have employed investigators for decades. In 1988 a number of districts formed judicial tasks forces to battle drugs and drug related crimes. The formation of the task forces resulted from Governor Ned McWherter's Drug Free Tennessee campaign. The judicial district task forces bring together the resources of multiple local, state and sometimes federal law enforcement agencies.

The most recent state agency created with law enforcement responsibilities is the Office of Homeland Security. It also depended of the resources of law enforcement and other agencies across the state. One program of the Office of Homeland Security, the Citizens Corps, consists of a broad network of volunteers to insure preparedness at all levels. The office was established on April 3, 2003, and given the mission to develop and coordinate the implementation of a comprehensive strategy to secure the state of Tennessee from terrorist threats and attacks.

Retired Marine Corps Major General Jerry D. Humble served as the first director of the office. In May 2005 FBI veteran David B. Mitchell was named to head the office. Mitchell began his law enforcement career with the Murfreesboro Police Department and more recently supervised the Domestic Terrorism Unit at FBI headquarters in Washington.

Metropolitan Nashville Police Department

P ioneers settled along the banks of the Cumberland River in the western territory of North Carolina in the eighteenth century. The most notable band of adventurers was led by General James Robertson. They left from the Watauga settlements in East Tennessee and established Fort Nashborough in the spring of 1779.

Government came to Fort Nashborough and its surrounding settlement in 1780 when General Robertson led the community to enter into "Articles of Agreement" or "Compact of Government." Concern for law and order was basic to the compact, which included a system of General Arbitrators. These thirteen individuals were charged to guarantee rights and resolve disputes among the settlers.

Three years later the state government of North Carolina established the Inferior Court of Pleas and Quarter Sessions as a part of the newly designated Davidson County. This legislation provided for the building of a courthouse and a jailhouse. The seven commissioners of the new county were empowered to call upon residents of the community to enforce its laws.

The following year, 1784, Nashville was incorporated as a town by the North Carolina legislature and was given the authority to build "a court house, prison and stocks." The town was not given authority to establish a police or to create ordinances. The

Davidson County sheriff provided law enforcement for the town.

The first reference to the town Square mentioned a stone courthouse and a whipping post along with a stone jail house. Punishment for crime in the early years of Nashville was public and corporal, much as in other areas of the country. Murderers were hanged. The penalty for a thief who stole a horse or other property valued at $30 or more was to have his ears clipped or cut off. For lesser crimes the offender had to stand in the pillory, stocks set on the top of a post; or was taken to the whipping post, his shirt removed and given up to thirty-nine lashes with a cowhide whip. The sentence of the court for one horse thief in 1799 was typical.

> The said Andrew Pierce shall stand in the public pillory for one hour and shall be publicly whipped on his bare back with 39 lashes well laid on, and at the same time shall have both his ears cut off, and shall be branded on the right cheek with the letter H and on the left cheek with the letter T.

Tennessee entered the union in 1796 as the 16th state. The Tennessee legislature passed an act to incorporate Nashville on September 11, 1806. The act gave town officials the authority to establish night watches or patrols and to appoint a "high constable." They

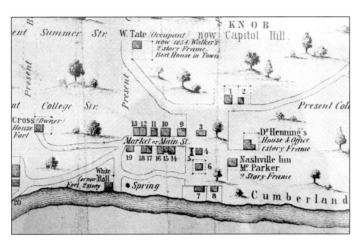

Nashville in 1804. Number 3 is the Market, 4 the Court House, 5 the stocks and 6 the jail with a picket fence around it.

were also authorized to pass laws and ordinances to regulate health and safety, to license business activity, to prevent and remove nuisances, to restrain and prohibit gaming and to regulate and restrain tippling houses.

A constable served as the law enforcement officer of early towns in Tennessee. In most cases his title was Town Constable and this title was used in later acts of incorporation of Nashville. But the title High Constable, used in the 1806 Act, continued to be applied popularly to Nashville's chief lawman until 1850. The high constable was responsible for civil and criminal law enforcement in the town. High Constable John Deatheredge was first appointed to the office and served from 1806 to 1808.

The high constable was appointed to one year terms by the mayor and aldermen of Nashville. The office was a part-time position and the high constable was paid from fees and fines generated from performing his duty. High Constable David Moore served from 1808 to 1814. As high constable he also held the position of clerk of the market house.

The town also established a night watch. The citizen police force served part-time and patrolled the town at night. They were appointed as needed and reported to the mayor. Insight into the activities of the night watch was given in the book, *Old Days in Nashville*.

Old Mr. Cruff, who had a vineyard just across the river, was the watchman of the town. After nine o'clock at night he used to walk up and down the streets and cry out the hours. If it was a rainy night, he would say: "Past eleven o'clock, and t'undering and a lightening, and a tam [damned] rainy night."

Law enforcement during daylight hours was provided by the high constable, the sheriff, other county law officers and the citizens at large. The turnover of the high constable was frequent during the early decades of the town. James Condon served as high constable 1814-16, Edmond Cooper 1816-18, R. Garrett 1818-20, Allan McDean 1820-21 and J. Grizzard 1821-24.

The need for a law enforcement presence to prevent the disturbance of weekend church services led to the appointment of the city's first patrolman in 1823 for the Sunday patrol. Wooldridge, in his history of the town, recorded that "On October 7, John Job was employed to patrol the town on Sundays, and was required to keep the streets clear of all assemblages of negroes, and to prevent all noisy and riotous conduct."

The process for selecting the high constable changed in 1826. An act dividing Nashville into six wards with two alderman to be elected for each and provided that the town constable be elected by the voters of the town. Town constables or high constables elected in the late 1820s and 1830s were C. Brooks who served from 1824 to 1828, William L. Willis 1828-29, George S. Gross 1829-32, Jefferson Cartwright 1832-33 and E. B. Bigley 1833-40. Bigley had the longest tenure in the position of anyone to this date and after a one year term by M. E. DeGrave in 1840-41, Bigley served again 1841-44.

By 1837 there was a night watch in each ward and a captain of the watch. The work of the watch was mostly hauling the drunk and disorderly to the recorder's office. From time to time the watch was overwhelmed. On one occasion "An eggnog party at the University of Nashville wound up with a fight with the night watch on the public square; the mayor and a mounted company were called on when the fight spread to the wharf, where students took on the boatmen." Sporadic clean-up campaigns ordered by the mayor and aldermen sent the constable to shut down faro dens and bawdy houses.

James Morgan was elected high constable in 1844 and served until 1846. He was followed by R. A. Cole 1846-47 and Spencer Chandler 1847-54. By the middle of the nineteenth century the population of Nashville had grown to over 10,000 and the city fathers upgraded aspects of city services. Ordinances adopted on February 26, 1850, changed the title of Nashville's chief law officer from Town Constable to City Marshal. City Marshal Spencer Chandler was the first Nashville lawman to serve under the title.

The 1850 ordinances also revised the structure of the night watch. The law provided that the Board of

Mayor and Aldermen elect a night watch every six months and choose one as captain of the watch.

Section 1. That at the first regular meeting of the Board, in the months of January and July of each year, there shall be elected a Night Watch, a suitable number of discreet and trusty persons, citizens of said city, who shall continue in office for the space of six months, or until their successors are elected and qualified—unless sooner removed—and shall receive from time to time such compensation from their services as the Board shall determine upon by resolution, or otherwise; the Board shall, at the same time, elect one of said number, who shall be styled and known as captain of said watch.

Night watchmen gave bond and security to serve and took an oath, "I, A. B., do swear that I will faithfully and impartially do my duty as watch in the city of Nashville, agreeably to the laws of this corporation and to the best of my skill and ability. So help me God."

The night watch reported to the mayor, who had the power to add watchmen if he believed "the safety of the city requires an increase." The size of the force varied. During one six-month term records indicated a total of forty-three men served including night watchmen, day policemen (created in 1851) and the city marshal.

The captain of the watch patrolled the public square. He also divided the city into patrol districts and assigned watchmen. Besides supervising watchmen, he was to report those arrested during the night to the city marshal the following morning.

The night watch was charged with patrolling the streets of the city throughout the evening until daylight. Their duty was to raise an alarm in case of fire, to arrest lawbreakers and take them to the captain of the watch and on his instruction to escort those arrested to jail. The job of the night watch was made easier on February 13, 1851, when the first street lamp was lighted at Second Avenue and the Public Square. Street lights were installed after the Nashville Gas Light Company was founded the previous year.

The Board established the day police in April 1851. The duty of these policemen was the same as the night watchmen except that day policemen could make arrests and take the prisoners directly to court. Fewer day police were appointed than night watchmen. The night watch was soon being called the night police and in 1852 night watchmen were given the

Ephrim Foster Corbitt, born December 6, 1832, died May 25, 1922, was appointed to the police department in 1866. Corbitt served almost 50 years on the police force as a patrolman and sanitary officer with the city health department. He was a steamboat pilot before joining the police.

direct power of arrest "as Police Officers of the city." Night watchmen worked from sundown until dawn. Day policemen served from sunrise to sunset.

City Marshal J. L. Ryan served from 1854 to 1857. A number of special police were authorized in 1855 and 1856. The Spring Keeper, who watched over the city water works, was also given police powers as were the state capitol watchmen and the watchman at the depot of the Tennessee and Alabama Railroad. Additional duties were given to the regular police. The marshal and his deputies were given the responsibility in 1856 for health and sanitation enforcement and acted as health inspectors.

City Marshal W. Matt Brown served from 1857 until April 1862. During his tenure a number of important issues related to the police of Nashville were addressed. Nashville amended the day police ordinance in November 1858 to state that the city council "elect three Deputy Marshals to act, in conjunction with and under the order of the City Marshal, as Day

Police." The law specified that the deputy marshals each be paid a salary of $500 per year. The act also defined the insignia to be worn.

> Section 4. That the Chief Marshal and each Deputy shall, at all times while on duty, (unless on secret service,) wear upon the outside of the left lapel of his coat a crescent of silver or white metal, with the grade of his office thereon engraved, which shall be furnished at the expense of the city, and known as the badge of his office, and which is to be handed over to the Mayor upon such Marshal or Deputy going out of office.

Secret Service was the term applied to the work of detectives in plain clothes. Private detective agencies sometimes used the term in the title of their agency.

A few months later, January 1859, the Night Police ordinance was revised and established the size of the force. "The City Council shall elect one Captain, one First Lieutenant, one Second Lieutenant and sixteen Watchmen, who shall constitute the Night Police of the city." The term of office was also expanded from six months to one year. The insignia to be worn by the Night Police was also specified.

> Section 3. That the Captain, each Lieutenant and Watchman shall be furnished, at the expense of the city, with a star made of silver or white metal, which shall be the badge of his office, and which he shall at all times (unless on secret service) wear on the outside of the left lapel of his coat, and upon which shall be engraved the words "Night Police." When the Policeman goes out of office, he shall deliver the said badge to the Mayor.

The mayor continued to serve much of the oversight function later assumed by the chief of police. Early policemen did not wear uniforms, only their badge of office. Randal W. MacGavock, noted Nashville Lawyer and mayor of Nashville in 1858 and 1859, wrote in his journal on March 3, 1859, "The Police force of the City appeared today with their silver badges. The night force have stars, the day crescents." The crescent referred to by MacGavock was probably crescent shaped badge with as star in the center, similar to those worn in Memphis, New Orleans and elsewhere. The law carried penalties for anyone wearing a badge who was not a policeman.

On September 30, 1859, near the end of MacGavock's term as mayor he published an annual report on the state of the city, entitled *Communication from His Honor the Mayor, Randal W. MacGavock,* *Transmitted to the City Council of Nashville, Tenn.* This appears to be the first annual report to the city and the first comprehensive appraisal of the police department. MacGavock reported the success of the police during the year as well as his concern with the mayor's role as head of the force and the lack of rules governing its activity.

> POLICE. In this department we have had, probably, as little complaint as in any previous year, certainly far less than I anticipated under the present system. The Recorder's docket shows that the misdemeanors are one-third less than last year, which is pretty conclusive proof that there has been more vigilance than usual—as a general thing, order and peace have prevailed, except in certain quarters where we look for such things. During the present term we have expelled two, and suspended, for a short time, some five or six members of the night police.

> Although we have managed to get through the year without any very serious troubles, I am fully satisfied that our present system is radically wrong. The Mayor is nominally the Chief Executive of the police, when really it amounts to a mere nullity. If he is to be held to a proper responsibility for their action, he should have the powers that our laws do not give him. Under the present system the dictum of the policeman is equal to that of the Mayor, and he performs his duty or not at his own pleasure. We have no rules for the government of our police, and the consequence is, that they frequently do things that the Mayor condemns in his own judgment, but has no power to reach it. As a body our present force are equal to any we have had, but the best men will work badly under a bad system, while the meanest men would do well under a good system.

The members of the police department in 1859, other than City Marshal Brown, were three deputy city marshals as the day police, James H. Brantley, John Chumbley and W. H. Wilkinson, two of whom would later serve as city marshals. Twenty men served on the night police, Captain W. H. Sturdevant, First Lieutenant William E. McAlister, Second Lieutenant R. M. Cavitt, John Baugh, A. Brannon, W. W. Calvert, G. W. Cotton, W. H. Craft, John H. Davis, W. T. Hughes, William Jackson, W. H. Lanier, Fred Marshall, J. B. Parrish, R. S. Patterson, Joel Philips, S. J. Starkey, A. C. Tucker, R. W. Watson and William Yarborough.

For a good many years prior to the Civil War the police station was at the south end of the market house on the public square. The city workhouse was located four miles away on Front Street. In his 1859 report MacGavock described the city jail and workhouse and steps he had taken to reform it.

At the beginning of the present year the Work House was an institution not at all creditable to the city. The prisoners of the city, amounting sometimes to forty or fifty, were crowded, without respect to sex or color, into two small rooms badly ventilated. During the present year an establishment has been erected, equal, if not superior, in all its appointments, to any similar institution in the country.

The sexes are now kept in different apartments, and ample provision made to protect all the inmates during inclement weather while at their work. Every Sabbath afternoon divine services is held in the prison by preachers of the different denominations, and its effects have proven beneficial. The whole establishment is kept in perfect order, and the health and comfort of its inmates were cared for.

The city stables were located adjacent to the workhouse and the workhouse staff was responsible for the city's steamboat and gravel boats. The river vessels were used to bring street building materials as well as wood, coal and other essentials transported on waterways to the city.

The budgets for the police and the workhouse were larger than any other city department except the water works. The budget for the police department in 1859 was $15,503.98 and the workhouse budget was $21,847.84. The total city budget was $225,399.12.

MacGavock reported a number of shootings and killings in the city. Political rallies and speeches often became violent due to high emotions preceding civil war. Reporting on one speech MacGavock wrote, "he made a most eloquent speech but as usual a man was killed. Pacoe an old policeman was shot by Bill Horn." "Pacoe" was former Policeman William Pacaud who was shot and killed on September 3, 1856. In an 1858 entry he wrote, "The Capt. of Police shot a man this morning who resisted arrest." He also reported a confrontation between police and armed robbers, "Quite a diabolical affair took place on our streets last night. Capt. Dismukes was going home from the Theater with his wife, and was knocked down by one of four men with brass knuckles and badly shot. The Police

was on hand pretty soon, and exchanged shots with the rascals, but they made their escapes."

Policeman John Davis broke up a fight between two men near the Commercial Hotel about 1:00 the morning of September 7, 1859. One of the combatants turned on Captain Davis and began beating him with a stick. Davis fought back and was winning the fight when the brawler got the policeman's finger between his teeth and refused to let go. When the pain became too much to bear, Policeman Davis pulled his pistol and shot the man in his stomach. The ball did not penetrate deep enough to do serious damage, but Davis saved his finger.

The Civil War created an upheaval in Nashville's police force as it did in the rest of the social and political order. As the South prepared for war able bodied policemen were among the first to volunteer for military service. As the state was about to secede from the Union a meeting of Nashville's citizens declared the police force was "incompetent to exercise the vigilance that was needed in war" and decided to organize a Vigilance Committee of twenty-five members. Their charge was three fold, to cooperate with the present police in defending the innocent and bringing the guilty to punishment, to request that all complaints against any person be brought for investigation and to request that no rash proceedings be taken against anyone.

The Union army under the command of General Don Carlos Buell took Nashville in February 1862. City Marshal Matt Brown left office when federal troops occupied the city. Martial law was instituted and the municipal police did not function as an independent force until the war was over. During the war a branch station was established over the Washington Fire Company No. 5 at 630 South Cherry Street. A building at the corner of Cedar and Cherry streets that had been used as a barracks for slaves was converted by the Federal army into a city prison. The building was abandoned after the war.

The title City Marshal was changed to Marshal during the war and the position continued to be the chief law enforcement officer under the watchful eye of federal authorities. Marshal John Chumbley held the post from April 1862 until October 1, 1865. The force consisted of six deputy marshals and four day policemen during the daylight hours. The night force consisted of Captain Henry A. Chumbley, two lieutenants and thirty watchmen. James H. Brantley became Marshal in October 1865 and served through September 1867. He commanded a day force of eight deputies and, beginning in 1866, detective R. M.

Cavitt. The night force was commanded by Captain A. J. Herald with the same number of lieutenants and watchmen.

Following the war a long struggle ensued to reestablish local law and order. Lawlessness was rampant and life on the streets was often brutal for a policeman. Criminals were more likely to fight than surrender when they were confronted by law enforcement. Lawbreakers often resorted to gunplay. When one policeman was asked by a newspaper reporter about a very physical arrest, he replied, "If the manner of arrest appeared rough to your informants, it was only because of the resistance of the prisoner which rendered force necessary."

Governor William G. Brownlow, selected to lead the reconstruction government in Tennessee, gave an address to the state legislature in November 1865 in which he referred to the situation.

> The reputation being acquired by Nashville, the Capital of your state, and the great commercial emporium of Middle Tennessee, is humiliating to every friend of law and order. Murders, robberies, and burglaries are the order of the day. No man is safe, day or night within a circuit around Nashville, whose radius is eight or ten miles.

Similar evaluations of the situation were given in the local press. Despite the increase in crime the number of city law officers remained at pre-war levels. Of the forty-three on the force, thirty were on night duty, four on day duty and nine were supervisors.

The year 1866 was eventful for policing in Nashville and across the state of Tennessee. The legislature enacted the Metropolitan Police Act at the behest of Governor Brownlow. James H. Brantley continued as marshal in Nashville. The night police was under the command of Captain R. S. Patterson, who expanded the leadership of the force to four lieutenants.

A Police Committee was established and a number of reforms were implemented. The force was increased to fifty-two by the end of 1866 including Patrolman Ephrim Foster Corbitt, a steamboat pilot who joined the force. Each ward was authorized to elect additional "special" policemen. A new position of detective was established and R. M. Cavitt became Nashville's first designated criminal investigator.

In cooperation with General Whipple, commander of federal troops in Nashville, local police were authorized to arrest any man in military uniform who was misbehaving and bring him before the proper military authorities.

Passage of the Metropolitan Police Act came on May 14, 1866. The three commissioners, Henry Stone, James Davis and Fred W. Spaulding, were appointed to organize the Nashville force of Metropolitans. They intended to model the force after New York City's Metropolitan police. Superintending Police Commissioner Henry Stone selected patrolmen for the force and began training and drilling exercises. None of the existing policemen or watchmen was selected to serve. The Republican Banner reported the initial activities of the Metropolitans in June.

> The force will be drilling and instructed in their duties sufficient to take charge of the city on the first day of July. Applications for positions on the metropolitan police are numerous, especially for the higher places, where good pay, much glory, and little work are expected.

Nashville's existing municipal police force continued duty on the streets of the city. On August 2, 1866, Mayor Brown and the city government filed an injunction to prohibit the Metropolitans from taking office on the grounds that the act was unconstitutional and intended to "strip the people of all power." Chancery Court Judge Campbell granted a temporary injunction and the existing police force continued on duty.

The city council took action to improve the police department. The marshal was authorized to divide the city into patrol wards and appoint deputies to be in charge of each beat. These "police wards" were not the same as the political wards in the city and because more officers serve at night, the number of wards for night duty was twice the number of wards for day duty. A move to put the force in uniform was also made.

The injunction preventing the Metropolitans from taking office remained in place until after the city elections in September 1867. Governor Brownlow ordered the state militia to insure the peace of the elections and to enforce the franchise law, which meant no one could vote who had been loyal to the Confederacy during the war. As a result A. E. Alden, the candidate of the Brownlow faction, won a lopsided victory as mayor. Within a month the suit brought by the city against the Metropolitan Police was dropped.

John Chumbley returned briefly as city marshal effective October 1, 1867. The title reverted from Marshal to City Marshal. Deputy marshals were Alexander Carter and W. J. Harrison. Captain William E. Danley commanded the night watch.

The existing municipal police force did not voluntarily resign. Approximately 50 members of the department petitioned for their pay to continue through the end of the calendar year. Night Policeman Edwards sued for being unjustly fired when he had been elected to serve for the full year. The court ruled against Edwards and the petition effort failed.

After fifteen months of inactivity the Metropolitan Police took office on October 17, 1867. William E. Danley, captain of the night watch, was named captain of the Nashville Metropolitans. Captain of Police became the title of Nashville's chief law enforcement officer for the next decade and a half. Danley had served on the police force during the war until he resigned in 1864 and entered the service of the United States Revenue Department. He returned to police duty following the war.

Commissioner Stone charged the force on their first day in office "to bear in mind that they must treat all persons, high and low, rich and poor, white and black, justly and impartially." The force wore military style uniforms and its training was similar to that of soldiers.

The Metropolitan Police began duty with 56 men including Captain Danley, Sergeant Isaac K. Jenkins, Sergeant Thomas Frame and 48 patrolmen. The balance of the force was the Sanitary Company composed of Sergeant William H. Sloan and four men. By the end of the first year the force was reduced to 46 men as a result of resignations, dismissals and one death.

The public was opposed to the force in the beginning. Even the city council, which was made up of Brownlow supporters, was opposed to the expenses involved. The act specified the level of pay for the force and the salaries were significantly higher than the men they were replacing.

Transition to the Metropolitan Police, referred to as MPs or the Metropolitans, marked the end of the night watch system in the city. It also marked the end of the city marshal as head of the police. Although city law enforcement was under the authority of the Metropolitan Police Board of Commissioners, the City Council elected Alexander A. Carter to the position of city marshal in 1868 and James H. Brantley to the position in 1869.

The position of city marshal continued into the twentieth century but after October 17, 1867, he was no longer Nashville's chief law enforcement officer. The city marshal retained police powers, but he functioned as a process server, insured payment of privilege and license fees, oversaw the market house, served as wharf-master, acted as clerk of the City Council, assigned hack stands and provided other civil duties.

The Metropolitan Police played a role in modernizing Nashville's police force. Personnel standards were improved. Applicants had to be at least 21 years of age, 5' 8" tall, of sound body and good character and citizens of Nashville and the United States. Literacy requirements were reaffirmed and officers were required to be full-time policemen.

Under the watch system many individuals had other jobs at the same time they worked on the police force. The department was now consolidated into one force rather than day and night patrols. Training emphasized discipline. Statistics of department operations were kept and regular reports were required.

As time passed in their two year period of existence, the Metropolitans made great strides in gaining respect from the citizens of Nashville. Although the opposition to Brownlow's control of the commission never relented, the *Republican Banner* commended Commissioner Stone for his conscientiousness and the policemen for doing a good job of apprehending criminals. The October 31, 1868, report of the commissioners to Governor Brownlow noted the change in attitudes.

> The feeling of hostility, which had been created in advance, against the Metropolitan Police System, soon passed away, and it is believed that the experience of the past year, and the manner in which police duties have been performed, have created entire confidence in the present system, among all good citizens. During its existence, the city has several times been the scene of unusual excitement, growing out of the heated political controversies which have taken place. Yet, without any addition to the regular force, by the energetic and efficient manner in which the Police have performed their duty, they have succeeded in preserving the public peace, under the most critical circumstances.

One of the near riots took place on the night of September 25, 1868. A torch light parade was in progress and was fired upon from the darkness. A riot was headed off when police officers moved quickly and decisively to take control.

An ongoing problem for the force was referred to as "the large floating population." This was a widespread situation throughout the South. Many individuals, both black and white, were without jobs and homes. They roamed the city and many incidents of petty larceny resulted. Many children from 10 to 16 years old were among those caught for such offenses, which further complicated the issue. No youth facilities existed to which they could be sent and they were too young for the penitentiary.

During their first year the Metropolitan Police made 4,707 arrests, 1,405 for offenses against persons, 534 for offenses against property and 2767 for violations of municipal ordinances. They also helped the fire department in fighting 25 fires and extinguished a number of small fires without raising an alarm.

Many of the repressive measures taken against the conservative white population of Tennessee during reconstruction came to an end in 1869, including the Metropolitan Police Act. Brownlow was elected to the U. S. Senate and resigned as governor of Tennessee in February 1869. The state elections in the fall of that year resulted in the defeat of the Brownlow faction. The act creating the Metropolitan Police was repealed on November 5, 1869.

Nashville reorganized the police department in December 1869 under an ordinance entitled "Appointment and Regulation of Police." Ironically, Nashville adopted the concept and organization of Metropolitan Police Commission. Although they ousted the commissioners appointed by the governor and the policemen selected under the reconstructionist regime, the city board utilized the structure and reforms that they implemented.

The reorganized department was under the control of three commissioners as was the Metropolitan force except the commissioners were not paid a salary. The command structure of the force was like the Metropolitan Police as well, with a captain in charge and sergeants supervising the patrolmen. Financial resources of the city were strained and the size of the force was reduced from 54 to 31 men, one captain, four sergeants and 26 patrolmen. Pay was also less than that of Metropolitan officers. The captain was paid $85 per month, sergeants $70 per month and patrolmen $67.50 per month. Officers had to furnish their own uniforms. The budget of the department dropped from $79,702 in 1869 to $29,386 in 1871.

The first three-member Board of Police Commissioners of Nashville selected in December 1869 by the city council consisting of James Haynie, A. C. Beech and Matthew McClung. Captain James Everett served as the first chief law enforcement official under this structure. Again a complete turnover of personnel in Nashville's police force took place. None of the Metropolitan policemen were on the new force. Seven individuals who had served as watchmen under the prior municipal force were hired as part of the new city police. The citizens of Nashville praised and supported their new police force.

Equipment and uniforms were the responsibility of each officer. Given the fact that most southerners had limited resources following the war, most police officers were poorly equipped. Mayor Kindred J. Morris proposed that the city council remedy this matter in a letter dated and submitted March 7, 1871.

Nashville's police force around 1870. Although poor in quality, the photograph was perhaps the earliest record of the department as a group. They were wearing military style uniforms with wide brim hats. Their breast badge was a shield with a star cut in the center and the only police insignia worn. Each carried a baton, which are clearly seen in the laps of those sitting and held under the arms of those standing.

Members of the Nashville Police Department in the 1870s. They were wearing a military style uniform and carrying an essential piece of equipment, a night stick. Batons carried by the day patrol were shorter in length. They wore the shield-cut-out-star style breast badge that was worn into the twentieth century. No hat badge was worn.

I wish to respectfully advise a limited expenditure of money which it seems to me would be most appropriate, and ought really to have been made at an earlier day.

If the Metropolitan Police were armed by the City, they took care to leave none of their pistols in our possession. The consequence is that the present police of the city have been left to their own resources for both pistols and maces, and the result is, there is neither uniformity nor certainty in either. Besides, I think it is unjust they should be expected to bear the expense of their own equipment in this respect. In view of these facts and the additional fact that several symptoms of serious riot have occurred, I have thought it worthwhile to recommend that each member of the Police be furnished with a six-inch Smith & Wesson pistol, branded by the manufacture, "Nashville Police," and numbered; and that a supply of cartridges manufactured specially under the direction of Smith & Wesson or their successors, be procured at the same time, and entrusted to the Captain of Police, to be issued by him as they are required, and further, that the Captain of Police be authorized to procure maces of the best material and of proper shape and size, sufficient in number to supply the entire force. The pistols and cartridges together would not cost much over $400, delivered, I suppose, and the maces but a trifle.

You will doubtless agree with me that the throngs of vagrants on our streets (most of them armed with concealed weapons) should be kept in partial obedience to the city ordinances at least; and you'll see to the propriety of having the conservators of the peace well equipped for their duty.

The board took action on Mayor Morris' request on the same day it was submitted and 32 of the S&W #3 revolvers were received in May. The sidearm was a .44 caliber single action with top break and plow handle grip. The back strap of each pistol was marked as specified, stamped "Nashville Police No. 5" for example, and numbered from 1 to 32. The city paid $579 for revolvers ($17 each), cartridges and shipping.

Nashville police patrol group circa 1875.

An additional $23.25 was paid to James G. Moore, a local saddle and harness maker, for 31 holsters. Southern Wheel & Handle Company at 94 North Market Street provided 40 "Police clubs" for $12. Police regulations were printed by the Ben Franklin Printing Co. at the same time. The payroll for the police department for May 1871 was $2,370.

General Rules for the police force were adopted by the mayor and Police Commission on April 15, 1871, that required policemen to work solely in law enforcement and not hold other jobs and that they work for salary alone, not for fees. The Captain of Police was in command of the force and answered to the mayor. Sergeants were responsible for the good order and discipline of their platoon. The main duty of Patrolmen was the prevention of crime by constant vigilance. A specific duty of the patrolman was to "carefully examine (in the night) all doors and low windows of dwelling houses and stores, to see that they are properly secured." Patrolmen were not to talk with each other or any person while on duty unless it related to police business.

Police headquarters was moved in 1871 from the market house on the public square to the city workhouse on Front Street four miles away. This was another cost saving measure, but one that was not well received by the police force. It was objectionable to the policemen both because of the extra travel involved and because of the poor health and sanitary conditions at the workhouse. A number of chiefs pointed out over the next several years that officer were exposed to typhoid, yellow fever and a number of other dangerous maladies. They in turn exposed the public with whom they came in contact. The matter was studied, but city officials decided the financial savings were worth the risks.

Captain of Police W. H. Yater succeeded Everett in 1871 and served in the position for 12 years. The department grew from 31 policemen to 47 during his tenure as chief. He established a good record for the department and for himself, becoming one of the most respected and well liked police chiefs in the city's history. On his retirement Yater became the city's Food Inspector.

The force lost an officer in the line of duty on April 30, 1875. Policeman Robert T. Frazier went to a residence on Whiteside Street near Front about one o'clock in the afternoon to arrest a man who had been beating his wife. The man drew a pistol from his pocket and shot the officer. Frazier died at the scene.

Policeman Robert Frazier joined the Nashville force in January 1874. He was six feet tall, well built and 48 years old. Frazier was a pleasant and well liked officer.

The killer was soon apprehended by Policeman Schneider and taken to jail. At the 8:00 p.m. roll call Captain Yater, the mayor and the force passed a resolution expressing sorrow and support for Frazier's widow. The mayor noted that citizens were aroused by the murder and that the force would have to quell any disturbance.

As dark fell on the city, a group began to grow on Broad Street in front of the Maxwell House and on the south side of the Public Square. At 9:00 p.m. a large mob began to move toward the jail. Soon after, the bell atop City Hall sounded the riot signal. Eight or ten policemen gathered at the front door to the jail, the mayor and others tried to talk the mob into disbursing.

The mob jeered and forced their way into the jail. They pushed the inside guards aside and found the murderer of Officer Frazier in Number 5 cell. The mob dragged the killer to the suspension bridge over

The city council authorized the purchase of 32 Smith & Wesson Model #3 revolvers for the Nashville Police Department in 1871. The sidearms were .44 caliber, single action, top break, with plow handle grip. The back strap of each weapon was stamped "Nashville Police" with a sequential number, "No. 3" on this example, shown above at the lower left. (Courtesy of Lyle Larkworthy, The Woodlands, Texas)

Captain W. H. Yater served as Nashville's chief law enforcement officer from 1871 to 1883. The force grew from 31 to 47 men during his tenure. Supervisors consisted of Yater and three sergeants.

the Cumberland where they shot and lynched him.

Such mob violence was another aspect of the lawlessness pervasive in the decades following the Civil War. The small size of the police force and the unavailability of other agencies to assist meant mobs usually acted with impunity.

Captain Yater's report for the year ended September 30, 1877, indicated that the force grew to one captain, three sergeants and 34 patrolmen, for a total of 39 officers. The patrol area was three square miles with 51 miles of streets and 29 miles of alleys. The city was divided into six watch-wards for day duty and ten watch-wards for night duty. Yater reported the "Distribution of the Police Force" in the city's annual report.

At a meeting of the Mayor and Police Committee, on the 21st day of August, 1874, I was ordered to divide the police force into three reliefs. The Captain is supposed to be on duty at all hours. One Sergeant, on day duty, in charge of the police office, and six Patrolmen, one to each day ward, comes on duty at 4 A.M., and are relieved at 12 M. by the second relief, consisting of six Patrolmen, one to each day ward, that are relieved at 8 P.M. by the night force. One Sergeant and one Patrolman are detailed in the Health Office. (This Sergeant has heretofore been in charge of the Police Office.) The third relief constitutes the night force, comes on duty at 8 P.M., and relieved at 4 A.M. It consists of one Sergeant in charge of the Police Office, one Sergeant acting as roundsman, and twenty Patrolmen, two for each ward for night; also one Patrolman on the Public Square at night.

The move to eight-hour shifts was temporary. The length of the work day for policemen was not finally changed from twelve hours to eight until 1890.

The total number of arrests in 1877 was 3,549. Yater reported no crime of a "serious nature" except "one bold robbery." "On the 20th April, 1877, at or about twelve o'clock in the day, parties entered the jewelry store of the firm of Gates & Pohlman and stole ($5,000) five thousand dollars worth of jewelry. They were caught and a portion of the jewelry recovered."

In 1880 the force was up to 45, one captain, four sergeants and 40 patrolmen. The patrol area had expanded to five square miles. Even the most routine of duties were often labor intensive. Patrolman Michael Ryan walked his beat one hot summer night when he observed one of his regular Saturday "customers" pass out in a doorway after too much Barleycorn. With no vehicle available and no way to contact the station house, Officer Ryan found a wheelbarrow, hoist the dead weight of the sleeping drunk into it and began the long trek to headquarters.

Two Nashville policemen who served during the 1880s.

Chief of Police J. Hadley Clack was appointed in 1887 and served through 1897.

The first trio of commissioners served through 1882. Others who served as commissioner during this period were P. Walsh, W. M. Duncan, Thomas Parkes, W. H. Ambrose, George Stainback, C. B. Kuhn, J. F. Turner and J. H. Wood. Captain W. H. Yater in his final report, dated October 1, 1883, repeated and stressed his recommendation for a new and more centrally located police headquarters.

Before Yater left office his title changed and the commission was abolished. On March 27, 1883, the General Assembly granted a revised charter to Nashville. The act authorized the establishment of a Board of Public Works and Affairs. The board was composed of three members elected by the City Council and had exclusive power over the personnel and functions of the Water-works Department, Police Department, Fire Department and Work-house.

The first members of the board were Robert Ewing, Dr. T. A. Atchinson and Michael Nestor. Chief of Police became the title of Nashville's chief law officer. The chief of police continued to carry the rank of captain for salary and other administrative purposes.

Martin Kerrigan was selected Nashville's first chief of police in October 1883 and served there through September 1887. Under his command were sergeants William E. McAlister, D. U. Burke, B. M. Hawkins, Henry Curran and fifty patrolmen. Sergeant Samuel H. Fields and Patrolman R. M. Porter were added to the force to serve as detectives.

William McAlister was one of the longest serving members in the department. He began with the force as a special policeman in 1855 during the high constable and night watch era of the department. He served two years as a watchman and was promoted to sergeant. While on duty on September 7, 1861, he was shot in the leg by a Confederate soldier. He rejoined the department in September 1866 and served until the Metropolitans took over policing of the city. When the Metropolitan Police was disbanded he went back on duty and served until 1890. He left the department to become the Market Master.

Samuel Fields became head of the new Detective Department with the title Chief of Detectives. Fields accidentally shot himself and was disabled for active duty. He was assigned to "duty on the bridge" after his convalescence. William Patton Casteen, born in Nashville in April 1844 and appointed patrolman in 1880, replaced Fields as detective in 1884. Casteen was promoted to sergeant in 1885. Samuel Fields briefly returned as a detective in 1885 replacing Porter, but by 1886 William Casteen was the only detective in the department and was named chief of detectives.

A patrol wagon was added to the equipment of the department on April 15, 1885. It was a spring wagon painted black and called the "Black Maria." Chief Kerrigan reported, "It has proven to be of valuable assistance in attending fires; carrying ropes, axes, etc.; in transporting prisoners, the sick and disabled, besides being useful in many other ways."

A number of injuries in the line of duty were noted in the eighties. Officer A. H. Roberts was severely cut with a knife while making an arrest. Officers P. H. Lawrence and W. P. Casteen were slightly wounded while arresting a drunken desperado. Patrolman Owen McGovern was shot and seriously wounded arresting a desperado and ex-convict. McGovern was born in County Cavan, Ireland, in 1850 and immigrated to the U.S. with his family in 1864. He became a Nashville policeman in 1883.

Patrolman John M. Arnold was shot in the line of duty on January 6, 1885, by a notorious desperado he was attempting to arrest at the Chattanooga Railroad depot. Arnold died of his wounds at 12:15 on the morning of February 12 at his home on Broad Street.

His pall bearers were six of the tallest men on the force, Officers Kuhn, Bolton, Roberts, Scalley, McConnell and Holland. Policeman Arnold first joined the force in 1866.

By 1886 the number of officers on day duty had exceeded the number of officers on night duty. The department consisted of the chief, five sergeants and 52 patrolmen. Two sergeants, 24 patrolmen and one detective were assigned to night duty. Three sergeants and 27 patrolmen were on day duty. Of those on day duty, one sergeant and one patrolman were detectives, one sergeant and two patrolmen were on sanitary duty and one patrolman each was assigned to the Law Department, the Water-works Department and the Market-house. Four patrolmen were added to the department during the year.

Chief of Police J. Hadley Clack was appointed in October 1887. Clack was born in Williamson County on December 5, 1859, and went to Montgomery Bell Academy in Nashville. He served as Assistant Superintendent of the State Capitol for a year and a half before being appointed a Nashville patrolman on June 7, 1881, at the age of 21. He was assigned to the Detective Department in 1884 and moved to the Law Department the following year. During his time with the force he exhibited natural ability as a leader and dedication to service. His 1887 command included sergeants W. E. McAlister, D. U. Burke, B. M. Hawkins and Henry Curran; and Detective W. P. Casteen.

Chief Clack added six patrolmen in 1888 and created the rank of captain, to which sergeants W. P. Casteen and D. U. Burke were promoted. The rank title was short lived. Each captain was given command of a twelve-hour shift. Clack also kept the need for a new police station before the Board of Public Works and Affairs.

R. M. Porter was promoted to sergeant and chief of detectives. When Porter left the police department he formed the Porter National Detective Agency and brought former Chief of Police W. H. Yater on as his assistant superintendent.

The first record of a black officer in the Nashville department was the appointment of John Stuart as a patrol driver on March 1, 1888. Although it would be six decades before the first appointment of black patrolmen, Stuart performed police related duties in his position.

Four men who started their career with the Nashville police as patrolmen under Chief Clack were John Varley, Walter A. Gibbons, William J. Smith and Bolivar T. Cummings. Smith later became chief of the

Group of Nashville policemen circa 1890. Officers are wearing summer uniforms and summer helmets.

Supervisors in dress uniforms in 1897. From left to right were Lieutenant William Patton Casteen, Lieutenant Owen McGovern, Lieutenant (soon to be chief of police) Henry Curran, Sergeant Lucius Leonard Polk, Sergeant Richard Reid, Sergeant M. B. McKenney, Sergeant Mitchell Allen Marshall, Sergeant Etheldred J. Moore and Sergeant Robert Newton Long.

2. The full dress of the members of the police force shall be of navy blue cloth, indigo dyed, and all wool.

3. Each garment shall be inspected . . . An officer who neglects to replace any portion of his uniform that has been condemned within a reasonable time, will be suspended from duty, and stand suspended, with loss of pay, until he has conformed to the order of the inspecting officer.

4. The department will furnish buttons, badges, belts, and day clubs, all of which remain the property of the department, and must be surrendered when the officer leaves the service.

Rules and regulations did not prepare Nashville officers for a harrowing event in April 1892. The rape of three girls in Goodlettsville had outraged the town's citizens. One of the rapists was taken by the mob and lynched before he could be arrested. The other was taken into custody and secretly moved to police headquarters in Nashville.

When the mob found out where the second rapist was being held they headed toward Nashville. The mob swept down Second Avenue. A cordon of patrolmen were unable to hold them back. Chief Clack dressed the prisoner in women's clothes and sneaked him out of the jail. A short distance from the station the lynch mob discovered the man. Nashville policemen tried to protect their prisoner. They shot and killed two of the mob in their effort, but officers were overwhelmed by the number of vengeful citizens of Goodlettsville. The second rapist was beaten, stabbed and hanged from the Woodland Street bridge.

The department lament numbered between ninety and one hundred men during the 1890s. After the tumul-

tuous year of 1892 Chief Clack requested ten additional men because of the crowded streets of the city. He indicated to the Board of Public Works and Affairs that he found it "necessary to place officers on the principal corners to prevent accidents and keep the streets clear." This was the beginning of the "corner-men" that served during through the first half of the twentieth century. The department had also responded to a second mob fight during the year. In the second incident Chief Clack was badly hurt.

Chief Clack did not shy away from his duty. Renowned boxer John L. Sullivan fled from Mississippi authorities as the result of competing in a pugilistic exhibition, unlawful in the state. Chief Clack and two officer met Sullivan's train as it reached Nashville. Clack told the boxer he was under arrest, but when one of the patrolmen moved to take him into custody, Sullivan's right fist snapped back ready for action. Unperturbed, Clack pulled a Derringer from his pocket and said, "Touch that man and I'll blow a hole through you." Sullivan was then escorted to jail without incident.

Clack did not shy away from personnel problems either. In 1896 the chief reported turmoil within the ranks of the department. Direct action brought a quick end to the difficulty.

There existed among the patrolmen some dissensions, but the dismissal of a number of these officers by your Honorable Board promptly put a check to this matter, and now the department is working smoothly and in perfect harmony.

The chief also had a lighthearted side. Clack had one of the first high wheeled bicycles or "ordinaries" popular in the 1890s. It was reported that Clack was often seen riding down the street with his coat tails flying in the wind.

Once Chief Clack had convinced the Board of Public Works and Affairs to have a new police station built, he turned his attention to the next most needed item for the police department, an alarm system. The only way policemen or the public could communicate with headquarters was by personal or business telephones. Patrolmen who worked in the business district were virtually cut off from headquarters after businesses closed for the day.

The chief's recommendation was finally agreed to in 1897 and the Gamewell System was installed. The telecommunication system provided a method of raising a police alarm at the police station. Signal boxes throughout Nashville allowed officers to report in and to call for assistance. A switchboard at headquarters was the nerve center of the system and required that an operator be on duty around the clock. Sworn officers served as switchboard operators.

The National Union of Chiefs of Police of the United States and Canada met in Nashville during the Tennessee Centennial and International Exposition in 1897. Chief Clack greeted fellow chiefs of police from across North America to the city. To commemorate the event a souvenir of the department was published containing a brief history and information on Nashville and the members of the department.

The department was commanded by Chief Clack; three lieutenants, Henry Curran, W. P. Casteen and Owen McGovern; and six sergeants, Lucius Leonard Polk, Richard Reid, M. B. McKenney, Mitchell Allen Marshall, Etheldred J. Moore and Robert Newton Long.

Sergeant Polk grew up on a farm near Springfield until he was 21 and after working in that town for fifteen years, he moved to Nashville and joined the police force in 1888. A year later he was promoted to sergeant.

Sergeant Reid was born in Ireland and came to the U.S. with friends. He finished a course of study at a business college before the war. Reid joined Moorman's Battery (Pelham Battalion of Artillery) in the Confederate Army when the Civil War broke out. He was wounded at Malvern Hill in Virginia and patrolled at Appomattox. He was appointed a Nashville Patrolman in 1870 and promoted to sergeant four years later.

Sergeant McKenney was an officer with long service. He was born in Davidson County in 1841 and became a Nashville policeman in 1863. He resigned in 1866 because of the upheaval in the department and

Detective Department in 1897. Detectives Robert J. Sidebottom and Allay Hiram Dickens at the top, Chief of Detectives, Lieutenant Samuel Fields Turner in the center and Detectives Benjamin Anthony Crockett and Daniel Lynch at the bottom. Robert Sidebottom served briefly as chief of police in 1898 and for many years afterwards as chief of detectives.

worked as a butcher until November 15, 1869, when he rejoined the police department. He was promoted to sergeant in 1893.

Sergeant Marshall was born in Davidson county in 1855 and became a policeman in 1883 after a number of years with a business firm. He was promoted to sergeant in 1892. Although never a detective, he was detailed on several cases where he demonstrated effective investigative skills.

Sergeant Long was born in Lawrence County in 1855. After a number of years in the mail service and mercantile employment, he was appointed a patrolman in 1885. He was commissioned a sergeant in 1893.

Sergeant Moore was born in 1850 in Davidson County. He worked in the livery business and real

Policeman Joseph Barnes Patrick, pictured with his family in 1897, was the first of five generations to serve on the Nashville force. The lad on the right, James Patrick, joined the force as the second generation. He was followed by Henry "Junior" Parrish and Robert Parrish, a third generation. The forth generation consisted of Kenneth "Pappy" Parrish, Ronald L. Parrish and W. Thomas Jones; and officers of the fifth generation were James Jones and Jeffery Brown.

estate business for twenty-one years before joining the police department in 1888. He was promoted to sergeant on October 29, 1894.

The Detective Department consisted of a chief and four detectives in the late nineteenth and early twentieth centuries. The department in 1897 was Chief of Detectives Samuel Fields Turner, Robert J. Sidebottom, Benjamin Anthony Crockett, Daniel Lynch and Allay Hiram Dickens.

Lieutenant and Chief of Detectives Turner was born in Williamson County in 1853. His family moved to Nashville when he was seven. Turner worked as a carpenter and in commercial pursuits until 1881 when he joined the department as a patrolman. He was appointed a detective in 1884 and on April 17, 1894 was promoted to chief of detectives. Turner gained a reputation throughout the South as a natural born detective, know for his shrewdness, bravery and integrity.

Detective Sidebottom was born in Alexandria, Louisiana, in 1860. His parents moved to Nashville in 1871 and following his education in public schools, Sidebottom worked for the city Street Department. He was appointed police patrolman in 1884 and named detective in 1887.

Detective Crockett was born in 1859 at Murfreesboro. He worked as a salesman until he joined the police department in 1890. On April 27, 1893, he was detailed to do detective work. He proved successful and became a regular member of the detective force.

Detective Dickens was born in Rock City in 1854 and was involved in commercial pursuits until March 1887 when he became a Nashville patrolman. He was appointed to the Detective Department in May 1894.

Detective Lynch, born in Nashville in 1860, worked in the shops of the Nashville, Chattanooga and St. Louis Railway and in the grocery business before entering law enforcement. He was elected City Constable from the First District in 1886. He became a Nashville patrolman in 1890 and was appointed to the Detective Department in 1894.

Completing the department roster in 1897 were 76 patrolmen, five sanitation officers, a humane officer, two patrol wagon drivers and a janitor. The department made 7,185 arrests during the year, a record number, and captured 60 fugitives from justice in other jurisdictions.

Eighteen-ninety-eight was a tumultuous year for department. Leadership changed twice in just over six months. Speculation regarding a change in the chief of police began soon after William T. Smith was elected chairman of the Board of Public Works and Affairs. In a meeting of the board on February 11, 1898, Detective Robert J. Sidebottom was appointed chief of police. The board also dismissed detectives Dan Lynch and Ben Crockett. In their place the board appointed W. S. Waddell and Alex Barthell.

Soon after Chief Clack lost the job he was selected to serve as city judge by the Nashville city council. The council had recently separated the responsibility of serving as city judge from the duties of the city

The Gamewell System was originally installed in 1897 to provide police alarm communications to the police station house from signal boxes through-out Nashville. The system was staffed with three Gamewell operators, one on each shift and a supervisor. The switchboard at headquarters was the nerve center of the system that was cutting edge technology in the twenties. (Nashville Banner photo, January 2, 1921)

recorder. Judge Clack continued distinguished service to the city.

New Chief Sidebottom was 38 years old with a distinguished record in more than ten years as a detective. He was an imposing figure, standing over six feet tall and weighing 250 pounds and had a reputation for hardwork and an easy-going demeanor.

Two months later leadership of the Board of Public Works and Affairs changed again after the untimely death of Chairman Smith. Forty ballots were required for the city council to select a new board chair, John L. Kennedy. With the change the political fortunes of Chief Sidebottom were reversed.

Chairman Kennedy called the chief before the board and ordered him to shut down gambling houses and close saloons doing business on Sunday. The board also raised concerns about department morale and discipline.

Chief Sidebottom began an assault on gambling the next day. On Sunday he put the entire force on extra duty to close saloons. Sergeant Marshall and Patrolman Woosley began in the morning by arresting a barman who opened his saloon on the Public Square. Bar closures and arrests continued throughout the day.

The chief was called before the board again three weeks later. This time they instructed him to put an end to the boldness of the city's prostitutes.

A rash of complaints by saloon owners and their supporters, along with the Chairman Kennedy's lack of confidence in Chief Sidebottom's ability to bring harmony to the department, created a growing upheaval among policemen and the public. The situation precipitated a mass public meeting of around 600 men to discuss the matter and support Chief Sidebottom.

Chairman Kennedy became convinced that the

Chief of Police Henry Curran served in the position from 1898 through 1914, serving longer than any other individual in the post.

they treated the new chief to a traditional congratulatory club ride. They placed a nightstick between his legs and rode him around the drill room. The event was reportedly uncomfortable to the dignified Curran in more ways than one.

Chief Curran was born in New Castle, Ireland, in 1849 and was brought to America at the age of three. He moved to Nashville in 1865 and worked as a boiler maker in the Nashville, Chattanooga and St. Louis Railroad shop. Curran was appointed a patrolman on the Nashville force on January 1, 1874. Six years later he was promoted to sergeant and less than a year later was named to the rank of lieutenant.

Chief Curran gained a reputation as an able and effective chief of police. He believed an officer was the personification of the law and that no person was entitled to wear the uniform of a policeman unless he deserved the respect of the public. He served 16 years as chief, longer than any other Nashville chief of police.

Lieutenant Mitchell Allen Marshall was made Chief of Detectives in 1898 following the death of Lieutenant Samuel Turner. The three patrol lieutenants were McGovern, Cartwright and Tanksley. The department consisted of 99 officers, 76 of whom were on patrol duty. Total arrests during 1899 were 6,269 including nine of the twelve people charged with murder. Arrests in 1900 grew to 9,795.

The department lost an officer in the line of duty in the spring of 1899. Patrolman Daniel Summitt was on patrol about 1:00 Sunday afternoon, April 30, when he came upon the owner of a grocery and saloon at the corner of Lischey and Foster. The man was intoxicated and cursing someone on the sidewalk outside his business. Officer Summitt knew the barman because he had closed down the saloon in the past for selling liquor on Sunday.

Patrolman Summitt told the drunken bar owner to stop the cursing and abuse or be arrested. The drunkard then began cursing the policeman and backed through the door saying, "I won't go any place with you." As the officer entered the building the owner retrieved a .38 caliber revolver and fired three shots. Patrolman Summitt was able to get one shot off before he stumbled out the door and fell. One bullet had torn through the policeman's right breast and lung.

Sergeant Robert Long soon arrived at the scene and had Patrolman Summitt moved to his home on Treutlan Street. The sergeant then went to the house of the gunman and made the arrest.

Although bleeding profusely and in severe pain, Patrolman Summitt was able to give a statement to Lieutenant M. A. Marshall. Daniel Summitt died

board had to name a new chief. The two candidates were former chief and now Judge Clack and Lieutenant Henry Curran. Judge Clack sent a letter to members of the board saying he had no interest in returning as chief of police.

The Board of Public Works and Affairs met on August 18, 1898, and appointed Henry Curran chief of police. Chief Sidebottom was demoted to the rank of detective. Other actions included the demotion of Lieutenant W. P. Casteen to sergeant and Sergeant L. L. Polk to patrolman. Polk continued with the department but Casteen resigned rather than be demoted. Ex-chief Sidebottom continued his police career and later served many years as chief of detectives.

Two new lieutenant were appointed, Mitt Marshall and Thomas Cartwright. Lieutenant Marshall was placed in command of the night detail and Lieutenant Cartwright assigned the morning detail.

Chief Henry Curran's appointment was happily received at police headquarters. The enthusiasm of officers reporting for duty at mid-day was such that shortly after midnight, May 1, 1899. The 55-year-old officer was a veteran of the Civil War and had been a member of the Nashville department for ten years.

Nashville reached a population of over 100,000 by the turn of the century. City utilities included electricity as well as gas, an extensive water system, a "hello" system provided by Cumberland Telephone and Telegraph and the Nashville Street Railway, an electric railway system that carried riders across the city for five cents.

Chief Curran reported that 1901 was not "marked by anything of a special nature," but noted 9,837 arrests. The value of stolen property recovered was a record $18,176.68. The department was referred to as the Metropolitan Police Department of Nashville in reports to the mayor and the Board of Civil Service Commission.

Nashville and the nation was becoming entangled in a social and moral struggle over the harmful nature of intoxicating beverages and their role in the cause of crime. Tennessee and other states later passed legislation to limit the sale and use of liquor and finally the U.S. congress passed the Volstead Act and prohibition began nationwide.

At the turn of the century saloons were spread across the city. One of the most notable was the Southern Turf on Cherry Street. Whiskey and beer was not only available in saloons, they could be purchased on the street of downtown Nashville from push carts. The city began to pass laws to restrict the sale of liquor. Increasingly the police department was in a no win situation. The "dry" proponents, opposed to alcoholic beverages of any type, called on the department to enforce the letter of the law while even a larger segment of the population of the city did not want the laws enforced again them.

In his 1903 annual report Chief Curran answered charges that the police were over zealous in enforcing unpopular laws.

The citizen should recognize that, no mater how objectionable a law may be to him, the police officer is not responsible for the law, but is responsible to his superiors and to the community for the enforcement of it. Therefore a policeman at times receives unjust censure when he come in contact with the unreasonable citizen.

The level of enforcement of the various illegal liquor laws often depended on who was serving as mayor. The police were attacked by both sides. In one instance in 1906 a resolution was introduced to dismiss the entire police force because of lax enforcement of the liquor laws, which at that time were minor in comparison to those passed over the next few years.

Enforcement of the liquor law was not only unpopular but dangerous. Incidents in which the majority of officers killed in the line of duty from the turn of the century until prohibition was repealed related to enforcing provisions of the "dry" laws. Such was the case of in an incident that occurred on a cold winter night in 1903. Many people objected to saloons being closed on Sunday and many saloon keepers broke the law to keep their establishment going on Sunday. Policemen Benjamin Franklin Dowell enforced the law and gave his life as a result.

Shortly before 8 o'clock on that Sunday night, December 6, 1903, shots rang out at the corner of Market Street and Lindsley Avenue. A few minutes later Patrolman Ben Dowell staggered through the door of Grace Cumberland Presbyterian Church, fatally wounded.

About 4 o'clock that afternoon Patrolman Dowell had arrested a female lookout at McDonough's saloon, which was illegally open. Nellie McDonough followed the officer out and demand in vile terms that the prisoner be released. Dowell arrested her as well. Mrs. McDonough's brother Thomas Cox made her bail and made threats against the officer.

That evening Patrolman Dowell stood at the corner where he was to be relieved by the night officer in the Fourteenth Ward. Tom Cox, in the company of two others, walked up to Dowell, pulled a pistol and began firing. The patrolman tugged at the buttons of his uniform coat trying to draw his revolver. Both Cox and Dowell emptied their weapons.

Ben Dowell was struck three times. One bullet hit his abdomen and passed through his body, a second tore away the end of his right thumb and the third entered the back of his right side, lacerating his liver. Cox was struck in the right arm, but not seriously.

Officer Dowell entered the church holding out his revolver and reeling in pain. "Gentlemen," he gasped, "I'm shot, take my gun please." As men eased him onto a bench, he asked them to reload his weapon. "Oh, My God! I'm shot. He shot me for nothing. He did not say a word." An ambulance was called to take the officer to City Hospital while doctors at the church tended him.

Patrolmen Bennett and Carlew arrived to relieve him and were directed to the church. Dowell told them Cox was the shooter. About the time they left to hunt for the gunman Lieutenant Long received a call at police headquarters that Cox was in a grocery on Cherry Street asking to be taken to the hospital. Long detailed patrolmen McGuire and Drake to make the arrest.

Policeman Dowell was mortally wounded and his condition steadily deteriorated. Chief of Police Curran and Chief of Detectives Marshall along with a magistrate came to the hospital and took Dowell's dying declaration on Monday, December 7. The officer died at 7:05 that evening.

At age 27 Ben Dowell was one of the youngest officers in the department. He joined the force two years earlier and had married the year before his death. Dowell was considered a capable officer and "fearless in the discharge of the duty."

An outcry arose in the city over the blatant act of assassination. In the newspaper citizens called for hanging and proclaimed the act was an outgrowth of "a class of lawlessness allowed to go flagrantly on without hindrance." Tom Cox had killed before and had attacked a law officer before, firing a gun at and brutally beating Special Policeman F. M. Erwin and attempting to stab Patrolman Sol Lucats. Talk of lynching was so prevalent that Cox and his two accomplices were removed from jail and taken to another city.

Cox was convicted of murder in the first degree and sentenced to hang. Two days before he was to go to the gallows he took poison. The death from twenty grains of red oxide of mercury was prolonged and agonizing.

Two ranking officer in the department died of natural causes during 1904, Sergeant A. N. Davis after five year on the force and Chief of Detectives M. A. Marshall after twenty-one years on the force. Robert J. Sidebottom replaced Marshall as chief of detectives with the rank of lieutenant.

Nashville's police officers found diversion from the tragic events of their occupation as well as the day to day grind of police duty. Baseball was becoming a favorite pastime throughout the nation and the Nashville Police Department fielded a team to compete with other groups in the city. They played at the Sulphur Dell in sight of the state capitol building.

New annexation and the expansion of the city's patrol area in 1906 brought a plea from Chief Curran to add at least 25 patrolmen. He also requested two substations in outlying areas. The board did not act on the recommendation and he renewed his request in subsequent years. The patrol area of the force had expanded to eighteen square miles by 1908 and in 1909 preparation of one new substation began.

A few of the cases solved by the Detective Department in 1909 were the capture of Jim Swain,

Nashville Police baseball team of 1905.

alias Jim Sweeney, a highwayman who terrorized travelers along Gallatin and Lebanon Pikes; the arrest of John Gilcrist, a notorious hotel thief; and the arrest of Jim Hooper, ex-convict and "all-round thief." Detectives made 748 arrests during the year and recovered $25,106 in lost or stolen property.

In another case Chief of Detective Robert Sidebottom single-handedly tracked down Josh Belt. Sidebottom later commented, "Old Josh Belt was one of the smoothest crooks I ever ran upon." The thief took around $10,000 from houses in Nashville. Sidebottom tracked him down in the edge of North Nashville and recovered the loot as well.

Detective Bolivar T. Cummings was one of the most noted Nashville police detectives in the early twentieth century. His gentle and kind disposition became stern when he faced law-breakers and he was fearless in the face of danger. The Detective Department was still made up of a chief and four detectives, who worked in pairs. Dick Jones and W. E. Jacobs were two detectives that worked with Cummings.

Four notorious gunmen and "safe-blowers" had cracked safes across Nashville and frustrated the police force for months. One night Bolivar Cummings and W. E. Jones marched into headquarters with the dangerous felons in tow. It was a great event in the annals of the department. On another occasion Cummings and his partner pursued a nationally known swindler to Canada and returned him to Nashville for prosecution. Cummings retired in 1921.

The police department was growing and modernizing by the end of the first decade of the century. Personnel

Nashvilles Detective Bureau in 1910. Seated in the front row from left to right were Tom Murray, Manner Bracy, George Redmond, Chief of Detectives Robert J. Sidebottom, Gus Kiger, Earl Kiger and William Irwin. Standing in the back row left to right were W. B. Wenfry, Walter Reece, John Varley, Pat Dowd, Henry McCarver, Sam Giles, Charley Woosley and Robert Vaughn.

included 117 officers in 1910, one chief, one chief of detectives, three lieutenants, six sergeants, eight detectives, three turnkeys, three patrol drivers and 92 patrolmen. In 1911 the first motorized vehicle was added to the force, an "auto patrol wagon." The chief requested a variety of other equipment to enhance the department's capability. The position of "Automobile Driver" was added to the positions on the force.

The policies of the department were revised and published in the "Rules and Regulations of the Metropolitan Police Force, Prescribed by the Mayor and Approved by the Civil Service Commission, January 31, 1912" section of the manual *Rules and Regulations Governing All Departments*. Changes from the 1891 manual included the expansion of police districts to three. District No. 1 was composed of the portion of the city south of Broadway and east of the river to the corporation line. District No. 2 was the area north of Broadway and west of Fourth Avenue North to the corporation line. District No. 3 was east of Fourth Avenue North and north of Broadway to the corporation line on the west side of the river and all the territory lying east of the river.

The force expanded to 140 by 1913 including 101 patrolmen. The other officers were the Chief Curran; Chief of Detectives Sidebottom; three lieutenants, Owen McGovern, R. N. Long and William J. Smith; nine sergeants, Richard H. Ried, J. R. Sadder, Walter A. Gibbons, W. A. Waddell, J. W. Longhurst, G. L. Smith, G. E. Wilson, John Milliron and E. A. Wright; ten detectives, W. E. Irvin, Pat F. Dowd, B. T. Cummings, John Varley, C. R. Wourley, B. F. Norton, W. E. Jacobs, R. K. Vaughan, Gus A. Kiger and Frank Carr; two auto detectives, N. P. McCaiver and M. L. Dawson; Wharf Master W. H. Burns; Market Master J. W. Fly; three turnkeys, three chauffeurs, three humane officers and a clerk. Police Matron Mrs. C. O. Smith was added to the force. Police headquarters underwent major repairs and repainting in 1913.

The position of Emergency Officer was created February 14, 1914. Emergency officers responded to urgent calls received at headquarters, driving the emergency car. Three patrolmen, Sanford Eagan, W. H. Patton and J. D. Ferris were assigned the duty.

Auto Patrolman John Thomas Ryan was assigned the responsibility of teaching other members of the department to operate the automobile acquired by the department. Ryan was called "Driver John" because of his efficiency with vehicles of the motor age. Ryan, age 28, drove the motorized patrol wagon and was an excellent "mechanician" when a motor car needed repair.

Driver John Ryan set out from headquarters about 9 o'clock on a cloudy Wednesday morning, March 4, 1914, with one of his driving students, Patrolman Washington Irving Wright. They were in the department's newly acquired five-passenger emergency car. Wright was 48 years old and a 10 year veteran of the department. Ryan drove the car to the country section of Franklin Road and turned the wheel over to Wright.

Officer Wright drove along the curving road until they reached a temporary bridge spanning the cut of the Lewisburg & Northern Railroad. The road angled at about 90 degrees at the bridge. Wright choked the engine and the car stalled. Ryan got out, cranked the engine and got back in the car. Wright threw the clutch in before straightening the wheels of the vehicle. The car leaped forward, crashing through the wooden railing and falling 30 feet. The two officers were trapped inside as the car landed on its top.

Patrolman Irving Wright breathed a few times and died. Ryan was taken to City Hospital. He had minor external injuries, but intense pain in his chest and abdomen. Ryan never lost consciousness. He asked about Wright's condition, but was not told of his death. Driver John Ryan died of internal injuries at 3 p.m. the following day. Ryan and Wright were the first Nashville officers killed in the line of duty as a result of an automobile crash.

Patrolman Andrew Harrison Roberts died on July 15, 1914, as the result of injuries he received three days earlier while on duty. The 77-year-old officer and his partner Patrolman Rainey were walking their beat at Eighth and Taylor just after 10:00 p.m. when Patrolman Roberts misjudged the speed of an approaching street car. He stepped directly in the path of the St. Cecilia street car. He was stuck and thrown several feet. Roberts joined the Nashville force in 1880 after serving a number of years as a guard at the state prison.

Alexander J. "Alex" Barthell took office as chief of police on January 1, 1915. Chief Henry Curran retired after 41 years on the force and seventeen years as chief, the longest tenure of any chief in the history of the department. Barthell was a trustee of Davidson County. The new chief began his law enforcement career as a Davidson County deputy sheriff and had served as a Nashville detective for several years. Afterwards he was chief special agent of the Nashville, Chattanooga & St. Louis railroad. Chief Barthell

entered the office with a great deal of fanfare and was presented with a gold badge decorated with gems.

A departmental reorganization included the promotion of J. L. "Lon" Redmond to lieutenant, succeeding Owen McGovern. Lieutenant Redmond joined the department in 1907 and in 1913 became an automobile detective as a member of the Automobile Bureau of the Detective Department. At 36 he was the youngest ever promoted to lieutenant. James W. Hurt was made sergeant to replace Richard Reid. Sergeant Hurt also joined the department in 1907

Chief of Police Barthell gave the city board an evaluation of the department. His report generally depicted a department in need of both equipment and administrative structure.

> I found the department in an impoverished condition being nothing there except a skeleton. There was not a lock for the prison door, nor a pair of handcuffs, not a horse, not an automobile, not a motorcycle, not a shotgun, no effective method by which to measure or identify criminals, there was no file cases and no records of any value.

Chief Barthell implemented a number of new programs and installed state of the art equipment. A Bertillion and Finger Print System was installed and an identification bureau created. In the first full year of operation of the Bertillion Bureau the identification unit photographed and fingerprinted 250 criminals resulting in the identification of 49. The chief purchased an emergency car and built a detention room for run away girls. He also implemented twice a week drills for the officers and once a month target practice. Matron Smith began using female prisoners who were unable to pay their fines to clean the city court, drill room and offices of the station house.

The new chief cracked down on vice operations in the city. Officers made 666 arrests for violation of the prohibition statute, arrested 155 gamblers and closed 21 gaming houses. Automobile theft continued to be a major problem in the city, although the department recovered all but one of the 62 cars stolen in 1915. The department made a total of 13,344 arrests in 1916.

Additional police duties accompanied the beginning of World War I. The department registered aliens, tracked down soldiers and sailors absent from duty, investigated plots against the government and did other investigative work. When the powder plant opened in Nashville police took on extra security duty.

The dangers of policing led to the death of three officers in the line of duty in the second half of the

Police Chauffeur John R. Leathers stands in front of police headquarters in 1914 by the Patrol Wagon that was draped to transport the pallbearers for the funerals of Auto Policeman John Ryan and Patrolman Irving Wright.

decade. Detective Lem G. Thompson died at 5:23 Sunday morning December 12, 1915, from multiple knife wounds that pierced both of his lungs and slashed his upper torso and face. He and his partner Detective J. D. Farris were on duty Saturday night gathering evidence against businesses breaking the "four mile" law, which made it illegal to sell drink liquor within four miles of a schoolhouse. The law meant no saloon was legal within the city limits of Nashville.

They arrested a disorderly drunk on Eleventh Avenue near Pearl Street. They headed to the corner of Twelfth and Pearl to call the paddy wagon. Thompson held the prisoner by the back of his belt. They took a short cut through an alley where they found a second drunk and Farris stopped to arrest him. Thompson moved ahead with the first drunk. The night was cold and the alley was dark. Only the crunch of the frozen ground told Farris of his partner's position when he heard a struggle.

Farris ran to where Thompson was trying to get his gun out as the prisoner stabbed him again and again. Thompson fired in the close quarters combat until the gun was empty. The knife-wielding drunk fell back against a stable door and Thompson sank to the ground. Farris had bent over to help his partner when Thompson saw the drunk lunge again with his knife raised. The wounded detective got to his feet, grabbed the loaded gun from Farris' hand and ran forward, shooting at the head of his assailant and killing him. Thompson was taken to City Hospital mortally wounded.

The following year the "dry bone" law replaced the "four mile" law and liquor was illegal anywhere in the state. The owner of a residence on Charlotte Avenue in northwest Nashville was suspected of running a disorderly house for "assignation purposes" where both prostitution and liquor laws were being violated. Sergeant Tige Milliron was assigned to investigate the house. Sergeant John B. "Tige" Milliron was a well respected officer. He was given his nickname because of his tiger-like courage.

On the night of July 12, 1916, emergency officers J. D. Farris and Manner R. Bracy went to the house in plain clothes with two women seeking a room. Sergeant Milliron, in uniform, waited in the car. Farris and Bracy were told all rooms were occupied for undergoing repairs, but to come again.

After conferring Milliron decided to enter the house and investigate. Farris and Bracy went along the sides of the house and Milliron entered the front door. Milliron was greeted by the proprietor who was holding a shot gun. Farris heard Milliron say, "Don't flash your gun in my face." Farris moved to a window in time to see Milliron go into one of the rooms. He also saw the man raise the shotgun to his shoulder and fire.

Farris fired through the window at the shooter and ran to the front door as Bracy came through the back door. The proprietor still had the shotgun and was trying to reload. Bracy fired three shots and the man fell, but was not seriously wounded. The two officers found Sergeant Tige Milliron lying face down, dead from a load of buckshot to the back of his neck. His night-

Patrolman W. Irving Wright, left, was killed on March 4, 1914, when the department's emergency car plunged 30 feet from a bridge. Auto Patrolman John Ryan, who was teaching Wright to drive, died the following day.

Supervisors of the final of the three shifts in 1914 were Lieutenant J. William Smith, Sergeant Wilson, Sergeant Longhurst and Sergeant Richard Reid.

Supervisors of another of the three shifts in 1914 were Lieutenant Owen McGovern, Sergeant Smith, Sergeant Waddell and Sergeant Edward Wright.

stick in his right hand, his flashlight in the left and his pistol still in its holster.

Sergeant Milliron was 50 years old and had been on the force for ten years, four as sergeant. Both Milliron's son John B. Milliron and son-in-law John F. Griffin later served the department as chief.

Having a pistol drawn, however, was no guarantee of safety. Patrolman John Edward Friel and his partner Patrolman C. H. McConnell responded to a prowler call at 2021 Broadway on a Monday night in the autumn of 1918. About 11:50 p.m. they moved silently down an alley until they spotted two burglars breaking into a garage. With pistols drawn, they rushed the two. The burglars spun around and at least one had a revolver. Friel fired and the burglar fired. Friel fell to the ground with a bullet in his chest and another in his groin. Friel was bleeding badly as the

thieves ran away. At the hospital Friel regained consciousness and described the shooter who was later captured.

John Friel, 63-year-old father of seven and 23 year veteran of the police force, died of his wounds at 4:00 a.m. on Tuesday, September 24, 1918. His son John Jr. was with the American Expeditionary Forces in France when his father fell in the line of duty here at home.

Some of Nashville's finest found themselves in court charged with kidnapping as a result of an incident on the night of November 19, 1919. The Nashville Railway and Light Company was having a labor dispute. A labor union organizer who had created disruptions in other places came into the city to unionize street car motormen and other employees. Chief Barthell wanted to prevent a disturbance in Nashville. He called in Detective Gus Kiger and told him to escort the man to Springfield and suggest he not return.

The man did returned to Nashville, however, and swore out a warrant for detectives Gus and Earl Kiger, George Redmond, Walter Reese and Patrolman H. M. Bills on a charge of kidnapping. The trial was front page news the following April. The officers prevailed in court, but the city council took action to fire them. The civil service board did not sustain the action of the council and the well respected detectives were returned to duty.

By the late teens and early twenties automobiles were a growing nuisance and danger on the streets of Nashville. City ordinances were passed to establish standards for the operation of vehicles. The newness of the technology of motorized vehicles impacted both safety and resistance to enforcement. Automobiles presented dangers that did not exist with horse and buggy,

Supervisors of one of the three shifts in 1914 were Lieutenant Robert Newton Long, Sergeant Sadler, Sergeant Walter A. Gibbons and Sergeant John B. Milliron. Uniforms in 1914 were provided by Pettibone of Cincinnati.

Sergeant John B. "Tige" Milliron, left, was shot and killed on July 12, 1916, as he investigated violations of prostitution and liquor laws. Detective Lem G. Thompson, right, was stabbed to death while investigating an illegal saloon on December 12, 1915.

but people did not like new legal restrictions imposed for their safety. The lack of experience in the operation of motorized vehicles compounded safety issues.

In January 1920 Nashville policemen and detectives took the offensive against drivers who broke the automobile laws. A special group of officers was hired to chase down violators. Popularly known as "The Flying Squadron," motorcycle traffic officers Lowe, Carney, Baker and Drennan patrolled the streets day and night in pursuit of reckless drivers and other traffic violators. The first motorcycle was acquired by the force two years earlier.

The department's Traffic Squad grew to 15 officers in the early twenties. The squad was made up mostly of cornermen, traffic officers stationed at the busiest intersections in the city. Their duty was to keep traffic flowing, work any accident that occurred in their area and generally deal with traffic and congestion issues.

Criminal activity such as gambling and bootlegging also demanded vigilance. Sergeant Griffin and officers Pierce and Varner raided a downtown gaming establishment in September 1920, arresting eight. After transporting the prisoners they returned to the parlor on the second floor of 200 Sixth Avenue North and destroyed the equipment. Hauling away chips,

A 1912 wreck totaled the automobile. The advent of automobiles brought new carnage to the streets of Nashville. Traffic control grew in importance and the police department responded by creating the Traffic Division. Corner men were placed at the busiest intersections and traffic enforcement officers soon began using motorcycles to pursue offenders.

"The Flying Squadron" in 1921 included motorcycle officers Lowe, Carney, Baker and Drennan. The four patrolled the streets of Nashville day and night in pursuit of reckless drivers and other traffic violators. (Nashville Banner photo)

cards, dice, tables and chairs and a small safe took two trips of the patrol wagon. Detectives Gus and Earl Kiger rounded up a liquor gang and captured 49 gallons of white corn whiskey in February 1920. The bootleggers had earlier shot it out with Davidson county lawmen, seriously wounding Deputy William Carey.

The enforcement of liquor laws continued to be a dangerous enterprise for police officers. Prohibition was a federal law when Patrolmen James Henry Johnson and George Barcroft raided a house just before midnight on Sunday, July 31, 1921. Barcroft went to the rear of the house at Seventh Avenue South and Johnson to the front. When Barcroft entered the back door, a heavy-set gray-haired man headed out the front door and was met by Johnson.

As Johnson began to search the man's car for whiskey the patrol car approached driven by Brandon Whitney. Turnkey George Drennon, a 17-year veteran of the force, was in the car as well. Headlights of the police vehicle lit the scene. Johnson waved them in with his flashlight. The suspect was standing in front of his car and began to back away. When Patrolman Johnson reached for him the man pulled a pistol and fired. He fired again and again. Johnson fell, shot in the chest, stomach and side.

Barcroft ran from the house when he heard the shots. He fired at the fleeing gunman but missed. Johnson iden-

Traffic Officer Tilford W. "Jelly" Drennon patrolled Nashville's streets circa 1920 as one of the department's first motorcycle officers. Early motorcycles had an anti-flipover bar. Drennon later worked as cornerman at Fifth and Union for nearly 15 years before retiring after 20 years on the force.

Vaughn Woosley Irwin Giles Wenfry Reece Sidebottom G. Kiger E. Kiger Redmond

McCarver

Gibbons Chief Smith Bracy

Group photograph of the Nashville Police Department taken on November 20, 1921. Officer wore their winter uniform coats. The department command was seated in front. Chief of Police J. William "Bill" Smith was flanked by the two lieutenants who were shift commanders Lieutenant Walter A. Gibbons and Lieutenant Manner R. Bracy. On either side of them were the department's eight patrol sergeants and the traffic sergeant at the far right. Standing immediately behind the uniform commanders were the plain clothes detectives including from left to right Tom Murray, Robert Vaughn, Charley Woosley, William Irwin, Henry McCarver, Sam Giles, W. B. Wenfry, Walter Reece, Chief of Detectives Robert J. Sidebottom, Gus Kiger and his son Earl Kiger and George Redmond at the far right.

tified his assailant before the patrol wagon rushed him to the hospital. He was dead on arrival. He had been a policeman only 18 months. The killer of James Johnson was caught the following morning.

A day later sixty policemen formed a long blue line as they marched four abreast down North First Street, led by Bill Smith, their new chief. When they reached Johnson's small home where his funeral was to be held,

Nashville police Paddy Wagon or Black Maria, an early 1920s Dodge.

they filed one by one by the brier in tribute to their fallen comrade.

J. William "Bill" Smith became Nashville's chief of police in 1921. Smith was tall, solemn, soft-spoken and kind. He served a number of years as a lieutenant before assuming command of the department. Chief Smith's shift commanders were Lieutenant Walter A. Gibbons and Lieutenant Manner R. Bracy. Gibbons came on the force at the same time as Smith and served as sergeant under Chief Clack. Bracy had served as a detective and emergency officer prior to his promotion to Lieutenant. The three commanded the department through most of the twenties.

Chief Smith created the Woman's Protective Bureau to ensure that the female population of Nashville was protected from criminal exploitation. Policewoman Elizabeth Goodwin served as chief of the bureau and was assisted by Policewoman Gertrude Whitney. The two women patrolled the streets daily, checking motion picture theaters, dance halls, hotel lobbies, department stores, railway stations, community houses and public institutions. Mrs. Jean Gibson was added to the bureau in the mid-twenties to work in the office.

Nashville Police Department Traffic Squad in the early 1920s.

Chief Smith launched a campaign against traffic law violators in January 1923. It was not the first effort to promote safety on Nashville's streets, but many drivers continued to ignore speed limits and other city ordinances. The maximum speed limit in the downtown area was nine miles an hour and only eight miles an hour was allowed when crossing an intersection. The maximum speed in the rest of the city was 15 miles an hour.

Sergeant Paul Bush had recently been appointed Chief of the Traffic Department. Most officers in the department were assigned to specific intersections in the downtown area as cornermen. Cornermen kept the traffic moving at their intersection and directed traffic with the use of a manual stop and go sign atop a pole in the center of the intersection.

Traffic Officer Bob McKinstry was assigned as cornerman at 3rd Avenue and Union Street, J. I. Marshal at 4th Avenue and Union, G. D. Craig at 5th Avenue and Union, Harry Lester at 5th Avenue and Church Street, Oscar Hosrich at 6th Avenue and Church, W. D. Rash at 7th Avenue and Church, William Kennedy at 8th Avenue and Church and Archie B. Wood at 8th Avenue and Broad Street. The department had two relief men, Enoch Shelton and F. M. Smith.

In a four day period 118 individuals were arrested for a number of infractions designated as "violations of the automobile law." Among the violations were "running without lights," "running with the cut-out open" (cut-outs were devices affixed to an automobile exhaust between the manifold and the muffler; when

Patrolman John Friel, left, died on September 24, 1918, after being shot by a burglar. Patrolmen James Johnson, right, was shot and killed by a bootlegger on July 31, 1921.

204

The Nashville Police Masonic Team performed rites of the fraternal order throughout the area. Of the hundred and forty member force, fifty-three were Masons. Forty-one of those were in this 1923 photograph. On the front row, left to right, were J. F. Osborne, W. T. Lowe, W. Y. Smith, Lieutenant J. L. Redmond, Sergeant Archie B. Wood, Wheeler W. Darr, Sergeant J. W. Hurt, Marton Tucker, J. D. Eubank, W. G. Swint and J. H. Campbell. On the middle row were John Leathers, John Nichol, B. J. Martin, E. W. Inman, J. W. Hunnicut, A. A. Foster, Charles Buchanan, H. G. Dennison, C. C. Warner, Eugene Dillard, T. W. Drennon, Dave Rash, L. L. Borum, O. A. Bussell and Enoch Shelton. On the back row were Irwine Bruce, Elkin Lewis, Thomas J. Murrey, Chief of Detectives Robert Sidebottom, R. K. Vaughn, F. M. Smith, Harry Lester, Ernest Felts, E. E. Clifton, C. C. McConnell, J. W. Bills, John Steinhauer, W. A. McGowan, Robert Leonard and G. D. Craig.

open, it improved performance by releasing the exhaust directly from the engine, but the unmuffled exhaust was extremely loud) and "running without numbers" (no license plate). For those individuals who declined to go to court, bond for the violations ranged from $5 to $50. Individuals driving in excess of 20 miles an hour or driving while drunk were bound over to the criminal court.

Over 50 officers were involved in making the arrests. Seven officers made five or more arrests each. Motorcycle Officer Bearden led the group in arrests closely followed by Auto Detective McCarver, Patrolman Gore, Motorcycle Officer Chester Borum, Patrolman Estes, Patrolman Graves and Traffic Officer Leonard.

Two policemen and a keeper in the city workhouse lost their lives in the line of duty in the mid-twenties. Rookie Patrolman John F. True was on patrol on the hot night of August 4, 1924, with his partner Patrolman J. A. Tanksley. True became a Nashville policeman just over two months earlier on June 1. He punched his box at Second Avenue South and Peabody Street at 1:00 a.m. letting headquarters know all was well.

Patrolmen C. B. Buchanan and E. S. Goodrich, officers from an adjoining beat, met True and Tanksley in Howard Park for a brief rest. They saw two men coming out of the park. The two look suspicious and

one of the officers called out, "Halt." The order was answered with gunfire. The first shot pierced Patrolman John True's chest near the heart. He let out a sudden sigh and emptied all chambers of his revolver. The last shot went into the air as he reeled and fell backward onto the grass.

Nashville Police Headquarters circa 1920.

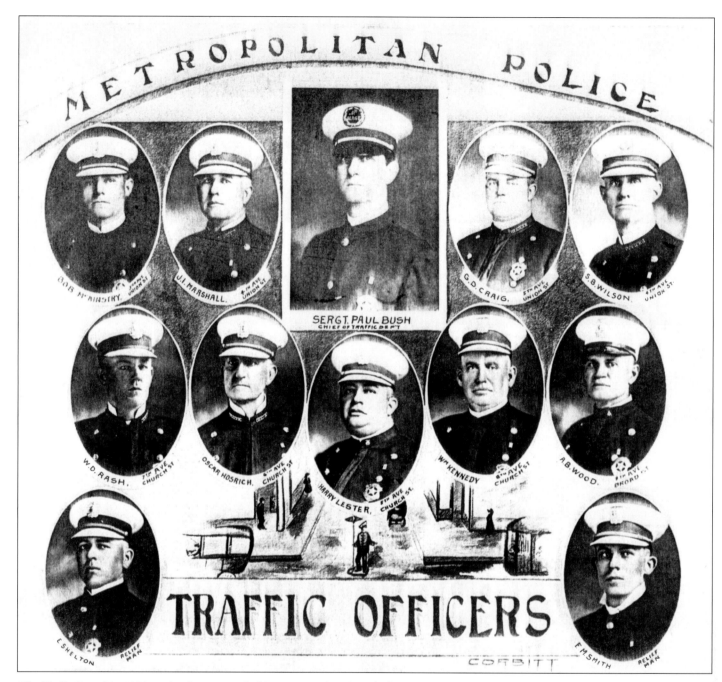

The Traffic Squad in 1923 under the command of Sergeant Paul Bush with the cornermen identified by the intersection they worked. Traffic officers began wearing white caps to make them more visible as they worked the most congested street corners in Nashville. The drawing in the lower part of the photo composite showed a cornerman on duty, his hand on the manually operated stop and go sign that he used to direct traffic.

A running gun battle ensued. A total of 21 shots were fired. One bullet struck the gunman who shot True, in the leg. The culprits escaped, but were later identified and tracked down. A Nashville patrol car drove to Columbia to bring back True's killer, the longest trip made to that date by a Nashville patrol car.

Thirty-three year old John True was taken to the nearby City Hospital where he died. There was no insurance provision for the families of officers killed on duty, but three years before over 300 members of the Nashville Chamber of Commerce had pledged $5 each, or more if needed, should such an incident occur.

Only three months later, November 12, 1924, Sergeant Archie B. Wood arrested four youths for auto theft. He ordered the four to drive to police headquarters. Sergeant Wood stood on the running board of the car as it proceeded toward the station. One of the two in the front seat drew a pistol, hit Wood in the head with the weapon and shot him in the stomach. A second gunman fired from the back seat, striking Sergeant Wood in the temple.

Archie Wood was taken to a hospital but died within a few minutes, at 1:25 a.m. Wood was a 12 year veteran of the department and served four years as sergeant. Fellow officers considered him a gentleman and said he was known to be fearless, fair and impartial.

The *Nashville Banner* reported, "Never was there such a manhunt in Nashville." Four Memphis boys between the ages of 15 and 18 were caught and confessed to the killing. Detectives Eugene Dillard, later to serve as chief, and Sam R. Giles drove to Murfreesboro to return the one who fired the first shot.

A call was received from the city workhouse on First Avenue North shortly after 10:00 p.m. on November 26, 1925, Thanksgiving evening. Emergency Officer Albert A. Foster, Detectives Henry Campbell and Elkin Lewis, Signal Superintendent Ed Blackburn and Patrolmen Dick McGrow and Jack Connors responded to the workhouse on the banks of the Cumberland River. They found seventy-two year old Charles H. Fudge, night keeper of the city workhouse, pinning J. E. Bond, another watchmen, to the floor.

Watchman Fudge had been shot twice by his drunken colleague, but managed to take the gun away and hold the assailant down. Fudge was shot in the head and abdomen and died in the hospital shortly before midnight.

This 1923 cartoon from the Nashville Banner was indication of the seriousness of the Nashville police in dealing with traffic law violators.

A similar fate almost befell state penitentiary guard Jack Orr in January 1926. Orr had taken two prisoners to a dentist in the Lambuth Building in Nashville. When he took their handcuffs off so they could go to the lavatory, the two attacked him with a blackjack one had concealed. Nashville Traffic Officer W. D. Rash heard the screams of the guard and rushed from the street, his weapon drawn and stopped the beating. Rash assisted Orr in returning the prisoners to the penitentiary.

Only months later the department had another run in with inmates from the penitentiary hospital. Eight convicts escaped. All but two were quickly recaptured. Two days later Lieutenant M. R. Bracy received a call of suspicious characters at Belle Meade Estate on Harding Road. Sergeants James Gennett and Ben Bracey, Patrolman Duke Purdue and Motorcycle Officers Jack Dowd and Leo "Lee" Flair captured the two pale and hungry convicts by the roadside.

The lack of available equipment slowed the response to a major crime in 1926. Shortly after one o'clock on Tuesday afternoon, August 10, a gang of five bandits pulled up in a Ford and walked into the East Nashville branch of the Fourth and First Bank and Trust on Woodland Street. The leader of the robbers stuck a large automatic pistol in the manager's

Rookie Patrolman John True, left, was shot in the chest and killed on August 4, 1924, when he and three other officer challenged two suspicious men in Howard Park. Sergeant Archie B. Wood, right, was killed on November 12, 1924, when he was shot by a group of car thieves.

Patrol Guard Uncle Jack Conners locked a prisoner up on cell roll at police headquarters in 1926. (Nashville Banner photo)

haunting the streets and alleys of the city, hitting victims over the head with a blackjack and robbing them. The two detectives were desperate to catch him before he killed someone. They finally rounded him up, finding his blackjack in his back pocket. They charged him with five counts of intent to commit murder and five counts of highway robbery.

Police took action against one of Nashville's best known centers of illegal active in September 1927. Nashville's red light district was located in the shadows of the Capitol building and had been there for as long as people could remember. Chief J. W. Smith told his officers that the slot piano, dimmed lights and all the activity that went with them were to be shut down.

The word went out to the madams and their employees. Chief Smith said to reporters, "I told the sergeants to tell them that they cannot run." One lady of the evening said she had been given 24 hours to "close up and leave town."

Other police operations were less overt. In one case Patrolman Sam Taylor was contacted by the proprietor of the Nash Hotel and Turkish Bath House on Third Avenue North about a suspicious guest. Patrolman Taylor dressed in civilian clothes and took the room next door to the man in question. Taylor knew something about outlaws, having spent much time in his youth in the company of famed desperado Frank James.

Taylor quickly gained the confidence of the fellow and discovered the hotel owner's suspicions were well founded. The following morning Taylor donned his police uniform and arrested the man for six robberies committed in Springfield. A thousand dollars worth of goods was recovered.

In other quick work by Sergeant James Hurst and Detective Lee Sanders, two payroll bandits were arrested for highway robbery and $2,600 in cash was recovered only two hours after the armed holdup. One of the bandits was found perched in a bath tub with cash stuffed in his trouser pockets.

The case of the "Dinner Burglar" was solved in December 1928 using one of the technological advances made in police investigation. Detectives Campbell and Flair used the Bertillion fingerprinting system to identify the thief, who entered and looted homes during the dinner hour. Fingerprints linked the sneak thief to fifteen burglaries.

Nashville police officers were active in their off-duty hours as well. They took a break each summer to participate in the City Policemen's Field Day. Six thousand people attended the 20th annual field day in 1928. The events were held at the State Fair Grounds in Cumberland Park on the 4th of July. Festivities began with a parade down Broad Street led by a mounted horseman, Patrolman Sam Taylor.

A wide variety of events were held including airplane stunts, fireworks, boxing, wrestling, dancing and a bathing beauty parade. Members of the force were the main competitors in the boxing and wrestling matches. An ample supply of old fashion barbeque and corn bread was available for hungry attendees. All funds raised at the field days went to the Policemen's Benefit Association for families of officers who died in the line of duty and for officers wounded in the line of duty.

Two of the most exciting events were motorcycle polo and automobile races. Those participating in motorcycle polo matches were "Fats" McCullough, Jack Dowd, Walter Draughn and Tennessee State Policeman R. Willard Jett. Additional officers involved in automobile races were Martin Stephens, Gus Kiger, Charley Paddock, Chester Borum and Tim Raspberry.

A number of significant personnel changes took place in the late twenties. Lieutenant M. R. Bracy resigned in August 1927 following a six month leave of absence. Sergeant Edward Wright served as acting lieutenant during Bracy's absence. Bracy was a respected member of the force with a long tenure. He resigned to pursue a career in business.

Nineteen-twenty-eight was a pivotal year for the department. The rank of Inspector was created in January 1928 to provide additional executive command within the department. J. Lon Foster and Elkin

Lewis were promoted to the new rank. Chief of Detectives Sidebottom was also given the inspector rank. Two new wards were annexed into the city during the year, creating a marked increase in officer work load and arrests.

J. Lon Foster was named chief of police in December 1928. Foster, fondly called the "Old Gray Ghost," was born in Nashville in 1879. He worked as a special agent for the N.C.R.R. for four years before joining Nashville's police force early in 1913. Foster progressed through the ranks from patrolman to sergeant in September 1919 and a short time later moved upstairs at headquarters to the Detective Department and had an illustrious career as an investigator. On January 3, 1928, Foster became one of the department's two inspectors. He served at the rank only 11 months before being selected chief.

Inspector Lon Redmond filled the position Chief Foster had held. Redmond was voted the most popular man in the Nashville Police Department in 1928, getting over two-thirds of the votes. Redmond's wife Martha Ida was no shrinking violet either. One night she captured two house breakers single-handedly in the alley next to their home while the inspector was putting on his pants and wrestling with his galluses.

Another significant personnel change took place on September 2, 1929, when Inspector Elkin Lewis was appointed chief of detectives. Long-time Chief of Detectives Robert Sidebottom applied for his pension, the process by which an individual retired. Pensions were typically one half of the salary of the officer. Sidebottom was making $3,600 a year as chief of detectives. He served on the police force for 45 years, the last 25 years as chief of detectives. Sidebottom reflected on his career in policing.

Times have changed a lot since I was a green rookie on the patrol. Why we used never to have any way to go after a crook except run him on foot, or sometimes chase him a horseback. It was just a case of outwit the crook or he'd outwit you.

Sidebottom was 69 years old and had been ill. Assistant Chief of Detectives W. Bate Winfrey had commanded while the chief was ailing. Sidebottom said he planned to move to Florida.

Chief of Detectives Elkin Lewis joined the department on September 10, 1918, and later served as an emergency officer. Two years after making detective in 1926 Lewis was promoted to inspector.

The department had only one automobile when Foster took over as chief, besides the motor driven patrol wagon. The car was old and scarred by long years of use. It was used by both the detective department and the patrol. Much time and effort was spent keeping the vehicle running. Foster campaigned to motorize the department which resulted in the purchase of an automobile for the detectives and an emergency car equipped for quick runs and emergency calls.

Chief Foster continued to press for a substantial fleet of automobiles to cope with the growing use of cars by the criminal element. In his 1929 annual police report he pointed out that the day of the walking patrol was becoming passe, "A 'beat' is slowly becoming an antique word in the more up-to-date departments in the county." The city leadership responded well to Chief Foster's proposals and by the early thirties the department owned 20 automobiles and 10 motorcycles.

Qualifications of policemen was also a concern for Chief Foster and guided his hiring practices. "In the old days, brute strength and bulldog courage were considered by all as the only essential attributes of a policeman, but that day had passed. The public demands more of its policemen than it did in years gone by and while courage is still essential, a policeman should possess tact, good judgment, and a wide sympathy; have ambition, be observant, exercise common sense."

A new badge was adopted by the Metropolitan Nashville Police Department in 1930. The badge of the basic uniform ranks was a circle with a six-point cut-out star and the state seal in the center of the badge. "Nashville" was stamped at the bottom of the circle. At the top of the badge was a number panel and a panel containing "Police" set in an art nouveau design. The hat badge was a circle around the state seal and similar panels, except the number panel was at the bottom. Traffic officers also wore an arm patch as insignia, sewn to the jacket mid-way between the shoulder and elbow. The patch was in the form of a spoked wheel and continued to be worn into the fifties.

Detectives and related personnel carried a smaller medallion style badge with the rank in the center in place of a seal. The badge was sometimes called the "lapel badge" because detectives often wore it pinned to the back of their jacket lapel and flipped the lapel to show the badge for identification. Supervisors wore a number of other styles of badges. Sergeants wore an eagle-top pinched shield breast badge with the state seal in the center. Hat badges of most supervisors were eagle-top wreath-encircled shield with the state seal embossed on it and a rank panel below. Some inspectors and other command officers wore unique, custom or jeweler made badges.

Traffic enforcement remained a major safety issue. Dedicated traffic officers were making an impact on congestion. By 1930 speed limits were increased and it was legal to drive a car 15 miles per hour through an intersection. Almost 50 traffic lights were installed by 1932 along with 275 stop signs. The most dreaded traffic accidents involved school children. Lieutenant R. B. Leonard led a safety campaign in 1932 and 1933 and school zones were patrolled when schools opened and closed. A School Boy Patrol was implemented in 1934. By the end of the decade automobile accidents involving school children were reduced to zero.

The Detective Department expanded to almost 30 officers in the early thirties. They answered over 4000 complaints a year and make over 3000 arrests a year. Detectives made more arrests in 1931 than in any previous year in Nashville's history to that date. Lead by the efforts of the six automobile detectives, for four years straight the department recovered over 96% of the nearly 500 cars stolen annually.

During the last years of prohibition Nashville police captured a record amount of contraband liquor. The department turned over more than 150 automobiles to federal authorities for confiscation. More than 4000 gallons of whiskey were turned over to the Davidson County Sheriff's Office for destruction.

The danger of policing continued. Rookie Patrolman Michael J. Mulvihill, only three months on the job, and veteran Patrolman Theodore Cook were in a store at the intersection of 28th Avenue North and Clifton Avenue. It was May 9, 1931, about 10:15 p.m. Their conversation was interrupted by shouts that H.G. Hill's grocery store across the street was being held up. The two officers rushed to the grocery. As Officer Mulvihill was about to enter the store, two armed men burst through the doorway. A third man came around the corner of the building and fired buckshot from a sawed-off shotgun at the officers from point-blank range.

Patrolman Mulvihill fell to the ground, dead on the scene. A running gun battle ensued, as Officer Cook, blood running down his face as a result of buckshot tearing his scalp, chased and fired at the three armed robbers. Cook struck one of the gunmen in the shoulder. Two escaped in a canvas-topped Ford, the other fled on foot.

Chief Lon Foster assigned Inspector E. A. Wright to head up the investigation. A massive manhunt involving more than fifty officers was conducted without an arrest. The next day two major breaks were made in the case. The getaway car, which had been taken in a previous robbery, was found abandoned on

33rd Avenue North near the scene of the crime. Also, a man went to the hospital with a gunshot wound to the shoulder, claiming that he was robbed and shot by two men.

The ensuing investigation led to the identification of five suspects. The owner of the stolen roadster positively identified two that had robbed him. They gave full confessions to the crime. The man in Vanderbilt Hospital died and the FBI matched the bullet taken from his shoulder to Officer Cook's duty weapon. The gang was responsible for numerous robberies in the Nashville area. Its leader compared himself to Al Capone. Detective Leo Flair tracked Mulvihill's killer down in Chicago and all surviving members of the gang were convicted of murder.

Detective George W. Redmond was killed in an ambush on September 25, 1933, as a result of his investigation into the activities of a "torture mob." When banks closed as a result of the Great Depression many people hid their money at home. This mob of bandits attacked and tortured elderly victims for their hidden savings. In one case the mob tied an elderly couple with bailing wire, burning the feet of the man until the skin fell off and choking his wife. Both fortunately survived.

The crimes were hideous and George Redmond work long hours over a wide area around Nashville and made the case against six individuals in the mob. Some of the crimes were perpetrated in adjoining counties and Redmond was scheduled to testify before the Williamson County Grand Jury. A few days prior to testifying he was lured to a Flat Rock barbeque stand. Redmond and the two detectives with him, Leo Flair and Ed Badacour, arrived and heard dance music coming from the darkened interior of the Dew Drop Inn.

Redmond went to the door and said, "Buddy, open this door." A shotgun blast exploded through the door. Redmond staggered and slumped to the ground. Detective Flair took cover in a cornfield and returned fire. Detective Badacour called headquarters from a nearby house. Twenty-six-year veteran of the force George W. Redmond was dead at the scene.

Reports on the whereabouts of the killer came into the station. About midnight Chief of Detectives Elkin Lewis and thirty-five officers surrounded the house across the street from the barbeque stand. The killer stepped onto the porch with his shotgun in hand and the officers fired. Redmond's assassin died of his wounds a few hours later.

Fifty-year-old Patrolman Charles B. Sanders died a violent death at the hands of another gang. Sanders

Patrolman Michael J. Mulvihill, left, was killed instantly on May 8, 1931, from the blast of a sawed-ff shotgun as he chased armed bandits. Detective George W. Redmond, right, was killed from ambush on September 25, 1933.

quietly to the woman beside him, "Duck. I'm going to shoot it out." She slipped to the floorboard.

Sanders sat motionless with his gun in his hand as the bandit reached his running board. Sanders fired twice, striking the masked man in the temple and the throat. The leader of the Blue Sedan Gang sprawled dead on the freezing ground. Another of the gang stood from the roadster's rumble seat and fired a shotgun at Sanders' car, hitting the post that held the windshield.

Sanders fired back at the volley of pistol shots that came from the bandits' car as he turned his vehicle around. His windshield cracked as a bullet entered the car. He drove the car back in the direction of his friends house. His companion moved back to the seat beside him and asked, "Are you hit?" Sanders said, "Yes, in the stomach." He was actually shot in the chest; the bullet severed an artery. As the officer slumped, his companion took the wheel. By the time they reach the house of his friend, Patrolman Charles Sanders was dead.

was on a date with a pretty grey-eyed widow when criminals tried to rob him.

A crime spree began on March 2, 1934, when a four-member gang of thugs in a stolen blue car did its first holdup. The leader of the gang, an ex-convict, stuck an automatic pistol in the face of the victims and said, "Put your hands up or I'll blow your brains out." A second gangster stood at the door with a shotgun, a third stood by with a pistol and the forth kept the car running. The Blue Sedan Gang pulled 17 robberies in four nights and reigned terror on Nashville over the following weeks as 60 policemen combed the city with riot guns.

Saturday, March 17, 1934, was St. Patrick's Day and 24 policemen led the parade, even though only a small percent of the force were of Irish descent in the thirties. The Blue Sedan Gang had stolen $1,300 in 22 holdups and officers had riot guns at the ready as another Saturday night approached. As the temperature dropped and icy gust of wind began to blow, the gang resumed their crime spree by robbing a taxi driver and stealing his cab. A short time later near Germantown, the gang stopped a yellow roadster, robbed its occupants and took the car.

Patrolman Charles B. Sanders, in the company of a lady friend, spent the evening visiting a friend at his home on the Clarksville Highway near Germantown. About 11:00 p.m. Sanders and his companion began the trip back to Nashville. Sanders' foot came off the gas when the approaching car swung sharply across the road in front of him. A man jumped from the yellow roadster wearing a mask and holding an automatic pistol and ran toward to patrolman's car. Sanders said

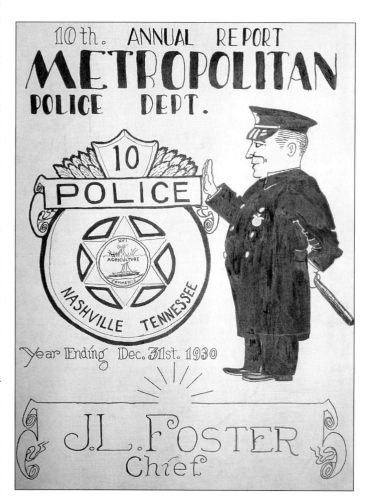

The cover of annual police report for 1930 featured the new style badge made by G. C. Dury Company of Nashville.

213

By midnight, 30 officers were searching the area. The leader of the gang was identified. Detective Sidney C. Ritter and other investigating officers searched the home of the brother of the dead gangster. They found freshly sawn flooring and beneath it a six foot square hole with loot from the robberies. The remaining gang members were convicted of the murder of Patrolman Sanders.

The following week the name "Charles B. Sanders" once again appeared on the roster of Nashville's police force. Charles B. Sanders Jr., son of the slain officer, was appointed to the department and served Nashville long and well.

Bravery exhibited by Nashville's policemen was not limited to facing criminals. Patrolman George Buchanan was recognized for his bravery during a tornado that struck East Nashville in March 1933. Buchanan spent three hours with victims of the tornado who were pinned under the wreckage of their home, saving the life of one young man. It was not the first time Buchanan demonstrated his bravery. The decorated World War I veteran risked his life a few years earlier by rushing into the flames of a burning house to save two people trapped inside.

The Nashville Police Department in 1936 was under the leadership of Chief of Police J. Lon Foster and Chief of Detectives Elkin Lewis. The remainder of the command were three inspectors, Eugene Dillard, E. A. Wright and John Griffin; four lieutenants, Walter A. Gibbons, J. W. Hurt, Robert Leonard and G. L. Scott; and six sergeants, R. L. Shirley, Sam Morrell, Frank Osborne, H. M. Bills, J. G. Gennett and J. A. Curley.

Inspector Dillard joined the department in 1918 and became an inspector in 1929. Inspector Wright became a Nashville policeman in 1907 and was promoted to sergeant five years later. Wright made lieutenant in 1928 and inspector in 1930. Inspector Griffin joined the department in 1911, was promoted to sergeant five years later, and remained at the rank until he was named an inspector on January 16, 1932.

The three desk lieutenants managed booking and other functions at headquarters on the three shifts. Lieutenant Walter A. Gibbons joined the force in 1896 and had served as lieutenant since 1915. Gibbons was one of the best known and best liked members of the force. He was a fierce-browed, hard-talking, yet kindly Irishman. Lieutenant Hurt came on the force in 1907, made sergeant eight years later, and became a lieutenant in 1928. In contrast to Gibbons, Hurt was a man of few words and mild in demeanor.

Lieutenant Walter A. Gibbons joined the force in 1896, served as sergeant under Chief Curran and was promoted to lieutenant in 1915. He had a forty-year-plus career with the department. This circa 1930 photograph showed Gibbons wearing the breast badge worn by commanders from the late nineteenth until 1952. The hat badge was adopted in 1930 and worn until 1952.

Desk Lieutenant Scott entered the force in 1918 and promoted to sergeant in 1931. He was promoted to lieutenant at the end of 1932. Lieutenant Leonard, the fourth lieutenant, was in charge of the traffic squad. He joined the force in 1918 and became a traffic officer in 1923. Five years later he was placed in command of traffic.

The department activated a new communication system on January 7, 1936. Chief Foster had campaigned five years for the radio system. The $30,000 system made Nashville as well equipped as any other department in the South. The central control unit was installed at headquarters and the antenna was located atop the National Trust Building. The system had two remote receiving stations. Call letters of the system were W4xAU.

Eleven of the police department's fleet of cars including the patrol wagon were outfitted with two-way radios for communication between headquarters and patrol cars. The radio cars were composed of a number of automobile makes, each capable of a speed of 90 miles per hour. Doors on patrol were marked "Radio Motor Patrol." The *Nashville Tennessean* summed up what the technology meant to patrolmen, "No pausing at call boxes. No delays while waiting to use a pay station. The dispatcher can be reached instantaneously—as though he were in the same room."

The city was divided into ten zones, each patrolled by a "scout car." Scout cars stayed in their zone unless there was an emergency. Four police cruisers supplemented the scout cars. Cruisers roamed the entire city. Scout cars were manned by two uniformed officers equipped with a riot gun. Cruisers were each under the command of a sergeant, two were manned by uniformed officers and two by plain clothes officers. Uniformed radio motor patrol officers, Radio Patrolmen, wore an arm patch in the form of a pinched shield mid-way between the shoulder and elbow.

An interesting feature of the patrol cars was a gun port on the passenger side of the bulletproof windshield. The device was a metal insert placed through the windshield and often called the "sardine can" because of its shape. A small button on the inside released the cover so that the officer could stick the barrel of a shotgun through the port.

Shotguns used by the department were 1897 Winchesters. They were military-issue trench guns and a number still had cooling flanges and bayonet lugs. They had been acquired by the Nashville Railway and Light Company during a strike that became violent. The company had their own police force and the shotguns were issued to guard plants and other facilities. The shotguns were given to the Nashville Police Department after the strike. Officers called them "knuckle busters" because they had a straight stock rather than a drop stock and when the slide came back if you didn't grip the weapon correctly. you got your knuckle peeled.

The department negotiated with General Motors to provide an armored emergency car. The 1935 Buick Model 90 Seven-passenger Sedan had bulletproof glass able to stop .45 caliber rounds on all windows, steel plates on all sides, fender guards to protect the tires, an armored window port to fire from, and heavy armor over the grill to protect the radiator.

To keep track of scout cars and cruisers an electrified control board was installed at headquarters. The board was a seven by ten foot map of the city, showing the ten zones, and located in view of the dispatcher. In each zone were 10 to 12 tiny green lights representing areas of the zone and a single red light. When a call came in of a problem in the zone, the red light was switched on indicating the scout car was out of service. The green light in the neighborhood where the problem occurred was turned on when the car went back into service and the red light was turned off. This allowed the dispatcher to keep track of activity throughout the city.

In the initial years of the new radio system the radio motor patrol responded to over 20,000 call per year with an average response time of less than three minutes. The patrol cars traveled over 500,000 miles a year. Over the next few years the radio division established a radio maintenance facility and expanded the number of radio receiving stations to five, giving better signal coverage over the city.

Expansion of the department fleet of motor vehicles also meant greater exposure of officers to the dangers of high speed traffic. Three officers were killed as a result of automobile and motorcycle accidents in the late thirties.

Patrolman Paul W. Cavender, age 60, died May 7, 1935, after he was struck by a speeding vehicle at 8:27 p.m. Cavender was crossing Eighth Street to make his 8:30 telephone check with headquarters. He and his rookie partner Patrolman Douglas E. Hosse, a future chief of police, had just relieved the Twenty-second Ward. Cavender was struck by the right front fender and hurled over the hood, shattering the windshield. He went over the top of the car and fell to the pavement behind it. Patrolman Cavender died at the hospital an hour later.

Detective Albert A. Foster and three others were on the way to Florida on March 20, 1936, to extradite a prisoner held on murder charges. It was a cold, snowy night about 8 o'clock. Detective Foster steered along the crown of a "turtle-back" road near Manchester, Tennessee. As he came over a rise he saw a coal truck, also driving along the crown of the road. Foster lost control of the car on the slick roadway and hit the truck almost head on. Foster was dead at the scene, his skull crushed. Others in the car, including future mayor Ben West and Davidson County Deputy Sheriff William Corcoran, were seriously injured. Albert Foster, second cousin the Chief Lon Foster, was 43 and a 14 veteran of the police force.

Thirty-one year old Motorcycle Officer William Ray Holbrook was one of the most capable officers on the force and an example of courtesy to the public. Holbrook loved hot apple pie with plenty of butter on top, fast motorcycles, and chasing bootleggers. He so

Sixty-year-old Patrolman Paul Cavender, left, was struck and killed by a speeding vehicle on Eight Street on May 7, 1935. Detective Albert A. Foster, right, was killed in an automobile accident on April 30, 1936, while in transit to pick up a prisoner.

enjoyed riding his motorcycle that he had returned to work after breaking his back in a line-of-duty accident two years earlier. He still wore a cast on his back from the injury.

Ray Holbrook, age 31, began his last motorcycle ride on Thursday morning, March 9, 1939. The nine-year veteran of the force left his home at 3600 Nebraska Avenue and headed to the station along Charlotte Avenue. His motor hit a hole in the pavement in front of the NC&StL Railroad shop near Twenty-sixth Avenue. Holbrook lost control on the streetcar tracks and crashed into a parked automobile.

The motorcycle officer suffered a severe brain injury, broke his right leg in two places, and dislocated his shoulder. He regained consciousness on the fourteenth and talked with his brother, telling him, "I'm going to ride that motorcycle again." Holbrook lost conscious again late that night and died at 7:25 on the morning of March 15, 1939. He was the first officer to die in the line of duty as the result of a motorcycle accident.

The Nashville Police Department moved to a new headquarters in 1938. The building on Second Avenue had been used as the county jail until the new courthouse was built in 1932. It was on the same parcel of land on which the Criminal Justice Center was built in 1982. Records, short-wave radio system, and prisoners were moved across the street from the old police station in November 1938.

The office of the chief of police was located on the first floor of the new headquarters, just to the left of the center entrance. The chief parked his car in an alley on that side of the building and often departed through a side door. The radio room was located on the same side of the building behind the chief's office. The Traffic Division was located on the first floor to the right of the entrance.

City Court was located on the second floor above the Traffic Division and patrol officers assembled in the center of the second floor. The Detective Division was to the left on the second floor above the chief's office complex and booking room. The building had a third floor in the center of the building that contained a property room and remnants of the old gallows.

Drive-in access located in the center of the building allowed the Black Mariah or paddy wagon to deliver prisoners. The door to the booking room was directly behind the entrance. Drunks and others arrested were placed in a large "bull-pen" in the jail area and were called up for appearance before the judge or other disposition.

The Bureau of Records and the Identification Bureau were combined into a single unit in 1938. The department had 32,693 individual criminal records on file in the bureau. Two men were dedicated to fingerprint work. Efficiencies of the reorganization resulted in five convictions based solely on fingerprint identification in the first year.

John F. Griffin was appointed chief of police on November 7, 1939. Chief Foster retired at age 60 after 27 years with the department and 10 years as chief. Detective Ed Burgess was promoted to inspector replacing Griffin.

Chief Griffin began a series of major improvements to the department. He began by expanding training and sending senior men to FBI schools. Sergeants John Milliron and H. A. Grizzard attended a two-week FBI school in Knoxville. An internal training program was initiated to instruct officers in first aid. Classes of 25 patrolmen were instructed by Sergeant Douglas E. Hosse.

Traffic Lieutenant Emmett Franklin posted six city maps in the Safety Bureau and tracked traffic accidents. Each map represented a four hour period. Colored pins marked the location of each accident, black denoted property damage, red denoted a personal injury and black with a white cross represented a traffic fatality. The greatest number of accidents occurred between the hours of three to seven.

FBI Assistant Director Hugh H. Clegg consulted with Chief Griffin in an evaluation of the department while he was in Nashville. The chief ordered a mandatory pistol drill for city officers, the first since 1916.

Line up of Radio Motor Patrol cars in 1936. Note the "sardine can" gun ports on the passenger side of the windshield and spot lights mounted above windshield. A single red emergency light was located in front of the grill and attached to the bumper by a metal bracket arm.

The drill was conducted by Sergeant John Milliron. Ammunition reloaded by Milliron was furnished to officers with .38 caliber sidearms. A number of patrolmen purchased new weapons. Sergeant Milliron had a perfect score in the drill. He was followed by Radio Patrolman Ivey Steele with a 99 and Radio Patrolman Bob Clark with a 98.

A new police record system was initiated by Sergeant Martin Stephens who had recently attended an FBI school in Washington. Booking cards were used to record details of the crime, name and address of the perpetrator, previous criminal record, marks of identification and the charge. The cards were stored as a permanent record.

R. Willard Jett joined the Nashville Police Department's Motorcycle Division on March 1, 1940,

Detectives "mug" for camera during photo shoot of Radio Motor Patrol cars.

The newly installed Radio Room at police headquarters became the communications center for radio patrol cars across Nashville.

The department's armored emergency car, a 1935 Buick Model 90 seven-passenger sedan with bulletproof glass able to stop .45 caliber rounds in all windows, steel plates on all sides, fender guards to protect the tires, armored window port to fire from and heavy armor over the grill to protect the radiator.

at the rank of sergeant after more than 10 years with the Tennessee Highway Patrol. He began his law enforcement career as a member of the Tennessee State Police in the late twenties.

Sergeant Jett was named director of safety in the traffic division of the Nashville department on November 15, 1940, and promoted to the rank of inspector. A vinyl-coated white cap was adopted for traffic officers. The headwear made officers more visible and the coating resisted rain and snow.

In other actions the motorcycle patrol was increased from six to ten officers with Inspector Jett in charge. The motorcycle unit worked funerals and parades as well as patrolling. A PBX switchboard was installed in the dispatcher's room and staffed by patrolmen Vic Williams, E. C. Marshall and J. A. Carter. A "showup room" was constructed on the second floor of police headquarters to allow officers to view city prisoners without being seen.

A new patrol routine was established for downtown Nashville. Beginning in August 1940 patrol beats were expanded from seven to 14 and patrolmen began to walk beats alone instead of in pairs. Shift times were also changed. The existing details patrolled from 3:00

a.m. to 11:00 a.m., 11:00 a.m. to 7:00 p.m. and 7:00 p.m. to 3:00 a.m. In order to eliminate the middle of the night shift change, details were changed to 7:00 a.m. to 3:00 p.m., 3:00 p.m. to 11:00 p.m. and 11:00 p.m. to 7:00 a.m.

Radio cars in the ten zones of the city were tracked on a map in the radio room that contained lights to indicate the car's status.

Radio equipped patrol units in 1936 were marked "Radio Motor Patrol, NPD" on the front doors. The patrolmen wore the uniform of the period, including the circle/six-point star style breast badge and corresponding hat badge. The officer on the left was Radio Patrolman Carmen Earsel "Big Jim" Dorman who wore badge number 13. The shoulder patch was a shield with the same design as painted on the door of the partol car. The patch was worn halfway between the shoulder and elbow, where most early law enforcement patches were placed. Radio patrol cars were standard models with standard shift, no power equipment and no heaters. Two large batteries in the trunk powered the radio and were plugged into a recharger at headquarters. The only emergency light was a red light attached to the bumper arms in front of the grill. Big Jim Dorman retired from the department in 1857 after 25 years and had two sons, Lieutenant Thomas M. Dorman and Sergeant Gary W. Dorman, who also retired from the Nashville force.

The Detective Department was divided into eight details, holdups, bootlegging, burglary, bad checks and shoplifting, automobiles, pawn shops, second-hand and junk dealers and general crimes worked by "field men." A Missing Persons Bureau was also established by Detective John Eubank.

The police radio system, under the management of Chief Radio Engineer F. E. Travis, was upgraded in 1941 to take advantage of new FM (frequency modulation) technology. Only two other police agencies in the nation had fully implemented FM radio at the time. In addition to providing enhanced clarity in communication, the change allowed car to car communication. Twenty-four police cars were equipped, doubling the number of the old system. A new transmission building and tower were built atop Love Circle Hill.

During the first years of radio communication patrol officers were sparing in the use of the radio to call headquarters and only called about important issues. One patrolman got the nickname "Dominiquer" Jones because he radioed the sergeant complaining about a chicken in the road that would not get out of the way.

The department purchased 15 new cars for patrol in 1942, eight Chevrolets and seven Plymouths. Most were used to replace worn out vehicles. Two new Hudson sedans and six new Harley Davidson motorcycles were purchased for the traffic division later that year.

An Auxiliary Police was organized in 1942 to work under the Nashville Civilian Defense Council. The force of 324 men was trained by Inspector Willard Jett, Sergeants Martin Stephens and Douglas Hosse

The old county jail, located on 2nd Avenue where the current criminal justice center is now built, would served as Nashville police headquarters from 1938 to 1958. The paddy wagon drove through the center arch to disembark prisoners. After entering the left side of the first floor, the door to the right led to the chief's office and the door to the left was the radio room. The traffic department was on the right side of the first floor. The detective bureau was on the left end of the second floor. The patrol assembly room was on the second floor in the center of the building. City court met on the far right side on the second floor.

and Motorcycle Officer Tom Scardina. Jett included security topics from a 10-day FBI school on sabotage and espionage he attended in Washington in 1940.

Inspector Jett took military leave from 1942 through 1946 and established an illustrious record of service in World War II, achieving the rank of lieutenant colonel in the U.S. Army. He served as a provost marshal at the Nuremberg war crimes trial and was in charge of security for Nazi Reichsmarshall Hermann Goering. Jett also took military leave in 1951 during the Korean conflict. In later years, after he retired from the police work in Nashville, he became an aide-de-camp to the adjutant general of the Tennessee National Guard.

The war years left two Nashville police officers killed in action on the home front. A drunken ex-con-

vict caused the death of a young Nashville detective shortly after midnight, June 25, 1942. The felon had been released from a Kentucky prison. He served only six years for killing two Kentucky State Police patrolmen when they tried to arrest him and his brother for operating a whiskey still. The drunk became belligerent with the staff of George's Restaurant on First Street North when they refused to serve him more alcohol.

Davidson County Deputy Sheriff Melvin Cooper Fleming arrived on the scene and tried to arrest the man. The felon drew a German Luger and shot the lawman three times, killing him. The gunman then turned the pistol on others in the restaurant, wounding a 16-year-old boy.

Nashville police Sergeant Martin Stephens, who later served as chief of detectives, had just driven up the hill from police headquarters. Also in the car were homicide officers Charles Dow Mundy and Robert Kimbro. The car was stopped for a red light when the policemen heard the gunfire. As they exited the car the killer ran across First Street. Sergeant Stephens told Mundy, "Catch that man."

Stephens and Kimbro were near the door of the restaurant when they heard two more shots behind them. They turned and ran to the shots. They saw Mundy down and they also saw the killer coming at

Detective Jack Dowd, left, was a member of the detective department in the thirties and forties. Policewoman Lillian Pomeroy Fuller, right, joined the Nashville force in January 1943 at age 37 and served in the city's playground program and venereal disease control program before she began work as a detective where she spent most of her career. Among many high-profile cases she captured the infamous Capitol Hill Rapist.

Traffic officers came to the station 30 minutes early one morning in 1942 to pick up March of Dimes coin containers for distribution throughout the city. Seated from left to right were John Leathers, Robert Maynard, Frank Graves, Ed Jordan, Richard Norris, Bruce Herndon and Gary Cooper. Standing from left to right were Sergeant Lonnie Martin, Sergeant Horace Bills, Lonnie Harper, Sam Stafford, Charles Sanders, C. W. Welch, Sonnie Johns, Charlie Womack, Will Whitehead, Robert Holt, Edgar Howse, John Steinhauer, Robert Rucker, David Bruce and Lieutenant Emmett Franklin. (Nashville Tennessean photo)

them firing his weapon. Kimbro was hit in the hip. Sergeant Stephens emptied his revolver into the gunman and dropped him.

Stephens went to Mundy and asked, "Are you hit bad?" Mundy answered, "Right in the chitlin's, Sarge."

Mundy's arms were spread to hold him in a sitting position. Stephens helped him stretch out on the sidewalk as his face turned white. The fallen officer was dead on arrival at the hospital. Homicide Detective Charles Mundy was tall and broad shouldered. He was 35 and had been with the department for four years.

Patrolman George "Silent Sam" Griffin with Accident Car used by the department in the early forties.

Traffic officers of the 1940s included Lieutenant Emmett Franklin circa 1940, left, who first tracked Nashville traffic statistics by time of day; and Officer Ernie Felts shortly before his retirement in 1947.

Homicide Officer Charles Dow Mundy, left, was shot and killed by a drunken felon on June 25, 1942. Patrolman Robert Burns "Bob" Sandefur, right, was hit by a shotgun blast on July 3, 1943, after responding to a domestic violence call and bled to death.

He was promoted to homicide the year before his death.

Just over a year later another Nashville officer died in the line of duty. Patrolmen Robert Burns "Bob" Sandefur and Sidney C. Ritter received a radio call, "A drunk at 37 Lindsley Avenue." It was Saturday, July 3, 1943. The address was the home of a 54-year-old city sanitation employee, a close friend of Patrolman Sandefur. The man had been drinking all day and abusing his wife. He was jealous because a man gave her a seat on the city bus earlier that morning.

The two patrolmen walked to the front of the house. Sandefur was on the left. Ritter reached for the screen door handle. A shotgun blast erupted through the screen door, striking Sandefur in the lower abdomen near the groin, severing a large artery. Sandefur drew his pistol and struggled for balance as he tried to raise the gun. The wounded officer reeled backwards and collapsed in the yard. Ritter, wounded in the side, rushed to a double window to the left of the doorway. He saw the gunman and emptied his weapon, hitting the shooter with three of the six bullets. The drunk gunman was arrested and taken to the station house.

Officer Sandefur was dead on arrival at General Hospital, killed by a friend he had played with as a boy in South Nashville. Sandefur was 39 years old and a patrolman for four years. A fellow officer said he was a "quiet and easy-going man, not afraid of the devil himself."

A non-sworn employee of the department lost his life on July 23, 1943. Dan Elam Crick was a police department electrician, who had transferred from the city's street light division at the beginning of the month. A violent storm did citywide damage and Crick responded to a call for assistance in making repairs. He was at the top of a pole working on an insulator when a live wire whipped free and made contact with the line attached to the insulator. Crick died instantly from the 2,300-volt surge of electricity.

The department remained relatively small and uncomplicated through the war years, with total personnel of 213. Command consisted of Chief John Griffin and four inspectors. Chief of Detectives Elkin

Nashville officers arrested an armed robber and hold the two weapons they took from him. Officers from left to right were Lieutenant W. F. Cuthbert, Patrolman R. L. Farmer and Patrolman W. S. Davis. (Nashville Tennessean photo)

Chief John Griffin and Police Commissioner Seth Mays are not pleased with a decision of the Civil Service Board in 1946.

Nashville motorcycle unit in 1948. From left to right are Johnnie Kittrell, Tom Phelps, Charles W. Flanders, J. W. Swafford, Inspector Willard Jett, J. W. Irwin, Leonard Irwin "Abe" Miller, Sergeant W. E. "Ted" Nannie and Officer Preslar. The two-wheel Harley Davidson's were painted blue. The color of the motorcycles changed to white in the fifties.

Lewis had 23 detectives under his command. Six lieutenants and 11 sergeants supervised 104 patrolmen, 12 traffic officers, 8 motorcycle officers, 15 identification officers and clerks, three matrons, two policewomen, five radio operators and dispatchers, and 19 other employees.

The Vice Squad consisted of two officers. Sergeant Herman Cobb, one of the best-known officers on the force, headed the unit. Red Cursey was the second man on the vice squad. Officers called him "the polygraph man" because when he got through talking with a suspect, the suspect would tell you everything.

A program of investigative training was provided to members of the force beginning in 1943. Sergeant Martin Stephens, head of the Homicide Squad and graduate of the FBI school, taught sessions on crime investigation to groups of 12 officers.

Detectives Howard Deck, left, and Harry Mott get the engine number from a stolen automobile they recovered in 1948. (Nashville Tennessean photo)

Detective Sergeant H. Allen Murray, head of the auto theft bureau in the 1940s, checked the card file of automobile transactions to get information on stolen vehicles. (Nashville Tennessean photo)

Ernest F. Underwood joined the force in 1943 and as other rookies learned the job from older officers and experience while working the streets. The force worked seven day a week without off days and with no overtime for court appearances. The city was small enough that Traffic Officer Underwood served for a time as Nashville's only motorcycle policeman. Later Underwood spent 12 months in the hospital when he answered a call at a break-in and was pinned to his patrol car by another policeman's car.

Beginning July 1, 1943, the department initiated a six-day work week for the first time in its history. Officers were divided into six groups and each group given a day off. Detectives already had a day off each week but were working 10 hour days. Their hours were reduced to eight hours per day.

World War II had an impact on all aspects of the Nashville Police Department. Most police recruits in the late forties were military veterans. Leonard Irwin "Abe" Miller began duty with the police department on January 16, 1946, fresh out of the army. He served as a battlefield mechanic and rode a motorcycle as a convoy escort. Miller quickly became a motorcycle officer.

New officers were given a set of badges, breast badge and hat badge and little else. The recruit had to buy his own gun and scrounge up a uniform. Uniform manufacturers were focused on producing military uniforms and police uniforms were scarce. Rookie policemen either found someone who had left the department or an officer who had an old uniform. Uniform shirts were gray and pants legs were plain with no stripe. Sam Brown belts were worn over the uniform jacket. In the summer the leather shoulder strap was worn with the long-sleeved shirt. Abe Miller bought a .44 Colt Special with bone-handle grips from Sergeant Hubert O. Kemp, who later became chief.

A group of officers in the late 1940s examine equipment for use in tactical situations. Standing from left to right were Carl Dickson, Johnnie Kittrell, Sergeant Carney Patterson, unidentified (officer in white cap behind Patterson), J. W. Irwin, Ed Burgess (in suit), Sergeant Roy Morgan, Commissioner of Police Seth Mays (in suit), J. W. Swafford, Detective Sergeant Luther, Inspector Eugene Dillard (in suit), Lynwood Neeley, Lieutenant Willard Jett and Sergeant Ted Nannie. Kneeling and sitting were, left to right, Charles "Snooks" Cardwell, unidentified (seated facing away from camera), Bill Donoho (holding tear gas gun), Sergeant Red Searcy (seated facing away from camera), Tom Phelps and unidentified (kneeling motorcycle officer).

Inspector Douglas E. Hosse, left, looks on as Patrolman W. S. Davis searches a burglar caught on a fire escape in downtown Nashville. (Nashville Tennessean photo)

The Harley-Davidson motorcycles used by the department were blue in color. They had a battery box over the rear wheel and red lights on the front. The mechanical or friction siren operated by a spindle that dropped onto the wheel when a pedal was kicked. The wheel turned the spindle and the siren wailed. The gear shift was on the tank and the motorcycle had a foot clutch. Motor officers wore a cap that quickly got the "fifty-mission-crush" appearance of a pilot's cap.

Department personnel was becoming more diverse in the forties. Lillian Pomeroy Fuller was the first woman to work in more traditional law enforcement

Nashville's first black police officers of the modern era joined the department in May 1948. The first seven black policemen were, left to right in the front row, patrolmen Otto Willis, Gentry Buford Bledsoe and William Latham. From left to right in the second row were patrolmen John Wesley Smith, Ernest Stamper Ford, Herman Lott Paskett and James Thomas Booker.

on the Nashville force. She became a policewoman in January 1943 at age 37 and served in many capacities until her retirement at the rank of sergeant in 1981. She had worked in the city's playground program. Fuller was initially assigned to the venereal disease control program and did not wear a uniform or carry a weapon or handcuffs. Later she served in most positions in the department with the exception of traffic. Most of her years were spent as a detective. On the vice squad she helped break up prostitution rings. She was involved in many high-profile homicides as a detective and captured the criminal known as the Capitol Hill rapist in the fifties.

A city ordinance chartered a reorganized police department effective at 10:00 a.m. on June 3, 1947. It authorized 269 total staff including 204 sworn officers. The organization and monthly salaries were 1 chief of police, $223.33; 1 assistant chief of police, 170; 1 chief of detectives, 170; 1 assistant chief of detectives, 135; 4

The planning committee for the November 2, 1948, Policeman's Ball included seated from left to right Sergeant William A. "Mickey" McDaniel, Chief Eugene Dillard and Detective Dave Beasley; and standing from left to right Traffic Officer Frank Graves, Lieutenant W. E. "Ted" Nannie and Sergeant John M. Steinhauer. (Nashville Tennessean photo)

Traffic Officer Raymond Marler was one of those trained by Sergeant Johnny Wise in 1951. Note the wheel patch worn by traffic officers and its location half way between the shoulder and elbow. (Nashville Banner photo)

police inspectors, 145; 4 lieutenants, 135; 13 sergeants, 122.50; 1 secretary to chief of police, 140; 1 sergeant at arms, 130; 1 chief homicide officer, 122.50; 1 court officer, 120; 1 secretary to chief of detectives, 117.50; 31 detectives, 117.50; 3 identification officers, 117.50; 23 traffic officers, 115; 13 motorcycle officers, 115; 104 patrolmen, 105; 1 radio engineer, 120; 3 radio operators, 105; 1 superintendent of maintenance, 117.50; 2 radio maintenance men, 105; 5 electricians, 105; 8 clerks, 105; 3 PBX operators, 85; 3 turnkeys, 105; 3 patrol drivers, 105; 2 matrons, 85; 1 head porter, 72.50; and 2 porters, 66.25.

The department was authorized to hire 15 apprentice policemen and an airport officer. Jim Singleton and Graham Anthony "Snookie" Miller, Abe Miller's brother, were among those who joined the force in August 1947. The City Workhouse and City Dog Pound were part of the department and staffed by one superintendent, five inside guards, one cook, three outside guards, two supervisory guards, one pound master, one dog catcher and one assistant dog catcher. The ordinance also gave officers one day a week off and 20 days a year vacation.

Nashville's first black police officers joined the force on May 1, 1948. They were assigned to duty in the predominately black districts of the city where they were considered better able to preserve order and enforce the law than white officers. The first seven black officers in the city were patrolmen William Latham, Otto Willis, Gentry Buford Bledsoe, John

Group of motorcycle officers during training session in 1951. (Nashville Banner photo)

Wesley Smith, Ernest Stamper Ford, Herman Lott Paskett and James Thomas Booker. Robert Lee Alexander was appointed on July 1, 1948.

The first assignment of the black officers was crowd control at the Ryman auditorium for a speech by Roscoe Conklin Simmons on May 2, 1948. William Latham carried the distinction of being the first black officer, since he was the first of the group to be hired. Latham had served nine years as a special police officer and was a member of the black military police during World War II.

The black officers and a number of other policemen were appointed under Mayor Thomas L. Cummings' apprentice policemen program. The mayor appointed policemen and firemen to serve at his "will and pleasure." Appointments were openly political in nature and the practice was ended by action of the state legislature in 1949.

The department sometimes depended on outside personnel for services important to police work. News photographers assigned to the police beat provided crime scene photographs to the department for use in investigation and prosecuting crimes. Jack Gunter was hired by the *Nashville Banner* as a photographer in 1947. He and other newspapermen were allowed to walk into a crime scene along with members of the department. Since the department did not have photographers of their own, Gunter and others routinely provided the police with prints for their files.

Chief of Police John F. Griffin retired on September 30, 1948, after 37 years of service to the Nashville Police Department. He joined the force on October 20, 1911. Two other retirements were tendered at the same time, Elkin Lewis as chief of detec-

tives and W. B. Winfrey as assistant chief of detectives.

Inspector Eugene Dillard was appointed chief of police by Mayor Cummings. Dillard was 57 years old and a 30-year veteran of the Nashville police force. Dillard's tenure as chief was brief.

Ed C. Burgess was appointed chief of police in 1949. Chief Burgess was a leader on the streets as well as behind a desk. Burgess showed his mettle in a gun battle that developed in downtown Nashville at 3rd and Jackson. A hoodlum barricaded himself in a beer joint and seriously injured two patrolmen. He shot one officer in the leg and crippled him for life; another officer, working in Car 1, was shot in the chest and nearly died. Burgess moved in and shot the gunman with a shotgun.

Mayor Ben West took office in 1951 and became actively involved with the police department. Soon after taking officer the mayor worked with Chief Burgess to create the School Mother's Patrol. Ernest F. Underwood organized the unit, one of the first such in the nation. The female officers were often referred to as the "Guardian Angels." Safety efforts of the department gained national attention in 1956 when the National Safety Council presented Nashville a special award for its school traffic safety educational program including the work of the School Mother's Patrol.

By 1951 the department consisted of approximately 350 policemen to patrol the 48 square miles of Nashville. Chief Burgess worked days and the one assistant chief worked nights. When Burgess took over the department was in need of a better way of hiring and training officers.

Chief of Police John B. "Johnny" Milliron talked with a traffice officer on Tri-Wheel duty in downtown Nashville in the early fifties.

Patrol Units 51 and 52 in 1950 with officers, left to right, George Herron, "Tink" Mulligan, Charlie Flanders, Hubert O. Kemp and C. F. Williams. (Nashville Banner photo)

Traditionally the police department in Nashville filled vacant positions based on attrition. When an officer left the department by resignation, retirement or otherwise, the position was filled. Sometimes a few vacancies were held open and three or four officers were hired at one time.

New officers got on-the-job training. A rookie policeman was assigned to a car with a senior officer, who functioned as a training officer while the two patrolled and policed the city. "The senior man ruled the roost," according to Oscar Stone. The training officer concept continued even after more formal training became standard for the department.

Many officers who joined the force through the years had only basic formal education. Some could not spell well and asked photographers or others they knew on the scene how to spell a difficult word and often looked to street signs for the spelling of street names. One time at a wreck between a train and a car, the officer could not spell engineer so he wrote "train driver."

Mayor Ben West and Chief Burgess created a formal school for recruits with instructors from both inside and outside the department. The first class began November 5, 1951. The school was located at Vanderbilt University in Kirkland Hall and held from Monday through Friday for two weeks. The school was run by Lieutenant Braxton M. Duke and Chief of Detectives Martin Stevens. In addition to sessions on policing, twenty of the eighty hours were devoted to the law. FBI Special Agent Benson Trembel, who later became juvenile judge, taught the law sessions.

The school had moved to headquarters at Second and Lindsey when Paul H. Uselton Jr. came on the department on September 16, 1955. Fifteen were in his class. Braxton Duke still led the school with help from FBI Special Agent Hank Hillin. Firearms training was conducted at the Hambone Range at the state penitentiary.

Forty-one individuals were hired from the civil service list for the 1951 class and 39 ended up in the class. Joe Dixon Casey, Oscar Roderick Stone Jr., Kerry A. Newman, King Ed Herndon, Glenn Bowers and William Dunaway were members of the class along with others who went on to have long and illustrious careers with the department.

Line up of new motorcycles on the grounds of the Parthenon in 1951. Traffic Lieutenant Braxton Duke was in the center in the overcoat. (Nashville Banner photo)

Mayor Ben West surrounded himself with local law officers in this Nashville Boosters event in 1953. The two officers on the left were members of the Davidson County Sheriff's Patrol. The three individuals in the center were, from left to right, Nashville Motorcycle Officer Charles Stoner, Mayor West and Nashville Motorcycle Officer William L. St. John. The two officers on the far right are members of the Tennessee Highway Patrol.

Joe Casey was an athlete. He played five years of professional baseball in the Boston Braves farm system and two years of professional basketball with the Nashville Vols of the Southern League. Casey passed the civil service exam and went to Mayor Ben West seeking a job as a fireman. Mayor West said, "Well, I happen to think you'd make a good policeman." Casey took the job and told the mayor, "When I get home my wife's going to kill me." Casey had never fired a gun, but made the pistol team.

Men with military service got five points toward their civil service qualification. Oscar Stone, a veteran of the Marine Corps in the Pacific Theater during World War II, was one of those who received the points.

Five black recruits were part of the 1951 class. Most patrol cars were manned by white officers, but

The Pistol Team in 1951 consisted of, from left to right, Johnny Milliron, Bill Donoho, W. R. Smith, W. A. McDaniels and Braxton Duke.

Department Electrician Dan Crick, left, was repairing storm damages on July 23, 1943, and was accidentally electrocuted. Special Policeman Dowdy, at right in a 1951 photograph, performed various duties for the department.

Chief of Police Ed Burgess has sign announcing Fire Prevention Week 1953 attached to the bumper of his car.

the patch to designate duty assignment. If the individual was assigned to inside office duty, for example in booking, the patch worn indicated "administrative." The patch replaced a generic winged-wheel patch worn by traffic.

The department began furnishing uniforms to the force. Burke and Company got the first contract. The athletic goods manufacturer was located at the corner of Church Street behind the Maxwell House Hotel. The uniforms were blue. Coats had a single vent in back and a vest was worn in cold weather. Mayor Ben West made the bow tie a part of the uniform.

Nashville police handled 45,474 cases during calendar year 1952, a record high. Chief of Detectives Martin Stephens reported 37 murders, 69 highway robberies and 21 burglaries. Because of the large number of military men who came to Nashville from Fort Campbell, Sewart Air Force Base and other bases, the Military Police maintained an MP Headquarters within Nashville's police headquarters building. The 12-man detachment covered the office around the clock.

The first female dispatcher, Mrs. Mary Hill, was appointed in April 1953. The following month she was joined in the role by Mrs. Martha Gibson and the following year by Mrs. Christine Morrell. The threesome provide dispatcher duty around the clock. All had previously been police telephone operators.

The women were seldom shaken by emergency calls and were better prepared to answer some calls

two cars were assigned to black officers. Car 2 patrolled South Nashville and Car 6 patrolled North Nashville.

The new recruits were issued the circle six-point cut-out star first used in the twenties. Being new on the force the rookies were given badges with high numbers. The badge number represented the seniority of the officer; badges were redistributed from time to time so that the officer with the longest service wore the badge with the lowest number. Stone, as the result of a request to the chief by his new partner, initially wore badge number four. The badge had been worn by his partner's father who was retiring from the force.

In mid-1952, about six months after the class graduated, Mayor Ben West authorized new badges for the department. The badge style was changed to the large eagle-top sunburst. The center of the badge had a city seal encircled with a blue enamel ring. Rank and other designations were either in a panel above the circle surrounding the seal or in the circle itself. The numbers was applied on a tab at the base of the badge. The hat badge was a sunburst with the seal in the center and an open panel for numbers at the bottom. The badge style was standardized for all ranks, with supervisory ranks in gold tone.

The shoulder patch worn with the badge was in the form of a shield with the department name and a multi-point star design in the center. The patch had "patrol," "traffic," or "administrative" at the bottom of

Airport Police Officers Steve Hailey, left, and Morty Dickens in 1954.

Traffic Department in 1955. Chief Milliron was standing front and center in a suit.

than the officers they dispatched. On one occasion officers were sent to assist a woman expecting a baby. The two patrolmen arrived about the same time that the stork did. After delivering the baby and getting the mother and child to the hospital, the officers returned to headquarters. Mrs. Gibson reported they were both shaking. One said to her, "Listen, robberies and mur-

ders are fine, but don't you ever send me out on a run like that again."

In October, 1953, John B. "Johnny" Milliron was named chief of police. The tall, easy going Milliron was 51 years old with 30 years on the department. He always had a smile on his face.

The Patrol Division had nine patrol zones with a car assigned to each. Car Number 1 patrolled downtown, a prized assignment. Car Number 2 and Car Number 3 were assigned to South Nashville; Car 2 was staffed with black officers. Car Number 4 patrolled Belmont along Hillsboro Road, referred to as "the silk stocking district." Car Number 5 was in West Nashville. Car Number 6 patrolled the northwest zone and was staffed by black officers. Car Number 7 was assigned to North Nashville. Car

Patrolman Tommy Dorman in a patrol car of the mid-1950s.

Motorcycle Sergeant John Hill tried out a new radio equipped motorcycle in 1956. Mayor Ben West and Inspector Willard Jett were observing. Hill later became the firearms instructor at the academy.

Number 8 and Car Number 9 patrolled East Nashville. A tenth zone was added in the early sixties. When officers heard the car number on the radio they knew exactly what part of the city was involved. If officers observed a crime and made an arrest, they transported the prisoner to headquarters. They called a paddy wagon when they served warrants or when a large number of prisoners was involved.

The Traffic Division had 4 zones with 4 cars plus a number of motorcycles. Cornermen, wearing white hats, continued to be assigned to major intersections in downtown. If an accident occurred in their area, they called a traffic car and worked the accident until the car arrived.

Many young officers who joined the department quickly sought assignment as a motorcycle officer. Thomas "Tom" Dozier started with the department in 1953 and after a short time in the patrol division became a motor officer. Dozier recalled that training was pretty straight forward, "We went out to Centennial Park. They started us out on the west side of the parking lot where they had the motorcycles parked, two-wheelers and three-wheelers. We went down the street and around the lake and came back and parked it where you got it. Then you were a traffic officer."

Motorcycle training was the same when James Roy Herald applied for one of ten openings three months after he joined the department in October 1956. He had never ridden a motorcycle and almost ran off the hill at Centennial Park, but it wasn't long before he learned to park the bike by locking the brake and slinging the back end into the curb. "If you couldn't do that you weren't a motorcycle officer," Herald said with a smile.

Riding a motorcycle had a number of perks in addition to the excitement and freedom of the duty. Starting salary on the force was about $250 a month and a motorcycle officer earned an extra $20 a month. Motor officers also got to take the motorcycle home. Since the number of patrol cars was limited, those assigned to cars drove them only on duty. Only the chief and the inspectors took cars home. Others assigned to cars were issued a bus pass to get to headquarters.

Motorcycle duty was considered by most officers the best time they had on the force, but it had painful moments. Motorcycle Officer Roy Herald carried sad memories of a 16-year-old girl killed in the first traffic case he worked. Other events were comical, such as the time he was working West End and got a pickup call on

Chief of Police Ed C. Burgess, left, was head of Nashville's police force from January 1949 until October 1953. Patrolman William Latham, left, in this mid-fifties photo was Nashville's first black police officer. He was appointed an apprentice patrolman on May 1, 1948.

a stolen car. About that time the car went by. After making a right turn on 19th Street and another right on to Hays Street, Herald pulled up beside him at a stop sign and said, "Hey, do you know your right rear tire is flat?" The guy pulled over and Herald arrested him.

Winter duty could be brutal. Sometimes the weather was so cold an officer's tears would freeze. If he didn't have a garage, when he tried to kick-start the motor on a cold morning he could stand up on it to kick it and it wouldn't move. By the time the officer got it started he was soaked with perspiration and then his clothes froze stiff.

Policemen worked six day weeks. The three shifts were the day shift, from 11:00 a.m. to 7:00 p.m.; the night shift, from 7:00 p.m. until 3:00 a.m.; and the morning shift, from 3:00 a.m. to 11:00 a.m. The shift hours were set to facilitate officers going to court, which was done on officers' time and without pay. Shift hours also provided continuous coverage when businesses opened and closed and when people came to and left work.

Patrolmen spent much of their shift riding the alleys of the city and checking buildings, especially doors, to be certain no one had broken into a business. When Patrolman Stone was later assigned to ride with Sergeant Morgan Smith, he became well acquainted with door knobs, "I had brass in my hands the first three months. I could tell you what alley I was in quicker than I could tell you the streets."

Sergeant Morgan Owen Smith Sr. was a legendary Nashville street cop from the rough and ready old school. The sandy-haired Irishman had steely eyes and

The first gunnery instruction was given by Gunnery Sergeant Bill Donoho shown here shooting at a target behind Berry Field with a Thompson sub-machine gun. The officers were, from left to right, Robert Titsworth (later to achieve the rank of major), Goose Warren, Harley Jackson, John Hutchinson, Donoho, Oscar Stone (partially concealed behind Donoho, soon became Gunnery Sergeant in his place), Red Johnson (who became a detective), Jimmy Goodrich (who made sergeant) and Glenn Bowers (who later served as chief of detectives).

Motorcycle officers in the late 1950s. The first four officers from the left were L. I. "Abe" Miller (as senior motorcycle officer, Miller wore badge #1), Bob "Mop Head" Coggins, Kerry Newman and Harley Jackson.

a quick temper. He joined the force as a motorcycle officer in October 1940 after service as a Davidson County deputy sheriff and a special policeman at the Municipal Airport. He chewed cigars, spoke with a gravelly voice and had a menacing scowl. He made sergeant in 1950.

Smith was considered a "policeman's policeman" by those who knew and worked with him. He had common sense and a keen sense of what was required to be a policeman. Oscar Stone said of Smith, "He taught me the first lick is 90% of the fight. He was tough as a dollar steak, but he wasn't abusive." Sergeant Smith was expert at finding break-ins as they searched the streets and alleys of Nashville for lawbreakers.

Sergeant Smith was dependable, capable and fearless. Joe Casey remembered, "Morgan Smith was never afraid of nothing or nobody." Once Smith was asked

Motorcycle Officer Tom Dozier joined the Nashville force in 1953.

nent two months later. Hosse had twenty years on the force. He was promoted to sergeant in 1940 and inspector in 1948. In December 1940 Sergeant Hosse and his partner Patrolman Ed Bennett were shot in a gun battle with a South Nashville hoodlum. The sergeant's arm was badly splintered.

Patrol and traffic cars were two-tone with a light blue top and well marked. Patrol cars were marked "Nashville Police" in a large white oval on the front doors. Traffic cars did not include the oval in their marking, but specified "Traffic" on the door. The emergency light atop cars was a large red bubble.

Twenty six-cylinder, straight-block Ford automobiles were purchased in 1955. Performance was a problem with the vehicles. Oscar Stone said, "They wouldn't pull your pants off if you unbuckled your belt." The department installed seat belts or "safety belts" in all patrol cars in 1955. The move was intended both to protect the city's police officers in case of accidents and to set an example for other motorists.

The Harley-Davidson motorcycle was the primary vehicle for traffic officers. Parking enforcement was done on the three-wheel Harley-Davidson Servi-Car. The three-wheelers were often called "popsicle wagons." The color of motorcycles changed to white in the fifties and Harley-Davidson Hydra-Glide models were purchased.

Abe Miller wore motorcycle officer badge number one from the late forties into the early sixties when he was promoted to sergeant. Badge number one meant Miller was the senior motor officer in the department. The motorcycle unit entered into a friendly competition each time a noted actress came to Nashville. They met at headquarters and raced their motorcycles to the airport. The first one to get there won the right to give the actress a ride around town on his motor.

The first gunnery instruction for officers was held for the class of 1957. Gunnery Sergeant William J. "Bill" Donoho was the instructor. He trained recruits in a wide range of weapons including the Thompson sub-machine gun. The shooting sessions were held behind Berry Field.

Besides the "Tommy guns" the department arsenal included 35 Remington rifles and shotguns consisted of the old 1897 Winchesters and 31 Remington pumps. Ammunition issued to policemen was 200-grain lead. Later the department went to brass jacket or "gilded" rounds.

Oscar Stone was promoted to sergeant in 1957, one of the youngest sergeants in police department history, and assumed responsibility as gunnery sergeant. The position was designated Gunnery Sergeant but the same badge and stripes were worn as other ser-

to describe the duties of a police sergeant. He replied, "A sergeant has to do what others don't want to do—when you got a man gone crazy or in a building or something, it's up to the sergeant to shoot him."

On one occasion Sergeant Smith and Patrolman Stone responded to a robbery in the downtown district. The bandit made his getaway on foot. The two officers caught up with him at Fifth and Union. The felon raised his 9 mm German P38 and shot it out with the officers. The armed robber died at the scene. Following the incident Stone purchased a .44 Smith & Wesson Special identical to the weapon carried by Smith.

The leadership of the department changed in the mid-fifties. Sidney C. Ritter became chief of detectives in 1955 and held the position until his retirement in 1961. After joining the Nashville department in 1932 Ritter was wounded three time in the line of duty. He was instrumental in the investigation that led to the arrest of the notorious "Blue Sedan Gang" that terrorized the city during a long and vicious crime spree. Ritter was also key to the capture of the five members of the "ride-rape-rob" gang that preyed on couples in lover's lane and a number of other high-profile cases.

Douglas E. Hosse became acting chief of police on August 1, 1956. The appointment was made perma-

Sergeant Morgan Smith held his .44 S&W after he and Patrolman Oscar Stone shot it out with a 9mm wielding robber in downtown Nashville.

geants. The individual had responsibility for all firearms and related equipment of the department.

Former Gunnery Sergeant Bill Donoho was promoted to inspector in 1957. On the night of October 31, 1959, Inspector Donoho exhibited courage and a level head in a standoff between police and two men armed with shotguns. One of the men threatened his neighbors with a 12 gauge shotgun and took refuge in his house. Authorities were not aware of the second man in the house, who was armed with a 16 gauge shotgun.

Police were on the scene when Donoho arrived. He ordered the area cleared and the house surrounded. At a neighbor's house he phoned the subject, asking to talk with him directly. Donoho entered the subject's house alone and with no visible weapon. Three minutes later he came out of the house with the two gunmen and without any bloodshed.

Police headquarters moved in February 1958 to renovated facilities in the building that had contained the market house. The complex was renamed the Ben West Building after the mayor. In addition to departmental offices, the basement of the building was outfitted with training and exercise space.

A four station pistol range was set up in the basement, but it proved noisy. The ceiling was too low to install an acoustical system. Initially bare metal baffle plates were set between the four stalls. Gunfire in the stalls was deafening. Officers had to wear both ear plugs and headsets to protect their ears. The din was lessened when acoustic tiles were used to cover the metal. Bullet traps were installed at the end of each station. A steel plate deflected bullets into a sand pit. Prisoners dug the lead out and it was sold to the man that molded bullets for the department.

A gym and a classroom were also constructed in the basement. One of the first uses of the classroom was training on the department's first breathalyzer, which was acquired not long after the new building was occupied.

An electric shop for repair of radios, spotlights and other equipment was set up in the rear of the building. The workers rigged a chair to deliver a teeth chattering shock to anyone who sat in it. They had great fun trying it out on department rookies.

The organizational structure of the force in 1958 was the chief and an assistant chief in command of three major divisions, patrol, traffic and detective. The Patrol Division had an inspector in command of each of the three shifts.

The Traffic Division was under the command of an inspector with lieutenants over accident investigation, intersection and parking control and the School Mothers' Patrol. Before 1958 traffic officers wore the same uniform as patrolmen, except that the shoulder patch specified "Traffic" and the hat was white. A new distinctive uniform was adopted for traffic officers. Pocket flaps and shoulder straps on the shirt were changed to white to contrast with the blue uniform. Whites stripes were also added to the outside seam of trousers. Some traffic hats had white covers while others were white vinyl-coated. The hats were rounded on the edge as the old motorcycle hat had been. Cornermen wore eight-pointed hats like the patrol, except white. The headwear of motorcycle officers was changed to a white helmet. Officers were not completely happy with the change, because the helmets were hot to wear in the summer months.

The Detective Division was under the command of the chief of detectives and divided into auto theft, criminal investigation and homicide. Two additional organizational units were central records and other assignment, which included the workhouse, training, hospitals security and other details.

A rash of assaults by youths in the summer of 1958 that sent two victims to the hospital prompted Chief Douglas Hosse to crackdown on teenage "gangs and hoodlums." An 11:00 p.m. curfew was established for youths and night-time loiterers. Extra enforcement was focused on drag racing. Weekend patrols were stepped up, including plain-clothes officers and unmarked cars. "I don't care whose children they are," Hosse said, "If we can catch them, they are going to the juvenile detention home."

In the late fifties the department went to one-man patrol cars. The move provided greater coverage of the city, but required greater caution on the part of the lone officer. The department produced a 53-page document entitled "Manual of One-Man Car Procedure" to provide officers with a training guide to the safest tactics for handling calls, making arrests, performing searches and seizures and transporting prisoners. In it Chief Hosse reminds officers, "Three of the greatest killers in police work are carelessness, overconfidence and lack of training."

In 1960 the department began to issue sidearms to officers. The weapon selected was the Model 10 Smith & Wesson, 4-inch barrel for uniformed officers and 2-inch barrel for detectives. The move to standardize the sidearm had advantages for training and for stocking of ammunition and other supplies. Initially 300 4-inch barrel and 150 2-inch barrel sidearms were ordered; an additional 100 were ordered later.

The pistols were blue steel and had "NPD" and a unique number in addition to the serial number stamped on the frame under the cylinder at the factory. Later weapons were stamped on the back strap.

Sergeant Stone established a card system similar to that used in the Marine Corps to track the sidearms. With the help of Mrs. Jordan, the chief's secretary, the officer's name, rank and date of issue for each pistol was recorded on a card.

Chief Hosse declined to take the pistol numbered one. Instead he ordered it to be issued to Traffic Officer John R. Leathers, the senior man in the department, who wore badge number one. Leathers joined the department soon after the end of World War I and was a traffic officer. He was assigned to 16th and Broad as one of the last cornermen. Chief Hosse took pistol number 4 and Gunnery Sergeant Stone pistol number 29.

The sixties were pivotal years for the police force of Nashville and Davidson County. Chief Douglass E. Hosse retired in August 1961 and Assistant Chief Frank W. Muller Sr. was appointed acting chief. In October 1961 a major reorganization of the Nashville Police Department was proposed. It created four divisions of the department, each to be commanded by a division chief, who answered to the chief of police and assistant chief of police. The four divisions were patrol, traffic, detective and services. The plan also called for the force to be expanded to 723 officers.

The reorganization of the department was implemented in January 1962. Acting Chief Muller, a 21 year veteran of the Nashville force, was named chief of police. Muller joined the department August 1, 1940 and was promoted to motorcycle officer in 1943, to sergeant in April 1948 and to lieutenant in December 1948. Muller held the ranks of inspector and assistant chief of police before taking over as head of the department.

Inspector Carney A. Patterson was appointed assistant chief of police and in direct command of the four

| J. B. MILLIRON | G. L. SCOTT | P. D. MURRAY | S. C. RITTER | T. A. FOX |
| *Chief of Police* | *Assistant Chief of Police* | *Section Chief of Police* | *Chief of Detectives* | *Section Chief of Detectives* |

The senior command of the Nashville Police Department in 1956 were from left to right Chief John B. Milliron, Assistant Chief G. L. Scott, Section Chief Paul D. Murray, Chief of Detectives Sidney C. Ritter and Section Chief of Detectives T. A. Fox.

Traffic units and personnel at the municipal safety building in 1958.

newly-created division chiefs. Patterson began his career with the Nashville police as a emergency driver in 1934, became a regular patrolman in 1938 and a motorcycle officer in 1939. He was promoted sergeant in 1948 and to inspector in 1957.

Inspector William J. "Bill" Donoho was appointed chief of services division. Donoho began his career as a patrolman in 1941 and became a motorcycle officer in 1945. He was promoted to sergeant in 1948 and to inspector in 1957.

Inspector R. Willard Jett, who was inspector in command of the traffic division, was named chief of detectives. He replaced Sidney C. Ritter, who retired because of ill health a few months before. Jett previously headed the traffic division and was considered one of

the most popular officers in the department. Jett's brother was Leslie Jett, sheriff of Davidson County.

Inspector Hubert O. Kemp was selected chief of the traffic division. Kemp was appointed a substitute patrolman in 1940 and became a regular patrolman a year later. He was promoted to sergeant in 1946, to lieutenant in 1948 and to inspector in 1955 after serving as acting inspector for four years.

Inspector Oly T. Boner was appointed chief of the patrol division. Boner started in law enforcement as a City Workhouse guard in 1938. He became a patrolman in 1940 and was promoted to sergeant in 1946, to lieutenant in 1948 and to inspector in 1950.

Five lieutenants were promoted to inspector, Ramond A. Marler, Braxton M. Duke, L. F. Neeley,

Promotions ceremony in 1958 included, from left to right, Pete Harper, Mayor Ben West (in suit), Frank Hancock, David Thompson, Eugene Sage, Earl Cullum (in sport jacket), "Babe" Elkins (in sport jacket), Fred Cobb, Jack Smith (in sport jacket) Tommy Coke, Henry Nickols, Malcolm Akin, Gordon Bargatze, Marvin Wright, Roy Herald, Bill Meadows and Chief Douglas E. Hosse.

Motorcycle officers at the Municipal Safety Building early in 1958 were wearing winter uniforms. The mayor and department command stood in front of the entrance.

William A. McDaniel Sr. and W. D. Monohan. Paul Murray, executive secretary to the chief, was also promoted to inspector. Six men were promoted from sergeant to lieutenant, C. H. Marshall, J. B. Kittrell, J. W. Irvin, J. R. Norwood, C. P. Lynch and William L. "Bill" St. John.

Inspector William A. "Mickey" McDaniel became a policeman in 1932 and was gentle, quiet and dedicated. It was said, "No man on the police department was more universally respected or regarded with more genuine affection than Mickey McDaniel." He attended the FBI National Police Academy in 1943.

Traffic command in 1958 were from left to right Sergeant Jesse Moore, Sergeant Claude Williams, Sergeant Raymond Marler, Lieutenant L. F. Neeley, Mayor Ben West, Lieutenant Braxton Duke, Sergeant Scottie Lynch and Sergeant Johnny Wise.

Motorcycle officers in front of the newly occupied Ben West Building in the spring of 1958. Officers on the far right were still wearing old style uniforms and officers to the right had donned the newly adopted dark traffic officer uniforms and white helmets.

McDaniel was best known for his leadership and administration of the School Mothers' Patrol. The group was organized in the early fifties and established a record for safety in school zones that garnered national recognition.

The police force began a program at Christmas 1961 that provided help for those families in need during the holidays. Sergeant Joe Casey began the Christmas basket program. Instead of officers giving each others Christmas cards they began giving baskets of food and later toys to needy families. At first deliveries were made in a U-Haul truck, later officers delivered baskets in patrol cars. Over forty years later the program continued, delivering food and toys to 200 families and over 500 children.

Metropolitan Government united the city and county in 1963 including the police function. The city police and the county sheriff's patrol were joined under a single organization structure, the Metropolitan Police Department of Nashville and Davidson County. Other incorporated municipalities

Chief of Police Douglas E. Hosse, left, served as chief from August 1956 until October 1961 and Chief of Police Frank W. Muller Sr., right, from October 1961 until April 1963.

Chief Douglas Hosse present "NPD" pistol number "1" to Traffic Officer John R. Leathers, the senior member of the force. Leathers joined the force in the mid-teens and worked as one of the last cornermen.

Black officers of the Nashville force in the circa 1960 included from left to right Otto Willis, William Latham, John W. Smith, Jr., Oscar H. Claybrooks, Raymond Black, Motorcycle Officer William D. Bodenhamer, Carl J. Crain, Bobby M. Hill, Benedict J. "Ben" Cook, Jr., Wilburn Carroll, Walter C. Buck and James L. Johnson

within the county maintained their existing police force, but the Metro force had chief law enforcement responsibility for the whole county. Metro cars patrolled all zones in the county and investigated all serious crimes.

On June 17, 1963, newly elected Metropolitan Mayor Beverly Briley named the top posts in the Metropolitan Police Department. Chief of Police Hubert O. Kemp was named to head the department. Braxton M. Duke was appointed assistant chief. Duke was appointed a patrolman in 1939 after serving as a school zone watcher. He became a motorcycle officer in 1943, was promoted to sergeant in 1948, to lieutenant in 1953 and to inspector in the January 1962 reorganization.

Five other positions were filled. Lieutenant William R. Smith was appointed chief of the detective division; W. Donald Barton, former chief deputy sheriff, became head of the patrol division; Inspector John H. Wise, director of the traffic division; Lieutenant William L. St. John, chief of services; and Traffic Officer Charles W. Flanders, head of the School Mothers' Patrol.

Ten other officer were promoted to top ranks effective August 1, 1963. Oscar Harper, William A. Ogles,

E. T. Griffith, Glenn Bowers, Charles N. Kimbrough and W. A. McDaniel were moved to lieutenant. C. F. Williams, Joe Casey, Paul Gill and C. P. Lynch were made inspectors. Approximately fifty members of the disbanded Davidson County Sheriff's Patrol were trans-

Mayor Ben West authorized Chief Frank Muller to initiate a Meter Maid Patrol circa 1962. The uniform of meter maids was light blue with white blouses and navy shoes.

Nashville Police Department command following the 1962 reorganization. Seated from left to right in the first row were Inspector Oly T. Boner (chief of the patrol division), Inspector Hubert O. Kemp (chief of the traffic division), Assistant Chief Carney A. Patterson, Chief of Police Frank W. Muller Sr., Inspector William J. Donoho (chief of the services division) and Inspector R. Willard Jett (chief of detectives). Standing from left to right in the second row were Lieutenant J. W. Irvin, Inspector Paul Murray (executive secretary to the chief), Inspector Raymond A. Marler, Inspector Braxton M. Duke, Inspector Lynwood F. Neelley, Inspector William D. Monohan and W. E. "Ted" Nannie. On the third row were Lieutenant C. P. "Scotty" Lynch, Lieutenant William L. "Bill" St. John, Detective Lieutenant Red Johnson, Detective Lieutenant Rex White, Lieutenant George Balthrop, Lieutenant C. H. "Moose" Marshall, John Norwood and Lieutenant Johnnie Kittrell.

ferred to the Metropolitan Police Department and promoted to the rank of patrolman first class.

The implementation of Metro government was accompanied by a good amount of turnover in the police department. Quite a few veteran officers retired from the force. Steps were also taken to be certain the department was cleared of the perception of dishonesty. An investigation concluded in 1964 led to indictment and conviction of several officers for corruption.

Officer Charles Rueben Byrd was the first officer to lose his life in the line of duty after the Metro system was implemented and the first officer to die in the line of duty on Nashville's police force in twenty years. Byrd was killed in a car chase on September 26, 1963. He was 27 years old.

A tough street cop, John Mullane, had a bad day with a shoplifter in 1962. Mullane was born in New York City. He was tall with a big Irish smile and strong opinions. Mullane had been with the Nashville police for 16 years when he arrested a shoplifter that day. The thief was on narcotics and went crazy. He pulled a knife and slashed Officer Mullane under the arm, through his stomach and twice through the leg. "I was bleeding like a stuck pig," Mullane said, "but I held on to him." A lesser man would have released the suspect. John Mullane was later promoted to detective in homicide.

For approximately a year after personnel from the police department and sheriffs office consolidated, officers continued to wear the badge issued to them by their original agency. Former Nashville police officers wore the large eagle-top sunburst and Davidson County deputy sheriffs wore the six-point star.

The new Metro shoulder patch was quickly designed and was issued and worn soon after the combined government was implemented. The motif of the patch featured the Metro seal.

A new badge for the combined force was designed by Ruth Strube, who worked at the police department. The custom designed badge was an eagle-top shield with a stylized sunburst design and the Metro government seal in the center. Four rank and number panels provided for designation of the wearer. The badge style was the same for all ranks with supervisors wearing gold tone rather than silver tone badges. The first badge was presented to Sergeant T. R. "Trickey" Beehan, senior man on the force.

During 1964 the International Association of Chiefs of Police (IACP) was invited to do an exhaustive study of the Metropolitan force. The association indicated that the department was weak in training officers and in field supervision. The report also recommended moving to one-man patrol cars to prevent crime and increase services.

A change in rank titles was recommended to simplify and clarify departmental structure. The numerous assignment ranks such as Patrolman, Traffic Officer, Motorcycle Officer and Detective became Police Officer. Individuals holding the Police Officer rank were given duty assignments in traffic, patrol and so forth. The rank of Inspector was dropped and the ranks of Captain and Major were created.

The department was reorganized as a result of the IACP study. Four bureaus were created under the chief

After the department originally installed seat belts in patrol cars in 1955, officials frequently encouraged the citizens of Nashville to do the same.

of police, field operations, services, inspections and personnel and training. A Vice Division was created separate from the bureaus. The Bureau of Field Operations was under the command of Assistant Chief of Police W. Donald Barton and was divided into three divisions, patrol, traffic and criminal investigation. Unifying all field operation under one head was intended to better utilize personnel and improve com-

Law enforcement officers accompanied a "Nashville Boosters" tour of the state in 1962 and promoted County Judge Beverly Briley's concept of the metropolitan form of government. The lawmen from left to right were Tennessee Highway Patrol Major Johnny Joe "J. J." Jackson, an unidentified Nashville traffic officer, Davidson County Sheriff's Patrolman Tommy Elder, Sheriff's Patrol Sergeant Harold Holt, Sheriff's Patrolman Melvin Hailey, Sheriff's Patrol Chief Deputy Donald Barton, Nashville Traffic Officer Charles Stoner and THP Lieutenant Arthur Lashlee. The two Nashville officers and the four members of the sheriff's patrol became a part of the Metro force the following year.

Metropolitan Nashville Chief of Police Hubert O. Kemp meets with officers at roll call soon after his appointment as head of the department in 1963.

munication and cooperation. Three captains commanded the three sectors, East, South and West. One of the captains functioned as the duty officer for the night shift.

Department staffing reported in the 1964 annual report numbered 574 employees including 517 sworn officers. Personnel classifications and monthly salary ranges were 1 chief of police, $1,000; 4 assistant chief of police, 785-824; 1 major, 714; 8 captains, 646; 12 lieutenants, 535-562; 14 sergeants, 461-483; 449 police officers, 400-441; 28 police officer trainees, 380; 2 auto mechanics, 420-446; 1 administrative secretary, 425; 8 senior steno-clerks, 325-355; 44 service technicians,

325-408; 1 senior typist clerk, 310; and 1 porter, 283.

The Bureau of Services was responsible for central records, communications, identification files, booking and equipment. The Bureau of Inspections was charged with continuing review of personnel and procedures, planning, budget preparation, intelligence operations and special security. The Bureau of Personnel and Training provided the functions of hiring, personnel and payroll and training.

Charles W. Flanders, commander of the School Mothers' Patrol, was promoted to captain. Lieutenant R. H. Hornbuckle served as second in command. The unit consisted of 266 school mothers in 1964 including nine supervisors and served 157 schools in the metropolitan area. No school child had been killed at a crossing patrol by the unit since its creation in 1951.

The Vice Division enforced gaming laws, illegal whiskey and moral crimes. Slot machines and other gambling activities were an ongoing problem and the division averaged destroying four to five thousand gallons of illegal whiskey every month.

An intelligence operation was created on April 1, 1964. Officer John A. Sorace, who joined Metro from the Davidson County Sheriff's Office CID, was selected to head the group. Sorace was given the rank of temporary lieutenant. Temporary rank was used frequently in the early days of Metro. Officers got the rank, the authority and the pay temporarily, but did not get civil service protection.

Senior officers of the Metropolitan police force in 1963 met in the basement classroom of the Ben West Building. Sitting from left to right in the front row were Paul Gill (head of traffic), J. W. Irwin, Raymond Marler, John Huffman, Red Wilson and Thomas A. "Tom" Dozier. In the second row were Ralph Peck, Lawrence Dickens, Charles W. "Charlie" Flanders, Gordon Vance, J. I. Johnson, Dave White, Blenn Bowers, George Balthrop and Chief Hubert O. Kemp. In the third row were Clyde Mangrun, Leonard I. "Abe" Miller and Ernest Underwood. In the fourth row were "Newtie" Barnes, John Calvo, Paul Uselton, "Duke" Edmondson, Claude Williams, "Pappy" Sills and Robert Titsworth. Note officers were wearing the badge of their former agency, eagle-top sunbursts of the police department and stars of the sheriff's office, but wore the new Metro shoulder patch.

Hubert O. Kemp	Braxton M. Duke	W. Donald Barton	William R. Smith	William L. St. John	John H. Wise
Chief of Police	*Assistant Chief of Police*	*Chief of Patrol*	*Chief of Detectives*	*Chief of Services*	*Chief of Traffic*

These were the first chiefs of the Metropolitan Nashville/Davidson County Police Department following the establishment of Metropolitan Government in 1963.

The Intelligence Division was started with two officers, Sorace and Detective Brode Pruitt and a secretary from central records. Initially the unit focused on organized criminal activity. An early case investigated a gang from St. Louis, Missouri, that pulled armed robberies. They were taken down just before they were to rob a shoe factory payroll.

The unit began to gather intelligence on groups that threatened civil unrest. In 1965 they gathered evidence on white supremacists trying to rejuvenate Klavern 13 of the Ku Klux Klan in Davidson County. The civil rights movement had begun to spawn radical groups. The unit gathered evidence on groups fomenting unrest and destruction in the mid-sixties.

Patrolmen Benedict J. Cook and Bobby M. Hill pulled off an investigative coup in the spring of 1964. The two became aware of a marijuana distribution ring working in Nashville the previous summer. They did preliminary investigation. By March Cook and Hill were sure the information was solid and went to Patrol Chief Donald Barton. Barton made Police Inspector Joe Casey and Sergeant Robert Titsworth, as well as state and federal narcotics agents, aware of the covert operation.

Cook and Hill were suspended for conduct unbecoming an officer and two days later they resigned, explaining they wanted "to prevent further embarrassment to themselves and their families." This was the cover story they used for the next two months. No one including their families knew the truth except for the few command officers. The two were in fact working undercover and within a week they had made their first buy from the drug ring.

Officers Cook and Hill faced embarrassment among family and friends and isolation while maneuvering into the gang's confidence, but they made a number of buys that resulted in cases against a number of individuals in the ring. The operation ended on May 22, 1964. Patrol Chief Barton made the public aware of the operation and the arrests, "We felt the men had accomplished what they had set out to do. We had good cases, thanks to these two officers, and we decided to spring the trap."

An alert Abe Miller quickly solved a robbery one afternoon while off duty. The report of a jewelry store robbery went out over the police radio and included the description of a get away car. Miller rode by a rental property he owned and then made a phone call. Detectives arrived a few minutes later and arrested his tenants for the crime.

Later as Miller cleaned out the apartment he found a quantity of meat in the freezer and gave it to a man who helped him maintain the property. Several weeks passed and the robbers confessed. They told detectives the jewelry was hidden in the meat. Miller learned the

"Drive Slow, Children on the Go" was the winner of the back to school safety slogan in September 1963. Standing by the safety van from left to right were Chief Hubert O. Kemp, Patrolman Newtie Barnes, Mrs. Mildred Strubie and Traffic Officer Fred Cobb.

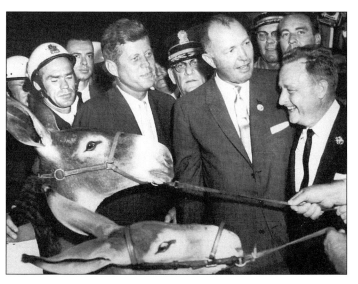

President John F. Kennedy was introduced to two Tennessee donkeys, the mascot of the Democratic Party since President Andrew Jackson was called a "jackass." Kennedy visited Nashville in 1963 before flying to Dallas where he was assassinated. From left to right were an unidentified Metro motorcycle officer (partially hidden), Motorcycle Officer Buford Hill, Motorcycle Officer Howard Lane (without hat), Kennedy, former Nashville Chief of Police Douglas E. Hosse, Governor Buford Ellington, THP Inspector J. J. Jackson, unidentified (partially hidden next to Jackson) and Metro Nashville Mayor Beverly Briley.

meat was still in his helper's freezer. Detectives recovered the stolen property and closed the case.

A significant step in the reorganization took place on January 1, 1965. Inspector Joe Casey became the first Nashville officer to hold the rank of major. Casey rose quickly to top ranks, promoted to detective on May 1, 1962, to sergeant on October 12, 1962, he was then promoted to inspector on August 1, 1963. Major Casey helped implement recommended training and supervision improvements. He was the highest ranking officer on night duty and reported directly to Assistant Chief Barton, head of field operations.

Fifty-five new sergeants were named at the same time to enhance field supervision and a training program scheduled for the following March under the direction of the IACP. Among those promoted to sergeant were Paul H. Uselton Jr., John A. Sorace, James Roy Herald, Malcolm C. Akin Jr., Charles L. Stoner and Kerry A. Newman.

Recruit training was redesigned prior to new officers being hired. Recruiting and in-service training programs were also introduced. No large recruit classes had entered the force in 1963. Two classes of cadets were trained in 1964, one graduating in April and one in August.

Robert E. Kirchner Jr. joined the department in March 1964 and graduated in the spring class. He

began as a patrolman and was transferred community relations by Chief Kemp. He was then assigned to planning and worked under Noble L. Brymer. Kirchner left the department briefly in 1978 to pursue a graduate degree.

Captain George Balthrop served as director of training during much of the sixties. The department also took advantage of the training program offered by the FBI. Lieutenant James A. York was invited to attend the FBI National Academy in 1966, becoming the third member of the department to go through the federal program. The other two graduates of the National Academy were Captain Balthrop and William St. John, soon to be assistant chief of police.

Over the next few years the number of Nashville officers graduating from the FBI National Academy grew to seven. Four officers, Oscar Stone, Paul Uselton, Charlie Hall and Don Rucker graduated from the police officer's administrative course at the Southern Police Institute in Louisville, Kentucky. Paul Uselton served as president of the school's alumni association in 1978.

Two substations were added as a part of the reorganization. The East Substation was located at 930 N. Hill Drive and the West Substation was at 3800 Charlotte Avenue. Both were in facilities provided by the public works department. Lieutenant Ernest F. Underwood served as the first commander of the East

The first Metropolitan Nashville Police Department badge was presented in 1964 to Sergeant T. R. "Trickey" Beehan by Chief Hubert O. Kemp. Standing behind the two was Assistant Chief Donald Barton, commander of the Patrol Division.

The Metro Nashville Police Honor Guard presented the colors at a city meeting in 1964, not long after Metro Government was enacted.

close friends and worked well together. They were assigned to the most dangerous traffic spots in the city. The Raiders moved from street to street every couple of hours to maintain the element of surprise in their constant enforcement presence. As the Raiders gained prominence, Tom Dozier and other motorcycle officers under the command of Sergeant Ramon A. Marler began calling themselves "Marler's Marauders" just to rib Newman.

Motorcycle Officer Jimmy S. "Jim" Ball was a member Newman's Raiders. The lanky, 6-foot 5-inch officer joined the Nashville police in 1962 from the Davidson County Sheriff's Department, where he was one of only two motorcycle officers. Ball began his law enforcement career in the Marine Corps military police. When he returned to Nashville after his hitch in the military, he raced motorcycles throughout the eastern United States. Ball's first assignment on the Nashville force was in the patrol division, but soon he moved to traffic duty and accident investigation.

Enforcement duty at the state fair was important for the protection of pedestrians and children. Newman had six officers, including Jim Ball and George Williams, playing hide and seek with motorists and ticketing violators during the fair. Raiders were known to issues over 100 citations a night. The unit got significant recognition and publicity because of their success. They also worked public events, parades and other functions as assigned by the mayor. "Motorcycle duty was good," Ball recalled, "except in the cold winter months when survival meant riding from one coffee shop to the next just to keep from freezing."

Substation. The substations were used as a site for roll call of the patrol division. Decentralizing patrol was important in order to cope with the broader service area created by the Metropolitan Government and to address the need for modernization. A lieutenant was in command at each of the substations and a captain on each shift was over both of the substations.

The traffic division developed an elite motorcycle enforcement unit to be assigned to areas where accidents were most frequent and where vigorous traffic enforcement was needed. The specialized group of motorcycle officers was called the "Raiders" and led by Sergeant Kerry A. Newman. The unit became know as "Newman's Raiders" and quickly established an illustrious record. The initial motorcycle officers in the unit were Ryman Buchanan, Paul Burris, Tony Cockran, Roy D. Cook, Mayo Craddock, Steve Harley, Peter J. Harper, King E. Herndon, and James C. Williams.

The members of Newman's Raiders were all volunteers. They were a strong group of officers who became

Officers deliver baskets to Nashville's needy during the 1964 Christmas season.

Duty was dangerous for all members of the department who were assigned to ride two-wheelers. Metro Motorcycle Officer Carroll Gordon Bargatze responded to a call of an officer involved accident on October 16, 1965. He was killed in an accident on 3rd Avenue en route to the scene. Motorcycle Officer Roy Herald, a friend of Bargatze, was two blocks away and the first on the scene. Officer Bargatze had been with the department for 17 years.

Newman's Raiders were disbanded in 1967 when the policy that allowed officers to take city vehicles home was abandoned. Within a year of dissolving the Raiders, Captain Paul Gill, head of the traffic division, was under pressure to improve traffic enforcement. Assistant Chief Barton announced plans for the formation of two motorcycle units of 10 men each and the acquisition of 20 new motorcycles.

The "law and order" image of the department was upheld in the mid-sixties by Traffic Sergeant Fred Cobb. Cobb established a reputation of enforcing the law the same for everyone. He issued traffic violations to a number of officials, including a deputy U.S. marshal, the city comptroller and a general sessions court judge. He also ticketed two meter maids for parking their scooters in a bus zone while they went into a drug store to eat lunch.

One Saturday night in July 1966, Cobb went to see "Who's Afraid of Virginia Woolf." On Sunday, Sergeant Cobb returned with a warrant and two other officers and closed the theater for violating the city's indecency and obscenity laws.

A number of new policies were implemented following the promotion of John A. Sorace to assistant chief in December 1967. He took charge of the seven areas of staff services, intelligence, internal security, inspections, internal affairs, planning and research, training and personnel. Training was extended from 6 weeks to 22 weeks and the training program revamped. Night shooting, instinct shooting and firing while running were made a part of the training. Officers were instructed that once they made the decision to fire their weapon, they should fire two shots and evaluate. Expanded background checks by the intelligence unit were begun and an IQ test, physical agility test, psychological test and polygraph were added to the civil service exam.

News conference on police issues in December 1965. Standing behind Mayor Beverly Briley, seated at the conference table, were Assistant Chief of Police Donald Barton, Roy Herald, J. W. Irwin, Glenn Bowers, Ralph Peck, Don Rucker (in suit), James Abernathy, Ed Herndon, James York, unidentified (behind Kemp), Chief of Police Hubert Kemp (in suit), Fred Cobb, unidentified (behind Brymer), Nobel Brymer (in suit), William St. John (in suit), unidentified (behind St. John), Bob Tittsworth and John Sorace.

Newman's Raiders was formed in 1965 as a special traffic unit of all volunteer motorcycle officers. Sergeant Kerry A. Newman supervised the unit. Members of the initial unit kneeling from left to right were Mayo Craddock, Sergeant Newman, Roy D. Cook and James C. Williams. Standing from left to right were Paul Burris, Tony Cockran, Peter J. Harper, Ryman Buchanan, King E. Herndon and Steve Harley.

Bobby Hill was promoted to lieutenant in 1967 and given command of the Intelligence Division, to which he was originally assigned in 1964. Lieutenant Hill was the first black officer in the history of the department to hold a division command and in 1965 was the first black officer promoted to sergeant. Hill made captain in 1972.

Assistant Chief Sorace appeared before two committees of the U.S. Senate in 1968, including the McClellan committee, the Permanent Sub-Committee on Investigations. He testified on intelligence gathered among descendent groups of the civil rights movement, their plans to make bombs and poison water supplies. He described vivid scenes of basements found with target shooting galleries and thousands of expended cartridges.

The impact of criminal activity by radical groups was felt by Nashville's police force in many and varied ways, but none so painfully as on a cold and raw January night in 1968. Officer Thomas E. Johnson was dispatched on Tuesday, January 16, to apprehend subjects who had just attempted to pass a forged money order. He spotted the suspect's vehicle and attempted to execute a traffic stop on Herman Street. The vehicle moved onto 15th Avenue North, which came to a dead-end at a railroad track. As Officer

Newman's Raiders in formation at the Court House and City Hall. Sergeant Kerry A. Newman stands at the head of his volunteer band of traffic officers.

Members of the Raiders motorcycle enforcement group. From left to right were Sergeant John Hill, who took charge of the Raiders, Jimmy S. "Jim" Ball, Mayo Craddock, Jenx Hackney, Robert "Puddin" Evans, Bill Bay, Roy Barnes, J. W. Davis and Melvin Hailey.

Johnson exited his patrol car, one of the five occupants in the suspect vehicle opened fire with a 30-30 rifle, striking him in the chest and killing him.

Officer Charles Wayne Thomasson, en route to back up Officer Johnson, was met by gunfire when he turned onto 15th Avenue. Officer Thomasson lay seriously wounded on the ground, when one of the suspects walked over and shot him several more times in the lower torso. The mortally wounded policeman struggled to his radio and called for help.

Officer Jim Ball heard the call and was first on the scene. He remembered the carnage when he arrived at the location of the incident.

> I was in a traffic car. I had a guy stopped, and I heard the call come out on the radio. It was like a voice from the dead. Thomasson came on the air and said, "Send us some help. We've been shot all to pieces." He was shot up real bad. Johnson, in my opinion, was dead when he hit the ground. When I stopped the car. I went to Johnson first. Thomasson lived two months and finally died. He was just shot all to pieces.

Thomasson was rushed to the hospital where he lay comatose with seven gunshot wounds and died on March 17. Officer Thomas Johnson, 39, was a ten-year veteran of the department. Officer Charles Thomasson, 29, was an Air Force veteran and had six years on the Nashville police force.

Emotions were high in the department. Everybody wanted to work the case. Five suspects were apprehended and found to be members of the Black Panthers, a militant group that advocated violence

Motorcycle officers Jim Ball, left, and Ryman Buchanan on night enforcement duty. (Nashville Banner photo)

against police officers. They were convicted of murder and sentenced to 99 years in the state penitentiary.

Following the incident, the department made an adjustment to the one-man car policy. Two officers were assigned to cars on night patrol in parts of the city considered trouble areas. One-man units continued day and early morning patrols.

Another Nashville officer lost his life in the line of duty in 1968. Officer Robert Lloyd Williams died on May 2 from injuries he suffered the previous day. His patrol car went out of control while responding to a call, struck another car and overturned. He was 34 and had joined the force in 1963.

A search for stolen property in a west Nashville home resulted in a gun battle that left two officers wounded and a felon dead. Major Joe Casey, Captain Raymond Marler, Lieutenant Paul Uselton and Patrolmen Robert White, Herschell Glenn, Morris McKenzie, Larry Jackson and H. T. Coleman served a warrant around 2:00 a.m. on February 8, 1968, to search for a items stolen in a weekend burglary.

The suspect was questioned about a car in his driveway. He admitted the vehicle was stolen by a friend. When he was told he was under arrest, he asked to put his shoes on before being taken in. Some officers exited the house to have the stolen car towed. Sergeant Burnett was searching the attic. Patrolman White stayed in the living room with the subject while Casey, Marler, Uselton and Glenn started into the kitchen. The arrested man reached under the coffee table for his shoes. Officers heard the man's wife yell, "Don't do that."

Officer John Wesley Smith III joined the department in 1962 and soon was working traffic. He was a second generation Nashville officer. His father was one of the first black officers on the force. As his father, he became a highly respected member of the force and reached the rank of lieutenant before he lost his life in the line of duty in 1980.

Members of the School Mothers' Patrol worked a booth at the fair to promote school zone safety.

Officers turned to see the felon holding a .25 caliber automatic pistol that was apparently hidden in a shoe. He aimed the weapon at Major Casey's head, about eight feet away and pulled the trigger. The pistol did not fire. The gunman jacked the slide and fired a bullet that went through Casey's arm. The shooter spun and shot Patrolman White four times. Officers in the doorway hit the floor and drew their weapons. Casey and Marler emptied their duty revolvers. Burnett exited the attic and fired. Patrolman Glenn had to reach over Casey to fire. Casey took his weapon and continued firing. Other officers fired as well. A total of 26 shots were fired. Major Casey was also shot in the side.

Major Casey was taken to General Hospital and Patrolman White to the Baptist Memorial, both in patrol cars. Casey returned to work later in the day and Patrolman White recovered from his wounds. The gunman was dead on arrival at the hospital with ten bullet wounds.

Nashville and the nation was rocked by a shot fired in another Tennessee city. On April 5, 1968, the day following the assassination of Dr. Martin Luther King Jr. in Memphis, civil disorder erupted in Nashville. Among the first injured was Assistant Chief John Sorace. Sorace was in an unmarked Ford sedan with a souped-up engine along with officers Bobby Russell and Roy Clark, members of the Intelligence Division. Sorace was the only one wearing a helmet. They were touring an area near the campus of Tennessee A&I (now Tennessee State University).

The car rounded a bend in the roadway and they were confronted by a large mob. As they sped away, a barrage of rocks hit the vehicle and smashed every window. One large rock came through the windshield, crushed Sorace's helmet and fractured his skull in two places. The assistant chief, bleeding badly, was taken to St. Thomas Hospital. He woke from a coma four days later.

A citywide 10:00 p.m. to 5:00 a.m. curfew was established and 4000 National Guardsmen were called up to assist the police in maintaining control of the city. They assembled at Centennial Park under the command of Adjutant General Hugh Mott, later to

Officers Thomas Johnson, left, and Charles Thomasson died as the result of a confrontation with militants on January 16, 1968. Both were shot multiple times. Johnson was killed at the scene; Thomasson died on March 17.

serve as Nashville police chief. Police, Highway Patrol troopers and guardsmen move onto the campus of Tennessee A&I and began patrols throughout North Nashville. Officers worked 12-hour shifts. The department was unable to get the headgear ordered from the Duco helmet company, but they were sent used Michigan State Police helmets in lieu.

Coordination of the policing efforts during the week of rioting was the responsibility of Major Joe Casey. After sniper fire from A&I, guardsmen and policemen searched men's dormitories, confiscating weapons, making arrests and wounding one individual who was firing from a sixth floor room. The curfew continued and was extended from 7:00 p.m. to 5:00 a.m. A small contingent of police led by Major Casey went onto the A&I campus a few days later when the ROTC building was burned. It was over a week before order was restored. The efforts of the police department and particularly the leadership of Major Casey were commended by all segments of the community.

The department faced a growing range of legal issues. Establishing prudent guidelines and protocols consistent with new legislation affecting police and reacting to lawsuits required additional legal resources. Senior Metro attorney Paul Bumpus was assigned by the city's legal department to work with the police department. In 1971 William L. "Bill" Parker Jr. joined the department as legal advisor to the chief, supplementing the Case Preparation Section and assisting field personnel. He served in the position for 25 years.

Major Joe Casey established a record for taking

Officer Tom Dozier bends over Officer Thomas E. Johnson, while Officer Jim Ball checks his pulse. The 1968 incident shook the police force and resulted in the death of two officers in the line of duty. (Nashville Banner photo)

Major Joe Dixon Casey became the first to hold the newly created rank on January 1, 1965. Casey later headed of the Metropolitan Police Department of Nashville and Davidson County as chief of police from 1973 to 1989.

command of situations, whether dealing with mobs or an individual. Casey placed himself in harms way on March 11, 1969, when a distraught husband walked into a downtown beauty salon with six sticks of dynamite rigged as a bomb. Major Casey walked into the building and persuaded the man to turn over the explosives.

Casey was selected to officiate the 41st National AAU Basketball Tournament in Gallup, New Mexico, in 1969. Casey officiated basketball for 25 years. He worked the first interracial game ever played in Nashville. During the rioting the previous year, Casey worked the demonstrations at A&I during the day in police uniform and then went back to A&I that night to officiate basketball games.

Thirty-three year old Joe Thomas McEwen Jr. barely escaped death during a murderous attack in 1970. McEwen joined the police department in January 1969, as a civilian employee in the booking room. Later that year he entered the police training

academy, conducted in the basement of the Ben West building and graduated in December. After the mandatory period of riding with a senior officer, he was assigned to zone 21 West, the Belmont/Hillsboro area, as a solo patrol officer.

McEwen was working the 5 p.m. to 1 a.m. shift on Friday, March 6, 1970. The report of a purse snatching at the Continental Apartments about 9:35 p.m. sent him in search of two perpetrators. McEwen spotted a man in a blue sweater sitting in a white four door Buick parked in front of a house near 26th and Blakemore. The occupant and the car matched the description of one of the bandits. McEwen approached the vehicle, flashlight in his left hand and his right hand resting on the butt of his duty weapon.

As McEwen questioned the subject in the car, the man's partner exited a nearby house, came up behind the officer and shot him four times with a .32 caliber pistol, once through his left elbow, once in his left side and twice in his upper right side. McEwen struggled to stay on his feet and fired two shots, striking the suspect in the car in the arm and stomach. McEwen took two more bullets to the neck. He fired again, hitting the shooter.

The two felons fled on foot. McEwen got to his car, flipped on the blue lights and radioed for help. Officer W. J. McKinley found McEwen lying on his back, next to the patrol car. He was rushed to the emergency room in critical condition.

One of the two would-be killers was taken into custody by Metro officers at 12:30 a.m. near the scene. The other was picked up in Marshall County at 12:45 a.m. by Tennessee Highway Patrol Sergeant Tom Edwards.

Officer Joe McEwen took medical leave for almost 18 months before returning to the force. He had been back on duty about six months when he found himself chasing an armed robber. The gunman grabbed a bystander and threatened to kill the old man. McEwen took a shooting stance and drew a bead on the felon. His bluff called, the bandit ran, taking a shot at McEwen. McEwen shot the gunman in the head and hit him with two more shots.

Joe McEwen policed Nashville for over twenty years, serving in patrol, Crime Analysis, the Training Academy, Auto Theft and finished up in Vice, specializing in outlaw biker gangs. He was promoted to sergeant in 1978 and to lieutenant in 1982, before retiring in July 1990.

Traffic Officer Jim Ball was promoted to the detective division and assigned to homicide. Sergeant and soon to be Lieutenant, Thomas E. "Tom" Cathey was in command of the Homicide Section. He had a solid reputation as a detective and a stickler for detail. Cathey was respected for his thoroughness and accuracy. He was also a good supervisor, discussing cases with his men, giving guidance and listening to their thoughts. Detectives worked long hours with no overtime pay.

All homicide men were deputy coroners. They worked all the hospitals in any incident of a crime against persons. Murder cases were worked by two medical examiners, either Dr. Core or Dr. Petroni. Dr. Simpkins later served as a medical examiner. Homicide also relied on capable identification people such as Willie Ray Arnold and Madison Waggoner. They were adept and stayed as long as it took to get the job done.

Detectives usually worked alone on cases. A case was usually solved as a result or either physical evidence or an eye witness. In one particularly violent crime Jim Ball worked, a bloody shoe print became a key to solving the crime. A French teacher had fought against her assailant all over her home in an upscale neighborhood. She was finally killed after being stabbed 18 or 20 times. Ball found the print of a shoe left in the blood-strewn house and cut out a section of the floor to preserve it. A solid case was built against the juvenile who killed the woman.

The investigation of the murder of a night watchman began with a witness description. A muscular assailant was raping a woman near a factory on Fourth Avenue South when a guard tried to stop him. The watchman wore his weapon in cross-draw fashion and as he was drawing the pistol, the rapist took the gun away from the guard and shot him. The woman's description led to the identification, arrest and conviction of the killer.

When a crime scene was compromised, the criminal often escaped justice. Detective Ball arrived on the scene of the murder of an Amway distributor to find that fellow policemen had violated basic procedures. The woman was found beaten to death in her product supply room. The scene had been tracked up by six patrolmen, a sergeant and a city councilman. One of the patrolmen had rubbed a pencil over an order form pad in an amateurish attempt to reveal a name or other clue. Evidence was contaminated or destroyed and the crime was never solved.

The key to solving a murder was driven home for Ball at a homicide school in Austin, Texas. A renowned detective/instructor said, "When you investigate a crime scene, especially a murder case, you got to keep in mind that the killer leaves something and that he takes something away. You have to find out what it is."

Detectives often put their life on the line in the process of an investigation. Homicide Detective Thomas N. "Tommy" Jacobs Jr. was in plain clothes, driving an unmarked car on February 11, 1971. He was investigating a series of rape and molestation cases with the Tactical Squad in the Green Hills area. Jacobs was shot three times and left beside a driveway on Oriole Place. One bullet struck his upper lip on the left side, passed through his sinus and lodged in the back of his neck. A second shot hit him in the back, grazing his spine and lodging there. The third shot passed through his shoulder.

Jim Ball was the first officer on the scene and found Jacobs lying on the street side of his car bleeding. Witnesses described a two-tone, black over blue, car with a man and a woman inside. Jacobs could not talk, but wrote for Sergeant Tom Cathey that he saw the man in the two-tone car pick up a female hitchhiker. Jacobs pulled the car over and the shooting occurred. Jacobs survived his wounds and his assailant was later captured.

A limited realignment of the top command was made on July 1, 1969. Assistant Chief William St. John took command of staff services and Assistant Chief John Sorace was placed over central services.

The department's armory at the Ben West Building was under the command of Lieutenant Oscar Stone. He had been joined by Patrolman Tom Dozier, a 14-year veteran motorcycle officer. The two worked

George Balthrop, standing on left; FBI Special Agent Bruce Hodge, standing on right; Oscar Stone, on left beneath sign; and Tom Dozier, on right beneath sign, at the Hambone Range on the ground of the Tennessee State Penitentiary.

together in various assignment for almost thirty years thereafter. In addition to weapons, they had responsibility for other inventory including cars. Before the motor pool was established, Stone and Dozier were responsible for equipping new automobiles for patrol service. The vehicle maintenance facility was also located at headquarters.

Stone and Dozier formed the department's bomb squad. They began with training and, as Dozier recalled, "about a dollars worth of tools." Later they were provided with a new vehicle, a steel cylinder on a trailer for detonation and transportation of explosives and other equipment. Bob Kirchner worked with them for a while.

Lieutenant Carl Dollarhide took command of the Bomb Squad in the early seventies as part of the Tactical Squad of Special Operations. In 1972 Sergeant Tommy Hibbs and Officer James Buford Tune were the first two to attend school. The unit dismantled the largest car bomb in Tennessee history in August 1979. Buford Tune and Jim Detlepsen disarmed the 300 to 400 pounds of dynamite and plastic explosives found near a Nashville nightclub only four minutes before it was set to detonate.

Technological improvements in the processing of information was needed in the department as well. Existing computers for all Metro departments were in the city's Finance Department. Central Services Assistant Chief John Sorace implemented a dedicated information system for the police department in July 1971, a UNIVAC 418 III mainframe computer and 20 terminals using a canned software package called LEAP (Law Enforcement Application Package). The system was paid for with a grant from the Federal Law Enforcement Assistance Act. Almost as soon as the department turned on the system, they caught a fugitive. A felon who showed up at the Vanderbilt emergency room was wanted for a long list of crimes.

The two officers were on hand around 10:00 p.m. on Sunday, September 19, 1971, when crime came to the Ben West Building. A call went out from the dispatcher, "10-52 [shooting] at headquarters, all units in vicinity report at once." The front of the building had been sprayed with seven gunshots, one bullet barely missing Sergeant W. D. McPherson at the glass-enclosed desk in the lobby. Lieutenant Oscar Stone and Officer Tom Dozier were in the lobby when the shots shattered glass around them. They found McPherson lying across his desk talking to the radio room.

Three men were arrested for the shooting the following Tuesday after an around-the-clock investigation led by Chief of Detectives Mickey McDaniel and homicide Lieutenant Kenneth Reasonover. The three, along with two women, had been drinking and one decided he would "shoot up the police station" as the car approached Memorial Bridge.

The Youth Aid/Vice Division was reorganized and split in the early seventies. The division had responsibility for investigations of crimes involving children, women and vice. Most of the female officers in the department worked in the division. Female officers included Lillian Fuller hired in 1943, Peggy Williams hired in 1966 and the first female officer to attend a formal police school, Flora O. "Sue" Klippstein hired in 1967, Jody Sacchinelli hired in 1969 and Arlene Moore hired in 1969. Moore was the Youth Aid investigator who worked the high profile kidnapping and murder case of a 12-year-old in 1969.

Women were required to wear skirts and high-heeled shoes and to carry their handgun in a purse. When youth and vice were divided Lieutenant Charles L. Stoner assumed command of the Vice Division and most of the existing staff including female officers stayed with vice.

The Youth Guidance Division was created in 1971 under the command of Major George H. Currey. Currey, a graduate of Peabody College, was teaching when he was persuaded to become a full-time juvenile officer by Davidson County Sheriff Tom Cartwright and started the first juvenile office in a sheriff's office in Tennessee. Currey later served as an investigator for the district attorney general and as assistant director of the state law enforcement academy before Mayor Briley asked him to design a juvenile division for the police department.

The division was funded from an omnibus crime bill grant and began operations in September 1970. It was staffed by about 55 people with college degrees. The prevention unit included three black officers, Emmett H. Turner, Charles Etter Jr. and Temore Willis. One unit was routinely in the schools, but up to 50 officers could be put into a school at one time if the need arose. The officers in the school were not in uniform; they wore blue blazers with a patch on the right pocket. The timing was right because over the next couple of years schools experienced major problems including riots and the Youth Guidance Division was credited with holding the schools together.

The division developed a Juvenile Warning Citation system that gave officers an option beyond giving a verbal warning or physically arresting the youth. The citation required parents of the juvenile to contact a youth guidance counselor for resolution of the matter without referral to juvenile court. Three counselors came to police headquarters to handle citations.

After eight years as a Youth Enforcement Officer and School Resource Officer, Emmett Turner was promoted to sergeant and briefly served as a patrol supervisor. Sergeant Turner returned to Youth Guidance Division in 1979 as supervisor of Sexual Abuse Unit, investigating child physical and sexual abuse cases. He served in the role for five years.

The unit also made an important contribution to encouraging degreed officers within the department. The Omnibus Crime Bill funded officers to go to school and the division allowed officers flexible hours so that they could schedule classes.

The department's emphasis on training and diversity remained strong. The largest recruit class in the department's history graduated in 1971. Ninety-eight rookie police officers were added to the force on December 17. The group included 19 black officers and 4 female officers.

Hugh B. Mott began duty as chief of police on February 1, 1972. Chief of Police Hubert O. Kemp retired effective April 1, 1972, but took accumulated time off. Mott was the only person to serve as chief who was not a law enforcement professional. He had served as Mayor Briley's head of public safety since the previous June, with responsibility for police, fire and civil defense. Prior to that, Mott took leave from the position of city treasurer to serve as adjutant general of the Tennessee National Guard.

General Mott served with valor in the U.S. Army during World War II. As a lieutenant, he led two sergeants on a mission to remove explosives from the bridge over the Rhine River at Remagen. Retreating Nazis planned to blow up the bridge to slow the allied advance. For his war-time action, he received a number of medals, including the Distinguished Service Cross, the nation's second highest citation for heroism.

Mott was intent on improving the image of the police department and increasing its visibility among the citizens of Nashville. He requested a review by the International Association of Chiefs of Police and subsequently reorganized the department using a more military model.

The new chief changed uniforms to solid blue trousers and shirts. Short-sleeved shirts were worn in the summer time and long-sleeved shirts in the winter with jackets. He also required that all officers wear whistles.

Chief Mott established a department-wide take-home-car plan to enhance basic coverage of the city and to increase visibility with the public. When shifts changed under the previous procedures, policemen had to bring the car in from the patrol sections to the police station. Then the new shift took the cars to be serviced before starting patrol. Many sections of the city were out of service for an hour or two on every shift change.

Having the patrol car to drive home meant the officer was essentially available for service from the time he left home until he returned after his shift. The car parked at the officer's home at night also acted as a deterrent to crime. Having the car all the time also meant the officer took better care of the vehicle, which cut down on damages to the unit.

A number of enforcement initiatives were taken during Chief Mott's tenure. Sergeant Kerry Newman was authorized to bring back Newman's Raiders. Also, the Tactical Squad was created to saturate areas of the city where crime was pronounced. Lieutenant Carl "Sonny" Dollarhide took command of the tact squad in 1973. The unit was composed mostly of ex-military officers accustomed to using firearms. Officers on the unit were at least six feet tall and weighed 180 pounds. Walking patrolmen were assigned in high crime areas.

Sergeant Kerry Newman was not happy when Chief Mott told him he would no longer be in command of Newman's Raiders. When Chief Mott told Newman he was being placed in charge of a new helicopter unit being created, Newman was "tickled," according to Mott. Newman, also a pilot, was sent to pick up the helicopters being provided by the Army and fly them back to Nashville.

Motorcycle Officer Gordon Bargatze, left, was killed in an accident on October 16, 1965, en route to an officer involved collision. He was killed in an accident on 3rd Avenue en route to the scene. Officer Raymond Leroy Wheeler, right, died on November 6, 1973, after being shot in the head by a juvenile he was transporting to detention.

Sergeant John Hill took command of the motorcycle unit. Although the unit was no longer called Newman's Raiders, the term "Raiders" stuck and became a designation on motorcycles officers shoulder patch.

A new substation was established in a converted doctor's office on Nolensville Road in 1972. The traffic and intelligence departments were moved to the new South Substation. A contingent of detectives from the burglary and property theft division also moved into the substation. The Ben West Building continued to house the detective department, located on the second floor, central records and the administrative bureau including all of the chiefs and Judge Doyle's traffic court. The other substations continued to be used only as a site for roll call of the patrol division.

The decentralization of departments at the South Substation lasted for only about a year because of limited space and logistics of getting reports to headquarters. Before electronic communication, reports had to be delivered by hand between headquarters and the substation.

At the encouragement of Major Malcolm Akin, commander of the South Substation, a K-9 Patrol was introduced. Canine officers and their handlers were trained and quickly proved their importance. When the training academy was established, a K-9 training facilities was setup and a K-9 cemetery dedicated.

The first K-9 Unit training was held in Nashville in 1973. The first class included Officers Ralph E. Key, Clyde Taylor, Charlie Hay, Tommy Gentry, J.R. Johnson and Johnny Ray. The trainer was Charlie Spain and the head of the unit was Jim Brown. The class was 14 weeks and the assignment was a seven day a week job for officers. The dog was the first thing on the officer's mind in the morning and the last thing at night. He fed, exercised and groomed his K-9 partner.

Officer Ralph E. Key with his dog Mr. Blu and Officer Clyde Taylor with Fritz did six weeks of narcotics training in Washington, D.C., in 1975. They became Nashville's first two certified narcotic K-9 Teams. In 1976 Nashville sent six K-9 Teams to the K-9 Trials in Ft. Wayne, Indiana, Officers G. Whitehouse and Officer R. Key finished at #1 and #2 Police Teams in the U.S. The departments four-man team won first place police department in the nation.

Improved personnel resources were introduced. The department created a standard operating procedures manual, documenting administrative and operational best practices. The campus of Bordeaux Tuberculosis Hospital northwest of the city was acquired as the future development of a training academy.

Chief Mott believed in educating community leaders to all sides of life in the city. On Friday and Saturday nights he invited six or eight ministers from churches around town, put them in squad cars and took them down to the "gay joints," the x-rated movie theaters, the massage parlors and to night court.

The police department's personnel director changed in 1973. Chief Mott appointed Captain Bobby Hill to the important position. Hill, a native of Sparta, had become a respected leader on the force as head of the Intelligence Division. Hill believed, as a black officer responsible for personnel, he could assure the community that discrimination was not a part of the hiring decisions of the department.

Chief Mott promoted nine other black officers as well. Samuel Sloss was promoted to sergeant and made a district commander. Oscar Claybrooks was promoted to sergeant in the intelligence division. Willie Williams was promoted to sergeant in the warrants division. Richard Ordway was promoted to lieutenant and made assistant commander of the Vice Squad. Thomas Claybrooks was promoted to sergeant and made a district commander. William Bodenhamer was promoted to lieutenant and made commander of the community relations division. Luther Summers was promoted to sergeant in command of the detective division's robbery detail. John Smith III was promoted to sergeant and made a squad commander. Richard Petway was promoted to sergeant.

The eyes of nation focused on Nashville and in November 1973 when the bodies of Grand Ole Opry regular David "Stringbean" Akeman and his wife Estelle were found at their home not far from the residence of his close friend Louis Marshall "Grandpa" Jones. Detective Sergeant Sherman Nickens and Detective Tommy "Jake" Jacobs Jr. were the first Metro homicide detectives on the scene. TBI Agent George Haynes was also at the scene. Metro Officer Clyde Taylor and Fritz of the K-9 unit searched the house and cars. Evidence recovered that was important to the case included beer cans, cigarette butts and weapons that belonged to the Akeman's.

Lieutenant Tom Cathey, commander of the Homicide Section; Captain Paul Godsey, head of the detective division; Chief Mott; and several other ranking officers were soon on the scene as well. They handled the press and others who gathered.

Many Metro detectives and other officers worked the investigation, but leads were few. The case began to break when a jailed arsonist contacted the district attorney general's office wanting to trade information on men who had talked about robbing the Opry star. Good detective work

Identification Unit van was a mobile lab unit used at crime scenes.

led to the arrest and conviction of two cousins of David Akeman for the double homicide. The killers were after money hidden in the residence by the Akemans.

The number of female officers in Metro were increasing, Shirley Davis, Diane Vaughn and Donzaleigh Heard were added in 1970 and Linda Gentry, Anita Lowrance, Wanda Uselton and Elizabeth Fox in 1971. Metro had 15 sworn female officers and their role in the department was changing. Women were allowed to wear slacks and to carry their weapon on their person. Judy Bawcum, hired in 1973, was the first female officer to wear a uniform. Sue Klippstein was the first female officer promoted to sergeant, also in 1973. Lillian Fuller was promoted to sergeant in 1978.

On September 1, 1973, Valarie Meece and Edith Langster began training to be the first female patrol officers. Training was held in the basement of old Bordeaux Hospital on the grounds of the future training academy. After graduation in January 1974 Officer Meece was assigned to the East Patrol Sector and Langster to the West Patrol Sector. Female officer hired afterwards were required to serve on patrol as their first assignment.

Deborah Y. Faulkner began a career with the department in 1974 as one of three new female officers assigned to the Patrol Division. Faulkner attended the FBI national academy in 1981 and was promoted to sergeant in 1982. Sergeant Faulkner was assigned to the team implementing a Computer Aided Dispatch system at the Communications Center. Faulker became the first female officer to head the department when she served as acting chief in 2003.

Monica M. Jett joined the Metro police in 1975. The daughter of former Davidson County Sheriff Leslie Jett and niece of retired Nashville Inspector Willard Jett followed a family tradition in law enforcement. She retired at the rank of sergeant in 1996.

A number of female officers began exceptional careers in the years that followed. Officer Honey Pike joined the force in 1977 and was promoted through the ranks to deputy chief. Officer Louise Kelton joined in 1980 and was named a precinct commander in the new millennium.

Carol Etherington became an intern with Metro while she studied psychiatric nursing at the Vanderbilt University School of Nursing. She counseled with rape victims and abused children. Etherington launched the Victim Intervention Program (VIP) in 1975 as a crisis counseling and victim advocacy program. Metro Nashville was one of the first departments in the nation with a victim counseling program. VIP was

Sergeant Tom Dozier, Officer Jimmy Forester and Lieutenant Oscar Stone at the Hambone range at the state proison. Park Police Sergeant Leon Whiteside looked on from the far left.

Vehicle acquired for the Bomb Squad that was composed of Lieutenant Oscar Stone and Sergeant Tom Dozier.

implemented under the Criminal Investigations Division and staffed by mental health professionals. The program grew to provide diverse services to anyone victimized by a crime.

Major Joe Casey and Major James A. York swapped duty assignment on October 16, 1973. York took command of the Patrol Division and Casey took command of the Administrative Services Division. Casey took a desk job for the first time in his 22 years with the police department. He had commanded the patrol division since 1966.

The next month, 47-year-old Joe Dixon Casey was named acting chief of police. He immediately called for a new police headquarters and at least 125 police officer to be added to the existing 800 member force. Casey was named permanent chief on May 28, 1974. Chief Casey served during the entire tenure of Mayor Richard Fulton, the head of Metro Nashville's government from 1975 to 1987. Mrs. Agnes Jordan served as Casey's secretary, as she had to the previous seven chiefs.

Chief Casey began to implement a number of changes to enhance the productivity and professionalism of the department. He implemented a new policy in February 1974 for officers responsible for the death of another. The officer would be put on administrative leave with pay until an investigation was completed. The regulation was not intended as punishment, but to allow the officer time to recover from the emotional strain.

A momentous step was taken to upgrade department training when Captain James A. York and Lieutenant Oscar Stone were assigned to organize the Metropolitan Nashville Police Training Academy. They and a small staff cleaned the recently acquired facility.

Three of the original K-9 teams trained at the academy from left to right were Officer Tommy Gentry with Max, Officer Charlie Spain with Rebel and Officer J. R. Johnson with Wolf.

Captain York was in a house on the grounds where the office was located. Tom Dozier soon moved to the academy with a promotion to sergeant, bringing the armory with him. The first class was held in the small chapel building and consisted of four recruits. The gun range at the penitentiary, the Hambone range, was used for firearm training and continued to be used for years.

The academy was formally dedicated on December 15, 1974. The refurbished facility contained four classrooms, a multi-purpose gymnasium, a firearms repair and storage center and nine offices. Captain Milton E. "Jack" Bowlin took command as head of the Metropolitan Nashville Police Training Academy. A class of 50 new recruits began a five month training program on January 3, 1975.

The first SWAT Team in was organized in 1975. Academy personnel formed the unit because they had the weapons and other equipment, had weapons certification and were the best trained. The first name given to the unit was Metro Unique Situation Team (MUST). The name was the idea of John Manning and was used to distinguish the unit from the "SWAT" television show that portrayed a false image of Special Weapons And Tactical units.

The team initially consisted of firearms and physical training instructors Kenny Barnes, William Bowlin, Richard Briggance, Phil Davidson, Tom Dozier, Tim Durham, John Hill, John Hoffman, John Manning, Joe McEwen, Chip Pearson, Ken Pence, John Ross and Phillip Sutton. The unit was formally incorporated into department functions in January 1976, membership spread to other department personnel.

The name of the unit was changed to SWAT in 1978. William Garner joined the unit in 1981 and

Chief Hugh B. Mott, left, headed the department from February 1972 to November 1973. Chief Joe Dixon Casey, right, served in the position from 1973 to 1989.

Richard Hillenbrand, Richard Holt and Robert Kirchner came on in 1982. In 1984 the team moved beyond academy personnel and began to bring members on from the field. Karen Krause joined the team in 1987 as the first female member of a tactical unit in Tennessee.

The most the team's time was spent in training. The first equipment was second-hand weapons and out of date protective ware. Team members bought a lot of their own equipment. The original response vehicle was a Ford stationwagon with a blue wooden box in the back for equipment. The team was issued .357 caliber revolvers, short barrel shotguns, M14s and M16s for long range protection, .45 caliber Thompson submachine gun and .45 caliber grease gun for entry and the 37mm granade launcher for gas and smoke canisters. Early call outs were individuals holding hostages, barricaded subjects and escaped prisoners. Most incidents were resolved without use of weapons. A MUST call out was initiated in the field by patrol or investigative officers in situation that called for the special resources of the tactical unit.

CID investigate high profile cases in the mid-seventies that were both difficult and dangerous. Homicide Detective Jim Ball set a record for the detective division in 1974. During a six-month period beginning in April, Ball arrested 35 persons as a result of his investigations. Second place in number of arrests in the six-month period was W. L. Birdwell with 32 arrests and third was George McNeill with 31 arrests. A promotion to sergeant put Jim Ball back in uniform as a commander in the East Patrol Sector. After about a year he told Mayor Briley he would rather be in the detective division than wear sergeant's stripes and was transferred back to homicide in October 1975.

The February 1975 homicide of a young girl captured the attention of the entire country. She disappeared while selling Girl Scout cookies in her neighborhood. She was last seen on February 25 walking down the street with two people. When she did not return home that night, a massive search ensued involving the police and hundreds of volunteers.

Thirty-three days later her strangled body was found in a Green Hills garage 150 yards from her home. Forensic consultant Dr. Bill Bass of the University of Tennessee—Knoxville determined that she was killed in the garage on Estes Road. As a result of the assault and murder, the Girl Scouts revised their guidelines on the selling of cookies.

Chief Casey formed two new units to focus on major crime problems. The Vice Control Division was formed in March 1974 by the reassignment of 34 offi-

Assistant Chief Paul Uselton, left, later became the second in the department to hold the rank of Deputy Chief. Captain Roy Herald, right, later served as major.

cers to concentrate on drug related crimes. In January 1975 a forty man burglary prevention squad was created to reduce residential burglaries. The program was named Operation Crime Control and commanded by Patrol Major Glenn Bowers. The department did stings and reverse-stings for the first time. Officers said the crooks would sell to anybody, so Chief Casey put on a big hat and a cigar in his mouth and made buys to prove the point.

Plain cloths investigators often found themselves in harms way. Metro Vice Squad Officer Phillip Levon Beene was shot and critically wounded on February 28, 1975, while he and his partner, Mike Nichols, investigated gambling activity in a North Nashville beer joint. A shootout erupted and Beene was shot in the groin area. He scrambled to a nearby porch and lost a lot of blood before he was discovered. The shooter was arrested the next day.

Sometimes good basic observant police work was better than investigative technique. One Friday night in November 1975, Officer Gary Mallory of the Tactical K-9 Unit stopped a car for running a red light at Fairfield Avenue and Lafayette Street. Moments earlier the dispatcher had broadcast the description of the bandit who robbed the Graystone Motel on Murfreesboro Road as wearing a toboggan hat. Mallory noticed one of the passengers in the car was wearing a toboggan hat. "That's when I reached back in my car and grabbed the shotgun," Mallory said. He arrested the men.

Investigation showed that the suspect in the toboggan hat did the robbery of the motel and nine other recent armed robberies. Fingerprint analysis by Identification Officer W. R. Arnold also connected the

Showing various tactical weapons were, from left to right, officers Tim Durham (retired at the rank of lieutenant), John Manning (retired as a major) and Marty Beauman.

man to a robbery and rape case. Detectives Morris McKenzie, Desmond Carter and William Rucker, who had been working diligently on the case, were grateful for the alert work of Officer Mallory.

Several officers of the Metropolitan Nashville Police Department were killed in the line of duty during the seventies and early eighties. Twenty-two year old Officer Raymond Leroy Wheeler died on November 6, 1973, after he was shot in the head the previous night by a juvenile he was transporting to detention. Wheeler was recognized as officer of the year by the Nashville Area Chamber of Commerce. Lieutenant Oscar Stone and the other member of the department's color guard served as an honor guard for fallen officers and at the funeral of Mayor Briley.

Two officers were killed in the line of duty in the first two months of 1976. Officer Curtis Jordan, 28, working patrol in South Nashville, was stabbed on January 12, 1976, and died the following morning. Jordan and his partner, Gordon Larkins, responding to a domestic call, entered an apartment just before midnight. The occupant said no one was going to take him away and lunged at the officers, stabbing Officer Jordan in the lower abdomen. Jordan was taken to the hospital and was given 60 pints of blood in the attempt to save his life. He was a veteran of Viet Nam where he served with the Rangers and had been a policeman for five years.

Officers George Howard Hall and J. L. Jones were on patrol in the South Sector shortly after 6:00 p.m.

on February 23, 1976. They responded to a complaint of thieves breaking into cars at the Hamilton Creek Boat Ramp. As they drove into the boat ramp area, they saw two teenagers run into a wooded area. The two officers gave chase, Hall about fifty yards in front of Jones.

Twenty-four-year-old Officer Hall found one of the suspects lying in the bushes. Hall ordered him to stand. The subject was facing away as Hall began to handcuff him. Suddenly the man reached into his waistband, pulled a handgun and fired over his shoulder. Officer Hall was struck in the upper right chest.

Officer Jones heard four or five gunshots and then heard Hall moan and yell. Seconds later Officer Hall stumbled out of the woods and fell into Jones' arms. Hall said he returned fire, but did not think he hit either of the youths. Jones made his partner comfortable and called for assistance. Hall was rushed to the hospital, where he died half an hour later. A massive manhunt was launched that included 50 Metro officers, 24 troopers of the Highway Patrol, a number of Civil Defense workers and two K-9 units. Two juveniles were arrested and the shooter was tried as an adult and sentenced to life in prison.

George Hall had been a policeman only 14 months. He was hailed as a hero a few weeks before his death. A woman in a burning second floor apartment dropped her infant out of the window to save the child and Hall caught the baby.

Chief Joe Casey announced later in the week of Hall's fatal shooting that the 750 Metropolitan

Officer Curtis Jordan, left, was stabbed to death on January 12, 1976, when he and his partner responded to a domestic violence call. Officers George Hall, right, died on February 23, 1976, from gun shot wounds sustained as he chased thieves near the Hamilton Creek Boat Ramp.

The original Metro Nashville Police SWAT Team in 1979. In the front row from left to right were Officer Tim Durham, Sergeant Tom Dozier, Captain Milton Bowlin, Sergeant Joe McEwen, Sergeant Richard Briggance and Lieutenant John Ross. In the second row were Officer Ken Pence, Sergeant John Manning, Officer Phil Sutton, Officer Kenny Barnes, Sergeant John Hoffman and Sergeant John Hill.

Nashville officers would begin wearing bulletproof vests as standard equipment. "The vest might have saved the life of Officer George Hall," Casey said.

Officer Steve Pinkelton, left, was killed on July 26, 1978, during the armed robbery. Officer Edward Tarkington, right, was shot while interviewing a burglary witness on December 17, 1978, and died on the way to the hospital.

Many officers were reluctant to wear the bullet resistant vests because they were heavy, bulky and slowed reaction. Light-weight vests were acquired from Armour of America.

An inmate riot at the Tennessee State Penitentiary in 1975 required a major force of Nashville police officer to assistance in putting down the unrest. The Tennessee Highway Patrol also became involved in the incident that was known as the "Pork Chop Riot" because of the steady diet fed at the prison that summer. The use of Nashville K-9 units was a major factor in ending the disorder.

Thirty-four members of the department assumed new job responsibilities on February 4, 1976. The reassignments were made to broaden the experience of the officers as well as bring fresh ideas and strengthen all area of the department. The range of transfers was from top commanders, including three majors, to civilian workers.

Major Glenn Bowers became head of the Criminal Investigation Division, swapping assignments with Major James C. Abernathy, who took command of the Patrol Division. Major James A. York was transferred

Firearms training conducted on the Hambone Gun Range at the State Penitentiary in 1973 prior to completion of the Metro Academy range. Before Metro firearms trainers were certified, the FBI provided a certified instructor to supervise. Pictured from left to right were FBI Special Agent Henderson "Hank" Hillin (later elected sheriff of Davidson County), Trainee Raymond Leroy Wheeler (killed in the line of duty before the end of the year), Training Sergeant John Hill, unidentified trainee, Training Sergeant Tom Dozier, Training Officer Sam Sloss, two unidentified trainees, Training Officer John Manning, Trainee Judy Bawcum (later an assistant chief) and Training Officer Tim Durham. These MNPD training officers became the first certified firearms instructors at the Metro Academy.

to the Planning Section and was replaced in the Personnel Section by Captain Ralph W. Peck. Captain Robert L. Titsworth became head of the newly created Special Operations Division. He was replaced as Chief Casey's administrative assistant by Lieutenant Robert E. Kirchner Jr. of the Inspections Division.

Captain Edward T. Griffin moved from the Equipment Section to command the West Patrol. He was replaced by Captain Donald S. Rucker of warrants. Captain King E. Herndon from inspections took command of the Vice Control Squad. Captain Raymond A. Marler was transferred from vice to inspections. Captain James T. "Tony" Gentry, former head of the defunct Alcohol Beverage Control, was moved to the Court Appearances Section.

A number of cost saving measures were adopted in the late 1970s as a result of the soft national economy. Expenses were reduced in January 1976 by eliminating 25 to 30 aging unmarked police cars. Accompanying the move, the drive-home privileges of 20 officers was revoked. Four administrative lieutenant positions were eliminated during the same month.

Chief Casey used new technologies to enhance police capabilities and services. He had a helicopter pad and air strip constructed at the training academy to accommodate police aircraft of the newly implemented air patrol.

Walking patrol units were assigned to the downtown area beginning May 1, 1976. Six to eight officers walked the center of the city as a deterrent to purse-snatchers, shoplifters and other criminals. The only policemen walking in the downtown area before the assignment were three traffic officers. Officer Charlie

Officer Merri Lee Puckett communicates with headquarters circa 1983. Officer Puckett was the first and only female motorcycle officer in the history of the department.

Metro Nashville Police SWAT Team in the early eighties. Kneeling were from left to right, Officer Joey Bishop, team commander Lieutenant Tom Dozier, Sergeant Phillip Sutton and Officer Richard Hillenbrand. Standing were officers Jimmy Hickson, Ken Pence, Mickey Garner and Richard Briggance. All of these officers later served in command positions, Bishop and Briggance as assistant chiefs.

Smith in planning wrote the first grant in 1976 to buy walkie-talkie radios for patrol.

Officer Steven R. Pinkelton, 30, was killed on July 26, 1978, during the armed robbery of a Pizza Hut. Pinkelton was waiting in line at the restaurant. He was off duty but wearing his uniform. One of the two gunmen grabbed the officer and shot him in the back of the neck. The two robbed the restaurant and made their escape. The murderer was charged in 1983.

Officer Edward Lovoyde Tarkington, 22, was shot on December 17, 1978, while interviewing a witness in a burglary investigation. The owner of the property where the interview was taking place began to interfere in the questioning. When Officer Tarkington attempted to arrest the property owner, he pulled a handgun and shot the policeman. The officer returned fire, wounding the shooter. Tarkington died after being transported to the hospital.

A similar tragedy was averted due to quick action by Lieutenant Fred Cobb on February 28, 1980. Sergeant David Eddings and Lieutenant Cobb reached the scene of an accident and saw that the car's passenger fit the description of the suspect in an armed robbery that occurred a short time earlier. As the officers approached the vehicle, the passenger leveled a .357 magnum revolver at Sergeant Eddings. Lieutenant Cobb fired his shotgun, striking the felon in the right arm with buckshot. The gunman was an escaped prisoner and had pulled that night's holdup.

Lieutenant John Wesley Smith III, 39, died in an

automobile accident on May 14, 1980, while en route to a murder scene. He lost control of his police car on a rain-slick street and hit an oncoming vehicle.

Smith had frequented police headquarters since 1948, when he was eight years old. His father was among the first group of black officers to serve on the force. The 18-year police veteran, with an ever present half-chewed stogie, was one of the most well-thought-of officers in the department. Black officers called Smith "the Godfather."

Officer William Lee "Billy" Bowlin, 27, was killed by a rifle blast to the head at close range on August 4, 1982. Bowlin and other officers responded to a report of shots fired inside a house following a break-in. As they arrived, the suspect, who had hidden outside the house, fired on the officers. The first bullet struck and killed Officer Bowlin.

South Patrol Officer Gary Summers was ambushed by two bank robbers on March 31, 1988, as he worked a roadblock at Ashley Drive and Bell Ridge Road. The bandits shot Officer Summers eight or nine times with a rifle and a shotgun and stole his cruiser to make their getaway. Officers Bobby Lawrence and David Justice rushed to the side of the seriously wounded officer and shouted into their radios, "Officer Down, 10-55." The 26-year veteran might have bled to death when the ambulance dispatched to the scene was delayed by traffic, but officers commandeered a nearby ambulance. Officer Summers survived his wounds.

Much of the crime and boldness of the criminal was the result of the growing drug problem. Chief Casey appeared before the U.S. House Select

Metro Officer Sylvia Taylor assists Nashville citizens during routine patrol duty. Officer Taylor left the force in 1991 after 13 years on the force. She was the first female officer serously injured on the department when she was stabbed while on duty.

Committee on Narcotics Abuse and Control in June 1981. He recommended cnactmcnt of the death penalty for habitual drug pushers and manufacturers. The strong law and order stand earned Casey the nickname "Hang 'em High Joe."

The chief was a tough disciplinarian. His insistence on discipline won him the respect of most people working under him and did much to improve morale within the department. He wanted officers to be their best and initiated a mandatory physical fitness program to reduce the weight of officers and improve their agility. At age 57, Casey passed the physical agility test in better time than officers 10 and 20 years younger. He also issued an order that all officers, regardless of rank, who did not pass their marksmanship test during in-service training were to be fired or forced to retire.

Among the significant actions in 1982, on June 1 Assistant Chief Richard Ordway became the first black officer to hold the rank of assistant chief following his promotion by Chief Casey. Ordway was also the first black major in the department. The department moved into a new headquarters in December 1982 upon the completion of the Metropolitan Criminal Justice Center. Ground breaking for the facility took place four years earlier.

Traffic became a stress point for the department in the eighties. The Traffic Division was working 30,000 traffic accidents per year and Traffic Lieutenant Michael Mitchell pointed out the division was staffed with fewer officers, 57, than were on the force thirty years earlier, before Metro Government expanded the

The Metro Aviation Division included from left to right Richard Thomas, J. W. Davis, Lieutenant Kerry Newman, James Stewart (mechanic) and Robert Milliken.

area to be patrolled. In 1957 Nashville had 90 traffic officers. Traffic Officer Jeff Ball and others in the division were overwhelmed by the growing traffic on Nashville's complicated interstate exchange.

Assistant Chief Robert Kirchner felt the traffic division was recovering from a 1981 survey by an outside consultant. Traffic investigators Lloyd Poteet and Ron Anderson pointed out the number of hit-and-run cases had steadily grown since the report and only four officers in the division were qualified to do accident investigation and reconstruction.

The Blue Light Police Band was organized in 1985. The musical group that included Chief Casey and other Nashville officers performed at school and community functions.

A number of significant personnel turnovers took place in the late eighties. Captain Carl "Sonny" Dollarhide took command of communications 1985. Major Abe Miller commanded of the Internal Affairs and Inspections Division in the mid-eighties. Deputy Chief Charles W. Flanders retired in the late eighties after forty years and an illustrious career with the Nashville police force. Assistant Chief Paul H. Uselton Jr. was named deputy chief, becoming the second to hold the post.

Flanders served five years in the U.S. Army during World War II and became a policeman at age 29. Flanders began with the department as a patrolman on January 1, 1947. Soon he moved to traffic as a motorcycle officer and later served as a cornerman. Flanders was given command of the School Mothers' Patrol in 1963 when the Metropolitan department was created and was soon promoted to captain.

Flanders completed his career as assistant chief over the Administration Bureau and as deputy chief, the first deputy chief in the Metropolitan Police Department. Flanders served the department with distinction and led by example.

Deputy Chief Uselton worked himself up through the ranks. He made lieutenant in September 1965, nine months after he was promoted to sergeant, and took command of the West Sector. Uselton took the lieutenant's exam only because a planned round of golf was rained out. After promotion to major, he was put in charge of internal security. Uselton made assistant chief and took over the Inspectional Services Bureau in August 1974 following the retirement of Assistant Chief William L. St. John. Uselton coordinated construction of the east, west and downtown precinct stations.

A number of Nashville organizations gave recognition for public service. The *Nashville Banner* gave

Lieutenant John Wesley Smith III, left, was en route to a murder scene on May 14, 1980, and was killed in a head-on collision. Officer Billy Bowlin, right, was killed by a shotgun blast to the head on August 4, 1982, as he investigated a house break-in.

Metro K-9 officers their public service award two months in a row in 1986. Officer Grady Pinchon and K-9 Bear III were given the award for teamwork in the capture of two on burglary and auto theft charges. Pinchon had been honored by the Oddfellows Lodge in 1979 for making a series of arrests, named "Police Officer of the Year" by the Chamber of Commerce in 1980 and honored for "distinguished and dedicated service to the community" in 1981 by the Downtown Optimist Club. The *Nashville Banner* cited K-9 Officer Ron Sloan and Sabre the next month for the capture of two armed robbers.

A special Vice Squad campaign against "numbers" gambling operations was initiated in 1986. The squad typically did mostly drug investigations, but the increase in gambling violation caused the unit to stage raids across the city. They also made a special effort to curb street prostitution in problem areas.

An event on August 17, 1986, again showed that even routine duty could turn dangerous for a police officer. Twenty-four-year-old East Patrol Officer William Randall Casteel observed a motorcyclist not wearing a helmet. The rider pulled in to a residence and ran for the house. Officer Casteel arrested him and placed him in the rear of the cruiser. At that point the policeman was attacked by four members of the man's family and brutally beaten before backup arrived.

The department lost its first K-9 officer in December 1986. Police dog Ingo was shot to death by a bank robber.

Metropolitan Criminal Justice Center was occupied by the police department in December 1982.

Carol Etherington established the Police Advocacy Support Services (PASS) in 1986 to assist officer and their families deal with the stresses incumbent to police work. Etherington joined the Vanderbilt University School of Nursing in 1995 as an assistant professor. She had provided the Nashville department with 19 years of innovations in professional counseling for victims of crime and law enforcement personnel.

A number of issues were impacting the police department when Mayor Bill Boner took officer in 1987. Chief Casey initiated a department-wide reorganization in 1988. Major George H. Currey was given command of the Metropolitan Nashville Police Training Academy. After 18 years at the helm of youth guidance, Currey headed the academy for the next two years. Captain Joe Anderson took command of the Youth Guidance Division, which became a part of the Investigative Bureau.

Major James Roy Herald was transferred from uniform services to command of the Special Operations Division. Herald had served as captain of the South Station since 1973. Special Operations included traffic, School Mothers' Patrol, K9s, flight, motorcycles, SWAT team, hit and run and DUI. East Station Captain Johnnie Griggs was promoted to major over patrol divisions.

The reorganization merged Inspection Services with the Internal Security Division to better monitor equipment management and maintenance. The Vice Division's anti-drug unit was split into three groups to identify and arrest major drug dealers, focus on street sales and improve undercover operations. The Crime Suppression Unit was created to target street gang crimes.

The Central Station was created on First Avenue in 1988. Emmett Turner was promoted to captain and took command of the new downtown substation.

The department added a female officer to its motorcycle unit in December 1988. Officer Merri Lee Puckett, 28, of the East Patrol Sector was a motorcycle enthusiast. She had 40 hours to learn to perform 14 motorcycle maneuvers in three minutes, seven seconds. Officer Jerry Coleman served as her instructor-partner.

Chief Joe Casey retired on September 1, 1989, after sixteen years in the position, the longest serving Metro chief of police and the longest serving Nashville chief in the modern era. His dedication to duty was such that in 38 years with the force, Joe Casey never missed a day of work. In addition to many other awards and recognitions, Casey was honored by the Tennessee Police Chief's Association with a newly created past presidents award, named the Joe Casey Award. Casey served as president of the association for seven years. The group also established a training award and named it the Cascy, Fowler and Williamson Award.

Casey served as president of the International Association of Chiefs of Police in 1987-88. In the role, he traveled extensively meeting with law enforcement and political leaders worldwide, as well as having an audience with Pope John Paul II.

Prior to his retirement, Chief Casey initiated the process of seeking accreditation of the department. Lieutenant Deborah Y. Faulkner, from the Internal Security Division, was placed in charge of the process to meet the accreditation standards. Chief Robert Kirchner promoted Faulkner to captain in 1990 and gave her command of the Professional Standards Division. The Commission on Accreditation for Law Enforcement Agencies, Inc. (CALEA) granted accreditation to the department in July 1994 and Deborah Faulkner was awarded the Chief's Exemplary Service Award. Captain Faulkner organized the department's Citizens Police Academy in 1995.

Robert E. Kirchner Jr. took command as chief of police on September 1, 1989. Kirchner had a varied background in the department, serving in patrol, community relations, planning and research and inspections. He held positions as administrative assistant to the chief, commander of the Training Division, commander of the SWAT Team and assistant chief of Uniform Services. The new chief completed a Bachelor of Science and masters degree with honors while a full-time Nashville officer. A number of the research projects he initiated were published in law enforcement journals.

Chief Kirchner claimed a worthy heritage in the department. His great-great-uncle was Chief of Detectives Elkin Lewis. Chief Lewis joined the Nashville department in 1918 and served as chief of detectives from 1929 until his retirement in 1948 after a distinguished career of 30 years.

Command of the Metro Nashville Police Department in 1990 consisted of Chief Kirchner, Deputy Chief John T. Ross and five assistant chiefs. Assistant Chief Johnnie Griggs headed the Uniform Services Bureau, Assistant Chief Richard N. Ordway commanded the Investigative Services Bureau, Assistant Chief Robert P. Russell was in charge of the Administrative Services Bureau, Assistant Chief Charles R. Campbell headed the Communications Services Bureau and Assistant Chief John A. Sorace commanded the Support Services Bureau. Lieutenant Steve Anderson was administrative assistant to the Chief Kirchner. Major Carl "Sonny" Dollarhide was made patrol major in 1989 and remained in the position until his retirement 11 years later. Jackie Watkins, who served in the chief's office for most of two decades, was named administrative assistant to the chief.

The reorganization of the department implemented by Chief Kirchner included a streamlining of personnel to improve efficiency. Sworn personnel was reduced to 987 in 1990, over a 100 less than the 1089 officers in 1988. The department had 1.93 officers per 1000 population in the metropolitan area. Kirchner expanded the use of civilian employees to allow more police officers to respond to calls and to patrol, the front line of police service.

The leadership of Metro Government changed in 1991 when Mayor Phil Bredesen took office. He lead the city for eight years and supported Kirchner in a major redirection for policing in Metro Nashville, decentralization of the police department.

The department had used substations for most of the twentieth century to organize the patrol function and provide a site for roll call of patrol officers. The full range of police services remained centralized at headquarters. Chief Kirchner advocated the precinct concept to make investigative services and other police functions readily available to Nashville's citizens. Precincts were intended to be a place for the public and the police to come together.

With the support of City Councilman Durwood Hall and the mayor, the precinct concept was approved, a budget prepared, land purchased and construction started on a new South Station. Chief Kirchner postponed his retirement for a year to see the implementation of the South Precinct completed. The precinct initiative was not fully implemented for a number of years.

Chief Kirchner made a number of changes in personnel policy including non-political promotions based on rank-order test scores, diversity training, two years of college as a requirement for police recruits, a intern program for college students and a police educational fund for officers. He directed the development of a strategic plan and preparation of annual goals and objectives by all department components and units. Chief Kirchner also instituted patrol committee meetings to encourage dialogue between patrol officers and commanders.

The department made a significant equipment upgrade in 1990 by trading its existing fleet of aircraft, three helicopters and an airplane for two McDonald-Douglas 500-E series jet helicopters. A local business also donated a boat for patrolling the river.

Captain Leonard Michael "Mickey" Miller, son of Abe Miller, was given command of the Personal Crimes Division of Criminal Investigations. The unit investigated homicide, rape and robbery. The murder squad was the unit within homicide that investigated crimes not solved within short time period and police officer involved shootings in which a person was struck by gunfire.

Major Tom Dozier was made Director of Training on July 16, 1990, and took command of the training academy. Dozier had been at the academy since its early days and made sergeant, lieutenant and captain while there. He remained director for nine years, giving him 28 years of duty at the training facility. Regular classes of new recruits trained in sessions that varied from 16 to 21 weeks in duration. Occasionally the academy offered a lateral class, for officers who had previous training and police experience. David Achord was a member of one such class in 1990. He served with the Rutherford County Sheriff's Office in Murfreesboro for three years and was hired on April 1, 1990, as a Metro officer. The lateral academy class trained for eight weeks at the academy. Achord became a homicide detective in 1995.

The recruit class of 1993, the 25th session of the Nashville police academy, was the most diverse in the history of the department. One third of the 64 recruits were minorities, including a number of Hispanics and Asians. Fourteen percent of the class was female. Twelve hours of diversity awareness training was part of the 21-week program. Paul Margulies, who later moved into federal law enforcement, was a member of the class.

Lieutenant Ronnie Woodard was killed on October 9, 1991, by a car thief. Officer Paul Scurry, right, was shot several times and killed as he and other officers served warrants on May 17, 1996.

It was also in 1993 that the department began to issue 9mm automatic service weapons. New officers chose from among makers Glock, Beretta, Sig Sauer and Smith and Wesson. Others in the department who wanted to swap to the 9 mm bought their own sidearm. They had the choice of the same makers. Some officer who had carried the .38 caliber revolver and qualified with it, stayed with the more familiar sidearm.

Chief Kirchner initiated a Bicycle Patrol on October 1, 1993, to be implemented by Assistant Chief Charlie Smith. The first bicycles deployed were two downtown working out of Central and two on Music Row. The bike patrol became a significant part of the department's Community Policing effort.

The Domestic Violence Division, designed to reduce homicides, assaults, officer injuries, spousal rape, hostage situations, stalking and other related crimes, began operations in April 1994. Detective David Miller of the Homicide Section had begun tracking domestic disturbance reports in the early nineties. The new division was organized as a part of the Investigative Services Bureau, with Captain Shirley Davis in command. Lieutenant Arlene Burris, day shift Sergeant Mark Wynn, evening Sergeant Kim Dillingham and midnight Sergeant Robert Williams supervised a staff of 25 specially trained domestic violence detectives. A separate counseling section for victims of domestic violence was also established.

The division was housed in the old Metropolitan Transit Authority land port at the end of Peabody Street. The Counseling Section was added under the supervision by Rhonda Harris. The unit soon gained national recognition for its work.

The division conducted a city wide warrant sweep in February 1995 code named Domestic Roundup I. The operation served backlogged warrants for domestic homicides, sexual offenses and stalkings. Twenty-five teams of officers and detectives hit the streets at 7:00 am that morning and served 27 people with 36 warrants. Other such sweeps took place in subsequent months.

Lieutenant Mark Wynn was selected 1998 Nashvillian of the Year. He was also given the National Improvement of Justice Award and recognized as one of the top ten police officers in the United States by the International Association of Chief's of Police and Parade Magazine in 1995. Wynn was a member of the SWAT Team for 15 years before his assignment to the Domestic Violence Division. He became recognized nationally and internationally as an expert on domestic violence and testified twice before the U.S. House of Representatives' Committee on the Judiciary.

Captain Valerie Meece, a 27-year department veteran, took command of the Domestic Violence Division in July 2000 and Lieutenant Danny Driskell was assigned to the unit in 2001. Lieutenant Rita Baker assumed temporary command of the unit on January 1, 2003, and upon promotion to captain in 2004 took permanent command. Leadership of the Counseling Section changed in the fall of 2001 when Dr. Carol Hughes Gipson, Ph.D. became its head.

Violence on duty remained a constant for Nashville officers. Lieutenant James Ronnie Woodard was killed on October 9, 1991. Woodard, an 18-year veteran of the department, was off duty, working an extra job, when he spotted a suspicious car and confirmed with the dispatcher that it was stolen. While investigating, the driver of the car shot Woodard five times with a handgun. Woodard was able to return fire and wounded the gunman. Patrol officers later apprehended the shooter in the area. Lieutenant Ronnie Woodard was pronounced dead at Vanderbilt Hospital.

Motorcycle Officer Ronald Ingram died on June 1, 1991, from injuries received in an off-duty accident the day before. Officer Ingram was traveling south on 21st Avenue near Garland just after 3:00 a.m. when a newspaper delivery van pulled into his path.

An attempt to stop a shoplifter almost cost Metro Officer James Glenn Duke his life on the afternoon of January 23, 1991. The lawman reached into the car to turn off the ignition. The thief raised the car window, trapping Officer Duke's arm in the window. The thief drove away, trying to sideswipe other cars, which

The South Precinct was established as the first decentralized sector of the Metro Police Department.

might have killed the officer. Officer Duke suffered a ruptured artery in his arm.

Leadership of the Metropolitan Nashville Police Department changed on January 15, 1996. Emmett H. Turner was appointed chief of police. Turner was a 27-year veteran of the department. The Haywood County native joined the force on January 1, 1969, and spent most of his early career in youth guidance. He was promoted to lieutenant in 1984 and transferred to the Planning and Research Division. Turner was given command of the new Central Station in 1988 at the rank of captain, was promoted to major in 1991 and assistant chief in 1993. Carrie Hudson served as his administrative assistant while chief. City leadership changed three years later when Mayor Bill Purcell took officer in 1999.

During Chief Turner's tenure two new facilities were built, Hermitage Precinct and North Precinct, dividing Metro into five precincts. A building was acquired on Trinity Lane for the Vice Squad.

One of Chief Turner's proudest accomplishments was the implementation of lap-top computer systems in patrol cars. Nashville became one of the first ten cities in the nation to use the mobile information system technology.

Chief Turner expanded the neighborhood watch program and reformed the internal affairs function. Participation in HEAT, Help Eliminate Armed Thugs, a joint federal-local effort to get guns out of the hands of felons, led to the destruction of almost 12,000 guns in a five year period. An important technology resource was acquired from AFT, the Integrated Ballistics Identification System (IBIS).

During the nineties, the department created a new model for patrolling trouble areas. The new patrolling

scheme, later known as the Flex Unit, was started in the West Sector by Captain Charles Smith in the early nineties. Officers with disciplinary or attitude issues were assigned to foot patrol in the Preston Taylor Homes housing projects during high crime evening hours. The West Nightwalking Unit or "West Walking" proved to be an effective tool for fighting street crime.

The success of the unit was such that in 1993 Lieutenant Bobby Dodson and Sergeant Randy Alexander began to assign highly motivated officers to the detail. By mid-year the unit consisted of ten officers and two cars. In 1994 five two-officer cars began patrol of the John Henry Hale and Edgehill housing developments where the unit made an immediate impact on drug related crimes. The unit also worked other crimes prevalent in the area and as a team served arrest warrants and search warrants.

Arrests and other statistics produced by the "Nightwalkers" surged and became comparable to the undercover Crime Suppression Unit. Occasionally West Walking patrolled into the Central Sector when all was quiet in West. This boarder patrol was justified because their work in West Sector pushed criminal activity into the Central Sector. Patrol opportunities of the unit further expanded when the Metropolitan Development and Housing Agency (MDHA) used grant monies to add officers to late night public housing patrols and Sergeant Alexander assigned officers from the walking unit to the duty.

Chief Robert Kirchner Jr., left, was appointed chief of police September 1, 1989, and initiated decentralization of the department. Chief Emmett H. Turner, right, was named to head the department on January 15, 1996. He directed the addition of two new substations and the installation of computers in patrol cars.

Officer Terry Burnett and his K-9 partner Aron. K-9 Aron was shot and killed by an armed bank robber on the morning of May 15, 1998 and Officer Burnett was wounded.

The outstanding performance of officers in the unit was recognized by numerous awards by civic groups. An Exemplary Service Award was given to the entire unit in 1996 for their work during the previous year.

The decision was made in 1997 that the West Walking unit should be used county-wide to focus enforcement wherever street crime was a problem. To enable the unit to strike not only wherever but whenever it was needed, the unit's shift was made "flexible." The unit was thereafter called the Flex Unit or Flex.

Flex became a central element in Chief Turner's comprehensive violent crime fighting strategy in response to a record number of homicides in 1997. A 35-member Flex Unit was created in 1998 with a team assigned to each sector. The chief also deployed Drug Activity Response Teams (DART) in all four sectors.

The chief's strategy included discussion of Metro-wide crime data in Criminal Intelligence Meetings, a predecessor to ComStat, and information systems that allowed precinct captains to look at crime statistics prior to monthly printed reports. Police also reached out to neighborhood organizations and put more resources in trouble areas. Homicides and other crime were reduced significantly.

A Mounted Patrol unit was created in May 1998. The Tennessee Walking Horse Association found out the department was going to create the unit and donated the horses so that the squad would use only Tennessee Walking Horses. The group also donated saddles and tack gear. The only thing they asked was that the blankets be marked, "Tennessee Walking Horse." Training for the unit included crowd control tactics, formation riding and police tactics.

All the resources of Metro police were needed on April 16, 1998, when three tornados hit Nashville. The first storm roared through downtown Nashville shortly after 3:45 p.m. The storms damaged and destroyed nearly 300 buildings including the State Capitol and police headquarters. At least 100 people were injured, one of whom later died. Numerous power outages left traffic lights out, debris blocking some roadways and rush-hour traffic was snarled. Nashville officers spread throughout the affected area to assist the injured and get traffic moving.

The backbone of the department continued to be the Patrol Division. Patrol officer handled over 6,000 "Shots Fired" calls in 1997 plus thousands of "Man with a Gun" calls. Their work continued to be the most dangerous as well.

The department had a death in the line of duty not long after Chief Turner took over. Homicide detectives and patrol officers went to an apartment complex on May 17, 1996, to arrest two individuals on outstanding warrants. The female occupant of the apartment finally opened the door. As they made a search, officers noticed a broken shelf near the access to the attic with bits of insulation on it.

Using a ladder, Patrol Officer Francis Paul Scurry entered the attic. Numerous shots were fired and Scurry was hit several times. The felon came out of the attic, still firing at officers. Two other detectives arrived on the scene and tried to extricate Officer Scurry. The gunman refused to surrender and was shot and killed by one of the detectives. Officer Paul Scurry was pronounced dead on arrival at Memorial Hospital.

The incident was one of a growing number in which a felon had weapons with more fire power than the police officer. Officer Scurry's sidearm was a 6-shot .38 caliber revolver and the felon had a Tech 9 plus another weapon. Following testing by the firearms training staff at the academy the department adopted the .40 caliber Glock as the standard sidearm for the force.

Officer Terry Burnett and K-9 Aron responded to the scene of a bank robbery on the morning of May 15, 1998, and with other officers pursued the lone bandit into a wooded area behind the bank. Aron located the armed robber, who opened fire with two semi-auto handguns. Officer Burnett was hit in the foot and Aron moved in front of his handler to attack the gunman and took the gun fire as other officers pulled Burnett to safety.

K-9 Aron was struck multiple times and his front legs were disabled from the wounds. Aron pushed his body with his back legs to where Burnett lay and lay on top of his handler. Officer Burnett refused medical treatment until they rushed Aron to a local emergency animal clinic. Aron died from his wounds. Officer Arthur Danner commented to the media, "The dog took the bullets for his partner. That's what they're trained to do but its like losing one of our own." The bank robber was killed in a gun battle with the SWAT Team.

Officer Robert Anthony Bristol, an 11 year veteran of the Metro police, was working off-duty as a security guard in West Nashville bank on November 6, 1998, when a masked gunman entered the bank. Bristol and the bandit scuffled and the two fired on each other. Officer Bristol took a bullet below his right shoulder blade and the bank robber was killed.

A second gunman was shot in the parking lot by other officers. Officer Bristol spend the night in the hospital and soon returned to duty.

Two officers lost their lives on Nashville roadways early in the new millennium. Officer Candace Ripp became the first female officer of Nashville's police force to die in the line of duty. On December 8, 2001, Officer Ripp was completing an accident investigation in the median of Ellington Parkway when she was struck and killed by a vehicle.

Nashville's second female officer died in the line of duty on July 19, 2004. Police Officer Christy Jo Dedman of the Hermitage Precinct was struck and killed by a tractor-trailer while she assisted a motorist. Officer Dedman and the motorist were out of the right-of-way on the side of Interstate 40 near the Stewarts Ferry Pike ramp with the cruiser's emergency lights on. The truck hit the cruiser and pushed the car into Officer Dedman and the motorist as they stood by a concrete retaining wall. Officer Dedman died at the scene. The 34-year-old officer had been on the force only 11 months.

A year later, West Precinct Officer Dan Alford was critically wounded by a gunman in the John Henry Hale public housing development. A drug dealer hid

Officer Candace Ripp, left, was struck and killed on December 8, 2001, while investigating an accident in the median of Ellington Parkway. Officer Christy Dedman, right, was struck and killed by a tractor-trailer while she assisted an I-40 motorist on July 19, 2004.

in an apartment from officers making a routine check of the area. Alford and other officers were clearing the building when the culprit opened fire on the eight year veteran of the force. A shot to the chest was deflected by Officer Alford's bulletproof vest; a second shot entered left lower abdomen.

The battle against drugs was not just fought with street dealers. A joint DEA-Metro Nashville Police Organized Crime Drug Enforcement Task Force code named "Operation Special K" was initiated in September 2001. Special Investigations Division Detective James "Benny" Goodman was assigned to the task force. Operation Special K targeted an international cocaine smuggling and distribution organization operating in Mexico, Texas and Nashville. The drug organization transported over 400 kilograms of cocaine into Middle Tennessee in 2000.

This case resulted in 13 arrests and the seizure of more than 71 kilograms of cocaine plus $3 million in assets. In November 2004, Detective Goodman, a 27-year MNPD veteran, became the first Middle Tennessee law enforcement officer to receive the DEA Director's Award in recognition for his work in Operation Special K.

Two venerable officers of the Metro Nashville force retired near the turn of the millennium. Lieutenant Oscar R. Stone Jr. retired on January 1, 2000, after 48 years of service as a Nashville police officer. Major Tom Dozier retired on January 1, 2004, with 50 years of service to the department. The careers of the two had intertwined through many of their years with the department.

The SWAT Team, a unit that Tom Dozier played an important role in, celebrated its 25th anniversary in 2001. The unit had grown in numbers and proficiency since its formation and had become a highly professional, award winning unit. Equipment improved dramatically to include an armored vehicle that was first used in an incident in which a deputy sheriff was killed. A mobile Tactical Operation Center (TOC) was added to the SWAT fleet to provide tactical intelligence for the unit command. A modified mobil home served as a Negotiator Command Post. Weapons improvements included a move from the UZI to the H&K MP5 and the issuing of Glock .40 caliber pistols, modified 870s as tactical shotguns, AR15 assult rifles and the 308 rifle for marksmen. Modifications to weapons were done by the department's armorer Joe Daniels.

The Cold-Case Squad was created as a multi-agency unit in December 2001 to work murder cases that had been inactive for five years or more. Detective Terry McElroy, a long-time murder investigator in command of the Technical Surveillance Unit, was the first man assigned to the squad. Detective Grady Eleam, a former member of the murder squad and partner of McElroy, transferred from Robbery as the second man on the squad. Detective Dean Haney took command of Technical Surveillance Unit.

A year later, the district attorney agreed to provide an investigator to the Cold-Case Squad and to provide space and equipment for the unit. The squad remained under the control of the police department but was housed in the district attorney's office.

Lieutenant Mark Wynn, left, was selected 1998 Nashvillian of the Year due in large part to his work with the Domestic Violence Division. Special Investigations Division Detective James "Benny" Goodman, right, became the first Middle Tennessee law enforcement officer to receive the DEA Director's Award in November 2004 as recognition for his work in the joint DEA-Metro Police "Operation Special K."

Chief Turner implemented a reorganization in 2001. The command structure included the chief of police, two deputy chiefs in command of field and support functions and five assistant chief responsible for the various bureaus. Deputy Chief Deborah Y. Faulkner was responsible for Field Operations. Reporting to her in field operations were Assistant Chief Mickey Miller in command of the West Patrol Bureau and Assistant Chief Judy Bawcum in command of the East Patrol Bureau.

Deputy Chief Steve Anderson was responsible for Support Operations. As captain, Anderson had been adminstrative assistant to Chief Turner. Anderson Joined the department in 1975 and served several years in the Planning and Research Division. In addition to other duties he was an instructor in criminal law at the training academy from 1985 to 1995. Reporting to Anderson were Assistant Chief Valerie Meece of the Administrative Service Bureau, Assistant Chief Joseph Bishop of the Investigative Services Bureau and Assistant Chief Richard Briggance of the Specialized Field Service Bureau.

Precincts were under the command of sector captains and included various functions. In addition to patrol units, each captain has school resource officers, a motorcycle unit, traffic cars and a few Directed Patrol (DP) officers who work in plain clothes. West and Central Sectors included bike patrols and Central a mounted patrol. Closed circuit television was installed to link night court to the Domestic Violence Division to ease the process of issuing warrants or orders of protection.

Deputy Chief Deborah Y. Faulkner, left, became a Nashville police officer in 1974 and served as interim chief of police from April 2003 until January 2004. Captain Louise Kelton, right, who joined the department in 1980 became the first black female to hold the rank of captain when she was name commander of the North Precinct in 2004.

Command of the Metro Nashville Police Department in 2005 included left to right, seated, Don Aaron, Public Affairs Manager; Chief of Police Ronal Serpas; and Deputy Chief Joseph Bishop, commander of the Field Operations Bureau. Standing from left to right were Dr. Lorraine Greene, head of Behavioral Health Services; Deputy Chief Steve Anderson, commander of the Investigative Services Bureau; Christine Ragan, Chief Financial Officer; Kennetha Sawyers, head of Professional Accountability; and Deputy Chief Honey Pike, commander of the Administrative Services Bureau.

Deborah Y. Faulkner was appointed acting chief of police on April 1, 2003. She had a strong educational background, with a masters degree in criminal justice and a doctorate from Vanderbilt University, both earned while on the Nashville force. Faulkner immediately began a review of several aspects of the department, including organization, technology and accreditation. The acting chief joined the force in May 1974 as a patrol officer.

Ronal W. Serpas was named chief of the Metropolitan Nashville Police Department and took command of the force on January 12, 2004. He had been selected after a national search. The 43-year-old Serpas was a 23-year veteran of law enforcement and held a PhD in Urban Studies. He began his career with the New Orleans Police Department in 1980 and rose through the ranks, retiring after twenty years at the position of Assistant Superintendent of Police and the Chief of Operations. Serpas then served as chief of the Washington State Patrol from 2001 until his resignation to become chief in Nashville.

Chief Serpas was a goal-oriented leader and began an intensive review of the 1800 member department. Within a few months the department was reorganized to streamline operations, reduce bureaucracy and save money. On May 16, 2004, the number of bureaus was reduced from five to three, Patrol Services, Investigative Services and Administrative Services. The Specialized Field Services Bureau was eliminated and the East and West Patrol Bureaus were merged.

At the same time Chief Serpas abolished the rank of assistant police chief. Deputy Chiefs Steve Anderson, Joseph Bishop and Captain Marjorie "Honey" Pike were appointed to command the three bureaus at the rank of deputy chief. Anderson, 56, was a 29-year veteran of the department; Bishop, 48, a 23-year veteran; and Pike, 48, a 27-year veteran of the force. Rose Loring was named administrative assistant to the chief. Three assistant chiefs retired and one reverted to the rank of captain.

Commanders of the organizational units were realigned, although not all assignments were changed.

Precinct captains were Rick Lankford at South, Danny Baker at East, Andy Garrett at Central, Louise Kelton at North, Michelle Richter at Hermitage and Mickey Miller at West. Other captain assignments were Anthony Carter over Special Operations, Gary Goodwin over Training, Tommy McBride over Youth Services, Karl Roller over Warrants, Chris Taylor over Criminal Investigations, Rob White over Identification, Anita Lowrance over Personnel, Ken Pence over Property & Evidence, Bob Nash over Strategic Development, Todd Henry over Vice/Intelligence, Rita Baker over Domestic Violence and Field Supervisors Joe Ogg and John Hoffman. Captain Mike Hagar took command of the Training in October 2005.

Commander Louise Kelton was the first black female captain in the department's history. She had also been the first black female lieutenant and along with Bonnie J. Malone as one of the first black female sergeant. Kelton, originally from Cardiff, South Wales in Great Britain, began in patrol in 1980 and served a stint in booking. As a sergeant, she was transferred from East Patrol to help create the new Central Sector under then Captain Emmett Turner. Kelton was promoted to lieutenant in October 1989 and assigned to Internal Affairs. She spent 15 years investigated complaints against other officers, an often lonely duty.

Additional personnel actions in 2004 included the retirement of over fifty officer as the result of a Metro incentive offer. The vacancies were filled by new recruits and lateral applicants from other agencies. To fill supervisory position, 46 officers were promoted to sergeants and lieutenants.

Chief Serpas took significant operational initiatives including regular ComStat meetings, using crime data and statistics to target delivery of police services in the areas most needing them. Beginning in January 2004 Investigative Services was decentralized. Seventy investigators and supervisors were distributed to provide each of the six precincts with a major investigative component including homicide, burglary and street-level drug detectives. The decentralization placed greater decision-making authority at the neighborhood level. One of the results was hundreds of drug arrests by undercover detectives in the months that followed.

At the same time, the department's nine-member centralized Narcotics Unit made 179 arrests between August 2004 and August 2005, seizing significant amounts of drugs and property. For this the unit was named Narcotics Unit of the Year by the Tennessee Narcotics Officers' Association (TNOA) in November 2005 and Metro Narcotics Detective Marti Roberts was recognized for making the largest Ecstasy seizure in Tennessee (5,400 pills).

The chief addressed traffic safety by initiating an aggressive driving enforcement program and actively using helicopters in traffic enforcement, particularly against speeders. The department received a Tennessee Lifesavers Award as a result. To enhance cooperation between citizens and the police, a new section was added to the department's web site with surveillance pictures of crimes in progress.

The Nashville Police Department was created in 1806 and Metro celebrates its 200th anniversary in 2006. Commerative badges are being worn by sworn personnel during the year and the department plans events and a publication to acknowledge the significance of the milestone year.

Under the leadership of Chief Serpas the department today is one of the most progressive departments in the nation. The Metropolitan Nashville Police Department continues to reinvent itself and the 1200-plus sworn officers of the department seek better ways to fight crime. The heritage of 200 years of dedication to duty and service to the community is a constant that remains at the heart of the force maintaining law and order in Tennessee's capitol city.

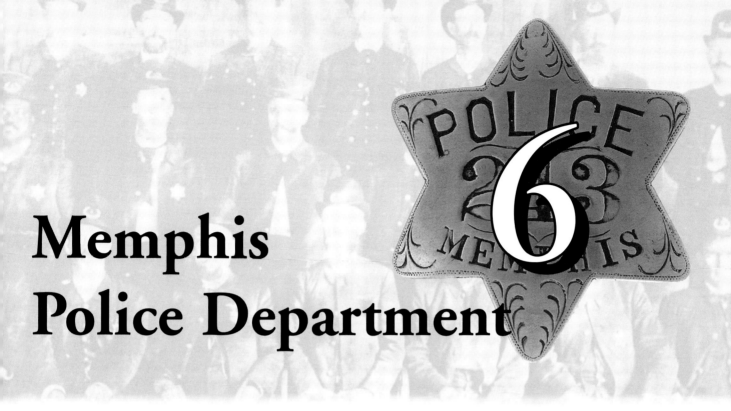

Memphis
Police Department

Memphis began as a rough and tumble riverboat town, second home to characters like Big Mike Fink and Davy Crockett. The city was incorporated in 1826, only a few years after General Andrew Jackson acquired the land west of the Tennessee River from the Chickasaws. Tennessee was part of the western frontier of the young nation.

Shelby County Sheriff Samuel R. Brown was elected when the county was organized in 1820. The first lawman for the new town of Memphis was Town Constable John J. Balch, elected on May 12, 1827. A town constable had the same power as other constables of the county.

The one man Police Department was a tinker by trade. Balch earned his living mainly by mending household pots and pans and other utensils. The job of town constable was a part-time position that included both criminal and civil law enforcement. Balch walked an area of less than one half of a square mile in his patrol of the young town and earned fees from fines and licenses.

During his one-year term as town constable, Balch was appointed deputy sheriff of Shelby County. He served as the county's only deputy until July 23, 1829, when he was appointed sheriff by the Shelby County court and served for seven years.

Other early Memphis town constables included David Banks, who served in 1828; William C. Doss, who served in 1831; and Lemuel P. Hardaway, who served from 1837 until 1839. The corporate limits of Memphis were extended in 1832. The act stated that the purpose for extending the limits related to "conferring of powers for the regulation of the police, or well ordering the good behavior of individuals." This is the first use of the word "police" in the acts of the Tennessee legislature.

Soon the need to maintain peace and quiet in the evenings resulted in the town forming a night watch to patrol the streets after dark. In March 1839 a night watch was created. James H. Cox and William Stockton alternated nights on the watch. They patrolled from 10:00 p.m. to daylight. In July Levi Matthews replaced Stockton as night watchman. In addition to his night watch duties James Cox was appointed Wharfmaster, a combination harbor-master, policeman and tax collector. Both Cox and Matthews resigned in October 1839.

W. W. Whitsitt was appointed town constable on September 12, 1839, upon the resignation of Lemuel Hardaway. The night watch was reorganized in March 1840 and watchmen were appointed by the political wards of the Memphis. Henry Randle was appointed from the first ward, M. M. Wise from the second ward and Charles Farrell from the third ward. Wards formed the basis for police deployment for the next 130 years.

The population of the town in 1840 was 1,799. Whiskey was two bits a gallon. The chief sources of crime and vice were the racetrack, "doggeries" or saloons and camp meetings where drinking bouts and orgies took place in the shadow of the preacher's pulpit.

The first record of equipment authorized by the Board of Mayor and Aldermen was on May 4, 1840, "An account to M. M. Wise for three dollars was also allowed, being for rattlers for the use of the night watch."

Rattles used by the police force were wooden noise makers. When the device was rotated by the handle, a flat piece of wood struck against a notched wheel making a clacking sound that could be heard for a good distance. Night watchmen used rattles to raise an alarm when they needed help. They also used lantern to light the way on the nightly rounds.

A September 1840 ordinance established the first supervisor of the Memphis police force, the captain of the night watch or night guard. The town constable did not supervise the night watch since he worked in the day time. The ordinance also described some of the duties and equipment of the night watch.

That a Captain of the Night Guard shall be appointed from among the number of Watchmen now in the service of this corporation, whose duty it shall be to attend to the ringing of the ten o'clock bell; he shall take charge of the badges, rattlers and other property in the hands of the Night Watch, belonging to the corporation, when not on duty.

The first official badges of Memphis law enforcement were the property of the town and were worn by patrolmen only while they were on duty. The nature or style of the badge was not noted and likely varied from time to time and from officer to officer. They were probably made of metal and in the shape of a star, but could have been cloth arm or hat bands in the earliest days. Since no uniforms were prescribed the 1899 publication *Memphis Police Department Illustrated* stated, "the star was the only insignia of office."

Night watchmen were part time and temporary and turnover of the force was frequent. A new night watch was appointed on March 15, 1841, consisting of Gabriel Haughter, David Veneman and Henry Wisener. Gabriel Haughter was named Captain of the Night Watch, becoming the first individual to serve in

that capacity. On March 19 Henry Wisener was dismissed and William R. James was appointed in his place. On April 1 Captain Haughter resigned, Samuel Whitsitt was appointed to the watch and David Veneman was promoted to captain.

Although some individuals served longer than others, the rapid turnover of personnel and duty remained consistent throughout the years of the night watch system. Individuals moved on and off the night watch depending on their availability and some individuals who served on the night watch moved on to become town constable or members of the day police in later years. The duties of the watchman was described in the 1899 publication.

The stalwart patrolman of that day made no reports to headquarters on his nightly rounds, but at each recurring hour tolled on the fire bells, would raise his voice, and sing out the hour, "one o'clock and all's well."

Gardner B. Locke was appointed town constable in 1841 following the removal of Constable Whitsitt. Locke resigned after only two months and Recorder James H. Lawrence was appointed to serve in the role of constable as well as recorder. Locke was again elected to serve during 1844. William D. Gilmore, the final town constable of Memphis, was first elected on March 1, 1845, and served for three years.

The state legislature granted Memphis a charter elevating the town to the City of Memphis in January 1848. Subsequently the Board of Mayor and Aldermen of the city passed a number of ordinances which restructured and expanded the police force. On March 14, 1848, the city board passed "An Ordinance Creating the Office of City Marshal." The office of city marshal replaced that of the town constable and continued to include duties related to sanitation, zoning and street maintenance in addition to more traditional law enforcement responsibilities. The first police station was a 12' x 20' brick calaboose or jail built at the corner of Main and Market at the cost of $185.

Samuel B. DeHart became Memphis's first city marshal, but resigned at the end of June. John Newsom and Thomas S. Brown briefly served as city marshal before William Underwood was appointed and remained in the office until mid-1852.

Other 1848 ordinances defined the police force, referring to the night watch as consisting of one captain and seven privates and divided the city into three police districts, each consisting of two wards. The restriction of the number of privates to seven was soon removed. The duties of the night force were spelled out and the use and importance of the badge and the rattle clarified.

It shall be the duty of the Captain of the Police, at the hour of 9 o'clock p.m. every night, to ring the bell, call the roll and assign the privates their respective beats, or districts, for the night.

Each policeman shall be at the town hall or police station at the time of 9 o'clock p.m. and from that time until daylight will diligently perform his duties.

Every policeman shall carry a rattler and shall, while on duty, wear a badge by which he may be distinguished, which badge shall be assigned by the Captain; and if he shall need assistance in the discharge of such duty he shall spring his rattle and those of the police who hear it shall answer the same and repair as speedily as possible to the assistance of the policeman who first sprang his rattle.

An ordinance was also enacted in 1848 to create a Day Police. The day police was commanded by a captain with the title High Constable with two assistants to be chosen quarterly as the watchmen. S. M. Champ served as the first high constable. The following year the position of Lieutenant was created. The lieutenant was in charge of the privates and answered to the high constable.

Although these entities, city marshal, night watch and day police interfaced, they functioned separately and independently. Over the next few years, city ordinances brought the police department into a more cohesive organization under the command of the city marshal. Other actions provided that the city marshal have an assistant and established a Board of Police composed of the mayor and three aldermen.

The population jumped from 3,990 in 1849 to 8,841 in 1850 when South Memphis became a part of the city. The consolidated population consisted of 6,355 white citizens and 2,486 black citizens, slave and free. Three men were hired, one for day service and two for night service, J. C. Williams, T. Wolf and Ben O'Havre.

In March 1850 the city board appointed 26 to the police force including the city marshal. This was a significant expansion of the force. Eight men were appointed to the Day Police, High Constable William

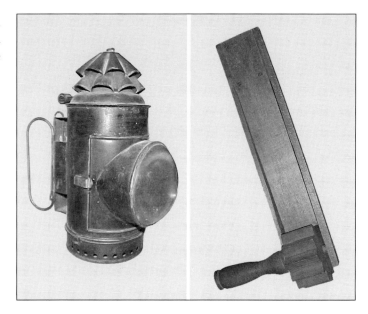

The Dietz Police lantern, left, was one of several types of lanterns carried by the night watch and night police. A wooden police rattle, right, used to raise an alarm by patrolmen on tour during the night watch in the early nineteenth century. (Rattle image courtesy of Walter E. Gist)

C. Causey, Lieutenant J. W. Dunn and Privates Joseph Aiken, John W. Causey, William T. Childress, B. Miller, John Rhome and William H. Sangster. Seventeen Night Police were appointed, Captain Benjamin O'Havre, Lieutenant Joseph C. Wilson and Privates H. Barclay, Andrew Brady, B. A. Carter, Patrick H. Duffy, R. C. Dunn, George Fryfogle, H. Hines, G. Malone, S. Miller, J. Morgan, Thomas Randall, W. Sheffield, J. V. Smith, L. K. Stone and P. Webbs. Before the end of the next month the force was reduced.

The Day Night and Night Police were uniformed in 1850, at their own expense. The city provided an allowance of $60 per year for uniformed officers and $50 per year for detectives.

Josiah Horn was appointed city marshal in July 1852 and served for two years. On October 5, 1852, a resolution was passed that day and night police be furnished with badges "to be worn in some conspicuous place." Soon after, the *Memphis Daily Appeal* confirmed the style of the badges, "The policemen have finally mounted their stars—the badge of their office. Both the Day and Night Police wear them."

The charter of the City of Memphis was revised by the state legislature in February 1854 and one of the new provisions required that the top three police officers, the city marshal, the captain of the Day Police (a title change from high constable) and the captain of the Night Police were to be elected directly by the voters of the city. Prior to this time they had been appointed by the Board of Mayor and Aldermen.

James M. Wilson was the first city marshal to be chosen in a general election in June 1854 with William C. Causey as captain of the Day Police and Benjamin G. Garrett as captain of the Night Police. Joseph C. Wilson was appointed assistant city marshal, five day policemen were appointed and nine night policemen.

Thomas Mynatt was elected city marshal in 1855 and re-elected the following year. J. F. Johnson was elected captain of Day Police at the salary of $70 per year, Benjamin G. Garrett was re-elected captain of Night Police at $60 a year and P. H. Duffy as lieutenant of Night Police. The day force consisted of John C. Davenport, Levi Hess, John R. Lester, J. Rienhardt, W. M. James and J. J. Hope. The night force was S. M. Thomas, A. W. Johnson, George Trump, R. G. Tucker, J. Chadeland, Robert Reid, B. A. Carter, C. N. Robinson, F. G. Butler, W. F. Barnes and George Schroyer.

James O. Reinhardt was elected city marshal in 1857, but was dismissed in November and William Underwood appointed in his place. Underwood won two subsequent elections and served through mid-1860.

An 1859 ordinance "authorized Captains and Lieutenants, both Day and Night, to be mounted on horseback to better supervise officers throughout the city." This was the first reference to mounted officers.

By 1857 city ordinances clearly spell out that the city marshal was the head of the police department, "The City Marshal shall be considered and held as Chief of the Police, and shall have general care of the peace of the city, and see that his subordinate officers do their duty." A new title was formalized when the city charter was amended by the state legislature in February 20, 1860. The title City Marshal was changed to Chief of Police, although the duties of the office did not change. The charter also provided that the selection of the two captain be returned to the city council.

Chief of Police Benjamin G. Garrett was elected in June 1860. The police roster included Day Police Captain J. J. McMurray, Lieutenant Samuel H. Moore, 2nd Lieutenant R. G. Tucker and 24 privates. The Night Police consisted of Captain J. T. Collier, Lieutenant Charles N. Robinson, 2nd Lieutenant Cyrus L. Morrison and 32 privates. Patrolmen were assigned by district. The roster also listed two Station House Keepers, one for day and one for night and one city jailer.

At the beginning of the Civil War many patrolmen enlisted and their places had to be filled by men not subject to military duty, which were men over 45 years of age. In this period the Vigilance Committee had oversight of the police department. They required that policemen be uniformed and be native-born or naturalized citizens.

An 1860 city ordinance gave design guidelines for an official police uniform and specifies "the badge of office shall be four inches long, one and a quarter inch wide, made of silver, and worn on the hat or cap, and fastened with a ribbon." This hat badge was to contain the number of the patrolman or rank of the supervising officer. White hats were often worn during this time.

A representative of the Memphis firm selected to supply the uniforms was sent to New York to acquire the outfits. Upon his return he reported the type, availability and cost of the attire worn by the police in that city. The Memphis city board decided to adopt the metropolitan style police uniform of New York City.

The fact that city police officers wore uniforms may have played a role in the fatal stabbing of Patrolman W. Stith Tucker at the Memphis Jockey Club on Monday evening, April 30, 1860. The racetrack was located where the fairgrounds and then Libertyland later stood at East Parkway and Southern. In 1860 the racetrack was outside the city limits, but venues in the county, especially racetracks, often turned to city police officers to provide security because their uniform was a symbol of authority. The practice of hiring city police officers at racetracks was prevalent throughout the latter part of the nineteenth century.

Patrolman Tucker was at the racetrack after the track closed and the grounds were essentially deserted. Tucker spotted a black man whom he believed to be a runaway slave. When he attempted to arrest the man, a white man who had a bad reputation and was thought to have a grudge against Tucker, interfered with the officer. In the altercation the white man drew a large knife and with both hands stabbed Patrolman Tucker in the forehead over the temple. Tucker pulled the protruding knife from his own skull. He spent the night at the racetrack with a young boy as his only company. Five days later he died of the wound.

The department lost another officer on New Year's Eve 1861. Patrolman John W. Causey began service with the Memphis Police Department in 1850. His brother William C. Causey was a detective with the department.

About 7 o'clock that December evening Patrolman Causey entered Sandy's Barber Shop on Main. A man who was getting a shave said he wanted to speak with the officer. The two stood at the corner of Main and Gayosa talking when suddenly the man drew a knife and stabbed Causey. The officer fell to the street, stabbed through the heart, and died in seconds. His assailant had been arrested three weeks earlier by Causey for stabbing another man.

Memphis struggled with war and its aftermath during the decade of the 1860s. On June 6, 1862, a fleet of Federal gunboats captured the city. The initial instruction to Mayor John Park by the Federal commander was to continue as usual the police protection of the city and he promised the cooperation of the military garrison. In August 1862 the mayor was authorized "to purchase 100 police stars at a cost of $75." The purchase of a new badge for the chief of police was also approved, at a cost of $2.50.

Memphis police functioned in this manner until July 2, 1864, when General C. C. Washburn issued General Order No. 70 removing all city officials and installed a hand picked city government. The police force was replaced by men loyal to the Union. Patrick M. Winters was initially appointed chief of police by General Washburn but was replaced by J. P. Foster on August 12, 1864, when Winters was elected Shelby County Sheriff. Foster served as chief of police until July 3, 1865.

Sergeant W. C. Stockham, one of the police officers appointed by the military government, was shot and killed on February 22, 1865, while he and other officers were attempting to arrest a drunk and disorderly barber. The drunk fired on two officers in the hallway of his apartment building and missed. When three other officers arrived the drunk retreated into his room. Officers moved into the room and the gunman fired at Lieutenant Somers Perry. The bullet passed over the head of the lieutenant and struck Sergeant Stockham in the side, exiting out his back.

The account in the Daily Bulletin said, "Stockham fell, and without speaking a word, groaned and in a few seconds died." Stockham, twenty-four, was from Illinois and had been on the police force about five months. He had served three years as a federal soldier. One of his brothers also served on the Memphis police force.

City government was returned to civilian control on July 3, 1865. Benjamin G. Garrett was elected chief

of the force of 95 men. Many men were continued from the force appointed by the federal authorities. The city was divided into 9 areas, each commanded by a sergeant and patrolled in two twelve-hour shifts.

Memphis was a powder keg in early 1866 and the police force was at the center of the pending explosion. Many of the same racial and socio-economic factors existed in Memphis that ignited the draft riots in New York City early in the war. The men who entered police service when the city was returned to home-rule were overwhelmingly of Irish descent. Of the 180 officers on the force, two were German, two were Italians, eight were "Americans," five were of unknown nationality and 163 were Irishmen.

Black Union soldiers from Fort Pickering were often assigned patrol duty in the city, which frequently put them in proximity and sometimes in conflict with the city police. After the black troops were mustered out of the army, relinquishing most of their weapons and while they were idle and waiting for their final military pay, violence erupted. Rioting began in Memphis on May 1, 1866.

A committee of the U. S. House of Representatives came to Memphis on May 22, 1866, and interviewed one hundred and seventy witnesses to the riots. In July the committee produced a 1200 page volume of their findings titled "Memphis Riots and Massacres." An excerpt of that report provided background into what caused the unrest.

> The causes which led to the riot, independent of the state of feelings which had been fostered by the press, was the animosity existing between the Irish population of Memphis, members of the city government, and the colored population, large numbers of whom had come into the city since its occupation by the Union authorities. A regiment of colored troops (the 3d heavy artillery) had been stationed at Memphis for a long time, and the families of many of the soldiers had gathered there. In the vicinity of Fort Pickering, where these troops were stationed, and immediately east of it, great numbers of these colored people had squatted and built their little cabins.

> Many of the families of the soldiers were living in these cabins. This was outside the corporate limits of the city of Memphis, and was called South Memphis. The natural hostility between the Irish and negroes seems to have been aggravated by the fact that it had been the duty of the colored

troops to patrol the city, bringing them into contact more or less with the Irish police; and it came to pass that whenever a colored man was arrested for any cause, even the most frivolous, and sometimes without cause, by the police, the arrest was made in a harsh and brutal manner, it being usual to knock down and beat the arrested party. Such treatment tended, of course, greatly to exasperate the negroes. The police waited with an evident anxiety for the time to arrive when the colored troops should be mustered out of the service, and should have no adequate means of defense. Unfortunately, when that time arrived the men were detained for some time after they were discharged waiting to be paid off. Their arms had been taken from them, but by some means quite a number of them had obtained possession of pistols; but having been mustered out, the restraints of military discipline having in a measure been removed, the soldiers, with nothing to do, would leave the fort in large numbers, and wander about in those parts of the city usually inhabited by colored people, congregating in saloons, and indulging, more or less, in drinking.

The killing of Patrolman William Mower heightened the tension. Officers Mower and Patrick Welch had finished their shift and were on their way home about 8 o'clock on the evening of February 22. The Daily Post reported the incident.

As Policeman William Mower was entering his boarding house on DeSoto Street, he was shot at by a colored soldier, who was armed with a musket. Mr. Mower attempted to draw his pistol, when the negro leveled his musket and fired a second time.

The first shot struck Mower in the abdomen and the second entered his back. He died on March 1, 1866. Mower had been first appointed on July 20, 1864, and reappointed in the city's annual process on July 11, 1865. He was in the command of Captain Daniel McMahon's watch as a uniformed walking patrolman.

The incident that ignited the riot took place on May 1, 1866, and also resulted in the line of duty death of a Memphis police officer. The day patrol of the seventh ward in the southern part of the city included twelve men under the command of Captain McMahon. Patrolmen John Stevens, James Finn, David Carroll and John O'Neil were walking patrol in the south most section of the ward. James Finn, who was wounded in the incident, recounted the events that led to the fatal shooting of John Stevens.

On Tuesday, May 1, 1866, about 5 1/2 o'clock p.m., John O'Neil, David Carroll, John Stevens, and myself were on Causey [Third] street. We heard a great noise in the direction of St. Martin's street, and we went in that direction. Near Morris cemetery I saw a crowd of about fifty or sixty negroes, which increased to a crowd of one hundred or one hundred and fifty, among whom were several negro soldiers. I asked one of them what the trouble was, and he said, "It's none of your God damned business, you damned white-livered son of a bitch; you got no business over here." This negro was dressed in citizen's clothes. This man said, "Go for Carroll, that white-livered son of a bitch." The negroes then formed a half circle around us, and two negro soldiers took hold of Carroll, who finally got away from them. Stevens and myself then commenced going east on South [Calhoun] street, and had reached the Bayou bridge, and were about twenty five yards from the crowd, when I heard pistol shots from the negroes and saw policeman Stevens fall, wounded through the thigh. O'Neil and myself then turned toward the crowd and commenced shooting at them. I fired four shots, and the whole crowd dispersed.

Thirty-six year old Patrolman John Stevens' upper right femur was shattered by a large caliber pistol ball. He was taken to a house on Causey Street and treated by doctors, but soon died.

The congressional committee concluded that the police officers acted lawfully and reasonably in the incident. The majority report stated that the mob's "behavior was riotous, and disorderly, and fully justified the interposition" of the police; and that when the police officers heard gunfire, they were justified in returning fire, "thinking the soldiers were firing at them." The minority report agreed, stating that the police "arrested two of the most noisy and boisterous discharged colored soldiers in a peaceable and orderly way, showing no arms," and as they left they heard shouts of "Shoot them! Shoot them!" and when shots were fired they fired back.

The rioting that followed the incident left large areas of the southern part of the city in flames and forty-eight people dead, forty-six black and two white. Although many Memphis policemen and the Shelby

County deputy sheriffs worked to restore peace, federal troops were called in to put down the rioting.

The riot gave Governor Brownlow a reason to press for passage of the Metropolitan Police bill then before the Reconstruction legislature and it was enacted soon thereafter. The "Metropolitan Police District of the County of Shelby" was formed to police Memphis and Shelby County. The Metropolitan Police force grew to about 140 strong. They became known to the populace as "The Metropolitans" or "Brownlow's Band." Reports said, "They were a law unto themselves, and a terror to the helpless citizen in dark reconstruction days, and frequently hauled innocent citizens before ignorant magistrates on ridiculous charges."

The city used the courts to resist the metropolitans. In addition the board refused to allocate funds from the city to support them. The third report of the Metropolitan Police Commission dated June 30, 1869, and addressed to Governor Dewitt Senter refers to the litigation as well as the working relationship with the Memphis city board.

> We regret that the agreed case submitted to the Supreme Court by the city authorities and ourselves, for the determination of all matters of dispute between us, has not yet been decided. We have been very anxious to secure the decision of that court, hoping that it might lead to a more intimate relation between our own and the other departments of the city government, as contemplated by the law originally passed. It was only in consequence of the refusal of the Board of Mayor and Aldermen to conform to the law, and to provide for the maintenance of the police force, that the Board of Police Commissioners were made independent of them, and such independence is still contingent upon the action of the city authorities.

> While there has been no difficulty whatever between the two Boards during the past year, but, on the contrary, a ready disposition to co-operate, it is yet clear to us that the public good would be promoted by the establishment of the relation between us originally contemplated by the law.

The same tactic was used by county authorities to resist Governor Brownlow's police force and no official county patrol was formed. A voluntary force was organized and proved successful.

> The law provides for the organization of a police force beyond the city limits, to be paid by the county, but it has been prevented by the refusal of the County Commissioners to make the necessary appropriation, and we would have been powerless to secure the preservation of order and the protection of property in that portion of the District, but for the voluntary service of citizens residing there. The result has exceeded all expectation, and the organized band of horse thieves and robbers infested the county has been driven out.

Suits and other court actions were taken to impede the efforts of the Metropolitan Police. The report indicated, "In these suits, injunctions have been procured restraining us from interference with gaming houses, lotteries and houses of ill-fame, which, though repeatedly dissolved by the Chancellor, have been as often renewed by the fiat of another judge."

Colonel Samuel B. Beaumont was appointed the first superintending commissioner, also referred to as the superintendent or chief of the Metropolitan Police and appointed approximately 100 policemen on June 14, 1866. The men selected were from northern states although they may have come to Memphis or the South prior to the war and some served with Confederate forces during the war. The Metropolitans began patrolling the streets of Memphis on July 1, 1866. Despite the often contentious nature of the environment in which they functioned, these policemen appeared to have taken their duty seriously and competently enforced the laws and ordinances of the city.

The Metropolitans wore Union soldier style uniforms. The coat of the patrolman resembled a line officer's coat, single-breasted and reaching to the knee. Supervisors' coats were double-breasted and resembled the uniforms of field officers. Buttons were imprinted with the Tennessee seal. A blue cap took the place of the white hat. On the front of the cap patrolmen wore a silver wreath enclosing their number and supervisors wore a golden wreath enclosing their rank. Patrolmen were referred to as privates and supervisors as officers.

The first black men to serve with the Memphis police were a part of the Metropolitan force. William Cook and John F. Harris were hired on November 18, 1867, and served for about two years as turnkeys at the two district station houses.

The Metropolitan Police was commanded by two captains, one in command of the First District (also called the Northern or Upper District) and one in command of the Second District (also called the Southern or Lower District). The captains alternated working 12-hour day and night shifts, so which ever captain was on duty had responsibility for the entire department. The only other rank above patrolman or detective was sergeant.

Two members of the Metropolitan Police force gave their lives in the line of duty in the first year of the force. Patrolman John M. Claridge was a native of Illinois who had resided in Memphis for twenty years. During the war he served in the 154th Tennessee Regiment of the Confederate Army. On April 23, 1867, he and his partner Eli H. Signor were walking a beat in the first district. Officers Cusick and Welsh were walking the adjoining beat. It was a rough area of the downtown and near the place where a murder was committed only a few weeks before.

About ten that evening Cusick and Welsh arrested four men for fighting in the Cotton Plant Saloon on Washington Street between Main and Front. They took the four to the station house. Around midnight Claridge and Signor heard another disturbance at the saloon and went to investigate. When they entered the saloon they were assaulted and shots were exchanged between the policemen and the rowdies. The two officers were thrown out but the firing continued. One shot tore through Patrolmen Claridge's uniform cap and into his forehead. A fireman was arrested for the killing, but as a result of conflicting testimony, he was found not guilty.

Less than two months later a second Metropolitan policeman was shot in the head in downtown Memphis. Patrolman Walter M. Rogers was killed on Main Street near the corner of Market between 4:00 and 5:00 a.m. A drunken fireman fired the fatal shot while a second fireman stood across the street and watched.

Patrolman J. W. Smith, who was on the same beat with Rogers on June 4, 1867, had confronted the two drunks earlier. He did not arrest them lest they be called on duty in case of a fire. Smith talked with them and thought he had persuaded them to go home, when one of the drunks fired his pistol twice in the air. Smith took the gun and accompanied them to a saloon for a last drink before they went home.

After the two had another drink they seized the officer by the throat and overpowered him. They took back the gun plus two other pistols the policeman was carrying, one a Derringer. The two then accosted two black men and made them get on their knees and beg not to be shot. When the two drunks saw Patrolman Rogers one crossed the street and told him to get on his knees. The officer refused and was shot in the head with the Derringer. Patrolman Smith watched the murder of his partner from across the street.

The incident, compounded by the recent killing of officer Claridge, created an uproar among the men of the police force. Superintendent Beaumont wrote a memorandum calling for restraint.

Office Superintendent
Metropolitan Police, Memphis, Tenn.
June 4, 1867

To the Officers and Patrolmen of the Metropolitan Police Force of Memphis.

The death of another of your comrades, stricken down by the hand of an assassin, for no cause, except that he wore the badge of an officer; following as it does so closely after the cold-blooded murder of the gallant and noble Claridge, has tended to arouse in you a thirst for revenge, which, if not checked by wholesome restraint, and a "sober second thought," would result in anarchy and the violation by you of the very laws you are sworn to uphold and execute.

It was for these reasons that upon learning at an early hour this morning of the assassination of Patrolman Walter M. Rodgers, and of your threats of vengeance, I promptly ordered you to use no violence upon the person of the murderer, should he fall into your hands. Your ready and strict obedience to that order, has served to increase the confidence I have heretofore reposed in you, and will be commended by all good citizens.

The failure of Patrolman J. W. Smith to promptly arrest the men concerned in the murder, when he found them disorderly and committing other violations of the ordinance, should teach you the danger of temporizing with known desperadoes, and the imperative necessity of prompt and firm action in the arrest and confinement of such offenders.

S. B. Beaumont
Superintendent, Metropolitan Police

Patrolman Walter Rogers was twenty-six years old and had been on the force only a month. He was a seaman before the war and served four years in the First New Jersey Infantry during the war. His killer was convicted of voluntary manslaughter and sentenced to five years in the penitentiary.

These incidents were consistent with the state of lawlessness throughout the South following the war. Lack of respect for authority was pervasive and whiskey and firearms readily available. The more desperate the character, the more deadly the situation was for the police. On Christmas Day 1867 another such incident took the life of Patrolman John M. Fenton, a native of Ireland.

Officer Fenton heard a disturbance inside McMahon's saloon. The twenty-six year old officer ordered three rowdy drunks out of the saloon. As he followed them outside he was jumped, knocked to the ground and beaten. One of the drunks pulled a gun. The first shot missed Fenton but fatally wounded a young boy standing nearby. Fenton was able to get off one shot, striking the gunman in his left arm, before a second shot pierced the policeman's lung. He died a week later.

A patrolman and one of the two captains of the force were killed in 1868 attempting to apprehend burglars. Patrolmen John Gear and C. P. Clinton were working the night shift on March 7. About 2:00 a.m. they spotted three men carrying bundles near Fourth and Jefferson. When the officers told the suspicious trio to halt, two of them turned and fired on the officers. Twenty-seven-year-old Policeman John Gear, a native of New York, collapsed. A bone in his leg had been shattered below the knee and he died six days later.

Captain Somers Perry, commander of the Southern District, met a similar fate on June 4, 1868. He was working the night shift and having a meal when burglars were spotted entering Price & Yeatman, a wholesale grocer at Monroe and Main. The incident was recounted by a private watchman named Telford.

Captain Perry was up in keno room getting lunch at a quarter to 12 o'clock; the negro boy, Henry, was standing at the window and saw two men go into the side door of Price & Yeatman; he went to Captain Perry and told him, and he got up from lunch, came down the steps alone, and met me at the foot of the steps; he told me to come and go with him; never said where he was going, and walked to the alley and turned down the alley until he got to the side door of Price & Yeatman; he pushed the door open, stepped inside, struck a match, and asked who was there; we were within six feet of the office door, and saw two negroes come out of the office door, each with a navy repeater in his hand; we stepped back outside the door as they advanced, and as Captain Perry stepped outside one of them snapped a pistol at him, but it did not explode. Captain Perry then drew his pistol, and poking it around the door fired, and the negro fired at about the same time, and Captain Perry fell, saying, "I am killed; follow them up."

The pistol ball passed through Perry's right arm, exited just below the elbow, shattered a rib and lodged in the right lobe of his liver. The burglars fired at Telford and fled past him. He chased them down the alley toward Union, firing at them and wounding one of the burglars in the neck. Patrolmen Allison Wright and Louis Barbierre, in whose beat the incident occurred, took up the chase along with another private watchman and two citizens. Patrolman Wright was wounded in the knee cap. The wounded burglar was captured and implicated four others.

Somers Perry was appointed to the Memphis police on August 5, 1862, as a part of the department's expansion. He was promoted to lieutenant in July 1864 under the military government, but was reduced to patrolman when the city government was restored on July 11, 1865. Perry was named to the rank of sergeant in October 1867 and then to captain on January 3, 1868, six months before his death, and was assigned as captain of the Second District.

The thirty-five-year-old Perry came to Memphis from Pennsylvania before the war, about 1860, and worked as a painter before he became a policeman. The Daily Appeal said of Perry, "Come what will, he is a brave and fearless officer, who, if he dies from this wound, dies like a hero doing his duty." The captain died a few days later. His killer was hanged the following year.

In the final year of the Metropolitans, Sergeant D. J. Finch was killed while assisting an Arkansas militia captain named Haynes apprehend a fugitive from Crittenden County, Arkansas. Haynes came to Memphis and asked Superintendent Pearne for assistance in the arrest of Cub Harland, a notorious "half-breed" Chickasaw. The desperado was holed-up, Haynes said, in Shelby County south of Memphis. Actually the outlaw was staying at a tavern at Horn Lake in Mississippi. Pearne assigned Sergeant John K. Brown and a patrolman to accompany Haynes to assist in the capture. When Sergeant Finch heard of the expedition he volunteered to replace the patrolman.

The three-man posse set out on Sunday morning, March 7, 1869. They reached the tavern at Horn Lake, and Haynes and Brown went inside while Finch waited outside. A gun battle erupted in the tavern and the fugitive was chased out. The fleeing outlaw and a hired man working at the tavern exchanged gunfire with the three lawmen. When the engagement was over, the outlaw had escaped, Haynes was wounded in the thigh and hip and Finch was shot twice in the chest. Sergeant D. J. Finch died at 2:15 the following afternoon.

The activity of the Metropolitan Police was mostly routine police work, enforcing the laws of the state and the ordinances of Memphis. The force made 6,595 misdemeanor arrests and 1,342 felony arrests in the year ending in 1869. The commissioners reported other activities in which the force was involved including 69 fires, 75 accidents involving injury and 61 cases of "lost children found on the streets and restored to their homes."

Reverend W. H. Pearne, an active Methodist minister from New Jersey, was the superintending commissioner or chief of the Metropolitans in their final year. Augustus P. Burditt was the financial commissioner and Channing Richards the clerical commissioner. The force was divided into two districts. Captain P. S. Simons was in charge of the First District assisted by Sergeants C. B. Smith and J. K. Brown with 46 patrolmen. Captain W. C. McMath commanded the Second District staffed by Sergeants G. L. Taylor and L. J. Hanson and 38 patrolmen. The Sanitary Department was under the command of Sergeant S. J. Atlee. Detectives were M. McCune, P. H. Connel, Benjamin G. Garrett, Samuel J. Ireland and George S.

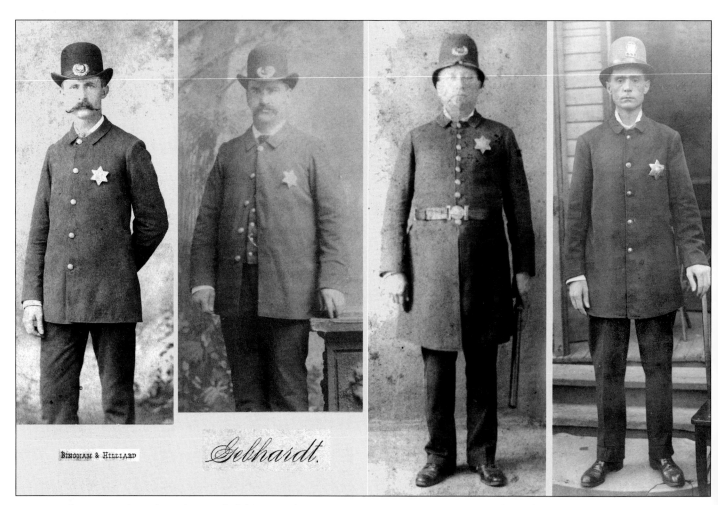

Four patrolmen in uniforms from the period of the 1880s through around 1915. The first two were cabinet photos by Memphis photographers, both made in the 1880s. The first from the left was by photographer Bingham & Hilliard. The second photo was Patrolman V. C. Russell, who served on the force for a brief period from January 31, 1888, until April 11, 1889, and was made by photographer Gebhardt. Patrolman John Breckinridge Clark was wearing the winter uniform and patrol helmet from around 1900 in the third photo. The patrolman in the fourth or right-most photo was wearing the insignia adopted by the department in 1912 and the summer uniform with the helmet worn only by patrol officers.

Hayden. Ireland and Hayden were Memphis's first black detectives.

The star continued as the badge of the patrolmen of the Memphis force. In fact Memphis policemen were often referred to as "stars." The practice of having the badge only while on duty was abandoned. The Rules and Regulations of the Metropolitan Police required that the badge be carried at all times.

> When on actual tour of service each member shall wear his shield on the outside of the outer garment, over the left breast, so that the entire surface of the shield shall always be distinctly visible. At all other times he shall carry it with him, and if called on to do active duty shall immediately place it over the breast, as above.

Decisions on police leadership and policy reverted to the Memphis city government in January 1870 following the repeal of the Metropolitan Police Act in 1869. Channing Richards was appointed interim chief of police for the month of January, after which Thomas O'Donnell was appointed and served for two years as chief.

The city leased a building on Adams between Main and Second for use as a police station, courtroom and offices. The station house was located on the first floor and the courtroom was upstairs. Uniformed patrolmen were divided into two watches or shifts. Each watch was twelve hours long from 6:00 a.m. or 7:00 a.m. until the same hour in the evening. Patrolmen worked the shift seven days a week. Captain Phil R. Athy commanded the day shift.

Initially the city placed the force in cadet-gray uniforms to distinguish them from the Metropolitans. Within six months the MPD returned to uniforms of blue navy serge accented by white Marseilles' vests, white caps and brass buttons. The city paid one-half the cost of the uniforms and policemen the other half.

Memphis policemen of the 1870s found that exposure to disease and the weather more deadly than desperados. Patrolman John Regan died of sun-stroke after walking his beat along the levee. On July 13, 1870, the thermometer reached 94 degrees in the shade. Regan left his beat around 1:00 p.m. for a lunch break. He had a serving of soup and said he wasn't feeling well. He asked for a pitcher of ice water and went to bed with instructions to be roused at 2:00 p.m. Regan was found dead on his bed. An inquest ruled that "the deceased came to his death from congestion of the brain, superinduced by the action of the sun."

Regan's funeral included full police honors. The *Daily Avalanche* described a police funeral of the day.

> The band was in front, followed by the Chief of Police and his Captains, on horseback, at the head of about sixty of the police, in uniform and mar.ching two deep; then came the hearse flanked on either side by the [eight] pall bearers.

> The funeral proceeded down Adams to St. Peter's Church. Arriving at the church the line of policemen halted and opened ranks through which the hearse passed, while the men uncovered their heads. The coffin was taken into the church and placed as usual outside the sanctuary railing and Father Carey read the funeral services and then preached a practical sermon.

Chief of Police Phil R. Athy served from January 12, 1872, to August 28, 1880. He headed the department during the yellow fever epidemics, one of the most difficult periods in the history of Memphis, and one in which the police force distinguished itself.

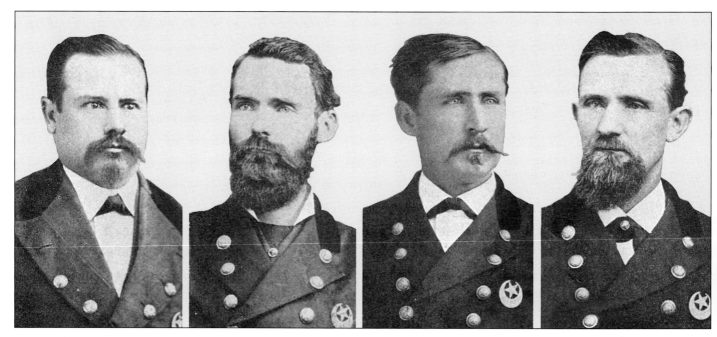

Chief Athy's commanding officers in the mid-1870s were Captain R. F. Arata, Captain William C. Davis, Sergeant George Thomas O'Haver, and Sergeant Charles Kunholz. Davis and O'Haver would later serve Memphis as Chief of Police. The commanders all wore a crescent-star style breast badge, while the majority of patrolmen wore six-point stars.

After leaving the church, the procession was again formed, and marched down Main to Beale, Beale to DeSoto, thence to South, where the line of policemen left the procession and returned through the city, headed by the band, playing gay airs. The pall bearers proceeded to Calvary Cemetery, and performed the last sad office for their departed brother.

Phil R. Athy served as chief of police from January 12, 1872, to August 28, 1880, except for a brief period in 1879 when the sheriff served as interim chief due the revocation of the city charter. Athy was an innovative chief who rebuilt the department after the days of reconstruction. The 1899 MPD publication said he was "a pioneer in the work which has given to Memphis the present efficient and satisfactory system of managing the police department of Memphis. Athy was a firm character and he succeeded in breaking up some of the most corrupt gangs that ever infested the city."

Chief Athy made an immediate positive impression with his leadership of the department. Only two months after becoming chief, March 15, 1872, citizens presented him with a horse, buggy, harness and whip as "a merited tribute to his worth to the city."

The Memphis Police Department was 77 strong in 1872 and included Chief Athy, Captain G. R. Weatherford, Captain C. T. Smith, Sergeants C. H. Braun, M. Dea, R. F. Arata and P. McElroy, Station

House Keeper W. Featherstone, three detectives, 60 patrolmen and seven in other capacities. A patrolman was paid $3 per day. The shift for the 25 day policemen began at 5:30 a.m. and ended at 6:30 p.m. The 35 man night shift covered the hours between 6:30 p.m. and 5:30 a.m. Captains and sergeants rode horses and patrolmen walked their beats.

The city remained divided into two police districts. The upper district contained the area north of Monroe and the lower district was south of Monroe. Police headquarters was located on Adams and a small facility on Causey [Third] Street at Linden served as a second station house.

On March 10, 1872, the force received new breast badges, wreaths for caps, and belts. The patrolmen's wreaths were of white metal in the shape of a half circle with a number corresponding to that of the breast badge. Breast badges were stars of German silver with the word "Police" and a number engraved in them. They were about one-third larger than the previous badges. The *Memphis Daily Avalanche* reported that the badges were engraved.

The engraving is the work of Mr. V. B. Thayer, of the Memphis Engraving Works, and reflects great credit upon his taste and skill. He says that a policeman can hang a prisoner on each corner of the star and convey him to the station without fear of breaking it loose from its fastening. Both the men and officers are well pleased with the work, as it could not have been executed better. In a few days the clubs will be ready, and then with their gloves and canes the police force will be in complete uniform.

Some policemen wore badges in the shape of shields or five-point stars, but patrolmen wore mostly six-point stars from the 1870s until shields were adopted in the late 1940s. Supervisory officers wore crescent stars in the 1870s.

Patrolmen were equipped with canes for their use in controlling disorderly individuals. The canes were finished with black lacquer and had a slung-shot for a knob. The slung-shot, leather covered lead shot, was an early form of the blackjack. A new style cap similar in appearance to that worn by naval officers was also adopted in 1872. Straw Panama hats and white gloves were worn in the summer. In 1875 come-alongs were provided to patrolmen. These devices, designed to clamp to a prisoners wrist with a handle to be held by the officer, were more typically called "nippers." Their use was described by the *Memphis Daily Appeal.*

> The patrolmen now use the steel nippers to over-come turbulent persons and convey them in safe-ty to the station house. The "nips" are placed on the wrist of the arrested, and with this lever the most unruly are soon tamed.

The decade of the 1870s was shaped by a deadly battle with the disease called "Yellow Jack." Yellow fever struck Memphis in 1873 and again in 1878 and 1879. The police force was honored by the city council in 1873 for "remaining on duty" during the epidemic when most well bodied individuals fled Memphis. This was one of the noblest and proudest moment of the Memphis Police Department. Of the 55-man force 50 were stricken with the fever and 10 died, Frank K. Birmingham, Patrick Cusick, John Campen, Detective William P. Brown, T. C. Cogbill, James Fitzpatrick, Thomas O'Mahoney, Thomas D. Franklin, Louis Servatus and Eugene McAuliffe.

The heroic efforts of Patrolman John J. Huber was of particular note. He remained at his post in the Happy Hollow district of the city, one of the areas most affected by the fever. Chief Athy wrote of Huber in his annual report dated January 8, 1874.

> I cannot but mention Patrolman J. J. Huber; he is a hero. All through the epidemic he was the only man on duty in the infected district. Alone, with no partner to keep him company, or cheer him, he walked his beat, when, at every step, the solemn stillness of the air would seem a warning that told him of the fate of his dead comrades.

The 1878 epidemic was the most devastating and claimed Huber as one of twelve policemen that died of Yellow Fever that summer, Morrison M. Allison, Michael Cannon, Captain William M. Homan, Timothy G. Hope, John J. Huber, Sergeant Reuben C. Manuel, James McConnell, Frederick Restmeyer, Patrick Ryder, Charles R. Staley, W. H. Sweeney and William Unverzagt. Two more Memphis officers died of Yellow Fever in 1879, Timothy Keefe and Thomas J. Maguire.

The department lost 40% of its strength. Commanders that survived the 1878 epidemic were Chief Phil R. Athy, Captain William C. Davis, Captain R. F. Arata, Sergeant George T. O'Haver and Sergeant Charles Kunholz. Fourteen other members of the department survived as well.

Pay during this time was slow for public servants and the *Memphis Daily Appeal* made a plea as winter approached in 1878 for help to uniform the force.

> The firemen and policemen who stayed here dur-ing the fearful yellow fever epidemic and survived this plague need new uniforms. Some good citi-zen ought to get up some uniform cloth for the boys out of which winter suits could be made.

The department hired a black officer in February 1878, Rufus H. McCain. The experience with Policeman McCain was so satisfactory that when white officers were lost to the disease, the number of black policemen were increased to a level proportionate with the black population of the city. Fourteen other black officers were added to the force in the August 1878. Most of these men stayed with the department for less than a year, but Townsend D. Jackson, Burrell Randolph, Moses Plummer, Howard Chastaine and Dallas Lee served as policemen over ten years.

The black patrolmen were kept on following the yellow fever outbreak and eight more black policemen were added to the force between 1879 and 1889. The force remained integrated until August 1895 when Dallas Lee left the department.

William C. Davis was appointed chief of police in 1880 and served until 1895; he and served again from 1908 to 1912 for a total of more than 20 years as chief. Davis was a capable chief and modernized the depart-ment. The 1899 MPD publication said that "his administration was one of the cleanest ever known in the history of the city. He was a man of great courage, an efficient officer, an elegant, high-toned gentlemen and his discipline was exceptionally good."

Davis introduced uniform collar insignia to commanding officers so that commanders were readily distinguishable from the rest of the force. Sergeants wore sleeve chevrons from the time the rank was created, but captains and the chief wore only their badge. The collar insignia consisted of an "MP" accompanied by a single star for captains and two stars for the chief. The insignia was sewed on each side of the collar in bullion filament.

The budget for the department was $64,533 in 1879. The pay scale for the officers in 1881 was $125 per month for the chief, $90 a month for captains, $80 per month for sergeants and $60 a month for patrolmen. In 1882 the force numbered 43, which meant only 22 officers were on duty at any time to cover the entire city from Chelsea to Fort Pickering and from the river to Estival Park. About one forth of the patrolmen were black and in 1883 black officers formed an association for their mutual benefit.

Police headquarters moved to a converted tin roofed, two story, cotton warehouse on Second at Washington in 1884. The first patrol wagon was acquired in 1890. The patrol wagon was used to transport prisoners, to convey large numbers of policemen when the situation required, to transport injured parties to the hospital and for other emergency needs. Wooden cells of the jail were also replaced with iron. An alarm system was installed that placed the department directly in touch with all parts of the city. The department made progress in many areas, but what was needed most was officers to patrol the streets.

The financial condition of Memphis in the late 1880s and early 1890s was such that the number of police officers was dangerously low. The number of policemen per thousand of population in 1870 was 16.2. This was reduced to 9.2 per thousand in 1880, a reduction of 43.2%. The department consisted of only 53 men in 1888 and in the spring of 1889 walking patrolmen were further reduced when ten officers were assigned as mounted patrolmen to provide coverage in the suburbs. Chief Davis pled his case for more police-

Chief of Police William C. Davis served as head of the Memphis Police Department from 1880 to 1895, and was again chosen to serve as chief of the department from 1909 to 1912. The "MP" on the uniform collar was frequently used to denote "Memphis Police" and the two stars were the rank insignia of the chief. Suspension badges were often the form worn by department heads. The eagle at the top attached the badge to the chief's uniform, and the crescent and star was suspended by chains from the eagle, with "Chief" on the crescent.

men in his annual report.

I urgently call your attention to the necessity of furnishing the department with more men, as you see from the roster we have only 38 patrolmen, 19 on each relief. We need at least 20 more men, which would be 29 for each relief, and

The composite of photos on the facing page was done as a tribute to the policemen who died during the 1878 yellow fever epidemic. Surrounding Chief Phil R. Athy in the center of the page were the twelve officers who died with the date of their death. Clockwise from the leftmost picture just above Athy were James McConnell (died Aug. 12, 1878), Mike Cannon (Aug. 22), William Unverzagt (Aug. 26), M. M. Allison (Aug. 31), Tim Hope (Sept. 17), Pat Ryder (Aug. 25), Charley Staley (Sept. 11), Captain William M. Homan (Sept. 25), Sergeant R. C. Manuel (Oct. 14), Fred Restmeyer (Sept. 9), J. J. Huber (Sept 2) and W. H. Sweeny (Sept. 10). Other members of the department were, clockwise beginning at the top left, Sergeant G. T. O'Haver, F. T. Couch, August Pante, J. H. Campbell, James Longinotti, Sergeant Charles Kunholz, Con Daly, T. Carmichael, P. Logan, John McPartland, Captain W. C. Davis, E. G. Forrest, City Recorder P. J. Quigley, T. N. Baker, Captain R. F. Arata, M. Mulowney, John Jenny, John Daugherty and Henry Wilson. A number of badge styles were used during the period, although the six-point star is the predominate form of insignia.

Sergt. G. T. O'HAVER.

F. T. COUCH.

AUGUST PANTE.

J. H. CAMPBELL.

JAMES LONGINOTTI.

Sergt. CHAS. KUNHOLZ.

HENRY WILSON.

JAMES McCONNELL.
Died Aug. 14th, 1878.

MIKE CANNON.
Died Aug. 22nd, 1878.

WM. UNVERZAGT.
Died Aug. 28th, 1878.

M. M. ALLISON.
Died Aug. 31st, 1878.

CON. DALY.

JOHN DAUGHERTY.

W. H. SWEENY.
Died Sept. 10th, 1878.

TIM HOPE.
Died September 17th, 1878.

T. CARMICHAEL.

JOHN JENNY.

J. J. HUBER.
Died September 8th, 1878.

CHIEF P. R. ATHY.

P. LOGAN.

FRED. RESTEMYER.
Died Sept. 4th, 1878.

PAT. RYDER.
Died August 25th, 1878.

M. MULOKNEY.

Sergt. R. C. MANUEL.
Died Oct. 14th, 1878.

Capt. Wm. M. HOMAN.
Died Sept. 25th, 1878.

CHARLEY STALEY.
Died Sept. 12th, 1878.

JOHN McPARTLAND.

Capt. R. F. ARATA.

T. N. BAKER.

City Recorder P. J. QUIGLEY.

E. G. FORREST.

Capt. W. C. DAVIS.

Memphis Police Force, Epidemic, 1878.

COTTAGE GALLERY, Memphis.

S. C. Toof & Co., Steam Printers and Lithographers.

which is less than three men to each ward. This is quite few enough considering the extent of territory to patrol and the time taken up attending to the wants of the public at the depots of Tennessee railroads coming into our city, where some forty passenger trains arrive and depart daily.

The general financial condition of the city was such that no action was taken on his request. The budget for the police force remained around $56,000 per year. No new officers were added and patrolmen's salary remain at $75 per month.

Salary was poor compensation for the danger officers faced at the hands of gunmen. Patrolman Rufus L. Parkinson was handsome in his uniform and handlebar mustache. He walked his beat along the southern levee from Front Street on the afternoon of November 1, 1894. A woman stopped him and pointed out a man who had robbed her in Osceola, Arkansas. As Officer Parkinson approached the robber fled, running toward Beale Street, The policeman gave chase.

At Beale and Clinton a citizen grabbed the bandit but he broke away as Patrolman Parkinson neared. The felon drew a revolver and shot the officer in the left side. Parkinson drew his sidearm and fired at the robber as he ran east toward Front. The patrolman continued the chase. At Beale and Front a rider stopped and offered his horse to Parkinson. When the policeman tried to mount the horse he was in such pain that he had to be helped to the ground.

The patrol wagon arrived filled with lawmen and Parkinson asked to be taken to his home on North Second Street. The Lincoln County, Tennessee, native had been on the police force only 10 months. He was bleeding internally and doctors were unable to help. Patrolman Parkinson died at around three in the morning.

Jerome E. Richards became chief of police in January 1898 following the tenure of Chief E. B. Moseley, who began his term in 1895. Richards joined the department in 1892. He was described in the 1899 publication as "probably the most rigid character who ever filled the office of Chief of Police in the city of Memphis. He is a natural disciplinarian. His word has the bark on it. He means what he says and he sometimes gives to his language a sulphuric coloring that makes it even more forcible."

The 1899 department headed by Chief Richards included watch commanders Captains John Joseph Mason assisted by Sergeant Oliver Hazard Perry and Captain George Thomas O'Haver assisted by Sergeant Thomas Joseph Cole. They supervised 45 patrolmen. Four detectives were under the command of Chief of

Central Police Station located at the corner of Second and Washington was used by the department at the turn of the century. The two-story, tin roofed building was a converted cotton warehouse acquired in 1884 to house the police.

Detectives Joseph A. Perkins. Department personnel also included a day patrol driver, a night patrol driver, a license inspector, a day station keeper, a night station keeper, two turnkeys, the chief's clerk, a matron, three rock pile guards and a pound keeper. A number of sanitary policemen were part of the health department.

The entire department including the chief wore six-point star breast badges. The uniform was a coat buttoned to the neck with brass buttons featured a five-point star. In winter a full-length coat was worn with a belt and military style belt buckle containing "MP" in raised letters. The headgear was a tall domed helmet, light colored in summer and dark in winter. Hat wreaths and breast badges stayed the same.

The patrol wagon or Black Maria acquired by the department in 1890 was the principle mode of transport for prisoners and others for over a decade.

Memphis policemen circa 1885 wearing dark brimmed hats with wreath insignia and six-point star breast badges. Some of the plain clothes officers wore fashionable straw skimmer hats.

Due to a large annexation by the city at the end of 1899 the department expanded to include Chief Richards, Captains Mason and O'Haver, three sergeants, six detectives, 54 regular patrolmen and nine mounted policemen. The budget to support the force of 83 men was $85,074. The monthly salary of patrolmen remained $75.

Communication was also improved between patrolling officers and headquarters when the Gamewell Police Telephone System was installed. The system provided 18 "signal boxes" with telephones on the streets for the patrol to communicate with headquarters plus another 37 telephones located in public buildings and private businesses available to officers. Officers were required to find a call box or business telephone and contact the station once every hour. They were also required to stay at the box for ten minutes so headquarters could call back with instructions.

Perhaps the change that most impacted individual officers was the reduction of hours in the work day. In 1900 the department moved from two 12-hour shifts to three 8-hour shifts. At the same time walking patrolmen extended into the "mounted districts" of

Nippers, left, or come-alongs were provided to Memphis patrolmen in 1875. The device was designed to clamp to a prisoners wrist and provide a handle for the officer to maintain control of the one arrested. Example above: Phillips Patent Police Nippers, partially open. A call box, right, of the Gamewell Police Telegraph system, installed in 1899, was an important technological advancement for communication between patrol officers and police headquarters.

Patrolman Rufus L. Parkinson was shot by a robber near the waterfront in 1894. He died of his injuries at his home a short time later. In this photograph Parkinson was wearing the summer uniform with a star breast badge and a wreath on the helmet, and was carrying a baton in his right hand.

Suddenly a shot echoed in the room as the killer fired from behind the bed. The next sound was the din of three shots, one from each of the detectives and a second from the murderer. Chief Detective Perkins cried, "I'm shot," staggered back to the door and fell mortally wounded. Detective Lawless emptied his gun except for one round, at the edge of the bed where the killer was hiding, but did not hit the gunman. The room was filled with smoke from the gunfire and Detective Lawless fell to the bed and waited. As smoke cleared Lawless caught a glimpse of the killer's head appearing above the bed rail. Detective Lawless stretched out his pistol and shot the murder in the head.

Chief Detective Joseph A. Perkins died 36 hours later. He was born in 1848 in Virginia and moved to Texas as a teenager. His first job was driving wagons between western Texas and Mexico, later he drove

Memphis Officer in the circa 1890 winter uniform featuring a dark frock coat and helmet. The sidearm was worn under the coat. The belt was of military design with "MP" on the buckle and the nightstick hung at the side. Breast badge number 31 was a six-point star worn by the department for a century or longer. The hat badge was a traditional wreath.

the city. The eight-hour shift was short lived, city budget restrictions brought back the twelve-hour work day.

For detectives those hours might be spread over the entire day. Detectives were referred to as the "secret service" of the police department because they wore no uniform to identify them as police. The dangers of police work was ever present for detectives the same as for officers in uniform.

In the early hours of July 15, 1900, Chief Detective Joseph A. Perkins and Detective Walter Lawless went to a house on McLemore Avenue in search of a murderer who killed a boy in Chulahoma, Mississippi. The killer's wife, who worked at the house, said her husband was not there. In a small, dimly lit bedroom the detectives saw a man's coat over the back of a chair and a man's hat hanging on a bed post.

Members of the Memphis Police Department in the 1890s. The officer in the front row, third from left, is wearing a suspension badge and is likely in command. Patrolmen are all wearing stars for breast badges and wreaths on their hats. The group includes a black officer, left end of the second row, believed to be Moses Plummer.

stagecoaches over the same area. He worked for the railroads both in Texas and in Memphis after he moved to Tennessee in 1877. He served ten years as a Shelby County Deputy Sheriff before joining the Memphis Police Department in February 1898.

Shootings normally grew out of officers stopping crimes or chasing a lawbreakers, but from time to time troublemakers came looking for lawmen. Such was the case with Joe Knight, the keeper of a notorious Memphis dive. Initially Knight seemed calm after Sergeant Oliver H. Perry arrested him. He paid his bail and left the station house.

The next morning, January 29, 1901, Knight returned to the Adams Street station. He waited outside until Sergeant Perry came out. Knight walked up to him, pulled a pistol, put the muzzle against the sergeant's stomach and pulled the trigger. The hammer snapped but the weapon did not fire. Before he could pull the trigger again Perry drew his sidearm and shot Knight dead. Captain O'Haver summed up the inci-

dent in his report to the mayor, "Joe Knight came to the station to kill Sergeant Perry. Knight's funeral will be held at 2:00 p.m. tomorrow."

Violence on city streets often resulted in death. The last known killing by an American Indian in the city of Memphis took place on the last day of 1902. Creeping Bear was a full blooded Cheyenne Indian from the reservation near El Reno, Oklahoma. He came to town with the Buffalo Bill Wild West Show in November and stayed. He was 17 years old, educated at the Carlisle Institute and sometimes used the English name Joe Weinbaum. He became a familiar figure around town, wearing a jacket, leggings, moccasins and wrapped in a striped blanket.

Creeping Bear was near the Fire Station #4 on North Main that New Year's Eve just before 8:00 p.m. An alarm was sounded and he came to engine house to watch the activity. George Millard was alone at the fire station after the firemen left. Millard, a Choctaw Railroad employee and frequent visitor to the fire house, had served two years as Memphis policeman.

When the two were alone Millard told Creeping Bear to leave and words were exchanged. Millard tried to hit the young Cheyenne. Creeping Bear pulled a tomahawk from his belt and struck Millard in the head. The weapon was the type with a blade on one end and a peace pipe on the other. Millard collapsed and the young Native American fled the scene.

A passerby helped Millard to a seat. It was reported that the two inch gash in his head was bleeding so badly they used a wooden bucket to catch the blood. He was rushed to St. Joseph Hospital in a horse-drawn ambulance. Millard died two weeks later.

Creeping Bear was captured at the Iron Mountain Railroad Depot by Patrolman Werkhoven and did not resist arrest. The young man said, "He called me a name that no man would take. He struck at me, and I at him. There were only two blows passed."

The young Cheyenne was tried twice for murder and both times the conviction was overturned by the Tennessee Supreme Court for irregularities. The state decided against a third trial and Creeping Bear was released.

John Joseph Mason followed Richards as chief in 1902. Mason began his career in law enforcement as jailer under Sheriff Phil R. Athy as the youngest jailer in the history of the county. In 1904 Mason requested an increase in resources to include 40 new officers, six new horses for patrol wagons and 20 additional signal boxes.

An incident on October 17, 1904, caused Chief Mason to require some officers to get sidearms with

The Memphis Detective Bureau at the turn of the century in front of Central Police Station.

more adequate stopping power. The incident left Patrolman Robert C. Jameson dead and two other officers wounded. Officers were called by Patrolman Sullivan to the scene of gunfire. Captain Oliver H. Perry with Patrol Driver Wells and Patrolmen Jameson, Montieth and Schmidt loaded into the patrol wagon and located the shooter on Mosby Street between Hill and High at 10:10 a.m. Patrolman Sullivan and Detective Price were observing the man who was armed with a Winchester repeating rifle.

Patrolman Jameson was the first to step from the wagon. The rifleman opened fire. The officer was shot in the neck and chest. He was able to return fire before he fell mortally wounded. The other officer began to fire as well, but the rifle fire continued, wounding two

The first Memphis chiefs of police of the twentieth century. Chief Jerome E. Richards, left, served from 1898 to 1902. Chief John Joseph Mason, center, headed the department from 1902 to 1905. Chief George Thomas O'Haver, right, commanded the department from 1905 to 1908.

Officers of the Memphis police force and the department's new patrol wagon acquired in 1905 to replace the old Black Maria.

other policemen. Finally Captain Perry charged the shooter and knocked him to the ground. Numerous bullets had hit the rifleman and he died at the scene.

Officers Jameson and Montieth were rushed to City Hospital. Five-year veteran Patrolman Robert C. Jameson died at 11:00 a.m. Patrolman John W. Montieth received a serious wound to his right leg but survived. Montieth was 28 years old and had been an extra policeman for only a month. Captain Oliver Perry was the third officer shot, getting a slight wound to the little finger of his left hand.

A few years later another officer died as he attempted to apprehend a criminal. A prisoner escaped from the police station on February 10, 1907, and around 10:00 p.m. was spotted in the Ninth Ward. Patrolmen W. Edwin Miller and C. W. Humphreys took up the chase that led them to the waterfront

The gasoline powered patrol wagon acquired by the MPD in 1910.

where the swollen Wolf River entered the Mississippi. The felon jumped from boat to boat to escape the clutches of the law.

Patrolman Miller was close behind and as he leapt from the wharf boat Patton Tully to the towboat Satellite he missed his footing. Despite the efforts of Patrolman Humphreys and the watchman of a nearby wharf boat, Miller sank beneath the waters and drowned. The body of the 45 year old officer was not found for over a week. Miller had been on the force for six years.

In 1905 George Thomas O'Haver was appointed chief of police. His father Benjamin O'Havre (the earlier spelling of the name) was a veteran of the Mexican War, wounded at Cerro Gordo, and was one of the early captains of the Memphis night watch. George T. O'Haver joined the force in 1878. Five months later he was appointed sergeant and less than a year later became Captain of Police. He served as chief until 1909.

O'Haver was recognized as an officer with great ability. Allen Pinkerton, founder of the famed Pinkerton Detective Agency, considered O'Haver the best detective in the South. Among his noted captures was hotel clerk Charley Tolbert who stole $30,000 in diamonds from actress Fanny Davenport while she was in Memphis on tour. O'Haver caught Tolbert in Kansas City before he could dispose of any of the loot. In the years following his duty with the police O'Haver formed a detective agency in Memphis.

O'Haver changed the uniform in 1906, changing the helmet to a bell-topped cap. Memphis patrolmen

Patrolmen Nelson, left, wearing badge #82 and Brett, right, wearing badge #83 with Flanigan the burro around 1912.

continued to wear a six-point star as a breast badge and a numbered wreath on the cap.

The department expanded to 146 policemen by 1907. The force included Chief O'Haver, a chief of detectives, three captains, eight sergeants, 14 detectives and 102 patrolmen. The budget of $149,886 included salaries for patrolmen of $85 per month. The Gamewell Telephone System was enhanced and expanded to 40 units.

A sub-station was opened at Webster and Wellington (Danny Thomas). Thirty-two men worked at the sub-station, a captain, two desk sergeants, four detectives, two patrol drivers, two turnkeys, a hostler and 20 patrolmen. Ten patrolmen worked days and ten worked nights.

A call came into the sub-station at Wellington and Webster on March 19, 1910, at 11:30 p.m. that a hold-up man who had been terrorizing the southern part of the city was spotted near the substation. Patrol Driver John H. "Johnnie" Ryan, Station Keeper Jimmie Davis and Turnkey David Schmitt ran from the station to catch the bandit. Ryan and Davis took Calhoun and Schmitt went down Elliott.

At Calhoun and South Fourth, Ryan and Davis spotted the bandit, who fled. After a short run the felon turned and began firing at the two lawmen. The officers shot back. Patrol Driver Ryan emptied his service weapon before he took a bullet to the chest. He staggered and fell exclaiming, "Jimmie, I'm shot."

Station Keeper Davis continued firing until he saw the gunman fall. Officer Davis then rushed to his wounded colleague. The patrol wagon that was normally driven by Ryan, sped him to the hospital but he died in route. The 30-year-old patrol driver had served with the department just over two years.

William C. Davis returned to the department as chief of police in 1908. Davis had last served as head of the department more than twelve years earlier. He was chief during an important period of change in city governance that had a significant impact on the police department.

The city changed to a commission style government on January 1, 1910. Civil Service was introduced for the first time in June 1910 and policemen were selected based on civil service certificates, without regard to political affiliations. The police force was expanded to 185 officers, composed of 143 patrolmen and 42 supervisors. The appearance and bearing of policemen were enhanced with the purchase of new metropolitan style uniforms and helmets. Patrolmen drilled under the direction of Major Deffry.

The department went through a major reorganization and took on a fresh look in 1912. Mayor Edward Hull Crump, formerly the police commissioner, named Chief of Police William J. Hayes to head the force in January 1912. Hayes served as chief through January 1916. Captain Joe Burney commanded the night relief and Captain John Couch commanded the day relief. The rank of Inspector was created to strengthen the command structure and Joe Burney was promoted. The new rank resulted in an expansion of the collar insignia for commanders. Captains continued to wear a one star designation, the chief began to

The Barksdale Station was constructed on Barksdale near Union in 1911, and served as headquarters for the mounted patrol. The station was used extensively for a number of functions through the following years.

An officer in the mounted patrol created at the Barksdale Station in 1911. In 1912 the uniforms of the mounted officers were changed to be the standard patrol style uniform, except for riding boots.

Chief of Police William J. Hayes served the department from January 1912 to January 1916. He implemented many of the changes which took place under the new commission form of government headed by Mayor Ed Crump.

wear three stars and the inspector wore two stars.

In addition to new uniforms, new badges were adopted in 1912. The breast badge continued to be a six-point star, but in the form of the large "pie-plate" star made famous in Chicago and purchased from Chicago makers. The Tennessee state seal was applied to the center of the star, a banner panel with "Memphis Police" was applied above the seal and brass numbers were applied below.

For helmet or hat insignia the department adopted a distinctive badge featuring the state seal on a shield surrounded by a wreath with numbers applied in an

Fifteen mounted patrolmen and two supervisors were assigned to the new mounted patrol in 1911. The unit was headquartered at the newly built Barksdale Mounted Police Station. In this photograph they were in formation in downtown Memphis.

Uniform styles and insignia adopted by the Memphis Police Department in 1912 when the commission form of government was implemented. The officers are, from left to right, Chief of Police, the new rank of Inspector, Captain, Sergeant, Traffic Officer, and Patrolman.

open panel at the bottom. The hat badge was later used by other Tennessee departments and the style continues to be used by Memphis into the new millennium. Sergeants and other supervisors wore a six-point, ball-tip star also similar to Chicago.

New insignia included the departments first uniform patch. Early arm patches were used to identify special units of the force. Traffic officers were the first to wear an arm patch. The patch was in the form of a wheel and sewn on the left arm of the uniform half way between the shoulder and the elbow.

Two new stations were constructed. In 1911 the Barksdale Mounted Police Station on Barksdale south of Union was opened with 15 mounted patrolmen assigned. Central Station at 128 Adams and Second opened in 1912. Amenities included a telephone system, a Gamewell Police Telegraph System and a Bertillon System in the Bureau of Identification.

The mounted police force was under the command of Sergeant Walter Lee and was drilled daily by the riding master Patrolman H. Morrison, a former member of the U.S. cavalry. Morrison was promoted to sergeant in 1912. The mounted force patrolled the more exclusive residential areas and eliminated a rash of suburban holdups.

Improvements in transportation technology brought changes to the department. Upon his appointment in 1908 Chief Davis implemented a bicycle squad for added mobility. In its first use of motorcycle officers the department hired Hubert Richmond in 1909 and Daniel W. Ward in 1910 to use their personal motorcycles for traffic enforcement. In 1911 the department purchased its first two motorcy-

Patrol officers in 1912 wearing new winter uniforms, helmets and insignia. The patrol was the only group of officers to wear the helmet.

The Detective Department in 1912. William Smiddy is pictured at the far left of the second row. He was later shot and killed by another former Memphis detective, who was a deputy U. S. marshal at the time.

cles. As the motorcycle division developed it was stationed at Barksdale.

The first two motorized patrol wagons were acquired in 1912, one was electric and the other gasoline. By 1920 the horse-drawn buggies that supervisors used to oversee foot patrols were replaced and sergeants were assigned Model-T Ford automobiles.

During Chief Hayes' tenure, the department lost three officers in the line of duty. Patrolman John M. Taylor was shot and killed about 4:00 a.m. on June 22, 1912, as officers were arresting a gang of street railway bandits. Two of the highwaymen surrendered to the party of officers. Sergeant McAuliffe with Patrolmen Walter Holt and John Taylor went across the street to 124 Illinois Avenue accompanied by Special Agent Charles Berry of the Memphis Street Railway Company.

McAuliffe and Holt went to the front door of the house and Taylor went to the back. Another of the felons surrendered at the front of the house. As Taylor reached the rear of the residence the fourth felon pushed the muzzle of a revolver through a broken window and fired. A .38 caliber bullet pierced Patrolman Taylor's heart. The officer returned fire, striking the wall with two rounds.

McAuliffe, Holt and Berry ran to the sound of the shots and saw Taylor fall. They fired at the escaping gunman. Patrolman Holt rushed to his fallen colleague. Taylor murmured, "They got me, Walter," and died in Holt's arms. Patrolman John M. Taylor was 42 years old and joined the MPD in August 1907.

Thirty-six-year-old Patrolman Andrew Jackson lost his life accidentally on morning of January 15,

The Memphis Police Department presented a new image in 1915. The department posed on the steps of the courthouse to show off new summer uniforms. Each officer wore a large flower on his right breast to greet the public.

1914. Jackson headed home after the night shift ended at 5:00 a.m. Thirty minutes later he reached the corner of Third Street and Chelsea Avenue near his home. He saw the rope that suspended a street light at the intersection was burning because of a sparking short circuit. The light was about to fall to the street.

Jackson called police headquarters and the Memphis Consolidated Gas and Electric Company from the corner grocery and told them to turn the power off. When he returned the light was in the street and other streets lights in the area were off. Officer Jackson picked up the fixture to move it out of the way of traffic. Suddenly the power came back on and electricity surged through the officer's body, killing the 36-year-old policeman instantly.

A 45-year-old supervisor was killed on the evening of August 30, 1915. Sergeant Julius S. Brett was making his rounds in one of the department's buggies when he came upon a burglar. The two exchanged

shots. Sergeant Brett was shot in the back and the bullet pierced his heart. His body was found about 2:20 a.m. in his buggy on Dunlap Street just south of Jackson Avenue.

Oliver H. Perry Sr. was appointed chief of police in January 1916 and served in the position until July 1917 when he resigned to run for sheriff of Shelby County. Oliver Hazard Perry was born in October 1861 and joined the Memphis police force in November 1887. Chief Perry had a number of dangerous encounters during his police career. He barely escaped death at the hands of Joe Knight and was injured by the gunman that killed Patrolman Jameson.

Another time Perry faced death out on the Mississippi from a shotgun blast. Perry and another officer chased river thieves onto the water in a skiff. As they approached the gang's boat one of the river pirates raised a double barrel shotgun loaded with buck shot and fired both barrels. Pellets buzz around Perry, but

Supervisors lined up in horse-drawn buggies used to oversee foot patrols in 1915. The vehicles at the end of the line are the first two motorized patrol wagons that were acquired in 1910, one was electric and the other gasoline.

none found their mark. Perry drew his weapon and captured the river bandits.

During Oliver Perry's term as chief one of Memphis' most notorious bad men was shot and killed by Patrolman J. C. "Sandy" Lyons. The incident happened shortly before midnight on August 22, 1916.

William "Wild Bill" Latura was known to have killed seven men in a seemingly unprovoked bar room shooting in 1908. The incident became known as the "Beale Street Massacre." He was also credited with a number of other killings. Latura had been arrested 35 times for liquor violations and was at the time of his shooting out of jail while he appealed a gambling conviction that carried a three-year sentence.

Sandy Lyons and Charlie Davis were walking patrol in the 23rd ward, which included Poplar and Dunlap where Latura's gambling house was located. The two officers had recently been fined 10 days pay by Chief Perry for allowing Latura to flagrantly run his illegal operation. Sandy Lyons told what happened that night.

We were out at Latura's place the first part of the night about 9 o'clock to 9:30. We had been told to keep people away from around there because he ran a blind tiger and gambling house. We saw Ben Morris come out the back door. We said, "Ben, you have been told to stay away from here.

Memphis motorcycle officers in 1915 at Adams and Third.

This group photograph of the Memphis police force in 1916 was labeled "Metropolitan Police Department, City of Memphis, Annual Inspection by Mayor Ashcroft & Commissioners, Nov. 24, 1916" and was taken by photographer C. H. Poland.

Why don't you do it." He said, "Bill told me to stay here and I am sleeping here." That was at 9:30.

We went down to Dunlap and Madison and telephoned to Headquarters and went over the rest of our beat, the 23rd Ward. We went back to Bill's place at 11:15. Bill was standing at the side door on Dunlap Street and his car was near him at the curb. We had come down Poplar Avenue; and as we turned the corner we saw him, and he walked toward us and we toward him.

Bill commenced talking at once and seemed to get mad the more he talked. He said, "You are running my help away from here. You are damned hard men and I don't like it." I said, "Bill, don't curse me that way." He had used some hard names to me. He said, "Aw, I'll kill you, you . . ." I said, "Bill, you are under arrest." He said, "Aw, you can't arrest me. I'll kill you sure enough." Then he started to draw and I beat him to it.

In falling to the ground a small automatic pistol dropped out of his pocket. After I fired the first shot, Latura made an effort to reach his automobile, where we had been informed he kept a Winchester rifle and a pistol.

Latura fell to the sidewalk about 11:50 that night gasping for air. Four rounds from Lyons' revolver had found their mark. Lyons and Davis left the scene fearing retaliation from associates of Latura. They reported the incident to headquarters and acting Captain Mike Kehoe sent the emergency car with Sergeant Pass in charge. Latura was placed in the car, but died as they reached City Hospital a few blocks away.

Grover E. McCarver, who joined the MPD two decades later, related some particulars of a patrolman's life in the teens to MPD historian Joe Walk. Night patrol was often cold duty for officers walking the wards and they often depended on the kindness of individuals on their beat.

About 1916 or 17 we lived at Orphanage and Pearle in North Memphis. My Daddy ran a saloon downtown and knew many policemen. In the winter time he would have mother leave the side door to the dining room unlocked at night and put a bottle of whiskey, two glasses, and a pitcher of water on the table. Late at night when businesses were closed and residents were sleeping, the walking wards had no place to get out of the weather, and about the only telephones available were a few outdoor "call boxes." Dad's hospitality was accepted but our sleep was never disturbed.

Joseph B. "Joe" Burney was appointed chief of police in January 1918 after James P. Quinlan and General Sam T. Carnes briefly served the force as chief during 1917. Chief Burney served as head of the department through 1927.

Chief Burney was born in Oxford, Mississippi, in 1866. He joined the Memphis Police Department on February 4, 1898. Patrolman Burney and his partner Patrolman Bill Hendrick walked their beat in the Third Ward, a troublesome district. Burney became a detective in 1905 and began his climb through the ranks. He held the rank of inspector and served as chief of detectives before being named chief of police by Mayor Harry H. Litty.

The teens and twenties were dangerous times for Memphis police officers, 17 of whom died in the line of duty during the two decades. In 23 months during 1921 and 1922 eight officer died beginning with the shooting of Patrolman Edward L. Broadfoot on February 23, 1918. Broadfoot and his partner L. D. Dowdy entered the Preferencia Cafe at 546 South Main Street and noticed three men sitting at a table with a black suitcase. They had reports that bootleggers were working the area. As the policemen headed toward the table one of the men started for the door. Dowdy moved to check the man.

Broadfoot continued toward the table. One of the two at the table stood, drew a automatic pistol from his belt and began to fire. The first shot hit Broadfoot above the right eye, the second entered his chest. The patrolman fell dead with his pistol still in its holster. Dowdy drew his sidearm but was shot three times before he could fire. Dowdy survived the shooting.

Patrolmen A. L. White and P. C. Hoffman went to investigate a stolen bicycle on April 13, 1919. The trail led the two to a shanty at the rear of a grocery near Deadrick and Lamar. Hoffman watched the front door as White entered the back. The room was dimly lit by an oil lamp and Officer White did not see the suspect reach for an automatic pistol in his belt. A single shot struck Patrolman A. L. White over the left eye, killing him instantly.

Two months later, June 13, 1919, Sergeant John C. Brinkley was shot and killed in a gun battle with a chicken thief. The sequence of events that led to the killing began when Patrolmen Dan McCarthy and Edward Crume traveled from the Barksdale Station to the Overton Park Market to check on a man believed to be selling stolen chickens. At the market they questioned the man and decided to take him in. The thief reached his wagon, got a pistol and wounded the two officers before getting away on McLean.

The shooter was stopped at Waldran and Jackson by a police car occupied by Chief of Police Joe Burney, Assistant Chief Edward Pass, Chief of Detectives Hulet Smith and Sergeant John C. Brinkley. A running gun battle followed. Detective Chief Smith was wounded in the hand and Sergeant Brinkley was mortally wounded in the face and chest. Brinkley's killer was captured by Chief Burney and Detective John Long.

It was about 3:15 a.m. on January 7, 1920, when Patrolmen Guy Saint said good night to his partner Thomas H. Smith. Smith had an early court appearance and was headed home for a few hours sleep. Officer Saint went to the corner of Vance and Lauderdale to call headquarters. He heard someone chopping at the side door of Sheely's Drug Store with an axe. Patrolman Saint pulled his service revolver and

Traffic Officer Vincent Lucarini, around 1916, was wearing the uniform and the arm patch of the Traffic Department.

stopped the burglar. Suddenly a shot was fired from behind Saint. The bullet struck Saint's shoulder blade and was deflected into his spine, paralyzing him from the chest down and making it impossible for him to fire his weapon.

A passing taxi stopped and the driver took Saint to Gaston Hospital. Saint was able to describe the burglar at the door but only saw his shooter as he ran down the alley. Patrolman Guy Saint died that evening at 6:25. The information he provided led to the arrest of his killer.

Memphis had a brief experience with the integration of the police department in 1919. Mayor Frank Monteverde had the support of the black community during his election campaign and promised he would appoint six black men to the police force. Upon taking office he kept his promise by first appointing three black detectives, Matthew Thornton Sr., F. M. Mercer and "Sweetie" Williams.

The three officers were doing well until a shooting incident. Thornton and Williams were tipped off that a wanted criminal was hiding in a black gambling joint on North Front Street. A white underworld boss ran the establishment and was enraged that the black officers searched his place. The next night the two detectives were attacked by a gang of white men and beaten with clubs and brickbats at the corner of Main and Market streets. Williams shot one of the men in the arm and the two officers managed to escape the mob.

The following morning, the three detectives were fired, ending their seven month tenure. Matthew Thornton Sr. later commented on his brief career with the department.

> I worked in fine cooperation with the white officers, who were my friends. I arrested a lot of Negroes for various offenses, and I never lost a case in court. I only had to use my gun once. That was when a Negro prisoner broke and ran when I was phoning for the patrol wagon. I fired into the air, but he got away. Only one time did I arrest a white man, and that was when I came upon a white man and a Negro who were fighting on South Fourth Street. Of course, I had to arrest both of them. The white man's case was not carried into court.

While patrolmen continued to wear the big stars the badge styles of supervisory ranks changed a number of times during the next two decades. Ranks above sergeant wore various styles of shields, plated with gold in the rolled-gold technique. These badges had a gold plated Tennessee state seal riveted to the center of the badge with the rank and "Memphis Police" in raised letters. Lieutenants and others wore a shield and captains a pinched shield.

A unique badge was created in 1922 for the rank of sergeant. The badge was a circle with three protrusions to give it the general shape of a shield. The shape resembled an acorn and was referred to as such. The acorn style badge changed through the years but remained unique to Memphis.

Age caught up with one famous outlaw in 1920 who had evaded capture by federal, state and local lawmen. His long career included the robbery of eight stagecoaches, 22 banks and 36 trains. Captain Kit Dalton, the last member of the Jesse and Frank James gang, died in Memphis on April 3. During the Civil War Dalton was a member of Quantrell's raiders, the Confederate guerrilla band, and following the war was a member of the Bass gang in Texas.

When amnesty was granted wartime raiders

The Memphis Traffic Department in 1917. They were wearing long winter coats which fully cover their sidearms. The badge and hat badge were of the style adopted earlier in the decade. The sergeant, at the far right, was wearing a smaller ball-tip star as a breast badge. His hat badge was a bullion wreath containing his rank, "Traffic Sergeant." Below his stripes was the wheel patch worn by traffic men.

Traffic Officer Vincent Lucarini worked a corner in downtown Memphis in the teens. The "cornermen" were essential to the flow of traffic since there were no traffic lights. The traffic signal was mounted atop a staff where Lucarini stood. "Stop" and "Go" instructions were painted on panels to signal drivers.

Dalton settled in Memphis and became a gambler. Later in life he became an evangelist and wrote the story of his life with the James gang. He walked the streets of Memphis wearing a Confederate uniform. Kit Dalton died at age 78, a footnote of a bygone era.

The Memphis Police Department in 1920 was struggling with technology of a new era, especially the automobile. The Traffic Department consisted of a single squad of men working during the day, mainly "corner men" and a few motorcycle officers. The corner man was essential to traffic flow on the increasingly congested streets of Memphis. These traffic officers were assigned to a specific corner in the downtown district. They managed traffic by manually turning a sign atop a staff in the middle of the intersection that told drivers when to go and when to stop.

In June 1920 Police Commissioner John B. Edgar announced a complete reorganization of the Traffic Department. Late afternoon and evening traffic had increased to the point that traffic duty hours needed to be expanded. The new organization divided traffic officers into two squads and provide service from 8:00 a.m. to 10:00 p.m., one squad working an 8:00 a.m. to 3:00 p.m. shift and the other squad working from 3:00 p.m. to 10:00 p.m.

No additional officers were to be hired, the traffic unit was expanded by transferring a number of uniformed patrol officers into the unit. The command structure was also expanded. Sergeant Vincent "Luke" Lucarini was in charged of the existing traffic force and was promoted to Lieutenant. New sergeants were named to supervise the two squads. The city also painted pedestrian lanes at intersections to control jaywalking and posted signs specifying parking time limits.

The dangers of automobile traffic was becoming a factor of life and death on the streets not only for the citizens of Memphis, but for its police force as well. The first death in the line of duty as a result of a traffic accident occurred in 1920. Three such deaths occurred that year. Two motorcycle officers of the Traffic Department died as a result of motorcycle collisions, Patrolman Vic Zambroni on March 23, 1920, and Patrolman James J. McNeill on December 14, 1920.

Patrolman James S. Holmes was killed on September 21, 1920, while directing traffic at the corner of Main and Gayoso. The corner man was assisting a large truck to make a wide turn. He raised his hand to stop traffic for another motorist and the sleeve of his coat caught on the bed of the truck pulling him under the wheels of the truck and crushing him to death.

Tragedy struck the Traffic Department again on Wednesday morning, August 10, 1921. The pay-car of the Ford Motor Company was in route to the Ford plant office on Union Avenue. Paymaster Edgar McHenry had just picked up $8,500 in payroll from the Central State National Bank. He was escorted by Ford Special Officer and Chief Inspector Howard Gamble and Memphis Patrolmen Polk A. Caraway and W. S. Harris.

As the pay-car pulled up to the Ford office at 9:45 a.m. a blue Cadillac occupied by four armed men crowded the pay-car to the curb. Something was yelled from the Cadillac and almost immediately shots were fired. Paymaster McHenry bolted from the car and almost crawling made it inside the office with the money. The barrage of bullets came so quickly from the Cadillac that the three armed officers had no time to draw their weapons. Gamble and Patrolman Caraway were killed instantly. Patrolman Harris was seriously wounded with shots to the stomach and shoulder.

Traffic Lieutenant Vincent Lucarini and one of his men, Motorcycle Officer C. L. Bonds, were at headquarters when the call came in. They took a two-passenger Model-T Ford and began to comb the Wolf River bottom and surrounding roads. Lucarini saw his friend Joe Robillio driving his big blue Cadillac eight. Another traffic man, Motorcycle Officer Al Rodgers pulled in. Lucarini asked Robillio if they could use his car in the pursuit. Ed Heckinger, owner of an auto repair shop, arrived and asked to join the group. The five got into the Cadillac and headed east.

At about 11:30 a.m. they were speeding along Poplar Pike approaching Collierville. Deputy Sheriff Morris Irby and a posse of about 40 citizens arose from behind the shrubbery on the south side of the road where they had crouched. The group was awaiting a blue Cadillac filled with the killers who had tried to rob the Ford payroll and fired volley after volley of

shotguns and rifles, not knowing they were firing at three Memphis police officers and two citizens. Motorcycleman Bonds told reporters of the *Commercial Appeal* the story from his vantage point inside the car.

The shooting happened as we were approaching Collierville. I was sitting in the back seat and did not notice the road particularly. All of a sudden it seemed as though hell broke loose and somebody spit in my face. The lieutenant sank down in his seat. Joe Robillio fell back also. I told him to stop the car, for God's sake, because somebody was shooting at us. He said, "I can't stop her; I'm shot." I reached over his prostrate body and kept the car in the road, and just as I was trying to apply the emergency brakes, I got a bunch of buckshot in the face and arms. But I succeeded in stopping the car after it had run about 600 feet.

Lucarini was hit first, six buckshot crashing into the back of his head. He died of his wounds at 1:55 that afternoon. The 36-year-old policeman was a first generation American and had been with the Memphis Police Department eight years. He started with the department on the liquor squad and was next assigned to the emergency police car. Lucarini was then assigned to traffic and soon took command of the squad.

The incident left two Memphis police officers and a special officer of the Ford Motor Company dead.

Sergeant John C. Brinkley, left, was shot and killed on June 13, 1919, in a gun battle with a chicken thief. Patrolman Guy Saint, right, was mortally wounded while investigating a burglary in progress at Sheely's Drug Store.

Mounted Patrolmen A. L. White went to investigate a stolen bicycle on April 13, 1919. The suspect pulled an automatic pistol from his belt and fired a single shot that struck Patrolman White over the left eye, killing him instantly.

Five others, two of whom were policemen, were wounded, two seriously. Heavily armed police patrols covered the city in search of the gang whose attempted robbery had led to the killing of their fellow officers. A group of volunteers who assisted the police from time to time, known as Colonel Roane Waring's Vigilantes, rode with policemen and other lawmen.

Detectives led by Detective Lieutenant Earl R. Barnard were also at work and later the same night they took three of the bandits into custody. The three confessed and implicated the fourth member of the gang who was arrested three days later. In a search of his room officers found four pistols and 700 rounds of ammunition. All four were convicted of murder and attempted armed robbery.

As a result of the incident Chief Burney acquired an automobile famed in the department's history. The chief decided a high powered, well built chase car was needed. A four door Packard touring car was purchased in August 1921. The car could seat eight and sported white wall tires and a water temperature gauge atop the radiator. "The Packard," as the department grew to call the car, could climb a hill at 54 mph in second gear and in high gear was unchallenged at 75 mph.

The awesome reputation of "the riot car" grew as its exploits multiplied. To the unlawful element the car became known by such terms as "the black hawk" and "the night hawk" because it swooped down with talons to catch criminals. It was called "de cryin' car" because of the plaintiff wail of its two tone sirens. Bootleggers

called it "the running devil." The name "the wrecking car" was coined one night when officer responded to a honky-tonk and shot it out with "Two-Gun" Charlie Pierce, leaving the desperado dead.

The automobile was used as an emergency car. A team of two officers responded to emergency calls received at the station. When a call for help came in the emergency team took the emergency car and sped to the scene with siren sounding. Emergency men were quickly on the scene of the crime, be it murder, robbery, or riot. They gained the reputation of quick response and captured many felons in the act of their criminal enterprise or caught up with them soon thereafter.

Two more officers died in the line of duty before the year was finished, the first on September 1, 1921, as the result of a group of drunks ganging up on an officer. Sergeant J. L. Bell had given Captain Kehoe a ride home and was making a last check of his district before returning to the station to sign off the shift. He drove past the corner of McLemore and Rayburn and saw a drunk creating a disturbance in the Greek Cafe.

The sergeant went into the cafe and arrested the man. As Bell tried to take the drunk outside another man grabbed the sergeant's sidearm and fled. Bell was chasing the man when a second man grabbed him from behind and a third man cut his throat and stabbed him several times in the chest and shoulder. Sergeant Bell was taken to the hospital but died several hours later. Before dying he identified the man who stabbed him. The three men, the one who took his gun, the one who held him and the one who stabbed him were convicted of murder.

A patrol wagon in 1923 was dispatched from headquarters to the scene when arrests were made and transported prisoners to central station. Patrol wagon details worked in pairs on 12-hour shifts. Patrol drivers from left to right, including those in the car, were Ike Williams, C. W. Peek, J. D. Brownlee, and J. C. Lyons.

Chief of Police Joseph B. "Joe" Burney was appointed in January 1918 and served through 1927. He led the department with distinction through very dangerous years for Memphis policemen.

Another Memphis policeman died on November 3, 1921. Patrolman P. T. Fleet and his partner Sam Emberton were sent to arrest a man who had just shot and killed his female companion. The murderer fled the house and hid in a railroad yard at Kansas and Carolina. Patrolmen Bridges and Maroney joined the hunt. In the search Fleet rounded the corner of a boxcar and found himself face-to-face with the killer. Fleet was shot, the bullet entering his right armpit and exiting his left side. Patrolman Bridges rounded the other end of the boxcar at the moment Fleet was shot. Bridges emptied his revolver into the shooter, killing the murderer instantly. Patrolman Fleet died en route to the hospital.

A disturbance in the same establishment where Sergeant Bell died indirectly resulted in the death of Patrolman Jesse P. Wooten six months afterwards. It was Tuesday evening, February 20, 1922, when Wooten observed a disturbance in the Greek Cafe. He ran across the street and was struck by a trolley car. The car spun him into another trolley going in the opposite direction and he was crushed between the two and died a few hours later.

The spate of line of duty deaths continued eight-

een months later, August 4, 1923, when a shootout with a murderer ended the life of Patrolman Charles F. Stevens. Stevens heard a shot and went to investigate. He found a man with a gun who had just shot and killed his drinking buddy. The killer refused to hand over his gun and shot Stevens in the chest. Stevens returned fire hitting the gunman in the head and the chest. Both Patrolman Stevens and his killer died as a result of the shootout.

Motorcycle Officer T. B. Knox lost his life to a crazed gunman on April 5, 1925. The incident began when a man kidnapped his ex-wife and her boyfriend. Knox passed a car parked at the curb near Beale and Front. He heard a woman scream for help. Knowing nothing of the kidnapping, Knox approached the car. The gunman jumped from the back seat of the car and fired three shots, all of which struck the motorcycle officer. Knox, mortally wounded, drew his weapon and shot the gunman five times, killing him.

The early twenties was a dangerous period for department. Commissioner of Fire and Police Thomas H. Allen and Chief Burney had policy and executive command responsibilities. The MPD was divided into the Patrol Division and the Detective Division. The Patrol Division of around 150 men included a day and a night shift, each under the command of a captain, and the Traffic Department. The Detective Division consisted of the Bureau of Identification, the Automobile Bureau to investigate vehicle thefts, the Women's Protective Bureau, the Morality Squad under the command of a captain, the Homicide Squad, the Pawnshop Squad and the Bad Check Squad.

Chief of Detectives, Inspector William T. Griffin, left, took command of the Detective Division in 1920. Inspector Earl R. Barnard, right, took command of the Patrol Division on February 15, 1922.

Captain Michael C. Kehoe, left, and Captain Will D. Lee were in command of the day and night shifts of the Patrol Division in the early twenties. They wore the newly adopted badge style for the rank, an eagle-top circle surrounded by a wreath with a state seal in the center.

Inspector William T. "Will" Griffin began his tenure as chief of detectives in 1920. Griffin was born in Springfield, Tennessee, in 1879 and worked as a special agent and inspector with the Frisco railroad before being named inspector with the MPD. Griffin was instrumental in quelling the violence during a railroad strike in 1922 during which a strikebreaker was killed.

Under Griffin's leadership MPD detectives broke up the Klusman Gang of house burglars. Detective Sergeants Phelan Thompson and Frank Clark responded to a call in the Packard and caught two members of the gang in the act on October 4, 1922. In the confrontation the detectives opened fire with riot guns, killing one of the burglars and capturing the other.

Inspector Griffin led the investigation into the killing of Detective Sergeant Edward Clark on July 28, 1922. Clark's wife said the officer had committed suicide, but physical evidence including the two bullets found in his head indicated that he was shot while he slept. The investigation proved that the wife killed the detective for insurance money and planned to put the children in an orphanage and elope with a "red-headed man." She pleaded insanity and was sent to Western State Hospital in Boliver.

A complete records system for the department was designed and implemented by Inspector Griffin. The index card system recorded pertinent data on crimes, perpetrators, missing property and included photographs and fingerprints. It was the department's first comprehensive records system and one of the best in the nation.

Lieutenants Dave Jamison and Joseph Bishop assisted Inspector Griffin in command of the Detective Division. The rank of these positions was changed to Deputy Inspector in 1923 and filled by Joseph Bishop and Edward A. Parker. Captain Walter Hoyle was chief of the Automobile Bureau and assisted by Detective Sergeants J. W. Hawitt, J. W. Taylor, H. D. Taylor and W. L. Clark. Lieutenant Paul Waggener, a fingerprint expert, commanded the Bureau of Identification. The

The Motor Cycle and Auto Department in January 1920.

Traffic Lieutenant Vincent "Luke" Lucarini, head of the Traffic Department, was killed in the line of duty while pursuing a murderous gang in an attempted robbery of the Ford Motor Company payroll.

Homicide Squad consisted of Detective Sergeants William F. Glisson, W. C. Lemmer and L. P. Fox.

Captain A. Lee Boyles headed the Morality Squad. He was assisted by Patrolmen B. P. Chatham and Bond Harmon in the operation of the Narcotics Squad. The Women's Protective Bureau was established in 1921 and Mrs. Anna Whitmore was its chief. The role of the department's matron was filled by Mrs. Matilda Wallace and Mrs. Olive Marshall during the period.

Inspector Earl R. Barnard took command of the Patrol Division on February 15, 1922. Barnard was well organized and a strict disciplinarian. He introduced a records keeping system that tracked arrests made by members of the division and used the information in making promotions. A training program was developed to teach officers criminal law, to inform them of methods for apprehending criminals and to instruct court conduct for witnesses. He also established a crime map and assigned special details to areas based on the density of criminal activity. Inspector Barnard required officers to keep their uniforms neat with buttons and badges polished and their shoes shined.

The inspector was a native Memphian, born in 1887, who began his law enforcement career at the age

of 21 as a Shelby County deputy sheriff. Later he worked for the railroad police and became a division chief special agent. Barnard joined the MPD on March 21, 1921, as a lieutenant of detectives and was soon placed in command of the Homicide Squad. He was instrumental in solving a number of murders and in making the case against the Ford payroll bandits.

The day and night shifts of the Patrol Division were under the command of Captains Michael C. Kehoe and Will D. Lee. Captain Mike Kehoe was born in Ireland in 1868 and came to the United States when he was 18. He began his law enforcement career in 1888 as night watchman at the county jail. He was appointed to the police force in 1890, made sergeant in 1905 and captain in 1916.

Captain Kehoe was respected for this prowess as a policeman. On one occasion early in his career a professional heavy weight boxer bragged that no policeman would take him before the desk sergeant. Kehoe caught up with the heavy weight in "Whiskey Chute Alley" near Madison and Main. The two fought bare knuckled for an hour and a half until Kehoe dragged the battered prizefighter before the desk sergeant.

Captain Will Lee joined the force on January 12, 1910, and was promoted to sergeant two years later. He became one of the first commanders of the Barksdale Station and in 1920 made captain. Lee was one of the department's best marksman. He was once credited with saving Chief Burney's life when he fired at a criminal who had the chief in his pistol sights, hitting the felon in the pit of the arm holding the weapon.

Lieutenants W. R. Ham and Ernest A. Oliver were each assigned to a patrol shifts. The three pairs of emergency men were Julio Vannuccio and Fred

The 1921 Packard purchased by the Memphis Police Department to use as a chase car following the tragic events of the attempted robbery which left three dead. The Emergency Car was called "the riot car" by officers on the force, but was given the name "the black hawk" and other appellations by the lawless element in the city. The group was in front of Fire Engine House No. 1.

The Emergency Car was dispatched from central headquarters when reports of a burglary, hold-up, riot, or other disturbance call was received. The detail worked in pairs on eight-hour shifts. The car was equipped with a siren and "repeating shotguns." Emergency car officers from left to right, including those in the car, were W. G. Jamison, E. H. Crume, F. L. Henderson, J. J. Vannuccio, W. M. Crogan, and S. T. Emberton. Emergency men often caught burglars or highwaymen still on or near the scene of the crime.

Henderson, Sam Emberton and W. I. Poole, and Eddie Crume and W. S. Record. Lieutenant T. Joseph "Joe" Cole was court officer and responsible for transportation of prisoners between their cell and the court.

Lieutenant W. J. Herrington commanded the Traffic Department. He was assisted by Sergeant Buell Yates and Motorcycle Sergeant Hal V. Allen. Approximately fifty officers were assigned to traffic duty including ten motorcycle officers and three mounted officers. Traffic officers began wearing white caps in 1923 to make them more visible while working on the busy streets of the city.

The police department created a visible presence in a number of residential neighborhoods in the mid-1920s. Grover McCarver recalled the small enclosures used by patrolmen in outlying wards. There were four or so of these outposts that provided shelter and a call box.

I remember at North Parkway and McLean, Snowden School was there and right across the Parkway where Overton Park is, there was a "Lighthouse" for police officers. This was about 1925, before radios, and there were a telephone and work counter inside. In those days policemen were held in high esteem and we kids would go

there to talk with them. We kids called it a "Lighthouse" because there was a bright spotlight on top of the small room-sized building. Officers told me they turned the light on at night if they went out on a call, to notify their partner or others in the area.

McCarver also knew John Levy. His wife was a first cousin to McCarver's mother. Levy had become a wealthy man starting with only a small tamale stand on Beale Street. He then owned a tamale stand and hamburger restaurant at Madison and Dunlap across from the Number 7 Fire Station. Levy became known as the "Hot Tamale King."

Shortly before 11 o'clock on the evening of November 21, 1927, Levy was murdered. The pursuit of his killer became known as "The Case of the Gray Fedora" and was the most notorious murder case of the twenties. Levy was a noted sportsman and gambler, known to carry large sums of money. As he drove into the garage behind his home at 70 North Evergreen a lookout in front of the house and two armed bandits inside the garage lay in wait for him.

When he stepped out of the car the two demanded his money. Levy threw the roll of bills into a dark corner of the garage enraging the bandits. One of them fired a single round from a .25 caliber pistol. The outdoor light came on and the two fled down the alley. Levy died from the gunshot. The only clue was a gray hat left behind by one of the robbers.

Patrolman Morris Solomon, who became the first Jewish detective in the Memphis Police Department, was a friend of Levy and requested that Detective Inspector Will Griffin assign him to the case. A few weeks later he was detailed to help solve his friend's murder.

Patrolman Solomon was born in Poland and brought to Memphis in 1900 at the age of six. He joined the department as a patrolman in 1919 and a few years later was assigned to the Mounted Patrol working the downtown district. Solomon took the gray hat found at the Levy murder scene and carried it with him almost all the time, often going door-to-door asking if anyone recognized the fedora. This continued even after he was pulled off the case as a full-time assignment.

While investigating a robbery at a lunch stand the proprietor identified the hat as belonging to Charcoal Johnny. As it turned out Johnny had an ironclad alibi for the night in question, but because of the considerate treatment he received from Solomon Charcoal Johnny promised to help the officer. Sometime later he informed Solomon that he learned from Missouri Mike, a cell-mate in the city lockup, that the hat belonged to a man named Bill who lived at Ft. Pickering.

Solomon took the gray fedora and continued his quest. He found the owner of a rooming house who recognized it as belonging to a former boarder, Freeman Thronbo Gunion. She also told Solomon that one of her current boarders was a friend of Gunion's female companion. The boarder said she was told that

Gunion had thrown a pistol wrapped in newspaper off a bridge the night of the murder.

The trail led to Fayette County, Kansas City and St. Louis. Gunion's companion said Gunion had told her that he killed Levy when he threw the gun away. She said he was currently in jail in Danville, Illinois, on a counterfeiting charge.

Gunion was returned to Memphis and after hearing statements against him admitted to the murder. He named Edwin Grace as the lookout and master-mind of the crime and George Prince as the second bandit. All three were convicted and given the death penalty in October 1928. Their sentences were later commuted to life.

Thanks to Solomon's tireless investigation, the case was solved and the guilty convicted less than a year after the crime. Solomon was promoted to detective sergeant as a result of his efforts and established an outstanding record prior to his retirement in 1942 following a heart attack.

Solomon was considered hard headed by some but Inspector Bill Raney later said, "He was a darn good officer. He was one of those fellows that never gave up. If he got an idea or clue, nothing would stop him from working even though it might look like he was butting against a brick wall." Morris Solomon died on Valentines Day, 1963.

Will D. Lee was appointed chief of police on January 3, 1928, and served the next 12 years. Lee took over leadership of the department as it was working to restore confidence after the "Bellomini payoff book" affair.

John Bellomini ran a sandwich and cigar store at 350 East Butler. The place was also a well-known bootleg joint. Federal prohibition agents raided Bellomini's place on March 20, 1927. During the

The Memphis Metropolitan Police Department on March 15, 1922, under the command of Chief of Police Joseph B. "Joe" Burney, Inspector Earl R. Barnard, and Police Commissioner Thomas H. Allen.

The Memphis Police Department Bureau of Identification around 1930.

search they found a ledger with names and dollar amounts under the heading "Legge," Italian for "Law." The names were those of 51 policemen, 4 deputy sheriffs and several constables. Amounts ranged from $5 to $20 and totaled around $84,000. The ledger was assumed to be a book of payoffs to local law officers.

Thirty-eight officers from patrolman to deputy inspector were suspended during an investigation on charges of "inefficiency, incompetency and conduct unbecoming an officer." Police Commissioner Thomas H. Allen convened a Trial Board and heard testimony from numerous witnesses. After four days of hearings the board determined the charges had not been proven. No criminal charges were brought.

The department under Chief Lee's command in 1928 had a patrol force of 80 officers. The patrol division was divided into two shifts or reliefs. Each relief worked 12 hours, days one month and nights the next, and was under the command of a veteran captain.

Captain Hulet Smith had been with the MPD on and off since 1903 and rejoined the department on January 1, 1928, as patrol captain. In the intervening years he served as a Deputy U.S. Marshal, as the Memphis PD chief of detectives and as assistant chief of special agents of the Union Railroad. Smith's relief consisted of 36 patrolmen under the supervision of Field Sergeants D. D. Stallings, W. E. Adams and

Martin Cleary.

Captain Phelan Thompson won the post of relief captain by competitive examination in June 1925. He replaced Michael C. Kehoe who was promoted to deputy inspector and who was a full inspector by 1928. Thompson joined the MPD in 1920. Thompson's relief consisted of 36 patrolmen under the supervision of Field Sergeants Joseph G. Kennedy, John Cannon and H. D. Turner.

The Barksdale Station was under the command of Lieutenants T. B. Wilson and W. R. Ham in 1928. The

Memphis police Adams Street headquarters in the twenties.

two had supervised Barksdale personnel since 1915. Nineteen ward patrolmen were assigned to the station in two reliefs.

The most hazardous job in the department was that of an emergency man. A team of two officers responded to emergency calls and were the first on the scene of a crime, be it murder, robbery, or riot. He was also the first to fires, wrecks, or other non-criminal emergencies. Emergency men were called "Five-year Men" because tradition was that the average life of emergency men was five years.

Sergeant Julio Vannuccio was commander of the emergency squads in 1928. Three teams of emergency men worked out of Central Station in eight hour shifts, Sergeant Vannucci and Patrolmen W. W. Herrington, W. A. Stocks and J. W. Pryde, and Patrolmen Louis Rochelle and Ernest Oliver. The remaining two emergency squads were located at the Barksdale Station, Sergeant R. D. Almond and his partner Patrolman Ben R. Hall, and Patrolmen L. E. Brister and Eddie Crume.

Twenty traffic policemen were under the command of Sergeant W. J. Herrington. Traffic violators became familiar with Room 16, the headquarters location for paying fines. Sergeant Hal Allen headed the 15-man motorcycle squad. The department also had a 10-man dog-watch patrol.

Memphis policemen assisted businesses with security for payroll transfers and during special events such as this ham sale at Seessel's.

Detective Inspector Will T. Griffin remained in command of the 1928 Detective Division. Assisting in the management of the division were Detective Lieutenant Granville Heckle, expert on safe robberies, and Detective Lieutenant Lee Quaianthy Sr., specialist in stick-ups and gangsters. Detective sergeants in the division were Morris Solomon, Mario Chiozza, John Long, Dave L. Jamison, William Raney, John Foppiano, Wilburn Smith, Melbourne A. Hinds, W. J.

The Motorcycle Squad of the Traffic Division in 1925. At the point of the eleven-member unit was Motorcycle Sergeant Hal V. Allen, commander of the squad. This photograph was used in a Harley Davidson motorcycle advertisement.

Memphis Police Department emergency men in 1927. The sergeant at the far right supervised the squad. He wore the acorn style badge created in the early twenties as insignia for sergeants.

Hendricks, Sam Philllips, J. Walter Holye, Louis A. Crosby, Thomas H. Smith and Lawrence Fox. Detectives included Lee Quianthy Jr., Ed Nuismer and A. I. Conrad.

Two major bureaus within the division were the Auto Detective Bureau headed by Deputy Inspector Joel Bishop and the Bureau of Identification under Deputy Inspector Edward A. Parker. Detective Lieutenant Clegg Richards was second in command of the Auto Detective Bureau. Detective sergeants in the auto bureau were Joe Hewitt and Jimmy Taylor and detectives were W. W. Billings, William Hagan, E. E. Wattam and E. M. Crumby.

Sometimes force was needed to apprehend criminals. Chief Will Lee was not an excitable man, but when a flurry of criminal activity hit Memphis early in 1929 Chief Lee pressed his men to extreme measures. On January 31, 1929 the chief instructed the force to "shoot to kill" and offered a promotion to the first man to bag a bandit. The department also began a roundup of vagrants and suspicious characters. Those arrested were held without bond until they could be questioned.

A number of high profile crimes preceded the chief's declaration. A highwayman had shot and killed a Memphis fireman the week before. The previous night a bandit attacked the niece of the sheriff and robbed the college coed of her jewelry before her screams scared him away.

Chief Lee was especially frustrated with two of his officers who were robbed along with others in a drug store. The chief suspended the two patrolmen for not performing their duty. An article in the *Nashville Tennessean* explained how the patrolmen got into the predicament.

Patrolmen J. B. Cummings and John F. Edgerly, suspended last night because they stood with

Lieutenants T. B. Wilson, left, and W. R. Ham commanded the Barksdale Station from 1915 to 1928. Nineteen ward patrolmen were assigned to the station in two reliefs in the later twenties.

call box or business telephone and contact the station once every hour. A crime could occur near the officers location and he might not know about it for up to an hour later. Both Central Station and the Barksdale Station had an emergency car that could be dispatched in case of a serious crime.

The lack of a more immediate mode of communication was another factor that placed a patrolman at risk. The force lost two policemen in 1929. Patrolman W. R. Bridges, who had shot the killer of Officer Fleet in 1921, was himself shot down on April 20, 1929, by a drunk at the corner of Third and Beale. Patrolman J. T. Mathis pulled his revolver and fired six bullets into the gunman, killing his partner's murderer.

Patrolman Walter H. McEwen was killed on December 30, 1929, when he chased down an armed suspect. The man wrestled McEwen's gun away and shot the officer below the right eye.

Chief Will D. Lee attended the International Association of Chiefs of Police convention in Atlanta in 1929. Detroit Police Commissioner Rutledge made a presentation on placing radios in police cars, the first such program in the country. Chief Lee told Memphis Commissioner Clifford Davis about the radio dispatch concept and Commissioner Davis visited Detroit the following year to view the system first hand.

The nationwide economic depression made it difficult to come up with the $12,500 needed to implement the system. Budget cuts from within the department were required to fund the equipment purchase and experts from local commercial broadcasters were used to implement the technology. The transmitter was located at the

Prisoner processing in the Identification Bureau included fingerprinting, photographing, and taking vital statistics such as weight and height.

upraised hands while two robbers held up a drug store, were reinstated today by Cliff Davis, commissioner of police. Davis was told by others in the store at the time that the policemen had no alternative. The officers had gone there to make their hourly telephone report to headquarters when the robbers took them by surprise.

Cummings and Edgerly said they were unable to draw their pistols because of the long frock tail coats of the regulation police uniform. "If we could have grabbed our guns, there would have been a different story to tell," they said.

The regulation uniform coat was designed to keep the officer warm, but the policeman's sidearm was buttoned tight inside of the coat. If the patrolman found himself facing a gun that was already drawn he was at a serious disadvantage. This circumstance resulted in the death of police officers in a number of cities.

The incident also demonstrated the inefficiency of communicating with headquarters or the Barksdale Station by means of the Gamewell System. Regardless of their mode of transportation, officers had to find a

Memphis police developed a forensics section in the thirties.

Motorcycle Sergeant Hal V. Allen, front and center, with the Motorcycle Squad of the Traffic Division around 1930 in from to the Adams Street Station.

Barksdale Station and the first aerial consisted of a wire strung out of a window to the top of a nearby tree. Receivers were placed in 12 ward cars. Communication was one-way from dispatcher to patrol officer. Captain M. A. Hinds was in charge of the radio room.

The radio car came to Memphis at noon on July 29, 1931, when WPEC went on the air. The call letters proclaimed "We Protect Every Citizen." Some officers joked that it meant "We Protect Ed Crump," referring to the powerful political boss. Crump had, in fact, served as Commissioner of Fire and Police early in his career.

The first broadcast over the system was in response to boys throwing rocks at a home on Mosby Street. Squad Car 18 was on the scene in two minutes. By the second anniversary of the radio dispatch system in Memphis 126,000 calls had been issued by WPEC. Commissioner Davis said, "The people of Memphis definitely know the value of radio by this time. With the reduced manpower and less money to spend, due to the depression, and the additional territory we have taken in, the Department would have been overwhelmed without the radio."

Patrolman Walter H. McEwen, left, was shot below the right eye and killed on December 30, 1929, after he chased down an armed suspect. Patrolman C. J. Redder, right, was run over and instantly killed by a fire truck at Second and Union on October 22, 1931.

MPD patrol cars in the early thirties were stock vehicles without radios or other special equipment.

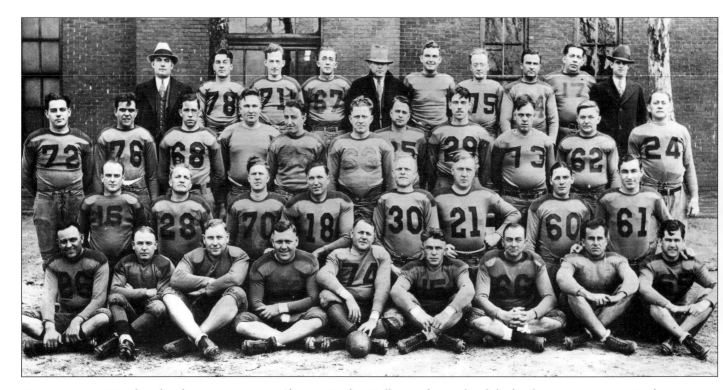

On January 1, 1932, the police department, wearing Christian Brothers College uniforms, played the fire department, wearing Southwestern uniforms, in a football game at the old CBC campus on Jefferson next to the present Juvenile Court. Playing on the police team left to right were seated in the front row, Toll Fowler, Pinkey Turner, Charles Todd, Everett Crawford, Bob Wilbanks, Pete Wiebenga, Roy Faught, D. H. Woolridge, and Lewis Muller. Kneeling on the second row left to right were Reagan, F. L. Gustavus, John Edgerly, W. T. Pilkington, J. D. Penick, Larry Fox, Eddie Thorn, and L. C. Williams. Standing in the third row left to right were John Getz, Jimmy Cox, Lee Quianthy, Ernest Johnson, Joe Feingold, Motley, Bill Raney, Wray, Harris, A. O. Clark, and Marquis. In the back row left to right were Clegg D. Richards, John Lucchesi, Hitchens, W. F. Clisson, Coach Edwin "Goat" Hale, Burt Hatch, Tom Hollahan, E. M. Crumby, H. D. Klyce, and Gordon Hollingsworth. (Photo courtesy of Judge John B. Getz, retired, son of player at the left end of row three)

The Great Depression had a dramatic impacts on the people of Memphis. The winter of 1931-32 was particularly hard on the jobless and needy citizens of Memphis. The Memphis Police Department and Memphis Fire Department met in friendly competition to raise money to assist their friends and neighbors in need. The two departments played a football game on January 1, 1932, called the Memphis Rose Bowl Classic, since it competed with the California event.

Spectators numbering 6,000 gathered at Hodges Field for the game, raising $6,100 for the jobless. The policemen scored first but the firemen won with a score of 7 to 6. Despite the police challenge to a game the following year the Classic was a one-time event.

A more serious confrontation occurred the following year with one of the depression era's most notorious gangsters. Dawn broke on the cool autumn morning of September 26, 1933, as local and federal lawmen moved into a residential neighborhood. Holed-up in a house at 1408 Rayner was one of Memphis' own, George Kelly Barnes Jr., a.k.a. "Machine Gun" Kelly. Kelly started his criminal life in Memphis playing

Memphis patrolmen in 1933 showed they were ready for criminals like Machine Gun Kelly.

hooky from school to bring a load of whiskey from Caruthersville, Missouri.

FBI agents from the Birmingham field office and members of the MPD stormed the house around 6:00 a.m. Kelly had been up all night sitting on the front porch with a .45 automatic pistol in his lap awaiting the authorities. When he returned to the inside of the house he left the door unlocked. Police found Kelly's partners in crime including his wife asleep as they entered the hide out, but Kelly was not among them.

As the lawmen searched, the bathroom door opened and out stepped Kelly in his underwear. Detective Sergeant William J. "Bill" Raney aimed a sawed-off shotgun at Kelly's heart and ordered, "Don't make a move." Kelly obeyed when Raney told him, "Sit down in that chair. Now put these handcuffs on." Newspapers reported that Kelly had come out sporting a .45 automatic but A. B. Randle who entered from the rear of the house said Kelly had been shaving and was unarmed. Nor did Kelly remark, "Don't shoot, G-man, don't shoot," as was attributed to him. The notorious gangster served time in Alcatraz and died on his 59th birthday in Leavenworth.

After the "Machine Gun" Kelly affair, the department determined not to be caught unprepared should a major criminal enterprise make a stand in Memphis. A 14-man Machine Gun and Tear Gas Squad was formed in 1934. This precursor of SWAT was armed with three Mauser submachine guns, two Thompson submachine guns, an automatic rifle, tear gas and bullet-proof vests.

Motorcycle Officer T. B. Knox, left, was gunned down on April 5, 1925, when he approached a car near Beale and Front. Patrolman W. R. Bridges, right, was shot and killed by a drunk at the corner of Third and Beale on April 20, 1929.

An expansion of the use of arm patches for specialized units took place in the mid-1930s. Motorcycle officers wore a winged-wheel patch. Mounted officers wore a patch with a horseshoe and horse head motif. These patches were worn approximately half way between the shoulder and the elbow. A number of decades passed before shoulder patches were worn department-wide.

The MPD continued to expand and improve radio communications. Radios were installed on motorcycles in 1934. In 1937 experimental two-way radios were installed in some cars. A 225-foot steel tower replaced the wire-strung-to-a-tree aerial.

Detective Sergeant William J. Raney was the first Memphis officer to attend the FBI National Academy as a student. He went to the Washington, DC, academy in 1937 during its early years, attending one of the first sessions. The first member of the Memphis Police Department to participate in the academy was Inspector William T. Griffin. Griffin was invited to lecture at the National Academy in 1936 on arrest, search, and handling of prisoners.

On April 1, 1937, soon after Raney's return from the FBI academy, he was promoted to lieutenant and opened the Memphis Police School now the Police Academy. The Memphis training program he organized was the first of its kind in the South. The first session was described as "the scientific methods of crime detection, evolved by J. Edgar Hoover for all G-Men." FBI Chief Hoover made the opening address at the Memphis Police School.

The department expanded as the economy improved in the thirties. The 201-man force in 1935

A patrol car rolls from the Barksdale station in the thirties.

consisted of a chief, two inspectors, two deputy inspectors, three captains, two lieutenants, ten sergeants, 29 detectives, 137 patrolmen and 15 others. Forty-one patrolmen were detailed to walking patrols, 72 to radio cars, 15 to traffic and nine to motorcycles.

Walking patrolmen worked downtown in pairs on two shifts. Their patrol area was Waterworks to Calhoun and the river to Lauderdale. Radio car patrolmen also worked in pairs, but on all three shifts and mostly in the suburbs. At night in 1937, 22 patrolmen walked the downtown in pairs from 6:00 p.m. to 6:00 a.m. Twelve squad cars with two-man teams cruised the suburbs on both the 4:00 p.m. to midnight and the midnight to 8:00 a.m. shifts.

Three Memphis officers lost their lives in traffic accidents while they were on duty in the 1930s. Patrolman C. J. Redder was run over and instantly killed by a fire truck at Second and Union on October

Radio dispatcher Beverly Boushe, later a city judge, issued call over the MPD's network, WPEC.

Patrolmen used the first two-way radio system installed by the MPD in 1937. Note the elaborate radio aerial on top of the squad car.

22, 1931, while working a fire. Patrolman George W. Ham was killed on February 27, 1936, as he and his partner chased a speeding car. The patrol car was broadsided when an automobile driven by a teenager ran a red light. Motorcycle Officer C. C. Musick was killed on July 2, 1937, when a DWI driver turned into the path of his motorcycle at Poplar and Tillman.

The department lost two patrolmen who walked the downtown beat, both from health related deaths. Patrolman Patrick T. Leahy, a native of Ireland, died of a heart attack on the afternoon of April 18, 1932. The 71-year-old officer had been with the MPD for 25 year when he collapsed on his beat near Main and Winchester. Patrolman Everett Scott, 58, was walking his beat at 10:45 p.m., December 16, 1939, when he began feeling ill. He stopped for a cup of coffee at The Shanty, South Court and Main, where he died of a heart attack.

Violent confrontations with criminals continued to claim the lives of policemen. Patrolmen Roy A. Scott and Charlie Zanone left headquarters on February 20, a cold Thursday afternoon in 1936. They reached 1409 Britton about 5:45 in search of a streetcar bandit. Zanone knocked on the front door while Scott watched the back of the house. The robbery suspect leapt from a window on the north side of the house. Scott, who had been a policeman for 51 days, ordered the thief to stop. The felon fired several shots and hit Patrolman Scott in the stomach. Scott stag-

Patrol units in the thirties were basic stock models without special equipment until the radio system was installed and receivers were mounted to the dash.

Chief Will D. Lee, left, joined the MPD in 1910 and headed of the department from 1928 to 1940. He implemented the first radio system of the Memphis force. Inspector William J. Raney, right, developed a nationally recognized training program for the Memphis Police Department. When he was a detective sergeant he captured the notorious "Machine Gun" Kelly.

gered and fell to the snow-covered ground. The young officer died as the gunman fled. Five hours later detectives located the killer. He admitted the shooting and was executed in the electric chair a year later.

Although John Cannon had left the police force he died as the result of an injuries he received on the job in November 1937. He and his partner arrested a drunk, and while his partner called for a patrol wagon the drunk kicked Patrolman Cannon in the chest. The impact ruptured Cannon's coronary artery. He succumbed to the injury on June 30, 1939.

Not all Memphis officer shot in the line of duty died of their wounds. Charles Rutland, who joined the force in 1916, was shot twice during the thirties, once in the leg while raiding a still and once in the arm while making an arrest. Rutland later served as a captain on

the vice squad. A few years before his retirement in 1945 he was seriously injured in a traffic accident and was assigned to traffic duty at Booker T. Washington High School. Rutland died in 1961 at age 88.

The department added 38 men in the month of December 1938. Police Commissioner Cliff Davis announced the hiring of ten new officers on December 1. "The new men were interviewed by Chief [Will D.] Lee, Inspector [Clegg] Richards, Captain [M. A.] Hinds, and myself. We have checked their references, observed their general demeanor and attitude. Each has a high school or equivalent education. We know the status of their families. They are all physically strong, under 30 and of good moral character. We feel that with proper police academy training they will make excellent young officers." The ten were, Eliko F.

MPD motorcycle unit in the late 1930s.

Recruits training in 1939, in the eighth class of the Memphis Police School established by Lieutenant William J. Raney, who stood at the back of the room. Seated from left to right in the front row were Whit Ables, Russell Barcroft, Richard Byrum, Bailey, and John Cannon; in the second row, B. O. Gilbert, Glisson, George Hughes, Charlie Hill, and Russell Jordan; in the third row, John Jeffries, Jamison, Roger Kinnon, Grover E. McCarver, and Max Milstead; in the fourth row, Patterson, Louis Rochelle, Gene Roach, C. O. Ritter, and Harry Spore; and in the fifth row, Trentham, Eddie Thorn, Bob Wilshire, Archie Wiseman, and J. D. Wortham.

Broens, Perry Hill, William P. Huston, Oliver F. Lambert, Roy McCoy, Adolph A. Meander, Charles T. Rhodes, Eugene Roach, J. W. Slaughter Jr. and Hiram E. Soule Jr.

Aubrey Epps, a former Tech High School football star and professional baseball player, was named a uniformed patrolman on December 5. L. J. Freeman and C. E. McNeil were hired as motorcycle patrolmen on the 14th.

Commissioner Davis announced the hiring of 25 more uniformed officers on December 16. Most were former athletes and scored over 90 on the Civil Service exam. "A few of the men have not taken the Civil Service examination and of course are employed only on a temporary basis. We have long been short of personnel, but with the addition of these men, this department will be able to increase its protection in every section of the city," Davis said.

Those named by Davis in this group were Whit Ables, R. J. Barger, Paul Barnett, U. T. Bartholomew, John Brasher, William R. Bryan, Everett Carter, L. W. Person, V. E. Ellis, C. W. Hill, F. T. Jenkins, M. J. Keely, Max Milstead, John Massey, William Moxley, R. L. Newberry, Woodrow Pierce, Cannon Roberson, T. E. Sanders, Harry Spore, J. W. Sumner, N. T. Vann and J. A. Wiseman. Two other officers were to be announced later. One of these was Grover E. McCarver.

The experiences and career of McCarver is an example of an officer's life with the Memphis Police Department through the middle decades of the twentieth century. Starting pay for an officer was $100 per

Recruit training in the Memphis Police School established by Lieutenant William J. Raney, kneeling at far right, included firearms training and time on the firing range.

month. Top pay for a patrolman was $165 a month. No hospitalization insurance was provided.

New officers had to provide their own uniform and equipment, including a pistol. Uniforms were ordered from Wolf the Tailor on South Main and cost around $100. A revolver ran about $35. The department provided his badge, the large six-point star. McCarver was given badge number 157.

The uniform was a dress type. Walking wards voted to wear coats even in the summer. Carrying a half pint of whiskey was typical for most walking patrolmen and the coat made it more easily concealed. White shirts were worn in the winter and light blue in the summer. Most men wore high top shoes. Summer hats had a ventilated frame; the frame on a winter hat was closed. Uniforms included a vest and the vest was required to be worn in the winter. Pea coats were optional winter wear.

It took three weeks for uniforms to arrive so McCarver was assigned with a team of generalist type detectives when he began work in 1938. He worked with

sergeants Turner and Willie King. Detective cruisers and ward cars had one-way radios. Calls were sent out three times to radio cars in case officers were briefly away from the vehicle. Telephones were used to get in service and otherwise communicate with headquarters.

When his uniform arrived McCarver was assigned

Patrol 1 was used to transport prisoners and to perform other duties requiring its capacity. Back of the paddy wagon had running board and hand rails.

to walk the 10th Ward from Front to Third and Beale to Calhoun. He worked the night shift, 7:00 p.m. to 6:00 a.m., seven days a week. During the day he went to school under Bill Raney at the Barksdale Station. There were no days off and no comp-time. McCarver's education was not all in the classroom. He made notes as he walked the ward and his partner pointed out law-breakers and places of ill repute.

McCarver rode the street car to get to work. The cost of the ride was seven cent unless he was in uniform, then it was free. The roll call for walking wards was held in the basement at headquarters. Patrolmen walked from headquarters if the ward was close or rode the streetcar to wards that were more distant.

Officers were seldom fed for free but were usually given a cup of coffee. Day walking wards got an hour and a half for lunch and were allowed to leave their partner and the ward to eat lunch. Night walking wards could eat but partners had to stay together in their ward for meals.

Patrolmen called into headquarters every hour, but did not wait around the telephone for return calls. When they called in, they frequently got instructions to respond to minor calls. There were no call boxes in the 10th Ward but the headquarters number, 8-9081, was a free call from pay phones.

Walking wards wrote traffic tickets, which were delivered by mail. They seldom wrote "short tickets" for parking violations. "Long tickets," written for moving violations, were turned into headquarters and mailed to violators. Tickets were not often challenged, so officers seldom made traffic court.

After a few days McCarver was transferred to Barksdale Car 38 and began patrolling suburban wards, with his partner Van Fletcher. He stayed in Car 38 until 1943. In the early 1940s the city had 13 two-man ward cars divided into north, south and east

Motorcycle officers Gene Meyers, left, and Adrain Taylor with one of the Indian Motorcycles used by the department.

zones, each zone supervised by a sergeant. Lieutenant H. G. Crum was located at the Barksdale Station and was in command. Besides the 13 wards patrolled by car there were 12 walking wards.

The department required that squad cars cover 50 miles per shift, day or night. The city gas station was located at Washington and Lauderdale and was the only source for gasoline. Midnight cars had to gas up

The motorcycle unit at Overton Park in the forties.

Mounted patrol around 1940. The officers wore a unit patch on the arm featuring a horse shoe with a horse head in the center.

between the time the station opened at 6:00 a.m. and the end of the shift at 7:00 a.m.

The department used all Ford cars. They were two door black sedans with no screen dividing front and back seats. Besides the one-way radio, they were equipped with red lights behind the grill and mechanical sirens but no spotlight. The cars were marked with a star on the door and the district number inside the star. A sawed-off shotgun was carried on the dash board.

In 1943 McCarver moved to Car 2 and was partnered with Dick Davis. The Nicholson/Kettlewell affair took place in 1943. All cars went to headquarters in a protest of what was generally considered the unfair dismissal of the two officers. As a result of the job action, patrolmen were given two days off each month. A uniform allowance also began in 1943.

McCarver took military leave from the force in 1944 and joined the Marines. He returned to the Memphis Police Department on January 1, 1946, and again partnered with Dick Davis, this time patrolling Midtown in Car 18 where McCarver remained until 1948.

A job action in 1948 led to the reenacting of Civil Service in the department. Commissioner Joe Boyle was angered by the affair and as a result partner and car assignments were changed every month or more frequently until 1950. Salaries were increased, improved the retirement plan and gave officers one day

off each week instead of two per month.

In 1950 McCarver was promoted to detective in the General Investigative Bureau (GIB). Three month later he was promoted to lieutenant. During his time in GIB he served in all squads of the bureau, but primarily he worked auto theft. McCarver retired from the department in 1964. He worked as a private investigator after his time with the MPD and died on February 1, 1990.

In part, the addition of officers in 1938 was in

Fifty-eight-year-old Patrolman Everett Scott, left, died of a heart attack walking his downtown beat on December 16, 1939. Motorcycle Officer C. C. Musick, right, was killed on July 2, 1937, when a DWI driver turned into the path of his motorcycle at Poplar and Tillman.

Criminal records were all on paper in the 1940s. Fingerprint cards were housed in filing cabinets, with mug shots of wanted felons were displayed above.

trucks. Honking horns except in an emergency carried a fine of $3.

Squad cars were increased from 13 to 15 in 1941. Detective cruisers were equipped with two-way radios and motorcycles were all furnished with one-way radios. Traffic equipment on the streets of the city was improved in the early forties as well. Traffic lights were changed from single overhead signals at intersections to pole mounted corner light with "walk" and "wait" pedestrian signals. Approximately 1900 parking meters were installed downtown.

Chief of Police Carroll B. Seabrook served as head of the department from September 1940 through January 1949. A number of significant achievement were made during his tenure. M. A. Hinds served as chief of detectives.

Inspector William J. Raney held the position of Director of Personnel and Training following World

preparation for the reorganization of the Traffic Division in 1939. Personnel increases were required for the new traffic configuration. The Accident Prevention Bureau had 23 officers and supervisors, most working in Accident Investigation. The Enforcement Unit included 14 officers in the Motorcycle Squad and 16 men in Congestion Control, most of them detailed as corner men. The division also had a one-man Safety Education Section. Speed limits were increased from 25 to 30 mph, 20 to 25 mph for

Patrolman circa 1940. The uniform jacket could be worn with the collar buttoned to the neck for cold weather or with lapels open to reveal a necktie. The winter hat had an enclosed frame, as the one pictured, and the frame of the summer hat was ventilated.

Accident investigation squad in 1941 with the scientific equipment used for traffic accident investigation.

War II. During the war Raney served in the army with a military rank of Captain. He became the Assistant Provost Marshal in charge of Criminal Investigations. His final wartime assignment was as Chief of Police in Manila, Philippines, in 1945 with the rank of Major.

The period following World War II brought innovations to all aspects of society including law enforcement. The Memphis Police Department changed badge styles in 1947. The star was replaced by a stock pinched-shield with the Tennessee state seal in the center. The uniform of the post-war years was long-sleeve shirts, navy blue trousers and a jacket in the winter. The hat had a one-piece navy top encircled by a concealed semi-rigid rim. The bill was black and the hat came with two frames, a solid fabric covered the frame of winter wear and an open cane-weave frame for summer.

In the winter the patrolman wore a white shirt and navy wool jacket. The jacket was fingertip length with an open collar and splayed lapels. A matching navy wool vest was available and a popular option. In the summer an officer wore a light blue shirt without a jacket. In the late 1960s the white shirt was discontinued and the light blue shirt was worn year-round. A

Mounted Officer Pete Zorzoli and his horse Tim partnered for over a decade.

navy wool tie was worn year-round. Navy wool trousers were available in summer and winter weights. Socks were navy or black and shoes were black plain-toed leather oxfords.

Beginning in 1948 new officers were required to complete two weeks of training before they were put on duty. Classrooms on the second floor of the Barksdale Station and the gym at headquarters were used for training sessions. Those who passed the first Saturday morning exam went on to the second week which included a day at the Penal Farm range. The results of the second Saturday test and duty assignment for successful recruits were posted on Inspector Raney's office door.

Memphis Patrolman Ed Sills used one of the mobile phones acquired in the late forties. The technology was developed by the military for walkie-talkies.

327

The first black officers in the modern era of the Memphis Police Department became policemen in 1948. They were from left to right Rufus J. Turner, Wendell L. Robinson, Claudius L. Phillips, Joseph E. Pegues, Daniel A. Evans, Jewel W. Jubert, Roscoe R. McWilliams, Ernest C. Withers Sr., and Marion C. Teague.

The first black officers of the modern era were hired in 1948. Nine men, Daniel A. Evans, Jewel W. Jubert, Roscoe R. McWilliams, Joseph E. Pegues, Claudius L. Phlillips, Wendell L. Robinson, Marion C. Teague, Rufus J. Turner and Ernest C. Withers, were hired to patrol sections of the city with predominately black populations. The men were trained separately from white officers. Training classes were not integrated until 1964.

Initially these officers walked foot patrol on Beale Street and provided security at black athletic, social and community events. Car 52 became the first squad car manned by black officers and patrolled Orange Mound from 6:00 p.m. to 2:00 a.m. In all, 19 squad cars were on patrol on each eight-hour shift with two extra cars from 9:00 p.m. to 6:00 a.m.

Claude A. Armour was named chief of police on February 1, 1949. Armour began his law enforcement career only eight years earlier when he was hired as a patrolman on the Memphis department in December 1941. Less than a year later he joined the U.S. Navy and served in the pacific from 1942 to 1945. He was wounded on Okinawa and cited for bravery under enemy fire. Upon return to the MPD he earned rapid promotions. He made lieutenant in 1946 and followed his graduation from the FBI academy in 1947 was promoted to uniform inspector.

Armour's tenure as chief was brief. He was appointed commissioner of fire and police on October 1, 1950, and was subsequently elected to four four-year terms as commissioner. Commissioner Armour had an illustrious 17-year tenure as commissioner in Memphis and serve four times as acting mayor. His reputation nationally was such that he was repeatedly asked to speak to graduates of the FBI National Academy. Armour was so popular that when he announced his retirement hundreds of off-duty officers staged a protest at city hall.

Armour's law enforcement career continued with service to the state as Special Assistant to Governor on Law and Order and as Commissioner of the Tennessee Department of Safety. He completed his career as Commissioner of Safety for the City of Murfreesboro.

Chief of Police Edward Hull Reeves was appointed in Armour's place in 1950 and oversaw the installation of a new FM radio system. The system designated KIC306 had three frequencies and two way radio radios were installed in 82 in automobiles and 18 motorcycles.

The second class of black officers graduated on May 28, 1951, and included from left to right Patrolmen James S. Persley, Elmo S. Berkley, Thomas B. Marshall, and Benjamin J. Whitney. Inspector William J. Raney, head of training for the department, stood at the far right.

The department totaled 341 men in 1951 including the chief, two assistant chiefs, 13 inspectors, 4 deputy inspectors, 6 captains, 48 lieutenants, 7 sergeants, 122 corporals and 139 patrolmen. Walking patrols continued in the city center, 13 black officers walked the Beale Street area and 16 white officers walked downtown.

The department lost a motorcycle officer on April 12, 1952. Department policy prohibited riding motorcycles on wet pavement and when it began to rain that day motorcycle officers James E. Walker and R. E. Felix proceeded to headquarters. As they approached the intersection of North Parkway and Avalon a driver pulled into their path. Motorcycle Officer Walker ran onto the median strip and struck a tree. He died less than two hours later.

Patrolman Joseph Palazolla lost his life on November 30, 1959. Palazolla was directing traffic on Bellevue in front of Bruce Elementary School. It was just after 3:00 p.m. and Palazolla was in the middle of the street with his hand up and blowing his whistle. A Memphis city bus struck the officer and dragged him over 50 feet. Palazolla died less than an hour later of massive internal injuries.

A number of specialized units were formed in the fifties. Additional detectives were hired in 1951 and the Hold Up Squad was created with four detectives on "cruise duty" at night. The Hotel Squad was created in 1952 so detectives could watch hotels and pool halls for gamblers and vagrants. In 1953 a two-man Racket Squad was formed to rid the city of gamblers and confidence men.

The department began using radar units for traffic control on March 20, 1953. Inspector Clifford Legg, head of the traffic department, reported that radar was directly responsible for the arrest of an additional 300 speeding drivers each month. Two Drunkometers were also acquired that year for use by traffic details.

Chief of Police James C. MacDonald was appointed in August 1954 and served through June 1968. Inspector Bill Raney retired from the department in 1955. He was a nationally recognized criminal investigator and created William J. Raney and Associates, which became a well-respected private detective agency. Raney briefly served as a special investigator with the Tennessee Bureau of Criminal Investigation in 1959 during the investigation of Hamilton County Judge Raulston Schoolfield.

Until 1956 patrolmen worked seven days on and one day off, which meant a different day off each week. Commissioner Armour and Chief MacDonald reduced the hours to be worked each week from 48 to 40, which resulted in a more stable duty schedule. Officers also began to receive one hour accumulated time for off-duty court appearances.

The Memphis Police Department grew to 520 officer in 1956, a significant increase from the 450 of the year before. Top pay for patrol officers was $331 per month. Door insignia on squad cars was changed from a six-point star outlined in gold and the car number in the center. New decals in the form of a solid silver shield-shaped badge with the car number were applied to the doors of marked units.

Short sleeve shirts were authorized in 1956 but were not well accepted by the command. They were authorized only if both officers in the car wore them and only if the officer had no tattoo on his arm. Officers who received first aid training wore a small patch with a red cross in a red circle. The patch was worn on the left shoulder of the jacket.

Memphis Patrolmen Wendell L. Robinson, left, and Ernest C. Withers Sr. with their patrol car soon after going on the job in 1948.

The Claude A. Armour Fire and Police Training and Communication Center opened in 1958. This facility replaced the Barksdale Station and Barksdale was closed, ending for a time the era of the mounted patrol. The last five horses were sold at auction and the stable on Washington closed.

The first female officers of the department were 10 Meter Maids who were hired in 1958 to take over the duty of ticketing parking meter violations. The ten were Betty J. Coats, Katie Ernestine Fitzhugh, Ossie Faye Fowler, Julia Claire Lester, Frances E. Marzioli, Bernice A. Parrish, Elsie L. Sanders, Rosie Sigler, Rita Thompson and Erma Z. Trent. They were under the command of Captain Fred F. Woodward. Not long after Woodward was promoted to inspector he died of a heart attack while on duty, on November 30, 1960.

The decade of the sixties was a dynamic period for the department. The formation of the Emergency Squad on May 15, 1960, provided the Memphis Police Department with special weapons and tactics capabilities. The original 15 members of the squad were Captain J. W. Slaughter, Lieutenant Sam Evans Sr. and Patrolmen B. A. Alfred, E. H. Arkin, S. O. Blackburn, C. H. Gamble, O. B. Holcomb, G. E. Mead, J. F. Molnar, Glen Moore, J. W. Owen, J. G. Ray, Phil Robinett, D. W. Williams and D. W. Zurka.

The Emergency Squad was intended to handle any adverse situation that might weaken the normal complement of the department. Its members were all experienced and specially trained. The four station wagons used by the squad were equipped with machine guns, rifles, shotguns, tear gas guns and projectiles, hand held radios, fire extinguishers, megaphones, oxygen, gas masks and riot helmets.

The department acquired its first aircraft in 1960. The twin-engine Beachcraft became affectionately

Chief of Police Claude A. Armour held the position only briefly, February 1949 to November 1950, before becoming commissioner of fire and police, a position he held for 17 years.

known as "933 Charlie" after its registration 4933C. Lieutenant Gene Barksdale served as pilot until the aircraft was retired in 1964. The Helicopter Squad was formed in 1969 with four pilots and a Bell Helicopter. The unit was commanded by Captain Glenn Moore.

Recruit training was expanded to five weeks in 1960 and to seven weeks in 1961. Training and other facilities improvements completed in 1962 included a new gym, firing range, print shop, microfilming center and an addition to the Central Police Station.

The Dog Squad was created in 1962 when four teams completed training in Kansas City. The squad was so successful that ten more teams were added by yearend. The canine unit was created as a direct result of the line of duty death of Patrolman Frank Bruno Jr. on October 7, 1960.

Patrolman Bruno and his partner W. E. Pierini responded to a complaint of breaking glass near South Orleans and East McLemore about 1:00 a.m. While Pierini talked with the complainant Bruno checked Ace Sundry and found the front glass broken out. Bruno entered the store and was struck in the chest by one of two shots that exploded out of the darkness.

Three Motorcycle officers circa 1950.

School safety patrol at Second Street and Adams Avenue in 1949. Police officers were assisted by safety patrol boys and eye-catching signage in the form of school children provided by businesses.

The officer staggered outside, his weapon still in its holster and fell to the sidewalk. Patrolman Pierini fired at the shadowy figure that fled the scene and went to assist his partner. Bruno died in the emergency room 30 minutes later. K-9 teams working similar incidents were certain to save officers lives and the department began planning for the Dog Squad.

A number of organizational changes took place in 1963. The Administrative Services Division was reduced from twelve bureaus to five, Planning and Research, Training, Communications, Identification and Special Services. The Vice Squad, a special undercover unit, was formed to ferret out prostitution, gambling and the illegal sale of alcohol and narcotics.

The title Detective Division was changed to Criminal Investigation Division and included Vice and Narcotics. The first black officers, Detective R. J. Turner and Patrolman W. A. Harris, were assigned to Vice and Narcotics in 1964. The first female officers were promoted to detective in 1965. Detectives Louise Dunavant and Mary Sample Fowler were assigned to Vice/Narcotics and Intelligence.

Officer Claudine Penn, employed September 16, 1963 as a meter maid, was commissioned in May 1968 as the first female black officer in the department. Other than the first class of meter maids, the female officers were not commissioned when they were hired. On May 15, 1970, all existing female officers were given 200 hours of re-training and were commissioned.

Julia Claire Lester was promoted to Lieutenant in July 1979 and became the first female 30-year captain

in 1988. Claudine Penn became the first black female sergeant in 1973 and the first black female 30-year captain in 1995 shortly before her retirement.

The Memphis Police Department graduated the first integrated class of recruits from the Armour Center in 1964. Four of the 24 members of the class were black officers. The top salary for patrolmen of $440 a month in 1964 increased to $535 per month in 1966.

Squad cars became "shiftless" in 1965 as the department acquired its first units with automatic transmissions. The following year the department purchased fifty new automobiles with air conditioning. Some of the autos were regular black patrol units, some white accident investigation vehicles and some detective cruisers.

Frank C. Holloman became the first Director of Fire and Police under the new Mayor and Council form of city government on January 1, 1968. The title was changed to Director because other divisions of the city were managed by a director. Holloman was a former FBI agent and served two years in the position. Henry E. Lux was appointed chief of police on July 1, 1968, and served four years in the position. The total number of officers in the MPD were 1,132, including 199 lieutenants, 45 captains, 33 inspectors and 7 assistant chiefs.

The MPD lost a number of officers to traffic accidents in the decade from the early sixties to the early seventies. Officer Morris E. White was killed in a head on collision at 8:55 a.m. on November 20, 1963. White spent the previous day in court and worked his full night shift without sleep. It was believed that he fell asleep on his way home after his tour.

On February 12, 1964, an automobile pulled into the path of a patrol car in an early morning pursuit of a speeder on Bellevue. Officer James E. Harper was killed in the accident. A similar incident on

Memphis traffic car, a 1950 Ford.

Motorcycle Officer Adrian Taylor wore the protective helmet adopted in the fifties to improve safety while on traffic duty.

Memphis began using radar units for traffic control on March 20, 1953. The radar unit was set on a tripod outside the car and connected to a monitor inside the car that displayed the speed of passing cars.

September 9, 1972, left Officer Michael D. Wright Jr. dead. A tractor-trailer turned into the path of his patrol car as he chased a speeder at 3:00 a.m. Officer Dennis J. Jobe lost control of his motorcycle during training at the Armour Training Center on September 22, 1970. He struck his head on the curb and died of his injuries.

Inspector J. Clifford Legg, head of traffic enforcement, employed the services of the media to promote traffic safety. Legg became the city's first airborne traffic reporter. His traffic reports started in 1965 and continued until April 1968. Legg was a familiar voice to Memphians as he mixed wit with warnings like, "fasten those cotton-pickin' seatbelts," and occasionally tripping over his tongue as when he reported, "very good traffic congestion at Union and Parkway."

Legg joined the MPD in 1935 as a motorcycle officer, later working in the detective and accident divisions before heading traffic enforcement. Major Louis Distretti served under Legg as a patrolman, "I remember his car leading every parade that went down Main Street. He was standing up on the running board with his door wide open, giving directions and keeping the parade coordinated."

Civil rights and other activism in the sixties brought a new level of scrutiny to the police department. The MPD recognized the need for improving communication with the public and involvement in the community. Captain William Carl Moxley was appointed director of a newly formed Community Relations Program.

Moxley joined the MPD in 1938. After military service in World War II, he worked in business until rejoining the MPD in 1964 as a patrol officer on the vice squad. He retired from the department in 1969 and became the West Tennessee regional representative of the Law Enforcement Planning Agency where he served for 13 years.

An event that shook the entire nation took place in Memphis on April 4, 1968. Dr. Martin Luther King Jr. stepped on the balcony walkway at the Lorraine Motel at 6:01 p.m. and the report of a rifle sounded over the gathered crowd. Dr. King fell dead of an assassin's bullet.

Officer James E. Harper, left, was killed on September 9, 1972, when a tractor-trailer turned into the path of his patrol car. Officer Dennis J. Jobe, right, lost control of his motorcycle during training at the Armour Training Center on September 22, 1970, struck his head on the curb and died of his injuries.

The Memphis Police Department Mounted Patrol in ceremonial duties at a Cotton Carnival parade in downtown Memphis in the mid-fifties. The unit was discontinued in 1958 and the department was without mounted officers for over two decades.

Homicide Detective Glynn King was one of the first officers on the scene of Dr. King's killing. He worked on the forensic team in the boarding house where the killer stayed across from the motel. Glynn King joined the Memphis force in 1961 as a traffic officer and five years later became a homicide detective. He worked violent crimes, including many high profile cases.

Patrolman Louis Edward McKay Jr. was a member of the Police Emergency Squad and one of the first to arrive on the scene. When the bundle was found containing the rifle that killed Dr. King, McKay was assigned to guard the bundle. McKay later admitted, "I was sort of frustrated because I was told to stand there and guard that weapon and don't let anybody touch it. I would rather have been looking in buildings, behind buildings. . . ."

Rioting followed in Memphis and in much of the rest of the nation. The Tennessee Highway Patrol and the National Guard were called in to assist Memphis and Shelby County law enforcement. Other law enforcement agencies responded as well. James Earl Ray was captured in June by officers of London's Scotland Yard. Ray pled guilty to first-degree murder in the killing and was sentenced to 99 years.

A number of changes were made at the MPD following the King assassination. The thirty-man Emergency Squad was replaced by a sixty-man Special

Services Unit. The Crime Scene Squad was created to gather evidence using the latest scientific methods. An In-Service Training Program was begun and five four-man Sniper Squads were trained.

John F. Molnar was placed in command of the Special Services Unit. Molnar was at virtually every major demonstration or protest in Memphis during the 1960s and early 1970s. He was always at the front with his trademark cigar stuck in the right side of his mouth and a blank expression on his face. He was usually the one to tell a group to disperse or face arrest. If they chose arrest it was usually orderly and low-key with Molnar even telling them how much bond was likely to be once they got to court.

Molnar earned the respect of some protest leaders for his willingness to talk calmly about what police would do in a confrontation. He said, "I'm a simple guy. I do what my superior officers tell me to do and I expect the men under me to do what I tell them."

Molnar began his career with the MPD in 1955. He got a taste for police work during his time in the Navy Shore Patrol. In 1960 Molnar joined the newly formed Emergency Squad that trained to lead the police response to riots and other civil disturbances or protests. Molnar led the Special Services Unit until it was disbanded in 1974. He retired in 1981 as a deputy chief of police.

In February 1968 Assistant Chief H. E. Lux raised the issue of forming a reserve force with Chief J. C.

The first female officers of the Memphis Police Department were ten Meter Maids hired in 1958. They were commissioned as police officers, but were not armed and told to avoid making arrests. The front row, left to right, included Bernice A. Parrish, Betty J. Coats, Julia Claire Lester, Ossie Faye Fowler, and Frances E. Marzioli; and in the second row were Rita Thompson, Katie Ernestine Fitzhugh, Rosie Sigler, Elsie L. Sanders, and Erma Z. Trent. Metermaids hired after the first group were not commissioned. Captain Fred F. Woodward, on the left, was commander of the unit.

Parade duty was a frequent assignment of motorcycle officers.

MacDonald. Following research into the various options of a police reserve it was decided that the department wanted a trained and armed group with regularly working members rather than an unarmed auxiliary force that worked mainly during extraordinary events such as riots. Implementation of the reserve program was delayed due to events surrounding the assassination of Dr. King.

Inspector Eugene Barksdale was chosen to plan and organize the reserve force. Police Reserve officers had to be between the ages of 21 and 45, in good health, and be able to work police duty 16 or 20 hours a month. They were required to complete a 22-week training course of 191 hours similar to regular officers and were assigned to regular duty with full-time policemen. Reserve officers worked for no salary and had to furnish their own equipment and uniforms.

Inspector H. H. Leatherwood was appointed to head the Reserve Program and on May 28, 1969, 41 Memphis police reservists graduated at the Armour Center. Their badges were the same as other officers, but contained the designation "Reserve." Reserve officers first went on duty on the evening of June 6, 1969, riding as a third man in patrol cars. Joseph E. Walk, who documented the history of the Memphis Police Department, was a member of this first class.

Robert H. Love, an attorney and former police officer, was appointed captain and commanding officer of the 41-man unit. James H. McCaleb and Harry L. Butler were made lieutenants. Reserve officers rode as part of the 3 or 4 man cars during the racial unrest. They also worked parades and the Mid-South Fair. In the early 1970s reserve officers worked in the detective division in plain clothes, in the radio room, sometimes as dispatchers, as well as vice and traffic.

In 1972 reserve officers served warrants in two-man teams and patrolled together in ward cars. The reserve had its own Traffic Division consisting of about 20 officers under commanding officers Lieutenant R. D. Lancaster and Warrant Officer E. J. Bowden and Douglas A. Ogilvie. Riding in unmarked cars, reserve traffic officers issued citations and made arrests for major violations such as DWI and reckless driving. The reserves had become a police department within the police department.

Patrolman Joseph Palazolla, left, was struck and killed by a city bus while directing traffic on Bellevue in front of Bruce Elementary School on November 30, 1959. Patrolman Frank Bruno Jr., right, was shot twice in the chest and killed as he investigated a burglary near South Orleans and East McLemore. The canine unit was created as a result of his death.

Commanding officers of the Reserve in 1973 were Inspector Robert H. Love, Captain James H. McCaleb, Executive Lieutenant Harry L. Butler, Lieutenants David H. Coombes, James E. Knauff and R. Don Lancaster and Sergeants Douglas A. Ogilvie and E. J. Bowden. They commanded 72 patrolmen and staff specialists.

From its inception in 1969 through 1975 the reserve force served 197,789 hours saving the city $1,242,286. The rank structure within the reserves faded in the late 1970s and reserve officers worked increasingly under the regular department command.

A number of reserve officers became regular full-time officers. A group of seven joined the regular ranks in May 1979. A waiver allowed the substitution of 200 hours of duty for the requirement of two years of college credit. The seven were W. I. Ashton, Gary W. Coleman, Mary L. Taylor, Joseph E. Walk, James Knauff, Gary T. Creasy and John R. Wright In September 12 more became regular officers.

A number of new regular officers were added in 1969. Among them was Walter E. Crews, a future director of the force. Officers rode two to a car, but the department was transitioning to one man cars. Single officer cars mainly took offence reports. More serious calls were taken by the two man cars. Three people were assigned to a car, two working and one off. Officers alternated days off, for example one took Sunday and Monday, another Tuesday and Wednesday and the third Thursday and Saturday. No one got both Saturday and Sunday off and Friday was "Kelly Day"

Members of the department get special recognition from one of Memphis' leading citizens and a well known supporter of law enforcement, Elvis Presley.

when all three officers worked. The junior officer worked wherever needed in the department.

Racial tensions remained very high following Dr. King's killing and social changes affected the operations of the police department. The MPD was mostly male and white. Two predominately black recruit classes went through the police training academy. When the rookie officers first started they rode together and cars were not racially mixed. The department set up community centers in small store fronts and similar spaces to improve communication in neighborhoods.

The city was divided into the East and North Precincts and soon the South Precinct was added. The North Precinct station was located at Fourth and Adams and included the area in the present West Precinct. All officers gathered at the Armour Station for every roll call. Officers of the East Precinct stood on one side of the room, officers of the North on another and officers of the South on a third. All of the commanding officers stood in the middle. Roll was called for officers in each precinct and the officers lined up and stood at parade rest in numerical rank

MPD created the Dog Squad in 1962.

order based on the number of their car. Car 1 first, then Car 2 and so forth. Car numbers were no more than two digits at the time.

Officers used the same cars as the previous shift. After the roll call officers drove their personal cars to the ward they patrolled, parked in a safe place and transferred to police cars. The vehicles were gassed up at a nearby fire station. Cars were two door with no screen partition and one officer had to ride in the back seat with the prisoner when an arrest was made. Cars were not air conditioned and commercial radios were not allowed. Officers rode with the window down even in winter so they could here gun shots or calls for help. Patrolmen rode the alleys at 3:00 or 4:00 in the mornings with the lights off checking the backs of buildings for burglars. Interior lights were disconnected so that when doors were open, the inside of the car remained dark.

Patrolmen Walter Crews, James Moss and Jim Anderson were assigned to one of the early integrated cars. Crews and Anderson were white and Moss was black. Moss was the senior officer of the three and passed on his experience to the younger men. Crews recalled, "Moss was low key and treated people fair, but didn't take any guff. Anderson was detail oriented and learned everybody in the patrol area. They were both honest, hardworking policemen." Patrolman Crews also rode with Officer Joyce Tuggle Pageant, the first female officers assigned to patrol car duty.

Patrol cars had two radio channels, North and East. A third channel was added when the South Precinct was formed. The traffic division had a channel and another channel was used for checking stolen cars and miscellaneous communications. Radios operated only when the car was running so engines were left on. Walkie-talkies were acquired in the 1970s.

Shifts for all officers changed every 28 days. Officers went from the day shift to the midnight shift

K-9 Officer Bill Highlander moved his partner along a special course designed to develop skills of the Dog Squad.

Patrolman Louis Edward McKay Jr. guarded the bundle found at 424 S. Main that contained the rifle that killed Dr. Martin Luther King Jr. A detective made notes. McKay was a member of the Police Emergency Squad that responded to the scene and he would rather have been hunting the assassin. (Commercial Appeal photo)

consisted of the former administrative bureau and services bureau. The Criminal Intelligence Squad was created in April 1971 to investigate organized crime.

A new role was created in the School Safety Unit in 1970. Officers Louis Edward McKay Jr. and Carl Mister were assigned duty as "Officer Friendly," working with children to give them a positive image of law enforcement. McKay spent 24 years of his 32-year career on the force as Officer Friendly.

Chief of Police Bill Price was appointed in 1972 and served for two years. The East Precinct was established to enhance police services to the growing population in the eastern section of the city.

A number of equipment enhancements and new technology were introduced in the late sixties and seventies. The fifty new squad cars ordered in 1968 were solid blue rather than black or white units. They were four-door with a screen dividing front and back seats and had hand-held instead of fixed spotlights. The department changed the paint scheme on squad cars in 1978 to phase out the blue units in favor of combination black and white units. Other equipment purchased in 1968 included six suits of body armor, eight Pepper Fog machines for riot control and television recording equipment for use in training.

Uniforms and insignia changed significantly in the period. An octagonal, soft-edged hat was introduced to the uniform in 1962 replacing the rigid flat-topped hat. The new hat was flexible and more casual. It was in used until 1986.

The city adopted a new seal in December 1962. The form of the seal was a rounded rectangle with "Memphis," "Shelby County," and "Tennessee" on its border. The new seal was made a part of the custom badge die when the department reintroduced the acorn style badge about 1967 for use by sergeants. The form of the badge changed slightly and was slightly larger than the 1922 version. The badge style had limited use among ranks other than sergeant.

The first department-wide shoulder patch was introduced in 1964 and worn on both shoulders. The form was a large pinched-shield with the department seal in red, gold and brown on a sky blue background. At the bottom of the patch were the words "Courage," "Knowledge," and "Integrity."

A casual and more functional fur-collar jacket replaced the suit-type jacket in 1968. The jacket was a zip-up with an elastic waist band and was made of a durable navy fabric. The shoulder patch was simplified and reduced in size. The new patch was a vertical oval in form, featured the department seal and retained the powder blue background.

and then to the evening shift. The system was effective for policing because officers learned everyone in the ward they worked and who was out on the streets at what hours. During the day house burglars were active and some auto thieves and truants, on the evening shift were mostly holdup men and domestic violence calls, and the midnight shift were the burglars, some armed robbers, pimps and prostitutes, and the growing problem of drug dealers and users. The frequent shift changes were stressful on the family of policemen and no matter what shift an officer worked, he went to court each day at 9:00 a.m.

In October 1970 the department was reorganized from five divisions to two. Field Operations took responsibility for uniform patrol, traffic, criminal investigation and special operations. Staff Operations

The use of badge numbers to indicate seniority and as the primary identification of the officer was abandoned. The number used to identify officers in the department's data bank became the more significant number and was called the "IBM number" or "funny numbers" by officers. The ID Number was required on each report.

When officers switched to winter uniforms in 1972 the light blue shirts of patrol officers were replaced with midnight blue shirts. Shirts had buttons for appearance, but fastened with a zipper. Supervisors soon discarded their white shirts for midnight blue as well. Initially the shirt fabric was a blend of cotton and synthetic in a lighter shade of midnight blue. Within a few years this changed to a fully synthetic material. Trousers followed a similar progression. The uniform became a permanent-press, all-synthetic, wash-and-wear fabric. Ties were changed to pre-tied synthetic wash-and-wear, although by the early eighties ties were no longer required, not even with long-sleeved shirts. Socks and shoes also took advantage of more modern materials.

With the introduction of midnight blue shirts, the department patch was worn on the right shoulder and a patch of the American flag was worn on the left shoulder. The small Red Cross patch was worn low on the arm near the cuff.

The supervision of the fire and police department had been under a single commissioner, later titled director, since 1910. In 1972 the position was split into a Director of Fire Services and a Director of Police Services.

Jay W. Hubbard was appointed as Memphis' first Director of Police Services in December 1972 by Mayor Wyeth Chandler. Hubbard, a career military man, fought in three wars. He was a pilot and retired as a brigadier general with 32 years in the Marine Corps. Hubbard agreed to stay for two years but stayed until 1975, during which time he labored to stabilize and modernize the MPD.

Two months into the job Hubbard decried the lack of black officers and the high number of brutality complaints. He created an internal security inspection system and worked to decentralize the department. During his tenure a six-man Metro DWI Squad was initiated, the helicopter unit became the Metro Aviation Unit and tripled its number of aircraft, the Special Operations Bureau was reorganized, the Police Cadet Program began, the Park Police Unit was started with eight officers, a twelve man Electronic

Memphis officers working downtown at the corner of Second Street and Monroe Avenue in 1957.

Surveillance Patrol was initiated using $100,000 worth of new electronic equipment and the Community Service Officer Program was begun in three public housing projects.

A number of important personnel actions took place in 1973. The Memphis Police Association was formed and recognized by the city as the official bargaining agent for officers below the rank of lieutenant. Temporary corporate officers of the association during the formation process including President Jack C. Carlisle, Vice President David Gallarno and Secretary-Treasurer Jim Holder, all of whom were warrant officers in the Bureau of Identification.

Sixty-five black officers formed the Afro-American Police Association later in 1973. The same month that Lieutenant W. L. Robinson became the first black officer promoted to the rank of captain.

The size of the department in 1973 was 1256 sworn officers. Top monthly pay for the patrolman rank was $890. Three female officers were assigned to patrol cars to ride with a male partner. It was only three years earlier that the first women recruits began training in the same class with men at the Police Academy. Sergeants Mary A. Fowler and Elsie L. Dunavant became the first female officers to be promoted to the rank of lieutenant. The next year, 1974, Lieutenant Fowler became the first female assigned to a field command position.

Chief of Police William O. Crumby was appointed in 1974 and was the last individual to serve in the position. The title Chief of Police was abolished in 1977 and replaced by two appointed Deputy Directors, one for operations and one for administration. On the resignation of Director Hubbard, Chief Crumby served as acting director until September 1976 when E. Winslow "Buddy" Chapman was named Director of Police. Chapman was not a law enforcement professional, but had some military training and was administrative assistant to a mayor. The North Precinct moved into a new building in 1976 and the West Precinct was established, becoming the fourth police precinct in the city.

An incident on October 3, 1974, brought national attention and a revision of deadly force policies throughout the United States. At about 10:45 p.m. officers responded to a "prowler inside call." At the scene a woman standing on her porch motioned to the house next door and told the officers she heard glass breaking. The two patrolmen heard a door slam and saw someone run across the backyard. The fleeing suspect's escape was halted by a chain link fence. The officers saw no weapon when then shined a flashlight on

Claudine Penn was employed on September 16, 1963 as a meter maid and was first black female officer in the department. Here she worked Beale Street, ticketing parking violators. Officer Penn was commissioned in 1968 and went on to a long and illustrious career, retiring as a 30-year captain in 1995.

the suspect and called, "Police. Halt!" as the figure crouched at the base of the fence. The burglar tried to escape over the fence and the officers, in accordance with department policy and Tennessee law, shot him. The bullet hit the thief in the back of the head and he died.

Suit was brought against the department and the case made it to the U.S. Supreme Court. In a 1985 decision, *Tennessee v Garner,* 471 U.S.1 (1985), the majority of the court found that the existing code that permitted shooting fleeing suspects was "unreasonable."

Tennessee Codes, House Bill No. 741, revised state law. An officer was authorized to use all necessary means to effect the arrest, but deadly force was authorized only after a warning was given and all other means of arrest were exhausted; and then based on probable cause of a felony involving the infliction or threatened infliction of serious physical harm and a belief that the subject posed a threat of serious physical harm, either to the officer or to others unless he is immediately apprehended. Deadly force policies across the state and in much of the nation were revised to comply.

A deadly incident on May 21, 1973, led to the development of a new specialized unit within the department. Ten minutes before the end of their tour

Motorcycle officers in the fifties from left to right were Inspector J. Clifford "Cliff" Legg, Captain Charles T. "Charlie" Rhodes, Bill Hart, Banks McCall, Ed Sills, Dave Zurka, Adrian Taylor, and Tom Hubbard. Officers wore the pinch shield breast badge adopted a few years earlier, and a generic motorcycle officer shoulder patch in the form of winged-wheel with an arrow through the center. Captain Rhodes wore an acorn style breast badge, and Inspector Legg wore an eagle-top acorn style badge.

Patrolmen David W. Clark and Joe Cottingham rolled on a call of a shooting in the 1700 block of Kansas. They found four bodies at the scene and a wounded federal probation officer.

Patrolman Clark chased the shooter to the rear of a frame house. From about 20 feet Clark fired his .38 caliber revolver at the felon, striking him in the shoulder. The fleeing killer was armed with a 30/30 rifle and Clark took cover behind the corner of the house. The felon fired his rifle. The bullet penetrated the frame wall of the house, striking the officer in the side of the head. Officer Clark was dead on arrival at John Gaston Hospital. Clark's killer was shot to death in a subsequent gun battle.

The department determined to reinstitute an emergency unit. Beginning in 1976 emergency response situations such as the incident that resulted in the death of Officer Clark were assigned to a newly formed the Tactical Apprehension and Containment Team or TACT Squad. The unit was composed of thirty-eight specially trained officers. A Hostage Negotiation Team was added to the unit in 1981.

Patrolman Edward J. Hammond Jr. was also killed in 1973. On November 23 he and his partner Billy Bandy were flagged down and told of a man with a shotgun outside the grocery at Chelsea and McNeil. They arrived at the scene and ordered the man to drop the weapon. The gunman fired one shot that struck Officer Hammond in the face. Bandy returned the fire. Both Hammond and his shooter were dead on the scene.

Patrolman McCord L. Springfield was the first black Memphis police officer to be killed in the line of duty. Springfield and his partner R. C. Sandidge answered a call at 11:30 on Saturday morning, March 12, 1977. As they neared College and McLemore, a woman flagged them down and told them she was shot

Officer Michael D. Wright Jr., left, was killed when a tractor-trailer turned into the path of his patrol car as he chased a speeder on September 9, 1972. Patrolmen David W. Clark, right, was killed on May 21, 1973, by a felon armed with a 30/30 rifle.

340

at from an apartment on College. Patrolmen H. L Thompson and H. C. Parker also reached the scene and covered the rear. Springfield and Sandidge entered the front. Springfield was covering a side door to the apartment when a gunman appeared and shot him point blank in the chest. Sandidge was wounded in the face during the gun battle.

Springfield was able to get off three shots before he went down. One of the shots hit the gunman and he retreated back into the apartment. Thompson and Parker entered the apartment and followed a trail of blood to a back bedroom where the gunman crouched beside the bed. As the officers entered the dimly lit room the gunman shot at them and Thompson fired three rapid shots. All three bullets hit the gunman and he was pronounced dead at the scene. Officers Springfield and Sandidge were rushed to the hospital. Springfield died of his chest wound in the emergency room.

In 1978 negotiations between the city and the Memphis Police Association went poorly. So much so

that most police officers went out on strike on August 10. The department was left in the hands of supervisors and a few officers. Law enforcement in the city was augmented by regular and reserve deputies of the Shelby County Sheriff's Office, the Tennessee Highway Patrol and 600 members of the National Guard. A contract was ratified by officers on August 18, ending the eight day strike.

The Criminal Investigation Division was restructured in March 1979. The criminal and special investigative bureaus were reorganized into Administrative Control, responsible for administrative duties; General Investigation, providing around-the-clock general investigation; and Special Investigation, providing in-depth investigations. Tom Marshall was promoted to chief inspector and named chief of detectives, becoming the first black officer to hold a top command post.

Chief Inspector Marshall joined the Memphis force in 1951 and was a member of the second class of black recruits. He walked a beat, served on the homi-

The first integrated class of recruits graduated from the Armour Training Academy on June 1, 1964. The class consisted of four black officers and 20 white officers. Those seated in the front row from left to right were Morris W. Biggs, Jessie C. Noe, Robert J. Lecuyer, Victory S. Thayer, Robert E. Cawthorne, James R. Acup, Michael B. Vaughn, and William S. Hardy. Standing in the second row were Academy Commander-Inspector J. K. Caughley, James W. Smith, Tommy L. McGowan, Frank A. Fracchia, Clayborne H. Manuel, William L. Srygley, Jerry R. Moses, Richard P. Furr, Mack Hughes, Cleveland Davis, Billy G. Cox, and Assistant Academy Commander-Lieutenant James L. Burgess. The third row were Odis E. Hoggard George T. Davis, Ronald L. McKinney, George E. Harris, Ervin Malone, and Arnold Speight.

Patrolman Edward J. Hammond Jr., left, was shot in the face by a man with a shotgun and killed on November 23, 1973. Patrolman McCord L. Springfield, right, answered a call on March 12, 1977, of someone shooting from an apartment on College. Springfield was shot point blank in the chest as he covered a side door. Springfield was the first black Memphis police officer to be killed in the line of duty.

cide squad and climbed through the ranks in various command roles. In 1981 Marshall was promoted to deputy chief for field operations in charge of the uniform patrol. He was third in command of the department when he retired from the MPD in 1984. Two years after he retired from the police force, he joined that Shelby County Sheriff's Office as assistant deputy chief and served in the position until 2000.

Deputy Director John D. Holt was appointed second in command in June 1979. He replaced Michael S. "Mickey" Jones, who had served in the position since 1977.

The badges of the Memphis Police Department were changed in 1979. The badge for the patrolman remained a pinched shield. The city seal replaced the state seal at the center of the new custom designed shield. The badge was silver tone with full color enamel seal and designations. The hat badge was changed as well. The form remained the same but the state seal was replaced with the city seal. The badge style of supervisory ranks, sergeants and above, changed to a new form of the acorn with the city seal in full color.

Wearing the badge continued to be a dangerous occupation. Seven officers lost their life in the line of duty from December 1978 to December 1982. Patrolman J. N. Bush Jr. was killed instantly when struck by a vehicle on December 29, 1978 as he investigated an accident on South Third Street. Motorcycle Officer James L. Jefferson was killed on August 18, 1979, after he was struck by an automobile. Motorcycle Officer Charles L. Harrison was killed when he was struck by an automobile in I-240 conges-

tion on May 6, 1782. Gawkers had slowed to watch activity on the expressway and Harrison collided with two cars, flipping him and his motorcycle.

Lieutenant Clarence P. Cox Jr. was found shot to death beside his patrol car on May 12, 1981. Cox had been shot in the head with his service revolver on North Lauderdale by an escapee. Cox's killer fled to Jackson, Tennessee, and killed a priest during a break-in before Jackson officers arrested him.

Lieutenant Ronald D. Oliver was killed a few months later, on August 5, 1981. Oliver responded to a silent alarm at Wendy's Restaurant on North Thomas about 10:30 p.m. Patrolman Aubrey Stoddard arrived on the scene as Oliver exited the restaurant with a suspect who was later shown to have robbed the business with a .45 automatic pistol.

The armed robber broke from Oliver and ran. The two officers wrestled him to the ground but he came up firing the .45. Oliver was hit in the chest and killed. Stoddard was knocked to the ground from an arm wound. The killer ran but was captured just over an hour later.

A few months later two armed robbers posing as plain clothes policemen, entered a house on Shady Grove, tied up the occupants and began to ransack the house. The night of January 14, 1982, was very cold with snow on the ground. Officers Larry P. Childress and James E. Knauff had stopped for dinner at 7:30 p.m. on Poplar. An occupant of the house on Shady Grove managed to free herself and call authorities. The two policemen pushed their food aside when they got the call and responded to the scene.

Knauff went to the front door and Childress moved down the side of the house toward the rear. The

Patrolman J. N. Bush Jr., left, was killed instantly when struck by a vehicle on December 29, 1978. Motorcycle Officer James L. Jefferson, right, was killed on August 18, 1979, after he was struck by an automobile.

armed bandits fled the back of the house and exchanged shots with Childress. Officers found Childress lying in the snow. He died about an hour later. His killers were captured that evening and later convicted of his murder.

Officer Charlotte Creasy and Police Trainee John Wesley Sykes Jr. thought they were making a routine traffic stop on December 31, 1982. They did not know that they were about to confront two desperate armed robbers. Sykes had graduated from the police academy only 13 days earlier.

Creasy and Sykes saw a beat-up Pontiac being driven erratically. When they attempted a stop, a high-speed chase developed. They lost sight of the car, but then spotted it in a dark cove with it's lights out. As they turned into the cove the lights of the Pontiac came on and the car sped directly toward them. Bullets tore into the squad car, one creasing trainee Sykes's bullet proof vest and entering his throat. He died less than two hours later.

The department reinstituted a Mounted Patrol in 1982. Duties of the unit included parades, crowd control and routine patrol of the downtown area. A garage located at Fourth and Jefferson was converted to a barn for horses.

The only horse of the modern unit to die in the line of duty was "Bay," an 11-year veteran of the Memphis Mounted Police Unit. Bay died while on duty at Madison and Danny Thomas Boulevard at 11:45 a.m. on Wednesday, March 4, 1998. The 18-year-old horse apparently died of a heart attack.

Lieutenant Ronald D. Oliver, left, was killed on August 5, 1981, as he wrestled with a bandit armed with a .45 automatic pistol. Lieutenant Clarence P. Cox Jr., right, was found shot to death beside his patrol car on North Lauderdale on May 12, 1981. Cox had been shot in the head with his service revolver by an escapee.

Officer Richard Millen had been Bay's rider for ten years. Six horses remained in the unit.

The new Criminal Justice Center was occupied in 1982. The command structure was realigned in 1983 and consisted of Director John D. Holt, Deputy Director Alva L. Williams who functioned as chief, four deputy chiefs and three chief inspectors who functioned as night chiefs.

The standard shoulder patch was redesigned in 1982. The new shield shaped patch had a navy blue background to better blend with duty shirts. Specialized unit patches were designed using the same shield form with varying motifs as insignia for the various units of the department such as the Dog Squad, Mounted Unit, TACT and others. Navy fabric baseball caps were authorized including an open-mesh version for summer wear. Shoulder patches were applied to caps as insignia. Navy windbreaker and black leather jackets were available as protect against the weather.

The line of duty death of Patrolman Robert S. Hester in January 1983 affected Memphis officers as much as any event in its history. A purse snatching was reported on January 11 and a suspect was identified that led officers to a house on Shannon Street. A dozen or more members of a self-proclaimed religious cult had gathered at the residence to drink wine and smoke marijuana.

At 9:04 p.m. Patrolmen Hester and Ray O. Schwill arrived at the small house and went inside. They immediately realized they were in the midst of a hostile, out of control group. They radioed for assistance and tried to back out of the house. Suddenly they were fighting for their lives. Schwill was shot in the face

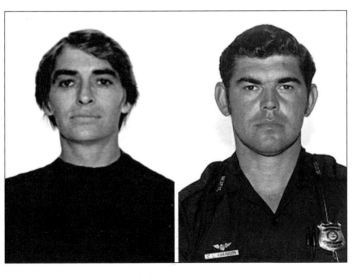

Officers Larry P. Childress, left, was shot and killed by armed bandits on January 14, 1982, while investigating a house where occupants were being held and robbed. Officer Charles L. Harrison, right, was struck and killed by an automobile in I-240 congestion on May 6, 1982.

with his own gun, but managed to escape the clutches of the mob. Officer Hester was overpowered, disarmed and dragged back into the house.

Patrolmen Thomas W. Turner and William R. Aiken arrived on the scene. Turner entered the house but was hit in the head and knocked back outside. Aiken went into the house firing. He retreated to reload and went back inside. When he was out of ammunition for his sidearm he retrieved the shotgun from his car and returned to the house. Other officers arrived on the scene but they were unable to reach Hester.

A thirty hour stand-off followed. Negotiators tried to communicate with the leader of the gang, but it was apparent he was mentally unstable and intended to kill the officer. Policemen outside could hear Hester calling for help as he was beaten by the group. Supervisors at the scene feared that attacking the house would lead to Hester being immediately killed. Soon the greater fear was that he would be killed if something was not done quickly.

At 3:05 a.m. on Thursday, January 13, 1983, TACT officers fired numerous Ferret tear gas cartridges into the house followed by several flash-bang grenades. The TACT Squad forced entry through the rear of the house. As they swept the house they were fired on and returned fire. Hester's body was found in the front room and he was carried to the porch for medical attention. TACT officers again swept the house returning fire on those inside. When the tear gas cleared the seven culprits who had remained in the house were found dead.

Examination of Patrolman Robert S. Hester's body revealed that he had been dead for some twelve hours

Officers assigned to the new MPD Crime Scene Squad gathered evidence as a specialized part of crime investigations.

before the assault on the house. He had been severely beaten with his own weapon and flashlight.

Police Service Technicians began service in 1984. This cadre of civilian employees wore khaki uniforms and worked traffic details and accidents. The group was an entry level opportunity for individuals interested in becoming sworn officers. Only a year later the first PST lost his life in the line of duty. PST Booker T. Shaw Jr. was struck by a truck in November 1985 and died the next month.

The rank structure for uniformed patrol officers was revised in 1985. Police Officer I rank was assigned to new officers in training, Police Officer II became the rank for basic police officers and Police Officer III specified officers with greater investigative or other work responsibility.

The Memphis Police Department included 1173 sworn officers in January 1987. The department was composed of a director, a deputy director (chief), 4 deputy chiefs, 3 chief inspectors, 8 inspectors, 57 captains, 138 lieutenants, 8 police technicians, 240 sergeants/investigators/police officer IIIs, 692 police officer IIs and 21 police officer Is (recruits).

Dress uniforms for staff level commanding officers, inspectors and above, changed from navy pants, shirts and jackets to navy two-piece uniform suits with white shirts. A fourth shift of uniform patrol was implemented and given the radio identification code Delta. The code was previously used by the Dog Squad, so canine units adopted the code Kilo.

The dangers faced by a street cop never relented, not even for the holidays. On Christmas Eve afternoon 1987 Patrolman Timothy A. Beacham stopped someone he suspected of driving under the influence. The subject suddenly attacked Beacham, seizing his pistol and shooting him four times. The shooter fled to a house at 4414 Ernie and barricaded himself inside. Forcible entry was made early Christmas morning after a 12-hour siege. The suspect was fatally shot. The incident left Officer Beacham permanently paralyzed from the waist down.

Leadership of the department changed on January 5, 1988, when the City Council appointed James E. Ivy director. Ivy was the first black officer to serve as director of police services and held the post for four years. Deputy Director Don O. Lewis, appointed in February 1986, continued as chief of the force. Director Ivy and Deputy Director Lewis promoted Inspector Eddie Adair to deputy chief of Uniform Patrol and Chief Inspector W. J. Craven to deputy chief for Special Operations.

Other command promotions made in 1988 included that of inspectors James R. Aylor, George

The Memphis Police Department Helicopter Squad was formed in 1969 with four pilots and a Bell helicopter. Insignia was painted on the engine cowl of the aircraft. The air unit of the force quickly became important in tasks from enforcement to search and rescue.

Harris, H. E. Randle and William L. Reed to chief inspectors. R. L. Brown, D. L. Dugger, H. A. Embrey, W. P. Oldham, G. L. Stacy and D. A. Moore were promoted from captain to inspector.

A number of firsts for female officers occurred in 1988. Lieutenant Armer Jean Torrance was promoted to captain and assumed command of the Sex Crimes Squad. Captain Torrance was the first black female captain and the first woman to head a major detective unit. Police Officer II Jane T. Martin completed specialized training and went to work in the Dog Squad as its first female officer. Dawn E. Anishanslin completed specialized training and became the first female TACT Squad member.

The John D. Holt Training Academy opened in 1988 to provide state-of-the-art training for Memphis recruits and officers from surrounding agencies. The facility included several classrooms, a 150-seat auditorium, gymnasium, weight room, driving range and indoor-outdoor firing range. Inspector Bill Oldham was named commanding officer of the academy. Oldham joined the MPD in 1972 and was executive captain of the North Precinct.

Among actions directly affecting the public Director Ivy appointed a 15-member Police Advisory

Patrolman Robert S. Hester, left, was taken captive by a mob in a house on Shannon Street, and was beaten to death on January 13, 1983. Police Trainee John Wesley Sykes Jr., right, graduated from the police academy 13 days before he and his partner make a routine traffic stop on December 31, 1982. Two armed robbers shot the young officer in the throat.

The Memphis police Helicopter Squad was formed in 1969 using a single Bell Hilicopter. The unit included pilots kneeling from left to right Lieutenant Larry Joe Cook, Commander of the squad Captian Glenn Moore and Lieutenant Jimmy A. Dungan; and officers standing from left to right Lavern "Larry" Childers, Larry Childress, Joe Bixler, Don Smith, Carroll Langston and Leonard Biggs.

Council to advise him on citizen concerns. The group did not review police actions. Implementation of countywide 911 emergency reporting was completed on February 2, 1988. Operation HEAT, Help Eliminate Auto Theft, began in 1989. Participating motorists were provided a bright yellow sticker for their car and any stickered car on the street between midnight and 6 a.m. was stopped and checked to be certain it was not being stolen.

A number of units were created or reorganized in the late eighties. The Child Abuse Squad became operational in 1987 when the detail was separated from the Adult Sex Crimes Squad. Walter Crews was one of two lieutenants in the Child Abuse Squad and upon his promotion to major he took commanded the unit. Crews worked patrol for over a decade before promo-

tion to sergeant and assignment as a homicide detective in 1980. He also served in internal affairs and as an instructor at the academy.

The Crisis Intervention Team was formed in 1988 under the leadership of Major Walter Crews to respond to calls involving mentally ill persons. Team members were volunteers and were trained by mental health professionals. The team was equipped with stun guns, Velcro wraps, extraction hooks, shields and other items necessary to control mental case calls with minimal force. The team became a national acknowledged as the "Memphis Model" and received many citations for its success. A year later the Family Trouble Center was opened to assist victims of spousal abuse. When Crews was promoted command of the unit was given to Lieutenant Sam Cochran. By 1991 the Crisis

All of the female officers of the Memphis Police Department, commissioned and noncommissioned, were given 200 hours and re-commissioned on May 15, 1970. Women in the front row of the class from left to right were Betty J. Coats, Kathleen N. Henry, Eva Gatlin, Frances Weyerbacher, Ann Felts, Joanne Moore, Louise Dunavant, and Ina A. "Billy" Bruno; and in the second row Sue Siko Hester, Katie Ernestine Fitzhugh, Mrs. Eichelberger, Elsie Whitten, Claudine Penn, Mary Sample Fowler, Elzeta Warren, and Parlie Douglas. Claudine Penn was the department's first female black officer, employed as a metermaid on September 16, 1963. The commanding officers standing from left to right in front of the group were Lieutenant Tom Moxley, Inspector H. H. Leatherwood, and Captain Earl Clark.

Intervention Team grew from 32 members to 88 members and answered about 5,000 calls a year

The Psychological Services Bureau was reorganized under a new director, Dr. Jerry Sparger, who was chairman of the Memphis State University Criminal Justice Department. He and two of his associates worked on a part-time or as-needed basis.

The Violent Crimes Squad was divided into the Homicide Squad and the Robbery Squad. The Homicide Squad investigated kidnapping for ransom with threat of death, conspiracy to murder, homicide and major extortion. The Robbery Squad handled all robberies of businesses, residences and individuals. Working hours for both units was 8:00 a.m. to 4:00 p.m., seven days a week. The MPD withdrew from the 17-year old Metro Narcotics Squad and shifted responsibility and personnel to the Organized Crime Unit.

The Special Services Branch of the Special Operations Division was restructured to include Aviation, Court Officers, Dog Squad, Harbor Patrol, Mounted Patrol, Reserve Bureau, Specialized Patrol and the TACT Unit.

The 12-team Dog Squad was under the command of Lieutenant Bo Wheeler. Dogs used were German Shepherds, Labrador Retrievers and similar canines, often mixed breeds. They were often selected from dogs found at the pound and showing alertness, persistence and a keen nose

Dogs were trained to sniff out drugs and bombs, run toward live gunfire, search darkened buildings and apprehend armed suspects. It took 14 weeks to train a dog for police work and 10 weeks for the canine to learn to find hidden drugs and explosives.

Canine officers were often even more exposed to danger in the line of duty than their handlers. Fido, a German Shepherd, was killed in 1982 and his handler Officer Al Pinnow wounded when they were shot during an altercation. A number of years earlier Samson was killed when he collided with a passing car while chasing a suspected auto thief across a street.

Bandit, a black German Shepherd, and Patrolman Andy Trautman were chasing a pair of suspected auto thieves through an alley in 1988 when one of the fleeing suspects turned and fired at Trautman. Bandit leapt and sank his teeth into the man's arm. The gunman pressed a .357 Magnum against the dog's side and pulled the trigger.

Bandit limped out of the alley and lay on the ground. Both suspects were captured and Trautman rushed Bandit to an emergency veterinary clinic. The bullet had passed through Bandit's chest without hitting any bones or vital organs. He was back on the job in two weeks. Lieutenant Wheeler reported, "The only thing different about Bandit now is that he absolutely hates gunfire. If you're out there firing a gun and Bandit hears you, you better get rid of that gun in a hurry."

Two bloodhounds, Elvis and Red, joined the Dog Squad in February 1998, the first bloodhounds in the squad since 1960. Patrolman Bob Davis was Elvis' handler and Patrolman Wayne Murdock handled Red.

Rank titles for all officers with the title Patrol Officer III, Investigator I and Police Technician were changed to the more common title of Sergeant in April 1989. Use of the rank Commander began the following year to distinguish those with the rank Captain from the 30-year captains.

The department went through significant changes in personnel and organization in the nineties. Deputy Director of Operations Don O. Lewis, second in command of the department, retired in 1990 at the age of 50 after 30 years service. Lewis was promoted to deputy chief in 1986 after being in charge of police administration and prior to that commanding the violent crimes squad and the South Precinct.

Deputy Chief for Administration Ted Beasley was named deputy director in February 1990. Other deputy chiefs were Fred Warner, Al Embrey and Eddie Adair. Chief Inspector Josh Randle was promoted to deputy chief for administration. Other promotions included East Precinct commander Inspector Sam Moses to chief inspector, Organized Crime Unit Commander Larry Goodwin to inspector and Lieutenant Curtis Williams of crime prevention to commander. Lieutenant Vic Thayer, a 27-year veteran of the MPD, was named administrative assistant to Director Ivy replacing John Bennett.

Another round of reassignments was prompted by the retirement of Deputy Chief Al Embrey in February 1991. Inspector Bill Oldham was promoted to deputy chief and Inspector Larry Goodwin was named commander of the MPD training academy in Oldham's place. Goodwin, with the department since 1970, was previously head of the organized crime and specialized patrol units. Commander Joseph Laurenzi was promoted to inspector over special operations.

Equipment changes were intended to aid officers in doing their job more effectively and to improved

officer safety. Following a yearlong study the department adopted 9mm pistols with 15-shot clips to replace 6-shot revolvers as the standard sidearm for Memphis officers. The weapon was selected for dependability, reliability, better accuracy and firepower. The expense for purchase of the new handguns was included in the 1992 city budget.

Patrol car markings were redesigned in 1992 to make vehicles more contemporary and increase their visibility. A blue and gold horizontal stripe was applied to the length of white squad cars. "Memphis Police" was imprinted on the vehicle and "911" placed at the top of the rear fenders. Cars were routinely replaced after they had been in service for 60,000 miles or 3 years. New vehicles were prepared for service at the Armour Center on Flicker.

Dave Ashmore, manager of technical services for the MPD, prepared new patrol cars by adding decals, roof lights and prisoner screens. Back seats were replaced with seats that sat nearly on the floor, were easily cleaned and hard to hide weapons or evidence behind. The 1993 budget included $3.1 million for the purchase of 250 new marked police cars. The Metro DUI unit got 12 video cameras and recorders for gathering evidence against suspects in traffic stops. The unit already had three cameras.

Police Inspector Melvin Thomas Burgess was chosen by Mayor Willie Herenton to become police director in January 1992. Burgess started as a beat officer on Beale Street 30 years earlier. He served in homicide, robbery, juvenile crimes, and vice and narcotics squads. Burgess stated his creed "work hard and take chances" when he assumed command of the 1,448 commissioned officers, 868 in the uniform patrol.

PST Booker T. Shaw Jr., left, was struck by a truck in November 1985 and died the following month. Officer John E. Reeve, right, was responding to a burglar alarm on September 9, 1991, when he lost control of his patrol car on Chelsea at Peres and crashed into a utility pole, killing him.

The remainder of the MPD command in 1992 were Deputy Director Eddie B. Adair, Deputy Chief of Investigative Services Fred Warner, Deputy Chief of Special Operations Jim Music, Deputy Chief of Administration Bill Oldham, Deputy Chief of Uniform Patrol Walter J. Winfrey and Chief Inspectors John M. Johnson, George Larry Stacy, Samuel M. Moses and George E. Harris.

Director Burgess eliminated the Vice Squad, the Specialized Patrol and reduced the Motorcycle Squad from two shifts to one. The department set a new policy to limit high-speed vehicular chases. The new policy authorized officers to initiate a high-speed chase only if the suspect was a violent felon. Under the new policy chasing a stolen vehicle was prohibited but a high-speed chase of bank robbers was allowed.

One bank robber was chased down by members of Memphis' bike patrol on August 31, 1993. Bicycle Patrolmen Mark Winters and David Parks were on patrol downtown when a bank robbery call went out. The two chased the bandit for three blocks and captured him in a downtown fast-food restaurant only 9 minutes after he did the robbery. "He had that surprised look on his face," said Patrolman Winters. Bicycle officers had recently began patrolling downtown on 21-speed mountain bikes paid for by downtown merchants.

A January 1994 reorganization created two patrol districts. District One included the North, South and East precincts and District Two included Central and West precincts. Deputy Chief William P. Oldham took command of District One, TACT, Aviation, Mounted Patrol, Dog Squad and the Harbor Patrol. Deputy Chief George L. Stacy headed Division Two, Traffic, DUI Squad, Warrants, Reserves and the School Safety

Night patrol on Beale Street.

Unit. Deputy Chief John M. Johnson headed Administrative Services and Deputy Chief Walter J. Winfrey commanded Investigative Services.

The Downtown Precinct was created and designated the Sixth Precinct. It operated out of the Beale Street Station along side the Police Museum and began operations on January 3, 1994. Command of the Downtown Precinct was given to Major Tommy Tabor who helped lead the push for the new one-on-one policing. He began Operation Saturation, a business version of Neighborhood Watch, and emphasized the bike patrol and walking patrol. He also stressed the importance of the police being the "ambassadors" of the city to tourists.

Tabor was transferred to the South Precinct, the department's busiest territory, in May. Major James Campbell, a 24-year veteran and native of Whiteville, Tennessee, took command of the 52-officer Downtown Precinct, moving from the West Precinct. Major Bob Wright took command of the Downtown Precinct in April 1995.

The department adopted community-oriented policing citywide. The first COACT unit was established in the Orange Mound/Binghampton area as a part of the Community Police Program in 1994.

In May 1994 Mayor Herenton named Deputy Chief of Investigations Walter J. Winfrey as interim director of police. Winfrey joined the MPD in 1968 and had formerly headed the uniformed patrol division and internal affairs. Augustus F. Brown was named deputy chief of investigations, S. M. Moses became deputy chief over the West, Central and Downtown precincts, Traffic Division and Harbor Patrol.

The department lost a command officer to gunfire in 1994. Major Rufus Gates, assistant commander of

Mounted officers and bicycle officers of the Memphis police escorted a neighborhood 4th of July parade.

Memphis police units respond to a call in a residential district. The cruiser on the left had the markings adopted in 2000 and the car on the right bears the 1992 design.

the organized crime unit, was shot five times by a South Precinct patrol officer on Friday, November 4, 1994. His injuries included wounds to the chest and abdomen. The incident grew out of a confrontation between Gates and the occupants of van that had struck his SUV outside a football game. Gates, in street clothes, got out of his car and took out his gun when he thought he saw someone in the van with a gun. When a uniformed patrolman arrived on the scene, Gates approached the patrol car with his gun in hand. The patrolman fired thinking his life was being threatened. Gates died three days later.

Director Winfrey appointed Walter E. Crews to the post of Deputy Chief of Special Operations in 1995. Crews had served in the Office of Drug Control Policy, as a shift commander at the West Precinct, and as Commander of the Office of Drug Prevention and Awareness. In 1997 Crews made a lateral move to Deputy Chief of Detectives.

New units were created in the mid-nineties included a Cold Case Unit formed early in 1996. Although an Old Mystery Team existed for years, Captain Mike Houston, a 54-year-old detective and 31-year department veteran, was assigned the specific duty of investigating cold cases. Houston focused on cases over a year old. The one-man unit solved six cases in its first year.

The Metro Domestic Violence Unit, a joint Memphis and Shelby County unit, began operation on Monday, October 27, 1997. The unit was housed on the first floor of the Criminal Justice Center and consisted of six investigators. Lieutenant Brenda Maples supervised the unit.

In June 1998 Deputy Chief Brenda Jones, age 41, became the first female officer to be named deputy

chief. She was given command of specialized units, Street Crime Abatement Team (SCAT), TACT, the newly formed Special Traffic Enforcement Unit (STEU), aviation and canine. Jones joined the department in 1974 as a civilian and became a sworn officer in 1978. She patrolled in the South Precinct, served as a detective in sex crimes and general investigations and headed the Organized Crime Unit as a major.

Two new precincts were opened in the late nineties. The Southeast Precinct was opened in July 1998 at the old Defense Depot on Airways near Ketchum and became the city's seventh precinct. The new precinct had 58 patrol officers and 18 supervisors under the command of Inspector J. W. Laurenzi. In July 1999 the Northeast Precinct's 15,000-square-foot station was constructed near Whitten Road and I-40.

The department lost four officers in traffic accidents in the nineties. Officer John E. Reeve was in a one-man squad car responding to a burglar alarm at 5:45 a.m. on September 9, 1991. He lost control of his patrol car on Chelsea at Peres and crashed into a utility pole. The call was a false alarm.

Officer Dannael James "Danny" Weekes died as a result of an accident on March 7, 1997. The patrol car crashed on wet pavement while he and his partner Patrick Joynt responded to an "officer needs assistance" call. Weekes died six days after the accident. The call was a miscommunication.

A gang of four shoplifters fled from police on October 12, 1999, after being spotted with stolen goods at a shopping center. The time was around 1:00 p.m. and they were driving a stolen Chevrolet Malibu. Officers Tom Warrick and Don Lee Overton in separate cars responded to the call and intercepted the

Major Rufus Gates, left, shot five times by a fellow officer on November 4, 1994, after failing to identify himself. Officer Dannael James Weekes, right, died on March 7, 1997, after a patrol car crash.

chase in progress at Staten and Hollywood. The getaway Malibu barely missed colliding with Officer Warrick and struck the squad car driven by Officer Overton. Firemen had to extricate occupants of both cars. Officer Don Lee Overton died within minutes of reaching the hospital. All four members of the gang were charged with murder.

Less than two months later, early on the morning of December 1, 1999, Officer John H. Robinson Jr. met his death in much the same circumstance as Officer Overton. Two felons robbed a man at a topless club, fired several shots at him and fled in a blue Mazda. Officer Robinson sighted the robbery car and initiated chase at Range Line Road east on Frayser and north on New Allen Road. The felon cut in front of the patrol car and slammed on the brakes. Officer Robinson veered to the right, lost control of the car and crashed into a grove of trees. The chase lasted less than a minute.

Officer John Robinson Jr. had to be extricated from the squad car and was pronounced dead of massive head injuries upon arrival at the hospital. The felons crashed into a metal guard rail and were arrested at the scene. The long-time felons were charged with robbery and murder.

Director Walter Winfrey retired effective April 1, 1999, and Deputy Director Bill Oldham was made interim director of the force. Deputy Chief David Dugger was named second in command and Inspector Mike Dodd was promoted to deputy chief. In December the interim leadership was replaced when the mayor named Deputy Chief Walter Crews as interim police director.

On Thursday, July 13, 2000, Walter E. Crews was appointed director of 1,900-member MPD. The mayor

Memphis Police Department command officers inspect a new helicopter in 2005.

said it was Crews' desire for change that won him the post. Crews was 58 years old and a 31-year veteran of the department. He quickly initiated a reorganization that changed most of the top command positions.

James Bolden, 52, was named deputy director and second in command. Bolden rejoined the department from his position in state government. Dr. Rita Dorsey

Officer Don Lee Overton, left, was killed in high-speed pursuit of thieves on October 12, 1999. Officer John H. Robinson Jr. was killed when his patrol car crashed on December 1, 1999, as he chased two armed robbers.

Officer Anthony Louis Woods entered an apartment near Getwell and American Way on April 26, 2003, in response to a domestic dispute. Officer Woods was shot in the head as he struggled with a gunman who had already killed his girlfriend.

The first Directors of Police Service of the Memphis Police Department in the new millennium were Director Walter Crews, left, who began as acting director in December 1999 and served as director from July 13, 2000 to March 1, 2003. Director James H. Bolden, center, served from March 2003 to November 2004. Director Larry A. Godwin, right, began his tenure as director in November 2004.

was appointed to command the training academy, the first female at the post. An immediate personnel policy change benefited uniformed officers and businesses alike. Police officers were given permission to work second or "moonlighting" jobs in uniform.

The department had recently lost an officer who was moonlighting. Patrolman Don Williams was working as a security guard at a local comedy club on Friday, December 26, 1997. A man that Williams ejected from the establishment returned with a handgun and shot the officer at pointblank range. The bullet hit Williams in the neck, severed his spinal column and left him paralyzed. The 38-year-old policeman with sixteen years on the force died a month later on Thursday, January 29, 1998.

An off duty incident resulted in the death of Patrolman Clayton Wayne Hicks Jr. after only two years on the force. Officer Hicks was at a social gathering on November 14, 2000, when he was confronted about a call he had made earlier while on-duty. The situation led to a physical encounter and Hicks left the house, getting struck on the back of the head as he left.

Officer Hicks went to his car, retrieved his police radio and service weapon and returned to the resi-

dence. Hicks' weapon was at his side as he approached the house. One of the individuals who had confronted him stood in the doorway. As the officer approached the man raised a AK47 assault rifle and shot Hicks multiple times. Policeman Clayton Hicks stumbled approximately 40 yards, collapsed in the driveway next door and died.

Director Crews was concerned about the growth of crime among the youth of Memphis and brought in programs such as Drug Abuse Resistance Education (DARE) and Gang Resistance Education and Training (GREAT). The department also started the Juvenile Violence Abatement Program (JVAP) to work with troubled youth. The program consisting of a 16-hour hotline young people could call to talk about any difficulty they were experiencing. Phones were answered by young people who were able to refer callers to professional help.

One of the major operational changes implemented by Director Crews was the expansion of the overnight detective bureau. The evening shift of the Felony Response Unit that responded to serious crimes was expanded from ten to thirty and the late night/early morning shift from seven to twenty. The action meant cases were investigated while they were still fresh and arrests made more quickly. This reduced the number of probable-cause prisoners following the decision by the county jail not to take probable-cause prisoners due to over crowding. The additional detectives were divided into two groups, property crimes and crimes against individuals, each under the command of a captain or lieutenant.

Patrol cars were given a new look in 2000. The new design featured a diagonal, tomato-red stripe and a much larger "Police" written atop it in blue and yellow. The phone number "545 COPS" was substituted for "911," and a new slogan "Helping people is our business" featured. The design increased the visibility of the units. The helicopter squad was also enhanced.

The department improved communication with the growing Hispanic community in Memphis. Officer Marco Yzguirre was designated as the department's Latino Liaison in February 2001. He was the first officer to hold the position.

Director Walter Crews retired on March 1, 2003. Crews was named executive director of Crime Stoppers in May.

Deputy Director James H. Bolden was named the new director. Bolden was well respected in the department. In 1970 he and his partner Robert Jones were the first black and white officers who rode together in a patrol car on a continuous basis. In 1973 Bolden became the founding president of the Afro-American Police Association and authored the group's motto, "Save ourselves from ourselves."

The new deputy director named was 28-year veteran Deputy Chief Ray Schwill. The South Precinct commander was strong on community policing and a decisive leader. Other command staff included District 1 Deputy Chief Charles Cook, District 2 Deputy Chief Janice Pilot, Investigative Services Deputy Chief Alfred Gray, Special Operations Deputy Chief Larry Godwin, Administrative Deputy Chief Mary Wright and Training Academy Commander Jimmy Kelly.

An incident on April 26, 2003, once again demonstrated the danger of a domestic violence call. Police Officer II Anthony Louis Woods, age 35 and a 7-year veteran of the force, entered an apartment near Getwell and American Way. The resident of the unit had been shot by her boyfriend. Woods struggled with the gunman and was shot once in the head. The shooter then turned the weapon on himself and committed suicide.

Less that a year later, March 30, 2004, at 1:42 a.m. Police Officer II Marlon Allen Titus was killed while on patrol on Park Avenue in Orange Mound. The 28-year-old officer was responding to a call to meet his

partner related to an incident at a convenience store. His car went out of control, hit a metal sign, crashed into a restaurant and spun into another building. The gregarious young officer was only two years on the job and had transferred to the Southeast Precinct the year before.

The senior command of patrol was all female for the first time following the assignment of Deputy Chief Mary Wright as commander of the District One uniform patrol in May 2004. She replaced Deputy Chief Charles Cook on his retirement. Deputy Chief Wright joined with Deputy Chief Janice Pilot, commander of District Two, to command the entire 1,400-member patrol force.

A significant equipment decision was made in 2004. The 89th and 90th Basic Police Session was the first group of officers to be issued the newly adopted .40 caliber SIG P229 pistol as the department's official duty weapon.

The top command of the department changed in November 2004 with the appointment of Larry A. Godwin as director of police services. Director Godwin joined the MPD in 1973 following his service with the Marine Corps in Vietnam. He began his law enforcement career as an officer in Metro Narcotics. Godwin later served as a uniform patrolman, member of the tactical unit, training academy instructor, homicide investigator, and fraud and document investigator.

Director Godwin was promoted to lieutenant in 1992 and served as shift supervisor in the Crime Response/Bomb Unit. On promotion to major in 1998 he took command of the unit. In 2001 Godwin was promoted to inspector and made Commander of Special Services and in April 2003 he was promoted to Director of Special Operations for the department.

Major Ernest Dobbins, commander of the Tactical Unit, was named Deputy Director. Dobbins established his leadership abilities in supervising major, multiple-agency drug operations. He also organized and trained the Street Crime Abatement Team (SCAT) and the Gang Unit. Other members of the MPD's senior command were Deputy Chief Uniform Patrol Janice Pilot, Deputy Chief Investigative Services Michael Lee, Deputy Chief Special Operations Annette Taylor, Deputy Chief Uniform Patrol Bobby Todd and Deputy Chief Administrative Services Jim Tusant.

The men and women who wear the badge of the Memphis Police Department have a venerable history of service and sacrifice. Today the Memphis force is the largest police agency in the state of Tennessee with total personnel of nearly 3,000, including about 2,000 sworn officers. The department responds to nearly a million calls each year and makes over 80,000 arrests.

Town Constable John J. Balch, the tinker and part-time lawman that kept the peace in the frontier river town of 1827, would undoubtedly be amazed by today's well trained professional police officers and the technology they use to enforce the law. Yet much of the rough and tumble of police work continues and Constable Balch would well understand the bravery and dedication to duty of today's officers.

Knoxville Police Department

Knoxville was an infant settlement in 1791 when Governor William Blount took up residence on the banks of the Watauga. Blount was commissioned "governor of the territory south of the river Ohio" by President George Washington. Governor Blount decided to make the settlement the seat of government and named it Knoxville in honor of Major General Henry Knox, Secretary of War.

The settlement was a thicket of brushwood and grape vines except for a small area on the river front where business was done. Lots were marked off and offered at public sale for $8 each. Families lived mostly in forts and when they went out to cultivate the fields, a guard was stationed for protection from the Cherokees.

The village outpost grew when a two-story blockhouse fort was built after the Cherokee declaration of war in 1792. The young town was described by a visitor in 1794, "Here are frame houses and brick chimneys. There is in it ten stores and seven taverns, beside tippling house, one Court House. No prison which they boast of as not being an article of necessity." When Tennessee was made a state in 1796, Knoxville became the state's first capitol and remained the seat of state until 1815 when the capitol was moved to Murfreesboro.

Law enforcement in the earliest day was under the responsibility of three commissioners who were appointed to establish "rules and regulations" for the town. The commission was expanded to five in 1794, Colonel John King, John Chisholm, Joseph Greer, George Roulstone and Samuel Cowan. After Tennessee became a state, commissioners were elected. The commission named citizen officers to enforce the laws of the town.

The first ordinances of Knoxville were written in four articles for peace and safety within the town limits. The first article required that streets be kept clear of filth; prohibited the building of slaughter houses, wooden chimneys and privies with pits less than six feet deep; and required that wells be enclosed. The second article prohibited the assembly of slaves in streets, kitchens, or uninhabited houses on Sunday or at night. The third outlawed running horses or carriages on the streets, allowing horses to run at large and prohibited the firing guns or pistols. The fourth restricted non-religious activity on the Sabbath and required that stores be closed. Breaking an ordinance was punishable by a fine in the amount of fifty cents for each offense.

By 1800, the population of Knoxville was 387. The Town Council met in 1802 to appoint a Town Sergeant to serve as the town's law enforcement officer. Joseph R. Reed was chosen. His duties included patrolling the streets at least two nights a week, seeing that Sunday church services were not disturbed, executing court processes and carrying out punishments as directed by the commissions. Town Sergeant Reed's salary was $80 per year, paid semi-annually.

Knoxville was incorporated as a city by the Tennessee General Assembly on October 27, 1815, with a mayor and aldermen style government. Seven aldermen were elected and they selected Thomas Emmerson as the city's first mayor. The title Town Constable was used for the law enforcement officer of the municipality, who was often referred to by the title High Constable as well. He reported to the mayor. The board of mayor and aldermen elected or appointed a town constable at the beginning of each year and other lawmen as needed. From time to time, the board also appointed night watchmen to patrol the town from 9:00 p.m. to dawn. Watchmen were required to call out the hour on each hour of their tour and state the weather conditions.

By 1815 town ordinances were expanded and penalties increased. Fines included $.50 for running or galloping on any street, $5 for tying a stud or jack to a mare on any street, $.50 for firing a gun, $5 for selling merchandise on the Sabbath, $10 for digging a well unless enclosed, $10 for carrying a torch or candle without enclosure, $2 for building a fire in the street, $.50 per 24 hours for leaving firewood, manure, or filth on street, $.50 per 48 hours for privy unless sunk 6 feet deep and $20 for keeping a gaming house. Activities that might cause a fire among the wooden structures of the town were serious matters. Penalties for offenses by slaves were either fines and lashes.

The title Town Marshal was given to the main law enforcement officer in 1840, although the title Town Constable continued to be used as well. D. J. Stacks was appointed town marshal in 1840 and continued in the position for a number of years. The town marshal was given the authority to collect taxes in 1842, although the duty was assigned to others at times.

Marshal Stacks was reputed to be an effective enforcer of the city's laws. He carried a cowhide lash inside a cane on his tour of the streets and used the whip to persuade lawbreakers to disburse. In the early years of his service, he was the city's only lawmen on duty during the day. A nightwatch continued to maintain peace during the evening hours.

The marshal was instructed in 1849 to "summon four responsible citizens" to assist in patrolling the streets. This citizen patrol of "assistant watchmen" was unpaid. The board also allowed Marshal Stacks to "hire a suitable place in the town at as low a price per month as he can for the convenience of the police or patrol during the night." The annual rent was $100 for this first police headquarters of Knoxville. Beginning in 1850, the calaboose or city lockup was located on the first floor of a building on Cumberland Street. The second floor was used for private parties. The calaboose was moved to Prince Street in 1858 and was used as a cage for unruly and disorderly prisoners until the late 1860s.

Growth of the city led to a need for more and better organized police. The Tennessee General Assembly expanded the power of the city board in February 1852 and gave them the authority "to regulate the police of the city." Fuller Ryan was appointed assistant marshal in 1854 to help Marshal Stacks but served for less than a year. Elijah Dunn replaced Ryan. A year later, James Nelson was selected to be a second assistant marshal to Stacks.

The marshal and his two assistants were the police force during the day and the nightwatch was the night police. With minor changes this structure continued until the Civil War. The police force in 1855 and 1856 consisted of Marshal Stacks and Assistant Marshals William Smith and Columbus Carliss. Charles Morrow was named the city's "lamp lighter" in 1855 and he also had the powers of an assistant marshal.

M. V. Bridwell was selected the city's chief law enforcement officer in January 1857 and given the title Chief of Police, although he was still referred to as marshal. Former Marshal D. J. Stacks and Assistant Marshal Charles Morrow were appointed Bridwell's assistant marshals. Bridwell's uniform was a gray cloth coat, with standing collar and long Prince Albert cut. It was adorned in front by a row of brass buttons. This was the first police uniform worn in Knoxville. The first breast badge worn by policemen was a shield with a star cut out in the center.

Two years later, 1859, the city decided to formalize the nightwatch into a night police force. Chief Bridwell took over responsibilities as night chief of police. The remainder of the night force were assistant marshals D. J. Stacks and Marshal Pesterfield. A new chief of police, S. P. Waddell, was selected for the day shift. He was assisted by Charles Morrow and Calvin Zachery.

The position of chief of police was combined with that of tax collector and market master in 1860 and assigned to Marshal Pesterfield. However, these duties were divided the following year. Chief of Police Pesterfield took the law enforcement duties and William Knott was elected tax collector and market zmaster.

Chief Pesterfield remained the city's chief law

enforcement officer until his death in June 1862 from a bullet wound sustained in the line of duty. The chief of police was on duty at the railroad depot when he was struck by an errant bullet. After Tennessee joined the Confederacy, soldiers were constantly on the move in the city. Maintaining law and order with masses of young soldiers in town was a challenge and the chief was frequently at the train station where troops congregated to be shipped out.

Chief Pesterfield was standing on the platform at the railroad depot when a soldier accidentally dropped his musket. The weapon fired and the shot struck the chief in the ankle. The ball lodged in Pesterfield's ankle and he failed to have it removed or get medical attention. Complications of the wound later claimed his life. William Knott, the tax collector and market master, took on the responsibilities of chief of police, but his service in the role was brief.

In October 1862 martial law was declared in Knoxville. Although both Union and Confederate sympathies were strong among the population in and around Knoxville, the Confederate Army made Knoxville its headquarters for northeast Tennessee. Colonel Woods of the Fifteenth Alabama regiment took command of the enforcement of martial law.

Civilian marshals continued law enforcement duty in addition to military policing, but jurisdiction and duty between the two groups was confused and muddled. The ever-present conflict on the streets of the city was often made worse by disagreements between the military and civilian police authorities.

The city employed additional police officers, but the situation did not improve. There was discussion among members of the Board of Mayor and Aldermen about city officers assisting military guards in keeping order. The mayor responded, "The Police of the city could not render the Military any service whatever in preserving the peace and order of the city."

Diminishing financial resources meant the city could no longer pay the full salary of the police force. The board considered keeping the four existing officers at half their normal pay but decided it was better to reduce the force by three. One marshal was retained by the city to collect taxes.

As the fortunes of the South's military changed, so did the occupation of the city. Confederate forces lost the city in August 1863 and moved out. Union troops moved in but provided no law enforcement function for the local population. Without the Confederate guards to maintain some semblance of law and order, crime became rampant throughout the city. Union

commanders allowed Mayor J. C. Luttrell and city officials to hire a police force. The mayor appointed veteran Knoxville lawman Captain M. V. Bridwell to serve as chief of police. Chief Bridwell selected thirteen officers to serve on the force, William Bice, Pat Cain, Benjamin Camp, W. W. Dunn, William Fischer, Larkin Gammon, John Griffin, John Jones, Thomas Jordan, John Kennedy, Rusus Kennedy, Lazarus Osborne and John Rice.

The wartime patrolmen were assigned two per ward and patrolled during the day. The size of the force varied during the war years and in the later years one or two "night watchers" were appointed in each ward to protect against crime. The city board requested that the military keep soldiers out of the city at night.

A curfew was established for both the civilian population and military personnel. Union forces placed a contingent of guards in the city to enforce the curfew and to assist in maintaining order. The ranks of the city officers declined as a result of increased military policing. The Board of Mayor and Aldermen pressed for cooperation between the civil and military police elements and the conflicts that developed in earlier years were avoided. Another former chief, S. P. Waddell, was selected in 1864 to head the police force.

The war ended and the military police left Knoxville in 1865. The city board immediately increased the police force to six officers on duty during the day and four to patrol at night. Even though Knoxville fared better than most other areas of Tennessee following the war, instability and a fragile economy encouraged crime.

Amid a large number of robberies in 1867, the board authorized the appointment of a "secret police." The force was composed of "discreet" persons in each ward who patrolled the streets at night. The secret police were employed for two weeks and paid $3 per night.

Captain Bridwell continued as a policeman after his tenure as chief, but his career and his life were almost ended in 1867. Bridwell exchanged shots with a man who resisted arrest. The gunman died of his wounds. Bridwell was shot in the right eye, which nearly killed him. The eye-ball was crushed and Bridwell lost his eye. He later served as a "merchant policeman" or security officer for a business on the west side of Gay Street.

During the late 1860s Knoxville and Knox County entered into an agreement for the city to take control of convict laborers for both the city and county. Labor provided by prisoners was important for rebuilding streets and other city infrastructure following the war. Convicts received thirty-three and a third cents per day toward payment of their fines.

When the city administration changed in 1868, L. H. Gamble became chief of police. He lasted less than a year in the position and two other men, S. C. Morley and W. A. Hooper, served short terms as chief in 1868 and 1869. A new city hall was built in this period and the calaboose and police headquarters were located in the facility until 1888.

The postwar years were dangerous for those charged to reestablish law and order. Two Knoxville policemen were killed as they attempted to make arrests and the two incidents were tragically connected. The first took place in 1868 at one of Knoxville's most rough and tumble saloons. The Dew Drop Inn was located among the raucous establishments on Gay Street. Patrolman William Dozier was on patrol when he was called to arrest a drunk in the bar room. As the officer approached, the unidentified rogue shot him through the heart. Policeman Dozier was killed instantly.

The following year, 1869, Thomas Dozier, the brother of the fallen officer was also drinking in a Gay Street saloon about half way between Main and Hill avenues. When he became drunk and rowdy, a policeman was summoned. Patrolman Nathan Haynes entered the bar and quickly found himself in a struggle. During the scuffle a pistol shot rang out. Policeman Nathan Haynes died of his wounds.

Chief of Police S. P. Waddell returned to head the police department in 1870-1871. Moses A. Claiborne was elected chief in 1871 and had twelve men on his force. Five policemen were on day duty and five at night, plus a watchman was on duty at the city hall during both day and night to answer calls. In 1873 James B. Pickens was made chief of police and William A. Harper in 1874. Claibourn, Harper and Pickens served as chief at various times in the 1870s and early 1880s. During Claiborne's administration and a portion of Harper's, Sanford C. Smith was a patrolman and considered one of the best men in the service. Smith was made chief of police in 1884 and served until 1885.

The first black policeman in the department's history, Moses Smith, was appointed by the city council on January 22, 1881. The board elected two policemen, Moses Smith and B. J. Reeder, to serve as the "patrolman or assistant police or marshal." The second black officer, James S. Mason, was appointed in 1884. Mason was a noted leader in the black community. He was the first black property owner and taxpayer in the city and founded a school for deaf black children in his

Patrolman James D. Selby in his formal photograph for the 1900 fire and police departments souvenir publication. The helmet was worn without a hat badge.

home. James Mason served as a Knoxville policeman until 1902. Knoxville continued to employ black policemen during the "Jim Crow" era of the early twentieth century when most other police departments in the state did not.

Knoxville created the Board of Public Works in 1885 as part of the system of municipal services begun by Mayor William C. Fulcher in 1883. The three-member board was responsible for the administration of all public services in the city and had the power to hire and fire employees, to organize the various departments of government and to set salaries of city workers. The first board consisted of Colonel Isham Young as chairman, Peter Kern and A. N. Jackson.

The Knoxville Police Department was under the Board of Public Works and the board appointed the police force. Chief of Police J. J. Atkins served as the first chief under the new system. The board form of executive administration allowed the police department the flexibility to grow and adapt to the changing needs of the city.

Chief Atkins was market master prior to becoming

chief of police. He paid strict attention to his duty and was known for his executive ability. Atkins remained in office until 1898, longer than any Knoxville chief law enforcement officer to that time, and earned the confidence and esteem of his men and the citizens of Knoxville. Atkins built the department from a handful of officers to a force of over thirty. Atkins' breast badge was shield-star with the designation "City Marshal." The badge was passed on to Atkins from Chief Smith and Atkins passed it on to his successor.

A group of Knoxville businessmen threw a party for the city's policemen on Thursday, May 20, 1886. They treated the 20-man force to a day of fun. The policemen formed ranks and marched, led by a band, from the Opera House to Turner Park. Hundreds of Knoxvillians joined them at the park to watch the festivities. The first event was a pistol-shooting match in which all officers participated. Officer Dewine won the match and was presented a gold badge with crossed firearms. A foot race and bicycle exhibition were also part of the event. The day ended with a dance at the park pavilion that lasted into the evening.

When Knoxville officers gathered three years later, it was for a funeral for one of their own. Policeman George Hoyle responded to a disturbance on Central Street in 1889. Hoyle arrested the subject and was walking him to city hall. As the two reached Logan's Temple on Commerce Avenue, the prisoner grappled with the policeman, wrestled away his pistol and fired a shot into the officer. Patrolman George Hoyle was mortally wounded and died a few hours later.

Walking continued to be the primary mode of transportation for Knoxville police. Policemen had to walk drunks and other lawbreakers to the city prison, unless an accommodating drayman gave them a ride. Frequently two or more officers were needed to carry a drunk. The state legislature passed a law in 1891 requiring cities to provide patrol wagons and Knoxville acquired one soon after. The horse drawn patrol wagon was used well into the twentieth century.

The Board of Public Works authorized the department to create a mounted patrol. Two horses were purchased and a number of policeman were assigned mounted duty. Although the men could patrol a considerably greater territory on horseback than on foot, it was soon decided that the costs of the horses was better spent on salaries. The mounted patrol was discontinued around 1910.

A new city hall was built in 1888 and police headquarters and the calaboose were relocated to the new building. The city lockup remained there until 1897 when a jail was constructed as part of the Commerce Avenue fire station building.

The Knoxville Police Department introduced the position of Police Matron in August 1890. Mrs. L. C. French was named to the position and served as police matron for about three months. Mrs. E. C. Wright became police matron in November 1890 and served for over a decade. She had an office in city hall and assisted the force with women and children who were in police custody. She wore a badge bearing the words "Police Matron." Mrs. Wright's efforts were credited with reclaiming many women, boys and girls from criminal careers. She also found homes and assistance for children and indigent women.

Chief of Police C. A. Reeder replaced J. J. Atkins as head of the department in January 1898. Reeder served for two years, 1898 and 1899. Chief J. J. Atkins returned in 1900 and served to 1905. The Knoxville chief of police held the rank of Captain as in most other departments of the era.

The command of the force in 1900 was Chief Atkins, Lieutenant W. P. Chandler who served as first assistant to the chief and Lieutenant George McIntyre who was the second assistant to the chief. Lieutenant Chandler had been a telegraph editor with *The*

Police Matron Mrs. E. C. Wright was elected to the position in November 1890 by the Board of Public Works and served in the position for over a decade. She wore a badge marked "Police Matron."

Sentinel (formerly *The Tribune*) before joining the force. Lieutenant McIntyre had been a private detective for the Southern Railway and was known for his skills as a detective.

Other supervisors on the force were First Sergeant Edward Conner, Second Sergeant W. P. Malone, Third Sergeant Edward Haynes, Day Police Desk Sergeant R. P. Williams and Night Police Desk Sergeant John L Austin. The force also included Police Matron Mrs. E. C. Wright, Day Prison Watchman Henry Davis, Night Prison Watchman B. F. Webb and Patrolmen Robert L. Saylor, Mike Wrenn, Pat Connelly, Joe Cruze, Garrett Mynatt, T. F. Ward, John Hubbs, Will Coleman, J. D. Selby, Oscar DeArmond, J. H. Freeman, James Montgomery, James Long, Dennis Finley, William M. Dinwiddie, S. C. Giles, Joe Reynolds (a black officer), F. H. Sterchi, Bart Childress and Dan Leahy. Sterchi, Childress and Leahy were fifteen-year-plus veterans of the force. Supernumeraries (special policemen) were R. J. McCroskey, Harve Swaggerty, Frank Dobson, William Lillison and I. H. Kyle.

The lawlessness of the nineteenth century did not go quietly and two of the old west's most notorious outlaws came to Knoxville in the new century. Harvey "Kid Curry" Logan and Ben Kilpatrick were former members of the Butch Cassidy and Sundance Kid Hole-in-the-Wall gang called "The Wild Bunch." Logan and Kilpatrick came to Knoxville in the fall of 1901 following their involvement a Montana train robbery. Superintendent Lowell Spence of the Pinkerton Detective Agency was hot on their trail.

Ben Kilpatrick was caught not long after the two came to Knoxville. He was tried and convicted in December 1901 and sentenced to 15 years in prison.

Logan, "Kid Curry," was the most infamous of the two. He was a killer wanted for fifteen murders and he was wanted in several states for numerous train robberies and other crimes. Logan stood five feet, seven inches, with jet black hair and dark eyes. Detective Spence wrote, "He speaks quietly but positively and is slightly bowlegged. He acts cool and collected." His body bore the marks of his life as an outlaw, with buckshot scars on his back, a knife scar, teeth missing from both upper and lower jaws and scars on his leg, right wrist and left forearm. Logan, now in his mid-thirties, was staying at a brothel under an assumed name and was wooing a respectable Knoxville girl.

Logan entered Ike Jones's Saloon on Central Street in the Bowery area of downtown Knoxville on December 13, 1901. He ordered a shot of expensive apricot brandy, lit a big cigar, took off his coat and began shooting pool with pair of local pool sharks. When the game of one of the pair suddenly improved after a large bet, Logan lost his temper and accused the man of being a hustler.

A hothead by nature, Logan had another apricot

Commanding officers of the Department in 1900. Captain J. J. Atkins, left, served as chief of police. Lieutenant W. P. Chandler, center, was first assistant to the chief of police, and Lieutenant G. W. McIntyre, right, was second assistant to the chief. Chandler became chief in 1906. They wore shields with cut out stars and rank panels on top. The chief's badge has an eagle-top.

brandy, returned to the pool table and began to strangle the hustler. The other pool shark stepped in and Logan, continuing to strangle the first hustler with one hand, pulled a pistol and shot him.

Patrolmen Robert Saylor and William Dinwiddie were walking their beat that cold night near Ike Jones's Saloon. They rushed into the pool hall and tried to pull Logan off the man he was strangling. The outlaw pulled his six-shooter and emptied it into the two policemen. Both officers were shot multiple times and slumped to the floor. Dinwiddie and Saylor lay bleeding on the floor as Logan made his getaway. A physician was called and the severely wounded police officers lived.

Two days later Logan was seen limping down a country road near Jefferson City, Tennessee. The man who spotted the outlaw used his newly installed telephone to gather a posse of his friends. They captured the notorious outlaw as he huddled over a small fire.

Logan was taken to the Knox County Jail and identified by Pinkerton Detective Spence. The outlaw was convicted of the Montana train robbery in November 1902 and sentenced to twenty years at hard labor. He escaped the Knox County Jail in June 1903 while waiting to be moved to the federal penitentiary.

Officers William Dinwiddie and Robert Saylor lived over twelve years following the shooting, outliving their assailant. However, the two lawmen never fully recovered from their wounds. At the time of the shooting Patrolman Dinwiddie had been with the force for ten years and Patrolman Saylor for four years.

Before the first decade of the twentieth century was over, two other Knoxville policemen faced death in the Bowery. The owner of a brothel was turned in by his bondsman for fines in the City Recorder's Office. Patrolmen Mike Wrenn and O. L. Jarnigan were sent to arrest the man on January 1, 1908. When the two reached the entrance to the brothel, the owner pulled a pistol. As the two wrestled with him for the weapon, he was able to shoot both of the officers in the head, killing them.

Patrolman O. L. Jarnigan was 35 and a member of the Knoxville force for three years. Patrolman Mike Wrenn was age 42 and a 10 year veteran of the department.

The incident happened during the last year of Chief W. P. Chandler, who led the department from 1906 to 1908. Chief J. P. Nichols commanded the department in 1909. From 1910 through 1915, E. D. Connors served as chief of police. Police headquarters moved to the upstairs of the Market House in the early 1900s, where it remained until 1930. The city jail

remained on Commerce Avenue.

Sergeant William A. Nelson, who began with the department in 1912 and retired after 46 years, told the *Knoxville News-Sentinel* in 1961, "Everybody walked in 1912. There were eight policemen on the day shift and 15 men each on the two night shifts." The day shift was from 8:00 a.m. to 4:30 p.m., the evening shift from 4:30 p.m. to 12:30 a.m. and the night shift from 12:30 a.m. to 8:00 a.m. The men walked in twos on the evening and night shifts to protect against attack from brawlers. Nelson continued, "If you hired for a night job you were stuck with it until some change was made in the department. We wore uniforms then summer and winter. Coats and all. We had high collars that buttoned."

Knoxville was a small town, with sleepy, tree-lined avenues in 1912. The textile mills hummed. Traffic problems did not exist because fewer than 25 Knoxvillians owned cars. The police department had less than 50 officers. The biggest job for the city police was keeping drunks off the street. Big-muscled farm boys and an occasional bully fought on Central Street, along with swigging corn liquor from a jug.

The paddy wagon was painted black with an overhead frame of heavy screen wire open to the weather. It had two long benches on each side. Doc Price was

Patrolman William M. Haley in 1909 with his son William Jr. (Photo courtesy of Captain Jack Lewis and McClung Historical Collection)

Knoxville mounted patrol in 1910. Patrolmen wore helmets with wreath insignia. Lieutenant W. L. Jack, second from right, wore a hat with no insignia. His breast badge was a shield with cut star and a top panel for rank designation. (Photo courtesy of McClung Historical Collection)

one of the paddy wagon drivers. Nelson said, "We had two horses to pull the Black Maria. Those horses stayed in harness. They pulled the wagon on every call, but they were always fat and slick." Police Headquarters and City Court were in the Market Square Building and the City Jail was under the Commerce Avenue fire station, so the horse drawn wagon made the trip from the jail to the court and back again for each session.

The individual credited with being the first detective of the Knoxville Police Department was Ed Haynes. Detective Haynes later served as chief of the force. His service as detective of the department began in the first decade of the twentieth century.

Uniform and insignia changes were made around 1914. The basic uniform continued to be a hip-length coat buttoned to the neck with the pistol worn beneath the coat. A double-breasted, knee-length top-coat was worn in winter months. Headgear of patrolmen changed from the domed helmet, which were introduced in the last decades of the nineteenth century, to a flat-top military style cap. The shield with a cutout star continued as the breast badge and a traditional wreath remained the hat badge. The wreath had been worn briefly on helmets. The wreath contained either the officer's number or the rank of supervisors.

The department lost two policemen in the teens, the first was forty-five-year-old Policeman Samuel C. Hickey. Patrolman Hickey and his partner Patrolman Charles Fox were going off duty on Sunday, April 19, 1914, when they encountered a domestic dispute on

Patrolmen William M. Dinwiddie, left, and Robert L. Saylor, right, responded to a pool game dispute at Ike Jones' Saloon on a cold December night in 1901 and found themselves face to face with notorious outlaw Harvey "Kid Curry" Logan. Both officers were shot multiple times. Although neither died that night, nor did they ever fully recovered from their wounds.

362

The Knoxville Police Department in 1910. The Board of Public Safety, seated on the bench, were from left to right James A. Hensley, John Fleeniker, and Sam E. Hill. Standing in the first row from left to right were Lieutenant W. G. Lee, Lieutenant J. L. Porter, Chief of Police E. D. Connors, Lieutenant W. L. Jack, Charles Walker, Matt Tillery, Orville Johnson, and Sam Hickey. Left to right on the second row were George Dearing, Mark Birdwell, James D. Selby, William M. Dinwiddie, William E. Haley, Charles Barbson, W. E. O'Connor, Jake Melton, Pete Yarness, and William Rowland. The third row were Dr. Cockrum, John Gleason, Charles Fox, W. E. Ball, James Walker, and Henry Sterchi. The forth row were Bill Rose, Mike Cross, Dan Leahy, William Coleman, Sam Whitlock, John Trouton, Horace Johnson, and Tom Waiugh. The fifth row were Bud Kyle, Bill Lillison, and John Singleton. In the rear were an unidentified janitor and Charlie Wardell.

Jackson Street. Officer Fox arrested a woman and was leaving the scene. Shots rang out and Fox ran back to his partner. Officer Hickey was shot twice. As he fell dead, he fired at the gunman, but the man escaped. Patrolman Samuel Hickey was in his third year on the force.

Patrolman James M. Tillery had been with the department for seven years when he and his partner, Patrolman Rice Witt, raided a house on Campbell Avenue in the red-light district on April 15, 1916. They were suspicious when they saw a young girl carry a package into the house, because the house had been raided before for illegal substances. Tillery went to the rear of the house and Witt to the front door. Witt heard four shots and ran to the rear where he found Officer Tillery lying face down. A man had jumped

out of a rear window and shot Patrolman Tillery twice. The mortally wounded officer returned fire but the gunman escaped. Witt held Tillery in his arms as he took his last breath.

Although the dangers of police work continued, technology was changing patrol duty for the Knoxville force. Patrol continued to be done on foot. A mounted patrol was sometimes used in more distant residential areas. A bicycle patrol was also created to help officer move about more quickly. From time to time bicycle officers even chased automobiles to catch traffic violators.

The Knoxville Police Department got its first cars in 1917 when six or seven Model T Fords were acquired. The city was growing and annexing new territory. The cars were used to patrol the suburbs, but in

Detective Edward M. Haynes, the department's first full-time investigator, in 1910 with his bloodhound and tracker. (Photograph courtesy of Barbara West, his granddaughter)

the down town area police cars were used for emergencies only. The horse drawn Black Maria was used for prisoners until 1923 when a "C" cab truck was acquired to serve as a police patrol wagon.

Officers were exposed to new dangers as the number of motor cars grew. Increased traffic and congested intersections heightened the danger for automobilists and pedestrians alike. Elevated traffic boxes were erected at major intersections and policemen climbed the structures to direct traffic. Being above street level, the traffic boxes gave officers a bird's eye view of the intersection and they were more easily seen by drivers and pedestrians. Hand paddles with "stop" and "go" printed on opposite sides served as traffic signals. Later, signal lights were mounted at the base of the traffic box. These were the predecessors of automated traffic lights.

Chief of Police Edward M. Haynes began his sixteen-year tenure as head of the department in 1916. He served until 1931.

Racial tensions in Knoxville erupted into violence in 1919 following an incident in the early hours of August 30. A black intruder entered a bedroom window and shot a white woman to death in her bed. The only witness identified Maurice Mayes as the killer.

Mayes, a mulatto, sometime deputy sheriff and rumored illegitimate son of the city mayor was arrested and jailed.

As the news circulated through the city, there was talk of lynching. Sheriff W. T. Cate had Mayes transported to Chattanooga. Even so, a white mob far too large for the police force and deputy sheriffs to constrain gathered at the Knox County jail. They broke down the door, freed a dozen white inmates, pillaged the liquor storage room and vandalized the jail.

The mob of white men remained outside the jail and grew to about a thousand. The mayor called in the National Guard. The first contingent of one hundred guardsmans began to arrive, but were unable to control the mob. The mob looted a number of businesses and armed themselves. A group of black men broke into one establishment.

The white mob moved to the black section of town and began shooting into buildings with black occupants. Black men returned the fire. Many were wounded in the violence. A National Guard officer was accidentally killed by his own men and one black man was shot and killed. The rioting was ended the following morning when several hundred additional guardsmen arrived and restored order.

The police force resumed its role as peace keeper. A change in insignia and uniform was introduced about 1920. A pinched shield with the city seal was adopted as the breast badge. Panels above and below the seal identified the wearer as "Knoxville Police" and

Knoxville cornermen worked from a raised traffic box mounted in major intersections. In this photograph, a crowd gathered on Gay Street to hear the World Series and watch the progress on a diagram on the side of the Knoxville Sentinel Building as the progress of players were moved about on the diamond. The traffic officer kept lanes available for automobiles and trolleys.

A patrol shift stood at the south end of the Market House in 1926. The sergeant, front row left, and captain, forth from the right in the front row, wore eagle top shields. The captain wore a large button on each lapel, an element of insignia that continued through the 1980s. Knoxville was the only major police department in the state with black patrolmen on the force during his period of history. (Photo courtesy of McClung Historical Collection)

the officer's number was in a small panel at the base of the badge. Supervisors wore the same style shield in gold tone with an eagle-top and a banner showing their rank. Some commanders chose to wear other style badges.

Uniform jackets with a short lapel and four buttons were adopted. Officers wore either a standard neck tie or a bow tie. The rigid top cap continued as headwear and the hat badge changed to a wreath encircled state seal with an open number panel at the base. Supervisor hat badges were gold tone with the rank cut into the bottom panel. Traffic officers soon added a generic shoulder patch featuring a winged wheel.

The same badge style and same basic uniform style were worn into the forties. One change introduced in the thirties was wearing the pistol on the outside of the coat with a Sam Brown belt. Another change was the adoption of a multi-point, soft-edged cap for patrol-

In 1923 a "C" cab truck replaced the horse drawn Black Maria used to transport prisoners. It was the first motorized paddywagon.

Knoxville Police Department emergency squad stood beside a large phaeton pursuit car in the 1920s.

365

Members of the Knoxville department from the 1930s.

men and traffic officers began wearing white caps.

As uniforms and equipment changed, the dangers of police duty remained. Patrolman Ross Ball Hinds lost his life in an accident as he ended his shift on Sunday morning, June 12, 1921. Hinds had been working a union strike with other officers at the Brookside Mill District. They were in the process of being relieved at 6:30 a.m. and were crossing the railroad tracks at Baxter Avenue. Hinds was the last of the group to cross the track and apparently misjudged the speed of an on-coming freight train. He was struck by the train and killed instantly.

The Knoxville Police Department established a women's unit in December 1924 soon after the city manager style of government was adopted by the city. Three policewomen, Sergeant Annette Steele and Patrolwomen Katherine Dooley and Daisy McLin, were hired by Safety Director J. Otey Walker. They had no regular beat, but operated in any section of the city where they were needed to work with women who were either arrested or abused. They worked with children as well and could be considered the first juvenile unit. The longest serving of the three women was Patrolwoman Daisy McLin, who served for seven years until her death in 1931. She establishing a reputation for self assurance and respect among her fellow officers and gratitude from those with whom she worked.

Retired Sergeant C. C. DeVois, who joined the force in 1924 under Captain Levi York and served for 33 years, described the method of communication between the station house and the patrolman in the early twentieth century. A large bell was located at headquarters that could be heard all over town. Each officer was assigned a certain number of rings and when the officer on duty at the station rang the officers number, the patrolman rushed to headquarters to get his assignment.

Safety Director Walker installed a Gamewell system in 1926. The system consisted of a call box attached to a utility pole in each police beat around the city. Also attached to the utility pole was a horn and a light. The light was turned on and the horn sounded by throwing a switch at headquarters. The patrolman then went to the call box and talked with headquarters by telephone. The system was a dramatic

Chief L. M. York, standing on the far right, oversaw the implementation of the department's first radio system. The one-way radio network allowed desk sergeants to dispatch calls to patrol units across the city. Officers continued to contact headquarters by phone.

Sergeant J. F. Gideon on one of the department's Harley Davidson motorcycles.

improvement in communication.

Another major enhancement to communication came in 1933 when one-way radios were installed in cars. The radios were basic AM transmitter and receivers. Operators at headquarters had to give the call letters, WPFO, every morning at 2:00 to meet FCC requirements. The radios only allowed headquarters to talk to officers in patrol car. It was still necessary for officers to use the telephones in call boxes or businesses to contact headquarters.

Two-way radios were installed in 1936 and patrol units could talk back to headquarters. Then, in October 1942, new FM radios were installed that allowed communication between patrol cars as well.

Police Headquarters moved to the new Public Safety Building at 409 N. Broadway in May 1930 under the leadership of Safety Director Chandler and Chief Haynes. The building was converted from a horse stable, but the remodeling did not completely hide the original layout or mask the fragrance. J. F. Montgomery was appointed chief of police for 1932, followed by Chief of Police Levi M. York who served from 1933 through 1942.

The tragic loss of another officer came in the late thirties. Patrolman Herman M. "Curley" Rollins, Patrolman Herman Wayland and another officer responded to a disturbance call at the Jenkins' Cafe on Walnut Street on March 13, 1939. When they entered the establishment, a nineteen-year-old waitress reached under the counter, pulled a pistol and fired three quick shots. One of the bullets went harmlessly through the coat tail of Officer Wayland, but Officer Rollins was struck in the back and mortally wounded. He was rushed to the hospital and died two days later.

Knoxville policemen provided their own service weapons through most of the history of the department. Most officers also carried a night club or "billy." Many patrolmen liked to have quick access to a scatter gun, a shotgun with a short barrel.

A policy was implemented in the 1940s that prohibited the use of shotguns without specific approval of a supervisor and shotguns were kept in the department's armory. The chief himself issued the weapons to supervisors who transported them to the scene of the incident for which they were needed. This procedure was cumbersome and soon six shotguns were maintained by the desk sergeant, who checked them out to officers when needed. In later years shotguns again became standard equipment in patrol cars.

The search for more current insignia led to the use of two breast badge styles for brief periods in the late forties and early fifties. In the mid-1940s the department adopted a circle medallion with decorative accents. The city seal continued to be featured in the center. The department returned to a pinched shield style badge around 1950, this time featuring an open panel in the center of the shield in which the officer's number was applied. The existing hat badge style con-

Patrolmen Mike Wrenn, left, and his partner O. L. Jarnigan were both shot in the head and killed on New Year's Day 1908 by a brothel owner. Patrolman Ross Ball Hinds, right, lost his life on June 12, 1921, when he was struck by a train.

The 1936 Traffic Division gathered in front of police headquarters at 409 North Broadway.

tinued to be worn with both of these breast badge styles.

New badge styles were adopted in 1955 and used into the twenty-first century. The breast badge was a full-sized teardrop with applied panels for department and rank in hard blue enamel. The state seal was used with "City of Knoxville" in reverse blue around the seal. The hat badge was a spread-winged, eagle-top medallion.

Newly adopted uniform shirts were gray and accented with dark epaulet straps and pocket flaps. Jackets were worn only in the winter and with the dress uniform. Custom shoulder patches were created some years later and featured the city seal. The department moved to solid navy blue uniform, including shirts and hats, on June 1, 1972. The chief and assistant chiefs wore a white shirt. A new shoulder patch was created to blend with the dark shirt that featured a spread eagle.

The year 1955 began with sadness for the depart-

Patrolman George C. Pace in 1939 standing beside one of the V-8 Ford patrol cars called the "Brown and Yellow Basket" because of their colors and shape.

368

Traffic Patrol in 1947 included Officers Earl Cronan, Frank Workman, Cecil McCubbins and John Farmer.

Patrolman Guy Vance riding a Harley Davidson ServiCar. The three-wheeler was used for enforcement duty as well as a utility vehicle.

ment. Patrol Officer Lester W. "Tarzan" Gwinn went to a home on East Scott Avenue on January 31 in response to a domestic disturbance call. Officer Gwinn completed his interview with the male occupant of the home and told the man he did not intend to arrest him. As Gwinn was on his way from the house, the man pulled a handgun and brutally gunned down the officer, shooting him five times in the chest. Policeman Lester Gwinn was rushed to Knoxville General Hospital where he died a short time later.

The first black female police officer was hired in October 1955. Policewoman Mrs. William Henderson was hired as one of the female school patrol officers. Henderson was a part of the traffic department under

Traffic Chief Joe Edington. The department was led by Chief of Police J. P. Kimsey at the time. He began his tenure as chief in 1943 and served for eighteen years, retiring in 1960. He was succeeded by Chief of Police F. Harris who served from 1960 to 1965 and Chief Harry Huskisson, commanding from 1965 to 1970.

The department formed a K-9 Unit in 1966 consisting of officers Bill Trusley, Floyd Patty, Doug Norman and John Lackey, along with their canine partners. The unit initially provided crowd control, building searches and tracking. This first K-9 group was retired in 1972. The unit was reorganized in 1979 beginning with Officer John Rose and K-9 Officer Ranger. The unit quickly grew to five teams. By 1988 the unit had grown to eight teams and started drug

Patrolman Herman M. "Curley" Rollins, left, was shot in the back by a cafe waitress on March 13, 1939, and died of his wounds two days later. Patrol Officer Lester W. "Tarzan" Gwinn, right, was shot in the chest five and killed when he responded to a domestic disturbance call on January 31, 1955.

Officer Bill Beck, later captain, in 1955 with a new Ford squad car. Beck wore the newly adopted insignia of the department. The door marking on the patrol unit remained a five-point star. Door markings on cars soon changed to the city seal under a banner reading "Knoxville Police."

Seated from left to right in this circa 1960 photograph were Detective William Golightly, Patrolmen John Williams, Patrolman and later Lieutenant James Rucker, and Detective James Guess. Standing from left to right were Patrolman Frank Cheatham, Traffic Officer and later Sergeant Theondrad Jackson, Patrolman Emmert Jackson, Patrolman and later Detective Sergeant Jeff Davis, Traffic Officer and later Captain Shields Minor, Traffic Officer and later Detective Ronald Osborne, Patrolman Zimmerman Walker, and Patrolman and later Lieutenant Jim Rowan. The shirt with dark packet flaps and epaulets were worn from the mid-1950s until 1972.

detection duty.

A major improvement in communications came in 1968 when all officer were given portable two-way "walkie-talkie" radios to carry while on duty. In 1975 officers were encouraged to carry their radios when off duty was well.

Knoxville lost two officers in vehicular accidents in the late sixties. Patrol Officer John H. Perkey was returning to Knoxville after a department related trip on December 8, 1967. The police cruiser struck a wet spot on Old Sevierville Pike and he lost control of the car. It left the roadway and struck a tree. Officer Perkey was thrown from the vehicle and killed.

A third Knoxville officer, George Michael Bradley, was involved in an on duty accident during the 1970s. The accident left Officer Bradley a paraplegic and he died of his injuries on September 12, 1993.

A new Safety Building complex was completed and occupied in 1969. The facility located at 800 E. Church Street contained the latest features and equipment. Chief of Police Joe C. Fowler, who began his

Patrol Officer John H. Perkey, left, was killed on December 8, 1967, when his cruiser hit a wet spot on Old Sevierville Pike and struck a tree. Motorcycle Officer John W. Phillips, right, died when his motorcycle struck an embankment and guard rail on the Clinton Highway on April 1, 1969.

tenure as chief in 1970, continued to lead the department until 1978. He was followed by Chief W. C. Fox who served from 1978 to 1980.

The Women's Bureau in the late sixties was staffed by policewomen Geradine Layden, Dorthea Sweeten and Eleanor Watkins. Each had an assigned duty, although their duties overlapped. Watkins worked with female prisoners, Sweeten's duties included mental case evaluations and referrals to Human Services and Layden worked in records. The uniform for female officers specified a skirt rather than slacks.

The duty of female police officers changed dramatically in 1973. For the first time female Knoxville police officers were given basic police training and assigned to patrol cars. The first four of policewomen trained at the academy were Ida Webb, Barbara Hopper Brock, Janice Adcock Ladd and Judie Cassetty Martin. They were not assigned to specific cars, but rode with a male supervisor who was on duty citywide. They were frequently called in to search female suspects and to assist with domestic situations.

The skirt and regulation shirt continued to be the uniform of all policewomen, including those patrolling. The uniform head cover for women was a female military style cap in white. The female officers carried their duty weapon in a small purse that was part of the uniform. The limitations of the uniform in a confrontation quickly became evident. In 1974 women were allowed to ware slacks, but during night duty only. The uniform head cover was change to the regulation police cap worn by the rest of the department. Soon women were allowed to wear slacks on all

Captain George C. Pace began his service in the department on April 8, 1937, and gained a reputation as "the policeman's policeman." Pace retired as an inspector on November 1, 1972.

shifts and a snub-nosed .38 caliber revolver was worn on a small belt. In 1978 policewomen moved to the standard sidearm.

The Criminalists Unit was formed in 1974 to provide specialized support to criminal investigations. The unit applied scientific techniques to preserving and processing crime scenes, used forensic methods to evaluate evidence and the documented their findings for court presentation.

An event on Gay Street in 1975 led to the formation of the Special Operations Squad. A mentally-ill man opened fire on a crowd on the busy street killing three. Sergeant Jim Lewis walked around the corner during the shooting and the gunman immediately surrendered. Although the incident was quickly ended, the potential of an even more devastating outcome focused on the need for a unit to respond to tactical situations. Officer Gary Shaffer, an ex-Marine Recon veteran, was assigned as leader of the unit. He selected team members and conducted training.

The primary equipment of the five-man team was

Policewoman Ida Webb and Sergeant William "Bud" Hawkins in 1973. Webb was one of the first policewomen on the Knoxville force to ride in shift cars and wore the uniform cap initially designated for female officers.

The department's first mobile crime unit was put into service in 1974. Inspecting the equipment used to collect and preserve evidence were from left to right Mayor Leonard Rogers, Captain Felix Maupin, and Sergeant Bill Smith.

Smith & Wesson .38 caliber revolvers and M-16 automatic rifles. The team was trained by the FBI SWAT team and the U.S. Marshals Service Special Operational Group in 1980 in preparation for the World's Fair. Not long after, the team was recognized by the U.S. Justice Department as the best SWAT team in the nation. Officer Shaffer was promoted to sergeant.

Lieutenant James Kennedy took command of the

Officer George Michael Bradley, left, was made a paraplegic by an accident in the 1970s and died of his injuries on September 12, 1993. Patrolman Mark Anthony Williams, right, was shot and killed while riding his motorcycle off duty on July 7, 1989.

unit in 1986. In 1988 the MP-5 submachine gun was adopted as the primary entry weapon and a mobile command vehicle was acquired along with other transportation and equipment. Subsequently a Bomb Squad and a Negotiation Unit were added to the department.

For most of the department's history no standard existed for service weapons. Officers carried a range of weapons that included snub-nose .38 caliber revolvers and .44 magnums. If someone reported for duty between 1967 and 1974 with no sidearm, the department would loan the officer a Model 10 revolver. The officer had to leave a $25 deposit. In 1978 money was allocated to buy sidearms and ammunition for the force. The standard service weapon became a .38 caliber revolver loaded with +P ammunition. The 9mm Glock was adopted in 1986 and later a variety of 9mm sidearms were accepted for use by the department.

The helicopter became important equipment for the department in the 1970s and 1980s. Police pilots reported traffic conditions, accidents and occasionally sat down to unsnarl traffic jams. The aircraft also grew to be important in patrol and pursuit and in other search situations.

Police cruisers were enhanced in a number of ways in the late sixties and seventies. Emergency lights on patrol cars were changed from red to blue in January 1968. The summertime comfort of patrol officers improved greatly in the seventies when patrol cars were equipped with air conditioning for the first time. Mesh screens were added between the front and rear seats of the vehicles, providing better safety for officers. In one incident just prior to installation of the screens a prisoner reached across the seat and grabbed the officer by the neck. He began choking the patrolman and almost caused the cruiser to wreck.

Walter Bearden became Knoxville's Safety Director following his retirement from the TBI. A reorganization followed that included a number of command assignment changes. Major George Tittsworth was transferred from the Juvenile Bureau to the Detective Bureau. Captain Bill Fox was promoted to major and placed in command of the Juvenile Bureau. Lieutenant Shields Minor was promoted to captain in the bureau, the first black officer in the department to hold the rank of captain. Leadership of the department was assumed in 1980 by Chief of Police R. A. Marshall. He served until 1988.

Chief of Police Phil E. Keith took command of the department in 1988. Keith became a Knoxville officer in 1970. He worked in a wide range of duties, patrol, traffic, records, communication, and planning and research. He progressed to sergeant and lieutenant before being named chief. Keith, who served as chief for 17 years, led the Knoxville Police Department to nationally accreditation.

The department lost an officer on July 7, 1989, when Patrolman Mark Anthony Williams was shot and killed while riding his motorcycle off duty. He was shot in the back at Cherry Street and I-40. It was suspected that Officer Williams was shot because he was a police officer.

Community service and officer support became increasingly important for the department. The Drug Abuse Resistance Education (DARE) program was introduced in Knoxville in 1990. Lieutenant Bob Wooldridge was the first to head the program and during the first year conducted the program in eleven area schools. A Chaplain Corps was formed in September 1993. Those who served in the corps gave spiritual and counseling support to officers and citizen victims in times of crisis. Each Chaplain served one 24-hour shift per month and was on call in crisis situations.

The department celebrated 2000 with a special badge authorized for wear in the first year of the new millennium. The badge was a oval with a center seal in the form of the shoulder patch.

Sterling "I.V." Owen IV was sworn in as Knoxville's chief of police on September 1, 2004. Chief Owen was a 22-year veteran of law enforcement with extensive experience in federal, state and local agencies. He established an exceptional record with the FBI and served as supervisory special agent in the FBI's Knoxville office before retiring and founding a security consulting business in Knoxville. Among

Chief of Police Phil E. Keith, left. retired in 2004 after 35 years on the force including 17 as chief. Chief of Police Sterling Owen IV, right, was sworn in as Knoxville's chief law enforcement officer on September 1, 2004. Chief Owen was a veteran FBI special agent with 22 years of law enforcement experience.

other recognitions Chief Owen was named National Criminal Investigator of the Year and received the FBI Merit Award as the result of the rescue of 13 hostages from the Talladega, Alabama, Federal Prison.

Chief Owen took command of a department with diverse and specialized organization and well trained law enforcement professionals. The Knoxville Police Department is divided into three divisions, operations, investigative and administrative, with 414 sworn officers. The department has a nationally accredited training center and a full range of specialized units. Knoxville officers continue to live up to the heritage of dedication to the service and protection of all the citizens of the city.

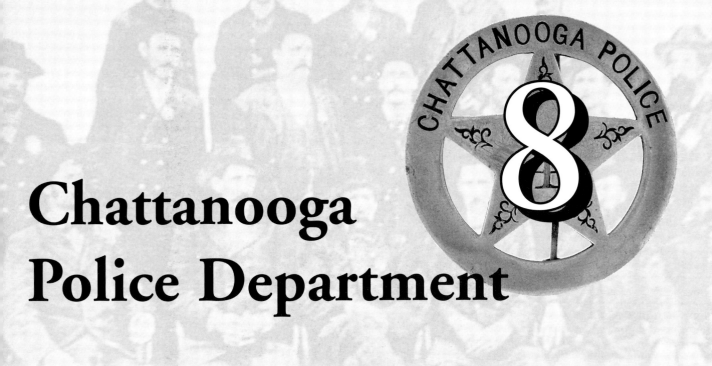

Chattanooga Police Department

The town of Chattanooga was created by act of the Tennessee legislature on December 20, 1839, on the site of a fledgling settlement called Ross' Landing. Town constables, appointed by the city council, were the first municipal law enforcement officers in Chattanooga. The identity of early town constables is not known due to the loss of records from the period.

A major reorganization of city government took place on January 5, 1852. The office of City Marshal replaced the Town Constable as the chief law enforcement officer of the city. The city marshal was empowered to hire assistants to be titled Policemen. Thomas McMinn was appointed as the first city marshal by the city's Board of Mayor and Aldermen. The board also appointed a small number of policemen and approved construction of a city jail at a cost not to exceed $220. The city lockup was completed in 1854.

The law enforcement duties of a policeman were basically the same as those of the town constable. Policemen were full-time and received a salary of $15 per month, with a $1 bonus for each arrest and conviction. The city marshal was allowed to patrol mounted, so long as he provided his own horse.

The force was divided into day and night squads. City ordinance required that the night watch cry the hour from 10:00 p.m. until daybreak. Failure to perform this duty resulted in the officer being fined $1 by the city recorder. Early policemen were not required to wear a uniform.

City Marshal Thomas McMinn, a prominent citizen, served three one year terms. The duties assigned to the city marshal made him virtually the chief executive officer of the city, second in authority and power to the mayor. N. P. Nail was selected city marshal in 1855.

The duties of the city marshal were expanded in 1856. In addition to his role as chief law enforcement officer, he became responsible for public works and sanitation. The city marshal also served as the market house master, tax collector, sexton of the city burial grounds and clerk of the recorder's court. The expanded duties were spelled out by city ordinance.

In addition to the prescribed duties of the marshal as a public officer under previous ordinance it shall be his duty to superintend, direct and control all officers and persons who may be placed by the city council under him for the preservation of peace and tranquility of the city, to collect all fines imposed by the recorder and to render an account to him every week of all public monies collected by him or the officers appointed under him; it shall be his duty to have the bell at the market house rung for five minutes at 9 o'clock every night except on Sunday nights at 10 o'clock.

In addition to his duties as police officer the marshal shall be street inspector and superintend the street drains and all other public works, unless otherwise provide for. It shall be his duty to remove all trash or filth which may be deposited in the streets, together with all dead animals and all impure matter from the streets, enclosed public grounds and improved lots of the city before 3 o'clock every day. He shall, at all times, remove any shavings, brick bats or other refuse of building materials which may have remained on any street for a longer period than twenty-four hours; it shall be his duty to attend the market house every day; he shall have charge and superintendence of the carts, horses hired by the council; it shall be his duty to fill up all holes on low places, to level and graduate the streets and place them in good condition, to keep the drains open and clean and to keep the small bridges in repair and prevent the settling of stagnant water in any of the streets of the city and do all other work on any of the public streets when ordered by the mayor and city council.

In consideration of his services he shall receive from the treasury, in addition to his fees, the annual sum of $600, provided the city be in no instance taxed in fees for the performance of any of the duties of his office.

Phillip Simmerman served as city marshal in 1856-1857, John J. Lowry served 1858-1859 and Jesse B. Allison served 1860-1863. The police force grew and the city marshal remained responsible for law enforcement until the Civil War enveloped the city. Martial law replaced the city's police force when Union troops occupied Chattanooga in 1863. For the duration of the war the military was responsible for law enforcement.

Military police kept basic order but conditions in the city quickly deteriorated when southern troops lay siege to Chattanooga. The longer the siege lasted, the more desperate conditions became. Rain and flooding made life even more miserable. The life of civilians was miserable and dangerous, made more so by overcrowding and constant foraging that often devolved into fights over scraps of food. Conditions improved after the siege was broken, but the population continued to be at the mercy of wartime dangers.

In 1865 the turmoil of war gave way to an uneasy peace as the days of reconstruction began. The period was marked by a boomtown atmosphere due to a doubling of Chattanooga's population during the war years, by tensions that carried over from the war and by pervasive lawlessness. The federal Provost Marshal returned municipal government to civilian control on October 9, 1865, and the last elements of Union troops left the city in April 1866.

A mayor and a board of aldermen were selected and the board passed a resolution establishing a voluntary police force.

There is in and about the city a large number of vicious, outbreaking persons, and thefts have become of such frequent occurrence, and burglary has become so common: therefore be it resolved: That the good people of the city be and are hereby requested to form themselves into a voluntary police force.

The voluntary police functioned for less than a year. Little is known about the force except that it apparently lowered criminal activity. When the Metropolitan Police Bill was passed by the state legislature in May 1866, it specified that the force controlled by the governor be in charge of Chattanooga's law enforcement.

The Metropolitan Police Act specified that "the quota of policemen for the City of Chattanooga shall not exceed twenty-four in number with one commissioner and two sergeants." The commissioner was not responsible to the city council; he functioned as chief of police and had absolute power over the police force. He also served as the ex-officio recorder of the city. Major Abel A. Pearson, an army officer, served as commissioner of the Metropolitan Police in Chattanooga. His salary was limited to $2,500 per year.

A photograph of Metropolitan Police Officer Hank Mayett survived from 1866. The uniform consisted of a dark three-quarters length coat and dark trousers. The coat had metal buttons, but no breast badge. The belt was military style and worn over the coat. A night stick hung from the belt. The cap was dark, brimless with a short leather visor, cylindrical crown with rigid frame and metal wreath insignia bearing the initials "M.P."

The Metropolitan Police system made progress in bringing crime under control, but was never well accepted by the city's inhabitants. The commissioner was so unpopular that the state legislature passed an act allowing him "to call to his assistance such number of good citizens of the city or county as may be required to execute the provisions of the act of 1866." This essentially allowed him an armed force to keep him in power. Commissioner Pearson quickly left town for points west when the era of the Metropolitans ended.

The legislature repealed the law creating the Metropolitan Police in February 1869 and control of the police department of the city was returned to the city council. The act abolished the office of City Marshal and specified that the city recorder function as Chief of Police and have direct authority over the police force.

A subsequent act in November 1869 re-established the office of City Marshal, to be elected biennially by the citizens of Chattanooga. City Marshal R. H. Croft served in 1869 and was followed by Captain Jesse B. Allison in 1870 and D. Charles Howell in 1871. N. W. Wilbur served as city marshal in 1872 and again in 1881-1882. John J. Lowry returned to service as city marshal in 1874, 1877 and 1879-1880. City Marshal D. M. Doty served in 1876 and City Marshal Eugene Balch in 1878.

Lawlessness was prevalent in Chattanooga after the Civil War. The police force faced desperados willingly to shoot with little or no provocation. During one encounter in December 1872 three officers were wounded in a gun battle with a murderer. The local hooligan stabbed a prominent Chattanoogan to death in a dispute and then escaped across the river in a skiff. Night Policeman J. H. Carver heard that the felon had returned to the city and was drinking in Kesterson's Saloon on Market Street, bragging that he would not be taken by the police.

Officer Carver along with Policemen George White and Sandy Templeton went to the saloon to make the arrest. The killer fled through the back when he saw the officers. He ran across a corral and hid behind a gate post. As the three lawmen chased him, he opened fire. Officer White was hit twice in the abdomen and Officer Carver was hit in the chest. Templeton was the last of the three to fall, with a bullet in his leg. The murderer was shot in the shoulder but managed to escape. All of the combatants survived their wounds.

City Marshal John Lowry became the target of gun fire around 10:00 one morning as he tried to arrest a ruffian for setting off a keg of gun powder under a bawdy house at Fourth and Broad streets. Marshal Lowry was on horseback when he called out to the man. The lawbreaker pulled his pistol and fired at the marshal. Lowry quickly dismounted and returned fire. The marshal was shot in the arm before policemen rushed to the scene and captured the shooter.

Ten policemen were on the force in 1878, under the command of the city marshal and a lieutenant of police. The police department was located at 182-184 Market Street and sessions court was held at Market

Metropolitan Policeman Hank Mayett in 1866 photograph, the earliest image of a Chattanooga police officer. Mayett wore a three-quarters coat with metal buttons, cap with visor and rigid frame, and a baton worn on the belt. The hat wreath contained the letters "MP" and was the only insignia worn.

between 6th and 7th streets. The first breast badges known to have been worn by Chattanooga policemen were large and plain pinched shields.

Police salaries in 1875 were $780 a year for patrolmen, $900 for the lieutenant and $1,000 for the marshal. The economy waned and by 1878 salaries were reduced to $540 for patrolmen, $720 for the lieutenant and $900 for the marshal. Arrestable offenses included fast driving, riding on the streets with lewd women, visiting a house of ill fame for lewd purposes and playing cards on Sunday.

Yellow Fever or "Yellow Jack" was the most deadly menace Chattanooga faced in the late seventies. The 1878 outbreak left 366 dead and drove many inhabitants from the city to avoid the epidemic. Special policemen were hired to guard the homes of wealthy citizens while they were away.

The first recorded line of duty death of a Chattanooga policeman was the killing of Patrolman James Wiggins while investigating a disturbance call in 1879. Around 8:30 Sunday evening, April 28, three men were drunk and disorderly at a bawdy house not far from the courthouse. The three continued the disturbance outside the house and brandished guns. The women in the house were fearful and blew a police whistle.

Officers Jim Wiggins and Charlie Davis responded to the house. Two of the drunks were arrested and taken to jail. Wiggins and Davis returned to the scene with Patrolman LeCroy to search for the third subject. Wiggins and LeCroy saw the man on a walkway. Wiggins approached him, words were passed and the drunk raised a pistol and shot the policeman. Wiggins grabbed his head and said, "Oh Lord, I am shot." He ran a few steps after the gunman and fell. Wiggins died moments later. The murderer was captured about 4:00 the following morning by Marshall Balch, Lieutenant Allen, Policeman Davis and Deputy Sheriff Stanley.

Patrolman Wiggins was from the Fifth Ward of the city. The Board of Mayor and Aldermen paid Officer Wiggins' family four months of his salary in a lump sum, an amount of $60.

Chattanooga grew in the 1870s and 1880s as railroads and industry expanded. The Chattanooga Street Railway Company provided mass transit for the city. A telephone network began service in July 1880 and electric lights were turned on in 1882. Between 1880 and 1882 the city grew from 13,000 to almost 18,000 in population.

The Chattanooga Police Department was a 12-man force in 1880. Policemen worked 12-hour shifts in the five wards of the city. Because of the growth of the city, the council expanded the force by two officers. The budget for police salaries in 1881 was $6,000.

Police headquarters was moved to Fourth and Market streets. The building already housed the county lock-up and the courtroom of the circuit judge was located on the upper floor. Police headquarters was only a block from the "restricted" section of town where brothels and saloons did business. The proximity meant officers were able to quickly respond to calls from these trouble spots.

Squire N. W. Wilbur was named city marshal in 1883. Lieutenant James A. Allen was second in command of the force of policemen that consisted of five white patrolmen and five black patrolmen.

The Tennessee legislature passed an act on March 29, 1883, to amend the charter of the City of Chattanooga and again remove control of the police from the city council and place it under a commission appointed by the governor. The legislation grew out of a power struggle between political factions in Nashville and Chattanooga. The act abolished the office of City Marshal and established a new metropolitan system of policing for the city to be commanded by a Chief of Police. The principles of new police system were defined in Section 4 of the act.

It shall not be lawful for the mayor and aldermen to elect or appoint any of the police force of the

Patrolmen John F. Hall, left, and Ebenezer I. Litz in the late 1880s wore uniforms that varied, which was typical in the period when uniform standards were less strict. A military style belt was worn by the officer on the right. Both wore the pinched shield as a breast badge. The officer on the left carried a shorter baton, the type often used for day duty and the officer on the right carried a longer "night stick." Offenders were more often drunk and rowdy at night and a longer baton delivered a more powerful blow. Many officers carried a longer baton whenever they were on duty.

city, but the same shall be appointed by the majority of three commissioners, which commissioners shall be appointed by the Governor; their terms of office shall be for three years, not more than two of whom shall be of the same political party; the said commissioners are fully empowered to exercise power and control over the police of the city; they shall appoint as policeman men of known integrity and character, fully competent to discharge the duties of policemen physically and mentally, and no person shall be a policeman who has not reached his 25th year; the commission is authorized to fix the salaries and establish rules and regulations for the government of the force; the office of city marshal is abolished and the commissioners shall appoint a chief of police in his stead.

The first commission appointed by the governor consisted of N. C. Ford, who served as president of the commission; G. W. Wheeland, the vice-president; and W. J. Golburn, secretary and treasurer of the commission. Three men were nominated to serve as chief of police, former city marshal N. W. Wilbur, former lieutenant James A. Allen and D. M. Doty, another former city marshal. On April 13, James A. Allen was chosen chief of police. D. M. Doty was appointed assistant chief.

Ten white policemen were named to the force, First Lieutenant W. P. "Dock" Mitchell, Second Lieutenant J. P. Kilgore, W. T. Douglas, M. F. Fitzgerald, R. A. Giles, J. A. Hogan, H. L. Longley, J. G. Prive, C. M. Rape and H. L. Sloop. Black officers would not serve on the force again until the modern era. Salaries established included $75 per month to the chief, $65 a month for the assistant chief and $60 per month for patrolmen. A month later R. French Lawson, J. Sullivan, E. J. "Abe" Litz, H. R. Williams and J. M. Davis were appointed supernumeraries or extra policemen.

Marshal Wilbur stated that he would not dismiss the old force until he was ordered to do so by the city council. On Monday morning, April 15, both the old force under Marshal Wilbur and the new force under Chief Allen walked their beats in the city. For two days the city had two police forces. The mayor and aldermen met Tuesday evening and dismissed Marshal Wilbur and his force.

Policemen on the new department remained divided into two squads and worked 12-hour shifts. One squad was on duty from midnight until noon and the other from noon to midnight. Patrolmen were required to make a complete circuit of their assigned districts during each shift. Officers had 60 days to acquire uniforms, at their own expense. The authorized arms were a pistol and a billy club, both to be worn outside the coat. The badge style was designated to be a circle-star, or "silver star and wreath," but the force continued to wear the large shield until the early nineties.

Disciplinary policy was established. Policemen were suspended for insubordination or disrespect, mistreatment of prisoners, neglect of duty, violation of department rules, absence without leave, immoral conduct and mental or physical incapacity. An officer had to get the permission of two commissioners in order to leave the city. The maximum age for an officer was 50 years.

One major source of crime in Chattanooga grew out of the hard times created by the depressed national economy. The extensive network of railroads made it easy for vagrants to travel into the city and panhandle or steal. The city council passed strict anti-vagrancy laws in 1885 and assigned the police force to make regular patrols of Union Terminal.

Police responded to a variety of incidents due to people traveling through the city. Policeman John Usery gained praise for action above and beyond the call of duty in tracking down a stolen horse and cart. Two men accosted an out of town visitor and took his rented rig. Officer Usery tracked the horse cart on foot. Night fell and he continued tracking by lighting matches at frequent intervals. Seven miles down Rossville Road he caught the thieves at a tavern and arrested them.

Chief of Police Tom J. Howard replaced James Allen in 1887 and within a year the force grew to 38 patrolmen. N. C. Ford, F. O. Wert and P. Lazard were commissioners. Chief Howard was the only officer with rank in the department and directly supervised the patrolmen. The mayor stated in his annual report that he "found Commissioners, Chief and Patrolmen ready at all times to render any assistance needed, and promptly to enforce all ordinances of the city." Chief Howard insisted that policemen present a neat and orderly appearance to the general public. The force drilled daily. Patrolman Joseph A. Pogue recalled the department in 1887.

To be accepted as a member of the department was considered a complement to one's physique and character. Headquarters was located at Fourth and Market and if you arrested a drunk in South Chattanooga you had to drag him all the way to the station. There was no patrol wagon then. All cases were tried before A. G. Sharp, who was mayor and city judge.

The Chattanooga police department in 1884. In the front row, left to right, were French Lawson, First Lieutenant and Assistant Chief W. P. "Dock" Mitchell (a future chief), Chief of Police James A. Allen, Second Lieutenant and Assistant Chief J. P. Kilgore (a future chief), Tom Russell, and "Dasher" Bates. Left to right in the second row were John Shelow, Tom J. Howard, Caleb Smith, Frank Duncan, W. F. Springer, John Usery, and Jenkins. The back row from left to right were an unidentified officer, John Hall, John Hankins, Cicero Rape, and Abe Litz. Uniforms were double breasted with brass buttons and a plain pinched shield breast badge. The wide brim hats had no insignia. Chief of Police James Allen was the first to hold the title Chief of Police. He was appointed to the position on April 13, 1883, and served for twelve years. Allen had previously served as a lieutenant on the force.

There were 33 policemen then who worked 12-hour shifts. Chattanooga was a rather wide-open town then. There was a saloon on practically every corner and gambling houses operating all night. It wasn't unusual to have to arrest everyone in those places every once in a while. There were plenty of free-for-alls.

Chief Pat Kilgore replaced Chief Howard in January 1890. At the same time the rank of Roundsman was established. The roundsmen patrolled and supervised patrolmen. Tom Russell and Robert Emory Baird were the first two officers to serve as roundsmen. The rank was later replaced by that of

Patrol Sergeant. Lieutenants John Hankins and D. C. Mitchell assisted the chief in command.

J. H. Cass, who retired as a captain 21 years later, joined the department on December 4, 1889, along with F. W. Hill, J. F. Carr, Marsh Doudy, Jerry Donovan, Joe Pogue and B. F. Carr. Cass recalled his days as a patrolman under Chief Kilgore, "Every officer wore a helmet, carried a club, and as much artillery as he wished. We had a two-horse patrol wagon, but it ran only at night." A patrol wagon was acquired late in 1887. Two new position were created, the Patrol Driver drove the wagon and the Patrol Guard was stationed at the rear of the wagon with a club to be certain no prisoner escaped.

Routine patrol could quickly bring an officer face to face with death. On the evening of December 19, 1890, Patrolman David C. Musgrove was working the beat called "Pat Row" and his partner Patrolman Joseph A. Pogue was working Main Street. A known thief had been spotted and Officer Musgrove proceeded to Irvine's Saloon to make the arrest. The saloon was divided into three sections, a sandwich shop in front was separated from the barroom by a swinging lattice door. Behind the bar was the gambling room with card tables. Musgrove arrested the thief at one of the tables.

As the officer and his prisoners passed through the barroom, the thief pulled away from Musgrove and drew a pistol. His first shot missed, but the second hit Musgrove in the left side. The bar owner tried to help until a third shot just missed the barman's head. Musgrove grabbed the gun and wrestled the shooter into the sandwich room. The gunman got loose, fired another wild shot and fled down the street. Officer Musgrove followed and was able to get off two shots before he faltered. He gave his gun to the bar owner and said, "Catch him! Catch him!" Two men moved Patrolman Musgrove onto a table in the lunchroom. The patrol wagon with policemen from headquarters soon arrived. Officer Pogue reached Musgrove's side just as he drew his last breath. David Musgrove died at 10:07 p.m.

Musgrove's killer was able escape Chattanooga, but Alabama & Great Southern Railway Detective J. B. Matthews headed him off. Matthews was a former policeman at Union Station and drill master for the Chattanooga Police Department. Chief Kilgore got a telegram from Matthews about 11:30 the next morning saying he had Officer Musgrove's killer in custody. A crowd gathered at the jail when the killer was brought back, but the police force was determined that he be tried for the crime. The killer of Patrolman David C. Musgrove was convicted of murder and hanged in the county jail on January 2, 1892.

The department purchased a horse drawn patrol wagon in 1887 that was used into the early twentieth century. The patrol wagon was used to transport prisoners and to transport officers to emergency calls. The patrol wagon was manned by a patrol driver and a patrol guard to oversee prisoners during transport. The wagon was destroyed in 1906 when a collision with a locomotive killed Patrol Driver May.

Patrolman Ben Kerr served as a Chattanooga policeman from 1889 to 1913. In cold weather he wore the full length winter coat which covered his sidearm. His insignia was the circle-star breast badge and a wreath on his helmet.

Chattanooga policemen began wearing the circle-star style badge around 1892. The five-point star cut in the center of the badge contained a number and the circle around the star showed the words "Chattanooga" and "Police" at the top and bottom. The insignia of the chief and other high ranking supervisors consisted of epaulets and sometimes lapel insignia; they wore no breast badge.

Uniforms consisted of dark coats with brass buttons and dark trousers. Hats were bell crown helmets for patrolmen and flat-top caps for the top ranks.

Lieutenant Fred W. Hill was appointed chief of police in March 1893 when Pat Kilgore resigned. Hill had a solid law enforcement background. He had been on the Chattanooga force four years and was one of the most honest and aggressive members of the department.

Hill was a businessman until 1885 when he was appointed chief deputy U. S. marshal by the Cleveland administration. Four years later he became a U. S. revenue collector, enforcing federal tax laws against East Tennessee moonshiners. He began his service in the Chattanooga Police Department as a supernumerary and was named a regular officer in 1889. One year later he was promoted to roundsman and to lieutenant in April 1891.

In a political move in April, Dock M. Mitchell was made chief. Mitchell's tenure ended when he died after being struck by lightning in July. Fred Hill was once again appointed chief and was unanimously elected chief of police by the police commission on August 1. Chief Hill was a capable manager and reduced the size of the force by increasing efficiency.

Thirty-three-year-old Chief Hill was the first "professionally" oriented police executive and during his term of office he concentrated on upgrading the department. He was a founding member of the National Association of the Chiefs of Police of the United States and Canada. This organization was to later become the International Association of Chiefs of Police.

The rank of Captain was created in 1893 and Lieutenant E. G. Huffaker was promoted to captain. The position of Chief of Detectives was created in 1895 and B. D. Haskins was appointed to the job. Haskins was serving as one of two sergeants on the force at the time. Creation of the new division of police was the result of the growing importance of plain clothes investigation. With police uniforms more distinctive and policemen less corruptible, crime went underground. Gangs used lookouts when they committed crimes. The work of detectives became important to ferret out criminals and criminal activity.

Police headquarters moved to the Market House where other city government offices were located on January 15, 1898. In February the new city jail constructed on E Street was opened and prisoners transferred there.

Chattanooga hosted the sixth annual convention of the National Association of Chiefs of Police of the

The Chattanooga Police Department in 1899. The force wore winter uniforms. Insignia included a breast badge in the form of a circle with a five-point star cut in the center, and a wreath hat badge. Patrolmen's uniforms included a coat with a single row of buttons and a helmet for head cover. Supervisors wore coats with a double row of buttons and a flat-top cap.

United States and Canada in May 1899. More than fifty chiefs of police attended the event. A souvenir publication of the event featured the personnel of the Chattanooga department. The 44-man force was headed by Chief Fred W. Hill, who was assisted in commander by Captain E. G. Huffaker and Captain T. C.

The command of the Chattanooga police force in 1899 included from left to right Chief of Police Fred W. Hill, Captain E. G. Huffaker, and Captain T. C. Russell. Chief Hill was selected chief at the age of 33. He served from 1893 to 1905 and raised the level of professionalism of the department.

Russell. Patrol supervisors were Day Sergeant William Clift, who also served as clerk to the police commission and Night Sergeant J. A. Hogan. Detectives were William H. Smith and Frank Wells.

The 26 patrolmen were R. E. Baird, V. M. Bell, S. H. Bennett, Will Burk, N. Carlton, John H. Cass, J. D. Croft, T. J. Dillard, J. T. Fry, G. M. Gilbraith, J. F. Hall, O. B. Johnson, B. F. Kerr, Ben Kessler, H. A. Krichbaum, G. L. Krug, H. C. May, J. T. Moseley, T. O. Musgrove, T. G. Newman, J. G. Parker, C. M. Rape, E. J. Scanlon, Frank Smith, R. A. Turner and John Woy. Part-time "supernumeraries" were M. M. Broxton, T. J. Chamberlain, C. C. Hixson, Frosty Johnson, I. C. Morgan and M. H. Poe.

Other department personnel included Patrol Guard T. J. Carlton, Patrol Driver W. R. Teppenpaw, Court Officer W. H. Light, Jailer P. A. Brandon and Night Jailer J. N. Hightower. Commissioners were W. E. Dyer, president of the commission; T. C. Latimore, vice-president; and Thomas McDermott, secretary and treasurer.

Captain E. G. Huffaker was the senior captain and considered the assistant chief. He joined the department in 1886 after wanting to be a lawman since his youth. Following six years on patrol he was promoted to lieutenant in October 1891 and to captain two years later. Huffaker served as secretary of the Police Benefit Association.

Captain T. C. Russell also aspired to be a policeman from his boyhood. He became a patrolman in 1884 after serving for a time as a supernumerary, substituting for patrolmen or working when otherwise needed. He was promoted to lieutenant in 1893 and to captain two years later.

Russell was shot in the left arm in an incident on the night of August 18, 1896, leaving his arm unusable for the rest of his life. He was making rounds on West Sixth Street when he came across a man standing in the shadows. When the officer confronted him, the man pulled a .45 caliber, 8-inch, double action Colt revolver and began firing. One of the balls tore through Russell's left arm. The shooter, an infamous highwayman, escaped but was surrounded by a detachment of policemen in January the following year. The outlaw opened fire and struck Detective Brock in the arm before other officers fatally wounded the felon.

Due to the efforts of Chief Hill the Chattanooga Police Department entered the new century with a reputation for integrity and professionalism. The state gave up control of Chattanooga's police in 1901 and a Board of Public Safety was established by the city council to oversee the department.

A new city prison was constructed on E Street in 1898.

Chief Hill understood the importance of keeping accurate records and created the position of bookkeeper for the force. The department established an identification bureau in 1901. The bureau initially used the Bertillion method of identification, which employed a series of complicated physical measurements taken by special instruments to establish a criminal's identity. In 1905 the department changed to the Henry system of taking fingerprints, making Chattanooga one of the first to adopt fingerprint identification.

Mrs. T. P. "Rachel" Marshall was hired in 1902 as matron for the police force. She was issued a buggy and returned errant children to their homes. The position of matron continued until 1941.

Chief of Police John T. Moseley took command of the department in 1905. Chief Moseley wore a jeweler-made breast badge that became the model for badges worn by command officers for almost a century. Moseley encouraged education and physical fitness for police officers.

Chief Moseley was a 15 year veteran of the department and familiar with the dangers of police work. On one occasion he was shot twice while making an arrest in an East Ninth Street saloon. Moseley barely escaped with his life another time when he was the lone officer in a confrontation with a number of lawbreakers. He was saved when a citizen, Will Nun, drew two pistols and backed him up.

The department purchased fifty Winchester Model 97 pump shotguns in 1905 for use in riots and guard duty. Many of the weapons remained in service until the 1960s. Prior to the purchase, the department had rented shotguns when they were needed.

Chief Moseley created the department's first mounted patrol unit, which was highly successful. He hired six patrolmen and purchased horses. Three mounted officers were assigned to each watch. Two horses and mounted officers stayed available at headquarters to respond to emergency calls. The horses were stabled in the basement of city hall.

A September 14, 1906, incident involving the department's horse drawn patrol wagon proved fatal for Patrol Driver Hugh May. The patrol wagon was returning from South Chattanooga with two prisoners under the watchful eye of Patrol Guard A. L. Clark. Normally May would have been riding guard, but the regular patrol driver was off. When the wagon reached

Chief of Police John T. Moseley, a fifteen year veteran, took command of the department in 1905 and served as chief until 1909. Chief Moseley created the department's first mounted patrol unit.

Captain J. D. Croft and Matron Mrs. T. P. Marshall circa 1905. Croft served as captain under Chief Moseley and Rachel Marshall was appointed matron in 1902 and worked with women and children. Croft and Marshall were later married.

the railroad crossing at Coward Street, May stopped and then proceeded when he was waved on by the railroad watchman at the crossing.

Midway of the crossing the wagon was struck by a train engine running backwards and pulling a number of cars. The wagon was destroyed and one horse killed. Clark and the prisoners were thrown clear. The impact threw Officer May between the wagon and the engine and he was dragged 50 feet.

"Uncle" Hugh May, who joined the department in 1887, died at 3:30 the following morning. May was known as a tough cop with a big heart. Sixteen officers, led by Captain Croft on horseback, marched from police headquarters to Policeman May's home, where he was given a police funeral.

Chief of Police Fred W. Hill returned to his former post in 1909, replacing Chief Moseley. The department's first communication system, a Gamewell

Examples of police department transportation in 1910. The engine driven patrol wagon was the first motorized vehicle acquired by the department. The mounted patrol remained the primary mode of non-foot transportation. The three mounted officer from left to right were Clarence Livingston, J. J. Irvins, and W. C. "Billy" Smith, who became one of Chattanooga's first motorcycle officers when the unit was formed in 1912.

Uniforms and insignia of Chattanooga policemen in 1910. Captain W. H. Hackett, far left, wore epaulets and bullion sewn hat insignia designating his rank. He wore the same breast badge as other officers, numbered and without rank designation. Patrolman W. E. Wann, second from left, wore the helmet of patrol officers and a metal hat badge with crossed batons. Mounted Policeman W. S. Baker, second from right, wore a visor cap with bullion sewn insignia reading "Mounted Police." Policeman B. F. Kerr, far right, wore a hat with full brim and no insignia, as did patrol drivers and other non-patrol officers.

Mounted Officer C. Ray Bryan talked with a patrolman at a Gamewell System call box about to report into the headquarters on the half hour. The Gamewell System was first installed in 1909 and served as the only communication between headquarters and the patrolman on the beat, unless the officer used a private or business telephone.

Fire and Police T. C. Betterton was the first to head the new department. The uniformed officers and the detectives functioned as two distinct and separate organizations within the police department. Each had a chief and both chiefs reported directly to the commissioner.

Eight-hour shifts were implemented for uniformed officers. Policemen continued to work seven days a week and they were required to work an extra four hours once a week. These extra hours enabled the department to maintain a reserve squad to be used in case of riots, major fires, or unusual circumstances.

The detective department was composed of Chief of Detectives William H. "Big Bill" Smith, at the rank of captain and six detectives. The investigative function of the department continued to grow in importance and detectives were considered the most prestigious positions on the force. The chief of detectives answered directly to the commissioner of fire and police, and was virtually equal in authority to the chief

Board, was installed in 1909. Prior to this policemen were summoned by police whistle or a runner. The introduction of telephone technology enabled citizens and officers to call headquarters to report an emergency or summon help. The Gamewell network gave the department a system dedicated to official communications.

The Gamewell Board system linked ten call boxes located throughout the city. Beat officers were required to call in every half-hour. Patrolmen were then given any calls for assistance on their beat that had come in to headquarters since their last call. Mounted patrolmen responded to serious emergency calls directly from headquarters.

A new badge style was also adopted in 1909. The silver-tone, pinched shield with a number disk at the center of the badge was the same style worn by the Cincinnati, Ohio, force.

Chief of Police Thomas P. McMahan took command of the department in 1910 and served until 1912. Police Headquarters remained at the Market House in 1910 when city government moved to a new municipal building on East 11th Street.

The Department of Fire and Police replaced the Board of Public Safety in 1911 as the governing structure of Chattanooga's police force. Commissioner of

Mounted Patrol Officer Fred Payne in 1911 was wearing a wheel patch on his uniform, the same as motorcycle officers.

of police. Fred W. Hill returned as chief of police in 1912.

Despite the best efforts of detectives, occasionally a case was not solved, even the killing of a policeman. Patrolman Clarence Livingston was killed on August 12, 1912, when he responded to a burglary call at Tom Dillard's Saloon on East Main Street. Livingston was one of the mounted officers at headquarters and rode to the scene on horseback. As he questioned a man standing in the alley at the rear of the saloon, a shot rang out from the building's basement. The bullet ricocheted off Livingston's flashlight and struck the officer in the stomach. He was not able to draw his service weapon as the two subjects fled down the alley. Policeman Livingston died a few hours later.

A wagon load of officers and Captain W. H. Hackett soon arrived and began the investigation and manhunt. They were joined by Chief of Police Hill and Chief of Detectives Smith. In an hour two suspects were in custody and a third soon after. With no real evidence against them, they were released. Two days later a mob intent on lynching Livingston's killers reached police headquarters in 20 automobiles

Policeman "Uncle" Hugh C. May, left, died on September 15, 1906, after the patrol wagon he was driving was struck by a train on Cowart Street. Mounted Policeman Clarence Livingston, right, responded on horseback to a call of a break in at a Main Street saloon on August 31, 1912. A shot fired from inside the building struck Livingston in the stomach and he died a few hours later.

demanding the suspects. Sergeant Frank Smith ordered Gamewell Board operator Tom Williams to sound the alarm. Bells in fire-halls all over town rang, calling policemen, on duty and off, to headquarters. Captain Hackett defused the rage of the mob by showing them the cells were empty. Despite an exhaustive investigation, Livingston's killer was never brought to justice.

Respect for Chattanooga's police force was heightened again in 1912 by the bravery of Patrolman Howard Peck. Peck was presented a gold medal for his quick action in stopping a runaway team and wagon on Market Street. The policeman boldly stepped in front of the team, grabbed the reins and stopped them, preventing property damage or personal injury.

The department got its first motorcycle in 1912. The Indian motorcycles were surplus from the army. P. C. Pennybaker and W. C. "Billy" Smith became the first motorcycle officers. They were instructed to ride through the city and warn bicycle riders to put bells and lights on their bikes and to stay off sidewalks. The motorcycles were so noisy they had to stay off some residential streets and were not allowed on Market Street because the noise frightened horses. Smith was the first officer to be injured on a motorcycle. He broke his leg when he fell at East Third and Palmetto streets.

Over the next few years motorcycles gradually replaced the horses of the mounted patrol until 1919, when horses were no longer used for patrol. The transition from horses to motorcycles was not always an easy one. Roy Hyatt, who would later command the

Chief of Police F. W. Hill joined the force in 1889 and was first appointed to head the department in March 1893. He served a number of terms as chief of police and chief of detectives until 1916. Chief Hill brought his experiences as a business man and federal law enforcement officer, and heightened the professionalism of Chattanooga's police department.

motorcycle unit, took mounted patrolmen to Warner Park for motorcycle riding lessons.

Even with training, old habits were hard to break. In one incident Officer R. H. Branson sped to an emergency call. Upon arrival, riding his newly assigned motorcycle, he yelled "Whoa" and pulled back on the handlebars. The mechanical horse did not respond and Branson crashed through a picket fence to his embarrassment and to the bemusement of the crowd at the scene. In a similar lapse, Officer Orville Bass pulled on the "reins" of his ride and drove under a mule, getting knocked off his two-wheeler and sending the mule galloping toward Main Street with the rider clinging to its neck.

Following his re-election in 1915, Commissioner Betterton named new leadership in the police department. Captain William H. Hackett was appointed chief of police and Robert Bass was named chief of detectives. Chief Hackett quickly set the tone for his tenure as chief of police, "The men on their beats must wear their uniforms. The captains and sergeants too,

Commissioner of Fire and Police T. C. Betterton, left, and Chief of Police William H. Hackett.

must wear theirs, and the chief of police will wear his. He will police with his men." Hackett was a strict disciplinarian, but was also fair and impartial.

The Chattanooga Police Department in 1922. Uniforms were similar to those worn by other departments of the era. Breast badges were pinched shields and hat badges for patrolmen are eagle-top shields with the state seal and a number panel at the base. Commanders continue to wear bullion-type hat wreaths showing the rank. Chief of Police W. L. Baker was standing on the lowest step at the right .

Department discipline was put to the test in August 1916 when civil disorder known as the "streetcar riots" erupted in the city. Streetcar motormen walked off the job leaving streetcars sitting in the streets where they stopped. A mob formed near Sixth and Market streets and became disorderly. The crowd was subdued by police using water hoses and guns.

Police salaries increased in 1917 for all ranks except the chief and assistant chief. Captains were increased to $1,500 per year and the new rank of Lieutenant got $1,320. Patrolmen earned $900 their first year, $960 their second year and $1,200 in their third year and thereafter.

W. L. Baker, a department veteran, was named chief of police in 1919 by newly elected Commissioner E. D. Herron. Chief Baker took pride in wearing his uniform to work every day. Disbanding of the mounted unit was completed soon after Baker became chief. The last members of the mounted patrol were Orville Bass, R. H. Branson, C. Ray Bryan, Charlie Hartness, Jack Neil and Lee Woy. All went to the motorcycle squad except Neil and Bryan, who were promoted to detective.

Chief Hackett became chief of detectives and served in the position for the next twenty years. New technology advanced detective work in the early 1920s. Detective C. Ray Bryan, a member of the department since 1911 and former mounted officer, demonstrated investigative ability and foresight. He was sent to Birmingham and studied scientific methods of investigation under a well respected criminologist. Bryan later created the bureau of criminal identification using fingerprints and other scientific techniques.

Emerging technology did not alter the dangers of police work. Officers James Willis Duggan and J. H. Gouldy were assisting Detective J. M. Gibson of the Knoxville Police Department in tracking down an interstate thief on June 22, 1921. Duggan was shot and killed when the three went to investigate a house on Adams Street. While Gouldy and Gibson sought entry through the front door, Duggan went to the rear of the house and entered through an unlocked door.

Duggan made his way down a darkened hallway as his two colleagues interviewed occupants in the front room. Duggan passed the open door to a dark room and two shots were fired. Duggan was hit and fell to the floor unconscious. Gouldy and Gibson ran toward the rear of the house. They too were fired on. Gibson took Duggan's pistol and the two returned fire. When the gun battle ended, the gunman lay dead.

Forty-one-year-old Policeman Willis Duggan was

Officers George Webb, W. C. Wheat, Bob Black, Lawrence Swanson, Captain Gober, and Lee Way stood in front of the departments Patrol Wagon and Model T Ford automobiles in this 1922 photograph of Chattanooga's "Tin Lizzy Squad."

The department's 1922 Motorcycle Squad included from left to right Bob Black, Ruben Branson, Ollie Alford, Roy Hyatt, Red Gang, Bill Garrett, Charles Hartness, and W. C. Wheat. They wore special hat badges and wheel arm patches.

pronounced dead on arrival at Newell's Hospital. He was a six year veteran of the department, the last three of which he served as a plainclothes "liquor raider." With passage of the Volstead Act, confrontations with rumrunners and bootleggers increased and often led to gunfire.

Detectives established a good record for the department. Of the 180 stolen cars reported in 1924, the detective division recovered 132. Additional stolen vehicles were recovered by patrol officers. The department answered 1,324 complaints and recovered more than $94,000.

Roy Hyatt was promoted to captain in 1922 and took command of the motorcycle squad. His reputation on the squad earned him the nickname "Tail Light Slim." Hyatt was a disciplinarian and under his command the unit developed the reputation as a "Spit 'n' Shine Motor Squad." The Motorcycle Squad was disbanded in 1934 when radios were introduced. Early radio units were too bulky to mount on motorcycles. Patrolman "Robbie" Robertson was one of the last members of Hyatt's unit and continued to wear the hat badge that read "Motorcycle Police" as long as he remained on the force.

Around 1925 the department changed breast badges. A "radiator" style badge, similar to those worn in the Boston area, was adopted. It was sometimes called the "church door" badge by officers because upside-down it looked like the front door of the Saints Peter and Paul Catholic Church on Eighth Street. A white shirt without a jacket was worn in the summer and the badge was so heavy that it frequently tore the shirt. For this reason officers usually wore the badge on their belt. Arm patches in the form of a wheel were worn on the left arm by traffic men. By 1927 the department numbered 97 officers.

Motorcycle officers A. R. Boles and Richard Paradiso were patrolling Chattanooga's south side on the morning of June 15, 1929, when they spotted a small roadster laboring under its load. They came along side the car and told the driver to pull over, but he sped away. The car was finally stopped at the corner of East Main and Madison. A gun battle erupted that lasted ten minutes and left the two liquor runners wounded. The fact that four such armed confrontations with lawmen took place in the same week was a sign of the lawlessness of the era.

Chief of Police W. L. Baker died of a heart attack on February 1, 1930. Baker remained a dedicated officer throughout his 11-year tenure as chief and participated in an all night stakeout of a bootlegger's establishment the day before his death. He was eulogized as a dedicated and honest public servant.

Assistant Chief C. Ray Bryan was appointed chief

Chief of Police W. L. Baker served from 1919 until his death from a heart attack in 1930.

of police on February 5, 1930. Chief Bryan had moved out west as a young man and became a cowboy. He returned to Chattanooga specifically to ride horses for the Chattanooga Police Department. Bryan had exceptional ability and proven himself the best pistol shot in the department, its best horseman and a criminologist without peer in the region. He was one of the first scientific policeman. He created Chattanooga's first crime lab and identification department and was instrumental in getting one-way radios in the patrol cars.

A double tragedy confronted Chief Bryan and Chattanooga's police force in November 1931. In a single week gunfire claimed the life of two policemen. Patrolman J. H. Cornett was walking his beat on the south side about 8:30 p.m. on November 4. As he passed the front of Magrill's grocery he saw a man and woman arguing. The man had a gun in his hand and Officer Cornett told him to drop the weapon. Instead, the man leaped behind a telephone pole and began firing at the officer at close range with a .45 caliber revolver. Cornett fired three shots before he fell, hitting the gunman twice. The shooter and his wife got in their car and drove away.

Headquarters received the call and Commissioner E. J. Bryan, Captain Roy Hyatt, Detectives H. F. Pane and G. B. Abercrombie and Officer C. L. Gardenhire came to the scene. Patrolmen Jesse G. Shirley and Clark came to the scene from their beats. Patrolman Cornett lay dead in a pool of blood, his cap to one side and his service revolver near his right hand. J. H. Cornett was 41 years old and had been a policeman for eight years.

The manhunt led officers to the house of the killer. Captain Hyatt, Detective Abercrombie and Officer Gardenhire caught the woman as she sneaked into the rear of the Popular Street home and arrested her as an accessory to murder. Officer Shirley and Detective Pane arrested the killer for first degree murder at his car in an alley between two houses. His wounds were minor. The force made the arrests within 15 minutes of the incident.

Three days later Motorcycle Officers Jesse G. Shirley and Aaron Robertson answered a complaint call of disorderly conduct and a shooting. They arrived at the house on North Highland Park at 10:50 p.m. and found a number of people drinking in the front room. They were directed to the middle room where they found a man with a .38 caliber revolver. The gunman said, "My gun is as good as yours," and began firing at the officers at point blank range. They both drew weapons and fired. Officer Shirley was hit by a bullet in the left side that went through both of his lungs. The gunman was shot and killed by the officers.

Officer Robertson transported Shirley to Erlanger Hospital. Shirley died of his wound at 5:30 the next afternoon. Officer Jesse G. Shirley had been on the force for six years.

Less than nine months later, July 15, 1932, Patrolman W. J. Mashburn was also gunned down. Officer Mashburn heard the report of a pistol at 7:30 p.m. as he walked his beat on Market Street near Fifth. He ran up the hill on East Fifth and saw a man with a gun. The gunman had fired a shot at a man with whom he was arguing and now fired at Mashburn. The shot missed and Mashburn cut through an alley to head off the gunman.

A gun battle erupted in a courtyard at the end of the alley. The first shot fired at the officer missed but struck two bystanders including a 12-year-old boy. Mashburn and the gunman continued firing. The gunman was mortally wounded with shots to the chest and left side. Thirty-one-year-old Officer W. J. Mashburn was hit in the both legs, hip and lower abdomen. He died the following evening after three years on the force.

Patrolmen C. Ben Butler, left, and Lloyd G. Goode with a department emergency car in 1933 wore Motorcycle Squad uniforms.

Police communication, an important safety factor for officers, was improving. After two years of planning and evaluation of radio systems for the police department, Chief Bryan oversaw the implementation of an RCA radio system in December 1933. A transmitter was installed on the roof of the Hotel Patten, the dispatcher located at headquarters and patrol cars equipped with receivers. The system was one-way with radio transmission from headquarters to patrol units. Officers in the field continued to communicate with the stationhouse by telephone.

Initially radio receivers were large and bulky and not practical for mounting on motorcycles. As a result the motor squad was virtually eliminated. The depart-ment changed to cars for motorized patrol of the city. When a call was put out, a bell was rung over the air to get the officers' attention and then the location and type of call was broadcast.

The early 1930s brought innovation in a low-tech piece of police equipment. Nightsticks were replaced by blackjacks. Nightsticks had become considered too dangerous and were seen as provoking violence.

Chattanooga police responded to an out-of-state call for help in 1937. Flooding inundated much of the Mississippi and Ohio river valleys. Louisville, Kentucky, was particularly hard hit and its police department requested assistance from other cities. Chattanooga sent fifteen officers under the command of Lieutenant Homer Edmonson to assist during late January and early February.

While Chattanooga was sending officers to assist out of state, criminals from out of state were plying their trade in the city. Chattanooga Detective O. O. Griffin found himself kidnapped by a foursome led by a Detroit ex-con. Headquarters received a call on June 21, 1937, that the gang had tried to sell stolen property and were parked behind the Grand Theater. Detective Griffin found the car, got in the back seat and told the driver to drive to the station house a block away. The driver turned and pushed a German Luger in the detective's face.

They disarmed the lawman and drove out Ringgold Road. Near Bald Knob, Georgia, they bound and gagged Detective Griffin, took $6 of the lawman's $11 in pocket money and half his pack of cigarettes, then dumped him beside the road. Griffin was able to free himself and hitched a ride to a telephone and reported the incident. FBI agents apprehended the

Traffic Officer T. L. Crowder, left, wore the traffic uniform of the thirties in a 1936 photograph. Patrolman Aaron "Robbie" Robertson, right, was one of the last members of Hyatt's motorcycle unit and continued to wear the hat badge that read "Motorcycle Police" until he left the force.

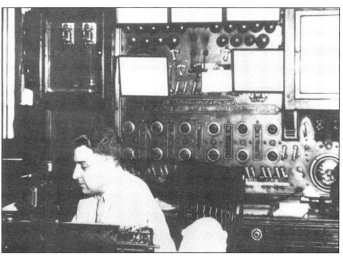

The Gamewell Board was still in use at headquarters in 1934, connecting the communications office with beat officers.

Patrolmen A. T. Atwood, left, and Tom Williams wore long-sleeve white shirts without jackets as designated for the summer uniform in the late thirties. They wore the "Church Door" style breast badges on their belts because the insignia was too heavy to wear on the shirt.

four at a tourist camp in Tampa, Florida, a week later.

A couple of years later Chattanooga police had their hands full with a pair of gangsters on the run from Minnesota. The two robbed the Sweetwater Valley Cafe at 2:30 a.m. on Christmas Day 1939. Within the next 24 hours the two, driving a black Buick sedan and wielding nickel-plated automatic pistols, held up three businesses in Chattanooga. A massive manhunt was launched. Public radio stations reported the events and citizens called in possible sightings. Officers in radio cars were busy following up on tips. Business owners and other citizens armed themselves.

Chief Deputy Claude Brown of the Hamilton County Sheriff's Office received a call at the jail around 5:00 p.m. on December 26. An employee of a Rock Castle roadhouse reported two suspicious men accompanied by two women staying in one of the double cabins at the motel. The caller said they arrived in a black Buick sedan and when he delivered meals to the group he saw several guns lying about.

Chattanooga police Captain Homer Edmonson and Detectives Clyde J. Shipley, Claude Knowles and John Carson proceeded to the motel. Since the roadhouse was located in the county the city officers were accompanied by uniformed county patrol officers Lieutenant Sherman Dyer and Patrolman Ira Hudlow. It was dark and drizzling rain when they arrived.

As the officer approached the cabin, lights on one side of the double unit went dark. Captain Edmonson, Detective Knowles and Lieutenant Dyer went to the front door. Detectives Shipley and Carson, and Patrolman Hudlow went to the back. The captain banged on the front door and yelled, "We're police officer and we want to look you over." The silence was finally broken by a female voice saying, "You will have to wait, I'm dressing." Then a husky male voice roared, "Come and get us, you damned coppers." With that a hail of gunfire came from the dark side of the structure. Edmonson pulled the trigger on his riot gun, but the weapon misfired and the officers took cover.

The three officers in the rear kicked open the back door on the lighted side of the cabin when they heard the gunfire. Detective Shipley entered the cabin. He reached the bathroom in the center of the unit and two shots were fired. Shipley was hit and fell dead on the floor of the bath, his pistol still in his hand. Gunfire forced Carson and Hudlow back. Carson ran to the front of the cabin and reported to Edmonson, "Be careful captain, they've killed Shipley! He never had a chance."

Captain Edmonson stationed the lawmen and the roadhouse worker, who had armed himself, around the cabin and a pitched gun battle began between the lawmen and the gangsters that lasted for twenty minutes. At one point the gunfire ceased and four figures ran from the cabin to the nearby garage and the gunfire recommenced.

One of the gangsters yelled, "They got one of the girls. Now I'm going to get one of them!" He then stuck his head out to get a shot at one of the officers. Captain Edmonson fired his rifle and the gunman slumped to the ground, a .45 automatic pistol in his right hand and a .38 special revolver in the left. The second gangster then ran from the garage into the heavy woods. The two "molls" came screaming from the garage with their hands in the air. One had a head wound.

Bloodhounds were brought to search, but without success. Captain Roy Hyatt took charge of the manhunt and organized a systematic search including stakeouts of train depots and bus terminals. Patrolmen Ben Susman and R. I Fraizier were off duty, but volunteered for the search. They were assigned to canvass the area around Main and Market. About midnight they roused the landlady of a rooming house on East Main Street. She said a man had checked in an hour earlier and directed them to the room.

They shined their flashlight on the slim figure lying in the bed asleep and were doubtful it was the killer until they saw the glint of a automatic pistol near his right hand. A second pistol was in reach of his left hand. Just then the eyes of the outlaw began to open. Patrolman Frazier jumped on top of the stirring form. Patrolman Susman followed and the two subdued the killer. It was later discovered that the automatic pistol on the bed was Detective Shipley's duty weapon.

Detective Clyde J. Shipley was an eleven-year veteran of the force and 41 years old. His father had also been a Chattanooga policeman. Before his promotion to detective, Shipley had been a member of Hyatt's "spit and shine" motorcycle squad. His killer was convicted of first-degree murder and three counts of highway robbery.

The 1940s brought significant changes to the Chattanooga Police Department. Commissioner E. R. Betterton, brother of T. C. Betterton, Chattanooga's first police commissioner, took office in January 1941. He replaced Commissioner Eugene Bryan, who resigned after fourteen years of service.

One of Commissioner Betterton's first acts was to introduce a coded call system for the police radio. He believed the public was better served if the nature of police calls was less overt. The following month, the transmitter for the police radio system was moved from the Patten Hotel to the top of Cameron Hill. The move increased the range of the radio system from seventeen to thirty five miles. In the summer of 1941 assistance from the federal government allowed Chattanooga to install a two-way police radio system,

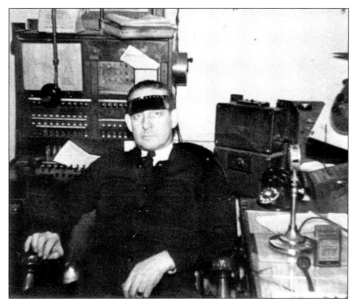

Jack Gilliland manned the headquarters radio and switchboard in 1941.

giving patrol units the ability to talk to headquarters as well as receive calls.

The Traffic Division was reorganized in 1941 under the command of Captain Homer Edmonson. The unit consisted of 15 men using automobiles. Motorcycles were not re-introduced in the department until the 1950s. Except for a brief time in the early seventies they have since been essential equipment for the department.

Uniform and insignia changes were also introduced in the summer of 1941. The department changed from the radiator style badge to an eagle-top circle with the state seal at the center of the circle and a number in a small panel at the bottom of the badge. Ranks above sergeant continued to wear eagle-top shields. Command officers often purchased solid gold badges handmade by Quarles Jewelers or other Chattanooga jewelers. The new uniform continued to be blue. The five-button jacket was hip-length with open lapels and worn over a gray shirt. Traffic officers were issued pith helmets for summer wear in lieu of the standard cap.

In the early 1950s the department adopted a shoulder patch for wear by all uniformed officers. The patch had a rounded top and featured a stylized state seal. The patch was worn on the left shoulder. Traffic and special unit patches were worn on the right shoulder.

Police insignia continued to symbolize an officer's dangerous duty as well as his authority. On the evening of October 24, 1942, another Chattanooga officer was

Detective H. H. Sully was in charge of the Identification Bureau in the 1940s, and demonstrated the use of a new camera equipped for photographing prisoners.

killed in the line of duty. Patrolmen A. E. "Toby" Carr and John Sheridan drove to 806 Green Street around 9:00 p.m. in response to a disorderly call. They found a man at the scene holding a rifle and told him to drop the weapon. The man fired at the officers while they were still in the squad car. Patrolman Carr was struck in the chest.

In the manhunt that followed, Captain Dan Grant and Patrolman A. C. Smith captured the shooter. They found a Swiss military rifle hidden in the leg of his pants. He was charged with murder when thirty-one year old Toby Carr died in Erlanger Hospital at 2:00 a.m. on October 27. Officer Carr had been a policeman for less that a year.

Chief Bryan retired effective December 31, 1943, after thirty years of service to the department. The chief was in poor health and had announced his intention to retire the previous August. Chief Bryan's last act in office was to pin the chief's badge on his successor, Chief of Police Homer Edmonson.

Cost cutting measures by Commissioner Betterton in December 1943 included elimination of the position of assistant chief of police. Assistant Chief Roy Hyatt was moved to the rank of captain with a $25 per month reduction in pay. The police department budget for the year was $302,385.07. Cost cuts resulted in a budget surplus of $11,836.90 at year end. The money was placed in the city's pension fund. The department published a 12 page book of rules and regulation for officers to carry as a guide in performance of their duty. Uniform shirts were changed in 1945 to gray and white.

Members of both the police force and fire department grew dissatisfied with working condition and pay in the mid-forties. The basic ranks of both departments organized and affiliated with labor unions. All police officers through the rank of sergeant joined the union with the exception of one man. Although the union charter contained no-strike clauses, many officials feared job actions. None took place.

The force was involved in a series of confrontations with religious snake handlers in the mid-forties. On September 24, 1945, Officer A. C. Floyd received a disorderly call that brought him to a faith-healing ritual being held by the clergy of the Dolly Pond Church of God. He saw nothing illegal and left.

A second call soon brought Floyd back along with Detective A. C. Smith and Captain Hartness. This time they were confronted by a clergy member of the church holding a large rattlesnake "in a threatening manner." Detective Smith brandished a riot-gun and

Detective Clyde J. Shipley, left, was shot and killed by an interstate gangster on the evening of December 26, 1939, as he entered a road house motel where the gang was hold up. Patrolman A. E. "Toby" Carr, right, responded to a disorderly call on October 24, 1942, and was shot in the chest with a rifle.

the snake was released on the ground. Smith quickly killed the reptile with a shotgun blast. For the rest of his career Officer Floyd was nicknamed "Snake" because of his involvement in the incident.

The Chattanooga Park Service was initiated in 1946. Park Policeman Harry Wilcox was the first officer hired and was soon followed by Harry Lindsey. Wilcox worked the night shift and Lindsey worked afternoons. They served as watchmen in Warner and Montague parks. As activities in the parks grew additional men were added. Ernest Hester was named the first supervisor in the early fifties.

Roy Hyatt was named chief of police in 1946, but the leadership of the department changed again in 1947 when Hyatt became commissioner of fire and police. Hyatt was a twenty-nine year veteran of the department and the first man to work himself through the ranks of the police force to become commissioner. Ed Ricketts, also a long-time member of the Chattanooga police force, was selected chief of police. The two did much to improve the efficiency and morale of the department.

The following year marked a significant personnel policy change in the department. For the first time since 1883, black policemen were added to the roster of the force. Thaddeus Arnold, Singer Askins, W. B. Baulridge, C. E. Black, Morris Glenn, Arthur Heard and Thomas Patterson were sworn in at 3:30 in the afternoon on August 11, 1948. The officers were assigned walking beats in black neighborhoods.

The first black officer in modern times went on duty on August 11, 1948. From left to right were officers Morris Glenn, Arthur Heard, C. E. Black, W. B. Baulridge, and Singer Askins. They made their debut in a ceremony attended by their families along with black and white community leaders.

Only four years later Chattanooga lost a black officer in the line of duty. Patrolman Ulysses Jackson was murdered in a most brutal manner as he struggled to control a prisoner. Jackson stopped, subdued and disarmed a man chasing a woman with a knife at Ninth and Cedar streets. He arrested the man, took him to a nearby filling station and called for the patrol wagon. It was against department policy at the time to handcuff prisoners and the hoodlum again attacked the officer. Using his blackjack, Officer Jackson subdued the prisoner a second time.

Moments later the prisoner, now sitting on the curb, grabbed the officer's legs and they began wrestling on the pavement. The event was observed by a small crowd that gathered. Some wanted to help the policeman but other held them back. While the two struggled, the prisoner was able to lift the flap on Jackson's regulation holster and pulled his duty weapon. He shot the officer once in the head. The felon then rose up as he straddled Officer Jackson and fired the remaining five bullets into the policeman's face and head. Before fleeing the scene the killer struck the dead officer on the head with the empty weapon.

Commissioner Hyatt personally directed the search for Officer Jackson's slayer. Detective Captain John Carson and Detectives G. R. Caldwell, G. T. Jennings, W. J. Patty and Clyde Russell joined in the manhunt. Patrolmen George G. Cline and Duke Hicks found the woman who had been chased with a knife by the killer and she told them where he lived.

Patrolmen B. C. Seahorne and Randall Rich had recently been assigned plain-clothes duty on the east side, patrolling for prowlers. Because they knew the area they were assigned to stakeout the residence and were armed with shotguns by Lieutenant P. R. Walker. Officer Rich watched the front of the Central Avenue house and Officer Seahorne hid in a garage on Tenth Street.

At 3:35 a.m. Seahorne heard footsteps and stopped a disheveled man matching the killer's description. The suspicious person wore torn and tattered pants, but a freshly laundered khaki shirt. When Seahorne asked for identification the killer ran. Patrolman Seahorne fired the riot gun, putting two loads of double-ought buckshot through the killer's neck.

Officer Ulysses Jackson was 29 years old. He had been a Chattanooga police officer for less than two years. Two thousand attended his funeral services including 100 policemen who form an honor guard for the fallen officer.

The dangers officer faced in even the most routine duty was again demonstrated on October 3, 1953.

Motorcycle Officer Jack Shasteen wore a generic winged-wheel traffic shoulder patch on the right shoulder in 1948. Shasteen was called "Little Jack" because his father "Big Jack" served as a Chattanooga policeman at the same time. The younger Shasteen later served as chief of police.

Patrolmen Harry T. Shipley and B. F. Holland stopped a car on East Third Street at 11:52 p.m. They were standing with the driver at the rear of his car when Holland spotted another vehicle headed toward them from the rear of the patrol car. He yelled to Shipley and pushed the driver to safety. Shipley was not able to move out of danger and was struck. The vehicle then sideswiped the stopped car and dragged Shipley 20 feet before it stopped. Forty-six-year-old Officer Harry Shipley, a nine-year veteran of the force, died at 8:00 the next morning.

Three other policemen narrowly escaped death in the fifties. Officer Joe P. Meredith was shot and seri-

ously wounded on November 10, 1954, by an armed robber fleeing a drug store at Rossville Boulevard and Central Avenue. Officer A. L. "Jack" Dempsey was struck by a fire engine on October 3, 1950. He was directing traffic at the intersection of Market and Eleventh streets. Dempsey stepped in the wrong direction as he tried to avoid the fire truck and was struck by the engine's headlight and right front fender and knocked 84 feet.

Patrol Officer Clifford L. Jackson was shot five times by a tavern owner on the night of February 12, 1955. Jackson and Patrolman A. C. "Snake" Floyd answered a complaint call at 7:12 p.m. reporting several drunks at the Riverside Inn on Manufacturers Road. The proprietor and his wife became verbally abusive when the two officers entered. Policemen Floyd and Jackson closed the club and arrested the couple for disorderly conduct. As the bar cleared, the woman went to the residence next door and the man gathered the night's receipts into a cigar box.

Officer Jackson noticed the woman had left and went to look for her. Officer Floyd followed the man as he went next door as well. The woman had hidden in a small bedroom. Jackson found her. When the bar owner reached the bedroom he pulled a .38 caliber pistol from the cigar box and emptied it into Jackson. Bullets struck the officer in his back, abdomen, left thigh and two in his right arm. Jackson fell across the foot of the bed.

The tavern owner was still firing when Floyd reached the room. Floyd drew his .357 magnum and shot the man in the shoulder; the bullet passed through his lungs and heart. Floyd's second shot struck the gunman's cheek and passed through his head. Officer Jackson's shooter was dead on the scene. Jackson was rushed to the hospital and recovered.

Occasionally new equipment made the police officer's job easier. New radar speed-detection technology came to the Chattanooga Police Department in late 1953. More than 800 speeders were cited during November 1953, the first full month the force used radar. Lieutenant Lamar Boyd of the traffic department noted the impact of radar beyond its ability to catch speeders, "The real value we find in the instrument is the psychological effect it has on drivers." Drivers slowed their vehicles just because they knew the radar units were in use.

Herbert P. Dunlap took office as the commissioner of fire and police in March 1955. Colonel Dunlap had a military and academic background. He was a graduate of the Citadel Military College and served as headmaster and commandant of the military department of the McCallie School in Chattanooga for many years. He served during the World War II and was on Iwo Jima when Japan surrendered.

After a period of evaluation Commissioner Dunlap appointed Edward H. "Ed" Brown as chief of police, replacing Chief Ed Ricketts. Ricketts transferred to the Detective Department where he served as chief of detectives until his retirement two years later.

Chief Brown was a 20-year veteran of the department who began his career walking the Main Street beat. He was physically imposing, standing six feet tall and weighing 225. He earned the title "the Singing Cop" while he was a detective and sang the role of

Patrolman Ulysses Jackson, left, was brutally killed on the night of September 27, 1952, after he interceded to save a woman from a knife wielding felon. Patrolman Harry T. Shipley , right, died on October 4, 1953, from injuries he received after being struck by a car at a traffic stop.

Escamillo the toreador in the Chattanooga Opera Association's production of Carmen. As chief of police Brown was a strict disciplinarian.

The morale of the force Chief Brown inherited was poor. A contemporary explained, "When Chief Brown took his new position, the department was in near-chaos due to dissension and lack of discipline. He worked with a firm hand and his usually pleasant demeanor could alter quickly to cold implacability." Brown began by requiring officers to look sharp and to act sharp in routine duty. Uniforms were to be clean and pressed and hats were to be worn at all times, even while in patrol cars and on lunch breaks. "When a supervisor called for an officer, he would stand at attention outside his vehicle. It didn't matter if it was raining or snowing either."

Patrol cars remained very basic. They did not have air conditioning and were not purchased with heaters. During cold winter weather officers often stopped at a construction site and picked up a flambo or smudge pot, a metal globe with a wick, filled with kerosene and used to mark roadway construction. The officer on the passenger side lit the flambo and held it between his feet for the heat. The impromptu heaters filled the car with smoke so officers drove with the windows down. Of course, they were required to have the windows down anyway so they could hear burglars breaking glass or shouts for help.

Commissioner Dunlap established a juvenile unit soon after he took officer. Initially one lieutenant and four traffic officers served part-time in the unit, but its success was such that on June 17, 1956, a full-time

Juvenile Division was created to deal with growing youth problems.

A recruit school was also established in 1956. The school consisted of two-hour classes held each night for nine evenings. All officers hired during the previous year were required to attend. In December 1962 the Law Enforcement Commission of Chattanooga –Hamilton County formed a joint venture with the University of Chattanooga to create a police-training academy. Classes held at the university also provided in-service training opportunities for current officers.

In January 1957 Dunlap announced a major reorganization. The detective bureau was placed under the command of the chief of police. For decades detectives reported to a chief of detectives who ranked equally with the chief of police and who was directly responsible to the commissioner of fire and police. The new unified organization made all policemen including detectives subordinate to the chief of police. Chief of Detectives Ed Ricketts retired at this time and Assistant Chief of Police John Carson took command of the detective bureau.

Nightsticks were re-issued to officers in 1958. Patrolmen had been issued only blackjacks for more than twenty years, which meant officers had to get very close to an attacker before the weapon could be used effectively. Nightsticks allowed officers the extra reach needed to safely subdue a lawbreaker resisting an arrest.

Two significant organizational changes were implemented in February 1960. Shifts were staggered to eliminate the 45-minute period at each shift change when the city was without any officers on patrol. Also, two additional police districts were created and black officers were assigned districts for the first time and worked in patrol cars. Patrolmen James Perry and Cletus Rogers were assigned to District 12, Alton Park, and patrolmen Morris Glenn and Joseph Jackson were assign to District 13, Bushtown or Highland Park. Patrolman Walter Maples Jr. was assigned as swing man to relieve officers on their days off.

The Dog Squad was created in 1961 to reduce risks during investigations and apprehension of suspects. The K-9 unit was fully operational within a year. The first police dog was Prince. A reorganization of the unit in 1965 began when officers Dick Kovacevich and Dean Gross participated in a 14-week dog training course in Memphis. The success of the squad was dramatized in the capture of the kidnapper of a 9-year-old girl. The kidnapper fled into a densely wooded area after the girl escaped. Patrolman Danny Rowland came to the scene with his dog Fang. Fang

Officer Johnny Russell patrolled in Car Number 12, a Ford, in 1953.

soon located the kidnapper and bolted into thick underbrush to capture the felon.

The department lost its first K-9 officer on March 29, 1966. Officer Kenneth Bowman and Apache were responding to a burglary in progress when the officer lost control of the car as he tried to avoid a road hazard. Both Bowman and Apache were injured. Apache's injuries were such that the police dog had to be euthanized.

The Dog Squad experienced both good times and bad times in 1971. Rebel with handler Officer Marvin Rhea became the first marijuana-detecting K-9 in the unit. However at mid-year Sergeant Dean Gross, the driving force behind the dog unit, retired and the squad became a part of the Special Services Division known as the David Squad. A number of officers subsequently transferred from the squad. Officer John Brown and Sarge was the last team when the unit was disbanded.

The investigation of a break-in at the American Legion on Lindsay Street on the morning of April 2, 1963, left a Chattanooga officer shot multiple times. Patrolmen Bill Dixon and Paul W. Lee responded to the call. While Dixon covered the rear of the building, Officer Lee entered to search. The burglar was hiding in a toilet stall of the women's bathroom. When Lee entered, the thief fired six shot striking the Legion's bookkeeper twice and Officer Lee four times, in his right jaw, right chest, left thumb and left side of his back. The burglar fled but was chased down by Merchant Officer M. Stroud, a former city policeman.

The department first established a dog squad in 1961. Among the department's earliest dog teams were Officer Dean Gross with Prince, left, and Officer L. P. "Skeet" Schoocraft with Jack, right.

Both Officer Lee and the bookkeeper were treated and recovered. Paul Lee retired from the force a short time after the incident.

The decade of the sixties was a time of turmoil for the Chattanooga Police Department. The top four officer in the department including Chief Brown resigned in April 1963 when James B. "Bookie" Turner took office as commissioner of fire and police. Turner was the former Hamilton County Sheriff and one of the most colorful personalities to serve as commissioner.

Turner did not initially appoint a chief of police but made Hamilton County Chief Deputy Sheriff Gene McGovern the assistant chief of police. Later McGovern was made chief of the force, John Henry "Jack" Shasteen named assistant chief and Leroy Kington chief of detectives.

Over the next few years a number of improvements were made, including the move from the city jail to a new facility in 1965. Administrative functions were housed in a new Information and Communications Center in the basement at city hall. A new squad room was constructed. Sufficient parking for patrol cars was provided near the public works garage at 12th and Park Avenue in the area known as "Onion Bottom."

Benefits for officers improved. The work week was reduced to 40 1/2 hours per week and salaries were increased for patrolmen to $466.66 a month in 1966, as compared to $400 per month in 1963. Officers were also given a uniform allowances for the first time, averaging over $10 per month and additional paid days off. A number of vacancies were filled and by 1967 the department numbered 214. New equipment was added to the department including a new radio system, 70 new cars, motorcycles and 40 riot guns. A Missing Persons Bureau was also established.

A number of officers were recognized for outstanding service. The Chattanooga Exchange Club named the first "Policeman of the Year" in 1966. Patrolman J. R. Farmer was selected for his attributes of alertness and dedication to duty as well as his off-duty work with youth. Officer Charles W. Gaston was awarded a Carnegie Hero Fund Commission bronze metal for rescuing two boys from a flooded creek in July 1967.

Officer Frank Harris was honored as Policeman of the Month by the Junior Chamber of Commerce for quick thinking in a robbery-kidnapping incident on July 1, 1966. Harris was on his first day back from leave due to a serious injury while on motorcycle duty. A call of a robbery and kidnapping at the By-Ryt Supermarket on Dodson Avenue brought him and others to the scene of the crime. Using a description of the car and the perpetrator, Officer Harris patrolled the

Motor Officer Leon Wilkey in 1965 riding Harley Davidson's new Electra-Glide.

Patrolman F. E. Smith, left, encouraged a young lad each Sunday when he did traffic duty at the youngster's church. Those words had a impact and led Officer Lon L. Eilders, right, to a illustrious career as a Chattanooga policeman.

emergency response unit. Captain Lee J. Hicks was called upon to organize the Multiple Action and Response to Special Situation Team, or MARS Team. Ten other officers were selected, Sergeant Lee R. Tate, Sergeant Alvin Capley, Jack Braunstein, Frank Otis, Barry Cole, Toby Gilliam, Fred Fuson, Herb Keedy, "Wild Bill" McCrary and Jackie Williams.

The team did rigorous training and physical conditioning. M16s were acquired from military surplus. The team learned techniques and weapons and most importantly to "think, act, and move as one." In the winter of 1977 Dr. Watson Rodney Fowler joined the team and introduced the "contain and negotiate" method.

Assistant Chief Clyde L. Wilhoit was named chief of police on October 8, 1976. Chief Pitts left the department to run for Hamilton County Sheriff. Chief

Aviation Section was terminated in 1984 when the aging helicopters became too expensive to maintain.

The Arson Unit was formed in 1973 and was staffed by Captain Jerry Evans of the fire department and police Inspector Amos Croft. The two worked out of their cars and investigated arson, explosions and fires of mysterious origin. Captain Roy Dickey and Lieutenant Charles Love, both of the police department, staffed the unit in 1977. By 1983 the unit had grown to six members.

A new $1.5 million Police Service Center was completed in 1974 on Amnicola Highway in the geographic center of the city. All divisions of the Chattanooga Police Department were under one roof for the first time in decades. A Teleprocessing Information Delivery and Exchange System (TIDE) was installed that linked Chattanooga to other law enforcement agencies including the National Crime Information Center (NCIC).

The department adopted a Sector Team Police model. The force was organized into four patrol teams and the city was divided into four sectors, Adam (North Chattanooga and Hixson), Baker (Brainerd, East Brainerd and Highway 58), Charlie (East Chattanooga, Highland Park and East Lake) and David (downtown, St. Elmo and Tiftonia). The sectors were headed by the deputy chief of patrol and two captains. One captain was in charge of Adam and David and the other Baker and Charlie. Each sector was commanded by a lieutenant with four sector sergeants to supervise patrol officers. Detectives also worked by sector.

By the mid-1970s growing incidents by radical and militant groups caused the CPD to reorganize an

The Aviation Section was formed in 1972 when two helicopters were made available to the department from the Civil Defense. Eleven years later the section was dissolved and the choppers retired. Helicopters later returned to become an important law enforcement resource for the Chattanooga Police Department.

The Blue Knights, a biker club formed by Chattanooga motorcycle officers, was formed in 1974. Kneeling were Terry Turner on the left and Mark Easley. Standing were Ken Hall, Terry Yates, Billy Sampley, and Craig Johnson.

Wilhoit served as a B-24 pilot in World War II and during 50 missions over Europe won a Purple Heart and the Air Metal. He joined the Chattanooga police in 1948 and worked his way through the ranks. One of his most important assignments was as Director of Planning and Development where he was key to obtaining federal funding for extensive building of police and fire facilities. Wilhoit proved to be a capable chief, combining discipline with fairness.

Insignia was changed in 1977. New custom breast and hat badges were adopted featuring the city seal. The copyrighted badge design was heavily enameled and the same badge was worn by all ranks. Some supervisors continued to wear jeweler-made presentation badges for a number of years after the new badge was adopted. The new shoulder patch was round and also carried a stitched, full color rendition of the city seal. The general patch continued to be worn on the left shoulder and special unit patches on the right.

The late 1970s were some of the most tragic years in the history of the force. The department lost its first female officer in the line of duty on September 17, 1975. School Safety Patrol Officer Elspeth K. Knox was killed when she was struck by a car at Bailey Avenue and Hawthrone Street as she directed traffic at the school crossing. Officer Knox had been a member of the school safety patrol since 1967 and had been injured in two previous accidents while on duty.

Four Chattanooga patrolmen were shot to death during the last three years of the seventies. Patrolman Clarence E. Hamler was killed during an armed robbery on August 17, 1977. Officer Hamler was on his way to begin his shift that hot Sunday afternoon when he stopped by to see his brother who worked at the Red Food Store on South Broad Street. Two career criminals had also entered the store leaving their automobile running. One was armed and the other took a revolver from a guard at the rear of the store. The two had quietly gathered the manager and other employees into the store office. Patrolman Hamler was unaware of the robbery in progress and was about to leave the store when a bag boy ran to him gasping, "It's a robbery."

The four-year veteran street cop told the boy, "Just be cool," and eased his service weapon from its holster. As Officer Hamler turned a corner he came face to face with one of the gunman who immediately shot the officer in the mouth, the bullet lodging in his neck. The felon shot the fallen policeman again in the back of his neck, killing him instantly.

The store manager pulled a .38 caliber revolver from his pocket and mortally wounded the second bandit. The officer's brother took the weapon from his limp hand and fired at the fleeing gunman, as did the store manager. At 1:35 p.m. a Code 400 went out to "block the city." Despite the citywide lockdown and search for the blue Galaxy, the killer was able to escape. He was put on the FBI's Ten Most Wanted List and was captured five months later in Georgia.

Less than a year later, June 12, 1978, two Chattanooga policemen died in a single incident. Officers David Friederichsen and Nelson I. "Nick" Hess V responded to a domestic call. A drunken convicted felon was threatening to kill his wife when both policemen pulled up to the Conner Street house at about 8:00 p.m. They went to the front entrance, stood on either side of the door and knocked. The door opened and the two officers entered to face the male occupant. A woman stepped into the room and said she wanted to leave the house. The man pulled a .38 caliber revolved from a counter. The two police officers backed toward the door and drew their weapons as the gunman fire three shots.

Both officers were hit. Friederichsen grabbed Hess and pulled him out of the room as he traveled backwards fifteen feet and fell. Hess also fell, but rose and fired four shots into the gunman before he collapsed and died. Friederichsen struggled to talk into his radio, "I'm shot. Baker 4, I'm shot. I don't know if 15 is shot or not." Dispatch Officer Esby Norwood directed backup to the scene.

Officer Elspeth Knox wore the uniform and insignia of the School Safety Patrol in the seventies. Officer Knox was stuck and killed by an automobile on September 17, 1975, as she directed traffic at a school crossing.

Patrolman Eddie Cooper, Baker 3, was the first to the scene. He called for ambulances, then pulled Friederichsen to a tree and moved Hess close to a wall. The house was dark and the door locked. Cooper kicked in the door. The woman fled the house and Cooper radioed, "The party's down. He looks 449 [deceased]." Other officers including Lieutenant Earl Wolfe began to arrive.

Officer Nick Hess was pronounced dead on arrival at Erlanger Hospital. Two days later the 35-year-old officer was buried. The next day, June 15, Officer David Friederichsen died of his wounds.

Officer Harry Wilcox was the first member of the Park Police to lose his life in the line of duty. Wilcox was killed on the evening of January 18, 1979, while on duty in Warner Park. The park policeman had not been seen by fellow officers Johnny McGhee and Carl Riddle, or others he normally met during his rounds. His body was found around 9:30 p.m. in a park bathroom. He had been shot with his own service weapon. Officer Wilcox's killer was arrested one year later following an extensive investigation by the Homicide

Division under the direction of Assistant Chief James M. "Pete" Davis. The killer was a paranoid vagrant and was committed to a institution for the mentally insane.

Major administrative changes in the department took place in early 1979. In January Governor Lamar Alexander appointed Commissioner Roberts to a state post as Commissioner of the Department of Safety. The city commission appointed Colonel H. P. Dunlap to fill out Roberts' term. In March Walter W. Smart was elected commissioner of fire and police. Smart was a retired FBI special agent with over 20 years of law enforcement experience.

Chief Willhoit resigned as chief of police to serve with Roberts in Nashville. Jack Shasteen was appointed to the position of acting chief of police for a second time. Following his election Commissioner Smart made John H. "Jack" Shasteen chief of police effective February 1, 1979, and began a departmental reorganization. One of the first changes he made was to beef up the department's Traffic Division, pointing out that "the city experiences more loss of life and property through traffic accidents than through crime." Twelve new Harley-Davidson motorcycles were purchased, together with 40 new police cars. The color of marked patrol cars was returned the more traditional dark blue with the image of the new breast badge as the door marking.

Department administration was streamlined by the appointment of two deputy chief, both veterans of the force. Deputy Chief L. "Tom" Kennedy was placed

Captain Morris B. Glenn, left, was killed when his vehicle crashed on the night of March 29, 1971, on his way to investigate a shooting. Patrolman Clarence E. Hamler was on his way to work on August 14, 1977, when he walked into a armed robbery and was shot to death.

in command of field operations and Deputy Chief Amos Croft headed the services division. Chief of Detectives Pete Davis was in charge of investigative functions.

The intervention of a citizen during an incident on October 3, 1979, may well have saved an officer's life. It was just after midnight when Larry Shell saw a struggle between a policewoman and a man on Market Street. Shell stopped his car to aid the officer as others stood and watched the man knocked the officer down. Shell reached the scene just in time to deflect the pistol that the felon was about to fire at the officer. Shell was shot in the shoulder as he wrestled with the gunman. Shell's quick action allowed the officer time to draw her weapon and shoot the felon.

The friends and relatives of Larry Shell were undoubtedly proud of his act of heroism. Likely none more than his father, retired Chattanooga police Sergeant Lester Shell. Larry Shell was given the department's first Citizen's Service Medal and was also honored by the Chattanooga Area Crime Alert and Law Enforcement Commission.

The eighties were a time of economic stress due to a national recession. Inflated gasoline prices led to officers being ordered to park their cars for ten minutes out of every hour in order to conserve fuel. The number of patrol cars was decreased and each patrol team was limited to seven cars per shift.

Racial tensions again shook Chattanooga in April 1980. The situation began when a shotgun blast wounded five elderly black women as they stood on a East Ninth Street sidewalk. The shooters were quickly apprehended by police and were tied to the Ku Klux Klan. After a week long trial three months later two of the defendants were acquitted and a third was convicted of a reduced charge. Less than 12 hours after the verdict, late on the night of July 22, violence broke out in Alton Park.

When police and firemen responded to fire bombings, rocks and bottles were hurled at their vehicles. The mayor imposed a curfew when incidents were repeated the next night. The sale of handguns and gasoline in plastic containers was banned. On the third night of the unrest police were fired on with shotguns while they investigated a fire at 38th and Alton Park Boulevard. Pellets wounded eight officers but none seriously. The officers were extracted by the SWAT team. Policemen worked 12-hour shifts and sealed off trouble spots as violence and civil disorder continued three more night.

Deputy Chief L. Tom Kennedy, a 19-year veteran of the Chattanooga force, was appointed chief of

Patrolmen Nelson I. "Nick" Hess V, left, and David Friederichsen, right, were shot and killed in the line of duty after answering a domestic disturbance call on June 12, 1978.

police upon the retirement of Chief Shasteen in 1980. Both Jack Shasteen and Assistant Chief Jack Robbs, chief of detectives, retired at the same time.

Chief Kennedy was a city court clerk when he joined the force in 1961. He was nicknamed "Juvenile" as a rookie because he looked so young. He worked in sectors and units throughout the department and established an exemplary record as a detective. After only a few years as chief, Kennedy took leave in January 1983 and won election as commissioner of fire and police, the second individual elected from the ranks of the force.

Eugene McCutcheon was appointed chief of police in May 1983 and the department initiated a plan to put more officers on the street. The four sectors were combined into two and in an unpopular move patrol sergeants were assigned to patrol duty rather than supervision. Lieutenants assumed the job duties previously performed by sergeants. The rank of major was created and the rank of assistant chief was abolished. Four were promoted to the rank of deputy chief in September 1983 forming the senior command of the department.

A Mounted Patrol was re-introduced in June 1983 to patrol the downtown area with increased visibility and mobility. The patrol began with Officer George Walden mounted on Pride and Officer Fred Layne on Courage. Pride, Courage and the mounts that followed were Tennessee Walking Horses. Officer were given 120 hours of riding instruction.

A number of officers were honored for outstanding service and valor in the eighties. Investigator Charles Dudley was presented the Medal of Valor in January 1984 after being shot in the chest as he chased an

The department uses all available resources to apprehend criminals. From left to right were Captain Lee J. Hicks, Sergeant Skip Vaughn, Lieutenant Lewis Guinn, Officer Bouchard, Chief Jack Shasteen, Commissioner Walter W. Smart, Lieutenant J. R. Farmer, Deputy Chief Tom Kennedy, and Sergeant Jimmy Tate. (Photo by Michael Payne)

armed bandit. Officer Charles Sivley received the Police Metal in May 1986 in recognition of undercover investigations into prostitution and burglary rings. Officer James Appugliese was shot in gun battle with a diamond thief in January 1985, the second time he was wounded in the line of duty and was presented the Metal of Valor the following year.

Chief of Police Ervin L. Dinsmore replaced McCutcheon in May 1989. Dinsmore's tenure as chief was brief. He was sworn in as commissioner on August 1, 1989, after Commissioner Kennedy retired due to health problems.

The Specialized Police Operations Team (SPOT) was created in the summer of 1989. Personnel for the unit was selected based on particular skills and high motivation. The team used advanced equipment including electronic surveillance technology and special weapons. SPOT provided support to patrol and

detective divisions as assigned by the chief. They worked drug and gang activities, armed robberies and similar high profile cases.

Captain T. E. "Skip" Vaughn took command of the SWAT Team in 1993 in addition to his duties as commander of Burglary and Robbery. The unit changed its name from the MARS Team in the early eighties and continued to develop expertise and recognition. Vaughn served as a lieutenant on the team in the period. When Captain Hicks left the unit in 1982 Sergeant Bill McCrary took command of the unit at the rank of lieutenant. On McCrary's retirement in 1988 Captain Bill Vincent took command.

The unit became a regional responder, answering call outs in the tri-state area of Tennessee, Georgia and Alabama. During the 1996 Olympics the unit was tasked with security for the water events in the Chattanooga area. The team was expanded to 24 men,

The SWAT Team was the successor to the Multiple Action and Response to Special Situations Team, or MARS Team, formed in the mid-1970s. Officers kneeling in the front row from left to right were Lee Robbs, Roger Blaine, Lee Stewart, John Stuermer, and David Frye. Standing left to right in the back row were Tim Carroll, Alan Franks, Paul Lee, Rusty Carnes, Randy Dunn, Mike Williams, unidentified, Mike Robbs, and Randy Dockery.

two 12-man detachments. Twelve was the combat load for a UH60 helicopter, which was used to move the unit quickly. When Vaughn was promoted to Special Operations Commander, which included responsibility for SWAT, the Bomb Squad, Traffic Division and other units, Captain Mike Williams took over as SWAT team commander. Williams was the first to serve full-time in the role.

After the Columbine High School incident in Colorado, SWAT implemented a plan for "an immediate response to an active shooter," which was accepted by the Chattanooga school board. LAPD and other agencies adopted and taught the Chattanooga plan.

The unit expanded its equipment, included acquisition of an M25 Dragoon light armored vehicle from the Marine Corps. Much of the equipment they acquired was funded from SWAT schools conducted by the team for other agencies. Chattanooga SWAT was organized to be a force multiplier. One team member was assigned to every sector on every shift to eval-

uate situations and advice on making a call out. The unit was divided into the Gold Team and the Blue Team so that the entire unit did not have to be called out unless needed.

Chief of Police Ralph H. Cothran was appointed on August 1, 1989, and became the first black chief of police in the history of the Chattanooga department. Cothran stood 6'6" and was well liked and respected by members of the force. Cothran died in office in November 1995 as a result of illness.

The department functioned without a chief of police until 1997 when J. L. Dotson was appointed by the mayor. Chief Dotson began the process of achieving national accreditation for the department. He pressed for increased salaries and educational opportunities for Chattanooga police officers in addition to upgrading the department's operating manual and computer system. A new command structure was introduced in early 2000. The number of deputy chiefs was reduced from three to two.

The first record of an individual designated by the title Policeman was in 1858. John Dodd served with the title Night Policeman. He had much the same duty as members of the patrol in the 1820s and 1830s and reported directly to the mayor. John J. McAlexander was elected town constable in 1858 and 1859. J. J. McAlexander served Jackson as a law enforcement officer into the 1880s. He also served one term as mayor.

One of the most famous mysteries in the history of Jackson centered on an incident on the night of February 3, 1859. Between the hours of six and nine that evening a clerk in the Jackson branch of the Union Bank was murdered and the bank was robbed of $20,860 in notes on out of town banks and $4,545 in gold, mostly in twenty-dollar coins. The bank was located across from the courthouse on the southwest corner of Shannon (now Liberty) and Baltimore streets. The mayor formed a citizens investigating committee chaired by one of Jackson's civic leaders to direct inquiries into the murder and robbery. Despite suspicions and the hiring of an outside investigator, the crime remained unsolved.

In October 1859 a "committee to appoint a police" was created by the town council. The committee appointed J. L. Tomlin, David McGraw, James Boyd and James Butler as lawmen. Two policemen served each night and alternated. Each was paid one dollar per night on duty. Boyd and Butler served only eight nights and resigned. McGraw and Tomlin continued, working every night. The policemen provided written reports to the city board.

> Mayor & Aldermen of the town of Jackson, we D. E. McGraw & J. L. Tomlin for service rendered as policemen 15 nights at $1.00 per night, the following arrests have been made: Oct. 13 Peter Brown arrested fined by Mayor $5.00 & cost, assisted the constable in arresting John Crawford who was fined by Recorder $5.00 & cost, on 23rd two arrests made for gaming, fined $5.00 & cost, Nov 7th four arrests made & no tryal.

Both the mayor and the recorder had the powers of a justice of the peace and alternated as judge in the town court. Reports show fines for such offenses as "fighting," "attempting to fight," "wanting to fight," "lewdness," "riding on the sidewalk," "contempt," "swearing," "gaming," "sneezing," and "halloing."

The Police Committee did not last long and the oversight of law enforcement once again became the responsibility of the mayor. J. J. McAlexander was reelected town constable in 1860 and his annual salary was set at $300, a salary higher than that of the recorder, mayor or aldermen. McAlexander was also elected tax collector. Policemen James W. Boyd and G. N. Allen were hired by the month and received one half of the fines collected from arrests they made as pay.

The structure of the police force was changed in 1860. Aldermen from each of the four wards of the town were authorized to select a policeman from their ward. The office of Captain of Police was established to supervise the night police and James W. Boyd was appointed captain. Siebert McAlexander, A. Whyte and H. H. Whitesides were appointed policemen.

Boyd was thirty-eight years old, stood six feet two inches tall and had blue eyes. He might be considered the first law enforcement officer in Jackson to function as chief of police. Until this point the force was supervised by the mayor.

Jackson was preparing for the war in 1862 when H. H. Whitesides was elected town constable. Policeman Edwards served until the end of March and enlisted as a confederate soldier with other Jackson men. Jackson's Board of Mayor and Aldermen met in a called session on May 9, 1862. Town Constable Whitesides and all but two aldermen resigned their office.

From June 6, 1862, to June 6, 1863, the town of Jackson was occupied by Union troops. No regular police existed until the war ended. Martial law under

Mayor Richard J. Hays, left, supervised the Town Constable and night patrol during his terms as mayor in the 1840s and 1850s. Hays resigned during his first term in 1846 to serve in the Mexican War. Confederate veteran General Alexander W. Campbell, right, served as the "chief of the police" for the special police force that served during elections in the post-Civil War years.

the military was primarily concerned with suppressing insurrection. Citizens took action to deal with crime as best they could.

Jackson reconstituted its government the month after Lee's surrender and held elections on May 30, 1865. Siebert H. McAlexander was elected town constable, tax collector and sexton at a salary of $600 per year. He was the brother of John J. McAlexander who served as town constable before the war. The brothers continued to be prominent members of the Jackson police force in the coming decades. A room in the courthouse was made into a lockup for town prisoners until a Calaboose was built on the Market House lot on the northwest corner of College and Market (now Highland).

Rebuilding the war devastated town was a challenge. In addition to law enforcement duty Town Constable Siebert H. McAlexander was assigned responsibility for public works projects including laying brick pavement on streets, repairing the cemetery fence and removing trees that were obstructing traffic.

John C. Cock and Lafayette Tanner were elected policemen and paid $50 a month with the incentive of receiving more based on the amount of fines collected from those they arrested. Policemen were still hired by the town council but the town constable began to take more responsibility for their oversight. John J. McAlexander, John C. Cock, John H. Clark, John G. Carver and C. Hamner served as policeman from month to month over the next couple of years.

Violence was routinely a part of elections in the years following the war. Special police were appointed to maintain order on election day. General Alexander W. Campbell, attorney and former Confederate leader, served as "chief of the police" for the cadre of special police on election day in the late 1860s.

By an act of the General Assembly on February 25, 1867, the Town of Jackson became the "City of Jackson." John G. Carver was elected city constable. Prisoners who were not able to pay their fines worked to rebuild or maintain the streets of the city. This helped to rebuild the city infrastructure and enabled prisoners to reduce their time in jail. The calaboose became a work house as well as temporary confinement for those awaiting trial.

Former Town Constable and Policeman John J. McAlexander was elected mayor of the City of Jackson in 1868. John H. Clark was elected city constable. The financially strapped city dissolved the police force for a time, but as crime increased. City Constable Clark demonstrated a police force could be supported by

court fines and he was authorized to hire night policemen.

The best record of day-to-day law enforcement activity was given in the reports policemen made to the City Council.

Jackson Tn Nov 10th 1868. The following is my official report since I have been in office. I have policed the city day & night, the usual hours except one night. Then I was unwell, and it was raining. I have made five arrests as follows, Jack Lyle for fighting, Fined $5 Costs $4. He worked the same out on the streets. Hal Yarbrough was released for want of evidence to make out a case. Turned over Dick Smith to City Constable J H Clark for fighting, Fined $5. Collected and paid to the Recorder. George Bussimar for drunkenness and disorderly conduct. Fined $5. Secured by Martin Walsh. I have also assisted in keeping down riots &c during Barbecue and Election times.

S. H. McAlexander, Policeman

The terms City Constable, City Marshal, and Chief of Police were used interchangeably in the late 1860s and 1870s. City Marshal William Frank McCabe was elected in 1869 and served as the chief law enforcement officer of Jackson for the next seven years. After his term as mayor, former town constable John J. McAlexander returned to the police force. John H. Clark, the immediate former city constable, and Lawrence McCafflin also served on the force. Newton C. Perkins soon replaced McCafflin.

Policeman during the 1870s faced their most challenging and risky duties in the city's saloons. Officer Robert H. Rawls was almost killed in one encounter. Rawls joined the police force in the fall of 1872 as night policeman and served during most of the decade. His career as a policeman almost ended on Tuesday evening, December 30, 1873, when he tried to arrest a disorderly drunk. The brawler struck a brutal blow to Rawls' left eye. Rawls survived. He was considered one of the best officers on Jackson's police force, "prompt and fearless" in the discharge of his duty.

In the decades following the Civil War people were usually armed and lawlessness was pervasive. Deadly or potentially deadly encounters were frequent for lawmen. Policeman J. J. McAlexander faced one such dangerous man on a Thursday evening in January 1874. When McAlexander confronted the man for assaulting a woman, the fifty-year-old officer was knocked down and attacked by the man. He would have been more seriously injured had a group of men not interceded.

Once the two were separated, the ruffian got on his horse and rode down Liberty Street. McAlexander pursued him on foot and fired at him. The man dismounted and with a brick in each hand moved toward the officer. McAlexander fired twice more, putting a hole in the man's hat and nicking his ear, but he did not slow his pace. When the two combatants were about fifteen yards apart, Sheriff R. M. May jumped between them. Officers arrested the man who assaulted Policeman McAlexander.

Despite the frontier style violence of the era, the department made improvements. Chief McCabe established a police headquarters in December 1873 in a room over C. P. Duncan & Co. drugstore on Main Street at the address "fourth door to the left." Prior to this if a citizen needed a policeman, he or she had to locate an officer on patrol or leave word at the calaboose. Officers were required to wear uniforms, but they had to buy them out of their pay. Uniforms were not consistently worn. The City Council adopted "An Ordinance to Define the Duties of City Constable and Police Officers of the City of Jackson" in 1875, which specified policies and procedures for the force. James D. Marks was elected city marshal for 1876, replacing McCabe.

The streets of the city remained dangerous and on a sultry Sunday night in the summer of 1876 when Patrolman Newton C. Perkins was killed in the discharge of his duty. At about 10:00 on the evening of July 13, 1876, Policemen Perkins and his partner Robert Rawls observed activity in Louis Eppinger's barbershop on Market Street. The shop was closed and they recognized the head of a prostitution ring.

The two officers pursued four individuals, two male and two female, as they left the shop. Patrolman Perkins intercepted the group at the corner of Lafayette and Liberty streets. The ring leader of the group pulled a pistol and shot the officer. Perkins staggered back along Lafayette Street seeking help and fell dead about half a block from where he was shot.

Policeman Newton C. Perkins was a veteran of the Civil War and a respected member of Jackson's police force. He was the younger brother of Madison County Sheriff George G. Perkins. His killer was hanged one year from the day of the incident at the Hanging Grounds south of the city.

The murder of another well known Jackson resident the following year caused a large group of citizens to call for an investigation. The mayor informed the City Council that he had "detailed police officer Ramseur, as officer to the Special Committee of Citizens appointed to investigate said murder." Patrolman John Ramseur was the first Jackson officer assigned specific duty as a detective or investigator.

The force was expanded in November 1878 to seven policemen, six white and one black. Marshal James D. Marks' officers were John F. Ramseur, S. W. Edwards, J. H. Sewell, W. Frank McCabe, Siebert H. McAlexander, W. W. Bruce and Milton Thomas. Fifty-two-year-old Milton Thomas was the first black officer to serve in the Jackson Police Department.

Subtle killers visited Jackson in the 1870s. Outbreaks of smallpox and yellow fever led to extraordinary policing measures. A standing force of sanitary police and a mounted patrol of sanitary guards were established to enforce health codes in the town and to check those coming into town for signs of illness.

Special Sanitary Policeman W. G. Wells was appointed to check all "trams" coming in at night and to intercept "tramps of suspicious character." Milton Thomas performed the same function in the black community. The sanitary policemen were under the control of the City Marshal as other policemen and other policemen assisted them when necessary.

The first undercover policeman, or "secret policeman," was appointed in 1882 to protect the city from arsonists and thieves. Officer A. Caradine worked nights "to aid in preventing incendiary fires and to arrest suspicious characters." His name was not revealed to anyone including the city council until two months after he was hired. Caradine later worked as a regular policeman.

Selection of the city marshal, previously determined by popular election, reverted to the Board of Mayor and Aldermen in 1882. James Marks was reappointed by the board. Siebert H. McAlexander, T. L. Hughes, Thomas C. Gaston and A. T. Nichols were selected as policemen. Salaries were increased from $60 to $75 per month for the city marshal and from $50 to $60 per month for policemen.

Badges worn policemen were purchased and owned by the officers until November 9, 1883, when existing insignia were purchased by the city and issued to policemen when they were on duty. Officers continued to be responsible for providing other equipment including batons, revolvers, nippers or handcuffs, ammunition and uniforms. The city did give a uniform allowance from time to time.

The City of Jackson purchased a cotton warehouse on May 30, 1884, to serve as a city hall. The two-story brick structure located on the west side of Church Street between Main and Lafayette housed the recorder's office, police station, fire station and calaboose.

An ordinance was passed on May 5, 1885, requiring police officers to give full time to their job with the city. This marked the end of an all part-time police force in Jackson. Policemen were prohibited from drinking intoxicating beverages during their term of office, either within or outside the city limits.

Thomas W. Murrell was unanimously selected to the position of city marshal in January 1887 and Thomas C. Gaston was made lieutenant of police. This was the first time a supervisory rank was used for the regular police force in Jackson. As lieutenant, Gaston was second in command to the city marshal and chief of the night police. The title of Jackson's chief law enforcement officer officially changed to Chief of Police by ordinance in December of 1889. His salary remained $75 per month.

Tom Gaston proved to be not only a capable commander, but a fearless and resilient lawman. He was nearly killed in an incident on August 13, 1889. Thirteen buckshot entered his body, mostly in his arms and one in his left eye. A Memphis Daily Avalanche story reported some of Gaston's exploits.

Gaston has been a policeman in Jackson about eight years, and has the reputation of being one of the bravest men who ever wore a star. He has proven himself a terror to the roughs, black and white, who infest Jackson in common with other large towns. Some of his experiences have been sensational in the extreme.

About two years ago, while Gaston was striking the 9 o'clock bell in the courthouse at Jackson, he was fired upon by an unknown party, the bullet barely missing his head.

Gaston lost his left eye in the incident, but soon returned to duty. In 1892 Gaston's rank was changed from lieutenant to captain.

On the Wednesday morning before Christmas in 1892 Captain Gaston again faced gunfire on the streets of Jackson. The owner of a saloon at 205 Market Street had threatened Gaston because of raids on his saloon for selling whiskey on Sunday. Gaston was passing by the saloon about eight o'clock that morning. The Memphis Commercial Appeal reported the incident under the headline "Game Gaston's Deadly Gun."

This morning Gaston walked down Market street past Strickland's saloon, into which he and his brother, Pat Strickland, had just entered. Gaston entered a feed store to order some hay. The proprietor was not in, and he turned back and passed Strickland's saloon. The latter was in his front door. Some words and oaths passed, and five or six shots were fired by Gaston and the Stricklands. Gaston was untouched, but W. C. Strickland fell forward on the pavement with a bullet in his left temple and his brains oozing out.

The saloon owner had prepared for the shootout and was wearing "a double copper shield, or protector," over his breast. Captain Tom Gaston, with only one eye, not only out-gunned the man clearly intent on killing him, but out-witted his opponent by shooting above the bullet proof vest.

James D. Marks was named chief of police for 1893 and 1894; and B. Alexander Person was chief of police in 1895 and 1896. Person had been sheriff of Madison County for five years. Tom Gaston served as policeman and chief of the fire department until 1897 when he and Alex Person switched places. Gaston was made chief of police. Person became chief of the fire department and policeman. The arrangement was brief; Person resigned in April 1897. Tom Gaston was then named both chief of police and chief of the fire department and served in both roles until 1915. He earned $85 a month as chief of police and another $20 for serving as fire chief.

Chief Gaston was again shot in the line of duty in May 1905 when the police were called to a home over a livery stable in the business district. The wound was to his hand.

The badge worn by Gaston was a large eagle-top shield. Patrolmen wore a round breast badge with a number soldered to the orange-peal textured center of the badge. Officers were still wearing this style badge into the 1930s. The hat badge was an eagle-top medallion with numbers soldered in the center on a similar surface to the breast badge and with the Tennessee state seal affixed at the bottom.

The first city ordinance regulating the operation of automobiles was enacted on July 15, 1913. Key parts of the regulations required that automobiles and drivers be registered with the police department, that cars have a "board" attached with an identification number, that cars have two lights in front and one in back, that drivers keep to the right and pass on the left and that speeds not exceed 12 miles per hour within the

Chief of Police Thomas C. Gaston with his badge partially visible beneath his jacket. The chief preferred to be photographed in profile because his left eye was lost from a shotgun blast.

city offices were relocated a number of years earlier. The building at 107 Church Street was designated Police and Fire Station Number 1.

As most of Jackson celebrated the end of World War I on November 18, 1918, Officers Tip Taylor and Tom Brown were on their way to Elm Flats to arrest a well-know local bad man who was terrorizing his family. The two lawmen reached the house about 7:30 a.m. Taylor went around to the back door and Brown knocked on the front door.

Officer Brown was met at the door by the subject who began cursing them. The ruffian resisted arrest and Brown drew his gun. The subject fled to the bedroom and found Officer Taylor moving toward him. When Brown entered the room, the ruffian was savagely attacking Officer Taylor. Patrolman Brown shot and killed the attacker to save his partner.

Conflict moved into the corridors of city government a few months later. One of the liveliest meetings of city government took place on May 9, 1919. Policeman Bud Shelton had known for some time that Chief of Police Jim Deming was guilty of indiscretions. The nature of his offense apparently involved the misuse of funds. After Shelton told Mayor Taylor, the matter came to a head at the next meeting of the Commission.

Patrolman B. H. Shelton appeared before the Commission as requested by Mayor Taylor, on account of charges that he, Mr. Shelton, had made against Chief of Police Deming. As the investigation proceeded, a controversy arose between Mr. Shelton and Mr. Deming, which resulted in an altercation between the two gentlemen, which terminated the meeting, after which the meeting was adjourned.

The confrontation became heated and must have become physical and perhaps a gun was drawn. Later that day the Commission met again in a called session. Jim Deming submitted his resignation as chief of police and it was accepted. Officer G. Thomas Brown was selected to fill the unexpired term of the chief. Officer Bud Shelton was suspended indefinitely for coming to the meeting armed, for failing to report the irregularities earlier and for using insulting language in an open meeting of the Commission. The indefinite suspension lasted for two months until the board's next biennial election of policemen when Shelton was put back on the force. Former policeman W. Alex Stegall was chosen chief of police at that time.

The eight-man force was divided into two shifts. Two officers stayed in the downtown business district

Fire Limits or 15 miles per hour in the balance of the city limits.

The department got its first automobile, a new Model T Ford touring car, in July 1916 at the cost of $463.40. The car was used only for emergencies. Patrolman continued to walk their beat and usually answered calls on foot or by streetcar. In cold weather the Ford often did not respond to the hand crank and had to be pushed south on Church Street until it started.

The charter of the city was revised in June 1915. The Board of Mayor and Aldermen form of government was changed to a Board of Commissioners. Under the new form of government, a three-member commission was responsible for governing the city. One of the first actions of the new Commission was to split the positions of chief of police and chief of the fire department. J. A. Deming was selected chief of police and Tom Gaston's long and illustrious career with the Jackson Police Department was ended.

City Hall was officially moved to the building at 308 Main Street where the recorder's office and other during the day shift. The other six officers were on night duty, two in East Jackson, two in West Jackson and two downtown. One of the primary duties of the patrolmen in the business district was to shake doors, that is to test the doors of all businesses to be certain they were locked and no thief had entered. Officers continued to answer most calls on foot or by streetcar.

Policeman M. W. Wilson was assigned to the East Jackson beat. On a typical tour he and his partner patrolled from 6:00 p.m. to midnight, then walked to the Illinois Central Restaurant for a cup of coffee, then to the Nashville, Chattanooga & St. Louis depot to meet the 1:30 a.m. train and afterwards went back to their residential beat. At 4:00 a.m. they returned to Police Headquarters. Half of the night force then went home and the other half remained on duty until 6:00 a.m. when they were relieved by the day shift.

When a call came into the deskman at the police station on Church, beat cops were given the alarm by means of ringing a bell located in a tower built near the front of the station house. When patrolmen in East Jackson heard the bell at night they went to the office of the old compress near Lane Avenue. The night watchman there let them use the telephone to find out where the alarm needed attention.

The police station had two telephones on the desk because two different telephone companies were competing for business in Jackson. The two systems did not link to one another and people with a telephone from one company could not talk to those with a telephone from the other company. Any organization or business that needed to be reached by everyone had a telephone from both companies.

Chief Stegall required that all policemen report to work in full uniform. Patrolmen each bought two uniforms, but typically when the uniforms were worn out, they returned to wearing civilian clothes and the uniform cap. "Patrolling was mighty hard on shoes and trousers," M. W. Wilson remembered. "Not only was there much walking, but streets were not well paved then. Most of them were either graveled or just plain dust or mud." D. L. Staley was appointed "motorcycle police officer" in May 1920 at a salary of $100 a month. He used his personal motorcycle to patrol. A month after he was hired the city purchased a motorcycle.

The roaring twenties produced a number of infamous characters. One day while making a routine round of the city Officer Tip Taylor met one of the most notorious. Taylor observed a car parked at the curb in front of Fox's Café on East Main Street. As two strangers walked into the café Taylor saw that the car

was from out of state and heavily loaded with boxes. On investigation he found the cases contained bonded liquor. Taylor arrested the two men, George Kelly Barnes and R. G. Hammond. Barnes later became better known as "Machine Gun" Kelly.

The city administration changed in 1923 and Andrew "Tip" Taylor was named chief of police. Outgoing Chief Alex Stegall was named "special park police." Chief Taylor reorganized the department and assigned each officer to patrol a specific section of the city.

Jesse T. "Crutch" Crutchfield became an extra policeman and gained the reputation as the fastest man on the force. Most calls were still made on foot and prisoners walked to the station. Crutchfield and another officer arrested one habitual lawbreaker who unknown to them also had a reputation, that of escaping by outrunning the police. They had gone only a block or so when the prisoner said, "Well, it's been nice seeing you. Goodbye." And with that he sprinted for freedom. The other officer headed after the prisoner while Crutchfield circled to head him off. Crutchfield caught him and this time put him in handcuffs. When they reached headquarters, the prisoner, with a sheepish grin, said, "That's the first cop that ever outran me." One of the pitfalls of walking a lawbreaker to headquarters was that many a drunk was walked sober before he could be booked.

The old Ford police car was traded in toward a new Dodge in October of 1923. The city got $210 for the Model T off the $985 cost of the Dodge. Eight months later Patrolman L. T. Mays wrecked the Dodge. The mayor investigated and reported, "Mr. Mays admitted the fault was all his but that it was an accident that he could hardly explain, that he was in a hurry to get Chief Warlick to the fire and was running too fast." Officer Mays agreed to pay half the cost of repairing the damages of $125.95. The police department paid $63 and Mays paid $62.95.

Jackson finished building a new City Hall at the corner of Main and Cumberland Streets in February 1924 and the ground floor was outfitted with space for the police department, city court and city jail. The lockup was divided, with three cells for female prisoners and six cells for male prisoners.

The move to the new City Hall changed the patrolman's routine little but added leg work to the deskman's duty. The police bell was installed atop the new City Hall and the desk officer had to climb stairs to the third floor to sound the alarm and summon policemen on duty in the business district. This finally became so troublesome and such a waste of time that two police

Chief of Police Andrew "Tip" Taylor served Jackson in this capacity for twenty years, 1923–1943, longer than any other chief.

officers were instructed to remain within a couple of blocks of the police station at all times. When a policeman was needed, the deskman would step out on the sidewalk and blow a whistle. The bell was still used to alert officers in the residential areas.

When J. E. Mays resigned as motorcycle policeman in February 1926 Robert A. Mainord Jr. was appointed to the position. He had been a deputy sheriff under his father, also named Robert, who was sheriff of Madison County. Mainord became one of the most respected officers in the department and later served as chief.

Chief Tip Taylor saw a need for better administrative oversight of the night police and appointed L. T. Mays night captain. Mays was also called the night chief of police.

Department personnel remained stable during the late twenties and thirties. For the two-year term beginning July 1927 the entire eighteen-man force was reelected. Tip Taylor as chief and L. T. Mays, W. H. Thomas, H. G. Utley, Charles W. Wooten, J. A. Mayo, M. W. Wilson, Wyatt S. Tomlinson, J. D. Cock, Thomas A. Garrison Jr., J. T. Crutchfield, Harvey J. Penn, Tom Parish, John T. Johns, Robert A. Mainord Jr., C. B. Blackmon, Robert A. Mainord Sr. and John W. Jones as policemen.

The second death in the line of duty of a Jackson policeman was the result of injuries inflicted during a hit and run on Sunday afternoon, December 20, 1931. Motorcycle Officer John Turner "Johnnie" Johns was directing traffic on South Royal Street below the Nashville Chattanooga & St. Louis depot. A car had run off the road and into the lake near the waterworks pumping station called The Wells. A wrecker was pulling the car out of the lake and had the road partially blocked. Traffic was down to one lane and Johnnie Johns, whistle in his hand, stood in front of the wrecker signaling cars to pass.

A green roadster came from the south traveling in excess of fifty miles per hour. The driver had been drinking and darted around waiting cars. The roadster struck Officer Johns with such force that his body came to rest sixty-three feet from the point of impact, breaking numerous bones and causing extensive internal injuries.

The driver fled the scene in the damaged roadster. Officers L. T. Mays, Harvey Penn and Robert Mainord Jr. quickly arrested him. All testified that they "smelled liquor on him."

Feelings against the hit and run driver ran high in the community when Officer Johns died two days later. The thirty-eight-year-old officer was a veteran of World War I and well-liked. Johns was gassed in France during the war and discharge from the Army. He served on the police force for eight years before he was killed.

Soon after Johns' death, Motorcycle Policeman Jake Steadman was suspended for drinking while on duty. Steadman and Johns worked side by side as motor officers and were close friends. Thomas D. "Tommy" McCord was given motorcycle duty on a trial basis in Steadman's place. McCord was born in Bemis and had worked for seven years as a railroad detective. Tyree Blackmon was also appointed on a trial basis as motorcycle policeman to fill the vacancy created by the death of Officer Johns. Steadman was reinstated to the force in February 1932.

A department reorganization was announced in the December 9, 1936, Jackson Sun under the headline "Police Force Is Shaken Up By Tip Taylor. Chief Gives Practically Every Man On Force a New Partner." Chief Taylor realigned the department and teamed partners on night duty, Landon Weir and Raymond Gaba, J. I. Carter and Homer L. Knowles, Robert Stedman and Tom Murtaugh, and Jesse T. Crutchfield and Kelly Mills. The day shift teamed P. Y. DuPoyster and M. W. Wilson, and Wyatt Tomlinson and Harvey J. Penn. Motorcycle Patrolmen Tommy D. McCord and Robert Mainord Jr. were not affected, nor were John D. Cock and Charles W.

Motorcycle Policeman Robert A. Mainord Jr. at the corner of Main and Shannon Streets in 1927, soon after he went on the force. He was talking with Chief Tip Taylor seated in the department's second automobile, a 1923 Dodge. The front bumper of the car was replaced with a pipe, possibly to assist stalled motorists with a push. The motorcycle officer on the right was likely Harvey J. Penn, who usually rode partners with Mainord.

Wooten, who had been working together for some time. Jesse T. "Crutch" Crutchfield was made assistant chief on December 15, 1936.

The long police career of Harvey C. Marcom began on August 24, 1937, when he was hired as a probationary officer at $100 per month. Pay for regular policemen was $125 per month. Marcom was a native of Crockett County and had graduated from delivery boy to meat cutter while he worked in a grocery store at the corner of Lambuth and Hatton Streets. Marcom had a good voice and sang as "The Singing Butcher Boy" on WTJS radio. Marcom recalled his early days on the force.

> I was issued a cap, cap badge, coat badge and a pair of twisters and became a policeman. I remember I paid $17.50 for a blue serge suit to go to work. They wanted 35 or 40-year-old men back then. I was 23 and one of the first young men hired. We used to hire a man and put him with an experienced man. That's how we got our training.

> Back then, you did the whole bit. If you started a case, you did it all. You made the investigation,

you made the arrests and you went to court with the case. We had a lot of fun and knew almost everybody in town. We had two patrol cars and at night we would use the city engineer's car. That gave us three cars at night. When the desk sergeant got a call, he would step outside City Hall and blow his whistle. We had a "whistle man" who walked the downtown area. The Fox Restaurant (at the intersection of Liberty and Main streets) was about as far as he could get away from the station. The "whistle man" would go to the station, find out what the call was, get a patrol car, go pick up another officer and answer the call. At night we had two men down town, the "whistle man" and another man who mostly worked around the picture shows and New Southern Hotel. Movies were big things back in those days and the hotel had a lot of business.

> We got one or two calls a night and we answered calls with two men. We had lots of bootleggers back then and were plagued with peeping Toms, but we didn't have any big problems. Then I got a $25-per-month raise and drew $62.50 payday every two weeks for a year. Then we went to a six

days a week and finally five days a week. That was a big improvement. I guess the biggest improvement was when we got radios. That was the best thing that ever happened to the department.

Robert Stedman trained Marcom and they became life-long friends. The twister to which Marcom referred was a chain with interlocking handles at each end. It was placed around the wrist of a prisoner to control him on the way to the station. A more dramatic piece of equipment was about to be added.

A series of robberies in the spring of 1938 prompted Chief Taylor to get serious with prowlers. All cars on patrol were supplied with sawed-off shotguns and the chief told officers to use the guns if they ordered a person to halt and he kept going. Officer Tom Murtaugh followed the chief's instruction one night and took a shot at a prowler as he fled through a yard on McCorry Street. The blast from the sawed-off shotgun may have hit the thief, but failed to stop him. When Murtaugh "cracked down," the prowler dropped his bundle, a box of fancy cakes and a pair of light grey trousers.

Patrolmen Carter and Stedman seized the first large supply of marijuana in the city's history in October 1938. They arrested a transient from Atlanta with several sacks filled with the grayish brown weed. He told them it was hemp and used as birdseed. Inspector Davis Hoke, a federal narcotic inspector from Memphis, was called in to verify it was a narcotic.

Two major changes took place in the Jackson Police Department in early 1940. The department moved to eight-hour shifts and installed a radio sys-

Patrolman Harvey C. Marcom soon after he joined the department. The circle-star breast badge and crossed-batons cap badge were worn during the thirties and forties.

tem. A couple of years after installing the radio, the microphone at headquarters had developed a sticky switch and didn't always stop transmitting when the switch was released. One day Chief Taylor was riding in a patrol car with Officer Rip Rampley. Desk Sergeant Connie Spain sent out a message and when he released the switch, it stuck, leaving the microphone open. An uncooperative prisoner had just been brought to the desk and Sergeant Spain spoke to the prisoner in very uncomplimentary terms.

In the patrol car Chief Taylor said, "Shut it off," and Rampley replied, "I can't shut it off, he has to shut it off down there. He's going out to the whole world." Chief Taylor mumbled, "I never wanted these damned radios anyway."

The second transforming change for the department, elimination of 12-hour shifts, required that three new patrolmen be added to the force. Dave Moore, E. Kelly Mills and James G. Davis were hired. Chief Taylor established the duty schedule for the three shifts with four men on duty between the hours of 5:00 a.m. and 1:00 p.m., six men on duty from 1:00 p.m. to 9:00 p.m. and ten men on duty from 9:00 p.m. to 5:00 a.m.

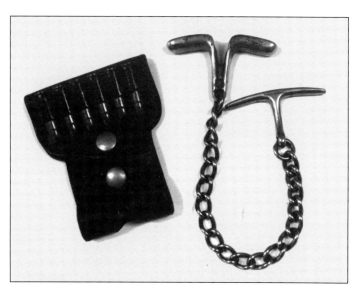

Chain twister issued to officers for restraining prisoners by the wrist. The leather case included loops for six .38 caliber rounds.

420

The new radio equipment quickly became an essential crime fighting tool. Two armed bandits created excitement across West Tennessee in June 1940. The two stole a car in Memphis and robbed a filling station a block from the Haywood County Courthouse in Brownsville. A BOLO (be on look out) was sent to surrounding towns and broadcast to radio cars in Jackson. Patrolmen Tom Murtaugh and Paul Kilzer were in a car on Highway 70 near the western city limits about 1:00 a.m. when they saw the bandit car.

Officers Murtaugh and Kilzer gave chase, firing at the bandit car with a pistol and a pump shotgun. The chase through the business district ended on East Lafayette Street when the robbers, trying to reach the Nashville highway, whipped the car around so suddenly that they overturned the vehicle. The Jackson policemen made the arrests.

Patrolmen Murtaugh and Kilzer, along with Robert Mainord and Raymond Gaba, worked a high-profile murder case in August 1940. The fifty-seven-year-old night watchman at the Coca-Cola Bottling Works on River Road was bludgeoned about 11 p.m. His pistol and keys were taken along with approximately $300 in cash from the plant office. The next morning at 5:20 a company salesman found the watchman just under the roof of the garage, his back to the wheel of one of the trucks parked inside and his head down. The watchman was taken to the hospital where he died later that day.

That afternoon Officers Tom Murtaugh and Robert Mainord arrested an ex-inmate of the reformatory and interrogated him into the evening. The prisoner confessed and implicated a former worker at the plant. Patrolmen James Davis and J. I. Carter arrested the second perpetrator about 4:30 Sunday morning. He took officers behind his residence where they retrieved the night watchman's pistol and part of the stolen money under a board in the outhouse. The caretaker at Riverside Cemetery later found the heavy iron bar that was used as the murder weapon. The two killers were convicted of first-degree murder and executed in Tennessee's electric chair.

Chief of Police Andrew "Tip" Taylor tendered his retirement letter on April 16, 1943, due to poor health. He served twenty-six years on the force. "Chief Tip," as he was known to many, served a couple of months shy of twenty years as chief, longer than any chief of police in the history of the Jackson Police Department. Robert A. Mainord Jr. was appointed chief of police to serve out Taylor's term.

When the city administration changed in July 1943, George A. Smith took office as mayor. He

Officer Wylie Buford McKenzie chalking tires in front of White Drug Company at the northeast corner of Main and Liberty Streets in the summer of 1941. John R. Long Jr., who took this photograph, said Officer McKenzie was well-liked by young people who frequented the soda fountain at the drugstore. The courthouse and Post Office/Federal Building were in the background. (Photo courtesy of John R. Long Jr.)

named Richard Jack Bowers Sr. chief of police. Chief Bowers was an ex-Marine and had worked as an inspector for the State of Tennessee Department of Finance and Taxation for twelve years. Robert Mainord returned to the role of second in command. Mayor Smith worked closely with Chief Bowers to set a new standard for law enforcement in Jackson. Smith, Bowers and the police department wasted no time in beginning a clean up of illegal activity in the city, raiding and arresting racketeers.

Chief Bowers instituted a platoon system with each of the three platoons under the supervision of a sergeant. Those named to the post of sergeant were Robert Stedman, Harvey Marcom and Raymond Gaba. Each platoon was assigned to one of the three shifts. Assistant Chief Mainord and Chief Bowers took on the role of the principal criminal investigators as well as dividing the overall supervision of the force.

With World War II at its height, an estimated 1,500 to 2,000 servicemen visiting Jackson each week. Mayor Smith requested that a detail of Military Police be assigned to Jackson. Army Sergeant Delmar Dixon and privates Lee T. Grissom and Joseph Sanchez reported to Chief Bowers in December 1943. The MPs immediately joined officers of the JPD in squad cars patrolling the city. The MPs were stationed at Police Headquarters in City Hall. The detail of MPs was enlarged in February. They began patrolling in military vehicles, since the majority of nightclubs frequented by servicemen were outside the city limits.

Patrolmen William T. "Tom" Parrish and Fred C. Smith were added to the city's force in December 1943 to bring it back to full strength at twenty-five men. The force consisted of Chief Bowers, Assistant Chief Mainord, three desk sergeants, three "field" sergeants and seventeen patrolmen.

A Thompson submachine gun was added to the department's arsenal in July 1945. The Thompson came equipped with a fifty-shot drum and several clips for its .45 caliber cartridges. The department already had the two Reising submachine guns. If the force needed more firepower, machine guns were available from local units of the Tennessee State Guard. The JPD arsenal also included ten shotguns, teargas guns and a full complement of revolvers. Each patrol car was supplied with shotguns, gas shells and other emergency equipment.

A major reorganization of the department took place January 1, 1946, following the resignation of Chief Jack Bowers. Robert Mainord took command of department. Sergeant Raymond Gaba was named assistant chief and Patrolman Mack D. Cozart was promoted to sergeant and placed in charge of a patrol platoon. Tommy D. McCord was made traffic supervisor, with rank of sergeant, to head the new Traffic Division of the department. Bill Cole was named special investigator or detective, with rank of captain, to head a new Special Investigation Department, soon to be called the Detective Division.

Chief Robert Mainord continued the modernization of the department and started the use of fingerprint analysis. Assistant Chief Gaba assisted with fingerprint and photographic work. The JPD worked with the FBI to upgrade records management within the department and to interface with the federal clearinghouse for identification records and nationwide crime statistics.

The Detective Division gave a good accounting of itself in the initial years of its existence. Over 73 percent of the crimes referred to the Detective Bureau during the first year were solved and of the twenty files that remained open, the majority were minor in nature.

Patrolmen Joe Cooksey, left, and Kyle Chandler chat with the driver of a 1941 Chevrolet during the war in 1944.

Alertness by a new officer was key to solving the robbery of the Ragland-Potter Wholesale Grocery Company. Officers Edwin Bacon Alderson and Joe Cooksey were cruising in a prowl car when they noted a car parked near the grocery firm. The robbery was reported shortly thereafter. Alderson, a rookie patrolman, remembered the license number and found that the car belonged to an employee of the company. An investigation quickly resulted in an arrest and the recovery of $1,200.

The nation's most famous gangster, Al Capone, came to Jackson on February 1, 1947. Capone posed no problem for the force when he rolled into town on the Illinois Central "Sun Chaser" at 9:30 that Saturday morning. He was well secured in an expensive bronze casket on his way to Chicago for burial.

The reorganization of the department was accompanied by a change of uniform and insignia. A silver-

City Hall circa 1947 and one of the 1946 Chevrolet four-door sedans, the first patrol cars purchased after the war. "Jackson Police" was painted on the doors, and a "Police Department" sign was over the front entrance to the station house.

The Jackson Police Department in its first group photo, taken in 1947. Front row, from left to right, were Chief Robert Mainord, Traffic Officer Joe Cooksey, Traffic Division supervisor Sergeant Tommy D. McCord, Traffic Officer Hugh Pegram, Traffic Officer Kyle Chandler, and Assistant Chief J. Raymond Gaba. On the second row were the "First" or "A.M." shift officers on duty from 5:00 A.M. to 1:00 P.M., with platoon leader Sergeant Robert Stedman and Patrolmen Charles Price, James Matlock, Ernest Oakley, W. Buford McKenzie, and Homer L. Knowles. On the third row were the "Second" or "P.M." shift officers on duty from 1:00 P.M. to 9:00 P.M., with platoon leader Sergeant Harvey Marcom and Patrolmen Floyd Roberts, Buddy Gaffney, Clint Sells, Fred Smith, J. T. McCann, and Edwin Alderson. On fourth row were the "Third" or "Night" shift officers on duty from 9:00 P.M. to 5:00 A.M., with platoon leader Sergeant Mack D. Cozart and Patrolmen Jesse B. Goodrich, Tom Parrish, Guy Usery, and Louis G. Burlison. On the fifth row were Detective Division supervisor Captain Bill Cole holding the recently acquired Thompson submachine gun, night Desk Sergeant M. W. Wilson, A.M. shift Desk Sergeant Connie Spain, P.M. Desk Sergeant Jesse T. Crutchfield, and Detective James Davis holding one of the department's Reising submachine guns. The photograph was taken on the front steps of City Hall on Main Street. The 1946 Harley-Davidson Servi-Car parked on the sidewalk was used by the Traffic Division. (Jackson Sun photo)

tone shield with the city seal at its center was adopted as the breast badge. The cap badge was an eagle-top medallion with a cutout number applied in an open panel. Badges worn by supervisory ranks were of different styles and gold-tone in color. Members of the Traffic Division were identified by a white uniform cap with a different style hat badge. Sam Brown belts were worn over winter jackets.

The department expanded significantly in the late forties and fifties. The Civil Service Act was applied to employees of the City of Jackson in January 1949 and police officers were no longer elected by the City Commission every two years.

An identification bureau was formed. Photographs and fingerprint records on felons and "suspicious characters" were maintained in permanent files at headquarters and copies were sent to the FBI in Washington. William Warren Jones was hired on January 1, 1950, as identification officer at the rank of sergeant and at a salary of $215 a month.

The Cold War once again raised the need for civil preparedness. Chief Mainord and Madison County Sheriff Emery O. Bruce were made members of the local Civil Defense Council. The Jackson Police Department formed an Auxiliary Police of approximately fifty individuals to augment the police force in times of emergency. The group functioned from the early fifties into the 1960s.

The department was increasingly faced with growing traffic issues and fatalities on city streets in the fifties. New technology aided enforcement. The first Breathalyzer was acquired in 1958. The first speed detection device used by the department, other than clocking a car with a cruiser, was an electronic timing device called "The Black Widow" because of the web spread by traffic officers to catch speeders.

The device was set up in the roadway by stretching two cables across the street exactly eighty-eight feet apart. When an automobile ran over the first cable, air pressure started a timer. When its tires hit the second cable the timer stopped and the lapsed time between the two cables determined the speed of the vehicle. Two officers were required to set up and run the operation. The cable device was transported in the rear compartment of a three-wheeled motorcycle and monitored by the traffic officer who rode the Servi-Car. A second motorcycle officer performed the chase duties.

The Detective Division consisted of Captain Bill Cole and Lieutenant James Davis. Patrolman Fred Smith solved a series of fires set in downtown garbage containers when he arrested a man in the act of starting two fires. Officers Eugene Jones and Tommy Marcom demonstrated the value of door shaking in 1957. On a routine check of East Chester businesses they noticed a side door open and arrested two men inside Hoot's Café in the process of a burglary.

Detective work almost became fatal for Detective Captain Bill Cole on July 27, 1951. Cole was shot at about 12:30 on Friday afternoon as he searched a

Desk Sergeant Jesse T. "Crutch" Crutchfield at the desk in the police station at City Hall on Main Street with radio mike on the left and telephones on the right. The oversized Pepsi-Cola bottle contained an AM radio. One morning around two or three A.M., Desk Sergeant Buford McKenzie was playing the radio and decided to share the music with officers on patrol. He held the police radio system mike button open and the music was broadcast into all the patrol cars. Chief Mainord called in and asked, "Where's that music coming from?" The radio bottle was not seen again.

house on Glass Street for a murderer. Detectives Cole and Davis received a tip and went to the house with Chief Mainord and Officers Bill McIntosh and Louis G. Burlison.

When Chief Mainord and Captain Cole entered the front room, they heard a noise and kicked open the door into a middle room. They were greeted by the shotgun blast which struck Cole. Chief Mainord emptied the Thompson submachine gun into the room and retreated to get Cole to the hospital.

Once Cole was on his way to the hospital in a taxi, Chief Mainord sent for tear gas guns. Officers Bill McIntosh and L. G. Burlison were at the rear of the house when Chief Mainord and Lieutenant Davis fired two tear gas shells into the house. The killer ran out the back door with his shotgun in his hands and headed straight for McIntosh. Officer McIntosh fired two rounds, hitting the gunman the left arm and in the chest. The murderer fell, almost at McIntosh's feet, digging the muzzle of the shotgun into the ground as he went down.

Captain Cole was partly protected by a door facing and the injuries to his head were not serious. The shooter also survived and was sentenced to 99 years in the state penitentiary.

Traffic Officer Gerald Parish worked a wreck at Main and Shannon Streets. James Shoe Hospital was on the northeast corner of the intersection.

Gerald Parish leads a parade west on Main Street passing the Liberty Street intersection. The third and fourth cars were 1948 Plymouth Special Deluxe sedan patrol cars of the JPD. These were the first patrol cars to have the front doors painted white.

Training was becoming an important aspect of modernizing the department. Detective Sergeant Edwin Bacon Alderson was the first member of the JPD to attend the FBI National Academy in Washington, DC. He participated in the intensive twelve-week program in 1957. Patrolman Tommy Marcom attended the National Academy in 1959.

Basic training continued to be provided on-the-job by an experienced officer as the training officer. Certain basic duties were assigned to all rookie officers. They rode the courthouse square when on night duty. When they worked days, they stood on the bank corners, regardless of the weather. There were three banks downtown and an officer stood at the corner nearest each bank entrance and blew his whistle every time the traffic light changed. Basic equipment issued

to new officers included a slapjack and, instead of handcuffs, a chain twister or come-along.

Policemen occasionally found creative ways to fill the hours of boredom. A good number on the force were hunters and a few officers did a little rabbit hunting on night duty. They went to open areas at the fairgrounds or near the city limits and killed a few rabbits, then took them to a cook at the Illinois Central Restaurant who barbecued them. Around midnight they had a rabbit supper. Chief Mainord stopped by roll call one afternoon and casually commented, "Well, I had a call today from the game warden, and he said he didn't want to arrest any police, but he could, if he had to." That broke up the rabbit hunting.

The 50-man force had two marked cars and one unmarked car used for patrol. Traffic had a GMC

Traffic Sergeant Carl Lee Johnsey with the cable-operated speed detector called "The Black Widow" because traffic officers spread a "web" to catch speeders.

department's first youth guidance officer. Castellaw worked with youth in an effort to prevent juvenile delinquency. Castellaw initially wore a different style uniform and after about two and a half years switched to plainclothes.

A Safety Patrol for school zones was formed on November 1, 1957. Four policewomen were hired for the unit, sometimes called the Patrol Mothers, Loretta Gillmann, Mrs. Louise Hudson, Mrs. Dorothy Kemp and Mrs. Mary Gadd. Their pay was $1 an hour or $60 per month each for their part-time duty at city schools.

Assistant Chief J. Raymond Gaba, a thirty-year veteran of the JPD, was selected chief of police on August 15, 1959, upon the retirement of Chief Mainord. Guy Usery was promoted from lieutenant to captain, Hugh Pegram, James Matlock and Bill O'Dell from sergeant to lieutenant, Warren Roberts from detective to detective sergeant, J. T. McCann from patrolman to sergeant and J. A. Eubanks from patrolman to night desk sergeant.

Jesse Leon Massey, 44, was appointed in August 1960 as a youth guidance officer and became the department's first black officer of the modern era. He joined Ike Castellaw in the youth division and worked with the city's black youth. Massey attended Lane College and had a perfect score on the civil service examination. The department had already elected Helen Porter as a policewoman, or patrol mother, for traffic duty at South Jackson Elementary School. She was Jackson's first black female officer.

Carryall, three motorcycles and a three-wheeler. The chief had a car and the detectives had a car. Sometimes there were only five officers working the night shift, four riding patrol and Sergeant Harvey Marcom working the desk. Twice a night the patrolmen working the square left their patrol car and walked the downtown area, shaking doors on every business establishment.

Two important personnel actions took place on September 1, 1957. Former FBI fingerprint expert Ray G. Pratt replace Sergeant Warren Jones as the department's identification officer when Jones joined the TBI. The records and identification division consisted of six filing cabinets, a fingerprint kit for dusting crime scenes and a camera.

At the same time the department created a Youth Work Division and hired Ike E. Castellaw Jr. as the

Traffic Officer Richard Ford enforced the city's speed limits to decrease traffic deaths in Jackson.

Youth Officer Ike E. Castellaw Jr. and the four school mothers who served as crossing guards, from left to right, Loretta Gillmann, Dorothy Kemp, Louise Hudson, and Mary Gadd. Castellaw wore a different style uniform than the rest of the department.

The period of the sixties and early seventies was an era of social upheaval and the police were at the center of the conflict. The first major challenge to segregation in Jackson came in October 1960 when Lane College students refused to sit at the back of the city's public transit buses. Nine students were arrested and charged with threatened breach of peace. A boycott of city buses brought an end to segregation on the Jackson City Lines, Inc. within a few days. Next the black students turned their attention to segregated lunch counters at Woolworth's and McLellan's department stores.

Plainclothes officers of the Detective Bureau, Bill Cole, James Davis, Ed Alderson and Warren Roberts were assigned to handle the disturbances related to the civil rights demonstrations. Roberts recalled, "My partner and I were stationed across the street, observing what was going on. They told us to keep the peace. It wasn't always simple." Jackson public schools were integrated in January 1962 when three black students entered Tigrett Junior High School. Warren Roberts and Ike Castellaw were assigned to patrol the halls of Tigrett to prevent any violence.

The police force effectively maintained order at demonstrations. Die-hards and agitators on both sides exacerbated the instability, but the community and the police department were less reactionary than many other cities.

Assistant Chief Harvey Marcom became chief of police on July 16, 1963, when Chief Gaba retired after thirty-five years of service to the department. The Jackson Police Department, under the leadership of Chief Harvey Marcom and with the support of Mayor George Smith, responded to the changing racial dynamics and added a black patrolman to the ranks.

James Neal Cherry Jr. joined the force in January 1964 as the department's first uniformed black patrol officer in the modern era. Cherry was 36 when he joined the force. Other black uniformed patrol officers were soon hired, including Officers William Wiley Hendrix in March 1964 and Alex Hunt Jr. in January 1965.

When these black officers came on the force, public facilities were still segregated. "I had a white partner. He'd go in one side and I'd go in the colored side," James Cherry recalled. The first black officers often got more respect from the white community than their fellow black citizens. In one instance Cherry arrested a black man for drunkenness on Sycamore Street, sometimes called the "Beale Street of Jackson" because it was so rough. The offender didn't take a good look at Cherry until he was in the car. He looked at Cherry, said no black man was going to arrest him and jumped out of the car. Cherry fought with the drunk in the rainy intersection and put him back into the car. Another call Cherry said he would never forget was to a house at 118 Tanyard Street. When the black woman answered the door, she said to him, "I don't want you. I want the real police." Cherry simply got back in the patrol car and drove away.

Police officers Jerry Lee Johnson, left, and Bobby Law, right, in a patrol car in front of Police Headquarters in 1963.

Department policies were adjusted for a time after black officers joined the force. Because no screen separated the front and back seats, one officer rode in the back with the prisoner. Sergeant Jerry Johnson was assigned as Cherry's training officer and when the two arrested a black man Cherry rode in the back. When they arrested a white man Johnson rode with the prisoner while Cherry drove. These practices were intended to prevent unnecessary racial conflict and were soon abandoned.

Loretta Gillmann, one of the original four policewomen employed for school patrol work, became the department's first full-time female officer in 1964.

Patrolman Danny Utley on "door shaking" duty on a downtown business to be certain it was locked.

Mrs. Gillmann was hired as parking meter maid and was frequently called on for other functions, such as frisking women prisoners and helping lost children.

The Detective Division went through a leadership change in August 1967 Detective Captain William W. Cole retired and Ed Alderson, who had been promoted to assistant chief in February 1966, took direct command of the Detective Division. Warren Roberts was promoted to captain of detectives in September 1970 and took operational command of the division.

An alert patrol officer, on or off duty, sometimes thwarted crime in process. Patrolman Eddie Roy Moore, 24 years old, with two years on the job, was off duty on the night of September 15, 1967. Driving up Highland Avenue just before midnight he saw two suspicious men at a phone booth outside of a drug store. A few moments later Moore drove back to the pharmacy and found the two men inside. The pair had committed a series of burglaries in the area. Moore was not in uniform, nor was he armed, but he entered the store anyway.

Patrolman Moore told the two they were under arrest. One swung a crowbar at the officer's head and barely missing him. Moore wrestled violently with the burglar and pinned him just outside the pharmacy. The second burglar fled and was later killed in a car accident. As Officer Moore struggled with the one thief, he yelled to passing motorists for help. Mike McCullar, a friend of Moore, happen to be passing and recognized Moore's voice. McCullar stopped to lend assistance and the two held the felon until other officers arrived.

Bootlegging continued to be a major law enforcement issue for the city. The largest seizure of illegal whiskey ever made in Jackson took place one afternoon on South Highland Avenue. Officers Thomas Acuff and Tommy Marcom were on patrol when they received a call that a U-Haul headed to Jackson from the south was weaving in and out of traffic. They stopped the truck near the Civic Center. The driver, an escapee from Parchman Prison in Mississippi, and the passenger got out of the truck staggering. Acuff saw a gallon jug on the front seat and asked the driver what was in the jug. The driver admitted that it was white whiskey. Acuff said, "That looks like a lot." The truck driver answered, "That's nothing; I've got 1,300 gallons of this stuff in the back."

In March 1965 Patrolman Milton Weaver and "Jaycee," a ninety-seven-pound German shepherd, became Jackson's first dog patrol. They graduated from a twelve-week police dog course at the Armour Police Training Center in Memphis and received two weeks of on-the-job training with the Memphis Police Department.

428

Officer Norman Pipkin prepares the department's "Pepper Fog" machine designed for riot control.

Detective Sergeant Robert W. Dailey Jr. became the department's third officer to attend the FBI National Academy in 1967. While there he presented FBI Director J. Edgar Hoover a plaque on behalf of the Tennessee State Lodge, Fraternal Order of Police.

The entire department was called on in March 1969 when rioting broke out at Lane College in Jackson. Officers had already been assigned to protect the president of the school before rioting occured and to enforce the curfew afterwords. Deputy sheriffs and troopers of the THP assisted in ending the riot.

The department often used FBI resources in working crimes. The manager of Hub City Clothing Company at 208 North Liberty was shot to death on the morning of February 6, 1969. Assistant Chief Ed Alderson, Detective Lieutenant Robert Dailey and Detective Sergeant Jackie Moore investigated and found a receipt made out to the twenty-year-old railroad section hand. He was arrested at Montezuma in Chester County five and a half hours later. A .45 caliber automatic pistol was recovered and Assistant Chief Alderson flew to Washington with the weapon and the bullet removed from the body. The FBI lab confirmed the murder bullet was fired from the gun and the killer was convicted.

The department upgraded both uniforms and equipment in the seventies. A stock eagle-top circle badge was adopted in 1974. A military-surplus helicopter was acquired from the Jackson-Madison County Civil Defense Unit in 1974 and a grant application was filed to equip the aircraft. Virgil Ray Russell, a twenty-three-year-old McKenzie native, was

employed in May 1974 as the department's first helicopter pilot.

The rank of Detective was changed to Investigator and the department name became the Criminal Investigation Division (CID). Captain Robert W. Dailey Jr. took command of CID on the retirement of Warren Roberts. Richard L. Higgins and Neil Morphis were transferred to CID.

The officers of CID kept busy. Three men held up the Perel and Lowenstein Jewelry store at the Jackson Shopping Plaza and were spotted within minutes. The getaway car and a patrol car wrecked on North Royal Street. Investigator Franklin Rice received a leg injury when he jumped over a car to catch one of the fleeing suspects. The following February a lone gunman robbed the North Highland branch of Second National Bank. A door-to-door canvass of the area by JPD officers and FBI agents led to the arrest of an unemployed Alabama man.

Officer Larry Price was near the Jackson Plaza Shopping Center just before 7:00 one Friday evening, when a call came over the radio that an armed gunman had robbed the Big Star Food Store. Price met the manager of the store near its entrance and asked for a description of the subject. "Description?" the manager said, "He's right there," pointing to a man moving down the open-air arcade of the shopping center. Price moved into the breezeway and called for him to halt The felon wheeled and fired at Price with a .38 revolver. Price returned fire, hitting the armed robber in the head and killing him instantly. The gunman was identified as an escapee from the North Carolina state penitentiary where he was serving twelve to fifteen years for armed robbery.

Patrolman Lavon Thompson, left, and Patrolman Jimmy Warren answer a call on Lafayette Street west of Liberty Street.

Father and son on the force. Patrolman Robert Dailey III, left, was called "Little Bob" and Lieutenant Robert Dailey Jr. was called "Big Bob." (Jackson Sun photo)

The department got a new home in March 1975 when the two-story Law Enforcement Center was opened at 234 Institute Street. Space for administrative, records, traffic, juvenile and CID personnel was on the main level along with interrogation rooms equipped with one-way glass. The communications section was located adjacent to central records. Booking and the lock-up were on the ground floor.

A Special Weapons And Tactics (SWAT) team was formed in 1975. The five-man SWAT team completed an intensive, weeklong counter-sniper course at the FBI Academy in Quantico, Virginia. Lieutenant Bobby Law led the team that included Patrolmen Kenneth D. Conway, Edmond C. Cepparulo, Jimmy D. Hardin and Robert W. Dailey III.

As the department expanded it implemented new training programs. Fourteen probationary police officers began basic training in the department's first police school on April 15, 1975. The class included five women, the first female patrol officers in the history of the department. The fourteen cadets were Melba Jo Kendall, Linda Dugger, Doris N. Jackson, Jana L. Childress, Anita D. Harrison, David L. Carter, Roger A. Gatlin, Douglas E. Frommel, Michael G. Shepard, Richard S. Staples, Jerry N. Priddy, Donnie E. Stanfill, James B. Flatter and Robert D. Williams. Two individuals of note in this recruit class were twenty-one-year-old Jerry Neal Priddy who would later head CID and twenty-two-year-old Richard S. Staples who would become one of the department's longest serving chiefs. Dennis Mays was the fifteenth member of the class, but few knew since he worked as an undercover operative for his first seven months on the force. Mays later became the department's first commander.

CID was called to one of Jackson's most high profile cases at 1:20 p.m. on December 20, 1975. Officers

Sammy Mullins and Donnie Stanfill responded to the Holiday Inn and in room 406 found the bodies of two nude men. They had stab wounds to the chest and one a slashed throat. Assistant Chief Ed Alderson said the slaying was "one of the worst I've seen in nearly 30 years of police work."

CID Sergeant Norman Pipkin and investigators Jack Wilson and Marvin Spencer collected evidence at the scene. Lieutenant Jackie Moore flew to Washington, DC, and delivered the evidence to the FBI laboratory. Fingerprints gathered at the scene, including one on a cigar band found under the bed and a stolen credit card led police to two hitchhikers who had committed the murders. Both murderers were convicted as a result of the extensive evidence gathered by JPD officers.

The robbery of the Northgate Rexall Pharmacy on Wednesday, October 3, 1979, led to a deadly encounter between two brothers from Benton County and JPD Officers Michael Shepard, Thompson Dabney and Rocky Acuff. The two robbers wearing ski masks were apprehended because of the quick thinking of the druggist who slipped out the back door, called the police and partially disabled the bandit's pickup truck.

Officers Shepard and Dabney spotted the slow moving pickup on North Highland. Their patrol unit was rammed twice as they tried to stop the pair. Acuff and Charles Cox arrived as the two felons exited the truck and fled on foot. The policemen were fired on by the robbers and a gun battle ensued. One robber died

Ribbon cutting ceremony at new Law Enforcement Center. From the left were Chief Harvey Marcom, FOP Ladies Auxiliary President Anne Elston, and Mayor Bob Conger.

The first full-time JPD Tactical Unit included, from left to right, JPD Officers Perry Hearn, Mike Turner, Mike Shepard, Wayne "Butch" Day, Madison County Deputy Sheriff Mark Caldwell, and JPD Corporal Edmond Cepparulo standing in front of the converted ambulance the unit used as a mobile command post.

at the scene; the other a short time later at the hospital.

Lieutenant Bobby Law arrived on the scene after the shooting. He sent the officers involved in the shooting to headquarters, telling them not to talk about the incident on the way. At the station CID Sergeant Richard Higgins secured their weapons and their statements were taken. Department policy required that officers involved in the use of deadly force be suspended without prejudice until an investigation was completed. The informal practice among officers to cope with such incidents was to gather with a few friends and a fifth of their favorite whiskey the evening after the shooting and then to never speak of it again.

Assistant Chief Edwin Bacon "Ed" Alderson was named acting chief on September 15, 1979, when Chief Marcum retired after 16 years as chief. Fifty-year-old Alderson, a 33-three-year veteran of the JPD, joined the force in 1946 after he returned from World War II. He was promoted to sergeant in 1951 and soon after transferred to the Detective Division where he made lieutenant in 1959. During his time as assistant chief, beginning in 1966, he supervised the Detective Division, the Juvenile Bureau, communications, cen-

tral records, community relations and training. He also had charge of federal grants and administration.

Alderson reorganized the department in January 1980 promoting Carl Lee Johnsey to the newly created position of deputy chief with administrative responsibility for the entire department. Deputy Chief Johnsey was a strong, no-nonsense leader, who had advanced under the tutelage of Tommy D. McCord. Johnsey was well respected by his colleagues. Jerry Lee Johnson recalls, "When Carl Lee wanted something done, he wanted it done then, and if you didn't do it, he would do it himself."

Assistant Chief H. P. Curlin retained his position as head of the night patrol. James Cherry was promoted to captain in the Patrol Division, Norman Pipkin to lieutenant in CID and Winston Dixon to lieutenant in the Patrol Division. Lieutenant Barney Crews became administrative assistant to the chief. As part of his reorganization Chief Alderson enhanced the rank structure with implementation of the corporal rank and revised shifts. Patrolmen Jerry A. Taylor, Varnell Womack and Charles W. Cox were promoted to corporal and became responsible for training recruits.

The 1975 recruit class was the first of the department's basic training police school. Recruits running as part of the physical training were, from left to right, Ricky Staples, Eddie Frommel, J. B. Flatter, Roger Gatlin, Anita Harrison, Donnie Stanfill, Mike Shepard, and Jerry Priddy. (Jackson Sun photo)

The Metro Narcotics Unit was formed in February 1980, made up of two JPD officers and one Madison County deputy sheriff. JPD Sergeant Bobby Holt led the squad. The unit began a four-month investigation that resulted in fifty-five drug indictments.

Traffic Patrolman Richard "Ricky" Staples was the first JPD officer to be accepted in the police traffic administration school at Northwestern University Traffic Institute in Evanston, Illinois. Captain Thomas Acuff recommended Staples in 1981 for the nine-month command school that drew officers from around the world. Acuff drove to Staples' 1982 graduation and presented Staples with a lieutenant's bar during the ceremony. When Staples returned, Deputy Chief Johnsey assigned him the responsibility as traffic engineer for the city.

A murder on May 14, 1981, drew the attention of both Jackson and Memphis officers. A call from St. Mary's Rectory at 8:26 a.m. that Friday brought Officers John Farmacka and Glen Penney to the scene where the priest's body lay on the floor. CID Lieutenant Richard Higgins, Sergeant Marvin Spencer and Investigator George Blanton were called and an investigation began. Captain Ray Pratt and Sergeant Gary Winbush gathered physical evidence including latent fingerprints, shoe impressions and a .38 caliber bullet.

The next day the owner of a bar called Chat's Place phoned Lieutenant James Cherry and gave him a gun that a man had pawned for $30 the previous night. The serial number of the revolver, a Smith & Wesson .38 special, showed it to be the sidearm of Memphis Police Lieutenant Clarence Cox who was murdered two days earlier. Palm and fingerprints of a known felon had been found on the roof of Cox's patrol car. Investigator Rocky Acuff took the gun and slugs from the murder scene to the TBI laboratory in Donelson. The revolver proved to be the murder weapon.

Chief Alderson called in Officer Edmond Cepparulo, who trained in 1975 at the FBI counter sniper school, and told him to gather men and equipment and be ready when the subject was located. Investigator Acuff and Patrolman James DeBerry joined others in the stakeout of the Highland Park Inn at Hicksville where the killer was reportedly staying.

About 8:30 Sunday morning they sighted the subject entering the Hut Restaurant, which was crowded with patrons. With his weapon held against his leg, Acuff moved through one dining area and into a section where the killer sat on a stool drinking coffee. The killer spotted Acuff in a mirror, put down the coffee and headed for the front door. Acuff did not want a shootout in the crowded eatery and moved close in

Captain Thomas Acuff, head of the Traffic Division, posted traffic statistics near the Law Enforcement Complex. (Jackson Sun photo)

behind the murderer as he neared the door, grabbed him by the belt and waist band, pulled him close and pushed the handgun into his lower back. The arrest was made without incident.

The situation resulted in the formation of a full-time Tactical Unit under Corporal Edmond Cepparulo in the summer of 1982. Officer Mike Shepard was second in command and Officers Perry Hearn, Wayne "Butch" Day Jr. and Mike Turner were the other members of the team.

The form of government in the City of Jackson changed in January 1989 from a three member City Commission to a ten member City Council. Mayor Charles Farmer was elected to head the new city government. The same year the Jackson Police Department became the first in the state of Tennessee and the 110th agency in the nation to receive national accreditation from the Commission for Accreditation of Law Enforcement Agencies. Captain Barney Crews led the accreditation process. He also led the selection of new insignia for the department including a custom shoulder patch and an eagle-top, teardrop style breast badge.

Deputy Chief Richard S. Staples was appointed chief of police on October 12, 1989, from among forty-nine applicants. Due to a number of retirements, Chief Staples reorganized the command restructure literally overnight. The department was organized into four divisions, Captain Roy Towater commanded the Patrol Division, Captain Richard Higgins headed the Criminal Investigation Division, Captain Barney Crews managed the Administrative Division and Captain Louis Fullerton was in charge of the Support Services Division.

Two changes to the command structure were soon made. Fullerton assumed supervision of both the Patrol Division and Support Services Division in October 1989. In November 1991 department Legal Counsel Dennis Mays took command of the Criminal Investigation Division with the rank of commander.

A community-wide crime problem faced the new chief in the early nineties. The number of homicides in Jackson grew at a disturbing rate and a large percentage of the cases were related to drug and gang activity. A cooperative effort between the police and community leaders developed in response to the epidemic.

"We had an epidemic we didn't realize," Shirlene Mercer, a well-respected leader in Jackson, recalled. "Crack-cocaine had such an addictive and psychological effect on people that they became lunatics. They would do anything for that drug. But you could make a lot of money and turf wars developed. People began killing each other to control selling it." Mayor Farmer called a citywide Crime Summit in 1993 to address the increased violence in Jackson. The department began to implement community-oriented policing and citizens led by Shirlene Mercer took to the streets in week-

Captains James N. Cherry Jr., left, and Richard S. Staples were promoted to deputy chief in October 1988. Deputy Chief Cherry was the first minority officer in the department ever to serve at the rank, and Deputy Chief Staples was the youngest officer ever to serve at the rank.

JPD command in the early nineties, from left to right, were Chief Rick Staples, Commander Dennis Mays, Captain Marvin Spencer, Captain Richard Higgins, Captain Louis Fullerton, and Captain Barney Crews.

ly neighborhood anti-crime marches. The department also formed a Gang Enforcement Team led by Lieutenant Patrick Willis and Sergeant Leslee Hallenback.

The killing of well-liked sporting store owner on Tuesday morning, May 14, 1996, resulted in bringing Jackson law enforcement together with the U. S. Attorney's Office to prosecute gang conspirators under federal laws. The sporting store owner was robbed as he worked alone in his store, then shot in the chest and killed. The following week four members of the Vice Lords gang were arrested. The murder became the seminal case in a joint effort between the Gang Enforcement Team and federal prosecutors. Both the murderers and gang leaders who were involved in planning the crime, although not directly involved at the scene, were successfully prosecuted under federal conspiracy laws. Other convictions for conspiracy at the street gang level followed.

A rash of bank robberies in 1997 and early 1998 proved to be a frustrating episode for the department. Within twelve months thirteen bank branches were robbed. Chief Staples tried everything including parking marked squad cars in bank parking lots. The string of robberies ended after officers chased down one of two bandits in a grove of trees about a half-mile from the bank. He had stripped down to his underwear before capture. All of the stolen money was recovered.

A restructuring of department command took place in January 1998 upon the retirement of Patrol Division commander Captain Louis Fullerton. Jerry

N. Priddy was promoted to captain and took charge of the Criminal Investigation Division and Commander Dennis Mays became head of the Patrol Division.

Shortly before midnight on May 4, 2004, for the second time in five years, tornados ravaged Jackson and Madison County, killing a number of its citizens. This time an F4 tornado made a direct hit on the center of the city. Among the hundred buildings damaged or destroyed were Jackson's Law Enforcement Center and the Madison County Criminal Justice Center. Jackson police officers and Madison County deputies worked frantically in the hours following the tornado and were on modified duty for months as the city worked its way back to normality. Officers from surrounding agencies assisted with traffic control and other tasks for weeks after the tornado.

Tragedy shook the JPD on Thursday morning, June 17, 2004. Sergeant Andy Thaddeus Bailey and other officers responded to a call that an armed felon grabbed a woman's purse at Old Hickory Mall and fired into the air as he fled. Law officers took up an eight minute, six mile, high-speed pursuit of the thief headed toward downtown Jackson.

The bandit rammed a police car when he was boxed in on West Orleans Street near Highland Avenue. He jumped from his car and fired three shots at Sergeant Bailey through the passenger side window before Bailey could exit his patrol unit. Andy Bailey was struck by two rounds, but managed to exit the car and provide cover to other officers before collapsing. The suspect was shot in a running gun battle and captured.

Sergeant Andy T. Bailey, left, was shot and killed on June 17, 2005, while pursuing an armed bandit. Chief of Police Richard S. "Rick" Staples, right, has led the department for over 16 years with commitment to cooperation between the police department and the citizens of Jackson.

Fellow officers gave emergency aid to Sergeant Bailey, one encouraging him to, "Stay with me, Andy." The 52-year-old lawman died later that morning at Jackson-Madison County General Hospital. The 31-year veteran of the department was planning his retirement for the following year. Sergeant Andy Bailey was posthumously awarded the department's Medal of Honor, the first in the history of the force to be so honored.

Today the Jackson Police Department under the leadership of Chief of Police Rick Staples is 250 strong. Its mission is "to improve the quality of life for all citizens of our community by reducing the problems associated with crime, through crime suppression and prevention, jointly educating our officers and the public and developing a co-active partnership with the community."

The Patrol Division is under the direction of Commander Dennis Mays. The Criminal Investigation Division is commanded by Captain Jerry Priddy. Captain Gerry Campbell is the commander of the Planning and Support Service Division. The Administrative Services Division is commanded by Captain Richard Higgins. The Jackson Police Department continues the tradition of valor and dedication to duty demonstrated throughout its history.

Clarksville Police Department

Clarksville was established in 1784 by the North Carolina legislature as the seat of Tennessee County. The town was part of a reservation set aside to compensate Revolutionary War veterans and was named for Revolutionary War hero George Rogers Clark.

The town grew quickly because of its access to navigation on the Cumberland River and rich soil that grew fine dark-fired tobacco. Steamboats first appeared at Clarksville in 1820 and the enhanced transportation added to the prosperity of the town.

Clarksville municipal law enforcement began with the appointment of Town Constable Lemuel Rogers in 1820. For his service he was paid $50 per year, plus a portion of fines and license fees that he collected. Two men were appointed as a night watch at the same time. They too were paid a stipend of $50 per year.

The duty of the "beat walkers," as they were referred to, was to work two nights a week and on Saturdays. They walked a prescribed beat once before midnight and once after midnight. Salaries were increased in January 1830 to $60 per year.

The Clarksville city council elected three night watchmen in 1858, A. D. Smith, Ike Barklett and J. W. Moore. Smith was appointed Captain of the Watch. The captain was paid $500 per year and watchmen were paid $450. The appointment as captain was not permanent and between 1858 and 1861 the cap-

tain rotated quarterly. Other watchmen elected prior to the Civil War were S. Woodrum, J. Crockett, Thomas Jackson, William Moore and J. J. Rawls.

The night watch was notified of emergencies by the ringing of a bell in the town square. Responsibility for listen and responding to the bell was assigned to one of the watchmen. That watchman then went to the scene of the incident, getting assistance from other watchmen or citizens as needed. Failure to respond to the ringing of the bell resulted in suspension by the city council for dereliction of duty.

Watchmen could find themselves in trouble for other reasons as well. Night Watchman J. W. Moore was tried by the city council in August 1859 for disturbing the peace and "outraging humanity." Details of his offense was not specified. He left the watch for a time, but later served as a watchman and as captain of the watch. The Moore incident resulted in the city council establishing a fine as penalty for neglect of duty by watchmen. The captain was fined one dollar for an infraction and watchmen fifty cents.

Clarksville established a workhouse in 1861 and J. Crockett was appointed Workhouse Keeper. Crockett was paid the same as a night watchman and was charged with keeping convicted prisoners confined for the length of their sentence. He was permitted to live in the workhouse and to charge prisoners forty cents a day for meals.

The city council decided in February 1862 that watchmen were to go on duty at dusk and patrol until dawn. Four watchmen were elected, J. W. Moore, William Moore, Thomas Jackson and I. N. Bartlett. Clarksville was divided into beats to provide uniformity to watchmen walking patrol.

No records were kept of any city government activity from June 1862 until March 21, 1865, the period of the Civil War. The nature of law enforcement, if any existed during the war, was left to the citizenry or whatever military force was in the area.

After the war Clarksville faced the rebuilding of the war torn city amid an economy that was also in ruin. Watchman Tarpley was the first law officer appointed following the war and took office on June 1865. The city had no funds to pay him, so he worked for the fines and fees that he collected. In October 1865, following interviews of candidates by a committee of the board, the city council selected four watchmen to be paid $500 per year.

A City Marshal was appointed by the end of 1865 and charged with selecting a police force of five "prudent citizens." Four individuals selected were Robert Gibson, T. J. Savage, John Goff and Moore. In 1867, M. W. Carkuff, James Walch, John Robinson and G. Yates were selected as the police force.

A police ordinance was passed by the city board on April 29, 1866. The ordinance provided that the number of policemen, their period of service and their rate of pay were to be determined by the Board of Mayor and Aldermen. The City Marshal was designated head of the police force and was required to submit a monthly written report to the board. The report was to contain the number of arrests and incidents of dereliction of duty by officers. Newly selected officers were required to take an oath of office. Lawbreakers were tried by the City Recorder for breach of city ordinances and by the Justice of Peace or City Recorder for breaking state laws.

The ordinance called on policemen to make arrests as gently and respectfully as circumstances permitted and to consider themselves "conservators of the public peace" intended to "prevent rather than redress offenses." The ordinance also specified that officers were "to be assiduous [tireless] in their vocations, exemplary in their conduct, sober in their habits, and to keep the laws, not permitting others to violate them with impunity.

Policemen were subject to discipline if they failed to perform their duty, failed to remain sober, treated prisoners harshly, or took money for not arrest someone. Disciplinary actions included being called before the Board of Mayor and Aldermen to be reprimanded by the mayor, being fined up to $50, or being dismissed from the force.

An event on April 13, 1878, left Clarksville a charred wasteland. In the period of a few hours the work of more than a decade of post-Civil War rebuilding was destroyed. The incident began when Patrolman Frank Phillips attempted to make an arrest. When the suspect resisted the policeman, a fight ensued. The law breaker was finally subdued. He died later that night in jail. The prisoner was popular and death threats were made against Policeman Phillips.

Sheriff James Mosley placed Phillips in a jail cell for his own protection. A mob gathered outside the jail and soon the fire alarm sounded. An arsonist had started a fire in a small building on Franklin Street. The blaze quickly spread to the center of town. The firehouse was destroyed along with other building in the path of the inferno. City officials wired Nashville, where fire fighters and equipment were loaded on a special train and sent to Clarksville. Nashville firemen arrived too late to save downtown Clarksville. The fire left 15 acres burned and 63 buildings destroyed.

Captain Madison Walter "Matthew" Carkuff served as head of Clarksville police in 1867 and perhaps earlier. The title Chief of Police was used to refer to Captain Carkuff, but was not his official title. Matt Carkuff served as chief again from 1875 to 1887.

Chief of Police Alexander C. Stafford took command of the Clarksville Police Department in 1888. Stafford was 37 years old and the city's first officially titled Chief of Police. Stafford began his career in law enforcement when he was elected constable in 1876 and later served as a deputy under Sheriff James M. Collier for 18 months.

Alexander Stafford was born in Lynchburg in 1851 and headed for Texas with a friend at the age of 20. The two reached St. Bethlehem outside Clarksville and his friend returned home. Stafford took work on a nearby farm. He married and moved with his wife to Clarksville in 1886 where he took a job as a city patrolman.

When Stafford became chief the department consisted of five officers with an average salary of $78 per month. The four patrolmen in the department were Granville Holleman, Joe Murphy, J. K. Smith and Pat Ginley. Former sheriff Charles Collier, William Rollow and J. E. Robinson joined the force in 1891 and Jack Stone was appointed in 1892. When Alexander Stafford failed to win reappointment in 1895 he remained on the force as a patrolman until 1900. Stafford was elected to three two-year terms as sheriff of Montgomery County and served as county trustee from 1906 to 1912.

Clarksville Chief of Police Alexander C. Stafford, seated in middle with cap, and the city's police force in 1891.

The forty-four year tenure of John Edward Robinson as Clarksville's chief of police began in 1895. The 32-year-old Robinson remained chief until he retired at the age of 77. He served as chief of police longer than any other individual in the history of the state of Tennessee. Robinson was a native of Bell Buckle and moved to Clarksville in 1886. He was 28 when he joined the police force in 1890. Chief Robinson primarily relied on his ability to communicate with people, rather than resorting to the use of force. He was proud of the fact that he was never shot and that he never shot anyone.

John P. Balthrop was appointed chief of police upon the retirement of Chief Robinson late in 1939. Balthrop had been hired in 1926 and walked a beat until he replaced retiring Lieutenant J. Q. Ellarson in 1935. Ellarson retired at age 65 after 31 years of service to the department. After retirement he was elected to the city council.

Chief Balthrop took command of a ten man force, Lieutenant George McCraw, Irvin W. Blackwell, Issac H. Buck, Adolphus D. Curtis, Robert I Hall, Louis B. Kirby, John Lee, William T. Milling, James A. Rinehart and Workhouse Keeper Carney Baggett. The rolling stock of the department consisted of two motorcycles and a 1938 Ford. In March 1940 the Ford was replaced with a black, 1940 model, four-door Chevrolet sedan.

The workhouse remained a police institution. People convicted of breaking city ordinances and were unable to pay the fine worked on the city street gang. Prisoners were paid $1 a day for the work and were housed in the workhouse while they worked off their fine.

The training of police officers was expanded beyond the on-the-job method by which an experienced partner serving as a training officer. Patrolman John Lee was one of three officers in Tennessee to

The Clarksville Police Department around 1910 standing at the entrance to the "Police Office" painted above the door. From left to right were Henry Cook, Alex Small, John Allsbrooks, Chief John Edward Robinson, Richard Perkins, H. Ellarson, and Walter Fowlkes.

complete the FBI School for local policemen in 1940. Lee trained other officers in the department when he return from the FBI school. Lee taught new scientific investigative skills he had learned and the city authorized the purchase of fingerprint equipment for $150. Patrolman Lee was a key witness in the first case in Montgomery County that depended largely on scientific ballistics evidence.

Chief Balthrop attended a 2-day FBI program on national defense in Memphis as the nation prepared for world war and possible invasion. Topics presented in the civil defense school included black-out enforcement, air raid precautions, looting prevention and general wartime law enforcement activity.

The attack at Pearl Harbor on December 7, 1941, plunged the United States into a second world war. The war effort had a special impact on Clarksville due to the creation of Camp Campbell. Construction of the camp and the flood of troops that followed brought growth to the city of 15,000 and a correspon-

ding need for additional police officers. Patrolmen H. T. Cook, Glen Morrow, Ervine Rinehart, Charlie Vaden and James Moore were added to the department to deal with the impact of the camp on the city. The police force was called on to deal with problems created by the spate of young soldiers including drunkenness, brawling, disorderly conduct, prostitution, burglary and robbery.

Prostitution became such a problem that the Camp Campbell command considered making the city of Clarksville off limits. Chief Balthrop publicly vowed to solve the problem with the assistance of the Health Department. The police made so many arrests that the City Jail was filled and prisoners overflowed to the County Jail.

The city jail was located in the basement of the police station. Those arrested were booked upstairs and walked the twenty or so steps down to the jail. The drunker the prisoner the more challenging the trip, for both the prisoner and the officer. There was one cell for women and several for men. Typical meals were donuts and coffee for breakfast, a bologna sandwich for lunch and a burger and fries from a nearby cafe for dinner.

Wartime brought turnover in department personnel in 1942 as the result of the need for experienced lawmen, the availability of well paying jobs and the desire of many young men to enter military service. Lieutenant George McGraw went to work at Camp Campbell and Jim Rinehart was promoted to lieutenant. Patrolman Issac Buck also took a job at Camp Campbell. Officer Charlie Vaden went to work in manufacturing. Patrolman James Moore enlisted in the army. Sergeant John Lee took a government job and was later assigned overseas.

The force was divided into two shifts of six officer each to patrol the city. Patrolmen walked the streets 12 hours a day, seven days a week and depended on blowing a whistle for emergency communication. To enhance the force, Patrolmen Lloyd Evans and W. T. Blackwell were hired and the city installed parking meters to limit the amount of time officers spent monitoring parking.

Policemen S. L. Wilson, Bayliss Seay, K. Leonard Nipple, R. I. Hall, Henry Cook and Howard Story joined the force in 1943. The department's budget in 1944 was $36,000, nearly double what it had been only a few years earlier before Camp Campbell was created. Fines collected in May 1944 amounted to $2,123, four times that of a similar month before the influx of servicemen into the city. The additional money was needed to maintain department personnel and equipment. The department traded for both a new motorcycle and a new patrol car. Workhouse Keeper Carney Baggett was allow an increase in meal allowance for prisoners from 25 to 35 cents.

A number of German prisoners of war were kept at Camp Campbell and from time to time escapes occurred. Clarksville Patrolmen H. T. Cook and Louis Kirby captured two prisoners who were trying to leave town by hiding on a railroad car near Fifth Street.

The Clarksville police force lost an officer in the line of duty about 5:30 a.m. on August 9, 1945. The incident followed a fire that quickly enveloped a two story brick building on Third Street that housed the Clarksville Laundry. The blaze threatened to spread to other downtown structures. The owner of the laundry told officials that he had recently installed new machinery and the fire obviously started in the boiler room. Patrolman K. Leonard "Cowboy" Nipple and two firemen were standing in the doorway of the laundry boiler room evaluating the scene when a wall collapsed. The three men were struck and Policeman Nipple was killed instantly. The 35-year-old officer

Lieutenant John Quency Ellarson retired from the department in 1935. This photograph was taken early in his career as a policeman.

was a native of Kansas and had been on the Clarksville force for three years.

Clarksville policemen began working 8-hour shifts in 1947. Officers had previously worked 12-hour shifts with one day off per week. Under the 8-hour shift plan, officers got no days off except for vacations. Three patrolmen, Leslie Suiter, Harlan Hogan and Maurice "Morris" Clark were added to the force at an annual salary of $5,000. In 1948 four more officers were hired, increasing the force to 16 men. The expansion allowed officers to have one day a week off. New uniforms were purchased for the force as well.

The FBI held its area police training school in September 1946 at the Clarksville city hall. Police officers from Paris, Erin, Dover, Springfield, Dickson, Waverly and Ashland City attended the event. Sessions were conducted on fingerprinting, treatment of prisoners, laws and mechanics of arrest, searches and

The Clarksville Police Department in 1930.

seizures, and investigative aids of the FBI. The entire Clarksville force attended the course of study.

New technologies were employed in the late forties to assist the police. A two-way radio system made by Bell Telephone Company was installed in 1947. WGTQ went into service on November 14 when Mayor Kleeman spoke into the microphone in a patrol car, "Mayor Kleeman calling Chief Balthrop, over." From police headquarters at city hall the chief responded, "Station WGTQ, time 10 o'clock a.m., go ahead Mayor."

The mayor completed the initial transmission, "Chief, this is a historic moment in the interest of Clarksville. The radio, I am certain, will do much toward reducing crime and increasing the efficiency of the police department. This radio adds much to the development and growth of Clarksville." Three days later, the police radio was credited with the speedy response that resulted in the arrest of at least three lawbreakers.

Traffic lights were installed and activated throughout downtown Clarksville in June 1948. Policemen were able

Patrolman K. Leonard "Cowboy" Nipple, left, was killed when a fire weakened wall collapsed on August 9, 1945. Chief of Police John Edward Robinson, right, led Clarksville's police force for 44 years, 1895 to 1939. He took over as chief at the age of 32 and retired at 77. He was the longest serving chief of police of any major police department in Tennessee.

Composite photograph of policemen serving in the Clarksville Police Department in 1944.

to manually control lights at primary intersections if required. A key provided access to a switchbox that allowed officers to hold traffic as long as necessary.

The police were faced with a number of violent crowd situations in the late 1940s. Strikes at two large manufacturing facilities, the Acme plant and the B. F. Goodrich plant, resulted in violence between strikers and non-strikers. The police were called in to keep the peace until the strike was settled.

City officers responded to shots fired in an East End cafe in 1948. A unruly crowd of nearly 100 surrounded the two patrolmen as they tried to arrest a Camp Campbell soldier. The policemen held off the mob with a sawed-off shotgun and a pistol until other city officers and several jeeps of military police arrived.

Clarksville patrolmen Ralph Turney and Louis Taylor made news throughout the southeast in November 1949. A fugitive who had recently been released from the federal prison in Atlanta, Georgia, stole a car in North Carolina and law enforcement officials in several states were on the lookout for him. He was on his way to Oklahoma when he passed through Clarksville and he was stopped. The felon tried to run down officers Turney and Taylor when they exited their patrol car, but they made the arrest.

New technology continued to aid law enforcement. An Alcometer was acquired in 1953 at a cost of $845. The instrument showed the precise blood alcohol level and the reading was used when drunk drivers were taken to court. The city paid for the unit by adding $2 to the fine of each convicted driver. Other agencies were allowed to use the device for a fee of $2 per case.

Sidearm policies and practices were altered in the mid-1950s. The city council began to provide ammunition that was previously purchased by officers. The mayor later recommended that the department use

Clarksville policemen attended a Red Cross class in 1953 taught by firemen of the city. Graduates were, from left to right, in the front row, S. Wilson, N. Townsend, J. Davis, V. McClain, and W. Jacobs; in the middle row, C. Douglas, M. Winters, B. Seay, and J. Smith; and in the back row, J. Rinehart, B. Swaffer, V. Emmett, R. Davidson, and L. Perigo. The first aid class was the first medical training given within the department, and graduates wore a small Red Cross patch on the left sleeve of the uniform jacket.

weapons of the same caliber. Officials at Fort Campbell also offered the use of the military target range to city police officer at no charge.

The department began to employ patrolwoman to provide school zone safety. The first female officer was hired in 1953 and four more were added in 1954. The patrolwomen earned $50 per month and were assigned to city recreation areas in the summer months. A sixth patrolwoman was hired in 1955 and the salary of the female officers was increased to $75 a month.

Other personnel improvements occurred in the fifties. Officer James O. Davis attended the FBI academy in 1954 and was promoted to sergeant soon after his return to duty. Charlie Vaden left his security job at the B. F. Goodrich plant and rejoined the Clarksville police force. James Rinehart was promoted to the reinstituted rank of lieutenant.

Salary increases in 1956 brought the pay level of patrolmen to $264 per month. The chief of police earned $400 a month, captain $330, lieutenant $308, sergeant $286, book keeper $240, workhouse keeper $165, chain gang boss $264 and patrolwoman $82.50.

Chief John P. Balthrop retired on February 1, 1957, after 18 years as chief. He received a pension of $200 a month. Other long-time officers who retired in the fifties were Lieutenant W. T. Milling, A. D. Curtis, Robert I. Hall, B. A. Seay and Leslie Suiter. Following

Chief Balthrop's tenure, a number of men served brief terms as head of the department.

James O. Davis was appointed chief of police later in 1957. Davis served in the air force during the war and was hired as a Clarksville beat officer in 1951, often working the midnight shift and often working alone. Louis Kirby was appointed to the newly created position of assistant chief of police. Charlie Vaden was promoted to sergeant and seven months later to the rank of lieutenant. The Clarksville Police Department also hired its first black officers, Patrolmen Henry Newell and Euless R. Pettus.

The department command consisted of Chief Davis, Assistant Chief Charlie Vaden, Captain James Rinehart and Lieutenant Joe Smith. Sergeants were Vester Emmett, Ed Groves, Calvin Louie, Lonnie Perigo, Gracey Farmer, George Blanton and Ervine T. Rinehart.

Patrolmen in 1957 were Kenneth Albright, Carney Baggett, Stanton Black, Russell Davidson, Sidney W. Davis, Andrew R. Earl, Luther Ellison, Jesse E. Evans, Wesley W. Herndon, Wesley A. Jacobs, Joe D. Kennedy, Robert W. Lucas, Henry Newell, Euless R. Pettus, Herschel Phillips, Sterling Pursell, Otis South, Benton T. Swaffer, Niles H. Townsend and Henry B. Wall. Patrolwomen were Annie S. Allen, Eura Fletcher, Buena Lee Mills, Evelyn S. Richardson, Dorothy E.

Smith and Lucille N. Smith. The workhouse keeper was Melvin Winters.

Department vehicles included five patrol cars, one unmarked unit and two motorcycles. During Chief Davis's tenure the Franklin Street firing range was established and summer uniforms were changed to short-sleeved shirts without neckties.

Louis Bertram Kirby was named chief of police in 1959. Kirby did military service in the cavalry during the first world war and learned to shoe horses. He worked as a blacksmith until he was 43 and joined the Clarksville police on July 7, 1939. He walked a beat for several years before making sergeant. He was appointed captain in 1953.

The two senior patrolwomen, Evelyn S. Richardson and Dorothy E. Smith, were selected in 1960 to serve as meter maids. They were paid $225 a month.

Sam A. Salerno took command as chief in July 1961 when Louis Kirby retired. Salerno was a career military man and was named chief because of his management expertise. He attended the Southern Police Institute at the University of Louisville and was the first chief to submit a formal budget to the city. Chief Salerno never carried a sidearm. Salerno resigned after serving for less than a year to join the Red Cross.

Charles Vaden became chief in March 1962. The department consisted of 43 employees, including jailers. Two additional black officers, Bennie Woodson and Robert Riggins, were hired in 1962. Patrolman Andrew Earl completed the 12-week course at the FBI academy in 1963 and became the sole graduate of the

James O. Davis served as Clarksville chief of police from 1957 to 1959.

school still with the department.

Financial difficulty in the sixties lead to a reduction in the police department budget and five officers were eliminated. The services of policewomen during the summer months were eliminated as well.

The Detective Division was created by city ordinance in 1965. The salary for detectives was set at $345 a month and detective sergeants were paid $372 per month. In 1966 the position of Crime Prevention Officer was established. Officer Charles Binkley was appointed to the position and served under the command of Assistant Chief Gracey Farmer

The annexation of New Providence in 1967 resulted in the hiring of six patrolmen. Command of the three shifts in the northern area of the city, including traffic control, was assigned to Captain Theodore "Ted" Seay. The three shifts in the remainder of the city of Clarksville were under the command of Ervine T. Rinehart.

Equipment additions in the late sixties included installation of the first dome emergency lights on cars in 1967, the acquisition of a radar unit, the acquisition of the first paddy wagon in 1968 and the purchase of two portable radios in 1969. Training was enhanced in 1969 when two federal grants enabled the department to send 11 officers to the recently established Tennessee Law Enforcement Training Academy at Donelson.

Traffic officers J. Evans, left, and R. Herndon with the department motorcycles in 1957.

The City Council Police Committee called for the creation of a manual for the department in 1970. *The Clarksville Police Department Rules and Regulations,* commonly referred to as the "red book," was created to provide guidelines for operation of the police force. The Juvenile Division was created the same year by city ordinance. Charlie Brinkley was assigned as director and Sammy Thomas as the juvenile officer.

The Clarksville-Montgomery County Vice Squad began operation in 1971 and focused on the growing drug problem. The squad was commanded by Chief Deputy Paul Neblett of the Sheriff's Patrol. Clarksville police Sergeant Jesse Dyce was second in command. After the unit had been in operation for only four months, one third of the cases before the Montgomery County Grand Jury were for drug violations and half of those were for hard drugs. Neblett resigned in 1972 to work for the TBI and Lieutenant Bill South became director of the unit.

Chief Vaden retired in 1972 after ten years as Clarksville's chief law enforcement officer. During his tenure as chief the city's police force grew from 25 to 70 sworn officers. The department was organized into five divisions, Patrol, Traffic, Detective, Administrative and Records, and Juvenile. The agency's jurisdiction had expanded to 21 square miles and patrol equipment consisted of 15 squad cars, one radar equipped and three motorcycles.

Lieutenant Ira C. Nunley, a seven year veteran of the department, was promoted to chief of police. Nunley served in the Army's 1st Airborne Division during the war and remained in the military until 1964. Ted Seay was named assistant chief and Gracey Farmer became chief of detectives. A number of other long-term officers retired in the seventies including Ervine T. Rinehart with 32 years of service, Ben Swaffer with 25 years, Willie James with 23 years and Jesse S. Evans and George Blanton with 22 years each.

Officer Kenneth L. Browning was shot and killed in the line of duty on February 13, 1974. He was the first officer in the Clarksville department lost to gunfire. At 9:20 that morning FBI Special Agent Frank Christina walked into the police station and told Officer Joe Mixon, the dispatcher, that a man was walking south on Second Street with a shotgun. Officer Browning was in the office at the time. Browning and Mixon took a patrol car and found the man with the shotgun on Second near the post office.

Browning turned on the car's emergency lights and stopped about ten feet from the armed man. He stepped from the car without drawing his weapon and told the man to freeze. The man pointed the shotgun at Browning and told him to get back in the squad car. The officer barely made it into the car when four shots from the shotgun were fired into the car. Mixon was struck in the right hand and shoulder and Browning was shot in the abdomen and gravely wounded. Browning was unable to drive the car. He opened the door of the patrol unit and fell to the pavement. Mixon was able to radio for help.

The gunman began to fire both the shotgun and a handgun, wounding several people. He reloaded his weapons just before officers Wade Harris, Billy Poor and Larry Thrower arrived on the scene. A gun battle ensued. Officer Harris was shot in the leg during the exchange. When the gunfire ended, the gunman was dead.

Officer Ken Browning died 28 hours later, on Valentines Day. He was 38 years old, a four year veteran of the Dickson Police Department and had been on the Clarksville force for only four months.

The mid-seventies was marked by growth and improvements in the city, which affected the police force. The department moved into new headquarters in 1976 following construction of the Clarksville-Montgomery County Criminal Justice Complex. The annexation of the area referred to as the North Annex

Chief Ira Nunley, left, and Lieutenant Bob Davis inspect new radar signs posted in the 1970s.

meant two additional officer on each shift were required to patrol the area. The department was also assigned security duty at Outlaw Field during twice a day flight arrivals.

The safety of police officers was improved when the department purchased 12 bullet-proof vests in 1976. Some officers also benefited in 1974 by the decision to give higher pay to individuals who earned college credits.

Several specialized units were formed. When the grant funding the city-county vice squad was exhausted in 1977, a Vice Squad was formed within the Clarksville Police Department and the important work of the unit continued. The Crime Prevention Bureau was established in 1979.

The creation of the Canine Unit in 1977 paired Officer Ralph Prost with Police Service Dog (PSD) King. King was killed while the two were pursuing a group of burglars on the night of May 22, 1978. PSD King took a bullet intended for Officer Prost and saved Prost's life. King, a four and half year old German Shepherd, had assisted in 1,366 backup calls and 42 apprehensions.

Two years later, February 1980, Officer Ralph Prost and his new canine partner Yankee were recognized by Mayor Ted Crozier for their extraordinary work. The mayor noted that Prost and Yankee were on call 24 hours a day and never applied for overtime. PSD Yankee died of hemorrhagic pancreatitis later that year.

Sergeant Doug Pectol and Detective Emmett Lilly were given the Mayor's Certificate for outstanding detective service. They identified and apprehended the perpetrators of a shocking double murder committed in the process of a house invasion. The department also solved the disappearance of a high school student and later a college student, both of whom were kidnapped and killed. Evidence collected led to the conviction of those who committed the murders. Other Mayor's Certificates were presented to Sergeant Pectol for organizing and executing a major sting operation and to officers Doug Glenn, Henry Lyle and John Young for rescuing a 2-year-old from a burning trailer.

The department formed its first tactical team in 1979. The unit was called the Clarksville Anti-Sniper Squad (CASS). The part-time 10 or 12 man squad did a lot of training before it was deployed. Five members of the squad, Lieutenant Bob Davis, Geno Grubbs, Richard Zimmer, Larry Thrower and Ernie Rice, went to Quantico, Virginia, for a week's training at the FBI Academy. The unit was short lived.

Soon after the unit was established, it was called out to a burglary in progress at Grand Pa's, a large merchan-dise complex with fishing and hunting equipment among other goods. Officers made an assessment and deployed into the large facility, moving down the aisles on their stomachs. Thieves had entered through the roof and filled shopping carts with rifles and other goods. One of the burglars broke an ankle on entry. When the second felon saw the police, he dressed in camouflage clothing available in the store and stood motionless like a mannequin as the CASS officers moved down the aisle. Officer Geno Grubbs looked up and saw an eye blink on the mannequin. Both burglars were arrested.

Chief of Police Ira Nunley retired in 1983 and a three-man screening committee began the selection process for a new chief. George Siegrist was chosen to head the department.

The forty-two-year-old Siegrist was well prepared to command the department. He enlisted in the army in 1953 and was commissioned as an infantry officer in 1964. He transferred to the military police in 1965 and retired from the army as Deputy Provost Marshall at Fort Campbell in 1978. Siegrist earned a bachelor's degree in law enforcement in 1967, a master's degree in criminology and corrections and was a graduate of the FBI academy.

Chief Siegrist made a number of personnel changes. Ted Seay continued as deputy chief. Paul Neblett came on the force as chief of detectives and David Blaize was hired as lieutenant. W. J. Souza was hired as the official police photographer. Reverend Bill Corley became the department's first full-time chaplain, on an unpaid status.

Chief Siegrist implemented a number of new units including the Intelligence Section, the Internal Affairs Section and the Street Crimes Augmentation Team (SCAT). Johnny Rosson was given command of the Intelligence Section.

The new chief also made changes to the evidence collection and storage process, and instituted a physical fitness program. He decentralized the department, establishing a North Precinct at the Outlaw Field terminal and a South Precinct at the Highway Patrol station on Madison Street. The Detective Division and the Vice-Narcotics Section relocated to Main Street across from the main fire station.

The department acquired a computer information system for maintaining police related records that also provided electronic communications with the county. The city began to provide sidearms to officers along with uniforms, allowing the department to standardize service weapons.

Maria Sayle became the first female uniformed officer of the Clarksville Police Department on

Shift photograph taken in front of city hall in 1976. In the front row, from left to right, were G. Elliott, E. Rice, Lieutenant J. Dyce, Captain C. Slayden, Sergeant W. Harris, and M. Mitchell; in the middle row were M. Taylor, B. Wilson, L. Cole, C. Linton, and P. Haynes; and in the back row were S. Poston, J. Harrison, J. Rosson, E. Crockarell, and E. Lilly.

October 1, 1983. The twenty-three-year-old graduated from the Donelson academy. Other women had worked as plainclothes officers in the juvenile and vice squads, but not as an accredited patrol officer. A few year later, on October 5, 1987, Cheryl Smith Anderson joined the department as the first black female patrol officer.

The department made the largest seizure of cocaine in the most valuable drug raid in its history in October 1983. Seventy-eight grams of cocaine with a street value of $50,000 were found hidden in a van.

Motorcycle Officer Aaron Douglas Glenn was killed in the line of duty on November 5, 1983. Officer Glenn was responding to a domestic disturbance call at 1:45 p.m. when a station wagon pulled into traffic from the entrance of Magic Wheels, driving directly in front of him. The officer was driving at a normal rate of speed, but was unable to avoid a collision. When his motorcycle hit the vehicle, Glenn was thrown 39 feet.

The 32-year-old policeman received serious neurological injuries. He lived for two weeks, dying on November 19, 1983, at 10:22 a.m. Officer Doug Glenn was given a police funeral including a 21-gun salute.

The creation of the Reserve Division in 1984 provided the force a significant group of trained men to supplement regular officers. The first class of reserves graduated in March. The Reserve Division continued

as a viable force until 1994 and contributed over 100,000 volunteer hours of service during its existence.

Paul E. Neblett became chief of the Clarksville department on March 19, 1985, when Chief Siegrist resigned after less than two years to become head of a larger agency in another state. Neblett began his law enforcement career as a deputy sheriff of Montgomery County in 1966 and was named chief of patrol in 1968. He was director of the Clarksville-Montgomery County Vice Squad after its creation in 1971. He became a member of the TBI narcotics strike force in January 1972, but resigned later that year to fill out the term of Sheriff Joel Plummer who was named Commission of the Tennessee Department of Safety. Neblett joined the Clarksville department in 1983 as chief of detectives. Chief Neblett brought the department back together in a single facility, The Old Booster Building.

Clarksville Police Officer Robert Hunt almost lost his life in the 1985 apprehension of three bank robbers. Early on the morning of June 28 three men wearing Halloween masks walked into the Commerce Union Bank in St. Bethlehem on the outskirts of Clarksville. A sheriff's deputy arrived within a minute after the call went out, but the robbers had fled.

A call was received that afternoon of suspicious subjects on a tractor in a field near exit 8 of Interstate 24. Numerous law officers from various agencies including the FBI and Clarksville Police Department responded. A helicopter was provided for the search by Metropolitan Nashville police.

Clarksville Police Canine Officer Robert Hunt and his canine partner Bear moved into a cornfield searching for the bandits who had ditched their getaway car. Officer Hunt and Bear found one of the robbers sitting in the middle of the cornfield. The felon dropped his gun and raised his hands. As Hunt reached his hand to secure the weapon, he felt something hard pressing into the small of his back. Hunt turned to see a second robber pointing a gun at him. The officer had his gun drawn and pulled the trigger. His service pistol did not fire.

Hunt knocked the bandit's rifle away and ran into the tall corn. He heard two shots and dove to the ground. The shots were fired by Deputy Sheriff Jimmy Worthington, Hunt's backup, and the robber fell to the ground wounded. Although the felon was wearing a bulletproof vest, Worthington's bullet found an exposed spot in the gunman's upper body. The two bank robbers were taken into custody and the third surrendered himself two days later.

St. Bethlehem was annexed the next year and nine officers were added to the Clarksville department to provide the police services to the area. Soon after annexation, the tactical team was called to the area after a subject barricaded himself in a business and took hostages. The team's negotiator brought the incident to a peaceful conclusion. In another confrontation in the newly annexed area in January 1987, the Drug Task Force had to use deadly force when a violent drug dealer fled a St. Bethlehem motel. Clarksville had joined the multi-jurisdictional, 19th Judicial District Drug Task Force, in June 1986.

Captain Charles W. Slayden was named interim chief of police when Paul Neblett retired in 1987. Slayden was a 21-year veteran of the force, who had quickly moved through the ranks. Lieutenant Johnny Rosson was promoted to deputy chief. A new department policy manual was issued and the traffic control was transferred to the department. Other important events during Chief Slayden's tenure included the first Tennessee Law Enforcement Training Academy session held in Clarksville in 1988, the return of the department to the Criminal Justice Complex in April 1989, the reopening of the North and South precincts and the introduction of the Drug Abuse Resistance Education (DARE) program.

Officer Tim Chandler was recognized with a Mayor's Certificate after the quick apprehension of the robber of the Sovran Bank on New Providence

Officer Kenneth L. Browning, left, was shot and killed on February 13, 1974, by a man walking the streets with a shotgun. Motorcycle Officer Aaron Douglas Glenn, right, was killed on November 5, 1983 as he responded to a domestic disturbance call and a station wagon pulled directly into his path.

Boulevard on August 30, 1988. Officer Chandler arrested the armed bandit seven minutes after getting the call.

Chief of Police Johnny Rosson took over as head of the Clarksville force on July 1, 1989. Rosson began his career under Captain Slayden fourteen years earlier. His initial training consisted of reading the "Red Book." Johnny Rosson's first case after he became a detective in 1977 was grand larceny of a dog. After he successfully solved the case, he got a call every time someone lost a dog. In 1984 Rosson was promoted to Lieutenant and became a Precinct Commander. He headed the 19th Judicial Task Force in 1986 and 1987.

Chief Rosson's most satisfying moment as a policeman was being on the scene when a young bicycle rider veered into the path of a truck on Madison Street. The boy had no vital signs when Rosson reached him. The officer began CPR. The boy was breathing by the time emergency medical personnel arrived. Rosson drove the ambulance to the hospital so medical technicians could continue life support. The boy survived.

The department made application for national law enforcement accreditation soon after Chief Rosson took command. The team assigned to lead the process was Captain Bobby Cushman, John Nichols and Steve Poston.

A number of new units were organized in the early nineties. The Special Operations Unit was formed in 1991 and affiliated with the 19th Judicial Drug Task Force. On August 23, the new unit arrested the "Ohio Boys" at a local motel with a quarter kilo of crack cocaine and two semi-automatic pistols. The group was prosecuted in Federal Court and the leader sen-

The Clarksville Anti-Sniper Squad (CASS) in 1979 team photograph holding M-16 rifles. Kneeling from left to right were C. Denton, Ernie Rice, and Larry Thrower; and standing were Bob Davis, J. Mann, Geno Grubbs, and L. Vaden.

tenced to 47 and a half years. The Special Operations Unit also arrested two drug dealers in February 1993 with crack cocaine, marijuana and $10,500 in cash. And, in cooperation with other agencies, the unit raided a Southside mobile home, confiscating 65 gallons of sour mash, a still, three weapons and almost $50,000 in counterfeit.

The Repeat Offenders Program (ROP) was started on November 1, 1992, under the direction of the Detective Division. The unit used computer technology to track known criminals. A new computer system was installed designed to manage law enforcement information. Over the next couple of years the department introduced an Alcohol Awareness Program to educate businesses about laws related to alcohol and the Combat Auto Theft (CAT) program that allowed citizen to identify their cars as part of the prevention plan.

A number of dramatic crimes were committed Clarksville in the mid-nineties. The first car-jacking in the city's history took place in January 1993. One of the most horrendous crimes in the history of Clarksville was committed on January 30, 1994. The employees of the night shift of Taco Bell on Riverside Drive were murdered execution style. Captain Doug Pectol worked with TBI Special Agent in Charge Jim Taylor to solve the crime. The killings were done by a Fort Campbell soldier who worked part time at the restaurant.

In the spring of 1994 the department initiated a program designed to help citizens better understand their police force. The Citizens Police Academy was developed by Lieutenant Mark Smith and Sergeant Gene Grubbs based on the model of the Orlando, Florida, program. Citizens were exposed to all elements of law enforcement in three hour sessions over thirteen weeks.

Operation No Refund combined the resources of several units of the department along with members of other agencies to conduct a reverse drug sting in the summer of 1994. Lieutenant Bill Carney led the operation that resulted in the arrest of 28 on drug charges.

The culmination of the departments work toward accreditation came in November 1994. The Clarksville Police Department was fully accredited by the Commission of Accreditation for Law Enforcement Agencies (CALEA) at its meeting in San Francisco. The process required the department to be in compliance with requirements of the commission in every aspect of police work.

Lieutenant Mark Smith was named deputy chief of the force in July 1995. At the time Smith was head of the department's Training Division, responsible for the computer system and a member of the Vice Squad.

The department lost two officers in the mid-nineties. Lieutenant Michael C. Barrett died of a heart attack on February 17, 1995. Barrett was one of the best liked and respected members of the department. Officer Tyler Barrett followed in his father's footsteps as a member of the Clarksville force. Just over a year later, April 24, 1996, Officer William O. Rucker died of a heart attack in his patrol car. Rucker was assigned to the North Precinct and was dedicated to the meeting the needs of children.

Community-Oriented Police Services became a focus of the department in October 1995 as the result of a federal grant to put more officers on the street. Four new officers were hired as part of the program.

In January 1996 the Street Crimes Unit was created. The unit consisted of Sergeant Ken Crews and Officers Vince Lewis, Eddie Chancellor and Robert Miller. Five more officers were added to the unit in May. The unit was quickly able to identify over 14 gangs in the city. Members of the unit testified before the state legislature in 1997, assisting the passage of Anti-Gang Laws. Officer Vince Lewis appeared on "The Leeza Show" on network television discussing gang activities.

The department was involved in a number of high profile cases with wide media attention. In one such case Clarksville officers assisted the FBI in apprehending a dangerous felon on February 5, 1996. The subject was an armed bandit who robbed seven banks in different states and said he would never be taken alive. An hour after he was featured on the television show "Unsolved Mysteries," the FBI got a tip that he was holed up in a Clarksville motel. FBI agents and Clarksville police surrounded the room and tricked the felon into coming to the door. He was taken without incident.

Sergeant Geno Grubbs, who had served 13 years as a training officer, was assigned duty as public information officer in 1997. He served in the position for eight years before his retirement at the rank of lieutenant in 2005.

One of Sergeant Grubbs first assignments as information officer was a double homicide. Two Baskin-Robbins employees were kidnapped from the business on April 23, 1997, as they prepared to close. Their bodies were found the next morning at Dunbar State Park. An arrest was made following an investigation that involved almost the entire force plus members of other agencies.

V. Lavoyed Hudgins accepted the position of chief of police in Clarksville on June 1, 1998. He served most of his law enforcement career in Alabama. Chief Hudgins initiated ComStat to use crime statistics to determine where best to focus enforcement resources.

Clarksville police headquarters was destroyed by a tornado in January 1999. The department was homeless and had to operate out of the south precinct. Officers worked long hours dealing with both the emergency situation in the area affected by the storm and providing routine service to unaffected areas.

Chief of Police Mark B. Smith took the helm of the Clarksville Police Department on March 1, 2002. Smith joined the Clarksville force in 1976 after completing a degree at Austin Peay State University in business administration. Two years later he took the position of chief deputy of the Stewart Count Sheriff's

Patrol officers David Scott, left, and Yamil Baez-Santiago were killed on June 7, 2002, in high-speed pursuit of a robbery suspect. Baez-Santiago was a recruit and Scott his field-training officer.

Department. He returned to the Clarksville PD on March 1, 1982 and was regularly promoted, becoming deputy chief in 1995.

Three months after becoming chief, Mark Smith led the department through the tragedy of losing two officers in the line of duty in a single incident. Patrol officers David Scott and Yamil Baez-Santiago were killed on June 7, 2002, while in high-speed pursuit of a robbery suspect. Baez-Santiago was a recruit and Smith his field-training officer. Their patrol car burst into flames after a severe collision at mile marker 11 of the 101st Parkway.

Today the dedicated officers of the Clarksville Police Department provide protection to the citizens of the city and their property. The force of over 200 sworn officer is divided into two major divisions, Administrative Services and Uniform/Investigators. The well-trained professionals in the department can well address virtually any law enforcement situation that might arise.

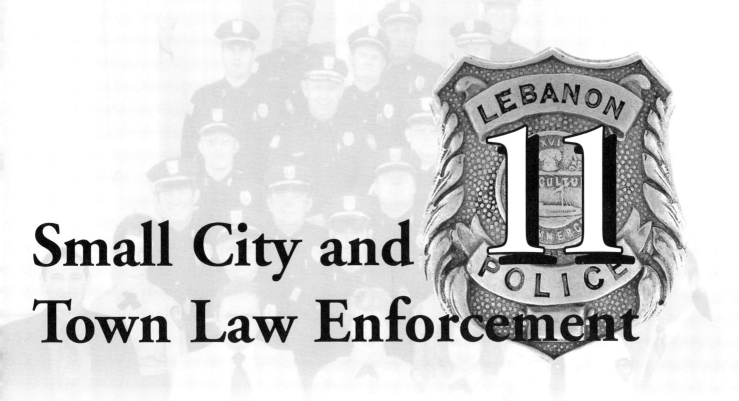

Small City and Town Law Enforcement

Smaller municipalities in Tennessee experienced the same general law enforcement history as larger cities. Typically a town constable served during the day managing legal processes for the town government, enforcing the law and often performing other duties such as tax collector and sexton. A night watch or patrol assured peace and order in the evenings and reported to the mayor.

By the middle of the nineteenth century the first night police replaced the night watch and the chief law enforcement officers took on the title of town marshal, although the use of the title town constable continued into the twentieth century in some locations.

When the nineteenth century ended the police department was organized along lines that continued through the twentieth century. The chief of police managed the force of officers that patrolled the town around the clock.

The City of Columbia was chartered on November 16, 1807, and the county court appointed the first "Patrollers" for the town in December 1808. The first patrollers were J. W. Craig, Perry Cohea and Samuel McClosky. The town charter was amended in 1850 and Columbia selected its first city marshal, John M. Cook.

The Columbia Police Department was officially established by the Board of Mayor and Alderman on June 13, 1883. The department consisted of Town Marshal R. H. Guest and two policemen. John Latta was appointed town marshal or chief of police in 1899 and was also appointed the first fire chief in 1901. A single individual heading both police and fire departments was not uncommon in smaller jurisdictions.

The Columbia force included six policemen in 1901. Two patrolmen were paid by the railroad since Depot Street was the roughest part of town. The first department policy, enacted in 1902, prohibited policemen consuming alcoholic beverages on duty.

Columbia had to call for assistance when racial conflict led to gunfire and the threat of rioting in February 1946. Sheriff J. J. Underwood arrested the leaders of the crowd of about thirty white men. Columbia Chief of Police J. W. Griffin with Patrolman Will Wilsford and two other uniformed officers walked into Mink Slide where around 200 armed black men gathered. The lawmen were met with shotgun fire when they passed through the lighted intersection a little after 8:00 p.m. All were hit, one seriously. They retreated without unholstering their weapons.

The Tennessee Highway Patrolmen and the Tennessee State Guard sent men to restore order to Columbia. All cities needed help for time to time to resolved widespread disturbances, but for smaller municipalities such situations were magnified.

One other issue fundamental to police departments of any size was that all police officers placed themselves in harm's way to protect their fellow citizens. Columbia Patrolman William Larry Whitwell stopped a vehicle for speeding on Sunday, April 5, 1981. Patrolman Whitwell did not know the two occupants had just robbed a local fast food restaurant. As he talked with the two the robbery call came over his radio and the officer saw a moneybag in the vehicle. In the struggle that ensued Patrolman Whitwell was shot and killed with his own weapon.

The loss of an officer is a tragedy in any department and in a small agency it could be devastating in many ways. In a single incident on the night of February 16, 1926, the Pulaski Police Department lost its entire night police force.

Pulaski Police Officer G. A. "Bud" Jackson and Officer George W. Dotson were on foot patrol near the town square when five assailants fired on them with sawed-off shotguns and other weapons. Both officers died at the mouth of an alley near South First and Flower streets not far from police headquarters.

Officer Dodson was shot six times, five in the back and one in the hand, and never had a chance to draw his sidearm. Officer Jackson emptied his weapon in the gun battle before he fell. Jackson had been a member of the Pulaski force only a month, but had been in law enforcement for seven years. Dotson had been a Pulaski officer for three years.

Davidson County Deputy Sheriff Pugh was called in with his bloodhound to track down the suspects from blood found in the alley. One of the suspects was tracked to his bed and arrested by Giles County Sheriff Nelson, Deputy Sheriff Ira Young and Pulaski Chief of

Harriman Chief of Police Wash Green in the late nineteenth century.

Police Aynett. The man confessed and named the other killers. Sheriff Nelson had to secretly transfer the prisoner to Nashville to keep him from being lynched.

The Pulaski department lost another officer on March 20, 1991. Patrolman James Myron Suggs and several other officers answered a domestic disturbance call. Thirty-eight-year-old Patrolman Suggs died of a heart attack as he struggled with a man he tried to arrest at the scene.

McMinnville City Marshal Enoch Cooksey entered a house of ill-fame in the town's Red Light dis-

Pulaski Patrolmen G. A. "Bud" Jackson, left, and George W. Dotson, right, were shot and killed by five felons on Tuesday night, February 16, 1926. They composed the entire night police force of the city.

trict about 10:30 on the night of November 15, 1873, to quell a disturbance. Marshal Cooksey was shot in the chest and killed. His body was found in an upstairs room of the brothel.

A shootout took place on Johnson City's Main Street about 11:00 p.m. on May 23, 1904, when a city policeman and a revenue officer tried to arrest two moonshiners. One of the culprits drew his pistol and Policeman John S. Webb grabbed his arm. The moonshiner fired four times and two bullets hit Webb in the stomach.

Shootouts between lawmen and criminals were frequent in the twenties. Night Policeman Cheatham Bates and a young farmer shot it out on Main Street in Dickson on January 23, 1927, when the drunken man pulled a gun on the policeman. On July 4, 1927, Gordensville City Marshal Bob Harrington shot two men who were drinking and provoked the encounter with the lawman.

Johnson City Lieutenant Thomas S. Church and Patrolman Manuel Dillow were wounded and a former chain gang guard killed on October 3, 1926. Over 30 rounds were fired in an incident as officers moved to arrest the ex-guard on a liquor charge. Tom Church was serving Johnson City as assistant chief of police on January 8, 1928, when he and Patrolman Linvelle went to arrest an ex-convict for drunkenness. The felon pulled a gun and shot Assistant Chief Church in the stomach. The mortally wounded assistant chief was able to return fire and kill the gunman before he slumped to the floor and died.

Two chief of police were wounded in a shootout with a gunman at a Jellico barbershop on May 12, 1926. The two lawmen went to arrest the man for firing a shot at his house in a domestic dispute. In the

The Cleveland, Tennessee, Police Department in 1939.

gun battle Chief of Police J. F. Gaylor of Jellico, Tennessee, and Chief of Police George Schmidty or Jellico, Kentucky, were both wounded and the gunman killed.

Jefferson City Chief of Police Tobias B. Younce was shot in the abdomen and killed on September 5, 1930, while investigating a disturbance near the railroad tracks. He was able to identify his killers before succumbed to his injuries.

Domestic violence calls were always dangerous and officers in many jurisdictions lost their lives in the line of duty while responding to family disputes. Johnson City Chief of Police George F. Campbell and another officer went to a home on September 16, 1914 about 9:00 a.m. When Chief Campbell tried to arrest the wife-beater, he shot the chief in the forehead, killing him instantly.

Tullahoma Policemen Charles Holt and E. C. Armstrong were both shot in the December 3, 1934, incident in which Tennessee Highway Patrolman Lindsley Smith was killed. A drunken abuser shot and killed Patrolman Holt instantly, Patrolman Armstrong died on December 10. Kingsport Patrolman Ira H. Burgess was killed by a shotgun blast on June 13, 1950, by a man who threatened to kill his wife. The gunman was shot and killed by a city workhouse guard.

On July 20, 1941, a mentally unbalanced man walked up to Sevierville Chief of Police L. Newton Bogart and opened fire with a .32 caliber pistol. Chief Bogart died almost instantly, struck once in the head, three times in the chest and a fifth bullet grazed his shoulder. The killer muttered, "I stood it as long as I could," but gave no reason why he killed the chief.

Sevierville Chief of Police L. Newton Bogart, left, was killed on July 20, 1941. Maryville Marshal J. H. Clemens, right, was killed when he tried to make an arrest on August 25, 1911.

Maryville Police Officer Barton Coker, left, and his partner approached two suspicious men exiting a lumber yard on January 2, 1938; one pulled a handgun and killed Officer Coker. Bristol Patrolman Clarence Luther Maines, right, was shot while walking an arrested drunk to jail on October 25, 1926.

Greeneville Police Sergeant John Lowery Freshour, left, was responding to an emergency on December 14, 1964, when his patrol car and a fire truck collided, killing Freshour. A losing candidate sheriff shot and killed Lexington Patrolman Arthur Gurley, right, with a .45 automatic pistol on the morning of August 6, 1954.

Twelve year veteran Bolivar Patrolman Hugh Everette Eubanks responded to a domestic disturbance call on March 17, 1975. When he arrived the two males at the scene told him there was no problem. He returned to his cruiser and was on the radio when one of the suspects shot him in the chest three times with a 30-06 rifle.

Sergeant Charles Lanny Bridges, a 25 year veteran of the Covington Police Department, was killed on August 14, 1997, when he responded to a possible suicide. Bristol Police Officer Mark Edward Vance was shot in the head and killed when he entered a residence on November 27, 2004, in answer to a domestic disturbance call.

Goodlettsville Police Detective Lynn Wayne Hicks was shot in the head from ambush and killed on May 22, 1999. The detective was near the location of a domestic disturbance and responded to the call. Hicks reached the scene and approached the residence. A second suspect, who had murdered his estranged girl-friend an hour earlier, was waiting for the man inside the residence to kill his wife and return to the car. When the killer sitting in the car saw Hicks' badge and sidearm, he shot the detective.

Police officers never knew what awaited them when they approached a vagrant, drunk, or suspicious person. Night Policeman Jack Bryant of Milan was killed on May 26, 1900, by two vagrants he approached on the street. Greenfield City Marshal Carl Right Grooms exchanged shots with a drunk he attempted to arrest on July 19, 1908. Both were killed. Maryville Town Marshal J. Henry Clemens was shot through the heart and killed when he tried to make an arrest for assault on August 25, 1911.

Hobos and other vagrants at railroad depots were frequently desperate and ready for a fight. Night Marshal Walter Gray Morgan of Martin investigated a suspicious person hiding in the shadows near the railroad depot on July 26, 1913. The 32-year-old lawman was shot and died two days later. City Marshal C. E. Hankins, of Paris, spotted a hobo riding a northbound L&N passenger train about 1:00 a.m. on April 4, 1914. When ordered from the train the rail tramp began to fire on the marshal. One bullet struck the lawman in the hip. He returned fire but the shooter escaped. Marshal Hankins survived his wound.

Drunken troublemakers were dangerous even if they were in church or under arrest. Kingsport Patrolman J. M. Carmack was called to deal with a drunken man creating a disturbance at a prayer meet-

Harriman Police Department officers Cliff Leffew, left, and Chris Hunley on night patrol in the 1940s.

456

Humboldt Police Officer Kenny Smith patrolled the downtown area in 1971.

ing on June 24, 1919. The drunk shot Patrolman Carmack twice and he died the next morning. Bristol Patrolman Clarence Luther Maines was shot while walking an arrested drunk to jail on October 25, 1926.

North Chattanooga Marshals James A. Houser and Bob Graham responded to the report of an intoxicated man brandishing a shotgun on Tuesday, June 11, 1929. As the two marshals approached the man's home the drunk ran from the house and shot Marshal Houser with a shotgun. Marshal House, age 63, died at the scene with 80 shot from a 16 gauge shotgun in his chest and stomach.

Social or labor unrest placed police officer in highly volatile situations. Alcoa Policeman Will M. Hunt was shot and killed on July 7, 1937, as officers became embroiled in a gun battle with striking workers at a sheet mill plant. The riot broke out when the plant reopened for non-striking workers and strikers kept them from entering. Eleven other officers were wounded and one striker was killed. Policeman Hunt was one of the officers hired when the strike began and was with the Alcoa Police Department only seven weeks.

The lawlessness of the era from the depression until World War II frequently placed law enforcement officers in harms way. Tullahoma Policeman James Flippo was shot and killed with his own weapon on January 1, 1935, by a prisoner he was lodging. Shelbyville Chief of Police Sumner A. Dillard Monday and another officer arrested two men on March 2, 1936. As they drove away a third man shot the chief in the back of the head with a .30 caliber rifle.

McMinnville Night Policeman Herman H. Kirby, 45, was killed on the evening of September 15, 1935, when he tried to arrest a man for disorderly conduct. The ruffian, on furlough from a CCC camp, grabbed

the officer's nightstick and beat him over the head with the club, fracturing the lawman's skull multiple times.

Maryville Police Officer Barton Coker and his partner approached two suspicious men exiting a lumber yard on McGee Street on January 2, 1938. One of the suspects pulled a handgun and killed Officer Coker. Two gunmen shot and killed Jamestown Town Marshal Oder Fowler and wounded Fentress County Deputy Sheriff M. A. Robbins on March 14, 1938, as the lawmen attempted to make an arrest. Town Marshal Fowler, 36, was killed instantly by a shot to the chest.

Gunfire claimed the lives of many law enforcement officers in the second half of the twentieth century. Lenoir City Patrolman James S. Hildreth was shot between the eyes in a hail of gunfire from occupants of a get-a-way car following an attempted theft. Patrolman Hildreth died the day following incident with the teenage felons, January 27, 1952. Other officer shot and killed as they attempted an arrest were Alcoa Patrolman Fred Guffey on August 31, 1952; Oliver Springs Patrolman Joseph E. Messer on July 29, 1967; Gatlinburg Patrolman Jerry Dean Huskey on June 14, 1975; Sweetwater Patrolman James Loyd Stapp on January 16, 1977; and Hohenwald Police Officer Alan Matthew Ragsdale on November 27, 2000. Patrolmen Guffey and Messer were killed with their own weapons.

Dyersburg Police Investigator Frank Thomas Maynard was in plainclothes in an unmarked patrol car on July 25, 1975, when he witnessed the fire-bombing of the federal building in downtown

Two Hendersonville Police Department sergeants killed in motorcycle incidents. Sergeant Richard L. Bandy, left, was killed by a motorcycle being driven recklessly on January 19, 1980. Sergeant Jody Benjamin Sadek, right, was killed on September 20, 1988, while chasing a speeder.

Bristol Police Officer Mark Edward Vance, left, was shot in the head and killed on November 27, 2004, when he entered a house in response to a domestic disturbance calls. Goodlettsville Police Detective Lynn Wayne Hicks, right, was shot in the head from ambush and killed after responding to a domestic disturbance call on May 22, 1999.

More challenging was the need to enforce speed and safety laws as motor vehicles grew in numbers and power. By the mid-twentieth century, the death toll on streets and roadways was at epidemic levels. Automobile accidents claimed the lives of policemen as well. Some of those killed in accidents while on duty were Loudon Police Officer Sam Robert Hickey on April 25, 1954; Greeneville Police Sergeant John Lowery Freshour on December 14, 1964; Tullahoma Patrolman Henry Travis on January 1, 1970; Maryville Police Officer John Michael Callahan II on February 21, 1981; McEwen Police Reserve Officer Larry James Tidwell on August 2, 1983; Bristol Patrolman Jackie Lewis Phillips on October 1, 1988; Shelbyville Police Sergeant G. J. Jordon on January 22, 1995; Winchester Police Sergeant Daniel Aaron Smith on May 31, 1996; Cross Plains Chief of Police Wallace Lee Clinard on November 4, 1997; Alcoa Police Sergeant Timothy Joe Hunt on April 20, 2000; Harriman Police Officer Jesse Matthew "Matt" Rittenhouse on September 16, 2004; and Decherd Police Drug Investigator Sergeant Michael Keith Buckner on March 17, 2005.

Murfreesboro Motorcycle Officer Kay Rogers died on November 9, 2005, from injuries received in a motorcycle accident the previous evening. Officer Rogers, the department's first female motorcycle officer, struck a vehicle that turned into her path.

Often police officers were killed while working incidents on the streets and highways. Some deaths involved officers working accidents or on their way to the scene of an accident. New Tazewell Police Lieutenant George Brooks was struck and killed by a car while he investigated a minor traffic accident on February 19, 2003. Red Bank Police Officer Gerald Warf was responding to an accident-with-injuries on June 28, 2003, and died when he collided with a broken down street sweeper.

Moscow Chief of Police Louis Dwane Snow was killed on July 19, 1973, when a freight train struck his patrol car at a crossing on Route 76. The chief was responding to the scene of another accident.

Two officers were killed in unusual incidents. Waverly Chief of Police Guy Oakley Barnett Sr. was overseeing the cleanup of a train derailment on February 26, 1978, when a derailed tanker car exploded, killing the chief and fifteen civilians. Parsons Patrolman Darrell William Drehman was directing traffic at an accident in which a fleeing felon struck a utility pole. A passing tractor trailer caught the wires and pulled the pole down on Officer Drehman's head. He died a week later on February 8, 2000.

High speed vehicular pursuit claimed the lives of two Hendersonville Police Department motorcycle officers. Sergeant Jody Benjamin Sadek was killed on September 20, 1988; and Officer Daniel Stanley MacClary on September 27, 2000. Both officers were chasing speeders. Another Hendersonville officer, Sergeant Richard L. Bandy was killed by a motorcycle being driven recklessly on January 19, 1980.

Vehicular assault took the life of Lenoir City Police Sergeant Jesse J. Buttram on August 31, 1972. He was struck and killed by a car while making a traffic stop. In a more egregious incident Mount Juliet Police Sergeant Jerry Mundy and Wilson County Deputy John Musice were run down by fleeing felons as they

Mount Juliet Police Sergeant Jerry Alton Mundy, left, was run down by fleeing felons near exit 226 of I-40 on July 9, 2003. New Tazewell Police Lieutenant George Brooks, right, was struck and killed by a car while he investigated a minor traffic accident on February 19, 2003.

were putting down stop sticks near exit 226 of I-40 on July 9, 2003.

The stress of police work resulted in a number of officers dying from heart attacks on the job. Kingsport Patrolman George W. Frazier had a heart attack and died on May 30, 1938, during a shootout. Rossville Patrolman Orville Franklin Evans, 50, suffered a fatal heart attack on June 27, 1989, at the Tennessee Law Enforcement Training Academy during a physical stress test that involved shooting at targets while negotiating an obstacle course. Other officers who died on duty of heart attacks included Millington Marshal John William Lowe Sr. on October 30, 1942; Hendersonville Police Officer James Gammons on July 13, 1974; Gallatin Patrol Officer Steven Harold Downing on April 12, 1985; Shelbyville Patrolman Melvin Claxton on February 17, 1999; and Gallaway Police Captain Elmer L. Dosier on February 26, 1999.

Other small Tennessee city and town police officers killed in the line of duty include LaFollette Police Chief of Police Samuel Henderson Smith on May 14, 1914; Monterey Chief of Police Alvah H. Countiss on March 19, 1916; Union City Patrolman Oscar T. Roper on July 16, 1919; Union City Patrolman Dave Yates on December 4, 1922; Bon Air Police Chief Sergeant Hugh Thomas Lowery on April 23, 1924; Selmer Town Marshal James Franklin Crocker on November 1, 1933; Crossville City Marshal George W. Young on June 27, 1934; Tiptonville Police Officer Millard Williams on September 26, 1936; Tracy City

Motorcycle Officer Kay Rogers was the first and only female motorcycle officer of the Murfreesboro Police Department when a car pulled into the path of her motor. Injuries from the incident resulted in her death on November 9, 2005.

Patrolman James Cagle on January 12, 1969; Lewisburg Patrolman Billy W. Blackwell on February 1, 1975; Vonore Police Officer Walter David Green on September 21, 1975; and Tullahoma Policeman Clifford Riddle on January 1, 1987.

Today police officers in communities across Tennessee serve to protect the lives and property of their neighbors. New technology and enhanced training has changed the dynamics of police work, but commitment to service and dedication to duty remain at the core of the men and women dedicated to law enforcement.

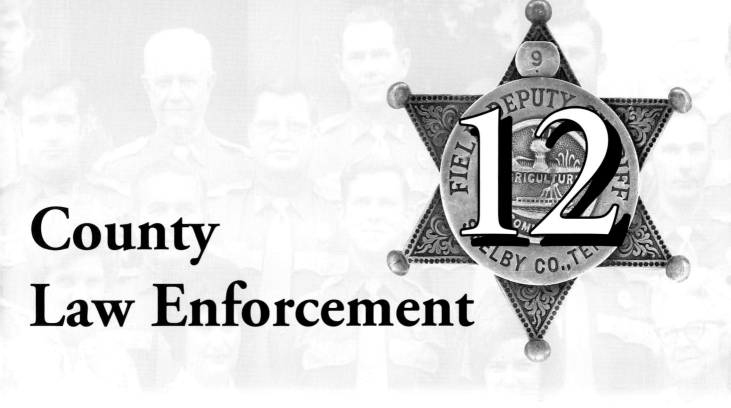

County Law Enforcement

The first law enforcement officers in Tennessee were the county sheriffs and constables appointed while the territory was still part of North Carolina. When Tennessee became a state the only two law enforcement officers designated in its constitution were the sheriff and constable.

The 1796 Constitution of the State of Tennessee provided that a sheriff and a sufficient number of constables be chosen for each county by the County Court. The revised state constitution of 1835 required that the sheriff and constables be elected by popular vote.

These officials were known to the colonies from England and became the recognized law enforcement positions in the newly independent United States of America. The sheriff was the representative of the Crown in each English shire and in the U.S. he became the law enforcement officer of the county. The constable served in the judicial districts of the county like the parish constable served in the English countryside.

The sheriff was elected to a two-year term and his duty was to suppress all affrays, riots, routs, unlawful assemblies, insurrections and breaches of the peace. The sheriff was also responsible to attend courts in the county and execute all criminal warrants issued as well as all civil process. The sheriff was also the keeper of the county jail.

Jailers and deputies who worked for fees assisted the sheriff to perform his duties. The state legislature passed an act in 1823 permitting the sheriffs of Knox, Davidson, Maury, Smith, Rutherford, Jefferson, Sumner and Washington counties to appoint up to three deputies, one more than allowed to other counties in the state. Sheriff often used constables to serve as deputies.

Before civil districts existed in the county, constables were appointed for each militia company or town. The militia was basic to society in the decades following the Revolutionary War. The men in each community selected a captain and formed a militia company. The General Assembly initially used the division of the county into militia companies to determine the jurisdiction of constables.

> The courts of the several counties which now are or hereafter shall be within the state, shall, at the court to be holden for each respective county next after the first day of January, nominate and appoint constables for the same, but no more than one for each captain's company, and one for the county town, which constables shall be persons of good character, and shall hold their offices for two years.

Civil districts were established in 1836 and constables were elected for each district. The constable

Prisoners were made to stand with their head and hands fastened in the pillory as public punishment. They could be branded or have their ears cropped while in the pillory. Lashes were administered at the whipping post.

although technology, training and growth have changed the dynamics of their work. One important exception has been the elimination of the sheriff's responsibility for carrying out the sentence of the court and punishing felony criminals.

Before the Tennessee state prison was built in 1831 criminals were not punished by confined for long periods. Punishment for crime was corporal and often left permanent bodily reminders of the sentence. In addition punishment was administered publicly in order to teach a moral lesson to the community. Punishment was also administered locally by the county sheriff. Punishment was swift in the early years of the state as well.

County jails were intended only to hold prisoners until trial and even though trials were held quickly, escapes were frequent Sheriffs moved prisoners from one cell to another to interrupt prisoners sawing bars or working at other forms of escape. Desperate criminals were taken to stronger jails in another county.

The main instruments of punishment were the gallows, the pillory and the whipping post. The sheriff carried out the punishment including hanging murderers. Hangings were public and drew large crowds of spectators. The pillory consisted of a set of stocks affixed to the top of a post or frame set into the ground and was used to secure prisoners for public punishment. The pillory was located at the courthouse and prisoners were sentenced to stand in the pillory in the public square.

Some crimes required that prisoners be whipped, branded or have their ears cropped. Whippings were given at the whipping post and consisted of no more than thirty-nine lashes. The British navy had found that floggings of forty lashes or more could result in death so when a sailor was "beaten within an inch of his life" he was given thirty-nine lashes.

Criminals who stole horses were often branded with an "HT" and carried for all time the sign of his offense. Ear cropping was another method of punishment that marked a criminal for life. While standing in the pillory the ear or ears of the offender were nailed to the pillory, or in the vernacular of the day "he had his ears pinned back." He then had part or all of his ears cut off.

Records of the Jonesboro court in 1790 as cited in *Dropped Stitches in Tennessee History* illustrated the typical justice meted out to a horse thief.

The defendant being called to the Bar and asked if he had anything to say why sentence should not be passed upon him Saith Nothing. It is therefore

had most of the law enforcement duties as the sheriff. Those who served as Town Constable were the chief law enforcement officer of the towns and cities within the county and together with the night watch provided the initial policing function for the municipality. In recent years some counties in Tennessee have eliminated the position of constable.

Another county officer who was appointed at the same time as the sheriff in frontier Tennessee counties was the County Ranger. Although not a lawman, the ranger had a quasi law enforcement function. The principle duty of the ranger was to ride the range of the county and round up stray livestock. The ranger apprehended runaway slaves and was the eyes and ears of the sheriff in the remote areas of the county. In some ways the ranger was the predecessor of the county patrolman, but as counties beame more populated in the 1840s and 1850s the office of Ranger was made obsolete.

The duties of sheriffs and constables have generally remained the same over the last two centuries,

Ordered that the said Elias Pybourn be confined in the public Pillory one Hour. That he have both his ears nailed to the Pillory and severed from his Head; That he receive at the public Whipping post thirty nine lashes well laid On; and be branded on the Right cheek with the letter H, and on the left cheek with the letter T, and that the Sheriff of Washington County put the sentence in execution between the hours of Twelve and Two this day.

The use of cropping of ears to mark criminals grew out of the use of ear cropping to mark livestock. Cattle and other livestock were given an owners mark by cropping or otherwise cutting one or both ears. Examples of stock marks recorded in county courts were "a crop and slit in left ear and a hole in the right," "a crop off left ear," and "a crop and under bit in the left and an half crop in the right ear."

An individual's reputation was in jeopardy if he lost part of an ear accidentally. In such a case it was important that the individual set the record straight, as indicated in another court proceeding.

Joseph Culton comes into Court and Proved by Oath of Alexander Moffit that he lost a part of his left Ear in a fight with a certain Charles Young and prays the same to be entered of record. Ordered therefore that the same be Admitted Accordingly.

Hanging was the final judgment for murderers, and was conducted by the sheriff. Hangings were major public events in the community throughout the nineteenth century and drew spectators for miles around. Hangings continued to be done locally by the county sheriff into the twentieth century, but by the turn of the twentieth century the death sentence was carried out in behind the walls of the county jail rather than in public.

A hanging event typically began with a procession from the county jail to the hanging grounds. The condemned man rode in a wagon often accompanied by a clergyman and surrounded by lawmen led by the sheriff. Religious ceremonies including singing and preaching preceded the execution. Once the prisoner mounted the gallows and the noose placed around his neck he was given an opportunity to say his final words.

Placement of the noose was essential for an efficient hanging. The hangman placed the rope leading from the noose on the side of the man neck so that when the trap was sprung death would come quickly from a broken neck. If the rope slipped to the back of the neck, strangulation brought a slow and agonizing death accompanied by thrashing of the body. Once the doctor on site verified that the condemned was dead the body was cut down and custody passed from the sheriff to the undertaker or the family.

Felony punishment that involved branding and whipping gave way to a term of incarceration following the construction of Tennessee's first State Penitentiary House in Nashville in 1831. In 1909 responsibility for executions also passed from the county sheriff to the state penitentiary staff. The method of execution was changed from hanging to electrocution in 1913.

Other twentieth-century changes, especially training and the adoption of technology, greatly enhanced the sophistication and effectiveness in the offices of sheriff across the state. The creation of the Tennessee Law Enforcement Training Academy in 1966 provided a major resource for sheriffs' offices in the state. A greater level of professionalism was reached as deputy sheriffs received training in the law, crime fighting, and investigation.

A dramatic change in funding of county law enforcement occurred early in the second half of the twentieth century. Prior to that time, the sheriff had full responsibility for the funding of his office. Fees from the service of papers, making arrests, and housing prisoners formed the base revenue for supporting the expenses of the sheriff's office. Payroll, automobiles, maintenance of the jail, food for prisoners, all expenses were paid from fees due by statute for the performance of specific duties. Deputies furnished their own sidearms and other equipment, and did not wear uniforms.

This began to change in larger counties before the middle of the twentieth century. Tax payers began to support the law enforcement efforts of county sheriffs and full-time deputies were paid from the general fund of the county. The title Field Deputy or Road Deputy was used for part-time deputies that continued to be paid from fees.

Smaller counties continued to depend largely on a fee-based revenue stream until 1973, when the state halted the practice, and expenses were hence paid from the county's general fund. Fees and other monies taken in by the sheriff's officer went directly to the general fund and salaries, equipment, jail operations and other expenses of the sheriff's office were included in the county budget. The change in funding had a major impact on the stabilization and uniform operation of the sheriff's office.

Additional stability of the county law enforcement function came with the extension of the sheriff's term of service. The term of office for sheriffs was two years and an individual could only serve three consecutive terms. The legislature acted in 1978 to make the term of office four years and to remove term limits. Thereafter, voters determined how long a sheriff served in office.

In the late twentieth century technology created an ongoing challenge to law enforcement. Computing and communications technology added to the ability of law officers to do their jobs, but financial investment and training required to implement new technology constantly strained the resources of the county.

Davidson County traces its history to a time prior to Tennessee statehood. The North Carolina Legislature established a "district county westward of Cumberland Mountain" called "Davidson County" in April 1783. In October the Inferior Court of Pleas and Quarter Sessions for Davidson County met for the first time and appointed Daniel Williams as sheriff of Davidson County. The court also appointed a coroner, a register and a ranger. The court ordered the creation of a "courthouse and prison." The jail was to be fourteen feet square and made of logs one foot thick.

Sheriff Daniel Williams arrived in Nashborough sometime in 1779 or 1780 as part of the Buchanan party from South Carolina and established a land claim of 640 acres. He and his son Sampson signed the Cumberland Compact, an agreement of cooperation among the settlers, in 1780. Fights with Cherokee, Creek and Choctaw warriors were frequent. Williams was a proven soldier and fighter and he remained in the area to defend Fort Nashborough when other men moved their families to less dangerous territory. His bravery and willingness to take a stand and fight was good reason to make him sheriff. Sheriff Williams died prior to January 1794.

The town's name was changed to Nashville in 1784 and John Mulherrin was sheriff of the county. He also traveled with the Buchanan party and received land in the county from the North Carolina legislature for his defense of Nashborough. In the same term of the court, Russell Gower "took the oath of a Deputy Sheriff." Gower was 29 and born in Virginia.

Thomas Marston and David Hays served as sheriff in 1785 and 1786 respectively. Thomas Hickman served as sheriff in 1788 and may have been killed in an Indian raid. If so, he was likely the first law enforcement officer to be killed in the line of duty in Tennessee.

Sampson Williams, Sheriff Daniel Williams' son, became sheriff in 1789 and again in 1791. He was a captain of the county militia and served as Andrew Jackson's commanding officer. Williams moved to Sumner County after his term as sheriff and later went on to Jackson County. Sampson Williams served three terms in the Tennessee Senate.

North Carolina transferred ownership of Davidson County and other western territory to the federal government in 1790. It became a part of the Southwest Territory under Territorial Governor William Blount. William Porter was Davidson County sheriff at the time.

Twenty-two-year-old Virginia native Nicolas Perkins Hardeman was appointed sheriff in 1794. He was age 13 or 14 when he arrived in Nashborough by flatboat. In 1797 the sheriff was made tax collector as well.

Wright Williams, son of Daniel Williams and brother of Sampson Williams, was named sheriff in 1799. Sheriff Wright Williams carried out the judgment of the court on a horse theft, that he "stand in the public pillory for one hour and shall be publicly whipped on his bare back with 39 lashes well laid on, and at the same time shall have both his ears cut off, and shall be branded on his right cheek with the letter H and on the left cheek with the letter T."

Joseph Johnson was named sheriff in 1800 and John Boyd in 1802. Sheriff Boyd arrived at French Lick with the Donelson flatboats and was a signer of the Cumberland Compact. A new jail was completed in 1807 pursuant to an act of the state legislature. The jail had three rooms, "one for the jailer, one for felons, and one for debtors." The act also created a system for jail inspections and established standards for handling of prisoners and for the cleanliness of the facility. Michael C. Dunn became sheriff in 1808.

Twenty-seven-year-old Caleb Hewitt was elected sheriff of Davidson County in 1816. On Thursday, September 9, Sheriff Hewitt was about his duty of serving papers of the court. While serving a writ he was attack with an adze, a wood shaping took with a thin arched blade at a right angle to the handle, and mortally wounded. Caleb Hewitt died four days later of his wounds. The notice of his death appeared in the September 10, 1816, issue of The Nashville Whig.

DIED - On Monday the 9th inst. CALEB HEWITT, Esq. Sheriff of Davidson county, of a wound he received from James Maxwell, on Thursday last, who struck him with an adze, while he was in the act of serving a writ on him.

Maxwell was apprehended on Friday night, and is now safely lodged in the jail of this county, to await his trial in November next.

Caleb Hewitt was born in Fayette County in western Pennsylvania on October 5, 1788. His family along with 18 others migrated by keelboat down the Ohio River to Davidson County in 1790 when Caleb was an infant. He was the son of Judge Robert Hazael "Hayes" Hewitt and Anna Shute Hewitt. His maternal aunt, Susannah Shute Harding, and her husband, John Harding, were the builders of Belle Meade Mansion.

Sheriff Hewitt died little less than four weeks short of his 28th birthday. The county court appointed Joseph Phillips to complete his term.

Sheriff Joseph W. Horton was elected around 1821 replacing Thomas Hickman who served from 1818. Sheriff Horton was age 29 and born in Davidson County. He served as cashier for the Bank of Tennessee before his election. Horton died on October 31, 1846. During Sheriff Horton's time in office the infamous West Tennessee land pirate John Murrell was convicted of stealing the mare of a Williamson County widow. Sheriff Horton carried out the judgment of the Davidson County court, which was described by a young man who witnessed the event in the March 21, 1821, issue of the Nashville Banner.

The sheriff took from his pocket a piece of new hemp and bound Murrell's hand securely to the railing [near the prisoner's box]. In a short while a big man named Jeffry came in bringing a tinner's stove that looked like a lantern and placed it on the floor. Being anxious to see all that was going on, I climbed upon the railing close to Murrell. Mr. Horton, the sheriff, took from the little stove the branding iron, a long instrument, which looked very much like the soldering irons now used by tinners. He looked at the iron which was red hot and then put it on Murrell's hand. The skin fried like meat. Mr. Horton held it there until the smoke rose probably two feet when he removed the iron. Mr. Horton then untied Murrell's hand. Murrell, who had up to this time never moved, produced a white handkerchief and wiped his hand several times. It was all over, and the sheriff took Murrell back to jail where he was yet to suffer punishment by being whipped and placed in a pillory.

Willoughby Williams began three terms as Davidson County sheriff around 1830. He was 32 and born in North Carolina, moving to Davidson County in 1818. Williams served as president of the Bank of Tennessee following his time as sheriff. The county built a new courthouse in 1830 and the sheriff's office was located on the main floor.

Phillip Campbell was elected in 1836, the first sheriff of Davidson County to be elected by popular vote. He was a major in the county militia at the time. Sheriff Campbell died in office on June 28, 1838. The County Court selected twenty-eight-year-old Felix Robertson Rains to complete Campbell's term of office on July 2. Felix Rains was born March 11, 1810, in Davidson County, a son of John Rains, one of the earliest settlers in the county. Rains was related through marriage to Michael C. Dunn, sheriff in 1808. At the time of his appointment, Rains served as a constable for the 8th district and as a deputy for Sheriff Campbell. He served three terms as sheriff and went on to serve as a director of the Bank of Tennessee. He died June 1, 1883.

Churchill Lanier, a farmer born in North Carolina, was elected sheriff in 1844. He had previously served as constable for the 24th district and as a constable for the Circuit Court. He continued as part of the sheriff's office and served as a deputy under Sheriff Barnes. Lanier died September 14, 1889. Sheriff Bartlett M. Barnes was elected in 1848 defeating Lanier by 235 votes. He was a 43-year-old native of Davidson County and had served multiple terms on the County Court as magistrate. After two terms as sheriff he moved to Arkansas and served in the 25th Arkansas Infantry during the Civil War. He later served a term in the Arkansas legislature.

Four men served as sheriff during the 1850s when the county build two major facilities. Littlebury W. Fussell, who had served as a deputy, was elected sheriff in 1852 at the age of 34. He oversaw construction of a new jail designed by Adolphus Heiman and built on the eastern edge of the public square at a cost of $25,000. Edward B. Bigley won election as sheriff in 1854. Fifty-four-year-old Bigley served as High Constable of Nashville from 1833 to 1839 and 1841 to 1843 and before that was a farmer.

John K. Edmundson, born in Virginia and also a farmer, was elected in 1856 at the age of 42. The Davidson County Courthouse was destroyed by fire in 1856 and was rebuilt at a cost of $30,000. James Hinton, elected in 1858 at the age of 31, served the next two-year term as sheriff. He appointed two deputies who had served as constables, and one jailer.

John K. Edmundson was returned to office as sheriff in 1860 as the county prepared for civil war. James M. Hinton took office as sheriff in March 1862 within a month after Union forces occupied Nashville and Davidson County. Hinton stayed in office through the remainder of the war. His deputies in 1865 were John D. Gower, A. Garnett and Thomas Hobson. Following his tenure as sheriff, Hinton was elected to the County Court and served in that body until 1894. He served as steward of the city workhouse for fifteen years until his death on March 7, 1897.

Elijah E. Patterson, the 34-years-old constable of the 2nd district, was elected sheriff in 1866. His three deputies were W. C. Shaw, S. T. Davidson and Thomas Shute. The jailer became an elected position in county government in 1867 and Davidson County elected its first black jailer, constable and justice of the peace.

The number of personnel in the Davidson County Sheriff's Office remained small. C. M. Donelson was elected sheriff in 1868 and selected four deputies, L. L. Soey, S. C. Marshall, R. T. Gains and N. C. Austin. Edward D. Whitworth, elected in 1872, had served as a deputy sheriff. Francis Woodall, elected sheriff in 1876, served six years as a constable and four as a deputy sheriff.

Confederate veteran John L. Price, member of Company G, 15th Tennessee Regiment, won election as sheriff in 1878. Tim Johnson, veteran of the 20th Tennessee Regiment, was elected in 1880. T E Moore, elected sheriff in 1882, oversaw construction of a new jail on First Avenue in 1884. A residence for the jailor was built next door. R. D. Marshall was elected in 1886, William J. Hill in 1890 and John D. Sharp in 1894.

Davidson County Constable Ed Manlove, left, was killed on December 15, 1894, as he attempted to make an arrest. Davidson County Deputy Sheriff Melvin Fleming, right, was shot and killed on June 25, 1942, by a drunken ex-convict in an incident that also left a Nashville detective dead.

Constable Edward Manlove was killed in the line of duty on December 15, 1894. Manlove was the constable of the White's Creek district and officer of the Grand Jury. He was attempting to arrest a man who attempted to murder a tollgate keeper on the White's Creek Turnpike. A gunfight ensued and Manlove was shot with a Winchester rifle.

Hermitage District Constable B. Lewis Hurt was 31 when he was elected sheriff in 1898. He appointed T. H. Scott, W. P. Moore, James Hurt and Sam Borum as deputies. D. A. Bradley served as chief deputy. Borum later served as sheriff.

Thomas E. Cartwright was elected in 1902 and began another dynasty of Davidson County sheriffs. Both his son and his grandson later served as sheriff. Cartwright was 46 and had served with the Nashville Fire Department and the Nashville Police Department. He was a lieutenant of police before his election. Charles D. Johns defeated Cartwright in 1906 by only 14 votes. Johns had served briefly as a Nashville policeman. He appointed D. A. Bradley as chief deputy. During Johns' term as sheriff the county erected a new jail on Second Avenue North.

Former deputy Sam Houston Borum won election for sheriff in 1908 after three previous attempts. He served as a deputy from 1894 until 1902. He campaigned on implementation of the state's "bone-dry" prohibition statutes. Borum was associated with the sheriff's department for many years. He served two terms as sheriff, served as chief deputy 1938 and 1940, and ran again for sheriff in 1942 but lost.

Former Nashville City Marshal Charles W. Longhurst was elected sheriff in 1912, accepting responsibility for 120 prisoners in the county jail. He had served as constable from 1901 to 1903 and was elected city marshal in 1904. Longhurst was elected to the state House of Representatives in the 61st General Assembly, 1919 to 1921, and was superintendent of the City Workhouse in the 1930s.

Between 1916 and 1928 Joe W. Wright, James R. Allen, R. Louis Camp and Bob Briley served as sheriff. Sheriffs were authorized to have as many as nineteen deputies. Louis Camp served as custodian of the county jail, as murder officer and later as chief deputy. Bob Briley also served as murder officer. In 1921 fees for service were established for the sheriff and constables at $1.50 for every capias, summons, or other leading process and $0.75 for service of a Justice warrant.

Nashville Police Department Detective Gus Kiger won elected as sheriff in 1928 by 10,000 votes. Kiger had twenty-six years of law enforcement experience as an investigator with the attorney general, deputy sher-

The first black deputies of the Davidson County Sheriff's Office with were added to the force by Sheriff Garner Robinson in the late 1940s. The deputies seated from left to right were Terry Dowdy, Sheriff Robinson, and John Bluing; and standing in the second row were Alvin Futrell, Lem Dawson, Pie Hardison, and Walter Swett.

iff, Nashville patrolman and detective. As sheriff, Kiger vigorously enforced prohibition laws. Kiger later served as deputy sheriff under Sheriff Marshall between 1940 and 1943.

Investigation of a reported drinking and gambling joint on September 29, 1928, resulted in a serious wound to Davidson County Deputy Sheriff Dewey Johnson. Deputies Johnson, D. Ledbetter and W. J. Walton ended up in a pitched gun battle with an ex-convict. Johnson was shot in the abdomen and the assailant was killed.

Sam Jones Shryer, elected sheriff in 1930, died in office on July 1, 1932. His term was completed by 71-year-old Coroner James Allen. Lawrence A. Bauman won the September 1932 election over fifteen other

candidates. During Sheriff Bauman's terms in office he consolidated the Belle Meade and Old Hickory police departments into the sheriff's office. The sheriff's salary was set at $7,500 per year in 1933. Both sheriffs Shryer and Bauman were elected president of the Tennessee Mississippi Peace Officer's Association.

On February 12, 1938, Sheriff Bauman died in office. The previous September he had overseen the opening of the new county jail located on the seventh floor of the courthouse. Coroner Leon Taylor succeeded him temporarily until the County Court appointed F. A. "Pete" Carter in April to complete Bauman's term.

Ivey Young, farmer and livestock breeder, won the 1938 election and took office as sheriff in September. The new sheriff was presented with a solid gold badge set with a large stone in the center. Sam Houston Borum returned to the sheriff's office as Sheriff Young's chief deputy. The pervasive crimes of the day were gambling and bootlegging, and Sheriff Young was a dedicated enforcer of the law. One night he made a single handed raid on a Nolensville Road grocery and confiscated three slot machines.

Sheriff Ivey Young installed the first radio system in the sheriff's office, and established a radio patrol. He cooperated with other agencies including the Tennessee Highway Patrol, allowing them to use the sheriff's office radio network.

Robert D. "Bob" Marshall, a World War I veteran and superintendent of the county highway department, was elected sheriff in 1940 and appointed Charles Smith as his chief deputy. Sheriff Marshall died in office in May 1941. Coroner Leon Taylor again temporarily filled the position until the July appointment of Claude Briley, brother of former Sheriff Bob Briley, to serve the remainder of Marshall's term. Sheriff Briley was subsequently elected to the post.

Deputy Sheriff Melvin Fleming was shot and killed around midnight on June 25, 1942. A drunken ex-convict who had served time for murder of two Kentucky lawmen became belligerent with the staff of a Nashville restaurant when they refused to serve him more alcohol. Deputy Fleming arrived on the scene and attempted to take the man into custody. The felon pulled a German Luger and shot the lawman three times, killing him. Before the violence ended in the death of the gunman, Nashville Detective Charles Mundy was also killed. Deputy Fleming was 32 and had been with the department for two years.

Garner Robinson resigned from the Quarterly Court and as coroner to run for sheriff in 1946. The part owner of Phillips-Robinson Funeral Home and World War II anti-tank unit veteran won the election and served three terms. Sheriff Robinson made many improvements in the office including upgrading patrol of the county and adding the first black deputy sheriffs. After he stepped down as sheriff due to term limits, he was elected register, state representative and county trustee.

Law enforcement in Davidson County outside of the City of Nashville was augmented in 1946 by a small County Highway Patrol. The following year Davidson County was authorized to purchase and maintain "motor vehicles" for the Sheriff's police patrol. The unit was a further effort to consolidate police services countywide. Badges of county patrolmen and fender signs on motorcycles were designated

"Police." The area was a large territory to cover with a force that stood at only sixty men in 1952.

Earlier, several suburban communities relied on private subscription police patrols as well as private fire companies. Belle Meade hired a county sheriff's deputy in the 1930s to help crack a ring of thieves who were operating in collusion with house servants. A small patrol was hired by residents and taken over by the city of Belle Meade sometime after 1938. Inglewood and Madison set up their won private police and fire company in 1940. Chief Raymond Cannon, formerly of the U. S. Forestry Service, hired seven patrolmen. They were paid a salary from the $10 a year fee paid by subscribers. Fees collected from arrests were distributed to local charities. In Goodlettsville one resident moonlighted after work each evening as a one-man police force.

These makeshift police patrols provided only a basic level of security. Crime grew in the suburbs after World War II, particularly bootlegging and gambling that was previously limited to the inner city. The inadequacy and tentativeness of the private subscription system was underlined when police were call upon to

Davidson County Sheriff Ivey Young, far right, was presented with a solid gold badge jeweler made badge at his swearing in ceremony on September 1, 1938. Friends also presented Sheriff Young with a pearl-handled revolver and an automobile.

Sergeant Elmer Craig of the Inglewood-Madison Police in 1943. Among his other patrol duties, Craig worked at school crossing duty. The private subscription police force was later incorporated into the Davidson County Sheriff's Office.

take action against their subscribers. Various issues encouraged the continued unification of police services for the entire county under the sheriff.

A new jail was opened behind the Safety Building in 1950. The Sheriff's Office worked with volunteer groups to open a library for prisoners. The facility was

Two members of the Davidson County Police on new Harley Davidson motorcycles in 1950. The photograph was taken on the grounds of the Parthenon.

later called the Urban Jail when it was operated by the City of Nashville as both the city jail and workhouse. The sheriff's office remained on the ground floor of the county courthouse.

Thomas Y. Cartwright, son of Sheriff Thomas E. Cartwright, was elected sheriff in 1952. He had worked as a farmer, grocer and payroll clerk before opening a farm implement store. His public service included four years in the Quarterly Court and two terms in the state House of Representatives. Sheriff Cartwright appointed Fred Lassiter of the Nashville Police Department as his chief deputy. He was authorized to hire up to fifty-eight patrolmen. During his two terms in office he abolished the fee system, in which deputies were paid for service of process or by arrest, as the primary method of paying deputies and moved to a salary based pay system. All fees collected by those deputies on salary went into the general fund.

The name of the Davidson County Highway Patrol was changed to Davidson County Sheriff's Patrol in October 1954. New uniforms were adopted and each deputy was required to pay for his own uni-

Davidson County Sheriff's Patrol unit, a 1950 Pontiac Silver Streak, in front of the Parthenon.

form at $141 each. Employees were given one day off per week. Pay in 1955 was between $312 and $325 per month and four former sheriffs were on the payroll as Criminal Court officers, Bob Briley, Claude Briley, Ivey Young and F. A. "Pete" Carter. Even as most deputies were placed on salary, the office continued to employ field deputies who worked for fees rather than pay from the general fund of taxpayer dollars.

The Sheriff's Patrol included fourteen cars, all recently equipped with seat belts. In a three month period 2,007 were arrested by the Patrol, 153 for "driving while drunk." Captain Leslie E. Jett, a former member of the Tennessee Highway Patrol and safety officer for the sheriff's office, was commander of the 55-member Sheriff's Patrol. Detectives were placed on around-the-clock duty, two officers paired for each of three shifts.

The Sheriff's Patrol completed the American Red Cross Advanced First Aid course and first aid kits were added to each patrol car. In December 1955, employees of the Sheriff's Office delivered food baskets to three hundred needy families in lieu of an office Christmas party. This began a tradition for the force.

Sheriff Cartwright died in office on March 26, 1956. Upon hearing of his death many patrol deputies removed their badges as a token of honor. His brother-in-law, County Coroner Everett Gourley, was appointed to serve the remainder of his term.

Sheriff Cartwright's son, Thomas B. Cartwright, won the election that year and took office in September. Sheriff Thomas B. Cartwright was a veteran of both the European and Pacific theaters during World War II and served in the Korean War as well. He was the business manager for Baptist Hospital before his election. He kept Fred Lassiter as chief deputy. Sheriff Cartwright implemented a promotional testing system for the all positions in an effort to remove political considerations from promotions.

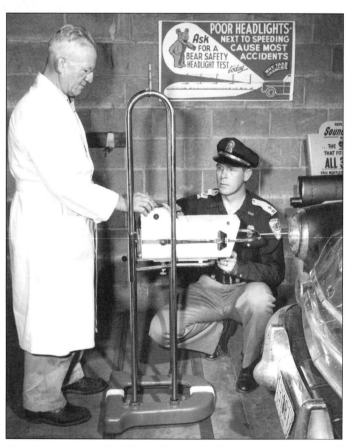

Davidson County Sheriff's Highway Patrol Captain Leslie Jett took charge of the county's safety program in the early 1950s. He checked out the equipment used to property direct headlight beams in this photograph.

Sheriff's Department, Davidson County, Tennessee

1959

Lt. R.E. FERRELL — Lt. M.A. BAKER — Lt. R.K. HILL — JAMES C. HESTER, Captain - Patrol — *TOM B. CARTWRIGHT, Sheriff — *FRED LASSITER, Chief Deputy — *J.H. KERKELES, Chief Investigator — *GEORGE CURREY, Juvenile Officer — L.S. LAWRENCE, Safety Director

.A. SESLER — Sgt. JAMES R. MALONE — Sgt. J.E. SAWYERS — Cpl. W.A. CROSSLAND — Cpl. C.E. VAUGHN — Cpl. D.L. WHITE — *JAMES T. GENTRY, Investigator — *NEAL JOHNSON, Investigator

MULLINS, trolman — R.D. BRUCE, Patrolman — *OSCAR DILLARD, Identification — *JAMES P. GOSSETT, Identification — *CHARLES M. HUNTER, Investigator — C.E. KEEF, Clerk — L.M. HALL, Dispatcher — F.M. WALDROP, Dispatcher — J.T. PRICE, Dispatcher — HUGH PERRY, Patrolman — D.A. COX, Patrolman

FINK, olman — *GUS STINNETT, Desk - Jail — *FRED McNABB, Desk - Jail — *R.B. RAY, Desk - Jail — *CHARLIE FREEDMAN, Jail — *WILL A. CORE, Jail - Kitchen — *GLEN SWAFFORD, Supt. - Jail — *WALTER BRUCE, Turnkey — *CLARENCE S. KELLAR, Turnkey — *LUTHER HARPER, Turn key — *J.E. SANDERS, Turnkey

ARNOLD, lman — JAMES H. MARABLE, Patrolman — W.J. HUNNICUTT, Patrolman — P.E. LEVER, Patrolman — H.E. STONE, Patrolman — E.A. JOHNSTON, Patrolman — EDDIE MARLIN, Patrolman — R.M. RESHA, Patrolman — W.E. ELLISON, Patrolman — G.W. SIMPSON, Patrolman — W.E. SMITH, Patrolman

ZELL, Jr., olman — A.V. BARNHILL, Patrolman — M.D. McCOOL, Patrolman — PAUL A. SHELTON, Patrolman — EVERETT T. WOMACK, Patrolman — Wm. M. BURKHARDT, Patrolman — A.A. LINDSEY, Patrolman — W.S. RUSSELL, Patrolman — A.W. THOMAS, Patrolman — T.P. CLEMONS, Patrolman — R.S. HAYNES, Patrolman

BARTON, rolman — R.J. YOUNG, Patrolman — E.D. SMITH, Patrolman — JAMES C. LESTER, Patrolman — DAVID T. FERGUSON, Patrolman — W.A. JONES, Patrolman — L.B. SILLS, Patrolman — P.G. GREER, Patrolman — E.L. MANIS, Patrolman — *JOHN A. CALVO, Jr., Field Deputy — *ERNEST PYLE, Field Deputy

*ROBERT WHITLOW, Field Deputy — *J.T. SNODDY, Field Deputy — *JOHN BOWEN, Field Deputy — *ED EDMONDS, Field Deputy — *L.E. JOHNSON, Field Deputy — W.S. WELCH, Field Deputy — C.E. MINTON, Patrolman — D.H. CRISWELL, Patrolman — JOHN M. ANDREWS, Patrolman — R.W. RIDGE, Patrolman

Salary not paid by Tax Dollars

Prepared by BUFORD LEWIS CO.

Former Sheriff's Patrol Captain Leslie Edward Jett was elected sheriff in 1960. Jett was a member of the famed Flying Tigers during World War II, served as lieutenant in charge of Safety Education for the Tennessee Highway Patrol, and was Director of Civil Defense for Nashville and Davidson County between 1956 and 1960.Sheriff Jett appointed W. Donald Barton as chief deputy.

The Davidson County Sheriff's Office consisted of 68 patrolmen, 97 in the School Mother Program, 10 field deputies, 9 investigators (2 of who also serve as matrons) and 1 administrator. Jim Ball joined the sheriff's office in September 1960 and soon took the place of former Deputy Bob Ridge as motorcycle officer. He and "Pappy" Simpson were the only two motor officers. Jett creating the phrase, "The life you save may be your own" for the School Mother's Program. The phrase was later adopted by the National Safety Council.

Among Sheriff Jett's early law enforcement activities was a series of raids on the liqour establishments in Printer's Alley. The Vice Squad was created in 1962 to suppress prostitution and illegal alcohol sales.

Davidson county schools were integrated in January 1961. Sheriff Jett assigned a patrol car to each desegregated school and assigned other cars to follow school buses. Jett personally manned the radio dispatch to issue quick response to any problem.

Sheriff Jett introduced new uniforms for deputies consisting of dark blue blouses with contrasting light blue pocket flaps and epaulets to match the slacks. The campaign hat had a wreathed circle badge and breast badges were six-point stars. Badges and buttons were silver tone for deputies and gold tone for supervisors. New substations were opened at Tusculum, Madison and Old Hickory.

Jimmy S. "Jim" Ball joined the Davidson County Sheriff's Patrol in 1960. Pictured here in 1961, Ball was one of the two motorcycle officers.

Leon Oldham was given regular motorcycle duty in December 1960. He was the first black deputy assigned to motorcycle duty. Sheriff Jett also promoted the first black deputy sheriff to the rank of sergeant, the first such promotion in the state.

Metropolitan Government of Nashville and Davidson County was formed in 1963 merging city and county governments. Law enforcement powers became the responsibility of the Metropolitan Police Department. The Sheriff's Office was charged with operation of the jail and service of civil process. Chief Deputy W. Donald Barton was made assistant chief of police and Sheriff Jett appointed Lafayette G. "Fate" Thomas to replace Barton as chief deputy.

The Sheriff's Office took possession of all jails and workhouses in the county including the city jail and urban workhouse controlled by the Nashville Police Department and the County Highway Department controlled workhouse. The workhouse staff moved to a forty-hour week and were required to wear uniforms. J. L. Harrison, a twenty-one year veteran of the U.S. Bureau of Prisons, was appointed warden of the workhouse at an annual salary of $7,200.

Davidson County Sheriff's Office Criminal Field Division.

Deputy Leon Oldham began motorcycle duty with the Davidson County Sheriff's Patrol in December 1960. He was the first black motorcycle officer on the force. Sheriff Leslie Jett stood beside him. (Nashville Banner photo)

The Sheriff's Office created a formal Civil Warrants Division replacing service of civil process by constables and others within the Sheriff's Office. The responsibility for prisoner booking and fingerprinting moved from the Sheriff's Office to the Metro Police Department.

Constable Robert Poe was elected sheriff in 1964 and took charge of 150 employees. He appointed Price Sain, a 20-year veteran of the Tennessee Highway Patrol, as chief deputy; and Herbert Jones as warden of the workhouse. Poe oversaw the desegregated of the Metro Jail in 1966

On May 22, 1966, Workhouse Sergeant Billy M. Stevens, 38, suffered a fatal heart attack after struggling with two inmates attempting to escape from Metro Jail. The inmates attacked guards with a makeshift knife and a mop handle. Sergeant Stevens was struck in the chest several times with the mop handle. Stevens had recently retired from 20 years in the Army and Air Force with tours of duty during World War II and Korea.

Sheriff John Frazier was elected in 1966. Frazier won the Bronze Star during duty with the U.S. Navy in Korea. He created the county's first work release program and served as the first president of the Tennessee Sheriff's Association.

Lafayette "Fate" Thomas, also a veteran of Korea, was first elected sheriff in 1972. His first duty with the

office was as a field deputy under Sheriff Robinson and the Sheriffs Cartwright before serving as Chief Deputy under Sheriff Jett. The Hill Building jail and administrative area opened in 1977 in the remodeled H. G. Hills Foods warehouse. The facility was designed to house juveniles and public drunks. The Criminal Justice Center (CJC) opened in December 1982. Sheriff Thomas appointed John W. "Billy" Lynch as chief deputy and Granville "Sonny" Lyons as administrator of CJC in January 1984.

Twenty-six-year veteran FBI Agent Henderson "Hank" Hillin won the sheriff's election in 1990. The Madison County native was heavily involved in the investigation of Tennessee Governor Ray Blanton. Sheriff Hillin temporarily closed the CJC's Intake Division in February 1992 because of jail overcrowding, preventing transfer of new inmates from Metro Police to the Sheriff's Office. To comply with a federal court order, he closed the workhouse and transferred inmates the CJC. Sheriff Hillin appointed his son Jim Hillin as chief deputy.

The first female sheriff in the history of Davidson County was elected in 1994. Sheriff Gayle Ray was an MBA graduate of the Massey School of Business, a council member from the 25th District and program coordinator for Vanderbilt University's Department of Mechanical Engineering. Sheriff Ray appointed James Daron Hall to be chief deputy. In 1995, female inmates were moved from the second floor of the CJC to the privately-managed Metro Detention Facility.

On September 22, 1995, Deputy Jerry Newson Jr., age 33, was killed in the line of duty and Deputy Johnny Spears was seriously injured. The two went out that morning to serve a warrant. The suspect came to the door of the house and began to argue with the lawmen. He then retreated into his house. The deputies were on their way to the patrol car to call for the backup when the suspect returned to the door and opened fire with a shotgun. Neither deputy was wearing a vest. Deputy Newson was struck three times and killed. Deputy Spears was wounded. Jerry Newson was a seven-year veteran of the sheriff's office

The former workhouse was converted to the Training Academy in July 1996. The Civil Warrant's Office moves from the Administration Building to the Training Academy. By the end of the year, Investigations, Transportation, Records Management and Dispatch had all moved most or all of their operations to the facility. The sheriff's office took over operation of the Booking Room at the CJC.

The Correctional Work Center opened in February 1997 providing 600 new beds and replacing the Work Release Center and DUI Centers. In December the sheriff's office unveiled VINE (Victim Information Notification Everyday) to provide movement or release information of offenders to victims. The Correctional Work Center became the first Davidson County jail, and only the second in the state, to gain accreditation by the American Correctional Association in 1998. Accreditation followed for the Training Division, the Administration Building, the CJC and the Hill Detention Center, making the Davidson County Sheriff's Office the first county agency in the nation to be fully accredited.

Sheriff James Daron Hall took office in September 2002. Hall was hired as a deputy by Sheriff Thomas in the Pre-Trial Release division. He later served as a counselor, classification officer, program director and assistant administrator before going to work for Corrections Corporation of America as a program director in 1993. He returned to the Davidson County Sheriff's Office in September 1994 as Sheriff Ray's chief deputy. Sheriff Daron Hall was the youngest individual elected Davidson County Sheriff in almost 200 years. He appointed John Ford III to the post of chief deputy and created two new divisions, Community Relations and Community Outreach.

The Davidson County Sheriff's Office has not only the longest traditions in the state of Tennessee, but has developed into one of the most professional agencies of its type in the nation.

Shelby County was among the first counties established by the state legislature following the acquisition of the land west of the Tennessee River. The county on the Chickasaw Bluffs was named for Isaac Shelby, hero of the battle of King's Mountain in the Revolutionary War and associate of Andrew Jackson in acquisition of the territory.

The county court gathered on May 1, 1820, to form a government. Along with other officials, Thomas Taylor was appointed sheriff pro tem. The next day an election was held to select permanent officials. Samuel R. Brown was elected sheriff. After a tie vote for constable, William Bettis and William Dean were both declared elected. Sheriff Brown was required to give a $5000 bond to insure faithful performance of his duties.

About twenty families were settled in the county. No roads existed, only the Cherokee Indian Trace. Most travel was by the river. When the county seat was selected by the legislature in 1824, Memphis was considered little more than a den of thieves and gamblers. The town of Raleigh, located on Sanderlin's Bluff north of the Wolf River, was selected as the county seat. A frame courthouse and jail was built initially and replace by a two-story brick structure in 1834. A whipping post was mounted in the court yard for dispensing justice.

Sheriff Sam Brown moved to Memphis in 1819 and built the first tavern in a double log cabin on the north side of Auction Street. The tavern of Colonel Brown was both a bar and an inn. He served as sheriff until 1828 when Joseph Graham was elected.

Sheriff John J. Balch, who had served as the first town constable of Memphis, was elected Shelby County sheriff in 1830 and served until 1836. He was succeeded by John Fowler, 1836-42; L. P. Hardaway, 1842-46 and J. B. Moseley, 1846-52. The population of Shelby County in 1850 was approximately 10,000. Sheriffs who served immediately prior to the Civil War were W. D. Gilmore, 1852-56; Robert L. Smith, 1858-60 and James E. Felts again from 1860-64.

With the 1862 occupation by Union forces, the elected officials of Memphis and Shelby County functioned under the close scrutiny of the Federal commander. In 1864 these officials were declared to be in revolt and Federal officials appointed a replacement government. After a brief tenure as Memphis chief of police, Patrick M. Winters was selected Shelby County sheriff by Federal authorities. Except for a brief period, Union soldiers policed Memphis and Shelby County from 1864 until the Metropolitan Police District of Shelby County was created in 1866. The county seat was moved from Raleigh to Memphis.

Sheriff Winters continued to serve, but the county law enforcement function, such as it was, was done by the Metropolitan Police. The county commissioners

The Shelby County Jail was a substantial sturcture.

refused to appropriate funds for the Metropolitans and little police work was done outside the city limits of Memphis. Organized bands of horse thieves and robbers flourished in the county. Winters was replaced as sheriff in 1868 by A. P. Curry, but little changed.

At the state level, the Brownlow regime was defeated in 1869. Traditional conservative leaders in the state quickly regained authority throughout the state. In 1870 Confederate General Marcus J. Wright was elected Shelby County sheriff. After one term, he was followed by Sheriff W. J. P. Doyle, 1872-74.

C. L. Anderson was elected sheriff in 1874 and appointed W. D. Cannon as chief deputy. Sheriff Anderson was in the office during the devastating yellow fever epidemics of the late 1870s and fell victim to yellow fever in 1878. E. L. McGowan was chosen to replace Anderson and served until 1880.

One of the most noted lawman in West Tennessee in the nineteenth century was Phil R. Athy. He served as Memphis chief of police from 1872 to 1880, during the difficult days following the Civil War and while yellow fever ravaged the city. Athy was elected sheriff in 1880 and died in office in 1884 shortly before completing his second term.

Chief Deputy W. D. Cannon was appointed sheriff to complete Athy's term. Cannon served as a captain in the Confederate Army. He served two terms as constable of the 18th Civil District before serving as chief deputy under three sheriffs. Sheriff Cannon comfortably won election in 1884 and served until 1888. Sheriff A. J. McClendon served from 1888 to 1894 and was the first sheriff to enforce the newly passed Tennessee "blue laws," restricting Sunday trade and activity. In one well-publicized incident three sportsmen were arrested for playing baseball on Sunday.

Sheriff J. A. "Arch" McCarver took office in 1894. He was a war veteran, serving in Company E 12th Tennessee Cavalry, and a butcher by trade with a market on Beale Street. Before serving as sheriff he was a meat inspector.

William Watts Carnes, another Memphis businessman and Civil War hero took office as sheriff in 1896. He resigned the Naval Academy at the outbreak of war and was made commander of the Confederate Navy vessel "Sampson." Carnes was able to escape with his ship when the Savannah was captured. Sheriff Carnes appointed Frank L. Monteverde as chief deputy.

Shelby County Deputy Sheriff Joseph A. Perkins joined the sheriff's office under Sheriff McLendon and continued through Sheriff Carnes' term. Perkins spent his early years driving wagons and stagecoaches between western Texas and Mexico. Deputy Perkins

Sheriff Frank L. Monteverde, left, served as chief deputy under two predecessors and later served as mayor of Memphis. Chief Deputy Ida O. Henry, right, was the first woman to serve as chief deputy. She organized civil procedures of the office and served the county for three decades.

demonstrated bravery in a dangerous incident during the Curve Riots.

A posse of sheriff's deputies went to the Curve, a notorious area, to raid a gambling place. Deputy Perkins along with deputies Charles Cole, Bob Harold and Avery Yerger went into the place and were standing at the bar. Gun fire erupted from behind a screen partition by several gunmen. Cole, Harold and Yerger were wounded. Perkins, assisted by other deputies, arrested eight of the shooters. Perkins joined the Memphis Police Department in 1898 and became chief detective before his death in the line of duty two years later.

Chief Deputy Monteverde continued at the post under Sheriff George W. Blackwell Sr. from 1898 to 1904 and was elected sheriff in 1904. Monteverde was the youngest individual ever elected sheriff in Shelby County. He was a renaissance man, a poet, an undertaker, a state legislator and the first Memphis-born mayor.

Although Sheriff Monteverde had a gentle personality and seldom wore a gun, he was a firm and fearless lawman and established a record of law and order. Monteverde was the last Shelby County sheriff to perform an execution, hanging three men at one time in the jailhouse yard.

Deputy Sheriff Thomas J. McDermott and Deputy Sheriff Houston Mitchell were killed in the line of duty on Monday, July 11, 1904. The two were members of a party that raided a gambling club and were killed by rifle fire. Over 40 suspects were arrested during the raid. Deputy McDermott was only 22 and

Shelby County lawmen captured a large, three-cooker moonshine still and brought it to the county jail in a 1921 Ford pickup. From left to right in the bed of the pickup were V. E. Brignardello and an unidentified trusty; and below were Sheriff W. S. Knight, G. P. Armour, S. A. Barbaro Sr. and A. B. Beaty.

been a deputy for one month. Deputy Mitchell was 46 and a five year veteran of the sheriff's office.

Sheriff Frank L. Monteverde's staff in 1910 included Chief Deputy Ida O. Henry, the first woman to fill that role in Shelby County. Ida Henry took charge of the civil procedure and brought order to the processing of papers for circuit, chancery and probate court. She served the county for a number of decades. Deputy sheriffs and court deputies included Victor C. Benner, W. F. Shelton, Samuel F. Bond, Joseph Farnbaker, L. A. M. Benner, Julius Rembrandt, Alvin Snowden, L. F. McConnell, L. C. Rutland, S. J. Rocco, W. C. Barrow and Major Kellar Anderson.

Sheriff T. Galen Tate took office in 1910. He was from Tate County Mississippi. His father, Captain Thomas Galen Tate, served with General Nathan Bedford Forrest during the Civil War. His grandfather

was one of the builders of the Memphis and Charleston Railroad. Sheriff Tate named his brother Michael G. "Mike" Tate as chief deputy. Following the single term of John R. Reichman, 1914-16, Mike Tate was elected sheriff and served until 1918.

Juvenile Court Detention Officer Charles F. Hooks was shot and killed on August 29, 1917, as he guarded youthful prisoners. Officer Hooks was in the mess hall overseeing the Wednesday evening meal. A 15-year-old prisoner drew a revolver and shot Hooks. The killer and seven other prisoners escaped.

Two deputies were killed in separate incidents as they tried to prevent escapes from the Shelby County Jail. Deputy Sheriff James C. Nelson was on duty the night of October 29, 1917, when he heard a disturbance. As he investigated, inmates told him that a prisoner had escaped. The fifteen year veteran deputy went to his office to retrieve his weapon. The escapee was in the office and shot Deputy Nelson with his own service revolver.

Jailer George Taylor Reeves, age 40, was shot and killed trying to stop three prisoners from escaping on November 30, 1920. The three convicts were killed in a shootout with officers in Mississippi.

The following month Shelby County lost 55-year-old Deputy Sheriff Phelan F. Appleberry to a line of duty shooting. On December 17, 1920, Deputy Appleberry took a horse drawn buggy to execute a warrant for the arrest of a man on the charge of disturbing the peace. The man was outside when Deputy Appleberry arrived and called out, "Come here, I've got a warrant for you." The man replied, "You ain't going to take me no where," raised a shotgun and fired. Deputy Appleberry was hit in the stomach. The shooter fled on foot. Phelan Appleberry died seven hours later.

A 32-year veteran of the Memphis Police Department, Chief Oliver Hazard Perry Sr., ran for sheriff and served three terms between 1918 and 1924. Sheriff Perry's two most significant appointments were Chief Deputy Charles B. "Charlie" Garibaldi and Miss Ida Henry, Chief Clerk of the Civil Department.

Garibaldi became desk sergeant with the Memphis police force in 1915 and served under Chief Perry. The *Commercial Appeal* described Garibaldi as a man "whose sparkling sense of humor and crackling repartee, had established him as one of Memphis' most colorful characters and popular citizens." He was an effective chief deputy and proficient crime solver. Garibaldi served as chief deputy for 19 years, under three sheriffs, leaving in 1936.

Ida Henry continued in charge of the Civil Department, maintaining order to the processing of papers for the courts. She was assisted by Miss Picket Mulcahy.

Sheriff Perry and Chief Deputy Garibaldi assigned each deputy to take a shift in the patrol car. The office had two squad cars to cover the entire county, one in the north county and one in the south. On Saturday nights an additional car was put into service. Part-time deputies throughout the county were used to serve papers, locate people and be available to assist full-time deputies. They were paid $50 per month.

Sheriffs following Perry were W. S. Knight, 1924-30; Colonel W. J. Bacon, 1930-36; and Guy E. Joyner, 1936-42. Emmett Armour served as jailer. The only place at the jail to interview a prisoner was in the jailer's bedroom. Sheriff Joyner purchased a camera and tripod in October 1939 and set it up on the fifth floor of the Criminal Courts Building for the purpose of "mugging" prisoners who did not pass through the police department's identification bureau. In addition to making mug-shots, the camera was used to photograph murders and major crime scenes. Homicide Squad Detectives Becker and Key served as photographers.

Guy Joyner was a member of the Chickasaw Guards and served on the Mexican border and during World War I. He appointed Oliver H. Perry Jr., son of the former sheriff, as chief deputy. Joyner spend a great deal of time in Nashville in liaison efforts with state legislators and officials.

Sheriff Joyner waged the "border wars" campaign against gambling in DeSoto County, Mississippi. A large, electrically lighted billboard was placed at the state line warning Shelby Countians against the "Gambling Dens & Dives." The sheriff assigned deputies to guard the sign, instructing them to "shoot the tires off any car" that tried to vandalize or destroy the sign.

Chief Deputy Oliver H. Perry Jr. was elected sheriff in 1942 and served until 1948. Hugh Bertchi was named chief deputy. Salaries were increased in 1943 to $170 per month for full-time deputies, $155 for court deputies and $225 for the chief deputy.

The sheriff's office had its hands full during the war years with the sailors and officers at Millington's

The Shelby County Sheriff's Office got its first traffic car in December 1958. (Memphis Commercial Appeal photo)

Shelby County Sheriff's Office K-9 Unit deputies in the 1970s.

was 31 and had been with the sheriff's office two years.

Deputy Sheriff Olney Benton Crawford was killed on March 24, 1946, when he was struck by a drunk driver. He and another deputy were investigating an accident when an intoxicated wrecker driver sped through the scene and struck 49-year-old Deputy Crawford.

Uniforms for deputies included light shirts with ties, zipper jackets for winter and soft-edge visor caps with a spread-winged, eagle-top medallion hat badge. The breast badge was a six-point, ball-tip star with an applied state seal in the center. Field deputies wore silver-tone stars, staff deputies and supervisors wore gold-tone insignia. No shoulder patch was worn.

The tradition of former Memphis policemen serving as sheriff of the county continued. James E. "Jimmy" Thompson, a six-year veteran of the MPD who served two years as an Army MP, was sheriff from 1948 to 1954. Following his time as sheriff, he briefly served as head of the TBI.

Edward Hull Reeves, former chief of the MPD, was sheriff 1954-58. His father George Taylor Reeves was killed in the line of duty in 1920 trying to stop a jail break and his mother served as a jail matron. Sheriff Reeves died while in office on May 7, 1958. Coroner Dr. J. R. Teabeaut served as acting sheriff until the election that year.

M. A. Hinds was elected sheriff in 1958. Hinds was the former chief of detectives for the Memphis force and served as sheriff until 1964. Chief Deputy John L. Carlisle assisted Sheriff Hinds.

Sheriff Hinds made uniform and insignia changes in the late fifties. Uniforms became light shirts with long ties, slacks and a brass buttoned jacket for winter and dress wear. A yellow and green shoulder patch was worn on shirts and jackets. The rigid-edged visor cap had an eagle-top wreathed circle in a teardrop form. The breast badge was a stock eagle-top wreathed circle with the state seal, gold-tone in color. Supervisors wore a different style insignia.

Radio equipment was upgraded in 1959 and 24-hour-a-day service began. A new tower was mounted atop the Sterick Building for a total height of 370 feet, giving county-wide coverage. Chief Dispatcher R. H. Morrison managed the radio system. Morrison became dispatcher with the sheriff's office after losing an arm while serving as a police motorcycle officer.

The first female deputies were hired in January 1960 for part-time traffic duty at county school intersections. The first five hired were Elizabeth D. Harris, Beverly D. Coleman, Mrs. Dickey M DeLoss,

Naval Air Tech Training Center and other military personnel. The force had 13 patrol cars when two-way radios were installed in 1943. They were set to the same frequency as the Tennessee Highway Patrol on WDBW. The dispatch room was located at the jail and a tower was mounted atop the water tower at the Colonial Country Club. Assistant jailers took turns handling the radio. Deputies on patrol no longer had to find a telephone to call headquarters after they received a call over the one-way radio system.

Two deputies were killed within a nine month period in the mid-forties. On June 26, 1945, Deputy Sheriff Edward W. Stelling and another deputy responded to a disturbance at a local business where a man was waving a shotgun. When Deputy Stelling arrived he was shot in the arm. The other deputy returned fire and killed the gunman. Deputy Stelling's arm was amputated, but he died four days later. He

Margarethe Hogue, and Doris E. Edwards. Two black deputies were also hired, Mrs. Armeter Johnson and Mrs. Murlese P. Tillman. The group wore green uniform jackets and skirts. They were supervised and trained by Chief Deputy Carlisle and Captain W. H. Hathcock.

The first black deputy sheriffs were added to the Shelby County force in February 1961. They were J. C. Benson, G. A. Whitney, William Hughes, and C. R. Venson. They were assigned to the predominately black sections of the county. Sheriff Hinds praised them for their work with the "still raiding squad."

William N. Morris served as sheriff from 1964 to 1970. He made Roy C. Nixon his chief deputy. Sheriff Morris initiated the Reserve force, the Junior Deputy program and created a sub-station.

Captain A. C. Gilless Jr., 34, took command of the Shelby County Sheriff's Office Homicide Department in March 1967. Gilless also remained head of the Bureau of Identification that he had commanded since 1964. Gilless joined the department August 10, 1959. He was promoted to sergeant in 1964 and to lieutenant in 1966.

Roy C. Nixon was elected sheriff in 1970. Gerald P. Proctor was appointed chief deputy, A. C. Gilless Jr. chief of the Civil Division, Dan L. Jones assistant chief of the Detective Division and H. L. Parker assistant chief of the jail. Twelve new cars were acquired with a new door design. The cars were the first four-door units with roll bars, prisoner screens and automatic transmissions.

A six-point star once again became the breast badge of the Shelby County Sheriffs Office. The new stars were gold tone with a full color state seal. The existing hat badge was retained. The stars were distributed at shift changes on Monday, July 6, 1970.

Sheriff Nixon served until his resignation at the end of 1975 to take the post of Shelby County mayor. Coroner James Rout Jr. briefly served as acting sheriff until Billy Ray Schilling was selected by the county court and took over as sheriff on February 2, 1976.

Gene Barksdale won the 1976 election for sheriff and served until 1986. Sheriff Jack R. Owens served from 1986 until May 1990. Ottis Higgs completed Owens' term.

The Shelby County Sheriff's Cobra Squad became a highly respected tactical team. They worked with the TBI and other agencies and gained praise for maintaining confidentiality so that pending raids were not compromised. Deputy Dave Wing commanded the unit.

A. C. Gilless was elected sheriff in 1990, becoming the first sheriff to have begun his law enforcement career as a member of the Shelby County Sheriff's

Office. Gillis joined the sheriff's office as a commissioned deputy in 1959, progressed through the ranks and was first named chief deputy in 1977.

Others with leadership roles in the early nineties included Chief Deputy A. Ray Mills, Chief Deputy Tom Marshall responsible for enforcement, Deputy Chief Don Wright responsible for operations, Assistant Chief Tom Lomax over Internal Affairs, Assistant Chief Lee Forbes over Staff Services, Assistant Chief Corbet Hart over the Narcotics Unit and Assistant Chief Neil Shea over the Training Academy

Specialized units expanded. The Narcotics Interstate Interdiction Unit was created in 1989. The Burglary, Robbery, and Auto Theft (BRAT) unit was established in 1989. The Automated Fingerprint Identification System (AFIS) was installed in 1990. The Detention Response Team was organized after the jail riot in 1991. The Crisis Intervention Team was started in 1992 to respond to incidents involving the mentally disturbed. The Violent Crime/Fugitive Task Force was formed in 1992. Research and Development was organized in 1993.

The Shelby County Sheriff's Office lost two officers in 1996. Deputy Jailer Sergeant Deadrick A. Taylor was shot and killed on Friday, April 19, 1996. The 9-year veteran of the force was ambushed as he returned home from work. Sergeant Taylor was shot several times with an AK-47 assault rifle and a handgun. The gang related attack was order by an inmate at the facility where Taylor worked.

Thirty-eight-year-old Patrolwoman Sherry Hopper Goodman was shot and killed after arresting a

Shelby County Deputy Sheriff Phelan F. Appleberry, left, died from a shotgun blast fired while he was serving a warrant for disturbing the peace on December 17, 1920. Shelby County Patrolwoman Sherry Hopper Goodman, right, was shot in the back of the head and killed as she transported a prisoner she had arrested on July 26, 1996.

Deputies of the Shelby County Sheriff's Patrol in the mid-seventies.

man on outstanding warrants. She apprehended the felon during a traffic stop in the early morning hours

Shelby County Patrolman Rupert Holliday Peete Jr., left, was killed on March 8, 2000, by a fireman who had murdered three others at the scene with a shotgun. Deputy Peete was shot before he could exit his cruiser. Shelby County Narcotics Unit Deputy Sheriff George Monroe Selby, right, was shot with a .357 caliber handgun when the unit served a warrant on December 4, 2002.

of Friday, July 26, 1996. She secured him in the back of her vehicle. Her backup unit was diverted to another call and she proceeded to transport the prisoner to jail. As she drove the prisoner pulled a pistol and shot Officer Goodman in the back of the head.

Patrolman Rupert Holliday Peete Jr. was killed on Wednesday, March 8, 2000, while responding to a shots-fired call. Firefighters had responded to a house fire and as two firemen approached the dwelling a man stepped out of the garage, fired a shotgun, and murdered them both. When Deputy Peete arrived on the scene he was shot before he left his cruiser. A fourth victim was found dead in the garage.

Sheriff Mark H. Luttrell, a Jackson, Tennessee, native, took officer in 2002. Following his army service from 1970 to 1972 Luttrell became public information officer/vocational training director at the Shelby County Penal Farm and held the position until 1977. Between 1979 and 1999 Luttrell was an executive at the U.S. Penitentiary in Leavenworth, Kansas, and warden at three other federal prisons. He then returned to West Tennessee as Director of the Shelby County Division of Corrections. Key members of

Sheriff Luttrell's staff were Chief Deputy William Oldham, Chief Administrative Officer Harvey Kennedy and Jail Director James Coleman.

The Narcotics Unit went to serve a warrant at a Frayser home around 10:00 p.m. on Wednesday, December 4, 2002. Deputy Sheriff George Monroe Selby, age 32, was a member of the unit. Deputies knocked on the door and identified themselves but no one responded. Suddenly shots erupted, fired from a .357 caliber handgun. Deputy Selby was struck in the shoulder in an area not protected by his vest. He was transported to Regional Medical Center where he succumbed to his wounds.

Forty-year-old Deputy Timothy Howard Dunn died on October 29, 2004, en route to speak at Bartlett High School on the dangers of criminal gangs. He collided with a pickup truck on Highway 70 at about 6:00 a.m. and was killed instantly.

Duty and sacrifice is a mark of the character of today's Shelby County Sheriff's Office. The strength of the force today is 1605 sworn or certified officers, 519 full-time and 13 part-time deputies, 1030 correction deputies, 22 process servers and 21 facility deputies, plus support staff. The force performs the full range of law enforcement duties and is one of the most professional and modern agencies of its type in Tennessee and the nation.

Madison County was established in December 1821 and named for President James Madison. It was among the first counties created in West Tennessee following the acquisition of the territory west of the Tennessee River from the Chickasaw by Andrew Jackson, the land that became known as the Jackson Purchase. Thomas Jefferson Shannon, age 35, was appointed the first sheriff of Madison County.

The Shannon family migrated from Williamson County and had a great deal of land and business interests. The land on the Forked Deer River south of the Town of Jackson, the newly laid out county seat, was known as Shannon's Landing. A major portion of the land for the town came from Thomas Shannon. Thomas had a tavern attached to his house on land just outside the initial town limits and next to the market house lot. Thomas' brother Samuel also resided in the county and his younger brother John David Shannon was the first town constable of Jackson.

One of the most important duties Sheriff Thomas Shannon performed was enforcing the collection of taxes. The continued existence of the new county depended on the flow of taxes to provide services to the growing population. Lists of unpaid taxes were published in the newspaper by order of the sheriff. Many land owners at the time resided outside of the county, in eastern Tennessee counties, North Carolina or other states. When taxes could not be collected, the property was sold at public auction to cover the tax obligation to the county. The sheriff conducted the auction process.

The initial counties of West Tennessee were established between 1819 and 1824. A number of the counties had too few residents to form a court and elect officials. Thomas Shannon, sheriff of Madison County, collected taxes in the counties of Haywood, Dyer and Hardeman until they formed county governments.

Law officers faced dangers from adventurous frontiersmen who were a rough and ready bunch as compared to most settlers, who were simply looking for a better life for themselves and their family. The most dangerous weapon of the day was the large knives carried by frontiersmen for defense. A number of stabbing cases and killings were tried in court during the early years of Madison County. The use of knives in brawls and confrontations was so deadly that the 1838 General Assembly of Tennessee banned the sale or use of "Bowie Knives and Arkansas Tooth Picks."

Sheriff Thomas Shannon carried out the judgment of the court as did other sheriffs. For the crime of "Horse Stealing" in 1824, the felon was taken to the public whipping post and given thirty-nine lashes, branded on the thumb with "HT," sent to jail for 30 days, made to stand in the pillory two hours for several days, "rendered infamous" and made to pay the cost of his prosecution. William Braden, Daniel Mading, Thomas J. Smith, and A. T. Gray served as deputies to Shannon at various times during this tenure as sheriff.

Sheriffs who followed Shannon were Mark Christian 1826-1830, Daniel Mading 1830-1831, Mathias Deberry 1831-1835, James Lyon 1835-1838, James McDonald 1838-1840, G. H. Kyle 1840-1846, J. S. Stewart 1846-1848 and J. R. Jelks 1848-1854. Deputy sheriffs who serve during the period of 1830 through 1844 included Lewis Carpenter, Elijah Haynes, Wyatt Epps, L. Coor Pender, Gale S. Kyle, Archibald M. Young, Fleming Welles, Joseph C. Stewart, Isaac C. A. Skillern and Charles D. Taylor.

Sheriff Jelks was instructed by the court to execute a murder in June 1849. The public nature of the event was reported in the local newspaper.

At 12 o'clock precisely, the prisoner was brought from the jail, amid a concourse of people surrounding the yard never before witnessed in the town of Jackson. As early as eight o'clock in the morning immense crowds were seen collecting around the prison and by the time the sheriff of the county was ready with his guard, it was with difficulty that any one could pass through the immense mass of living beings that blocked up the main street that led to the prison.

Sheriffs who served prior to the Civil War were J. J. Brooks 1854-1860 and J. R. Woolfolk 1860-1865. Sheriff Woolfolk served few of his normal duties after the war began.

George G. Perkins became Madison County sheriff in 1865 and served during a particularly tumultuous period in the history of the state and county. The sheriff's duty to oversee elections in the county was difficult following the war. Only those who signed a pledge of loyalty to the Union were allowed to vote and election days were filled with conflict and violence. Large groups of special police were sworn in to protect the ballot box in the city of Jackson. Still, in 1867, elections were postponed when Sheriff Perkins reported that he "was unable to procure competent and qualified persons to act as Officers of said election."

Sheriff R. M. May served from 1870 to 1876. The duty of an execution came in his final year in office. The hanging took place about a half mile from the courthouse and jail at the "hanging grounds" located at the end of South Liberty Street just outside the Jackson city limits on the banks of the Forked Deer River. The newspaper account of the 1876 execution gave details about the religious service.

When McLean's arms were being tied he laughed at the awkwardness and feeling displayed by Sheriff May. At 10 minutes to 12 o'clock, Dr. Slater, of the First Methodist church, and the Rev. E. McNair, of the Presbyterian church, entered the jail. At 12 o'clock precisely, the procession moved to the fatal grounds, guarded by the entire police force of the city, commanded by Mayor King. An immense crowd had gathered in front of the jail, and followed the funeral cortege to the gallows.

McLean walked out of the jail, mounted the wagon prepared for the occasion and seated himself upon his coffin. By his side sat upon the one hand Dr. Slater and upon the other the Rev. E. McNair. The sheriff upon a gray horse took position upon the left and the guard formed a circle

in which none were admitted except reporters. During the journey from the jail to the gallows, Dr. Slater engaged the doomed man in religious conversation.

The religious services of the occasion were very impressive. At twenty minutes past 12 o'clock the Rev. E. McNair read the ten commandments, facing the criminal. Dr. Slater then came forward and gave out that old and beautiful hymn, "There is a fountain filled with blood, Drawn from Emanuel's veins," which was sung by the crowd. The Rev. E. McNair then prayed a most fervent prayer. Dr. Slater then read the tenth chapter of Romans and prayed a most touching and eloquent prayer.

The sheriff read the legal sentence of the courts. Then the ministers of God bade a sad farewell to the criminal. They asked if he desired to say anything, and his reply was, "Nothing." With a feeling "God bless you," they retired.

At one o'clock the rope was tied about his neck. A black veil was then thrown over his face, and in an instant more the fatal drop fell. In the fall the knot of the rope turned from his left ear to the back of his head, and hence his neck was not broken, and he died the painful and lingering death of strangulation.

Dr. Collins, of the city, and Dr. Lanier, of Spring Creek, felt his pulse at ten minutes past one, and found it beating thirty to the minute. At fifteen minutes past one o'clock his pulse was still feebly beating. At twenty-five minutes past one all indications of life had ceases. He was cut down at thirty minutes past one o'clock, and his remains placed in a walnut coffin and turned over to his wife and friends.

Shortly before George G. Perkins returned to office as sheriff in 1876 his younger brother, Jackson Policeman Newton C. Perkins, was killed in the line of duty. Sheriff Perkins relinquished his duties as sheriff during the trial of his brother's killer in order to prosecute the case.

After the sentence of death was given by the court, Sheriff Perkins reassumed his duties to oversee the execution. One year to the day from the killing of Officer Perkins, his murderer suffered a painful death by strangulation on the gallows.

A large moonshine operation in or near Jackson. Chief Tip Taylor stands on the far left in the dark suit. (Photo courtesy of Andrew Thompson Taylor Jr.)

At 15 minutes to 12 o'clock, after a last opportunity to speak, the black cap was drawn over his head and face. At precisely 14 minutes to 12 o'clock, the proper was cut. The fall did not break the condemned man's neck. With agonizing energy he clutched the side of the scaffold, supporting himself by his hands and clinging to it. He died the terrible death of strangulation. Three times he drew up his legs and swayed his body. Thirteen minutes to twelve, his extraordinary muscle struggles ceased. There was a quiver of the pulse thirteen minutes after 12. At half-past 12 o'clock Dr. Arnold pronounced the condemned dead and his body was cut down and placed in a coffin.

Sheriff Perkins lost one of his deputies on March 3, 1877. Madison County Deputy Sheriff Jason W. Fussell was killed while attempting to make an arrest. Captain Fussell had served with distinction as a member of Jackson's 6th Tennessee Regiment Volunteers during the Civil War. Deputy Fussell and a posse including Deputy W. T. Anderson rode to the home of a family of armed ruffians in northeast Madison County not far from the Carroll and Henderson coun-

ty lines. Fussell and Madison County Deputy Jolly Rogers had arrested two of the clan the previous fall for carrying concealed weapons.

The posse confronted the father and three sons and the four began firing pistols at the lawmen. Deputy Jason Fussell was shot and killed in the exchange. Deputy Anderson killed one of the gang and the rest fled.

The following month, a posse led by Deputy Sheriff Garret Edwards and including W. T. Anderson, Harry Bowen, William Bowen, James Bowan, William Edwards, William Stewart, Taylor Macon and C. C. Cock captured one of the two desperados that remained at large in the cellar of a neighbor's house. Deputy Fussell's killer was captured the following morning by two citizens armed with a pistol and an empty shotgun.

During the last years of the nineteenth century Madison county was served by sheriffs W. F. Blackard 1878-1884, B. A. Person 1884-1890, B. F. Young 1890-1893, E. A. Brooks 1893-1899 and W. M. May 1899-1901.

R. C. Mayo was elected sheriff in 1901. Deputy Sheriff Doss Bond was a well respected fearless lawman under Sheriff Mayo. He confronted and arrested a

Chief Deputy Sheriff Edgar Lee "Edd" Stansell, left, served as Madison County Sheriff's Office chief deputy in the 1930s. Chief Deputy Fred Cunningham, right, served in the post in the late 1950s.

gunman who shot Jackson Chief of Police Tom Gaston and was active in enforcing the laws of the county during the first decade of the twentieth century.

Sheriff Mayo was assisted at the county jail at Liberty and Chester by Jailer Alex Stegall. Stegall later served as Jackson's chief of police. The jail was heavily populated in 1903, including a number of murderers. Sheriff Mayo hired a young man, Henry Douglas, to serve as night jail guard so he and jailer Stegall could get some rest. The duties of the night guard was to patrol all parts of the jail every thirty minutes. The new hire created some excitement in town on his first night of duty.

Before the sheriff could inform another young man who was rooming with the sheriff about the new night guard, he spotted night guard Douglas on the porch of the jail with a gun in his hand. The young man assumed Douglas was an armed jailbreaker.

The young man ran to Jackson Police Headquarters on Church. Guard Douglas heard the commotion of the running man and began a search outside the jail. As he returned to the Chester Street door, he saw three men running at him down Liberty Street. Jackson Policemen Ben Warlick, Tom Garrison and the young man staying at the jail were about to tackle the new guard when Patrolman Garrison recognized Douglas. Serious confrontation was avoided.

One of the murders in jail was a man convicted of killing his wife. Sheriff Mayo carried out the judgment of the court in July 1904 and hanged the killer. It was the last execution carried out in Madison County and was not a public hanging. The execution was done in an enclosure

built in the yard of the jail that was large enough to contain the gallows and a small group of witnesses.

Following tenures as sheriff by W. G. Person 1908-1914 and J. G. Perry 1914-1920, Robert A. Mainord was elected sheriff in 1920. Sheriff Mainord's son later served for many years a Chief of Police in Jackson and Chief Deputy of Madison County. A second son also served as a Madison County deputy. In the summer before Sheriff Mainord left office, a large illegal liquor operation was reported near the Haywood County line.

Madison County Deputy Sheriff W. L. Styers was mortally wounded late Friday night, July 9, 1926, while raiding the moonshine still on the Madison-Haywood line. In a fateful coincidence a group of Haywood County lawmen mounted a raid on the same still that night. Unaware of the presence of the other, gunfire broke out as the two groups of lawmen approached the still. Four officers were wounded. Haywood County Deputy Ike Curlin was shot in the hip and ankle but recovered. Deputy Styers, 39, was shot in the abdomen and died of his wounds on July 12 at 7:00 p.m.

Fred L. Exum won the 1926 election as sheriff and served until 1932. Sheriff Exum lost a deputy in the line of duty, and the loss was very personal. Madison County Deputy Sheriff Cliff C. Exum, the sheriff's brother, went to the Five Points Filling Station in Jackson on Thursday, May 10, 1928, to serve a capias changing a 24-year-old with carrying a pistol. Rather than submitting to arrest the man pulled a gun and murdered Deputy Exum. Cliff Exum was 38 years old.

Sheriff Tom Patton served his first term from 1932 to 1934. Sheriff A. S. Steadman served from

The 1942 Earnings Schedule for Madison County Deputy Edd Stansell illustrates how deputies of the early twentieth century earned a living.

Receipts	
Fees from General Sessions Court	$ 737.57
Fees from Circuit Court Clerk	306.12
Fees from Chancery Court	22.95
Graranteed salary from Sheriff	94.60
Salary from GM&O R.R.	103.00
Night patrol service	660.00
Total earned	$1,924.24

Expenses incurred		
Gasoline & oil	$210.00	
Repairs on car	211.00	
Depreciation on 1940 car, 20%	203.20	
Total Expenses		$ 628.20
Net salary and other compensation		$1,296.04

Madison County Sheriff's Office raiders, left to right, Sheriff Cecil Burlison, Chief Deputy Alfred Evans, Deputies Fred Cunningham, V. T. Dodd, Guy Thomas, Fleetwood Pratt, L. H. Crowe, and Billy Lewis. Cecil Burlison Jr. at far right. Part of the contraband from the raid was on the desk. (Jackson Sun photo)

1934 to 1936 and Tom Patton was again elected in 1936.

Madison County Fifth District Constable John L. Dalton was killed trying to break up a fight at the corner of Sycamore and Shannon streets in Jackson short-ly before midnight on Saturday, January 30, 1937. Two of the three combatants turned on Constable Dalton and brutally beat him, hitting him over the head with "some heavy weapon." He died a week later without regaining consciousness.

Madison County Sheriff's Office under Sheriff Lowell Thomas. Standing in the front row from left to right were Sheriff Thomas, Deputies James Richardson, A. C. Pollard, Sergeant E. E. "Fats" Haney, Fleetwood Pratt, and Chief Deputy Robert A. Mainord Jr. In the second row were Deputies L. H. Crowe, Sergeant Arthur "Barney" Mainord, and Marvin Wood.

Madison County Sheriff's Department about 1975. In the front row from left to right were Sid Perkins, Mrs. Sid "Dot" Piercey, Carolyn Williams, Nancy Miller, Mrs. Irby Thomas, and Sheriff James "Shug" Lewis. In the second row were Irby Thomas, Lee Stroud, Tommy Cunningham, Danny J. Phillips, Sergeant James H. Richardson, and Deputy Gullett. In the third row were C. E. "Buddy" Scruggs, Captain Bob Randall, Wayne Murley, Bobby Hudson, Richard Roe, Sergeant Marvin Woods, and Dan Marshall. In the back row were Brent Love, Chief Deputy James Eddlemon, Ed Dabney, Allen Chalker, Jack Hill, Larry Wright, Lieutenant Harold Smith, Paul Latham, and Joe Burton Williams.

Deputy Sheriff Edgar Lee "Edd" Stansell was one of most respected officers of the Madison County Sheriff's Office from the 1932 to 1942. He wasn't a large man, but he was stocky and had strong arms and hands from manual labor in his youth. Edd Stansell's great-grandfather, John T. Stansell, a pioneer who moved from Cocke County to West Tennessee, served as one of the first constables in Chester County after its created in 1879.

Prior to his years with the sheriff's office Edd Stansell served as town marshal of Bemis for two years. Bemis was a model town built for workers at the Bemis Cotton Mills, the largest industry in West Tennessee at the time.

Tom Patton owned the grocery store across from the mills when he ran for sheriff. Town Marshal Stansell supported Patton's campaign and became Sheriff Patton's chief deputy. Chief Deputy Edd Stansell quickly established his reputation as a firm but fair lawman, who always came back with the criminal he went after.

A part of his duty was to check "the strip" along Sycamore Street that included poolrooms, cafes and night-clubs. On a typical night Stansell and Deputy Armstrong knocked at an establishment, the doorman opened the door and told the patrons, "Everybody get up against the wall. Mr. Edd's here." The officers then checked the group for wanted men and illegal activity. Stansell kept track of what was going on in the county.

Chief Deputy Stansell also worked for merchants in downtown Jackson checking businesses at night. Seven days a week around 8:00 or 9:00 at night he walked the area checking doors to be certain they weren't open. He put a piece of masking tape on the door, so that the second and third trips around he could check it from the car.

Sheriff Ewing Griffin served from 1940 to 1944. Edd Stansell took a position as Special Agent for the Gulf, Mobile and Ohio Railroad in 1942, but retained credentials as a special deputy sheriff. He patrolled the IC, the GM&O and the NC&StL yards in Jackson in addition to looking after the private railroad car of GM&O President Isaac B. Tigrett who lived in Jackson. Stansell worked with the FBI and Secret Service and often transported prisoners from state to state for them.

Another noted officer of the period was Madison County Deputy Barney Lawson Cunningham. He served as a deputy under Sheriff Griffin and continued as a deputy sheriff under Sheriff Tom Lewis. B. L. Cunningham fostered a lineage of Madison County lawmen that extended for four generations.

Tom L. Lewis, a well-known farmer and magistrate, was elected sheriff in 1944 and served until 1948. Thomas

Deputy Dan Parr in March 1978 driving one of the first Madison County Sheriff's Office patrol car's with the green stripe down the side. The cars were purchased from a federal grant. Paar is across from Melesus School.

Acuff joined the force in 1945 and was joined by 21-year-old Frederick G. "Fred" Cunningham on August 1, 1947. They were the only two salaried deputies. B. L. Cunningham, Fred Cunningham's father, John Holloway, Curtis Duke at Beach Bluff and others worked on the weekend, the busiest time for the officers. Thomas Acuff joined the Jackson Police Department at the end of Sheriff Lewis' term.

After serving as a deputy for Sheriff Tom Lewis, B. L. Cunningham won office as constable in the Medon area of Madison County, serving in the position until his death in 1956. Constables worked closely with the sheriff's office, patrolling and performing other duties side by side with deputies. Tennessee Highway Patrolmen often rode patrol with sheriff's officers as well.

The sheriff had to buy everything necessary to run the office including cars, beds and mattresses for the jail and food as well as pots and pans to cook it in. He paid deputies a fee of $2 for each arrest and he got court costs and fines. After paying expenses, the sheriff didn't always make his own salary, which was $5,000 a year.

Beer joints and dance halls were scattered over the county and deputies Acuff and Cunningham worked them two or three times a night. When they brought a prisoner to jail and stayed at the office a couple of minutes chatting, Sheriff Tom Lewis sat back in his chair and said, "Well, you get out of here. If anything comes up in here, I'll take care of it." He didn't want the deputies sitting in the office, because revenue for the sheriff's office was dependent on the number of arrests made.

Sheriff Emery O. "Slim" Bruce began his first term in 1948 and served the maximum three terms or six years. Bruce was president of the Tennessee Sheriffs Association. Army Master Sergeant and war hero Fred Cunningham returned to his deputy duties in 1952. Cunningham was awarded the Bronze Star for his action in knocking out a North Korean machine gun position while he was under heavy fire.

Sheriff Cecil Burlison was elected and took office on September 1, 1954. He ordered the first uniforms worn by the Madison County Sheriff's Office. They were acquired from Beshires Department Store on Highland Street and arrived in December. The waist-length or Ike jackets were greenish-tan and worn with light tan trousers. Campaign hats were greenish-gray with no insignia. Stripes at the end of the jacket sleeves denoted the rank of the four full-time members of the force.

Sheriff Burlison's jacket sleeves had three stripes, Chief Deputy Alfred Evans' two stripes, Deputy Fred Cunningham's one stripe, and Guy Thomas' no stripe. The sheriff also provided the first badges issued by the

Madison County Sheriff Warren Roberts and Deputy Dan Parr test the new connection to the National Crime Information Computer (NCIC) in December 1984.

office. They were eagle-top circles. A large round shoulder patch was later added to the jacket.

Constable Marvin Woods worked part-time as a jailer and thwarted an escape one evening when he noted suspicious activity on the part of some inmates.

Madison County Deputy Sheriff Al Parrish worked the radio console as dispatcher in January 1987.

489

construct a jail acceptable to the sheriff. Specifications for the jail was a building "sixteen feet square; the logs to be one foot square, the lower floor to be laid of logs of that size, to be laid double and crosswise; the loft to be laid also with logs, and covered crosswise with oak plank, one and a half inches thick and well spiked down."

Settlers lived in forts and stationed a guard when they went out to farm the fields. The precautions were warranted. The Holston Treaty, a peace treaty with the Cherokee, did not hold and hostilities erupted. Sheriff Houston helped defend the town during the Indian attack on Cavet Station in September 1793.

Following his tenure as sheriff Robert Houston served in many other public posts including tax assessor, justice of the peace, county trustee, secretary of state, state senator and U.S. paymaster for federal troops stationed in East Tennessee. He also served as U.S. government surveyor for the treaty of 1819 with the Cherokee nation.

Sheriff John Love originally of Philadelphia served from 1802 to 1803, during which time a jail tax was levied so that a new jail could be built. Joseph Love served as sheriff from 1803 to 1814. He resigned before the end of his term and Coroner Thomas Brown was appointed to complete it. Sheriff John Callaway, an early settler at Ball Camp, held office from 1814 to 1826 and built a new jail on Walnut Street.

Sheriff George M. White, grandson of one of Knoxville's first commissioners and member of the first Knox County Court, served from 1826 to 1834 and later served as mayor of Knoxville. White was followed by Sheriff William Dunlap 1834-1838 and Sheriff Samuel McCammon 1838-1850. Sheriff William Craig, 1850-1856, oversaw completion of the fourth Knox County Jail, built at a cost of $10,000.

William Crippen served as sheriff 1856-1862 while civil war approached. He stood with the Confederacy and became a revenue collector after his term as sheriff. Sheriff William H. Swan, an attorney, served from 1862 to 1864.

Post-Civil War Governor William Gannaway Brownlow was a minister and newspaper publisher from Knox County and the state imposed less outside policing on the county than on most other portions of the state. The post-war transition was certainly difficult throughout the South, but in many ways it was less traumatic for Knox Countians.

Sheriff Marcus Bearden served from 1864 to 1870. Bearden was a veteran of the Union Army, having served as Captain of Company D of the 6th Tennessee

Infantry. He later served as Knoxville mayor and member of the Tennessee House of Representatives. Sheriffs that followed were V.F. Gossett 1870-1874, M.D. Swan 1874-1876, Alexander Reeder 1876-1880, C.B. Gossett 1880-1882 and Civil War veteran Homer Gilmore 1882-1886.

Sheriff Jacob Kimberlin Lones, 1886-1890, had served as a Captain in Company C, 1st Tennessee Cavalry Union Army during the Civil War and fought at the Battle of Mossy Creek in Jefferson County. Near the end of Lones' first term one of his deputies was shot and killed.

Two Knox County deputies went to a railroad camp to serve an arrest warrant on May 21, 1888. Deputy Sheriff D. A. Shipe, age 35, and another deputy found the robbery suspect lying in bed when they reached the railroad construction site. The bandit asked Deputy Shipe to read the warrant. As Deputy Shipe read the warrant, the robber pulled out a pistol, leaped at the deputies and shot Deputy Shipe. Shipe was hit in the chest and fell dead. The other deputy drew his gun, but it misfired and the shooter escaped.

The killer was captured and brought to the jail while Sheriff Lones was still out searching for him. As other sheriffs, Lones and his family lived at the jail. When a mob came to break the killer out and lynch him, the sheriff's wife was alone at the jail. She stood in their way and kept the prisoner safe until Sheriff Lones came home. The sheriff was reelected to a second term because "his wife made a mighty fine Sheriff."

Sheriff Tom Holloway served from 1890 to 1892. Matt Swann was elected sheriff and James W. Fox served as his deputy for terms in the years 1892-1894

Knox County Investigator James Kenneth Kennedy, left, was fatally wounded on March 27, 1984, while serving a warrant at a Knoxville hotel. Knox County Patrol Officer Angela K. Payne, right, responded to a 911 call on February 26, 2000, and was struck and killed by a vehicle.

and 1898-1904. Sheriff Jesse Groner served from 1894 to 1898.

Sheriff Harmon Kreis, 1904-1906, was born in Wartburg, Tennessee and served in the 9th Tennessee Cavalry Regiment of the Union Army during the Civil War. Sheriff Kreis cracked down on gambling while he was sheriff and appointed former Sheriff Jesse Groner as chief deputy. Chief Deputy Groner organized and commanded the famous "flying squadron," an armed group that demanded honest elections. Both Kreis and Groner later served in the state legislature.

C. A. "Lum" Reeder started his law enforcement career at the age of 21 as a Knox County Jailer and served as sheriff between 1906 and 1910. Reeder was the son of former Sheriff Alexander Reeder and had served as a deputy as well as Knoxville patrolman, detective and chief of police.

Deputy Sheriff William Walker, 38, was shot and killed on July 14, 1906, as he investigated the robbery of a well known physician. The incident began when a threesome broke into a private party. The hostess was struck on the head and her husband shot and killed by one of the three. A short time later the three robbed the doctor of his horse and buggy.

The doctor went to the Deputy Walker's home and they proceeded in search of the bandits, unaware of the preceding murder. When they found the trio, Deputy Walker told them they were under arrest. The killer opened fire on Deputy Walker, shooting him in the spine. Walker was taken to Lincoln Memorial Hospital where he died one week later.

Sheriff George Bolt, 1910-1914, was followed by deputy U.S. marshal John Blankenship. Sheriff Blankenship served from 1914 to 1916 and was known as "The Raiding Sheriff" because of his ongoing battle against bootleg whiskey and gambling. John Callaway was sheriff for the term 1916-1918.

Sheriff William T. Cate, 1918-1922, also a former deputy U.S. marshal, faced racial rioting in 1919 following a murder and the arrest of Maurice Mayes. When a lynch mob formed Sheriff Cate took the prisoner to Chattanooga. When the sheriff returned the next morning, he found the jail including his living quarters in a shambles. The mob had vandalized and robbed the facility. Rioters stole weapons and gun battles broke out between black and white citizens in Knoxville. National Guard forces were required to restore order.

Joseph W. Saylor, a railroad man, was elected sheriff for the 1922-1924 term. Sheriff Walter C. Anderson served during 1924-1928 and 1929-1930. He began a campaign to clean up the Copper Ridge

district north of Knoxville after Deputy U.S. Marshal Hughett was shot and killed by a notorious moonshiner. Sheriff Anderson was one of the organizers of the Tennessee and Mississippi Peace Officers Association and later served as Knoxville safety director. Sheriff Chester R. Hackney served two terms between 1928 and 1932. He later held the post of chief deputy U.S. marshal for 20 years and worked as a bailiff under Sheriff Paul Lilly.

Sheriff Wesley Brewer, 1932-1936, served while the Roger Toughy Gang was headquartered in the Knox county. He was followed by Sheriff J. Carroll Cate, 1936-1940, who also served in many other roles including chief jailer, workhouse superintendent and federal prohibition agent for East Tennessee.

Sheriff Hazen Kreis, 1940-1946, was a large man, 6' 5" tall and 365 pounds, with an extensive law enforcement background. He began as deputy and turnkey before serving as a Knoxville policeman. Kreis was one of the first officers to use a loudspeaker car to scold jaywalkers and other traffic violators. He served two years as Sheriff Cate's chief deputy and then three consecutive terms as sheriff, the maximum allowed by law.

R. Austin Cate, first cousin and first chief deputy of Sheriff Carroll Cate, served as sheriff 1946-1950 and 1952-1956. He implemented the two-way radio system. Sheriff Clarence Walter "Buddy" Jones, 1950-1952, a World War II Army Air Corps officer and gunnery instructor, had been warden at Brushy Mountain State Prison. Sheriff Jones once made the comment that he would not sleep until a murder suspect was in custody and earned the nickname "Sleepless Jones."

Former Tennessee Highway Patrolman and workhouse superintendent Paul H. Lilly served as sheriff for the 1956-1958 term. He was followed by Sheriff E. B. Bowles, 1958-1960. Sheriff Herman Wayland, 1960-1962, had almost 25 years of law enforcement experience. He joined the Knoxville police force in 1937, was a Navy shore patrolman during World War II and retired as a Knoxville detective in 1956.

During the term of Sheriff Carl Ford, 1962-1964, 17 moonshine stills were destroyed, 9 murders solved, 356 persons charged with assault and battery, 51 with felonious assault, 127 with illegal possession of whiskey, 96 with grand larceny, 42 with gambling and possession of gambling devices, 50 with embezzlement, 13 with rape, 15 with robbery and 28 with receiving and concealing stolen property. Stolen property valued at $22,090.33 was recovered and returned. He was followed by Sheriff Archie Weaver, 1964-1968.

Bernard L. Waggoner Sr. served as a deputy and

policeman before three terms as sheriff, 1968-1974. Sheriff Waggoner made progress in modernizing the department. When he was elected, deputies were still working seven days a week, twelve hours per day and had no paid vacation or sick leave. They could be fired at will by the sheriff. Waggoner established the Knox County Sheriff's Department Merit Council and reduced work hours to 40 hours per week. He secured significant pay raises, paid vacation and sick leave, insurance and a clothing allowance. Deputies trained for the first time at the Tennessee Law Enforcement Academy. Sheriff Ross Sims Sr., 1974-1976, brought experience as a Knoxville policeman, assistant chief of detectives, acting assistant police chief, and chief deputy sheriff.

The Knox County Sheriff's Department developed significantly during the tenure of Sheriff Joe Jenkins, 1976-1982. When he took office the department had nine cruisers and 35 employees. By 1981 the department had 150 cruisers and 300 employees. Sheriff Jenkins formed the Burglary and Auto Theft investigative divisions, Narcotics Division, Traffic Enforcement Division and programs in child abuse, crime prevention and safety education.

Sheriff Joe C. Fowler, 1982-1990, had a 28-year career with the Knoxville Police Department that began in 1950. He worked up through the ranks from patrolman and served as chief of police from 1970 to 78. Fowler was appointed United States Marshal for the Eastern District of Tennessee in 1994.

Knox County a Investigator James Kenneth Kennedy and another detective went to serve a warrant at a Knoxville hotel on Tuesday, March 27, 1984. Investigator Kennedy knocked on the door and the felon fired from inside the room, fatally wounding the investigator. Investigator Kennedy's murderer was shot and killed by other officers.

Sheriff Tim Hutchison took office in 1990. The long time member of the sheriff's office implemented the D.A.R.E. program in 1992 and formed the Family Crisis Unit in 1993. Sheriff Hutchinson established the Knox County Sheriff's Office Regional Training Academy and the Aviation Unit in 1996. The School Police Unit was developed in 1999.

In recent years Knox County has lost three officers in automobile accidents. Forty-eight-year-old Lieutenant Steve Keith McCulley, a 21-year veteran of the force, was killed when his cruiser was struck by an empty coal train at a double railroad track crossing as he was on his way to work on Tuesday, February 16, 1999.

On Saturday, February 26, 2000, Patrol Officer Angela K. Payne responded to a 911 call. The two lane roadway had no shoulders and the officers parked in the north-bound lane. They were standing in the southbound lane when another vehicle struck them from behind. Officer Payne, age 31 with three years on the force, was pronounced dead at the hospital and the other officer was seriously injured. Knox County Assistant Chief Deputy Keith Lyon was killed on May 9, 2006, when a vehicle crossed the center line and struck his unit head-on.

Today the Knox County Sheriff's Office is one of the major law enforcement agencies in the state and Sheriff Hutchison is the longest serving sheriff in Knox County history. Citizens of the county are served by 475 certified law enforcement officers, 450 correctional officers and 75 civilian support personnel.

Hamilton County, named for Alexander Hamilton, George Washington's secretary of the treasury, was formed on October 25, 1819 from parts of Rhea County and Indian lands. Hamilton County had 821 settlers in 1820 plus about 100 Cherokees. Charles Gamble was the first sheriff and served from 1819 to 1822. He was followed by Sheriff Terrill Riddle, 1822-1824.

The precise date served by some early sheriffs have been lost. The records shows the following served, Matthew Anderson, John Johnson, James Reddy, Alfred Rogers 1838-42, James Francis 1842-44 and further, James C. Connor 1848-56 and further, William Snow 1858-62, R. G. Campbell 1862-64, Milo Coulter, George W. Rider 1864-66, Asberry B. Connor 1866-68, R. G. Campbell 1868-70, Asberry B. Connor 1870-72, William H. Bean 1872-74, Charles B. Champion 1874-78 and H. J. Springfield 1878-82.

The Hamilton County Sheriff's Office lost two officers in a single incident on Thursday, September 14, 1882. Sheriff William T. Cates was newly elected. He and Deputy Sheriff John Conway boarded a northbound train with three convicted murders being transported to prison. The train stopped in Sweet Water, Tennessee, and three men boarded. One, the brother of one of the prisoners, walked up behind Deputy Conway, drew a pistol and killed the lawman. The gunman took the keys from the deputy and released his brother and the other two prisoners. Sheriff Cates rushed the men. He was shot several times and killed.

The three gunmen and the released brother went to the engine car forced the motorman to start the train. After passing through three towns without stopping, the four jumped from the engine and fled on horseback. In Knoxville, the other two prisoners surrendered to officers.

Hamilton County sheriffs in the late nineteenth and early twentieth century were H. J. Springfield 1882-84, S. C. Pyott 1884-86, John Emory Conner 1886-88, Azariah Shelton 1888-90, John R. Skillern 1890-94, Scott F. Hyde 1894-96, Samuel S. Bush 1896-1902, W. P. Hays 1902-04, J. F. Shipp 1904-08, Sam A. Conner 1908-14, Nick P. Bush 1914-18, Robert P. Bass 1918-20, Nick P. Bush 1920-22, Horace G. Humphreys 1922-24, Tom O. Selman 1924-28 and Charley C. Taylor 1928-32.

Deputy Sheriff John A. Snyder was a seven-year veteran of the sheriff's office and 35 years old. On Sunday, May 13, 1923, he responded to a disturbance where shots had been fired. His handcuffed body was later found with two gunshot wounds.

The department lost another officer in the line of duty on December 22, 1923. Deputy Sheriff William B. Gober, age 37, was shot twice while attempting to arrest a group of bootleggers in an old stable. Deputy Gober was taken to a hospital and died a short time later.

Sheriffs in the mid-twentieth century were John K. Tate 1932-34, Frank J. Burns 1934-40, Fred H. Payne 1940-44, Grady T. Head 1944-48, Frank J. Burns 1948-50, Rex Richey 1950-56, V. W. Maddox 1956-58, James Turner 1958-63, Judge Robert Summitt 1963-63, Frank Newell 1963-68, H. Q. Evatt 1968-74, Frank Newell 1974-76, Jerry Pitts 1976-78 and Sheriff H. Q. Evatt served 16 years from 1978 to 94.

An automobile accident claimed the life of Deputy Sheriff Lyle Armon Sneed on Wednesday, December 6, 1989. Deputy Sneed was en route to a fire when his patrol car left the roadway and struck a tree.

Sheriff John A. Cupp Jr. was elected in 1994 and remained in the office into the twenty-first century. Sheriff Cupp had been a member of the agency since 1970 and was a former minister and dangerous drug educator.

Deputy Sheriff Donald Kenneth Bond was brutally murdered in the early morning hours of Thursday, September 6, 2001. Deputy Bond responded to a call of suspicious activity at a produce stand. He cleared the call at 1:30 a.m. When the dispatcher tried to reach him at 2:20 a.m. he did not respond. Fellow officers searched for him and found his body at the produce stand. Deputy Bond had been shot nine times with an AK-47 assault rifle. The killer stole the front panel of the deputy's vest and his service weapon. The 34-year-old deputy had been with the agency two years.

Hamilton County Sheriff William T. Cates, left, and a deputy were killed on September 14, 1882, aboard a train to Knoxville as they transported three convicted murders to prison. Hamilton County Deputy Donald Kenneth Bond, right, was brutally murdered on September 6, 2001. He was shot nine times with an AK-47 assault rifle.

Informants gave investigators the name and address of the shooter. He was arrested the next morning as he left his house after he was seen throwing Deputy Bond's gun and vest panel from his back porch. The deputy's killer was convicted of capital murder and sentenced to death by lethal injection.

Other counties may have had fewer resources but their law enforcement officers had the same duties and were faced with the same dangers. For the small county sheriff, the job was particularly demanding.

When a man won election as sheriff in a smaller county in Tennessee before the middle of the twentieth century, it meant a commitment for his entire family. Such was the case with Perry T. Burnett in the fall of 1936 when he was elected sheriff of Wilson County.

On September 1, Sheriff Burnett, his wife and two daughters moved into the big white brick building just off the square in Lebanon. The building was the Wilson County Jail. The front part of the structure main floor was the living quarters for the sheriff and his family. It consisted of a living room and master bedroom with a hall between. The rear of the first floor held a dining room and the kitchen. Meals for the prisoners were prepared in the family kitchen. Between the kitchen and dinning room were the daughters' bedrooms and bath, and the stairs leading up to the jail.

The jail had a "bullpen" where a group of prisoners could be held in addition to a number of smaller cells. A trusty cooked for the prisoners. There was one woman who was frequently jailed for fighting. Inmates were happy when she was inside because she was a good cook. The sheriff got 25 cents a meal to feed prisoners. Dinner usually included pinto beans, a slab of cured pork, and cornbread. Food was better around hog killing time. The only jail staff was an old man who worked as the turnkey, but he did not stay at the jail at night.

A closet between the master bedroom and living room was used to keep whiskey until it was used at the court trial. The sheriff labeled the jars and jugs for identification. Whiskey not needed for trial was poured down the drain of the kitchen sink. The drain emptied into the town creek just behind the jail. A man who lived nearby and knew the sheriff's practice for disposing of whiskey, would wait nearby and get water from the "moonshine spiked" creek.

After quarterly court, prisoners sentenced to more than 11 months and 29 days were picked up from the jail by a long black car and transported to the state penitentiary. The families of some prisoners would come to the jail to tell them goodbye.

Sheriff Burnett's wife and daughters would entertain their guests on the front porch and in the front yard. Those who came to visit prisoners went to the back of the jail. The picture show was across the street from the jail and the sheriffs daughters were allowed to see movies at no charge. The family church was around the corner. Other than the occasional ruckus upstairs and being awaken in the middle of the night by the siren on the sheriff's car, the family had a near normal life.

Area lawmen worked closely. The Lebanon police force consisted of the chief and two patrolmen, and all were all on foot. The most numerous crimes were bootlegging and stealing chickens. Chickens were used by some in the community like currency to purchase goods.

Sheriff Perry Burnett carried his pistol in the glove compartment of his car and kept his blackjack hanging on a knob on the dashboard radio. He never handcuffed anyone and showed no favoritism to lawbreakers. One of the sheriff's daughters heard a prisoner call her name one night. Sheriff Burnett had arrested his nephew. The sheriff called his sister to say her son needed to spend a few days in Lebanon.

Burnett was even tempered by nature, but one Saturday night his patience was tried when a man he arrested ran away from him. Several days later the sheriff caught the same man and told him, "Now, if you run off tonight, I'm going to shoot you." The man knew the sheriff and didn't believe him. A few minutes later the prisoner took off running. Sheriff Burnett pulled his pistol and shot a hole through the man's britches, burning his leg. The ruffian stopped and yelled, "Hold it! Hold it! I'm not going to run."

Wilson County Sheriff Perry T. Burnett sat in his office at the county jail in May 1939. As other sheriffs in most counties, he and his family lived in the jail during his service as county sheriff from 1936 to 1940.

At the end of Sheriff Burnett's two terms in 1940, he continued as an honorary deputy the remainder of his life. He died in 1978 at the age of 90. Burnett was always thankful that he had to kill no one while serving as sheriff

Not all Tennessee sheriffs had a peaceful end to their life. Among a number of Tennessee sheriffs killed in the line of duty was Lauderdale County Sheriff Simmons D. Alsobrook. The newly elected sheriff was in uniform on November 1, 1860, when he was shot down in the street in an unprovoked attack.

Humphreys County Sheriff Edward Sam Stockard was killed by gunfire on September 15, 1914, when he and Waverly Town Marshal John Tankersley went to arrest a man on Duck River. The man had an automatic pistol and shot Sheriff Stockard ten times. A posse led by former Sheriff George Fentress shot Stockard's murderer when he resisted arrest.

Scott County Sheriff Richard Ellis was shot in the back of the head from ambush and killed on Thursday, August 13, 1925. He was in front of the county jail escorting a prisoner. Fentress County Sheriff Horace B. Taylor, 63, died on Wednesday, May 15, 1940, after being shot three times as he tried to arrest a rowdy miner in Zenith.

Warren County Sheriff Charles Walter Conlin Jr. accompanied Military Police Privates Earl Foreman and E. L. Roper to arrest an AWOL soldier for car theft. The three lawmen stopped the car and the sol-

Montgomery County Sheriff Alexander C. Stafford, seated on left, and his deputies circa 1900. The circle-star badges worn by the deputies were typical of insignia used by deputies of the area. Uniforms were not typically worn by members of the sheriff's office until the mid-twentieth century.

dier exited the car shooting, wounding Private Foreman and the sheriff. The car thief was killed in the shoot out. The MP survived but Sheriff Conlin died the following morning, January 10, 1942.

One sheriff from outside the state was killed in the line of duty in Tennessee. Sheriff Marion Louis Swords of St. Landry Parish in Louisiana was shot and killed on July 17, 1916, in Crockett County. The 16-year law enforcement veteran was attempting to arrest a fugitive. Two civilians who were assisting Sheriff Swords were also killed.

The most routine duties such as serving court papers often placed deputies and constables in harms way; even minor offences could generate deadly reactions. Loudon County Deputy Sheriff Edward N. Griffitts was shot in the chest and killed on September 26, 1903, and another deputy wounded. They went to arrest a man on a warrant for lewdness. Williamson County Constable Andrew Mattison Sullivan was shot and killed while serving civil court papers on October 29, 1933. Monroe County Deputy Sheriff Earl M.

Taylor was shot and killed on May 25, 1966, when he delivered a death notice.

Making an arrest for a felony crime was the most dangerous. Constable Jack Fraley of Hardin County's 10th District was shot and killed on July 26, 1890, as he delivered a prisoner to the county jail in Savannah. He had arrested the man for larceny and was helping him to dismount in front of the jail when the thief grabbed the constable's shotgun. As they tussled he shot Constable Fraley. The blast tore a chunk of flesh from the lawman's leg, severed the femoral artery, and Jack Fraley bled to death in a matter of minutes.

Monroe County Deputy Sheriff Charles E. "Charlie" Ray, 27, and other deputies went to arrest two brothers wanted for a murder on April 2, 1892. As the posse approached the house the killers opened fire. Deputy Ray was shot in the head and severely wounded. He lay where he was shot until the next morning when the other deputies rescued him. Deputy Ray succumbed to the wound on April 21.

Jefferson County Deputy Sheriff W. E. Alexander

was shot and killed on May 25, 1904, when he entered a store to serve a capias charging a man for carrying a pistol. The culprit drew his pistol and shot the 35-year-old deputy in the abdomen. Deputy Alexander said, "I am killed," and died twenty minutes later.

Fayette County Constable John C. Chambers served a warrant on Sunday, August 24, 1924. As he mounted his horse, a group of men beat and stabbed the constable. He died on August 31. Sullivan County Deputy Sheriff Hubert Webb and Kingsport Patrolman John Smith were both fatally wounded when confronting a fugitive with an arrest warrant on April 13, 1925. Sullivan County Twelfth District Constable Bruce Barker, 29, was killed in a shootout on Monday, May 30, 1938, as he and a group of officers tried to arrest a suspect near Kingsport.

Two Scott County officers were killed by shotgun fire on February 11, 1962. Deputy Sheriff Levi Harness, Fifth District Constable Alvin Jeffers and two other officers went to a darkened residence near Winfield to serve warrants on a man and his wife. Constable Jeffers and another officer entered the house. The husband and his son opened fire on the officers. Jeffers was struck in the chest and the other officer's head was grazed. The wounded officer got Jeffers outside and drove him to the hospital.

Outside, Deputy Harness took a position in the front of the house and a second deputy covered the rear. Minutes later the gunmen opened fire. Deputy Harness was hit three times and killed. Constable Jeffers died that evening.

Other deputies killed while attempting to serve warrants were Putnam County Deputy Sheriff Milton Otis Loftis on September 23, 1934; Fayette County Chief Deputy Olin B. Burrow on March 23, 1940; Franklin County Deputy Sheriff John Edward Penney on April 7, 1944; Scott County Deputy Sheriff Earl C. Koger on January 18, 1964; Bradley County Deputy Ken Wright Sr. on August 22, 1971; Sullivan County Patrolman Glayton M. Parker on May 31, 1990; and Hawkins County Deputy Sheriff Gerald Monroe "Bubba" Gibson on July 13, 2000.

Raiding whiskey stills and battling the illegal liquor trade was often a deadly duty for sheriffs and deputies in the late nineteenth and early twentieth century. The mountain counties of East Tennessee were in many ways the most challenging for law officers. The mountain people were independent and traced their fight against government control and taxation of liquor back to the Whiskey Rebellion of the 1790s.

Cocke County Sheriff Joseph S. Dawson was shot from ambush and killed on Thursday, April 20, 1899,

Bradley County Sheriff Israel L. Smith, left, was shot in the abdomen and killed on March 14, 1922, as he and deputies tried to apprehend bootleggers. Sullivan County Deputy Sheriff Hubert Webb, right, and a Kingsport patrolman were both fatally wounded by a fugitive on April 13, 1925.

just over the county line in Haywood County, North Carolina. The sheriff was with a posse led by federal Deputy Revenue Collectors J. B. Altom and J. A. Pearce that included Deputy Collectors W. H. Cadle and F. W. Brown, Deputy U. S. Marshal J. W. Justice and possemen R. H. Jones and Thomas Huff. The posse found and destroyed a number of stills and arrested one man.

The posse was using a lamp to search for whiskey in a narrow mountain gorge about 3:00 a.m. A shot rang out and a rifle ball struck Sheriff Dawson in the back of his neck. It passed through him and lodged in a book in the coat pocket of Deputy Collector Pearce. The round was fired from a rock ledge above the party. Sheriff Dawson was killed instantly. The Cocke County Sheriff's Office recorded more deaths in the line of duty than any other county agency except Shelby County.

Bradley County Sheriff Israel L. Smith was shot in the abdomen and killed on Tuesday, March 14, 1922, as he and deputies tried to apprehend bootleggers fleeing from a still near Cleveland, Tennessee. Deputies killed by bootleggers in the period included Bledsoe County Deputy Sheriff John U. Swafford near the foot of Walnut Ridge on June 19, 1929; and Robertson County Deputy Sheriff J. Mart Murphy in Springfield on July 23, 1931.

Thirty-eight-year-old Sheriff Cleve Daugherty left the coal mines to become a lawman. Daugherty was an unassuming, quiet man who was popular with the mountain people of Anderson County. His jail home was always open to visitors and on court days men from the hills ate at the sheriff's table. He was in his fifth year as sheriff on the night of July 19, 1933,

Obion County Deputy Sheriff Samuel Boyett, left, was killed in retaliation for helping capture a fugitive on July 1, 1930. Williamson County Constable Samuel Claybrooks Locke, right, was shot and killed in an ambush as he arrived home from work on March 7, 1925. Locke had been working with state and federal officers to raid shutdown 73 illegal whiskey stills in the county.

when he was shot in the back and killed by moonshiners carrying tow sacks of whiskey jars. Stewart County Sheriff Lucas Leon Ellis died on July 16, 1937, after having been shot on November 2, 1936, by a rum runner who pulled a pistol as he was searched.

Lawmen after moonshiners were often ambushed. One of the most egregious incidents was the killing of Deputy Sheriff Byrd Daugherty and his sons Willie and Fisher on Fork Mountain near the Anderson and Morgan county line. They were ambushed by a cousin of Daugherty whose son had been arrested by the deputy for moonshining. The arrest turned into a feud between the two families. An eye witness to the April 7, 1922, incident said Daugherty and his sons were headed across Waldens Ridge and near the fire tower when they were shot from ambush. Then one of the boys was shot and killed while on his knees praying.

Williamson County Constable Samuel Claybrooks Locke was shot and killed in an ambush on March 7, 1925, and Lawrence County Fourth District Constable Dan Smith, 35, was shot in the back from ambush on August 18, 1925. Both were killed by moonshiners for enforcement of prohibition laws. White County Deputy Sheriff Harkless Grundy Kirby was ambushed and killed by a shotgun blast on December 24, 1931, as he and another deputy destroyed a whiskey still.

Other criminal elements resorted to the cowardly act of ambush as well. Fayette County Deputy Sheriff David Dobbins died on January 27, 1915, after being shot in the throat from ambush the day before while he rode with a

posse pursuing several burglars. The sheriff was struck by two bullets but recovered. Fayette County Deputy Sheriff Leland E. Roper and another deputy were checking a local picnic grounds on July 22, 1949, when Roper was shot and killed by a man hiding behind a car.

Williamson County Deputy Sheriff John Morris Heithcock was assisting the Fairview police chief when he was ambushed from a ditch and killed by a shotgun blast to the chest on June 28, 1972. Giles County Deputy Sheriff Herbert H. Slayton was killed from ambush on January 24, 1978, while checked out a vehicle. Sumner County Detective James David Mandrell was working undercover on a cattle rustling case on June 28, 1988, when he was shot with a 30-06 rifle in an ambush and killed. The bushwhacker then walked up to him and shot him again in the face.

Roane County Deputy Sheriff Bill Jones and a civilian riding with him were shot and killed from ambush by two brothers with assault rifles on May 11, 2006. The 25-year law enforcement veteran died of 33 gun shots wounds.

Politics may have been behind the killing of two deputies outside of Copperhill, in a highly partisan section of Tennessee. Polk County Chief Deputy James Louis Wright and Deputy R. A. "Bob" Rogers were both killed by shotgun fire on March 8, 1958, when they stepped from their patrol car at the 69 Grill for a routine check. A third deputy, Carmel Gibson, survived.

Luckily many officers did survive assaults on them. Robertson County 1st District Constable Henry Roark

Lawrence County Sheriff Cleve O. Weathers, left, was stabbed to death by a prisoner on January 12, 1943. Sheriff Weathers entered the cell to break up a fight unaware that an inmate had a knife hidden in his boot. Sullivan County Deputy Sheriff Steve N. Mullins, right, was struck and killed on November 22, 1995, by a stolen van driven by three runaway juveniles. The vehicle struck Deputy Mullins cruiser, knocking the deputy into the grill of a wrecker 25 feet away.

Grundy County Sheriff John A. Cline, left, told an intoxicated man to go home and sober up on April 15, 1929. The drunk later returned, shot the sheriff's arm off with a shotgun, grabbed his pistol, and killed him with shots to the forehead and body. Sheriff Cleve Daugherty, right, was shot in the back and killed by moonshiners on the night of July 19, 1933.

survived a shotgun blast in his back from a bootlegger on October 12, 1929. Sullivan County Deputy Sheriff John B. Pierce survived a bullet below the heart in a shootout with a bootlegger on May 17, 1927.

Resourceful lawmen sometimes used trickery to bring in moonshiners. Humphreys County Sheriff J. L. Smith and his posse came upon a still in February 1926 and hid in the bushes. Soon a moonshiner came and lit the fire. He was arrested and held out of sight with the lawmen. When two others approached, they signaled by whistling. The sheriff returned the whistle and arrested the two when they reached the still. The lawman whistled in five moonshiners into custody for a stay in the county jail.

Lawrence County Sheriff Cleve O. Weathers was popular and well respected. Like many elected county lawmen he was strong willed and evenhanded in enforcing the law. He approached the citizens of Lawrence County as basically honorable but was caught off guard by a desperate and dangerous men.

Weathers was born in Loretta, Tennessee, the eldest in a large family. His father wanted him to be a doctor, but money was tight for the family in those years. Cleve managed the family business, Weathers General Merchandise Store at corner of Broad and Main streets in Loretta, before he ran for office. He was first elected sheriff in 1938. Sheriff Weathers was gregarious and dignified at the same time. He never wore a gun because he didn't think it was necessary.

Respect for Sheriff Weathers extended even into the community of law breakers. One bootlegger that farmed near Loretta made and sold whiskey to help through the lean times and Sheriff Weathers put him in jail many time. One cold winter day Weathers got word that a fresh batch of whiskey had been distilled and visited the moonshiner's house. The man was out and his wife quickly poured the whiskey bottled in the house into the wood stove created huge flames. When the sheriff got inside he remarked, "Mighty big fire you've got in that stove, Mrs. May."

The moonshining farmer came in about then and Weathers asked to search the barn. The man said to sheriff, "I just brought that corn crop in and I wish you wouldn't disturb it." The sheriff knew that a large part of the farmer's whiskey batch had been burned in the wood stove by his wife. The sheriff did not go to the barn to check for more whiskey that day. He knew the farmer needed some money to feed his family through the winter. Years later the moonshiner's son recalled that the only time he ever saw his father cry was when he heard that Sheriff Cleve Weathers had been killed.

A prisoner arrested at a local honky-tonk for assault and battery stabbed Sheriff Cleve Weathers to death at the Lawrence County Jail on Tuesday evening, January 12, 1943. The prisoner had been placed in a cell with another prisoner and hit the old man. The ruckus brought the sheriff to investigate. Tennessee Highway Patrol Corporal Greg O'Rear was at the jail at the time and followed Weathers to the cell block. O'Rear was in the "run-around" corridor when he heard a scuffle. Sheriff came from the cell and said, "He's hurt me, Greg." Weathers collapsed into O'Rear's arms and died from the five knife wounds to his chest. Cleve O. Weathers was in his third term as Lawrence County sheriff. His killer had smuggled a knife into the jail in his boot.

Two prisoners killed Williamson County Sheriff Milton Harvey Stephens with his own gun on Friday, June 27, 1919. The 76-year-old Confederate veteran was transporting the two horse thieves from Nolensville, where they were arrested, to the county jail in Franklin. The two desperados overpowered the sheriff on Wilson Pike, killed him with his own sidearm, robbed him and escaped in his buggy.

Prisoners attempting to escape or on the run were desperate and ready to kill rather than be incarcerated. Grainger County Sheriff Samuel Preston Greenlee died in the line of duty on Wednesday, April 10, 1889. The forty-nine-year-old sheriff was shot and killed as he attempted to arrest a man who had escaped from prison. One of Sheriff Greenlee's killers was arrested, but later taken from his cell and hung by angry civilians. The second was tracked down by a 16-year-old boy who shot and killed him.

A constable and his deputy were killed near Durhamville in Lauderdale County on January on January 9, 1900. Constable W. D. Turner arrested a man for not complying to a vaccination ordinance. When the man could not pay the fine, he was ordered to jail in Ripley. Constable Turner deputized Marvin Durham to assist him in transporting the prisoner to jail. At 11:30 a.m., about a mile and a half out of town, they were over taken by two brothers of the prisoner and shot to death. Later that night two of the culprits were lynched and a large mob was searching for the other.

Dickson County Deputy Sheriff Robert E. Mayo died of gunshot wounds on October 18, 1977. Deputy Mayo was shot on June 14 when he tried to arrest an armed robber who had escaped from the county jail.

Cocke County Deputy Sheriff Robert Scott Miller, 26, was shot to death on October 11, 1994, when he and two other deputies entered a house looking for two escaped felons. A second deputy was wounded. The two escapees set the house on fire and died in the blaze. Other county lawmen killed trying to prevent escapes or recapture prisoners included, Cocke County Deputy Sheriff Leonard Frazier on March 15, 1929; Coffee County Deputy Sheriff Ben McCullough on August 10, 1935; Hawkins County Reserve Deputy Sheriff John Wesley Wright on August 16, 1988; Johnson County Deputy Sheriff Allen Lipford on December 11, 1991; and Fayette County Deputy Jailer William Thomas Bishop on May 2, 1997.

Obion County Deputy Sheriff Samuel Boyett was killed in retaliation for helping capture a fugitive. The escapee from the Trimble, Tennessee, jail was captured on July 1, 1930. Later that night the brother of the felon went to the Mason Hall residence of the 55-year-old deputy. Deputy Boyett stepped outside his home and during the argument that followed, the fugitive's brother pulled a pistol and shot the lawman in the head, killing him.

Hancock County Deputy Sheriffs Alex Gary Morris Sr. and Alonzo Brownlow Tyler were shot and killed on April 22, 1961, attempting to arrest a county constable for drinking and driving. The constable led them on a pursuit to his home. Seven members of the constable's family opened fire on the two. Both deputies and the constable were killed.

Part of a lawman's job description was to insert themselves in the midst of conflict. The conflict could involve family matters, criminal disturbances or civil disorder, but it always involved danger. McNairy County Sheriff Samuel Lewis was killed by gunfire on Wednesday, July 31, 1867, during a riot at the voting polls in Purdy, Tennessee.

Election day was often violent following the Civil War due to the efforts of the governor to control the polls. The state militia was present and conflict arose with local residents. Gunplay erupted and Sheriff Lewis was caught in the crossfire. He received a mortal wound and died a few days later. Lewis served in the Civil War as a lieutenant in Company A of Fielding Hurst's Union Sixth Tennessee Cavalry. In 1865 he was elected the ninth sheriff of McNairy County.

An officer of the law never knew what awaited him when he went to investigate a criminal disturbances. Pickett County Sheriff George Winningham and his son Deputy Sheriff Floyd Winningham went to a lumber camp on Sunday, April 23, 1933, to investigate reports of a murder. When the Winninghams and another deputy reached the camp, they were told no murder had occurred, but that a drunk in a railroad boxcar was causing a disturbance.

The lawmen went to the boxcar and told the man to come out. He fired a .45 caliber pistol, killing Deputy Floyd Winningham instantly with two shots to the head. Sheriff George Winningham was shot in the abdomen and died the next day. The gunman fled, but weeks later turned himself in to a Scott County deputy. A few days after the arrest, a mob of citizens and lawmen took the murderer from jail and killed him.

Floyd Winningham was a WWI veteran. The other son of Sheriff George Winningham, Sheriff Willie Winningham of Clinton County, Kentucky, was also shot and killed attempting to serve a warrant on a drunk on July 29, 1933.

Pickett County Sheriff George Winningham, left, and his son, Deputy Sheriff Floyd Winningham, right, died at the hand of a drunk at a lumber camp on April 23, 1933. Deputy Floyd Winningham was shot twice in the head with a .45 caliber pistol and died instantly. Sheriff George Winningham was shot in the abdomen and died the next day.

Wilson County Sheriff Harold Griffin, left, was shot and killed with a .25 caliber pistol on April 6, 1954, as he served a warrant. Dickson County Deputy Sheriff Robert E. Mayo, right, died on October 18, 1977, from gunshot wound received four months earlier as he confronted an escaped bandit.

Cumberland County Sheriff Thomas Fenton Brown died on April 8, 1928, at a farm near Crossville. He was attempting to arrest a former sheriff who had been ousted from office the previous year. The ex-lawman was intoxicated and creating a disturbance. Sheriff Brown found a two-gallon jug of liquor. When Brown approached to make an arrest, his predecessor fired five shots, three of which hit Sheriff Tom Brown, killing him.

Even giving someone a break could have deadly consequences for a lawman. Rather than arrest an intoxicated man on April 15, 1929, Grundy County Sheriff John A. Cline told him to go home and sober up. The man later returned to town and went to Thompson's poolroom. When Sheriff Cline entered the pool hall, the culprit shot the lawman's right arm off with a shotgun, then grabbed the sheriff's pistol and shot him in the forehead and body, killing him. Deputies Kilgore, Guest and Griswold went to arrest the sheriff's murderer. They shot and killed him when he threatened them with a gun.

Polk County Deputy Sheriff John A. Gilbert was informed of a car parked on a sharp curve near the top of Little Sand Mountain on June 14, 1928. He went to investigate and found himself face to face with an armed bandit that shot him four times with a .45 automatic pistol. Fifty year old Deputy Gilbert fired one shotgun round before he died, seriously wounding the gunman.

Other county officers killed when they stepped into a violent incident or while investigating a violent act included Monroe County Deputy Sheriff Thomas S. Blair on January 29, 1911; Unicoi County Deputy Sheriff Frank Moore on January 30, 1922; Cocke County Deputy Sheriff Manuel Stuart on March 31, 1924; Cocke County Deputy Sheriff General J. Hall, on December 24, 1933; Johnson County Deputy Sheriff Conrad Franklin Bunton on April 9, 1936; Hawkins County Deputy Sheriff Drew Harrell on July 13, 1937; Monroe County Deputy Sheriff Ollie W. Harrell on September 24, 1939; Williamson County Constable Clarence Wesley Reed on January 28, 1944; Fentress County Constable Thomas Jefferson York on May 7, 1972; Cheatham County Deputy Sheriff Charles Frank Jordan on April 4, 1982; Roane County Deputy Sheriff Dennis Ray Armes on March 15, 1983; Johnson County Deputy Sheriff Ronnal Ralph Stanley on August 31, 1983; and Greene County Sergeant Ricky Dale Coyle on September 25, 1995.

Investigating disturbances involving domestic violence was especially dangerous. Unicoi County Sheriff Blake H. Head responded to a domestic call on Friday, September 18, 1942, and was shot with a rifle and killed as he stepped from his cruiser. Wilson County Sheriff Harold Griffin was shot and killed with a .25 caliber pistol on April 6, 1954, when the 40-year-old lawman went to serve papers to permit a woman to retrieve furniture from her husband's home.

Claiborne County Deputy Sheriff Elmer Taylor Singleton, 33, was shot on August 31, 1968, when a drunk opened fire him and three other deputies. The four lawmen stopped to help a woman calling for assistance. Deputy Singleton was hit in the chest and leg and died on September 13, 1968.

Others killed in incidents related to domestic violence included Weakley County Deputy Sheriff William T. Cross on July 1, 1926; two Obion County deputy sheriffs, Calvin Lee and John Wright, on September 27, 1942; Rhea County Deputy Sheriff Johnny Alford Swafford on November 13, 1975, and Loudon County Deputy Sheriff Jason Michael Scott on March 12, 2004.

One of the dark moments in the history of law enforcement occurred on August 1, 1946, in what became known as the "Battle of Athens." Political corruption was at the heart of the incident that pitted a World War II veteran's organization known as the GI Non-Partisan League against the McMinn County Sheriff's Office. To guarantee the election of the state senate candidate supported by Memphis political boss Ed Crump, deputy sheriff's absconded with key ballot boxes and took them to the jail.

A group of veterans took weapons and ammunition from the National Guard Armory and with several hundred others went to the jail, demanding the ballot boxes be returned. The deputies refused and a gun battle erupted. After several hours the veterans dynamited the front of the jail and the deputies surrendered. The mob then turned over police cars and burned them before finally disbursing. The incident contributed to breaking the statewide grip of Boss Crump's political machine.

Most sheriffs were honorable men who pursued their duty as a public service. One such man was Sevier County Sheriff Ray C. Noland. He established a reputation as a fair but stern lawman and served Sevier County as sheriff for six terms over three decades.

Noland came naturally to law enforcement both by his character and his heritage. An ancestral uncle, Phillip Noland, was elected sheriff of Loudon County, Virginia, in 1777. Almost a century later a second Phillip Noland was elected sheriff of Haywood County, North Carolina. Haywood County Sheriff Noland lost his life in the line of duty when he was shot from ambush on September 22, 1862.

In his immediate family, J. Reed Noland, Ray's father, was a Sevier County deputy sheriff as Ray grew up. His brother John P. Noland served as the first chief of police of Gatlinburg. A number of other relatives also served in law enforcement including Wayne Noland, his younger brother, and Charles A. Smith, his son-in-law, who served as Sheriff Noland's deputies.

Ray C. Noland began his law enforcement career as a Sevier County deputy sheriff and served briefly as a member of the Sevierville Police Department. He was first elected sheriff in 1946. On September 1, Noland was sworn in as High Sheriff of Sevier County. After having his gold badge pinned on, Sheriff Noland proceeded to the county jail, built in 1893, and received the keys from the former sheriff. Later that day he moved his wife and two young daughters into the living quarters at the jail. There was no paid cook, jailer or deputy. The sheriff's wife was responsible for cooking and keeping the books of the jail.

The sheriff used his personal automobile, a blue 1946 Ford bought soon after he took office, for road duty. The living room at the jail served as his office. He did his paper work on a roll-top desk and a black telephone served as his only communication system. Dave Smelcer became his first deputy.

The county sheriff dealt with all types of criminal activity, from investigating murder to stopping speeders. Sheriff Noland stood with integrity and bravery against individual hooligan and desperate men as well as organized bootleg operations. Perhaps his most dangerous activity was raiding moonshine stills. Moonshiners frequently fired at Noland, his deputies

Sevier County Sheriff Ray C. Noland in his blue 1946 Ford during his first term as sheriff. Noland established a record of bravery and integrity chasing moonshiners and murders during his six terms as sheriff in East Tennessee.

and state or federal agents who accompanied him. Sometimes shots were fired into the air in an attempt to scare the lawmen away. That was what one illegal distiller said he was trying to do, but Noland didn't believe the moonshiner because of the hole in the sheriff's black overcoat. Luckily the only injury in the incident was a deputy's broken foot.

Sheriff Noland served in three separate periods, a single term from 1946 to 1948, two terms from 1954 to 1958, and three terms from 1960 to 1966. When not in office he worked in a variety of jobs and locations including Washington state, Oak Ridge and as shift supervisor of guards at the Florida State Prison in Belle Glade, Florida. Even when he was not in office, he continued to take training in law enforcement.

Political campaigns and county budget challenges were frustrations the sheriff had to endure. Meeting people and asking for their vote was the pleasant side of campaigning, but the affects on his family of verbal attacks by his opposition were painful. Financial resources were often meager. Sheriff Noland was in debt after his first term as sheriff. A new jail was built in 1953, before his second term. No living quarters were included in the building and no money was included in the budget for the staff necessary to run the jail. Sheriff Noland had to convert space into living quarters so that he and his wife could run the jail.

Cocke County Deputy Sheriff Billy Walter Smith, left, and another deputy were killed instantly on December 20, 1974, when their patrol car was hit broadside as they turned onto an on-ramp for I-40. Tipton County Deputy Sheriff Michael Wilson Erwin, right, died on October 31, 1975, as the result of a vehicular assault.

Mutual respect and lasting friendships were established with fellow law officers who worked with Sheriff Noland. Deputies he worked with over his career included Albert Parrot, Herman Seagle, Wayne Noland, Kyle Cole, Wallace Moore, Charles A. Smith and Paul Galyon. Gatlinburg Chief of Police Wib Ogle, Sevier County Constables Lendell Hatcher, Wade Allen, Charles Allen and Ray "Ulerfish" Sutton worked closely with the sheriff and his deputies. State lawmen such as Highway Patrolmen Thomas J. Cantwell and Brownlee Reagan, TBI Agent Walter Bearden and other state and federal officers were allies in the war on crime.

Sheriff Noland balanced traditional hard fisted law enforcement with a progressive scientific approach to crime fighting. He participated in and hosted FBI training schools in the forties and fifties, learning modern investigation and crime analysis. Noland set up the first Sevier County Identification Bureau, keeping arrest records and fingerprint files. He appointed Cecil T. Patterson as identification officer for the county and kept the records at the Gatlinburg Police Department.

Although he was soft spoken and easy going, Sheriff Noland quickly responded to aggression with sufficient force to take control of the situation. Axing a still while bullets buzzed around him, chasing a souped up liquor-running car at high speed or facing down a knife wielding hooligan came naturally to Sheriff Noland. He employed both brain and brawn to bring burglars, bank robbers, murderers, liquor runners, gamblers, moonshiners and their like to justice.

Noland was twice invited to participate in the security detail at presidential inaugurals, President Dwight D. Eisenhower's in January 1956 and President John F. Kennedy's in January 1961. Sheriff Ray C. Noland ended his law enforcement career with integrity and the dignity of a job well done. Despite the dangers, he also ended his career without serious injury.

Fatal accidents ended the career of a number who pursued the fast and dangerous duty of a county lawman. Monroe County Sheriff James Pinkney Kennedy died on March 19, 1930, when he and a deputy went to investigate a store burglary around 2:00 a.m. The store manager arrived soon after and saw the sheriff exiting the rear of the store with his weapon drawn. The manager, blinded by the sheriff's flashlight, opened fire on the man he assumed to be a burglar and killed Sheriff Kennedy.

Scott County Sergeant Hubert Dean "John John" Yancey was in a party investigating a meth lab on November 28, 2003. He entered the house when he heard a scream, thinking a fellow officer was in trouble. The deputy inside saw his silhouette and, thinking he was an armed suspect, fired. The round struck Deputy Yancey just above his vest, killing him.

Lawrence County Deputy Sheriff James A. Lovelace was accidentally shot and killed on July 18, 1982, in a department training exercise. Other county lawmen killed accidentally in the line of duty included Cocke County Deputy Sheriff George Leon Wiley on Tuesday, May 17, 1927; Tipton County Deputy

Carroll County Deputy Sheriff Mark Thomas Pinson, left, tried to shut the engine off on a vehicle that crashed into a house on November 20, 1976. He was killed when the gas tank exploded. Roane County Deputy Sheriff Alan Wayne Shubert, right, was enroute to backup another deputy on March 10, 1979, when his patrol car was struck head-on by a driver who was drunk and high on PCP.

Sheriff Richard L. Rose on November 29, 1988; Bradley County Reserve Deputy David Allen McCollum on September 16, 1989, and Lawrence County Deputy Sheriff Jason Ellis.

Automobile accidents became a source of danger for twentieth century law officers. Loudon County Sheriff Theodore Virgil Garner was killed on Tuesday, July 31, 1951, in an automobile accident after transporting a felon to prison. Bradley County Deputy Sheriff Taylor Caywood was killed in automobile accident on January 27, 1932, also related to prisoner transport. Blount County Deputy Sheriff William D. "Bill" Nuchols died on October 7, 1956, from injuries sustained the previous day, when the vehicle he was riding in collided with another car that turned in front of him on Highway 411.

With the proliferation of automobiles and traffic congestion in the late twentieth century a growing number of line of duty deaths were the result of vehicular accidents. Unicoi County Deputy Sheriff Douglas Allen Arrowood on March 23, 1974; Cocke County Deputy Sheriffs Lloyd Clevenger and Billy Walter Smith on December 20, 1974; Henry County Sergeant Gilbert Walker Sr. on January 26, 1979; and Anderson County Deputy Sheriff William Cordell Scott on January 21, 1980; Cocke County Deputy Sheriff Larry Junior Thomas died on November 14, 1992 from injuries suffered a year earlier; Cannon County Deputy Ira Darby Prater on January 8, 1996, and Sullivan County deputy sheriffs Stephen Dwight Riner and Barry Shelton on September 30, 2001.

Many officers have been killed as a result of vehicular assault including Monroe County Chief Deputy Sheriff Aaron Holmes Mills on June 30, 1950;

Greene County Sergeant Ricky Dale Coyle, left, was investigating a hit and run in a remote area on September 25, 1995. Sergeant Coyle became involved in a gun battle at close range and radioed that he needed an ambulance. He was found slumped over his steering wheel, dead from three bullet wounds. The body of the assailant was found 30 yards away, shot five times. Loudon County Deputy Sheriff Jason Scott, right, answered a domestic disturbance call in a rural area at 8:30 a.m. on March 12, 2004. Deputy Scott was shot four times and killed as he exited his patrol car. The killer was a 16-year-old boy who had beaten his mother with a post because she refused to let him drive to school after drinking the night before.

Claiborne County Deputy Sheriff Ernest Doliver Duncan on September 12, 1965; Greene County Deputy Sheriff Emerson Shelton and Greene County Constable Beauford Rader on September 24, 1972; Tipton County Deputy Sheriff Michael Wilson Erwin on October 31, 1975; Marion County Constables O. V. Brazier and Andrew Winters on September 4, 1976; Roane County Deputy Sheriff Alan Wayne Shubert on March 10, 1979; Sullivan County Sergeant Arthur Carroll Lane on March 30, 1981; Cumberland County Deputy Sheriff Kenneth D. Nelson on January 17, 1988; Sullivan County Deputy Sheriff Steve N. Mullins, on November 22, 1995, and Wilson County Deputy Sheriff John Musice on July 9, 2003.

DeKalb County Sheriff W. H. Bing Jr. crashed into a bridge on Highway 41 in the Beech Grove community and was killed on Wednesday, June 8, 1966. He was transporting a mental patient to Nashville when the man reached over from the back seat and took hold of the steering wheel.

Carroll County Deputy Sheriff Mark Thomas Pinson was killed on November 20, 1976, while he tried to shut off the engine of a vehicle that had crashed into a house and the gas tank exploded. On April 22, 1980, Robertson County Deputy Sheriff Willard Pope Hill was killed in an airplane accident while transporting an inmate.

Cocke County Deputy Sheriff Robert Scott Miller, left was killed on October 11, 1994, as he and two other deputies tried to recapture for two escaped felons. Wilson County Deputy John Musice, right, was run down by fleeing felons near exit 226 of I-40 on July 9, 2003.

Perhaps the Tennessee sheriff with the greatest name recognition in the second half of the twentieth century was McNairy County Sheriff Buford Hayse Pusser, who held office from 1964 to 1970. His exploits have been the subject of books and movies and have been recounted to be point that it has become difficult to distinguish between fact from fiction.

Pusser served three years as Adamsville's Chief of Police before he was elected sheriff. He quickly came into conflict with the State Line Gang that ran gambling, prostitution and whiskey operations along the Tennessee-Mississippi state line. Sheriff Pusser's law enforcement activities frequently became violent. The gang tried to kill the sheriff in a 1967 ambush. Sheriff Pusser was seriously wounded but his wife was killed in the incident. Buford Pusser was killed in automobile accident in 1974 when his Corvette smashed into an embankment.

In the early 1970s young William G. Kelley of Fayette County was determined to become a law enforcement officer. He applied to be a deputy sheriff, but wasn't hired. He became a successful salesman, traveling five states selling automobile parts. In 1974 when the serving sheriff retired, Bill Kelley ran for the office and won. He found his time as a traveling salesman was good training to be a lawman. Kelley said, "I knew a lot about people and the job of sheriff is about people." Kelley continued as sheriff into the new millennium.

Sheriff Kelley saw a lot of changes over a third of a century as the county's chief law enforcement officer. His force in 1974 consisted of himself and four deputies. "We worked from can to can't," Kelley remembered. His turnkey lived in the jail and acted as a full-time dispatcher and a full-time jailer, working from 8:00 a.m. until midnight. In 2006 twenty people were doing the job of that turnkey and the sheriff's entire staff totaled 60.

When Kelley was first elected, the only training required for new sheriffs was a one-week "New Sheriff's School." With passage of the New Sheriff's Qualifications Act in the eighties new sheriffs were required to be POST certified. Sheriff Kelley was able to remain in continuous service when in 1978 the state extended terms to four years and removed term limits.

The major issue facing Kelley when he became sheriff was controlling the racial tension prevalent in the sixties and seventies. Sheriff Kelley recalled, "I did that by serving all the people of the county. I made no difference between anyone, be it white or black, poor or rich. If they needed to see me they could walk in my office and see me."

Drugs changed the whole complexion of law enforcement during Kelley's time in office. Some marijuana use was the extent of the drug presence in 1974, but by the mid-eighties crack-cocaine changed everything. When methamphetamine use reached epidemic proportions the impact on law enforcement grew exponentially. For Sheriff Kelley the most frustrating thing that has happened for law officers related to the sentencing act of 1989. Efforts to alleviate overcrowding in prisons reduced sentences of felons to the point that the criminal justice system seemed to have a revolving door.

Bill Kelley's desire to serve as a lawman resulted in a lifelong career as sheriff. At the completion of his term in 2006, Fayette County Sheriff William G. Kelley had served for 32 years, the longest tenure of any county sheriff in the history of Tennessee.

Another notable Tennessee sheriff in the last quarter of the twentieth century and into the new millennium was Sheriff Delphus Van Hicks of Hardeman County. Sheriff Hicks was initially elected in 1978 and was the first black sheriff elected in the history of Tennessee.

Delphus Hicks began his law enforcement experience as a part-time deputy with the Hardeman County Sheriff's Office for four years while working in private industry. In 1972 he joined the department as a regular deputy and two years later was named chief deputy.

Sheriff Hicks served as the chief law officer of Hardeman County for 16 years, 1978 to 1994. He then served as an investigator of the Tennessee Department of Mental Health/Retardation and as a senior correctional officer before his selection as the chief of police of Whiteville.

Delphus Hicks ran again for sheriff of Hardeman County in 2002. He won the election and began a fifth term in the office. Sheriff Hicks received many recognitions including Outstanding Sheriff of the Year and the Tennessee Outstanding Achievement Award. More importantly, he won the respect of local, state and federal law enforcement officers across Tennessee.

The day to day pressures of law enforcement often resulted in death in the line of duty from natural causes. Wilson County Sergeant Wiley T. Williams died of a heart attack on January 25, 1974; Loudon County Deputy Sheriff Frank Floyd McKenzie of a blood clot on March 26, 1977; Johnson County Investigator John Ralph Cunningham of a heart attack on January 15, 1986, and Sullivan County Patrolman Roscoe Teague of a heart attack on May 30, 1995.

Sometimes a law officer was killed because he was in the wrong place at the wrong time and simply because he was a law officer. McMinn County Deputy Sheriff Dan Mull was eating breakfast at a truck stop on August 20, 1975. Three armed robbers thought he was there to arrest them. One of the group walked up behind Deputy Mull, shot and killed him.

Henry County Deputy Sheriff Steve Russell was almost killed when he stopped to assist a motorist one Sunday afternoon in September 1981. The 20-year-old deputy stopped behind a 1965 Chevrolet pickup parked on the side of the road. He thought the truck was broken down, not knowing the two young men inside had just burglarized a house and stolen some guns.

Deputy Russell walked to the truck and recognized one of the individuals from high school. The man pushed a single barrel 410 shotgun in his face and said, "Don't go for your gun. I'll kill you." Russell began talking to him to calm him down. The man pulled the trigger. The blast hit Russell fully in the face. The deputy never heard the gun go off. Deputy Steve Russell escaped death, although he continued to carry 34 pellets in his face. Russell went on to an illustrious career in the Tennessee Highway Patrol.

A similar incident resulted in the death of two Lauderdale County deputy sheriffs, Kevan Maurice Ward and Bobby Joe Nolen. On January 2, 1990, the two officers gave a ride to an 82-year-old man whose car had broken down. The man shot and killed both deputies.

Other county law officers killed in the line of duty included Claiborne County Deputy William S. Thompson on August 11, 1931; Weakley County Deputy Sheriff Egbert Bullock on September 25, 1931; Lauderdale County Deputy Sheriff Will Hudson Evans on October 15, 1935; Fentress County Deputy Sheriff Casper Wood on May 15, 1940; Putnam County Deputy Sheriff John Morgan Bilbrey on September 7, 1941; Greene County Deputy Sheriff Thomas Melvin Ball on June 29, 1942; Grundy County Deputy Sheriff Oscar Ward on March 4, 1947; Grundy County Deputy Sheriff James Pascal Anderson on May 23, 1953; Greene County Deputy Sheriff Marshall G. Rader on January 14, 1967; Fayette County Chief Deputy Sheriff Daniel Bascomb Talley on December 11, 1969; Crockett County Deputy Sheriff Lloyd Johnson on January 1, 1972; Sequatchie County Deputy Sheriff Paul Schwiger on October 17, 1977; Anderson County Patrolman Ray S. Brown on June 9, 1981, and Rhea County Sergeant Bruce Owens on December 29, 1994.

County law enforcement today is more professional and better trained than at any time in history. Dedicated officers continue to protect and serve their fellow citizens, adding to the tradition of Tennessee's constitutional law officers.

Federal Enforcement in Tennessee

The first federal lawman in Tennessee was a United States Marshal. Tennessee became the 16th state June 1, 1796. The "District of Tennessee" was established by the federal judiciary January 31, 1797. Robert Hays was appointed U.S. Marshal of Tennessee on February 20, 1797. He continued as the sole marshal of the state until February 13, 1801, and was the only individual to serve as U.S. Marshal of the District of Tennessee.

The United States Marshal Service (USMS) had been formed by the Judiciary Act of September 24, 1789. The act specified that law enforcement was to be the U.S. Marshals' primary function. A marshal was appointed to each federal judicial district for a four-year term with the duty to attend the district, circuit, and supreme courts in the district and to execute federal judicial writs and process. He was empowered to enforce the laws of the United States and to appoint deputies to assist him. The role of the federal marshal was modeled on that of the county sheriff.

The Federal Judicial District of Tennessee was divided and the Western District of Tennessee and the Eastern District of Tennessee in 1801 and reorganized in 1802. The western most part of the state as known today was still Indian Territory at that time, so the Western District essentially included territory that is today the Middle District. Marshals for the Eastern District of Tennessee during this period were Charles

T. Porter, 1801-26; John Callaway, 1826-29; and William Lyon, 1829-38. Marshals for the Western District of Tennessee were Robert Hays, 1801-03; John Childress Jr., 1803-19; Robert Purdy, 1819-31; and Samuel B. Marshall, 1831-38.

The Middle District of Tennessee was created and the districts reorganized in 1838 and 1839 following the acquisition of the land between the Tennessee and Mississippi rivers by Andrew Jackson. The new area became known as the Jackson Purchase. The Jackson Purchase area of the state became the new Western District of Tennessee.

Marshals of the Eastern District of Tennessee since 1838 were Richard M. Woods, 1838-45; Arthur R. Crozier, 1845-50; Daniel McCallum, 1850-52; Joseph Parsons, 1852-53; William M. Lowry, 1853-61; Blackston McDannel, 1861-69; Samuel P. Evans, 1869-81; Thomas H. Reeves, 1881-85; Joseph J. Ivins, 1885-87; William M. Nixon, 1887-89; William S. Tipton, 1889-93; Stephen P. Condon, 1893-97; Richard W. Austin, 1897-1905; William A. Dunlap, 1905-10; James G. Crumbliss, 1910-14; John R. Thompson, 1914-19; J. Parks Worley, 1919-21; Frank W. Flenniker, 1921; Inslee C. King, 1921-33; James R. Worley, 1933-36; Chester R. Hackney, 1936-37; Henry R. Bell, 1937-53; Frank Quarles, 1953-62; Harry D. Mansfield, 1962-69; Leon B. Sutton, 1969-76; Bruce R. Montgomery, 1976-77; Harry D.

Mansfield, 1977-81; Bruce R. Montgomery, 1981-93; Donald R. Benson, 1993-94; Joseph C. Fowler Jr., 1994-2000; Donald R. Benson, 2000-02; and A. Jeffrey Hedden, appointed in 2002.

Marshals of the Middle District of Tennessee since its creation in 1838 were Samuel B. Marshall, 1839-42; Benjamin H. Sheppard, 1842-46; Jesse B. Clements, 1846-50; William M. Brown, 1850-53; Jesse B. Clements, 1853-61; Edwin R. Glasscock, 1861-70; Joseph H. Blackburn, 1870; Thomas J. Harrison, 1870-71; William Spence, 1871-76; Edward S. Wheat, 1876-83; George N. Tillman, 1883-86; George N. Wilson, 1886-89; Carter B. Harrison, 1889-94; J. N. McKenzie, 1894-98; John W. Overall, 1898-1915; Jonas T. Amis, 1915-19; George B. Witt, 1919; John E. Amis, 1919; Edward Albright, 1919-23; Reese Q. Lillard, 1923-33; James R. Jetton, 1933-38; Lonnie B. Ormes, 1938-39; Edward M. Baker, 1939; Reed Sharp, 1939-49; Larry M. Morphis, 1949-53; John O. Anderson, 1953-57; John H. Henderson, 1957-58; Herbert E. Patrick, 1958-61; Elmer W. Disspayne, 1961-69; W. Winsted Beaty, 1969; Leon T. Campbell, 1969-77; William J. Evins Jr., 1977-83; Charles F. Goggin III, 1983-94; Raimon L. Patton, 1994-95; Edward Scott Blair, 1995-2002; and Denny Wade King, appointed in 2002.

Marshals of the new Western District of Tennessee since 1838 were Robert I. Chester, 1838-50; Andrew Guthrie, 1850-53; Robert I. Chester, 1853-57; Hamden McClanahan, 1857-61; Thomas J. Gardner, 1861-66; Martin T. Ryder, 1866-67; H. M. Tomeny, 1867-70; Lucien B. Eaton, 1870-78; Milton T. Williamson, 1878-85; James H. Freeman, 1885-86; Thomas B. Yancey, 1886-89; James W. Brown, 1889-93; Joseph A. Manson, 1893-98; Thomas H. Baker, 1898-1902; Frank S. Elgin, 1902-10; J. Sam Johnson, 1910-15; Stanley H. Trezevant, 1915-22; W. F. Appleby, 1922-24; Terry Abernathy, 1924; Arthur Rogers, 1924-33; B. Money Bates Jr., 1933-37; Charles W. Miles, 1937-45; James M. Dixon, 1945; Ben L. King, 1945-54; William E. Smith, 1954-55; John T. Williams, 1955-60; George C. Harrison, 1960-61; Cato U. Ellis, 1961-69; George R. Tallent, 1969-75; Richard N. Moore, 1975-77; Willie D. Durham Sr., 1977-82; John T. Callery, 1982-94; David L. Stanton, 1994; Wesley Joe "Buck" Wood, 1994-2002; and David G. Jolley, appointed in 2002.

When the southern states including Tennessee succeeded from the Union, the United States of America continued to recognize the U.S. marshals appointed by the Lincoln administration in 1861. The Confederate States of America established districts courts and mar-

shals reporting to the Attorney General of the CSA in the Judicial Act of the 1861 Acts and Resolutions of the First Session of the Provisional Congress of the Confederate States.

Confederate States Marshals were named to serve the three Confederate District Courts of Tennessee and took office early in 1862. C.S. Marshal William H. Crouch was appointed to the Eastern District of Tennessee. Crouch had served as Post Master at Jonesboro in Washington County. C. S. Marshal Jesse B. Clements was appointed to the Middle District of Tennessee. Clements lived at Goodlettsville and had served two terms as the United States Marshal of the Middle District, 1846-50 and 1853-61. C. S. Marshal W. W. Gates was appointed to the Western District of Tennessee. Gates was a publisher in Jackson, Madison County.

Following the Civil War the activities of the Marshals Service increased dramatically across the war torn nation. Over two hundred deputy U.S. marshals made the supreme sacrifice in the enforcement of federal law since the creation of the Marshal Service. Fifteen or more of those died in Tennessee in the line of duty, mostly in the latter part of the nineteenth century.

Marshals Service activity in Tennessee following the Civil War included issues that grew out of the war. Elections were particularly confrontational during reconstruction and U.S. marshals worked to secure the polls and ensure the validity of the vote. They also were active in battling the Ku Klux Klan in the years following the Civil War.

Deputy Marshal R. T. Dunn died in Corinth, Tennessee, north of Nashville, as the result of being shot in the head through an open window as he slept about 11:00 on the night of August 8, 1873. One side of his face was shot off. Members of the KKK killed Deputy Dunn in retaliation for his participation in the arrest of other Ku Kluxers. Deputy Dunn and two other deputies had arrested several members for attacking a man. After the initial arrest the other two marshals left, leaving Deputy Dunn to complete the investigation.

In another run in with the Klan, Deputy U.S. Marshal William D. Hildreth was mortally wounded near Hillsboro in Coffee County on May 22, 1874. The 24-year-old deputy marshal went unarmed to serve a warrant, preferring persuasion to force. Hildreth came from Nashville to arrest one of a group who had beaten a black man for housing a black school teacher. The Klansman eluded him and Hildreth deputized a local man to help him search. They found the subject in a wooded area armed with a double-barrel shotgun. Hildreth borrowed his deputy's pistol and sent the deputy back for better weapons.

Deputy Marshal Hildreth continued to track his man and when he was within hearing distance told him he was under arrest. The Klansman turned and fired both barrels at the deputy marshal, striking him in the legs and groin. Hildreth tried to flee the assault but fell. The Klansman followed him and shot the lawman where he lay. Deputy U.S. Marshal W. D. Hildreth died a short time later.

Hildreth's replacement, Deputy Marshal James P. Everette, was shot and killed by members of the Ku Klux Klan on July 10, 1874. He was shot in the back of the head twice with a small caliber weapon. His killers then destroyed all of the arrest warrants he carried in his saddlebags.

Enforcement of tax laws was a significant duty for the USMS and dangerous duty. Deputy Marshal Felix H. Torbett of Memphis and Deputy Marshal Siebert H. McAlexander of Jackson rode to a Henry County farm on October 1, 1876 to arrest a man for defrauding the government by selling unstamped tobacco. The man was described as a "desperate character" and previous attempts to arrest him had failed.

As Torbett and McAlexander arrived, the culprit armed himself with a double-barreled shotgun and hid in the kitchen, a building separate from the main cabin. After they searched the house, they approached the kitchen. The lawbreaker confronted the deputies and leveled his gun at them. Deputy Marshal Torbett said, "Don't act foolish," but the subject fired. The lawmen jumped to the side, but the load of shot struck Torbett in the breast and he fell. The gunman fired at McAlexander, missing except for a few shot through the deputy's coat. The felon entered the house and soon fled.

Deputy Marshal Torbett lay writhing on the ground from the belly shot and said, "I believe I am killed." He died within the hour.

Another financial crime facing the nation was counterfeiting. Prior to the twentieth century and standardization of federal "greenbacks" as the official paper money of the nation, a large variety of banknotes served as currency. Counterfeiting was a serious problem and the Marshals Service pursued those who committed the crime. Deputy Marshal Albert Gibson arrested one counterfeiter and he was sentenced to two years in prison. Gibson also made a case against the man's father on the same charge. The father was about to go on trial as the son finished his prison term. On January 26, 1877, the just-released counterfeiter went to the home of Deputy Marshal Gibson at his board-

Wanted poster circulated by Eastern District of Tennessee U. S. Marshal William Nixon for the killers of Deputy Marshal Thomas Goodson, who was killed by moonshiners. (Courtesy of the U.S. Marshals Service Collections)

ing house on Poplar Avenue near Second Street in Memphis and shot the marshal in the face and back, killing the lawman.

Deputy Marshal Henry Seagraves fell prey to the banditry that was prolific in the late nineteenth century. Seagraves and another deputy marshal were returning from an assignment in Sumner County on April 8, 1881, when they stopped at a house in Macon County for the night. While there, two robbers fired shots into the air from a nearby cabin. The two lawmen went to investigate and were ambushed by the bandits. Deputy Marshal Seagraves was hit in the chest and killed. The bandits then robbed his body and fled.

Several deputy U.S. marshals were killed between 1872 and 1913, a period declared the Moonshine War by the Marshals Service. The Service lists 21 deputy marshals killed or wounded in the enforcement of the whiskey tax laws, six of whom were shot in Tennessee.

The production of whiskey was not in itself illegal in the nineteenth century as it became when prohibition was enacted. However, failure to pay state and federal taxes on distilled spirits was a crime that sent federal and state law enforcement officers after moonshiners and their stills since the time of the Whiskey Rebellion following the Revolutionary War.

Deputy Marshal L. J. McDonald was shot and killed near Mitchellville on July 12, 1884, during the arrest an illegal distiller. Deputy Marshal William Lee Miller was shot and killed on July 6, 1885, in the mountains near Goodlettsville while he searched for illegal stills. His body was found in a shallow grave that September with five bullet wounds, one to the right side, two to the forehead and two to the back of the head.

Deputy Marshal Miller Hurst and another deputy marshal arrested a man in Pickett County for moonshining and were returning him to Nashville on October 11, 1885. The two marshals were near Jamestown in Fentress County when they were ambushed. Marshal Hurst was struck by shotgun blasts and killed. The bushwhackers freed the prisoner.

Deputy Marshal Thomas Goodson was after a moonshiner in Carter County near Roan Mountain on December 1, 1888. He was clubbed and shot twice in the head with his own weapon. His body was found on the 11th concealed in a sink hole in a laurel thicket. Deputy Marshal Sam Hughes of Chattanooga was hit with eight buckshot while arresting a moonshiner on August 21, 1889.

Deputy Marshal Charles K. Stuart Jr. from Ducktown arrested a moonshiner in Polk County and with the help of his two brothers was transporting him to jail in North Carolina on March 4, 1892. Soon after they crossed the state line a mob of moonshiners confronted them. When Deputy Marshal Stuart refused to release the prisoner, a gun battle broke out. A .38 caliber Winchester ball crashed through the temple of the federal lawman, killing him.

A posse of three deputy marshals, B. C. Brown, A. W. Tilley and James H. Ballinger, a United States Store-keeper and Gauger, went to arrest the postmaster at Dry Creek for stealing money from the mail. As they approached his residence near Cookeville on July 21, 1892, a rifle shot from the second floor struck and killed Deputy Marshal James Ballinger.

Another posse of revenue agents was on their way to raid moonshiners near Monterey about 4:00 p.m. on Saturday, July 20, 1901, when they were ambushed. Two local police officers were wounded and U.S. Deputy Marshal Thomas Price was shot and killed.

Marshals had a broad range of duties and acted in any disorder that threatened the public peace. Deputy Marshals George W. Dillaway and Julius Rembrandt were assigned by Western District U.S. Marshal J. Sam Johnson to monitor an Illinois Central Railroad (ICRR) labor dispute in Memphis. The two lawmen along with ICRR Special Agent Victor C. Benner boarded a switch engine on December 7, 1911, to investigate trouble in the Nonconnah Yard. When they reached the scene, ICRR guards at the railroad yard mistook the three for armed strikers and opened fire. Railroad Special Agent Benner was struck in the throat by the first bullet and killed instantly. In the gun battle that ensued, Deputy Marshal Dillaway was shot in the chest. George Dillaway died of his wounds a week later, December 14.

A shootout in front of the Rosebud Cafe in Memphis on Friday afternoon, September 19, 1919, was due to a longstanding conflict over bootlegging. The incident left newly appointed Deputy U.S. Marshal Orville R. Webster lying dead on the pavement of Monroe Street. Will A. Smiddy, Webster's killer, soon breathed his last in the ambulance on the way to the hospital.

Orville Webster, born in Hicksville, Ohio, began his law enforcement career as a deputy sheriff in Dundee, Mississippi. He joined the Memphis Police Department late in 1918 as a walking patrolman. His success in ferreting out illegal liquor violations quickly earned him a spot on a special liquor squad and soon after a promotion to sergeant.

In one incident Memphis police officers raided a notorious bootleg joint, Kinnane's, and found only a small amount of amount of liquor. Webster and his squad hit Kinnane's a few hours later the same night and confiscated a wagon-load of whiskey. Such exploits earned him the enmity of Memphis bootleggers.

Webster was appointed a U.S. deputy marshal in April 1919 and around two o'clock on a Friday afternoon five months later he and Chief Deputy U.S. Marshal John T. Carrigan were driving by the Rosebud at 115 Monroe Street, a hangout for bootleggers and other unscrupulous characters. Someone among those sitting in a car parked in front of the Rosebud shouted an insult at the two federal marshals as they passed. This was not the first time the two had been taunted by a group of men outside the cafe.

On this occasion Webster stopped the car and confronted the group. Will Smiddy, who was sitting in a car, got out of the vehicle and exchanged heated words with Webster.

Smiddy, a native Memphian and half owner of the Rosebud, was also a former Memphis officer. He and his partner, Jack Klinck, were serving in the detective bureau when they both resigned to operate the Majestic Saloon at Third and Gayoso. Smiddy was considered a bootlegger and had been tried on the charged, but was never convicted of a crime.

Deputy Marshal Webster was carrying a blue Colt .44 with a six-inch barrel. Smiddy had a nickel-plated, four-inch barrel Smith & Wesson with the hammer filed off and the grips sanded smooth, so that it was easily concealed and came quickly from a pocket.

Webster and Smiddy met in front of the car and began grappling. Webster grabbed Smiddy by the coat and hit him over the head with his revolver. Smiddy grabbed Webster's right hand and drew his own gun. Both men, standing toe to toe, began firing. Chief Deputy Marshal Carrigan said, "Pistols were banging like machine gun fire." Both men emptied their weapons, Webster firing six shots, Smiddy firing five. Seven of the eleven shots found their target.

As the fight began Chief Deputy Carrigan came up behind Smiddy, and Memphis Detective Walter Hoyle and Patrolman Herrington ran up behind Webster. By the time these officers arrived the incident was over. Webster toppled backwards into Hoyle's arms. Smiddy's knees buckled and Carrigan caught him as he crumpled.

Another deputy marshal died in a bootlegging incident at the other end of the state. The Copper Ridge district north of Knoxville was known as a lawless area because of the moonshiners and bootleggers that lived and operated there. Deputy US Marshal Reuben LaFayette Hughett went into the district on June 13, 1930, accompanied by Knox County Deputy Sheriff J. Wesley Painter and Special Prohibition Agents Jones and Rogers to arrest a notorious moonshiner.

The moonshiner asked to get his hat and coat before going to jail. Deputy Marshal Hughett agreed and followed him into the house. Inside the prisoner pulled a pistol from the bib of his overalls and shot the marshal twice in the stomach as they grappled. Deputy U.S. Marshal Hughett died two days later.

The last marshal to die in the line of duty in Tennessee was Deputy Marshal Samuel Enoch Vaughn. He was assigned to Murfreesboro but was shot five times and killed in northern Georgia on August 8, 1953, while transporting two prisoners to the federal penitentiary in Atlanta. One of the prisoners had been leaning on the back of Deputy Marshal Vaughn's seat, talking to him as he drove. Near Cartersville, the prisoner grabbed the gun of the 20-year law enforcement veteran, told him to pull over, and when Deputy Marshal Vaughn refused, shot him.

The United States Marshals Service continues to provide exceptional services to the citizens of Tennessee. Fortunately no member of the Service has given his or her life in the line of duty in the last fifty years.

Internal Revenue enforcement officers were also very active in Tennessee following the Civil War because of the heightened need for tax revenue and the quantity of illegal whiskey production in the state. Internal Revenue collectors of the era did not have arrest powers and were assisted by deputy marshals when they made raids.

The Alcohol Tax Unit of the Bureau of Internal Revenue, predecessor of the ATF, lost several agents in Tennessee. Most of the collectors and agents were killed by moonshiners.

One of the best known revenue agents in the state was Deputy Collector James M. Davis. Davis served with distinction as a young soldier in the Confederate army and after the Civil War worked in law enforcement for the state of Tennessee. He joined the U.S. Internal Revenue Service as deputy collector in 1871 while in his mid-twenties and served under Collector W. M. Woodcock of the Nashville office. Another deputy collector in the office was John L. Eider.

James Davis was a large boned muscular man, standing over 6' 2" and weighing 210 pounds. Although Davis showed great courage and physical strength, he was kind-hearted and gentle.

Deputy Collector Davis established a reputation as a dedicated lawman. He made almost 3,500 arrests during his career and destroyed around 1,000 stills. In the process he was involved in frequent shootouts, wounded a number of times and killed several moonshiners in self-defense.

One on the most dramatic gun battles between government lawmen and moonshiners took place on August 23 and 24, 1878. Known as Peek's fight, because it took place at old man Peek's house in Overton County, the revenuers were surrounded for two days and nights without food or water by thirty moonshiners. The leader of the whiskey makers was Campbell Morgan, a noted moonshiner that Davis had previously dueled and shot in the shoulder. Firing was continual during the siege and several were wounded on both sides. Law abiding citizens finally stepped in and ended the clash.

Following the skirmish, moonshiner Campbell Morgan joined the revenue service and went to work under Deputy Collector Davis. Morgan became an effective agent for the government.

Four years later, about 2:00 p.m. on March 13, 1884, Deputy Collector Davis and his men were about three miles from McMinnville on their return from Beersheba when gunmen fired from ambush. Davis fell from his horse. He was able to regain his feet and moved toward the two men at the rear of his group when a second volley struck him, killing him instantly. Between twenty and thirty lead shot entered his body; his skull was literally shattered.

Three deputy collectors were killed in an ambush on October 7, 1892. Five federal lawmen traveled from Nashville to Flintville in Lincoln County as the result of an anonymous letter offering to lead them to a stash of contraband brandy. They were suspicious of the letter, but felt duty bound to investigate. The group included three Internal Revenue officers, Deputy Collector S. D. Mather, General Deputy Collector Creed S. Cardwell and General Deputy Collector Joseph L. Spurrier and two deputy marshals, J. E. Pulver and E. S. Robertson.

They were joined by a local, David L. Harris Jr., about 7:00 a.m. and set out along a wooded trail. Collectors Mather and Spurrier rode in front with Cardwell and Pulver about 25 feet back and Robertson and Harris bringing up the rear, 50 feet back. As the party was directly beside a large chestnut log on the right side of the road, a fusillade of gunfire tore through the posse. The three Internal Revenue collectors all went down. Buckshot struck S. D. Mather in the right side and back of the head, killing him instantly. Creed Cardwell took ten buck shot

in the back and side; he died at 2:45 p.m. at the train depot. Joseph Spurrier fell paralyzed to the ground with a Winchester rifle bullet in his spine. He died twenty days later, October 27, at his home in Nashville.

Horses and mules threw the remaining riders. The deputy marshals and Harris returned fire. Deputy Marshal Robertson shot one of the bushwhackers in the head and killed him instantly. The other three moonshiners fled.

Revenue Agent Irby U. Scruggs was shot and killed on April 30, 1921, while raiding a still in Knox County. The following year, July 6, 1922, Revenue Agent Howell J. Lynch died of gunshot wounds when a raiding party destroyed a still near Gainsboro. Revenue Agent William Franklin Berry tried to make an arrest in Chattanooga on March 18, 1938. The culprit resisted, drew a pistol and shot Agent Berry to death.

Like most federal lawmen killed in Tennessee, Alcohol Tax Unit Agent James L. Molloy was a native of Tennessee. Molloy died on January 31, 1939, as the result of his chest being crushed when his automobile fell from a bridge near Smithville a month earlier. Molloy was on the way to raid a whiskey still and his car skidded from the ice covered bridge. He had been a federal revenue agent for 21 years and was working out of Cookeville. Jim Molloy began his law enforcement career as a McMinnville police officer. He served as sheriff of Warren County from 1926 to 1928.

Revenue Agent Samuel Leeper was shot and killed while raiding a still in Marion County on July 31, 1940. On November 21, 1941, three alcohol tax revenue agents, William Milton Pugh, J. K. Howes and C. R. Rossner, went to the home of an ex-convict near Hale's Point to arrest him for running a whiskey still they had destroyed the day before. The moonshiner, on parole after a prison term for killing a Lauderdale County deputy sheriff, asked to say goodbye to his mother before being taken back to jail. Agent Pugh escorted him to the door of the residence. The felon returned armed with a shotgun and shot Pugh point-blank in the face. The killer was executed for the crime. Another revenue agent, Milton Rogers, suffered a fatal heart attack on July 12, 1948, while raiding a still in Knox County.

Federal Bureau of Investigation (FBI) agents have enforced federal laws in Tennessee since soon after the formation of the Bureau of Investigation in 1908. The activities of the Bureau expanded as a greater number of crimes entered the federal statutes.

The agency gained national recognition during the lawless years of the twenties and early thirties when

Postal Inspector Elbert Perry Lamberth, left, was shot multiple times and killed by a postal carrier in Gibson on August 16, 1917. Alcohol Tax Unit Agent William Milton Pugh, right, was shot in the face and killed by an ex-convict and moonshiner on November 21, 1941.

prohibition and depression era gangsters spread terror. The crime spree of one of America's most notorious criminals came to an end in the early hours of September 26, 1933, in Memphis. FBI special agents from the Birmingham Field Office and members of the Memphis police force captured bootlegger, bank robber and kidnapper George Kelly Barnes Jr., a.k.a. "Machine Gun" Kelly.

The FBI opened two Field Offices in Tennessee in the mid-1930s. The Memphis Field Office oversaw activities in the western part of the state and the Knoxville Field Office coordinated work in the eastern half of the state. Each Field Office has a Senior Agent in Charge (SAC). Resident Agency offices are located in larger cities throughout the state.

One of the early heads of the Memphis Field Office was Special Agent in Charge J. W. Vincent. He was transferred to Miami in August 1939 and replaced by P. Wyly. Memphis was under the command of Special Agent in Charge Donald S. Hostetter from 1944 to 1951. Hostetter established a notable reputation as a field agent, participating in many high-profile investigations, including the roundup of the Karpis-Barker gang in 1935.

Special Agent in Charge Julius M. Lopez Jr. headed the Memphis office from 1957 to 1959. He was followed by Special Agent in Charge Frank Holloman, who stepped down for health reasons in May 1960. Special Agent in Charge Marlin Johnson replaced Holloman. Johnson had been assigned to a number of high-profile cases including the Brink's robbery in Boston. Johnson was transferred to head the Washington field office at the end of October 1960.

Special Agent in Charge Clarence M. Kelley, 49, was then named to head the Memphis office. He served as Special Agent in Charge of the Memphis office until his retirement from the FBI on October 24, 1961. Kelley came back to serve as Director of the FBI from 1973 to 1978.

The FBI opened the Knoxville Field Office on May 1, 1937, with six special agents. Special Agent in Charge R. B. Hood headed the office and Special Agent Joseph Farley was stationed in Chattanooga. One of the first cases investigated by the Knoxville Field Office was the kidnapping of Chattanooga Police Officer O. O. Griffin in June 1937. Four suspects were identified and arrested in Tampa, Florida.

By 1942 Resident Agency offices were established in Johnson City and Chattanooga. As the United States looked toward the possibility of a second World War, the FBI geared up to fight the war against the enemy on the home front. Spying and sabotage were

primary assignments for the Bureau. Special agents assigned to the Knoxville Office arrested an enemy agent in July 1944. The spy had been trained in espionage in Germany in 1940 and had engaged in spying in the early forties.

Federal authorities recognized the need for local agencies to be prepared to assist in war related law enforcement as well as assistance with military training logistics and preparedness in case of military action in the United States. The FBI was assigned responsibility for the training of local departments in bombs and explosives, methods of sabotage, blackouts and air raids, traffic issues of military convoys and other wartime matters. Much of the training was useful non-wartime law enforcement.

The FBI started training courses for local police at the newly formed National Academy on July 29, 1935. The war-time training effort brought the training directly to local law enforcement agencies. Training was not only provided to large departments, but Quarterly Police Conferences were held that brought representatives of smaller departments together. The first conferences were held in Tennessee in 1941. Week-long conferences were held each quarter over the next several years. Police officers, deputy sheriffs and highway patrolmen across the state attended the sessions. Many agents participated in the training. One of the better known was Special Agent Glenn Trusty a firearms expert who assisted with training in Middle and West Tennessee.

In the years following the war, the course of study for local law enforcement officers at the FBI National

FBI quarterly conferences provided civil defense and law enforcement training in Jackson. Attending a 1942 conference were (front row from left): JPD Patrolman Robert Stedman, JPD Sergeant Robert A. Mainord, FBI Special Agent G. A. Wilson, THP Sergeant Ray Wheat, and O. D. Williamson of the Madison County Sheriff's Office. Back row from left: W. R. Wright of Bemis, J. B. Fry of Bemis, Edd Stansell of the Madison County Sheriff's Office, JPD Patrolman James Davis and James Phelps of the Tennessee Highway Patrol.

The FBI work closely with local police in making investigations, scientific evaluation of evidence, criminal identification and training. From left to right on the firing range at the Madison County Fair Grounds were FBI Special Agent George W. Hymers Jr., Jackson Assistant Chief of Police J. Raymond Gaba, FBI firearms expert Special Agent Glenn Trusty and Jackson Chief of Police Robert A. Mainord Jr.

"Rocky Top" ended in 1992 with numerous arrests. In 2005, operation "Tennessee Waltz" conducted by the Memphis Field Office and the TBI resulted in the arrest of six member of the Tennessee state legislature and others.

The support role of the FBI was as important to its heritage in Tennessee as the direct law enforcement efforts of its special agents. In the days when few Tennessee police departments or sheriff's offices had the expertise to gather basic evidence such as fingerprints, the FBI made its personnel and equipment available for scientific examination and assessment of crime scene evidence. Even after the TBI began to provide most scientific work not available locally, the FBI continued to provide assistance.

Training and information systems provided by the FBI, including Uniform Crime Reports and the National Crime Information Center (NCIC) that became operational on January 1, 1967, aided Tennessee agencies to track crime trends and identify criminals.

Director Hoover encouraged and rewarded agents who performed well in the field. One special agent stationed in New York City was standing in line at the bank to deposit his payroll check when the two men in front of him pulled a gun and proceeded to rob the bank. The FBI agent grappled with one of the robbers and was forced to pull his gun and kill the bandit. When Director Hoover

was informed, he transferred the agent to his home town, Columbia, Tennessee, as his reward.

FBI Special Agent Jerry Bastin returned to Tennessee in 1979 to begin duty in the Jackson Resident Agency. The Old Hickory native joined the FBI in 1967 and after training at the FBI Academy in Quantico, Virginia, spent a year in Omaha. Most agents spent their first year at a smaller office before gaining further experience in a major Field Office. Bastin moved to Baltimore and spent 11 years worked mostly political corruption cases.

In Jackson, Bastin joined Special Agent Joe Rasberry and later additional agents were stationed with them including J. Gary Boutwell, who retired from the FBI in Jackson and began a teaching career in criminal justice at Lambuth University. Boutwell was the son-in-law of Special Agent George Hymers. The Jackson Resident Agency office divided cases geographically rather than by the nature of the crime. The number of counties assigned to an agent depended on the number of agents in the office. Agents worked the full range of crimes from bank robberies to political corruption. Bank robbery, kidnapping and similar violent crime made newspaper headlines, white collar crimes often did not. Bank robberies were good for young agents to cut their teeth on, they were challenging and fun.

Special Agent Bastin was one of the federal investigators pressed into service in 1969 when the government placed armed security personnel on airliners due to increasing numbers of skyjackings. The group

Detective Sergeant Robert W. Dailey Jr. presented a plaque to FBI Director J. Edgar Hoover on behalf of the Tennessee Fraternal Order of Police.

worked flights for two months while the first federal Air Marshals were selected and given specialized training for the duty. In that period Bastin was constantly flying somewhere in the world.

No member of the FBI has been killed in the line of duty in Tennessee. A number of notable individual who have played key roles in Tennessee law enforcement began their career with the FBI.

Tennessee Valley Authority (TVA) law enforcement officers have functioned in many roles since the creation of the federal program in 1933. TVA was a part of President Franklin D. Roosevelt's New Deal intended to help lift the nation out of the depths of the Great Depression.

TVA was an innovative idea, creating a corporation with both the power of the government and the flexibility and initiative of a private enterprise. The Tennessee Valley was in sad shape even by Depression era standards. Farm land soils were depleted and eroded, the best timber had been cut and the area was without industry.

TVA built dams to harness power, control floods and improve navigation. It brought immediate jobs and assisted farmers to improve crop yields. Forests were replanted and habitat for wildlife and fish improved. Most dramatic of TVA's efforts was the generation of electricity. Life for residents of the Valley was made easier by electric lights and modern appliances and industries came into the region to take advantage of cheap power and brought desperately needed jobs.

The TVA law enforcement function began with a twelve-man Property Protection unit created in mid-1933. The name of the unit was changed the following year to Police, Fire and Guide Service. Responsibilities of the Service included life and property protection, fire prevention, traffic control, visitor escort and general policing duties. During the early years of the agency, TVA built towns for its workers and provided police and fire services to the towns. TVA police also provided protection to dams and construction sites, and staffed information posts at project sites. TVA-owned towns were sold at public auction in 1948.

TVA police officers wore utilitarian khaki uniforms and campaign hats without a hat badge. Breast badges were a stock pinched shield. The first sidearm carried by the TVA police was the .38-caliber, "pencil-barrel," model 10 Smith & Wesson, which was used until around 1971.

The name of TVA's law enforcement unit was changed again in 1936 to Public Safety Service (PSS). TVA PSS had a unit at each dam or project location. During construction, most units were under the command of a captain with at least one lieutenant, one or more sergeants and 25 or so officers. After the dam was finished the unit was reduced to eight or ten officers under the command of a lieutenant. The TVA system was divided into four districts with a chief of each district, two to four captains and a lieutenant over each dam.

The uniform of TVA PSS officers were changed in the forties to olive green trousers and Eisenhower jackets. Sam Brown belts were worn with the Ike jackets. Shirts were beige long sleeve with epaulets in winter and cream colored short sleeve in summer. Headgear became a standard eight-point service cap with a custom, art deco design hat badge. The breast badge remained a stock pinched shield. Some badges had numbers and some did not. When numbers were assigned, they were assigned by seniority.

The primary function of PSS offices was protection of TVA property. Many other duties were provided by the officers, including life saving and other emergency aid. PSS officers also staffed information booths, which later became visitors' centers throughout the TVA system.

PSS officers had law enforcement powers under the authority of an agency within whichever of the seven TVA states they were assigned. Their police power was limited to the state in which they served. PSS officers in each state had different jurisdictions. They might be under the highway patrol in one state and a sheriff's department in another state. In Tennessee, PSS officers' authority was under the county government in which the TVA facility was located.

During World War II espionage and sabotage concerns had TVA PSS officers on heightened alert. PSS officers were sworn in as Civilian Auxiliary to the Military Police. At the same time the all-male PSS was being drained as men were called to service in the armed forces. In a time when women were scarce in the work force of the nation, especially in law enforcement, TVA hired a select corps of women to serve as PSS officers.

On April 1, 1943, TVA announced that it would expand its PSS force to nearly 1,000 by creating the Women Officers of Public Safety (WOOPS). The female officers were uniformed and carried a .38-caliber revolver the same as male officers. WOOPS officers were between the ages of 21 and 39 and went

Tennessee Valley Authority Police, Fire, and Guide Service existed between 1934 and 1936, and enforced the law in worker communities created by the TVA at project sites in the early years of the federal program created in 1933.

through a course of intense combat training, including practice with riot guns and courses in judo.

The officers were eager for the opportunity but many had never fired a gun. Officer Winnie Wade, a new WOOPS, told the *Knoxville News-Sentinel,* "I want to learn to work with the dogs and to shoot." Some officers worked with German shepherd dogs in their patrol duties, as at the new Watts Bar Dam on the Tennessee River between Knoxville and Chattanooga which was assigned to WOOPS.

Many of the women were single, but a few were wives of PSS officers who were away at war. Kathleen Brown's husband guarded Chickamauga Dam. "He is overseas," she said, "I released him to the Army, as bad as I hated to, so I'm going to replace him."

WOOPS quickly gained respect. No incident of sabotage occurred at any TVA installation. In 1944, just over a year after the program began, the female corps won the coveted Army-Navy E for Excellence Award. Officer Rosemary Cross accepted the award on behalf of WOOPS.

When the men returned home from the war in 1945, the WOOPS went home as well. By the 1950s the TVA PSS was again all male. WOOPS officers were the "Rosie the Riveter" of law enforcement.

TVA also hired male PSS officers during the war. Ernest A. Smith joined the TVA force in 1943. Officer Smith and his family lived in a TVA house. One of the additional duties of PSS officers during WW II was spotting plane. Officers were given a deck of transparent cards with the outline of a different airplane on each. When a plane flew over their post, the officer held cards up until they identified the plane, then they called the FAA and reported it.

In the decades following the war the nation experienced unprecedented growth, creating ever larger demands for the energy produced by TVA. The responsibilities of the PSS expanded with the growth.

As the nation prospered, increased availability of free time for American workers led to major expansion of the use of recreational facilities related to TVA projects. For the PSS, law enforcement and safety issues

1974. Officer Hood was directing traffic at a TVA work site on U.S. Highway 11 south of Loudon.

TVA PSS officers in Tennessee were given state law enforcement commissions in the 1980s. PSS officers also began wearing a new style badge. A custom designed eagle-top shield similar to other federal badges became the insignia for TVA officers.

Lieutenant Charles Smith formed the Executive Protection unit in 1988. The unit was responsible for protecting the three federally appointed board members, and the presidents and vice presidents of TVA. Before the unit was formed, officers drove the officials on an occasional basis as needed. Later Steve O. Watson sent Captain Smith to a number of executive protection schools and Smith selected a number of

TVA Public Safety Service districts officers met at the Hiawassee Dam in North Carolina in May 1938. The chief is in the front on the left with a number of captains and other officers. They are wearing the pinched shield breast badge and the custom, art deco design hat badge.

expanded along with the increased use of TVA lakes and campgrounds. Incidents ranged from lost children and fishermen stuck on sand bars to serious violent crimes. The PSS grew in numbers and expertise to deal with the heightened demands on its resources.

Charles Alvin Smith followed in his father Ernest Smith's footsteps and became a PSS officer in 1971. The issue sidearm was changed that year to the .38 caliber Model 15 Combat Masterpiece revolver. Officer Charles Smith worked with his father until Ernest Smith retirement in 1973 after 31 years as a PSS officer. The younger Smith had begun his law enforcement career in 1960 working as a deputy for his father-in-law Sevier County Sheriff Ray C. Noland.

TVA lost its first officer in the line of duty when Public Safety Service Officer Thomas Harold Hood was struck and killed by a tractor-trailer on March 18,

Officer Elizabeth McCord, one of the TVA female officers hired during World War II. The armed officers of the Women Officers of Public Safety (WOOPS) had specially designed uniforms for summer wear, left, and winter wear, right.

good lieutenants to staff the unit. Smith also became a firearms instructor in the eighties and served as TVA's Master Armorer.

The East Tennessee Environmental Crimes Task Force was created in 1991 and based in Greeneville, Tennessee. Agents from the U.S. Department of Energy, the Tennessee Valley Authority, the Federal Bureau of Investigation, the U.S. Environmental Protection Agency and other state and federal agencies contribute personnel. The task force, later led by U.S. Attorney Harry S. Mattice Jr., was composed of five full-time agents and the 14 agencies responsible for environmental law enforcement.

By the mid-1990s, TVA had 500 Public Safety Service officers and a major reorganization of security and law enforcement responsibilities began. TVA out-sourced some security duties and reduced the size of the PSS force. Private security firms were contracted to protect TVA office buildings in Knoxville and Chattanooga and to provide armed security guards at TVA nuclear plants.

Law enforcement personnel of TVA were reduced to 150. The nature of the force was changed as well. The manner of getting police powers through agencies in the different states created limitations that had become untenable for the PSS.

Steve O. Watson initially joined the TVA Office of the Inspector General after he retired as deputy director of the TBI, but later became assistant director of

One of the ten boats used by TVA Police to patrol the lakes created by dam projects and used for recreation.

PSS. He was asked by Robert G. "Bob" Carter, director of public safety for TVA, to write a proposed law creating the TVA Police. The legislation passed congress as a part of the Crime Bill in 1994, giving the TVA Police uniform jurisdiction as a federal police entity no matter which state they served in, but limited to TVA properties.

The implementation of the TVA Police took place in 1995. TVA Police officers were sworn in as federal police officers on September 12, 1995. Captain Charles A. Smith was the first sworn that morning at the Federal Court House in Knoxville. Captain Smith was sworn in early so that he could receive the colors from the Color Guard at the ceremony.

That evening in a ceremony at Norris Dam, the other TVA Police officers and staff were sworn. Those sworn in were Director Robert G. Carter, Assistant Directors Steve O. Watson and Robert L. Thompson, Commanders R. DeWane Broome, James E. Carver, George W. Smith II and Sidney G. Whitehurst, Captains Charles A. Smith, Charles H. Cooper, Jimmy Davis, Kenneth R. Dix, Kenneth W. Lovingood, Ralph E. Majors, Robert D. Norman and Larry D. Sparks and Lieutenants Stephen R. Browder, Charles Robin Smith, Donald R. Andrews, Steve Caldwell, James R. Daughetee, John W. Draper, Nancy J. Martin, Jess D. Millsaps, Bobby R. Odom, Robert T. Parker, Thomas E. Phillips, Robert N. Porterfield, Robert C. Sterling and Gary J. Toomey. The remainder of the 125 officers sworn in was 15 sergeants and 81 officers. New officers completed a 16-week federal training program at the Federal Law Enforcement Training Center in Glynco, Georgia, and a 10-week field training program.

Assistant Director Steve Watson also developed the uniform and insignia for the force. The uniform was

TVA Police Special Services officers, assigned to executive protection and other special assignments for board members of the corporation, were sworn in as federal police officers on September 12, 1995. All were lieutenants except for Captain Smith, the head of the unit. Those seated in the front from left to right were Steve Bowers, Captain Charles A. Smith (commander of the unit), and Donald R. Andrews. Standing in the back row from left to right were Doug Milsaps, Robert Parker, James Daughetee and Mike Jenkins.

TVA Police Commander Charles Robin Smith, left, and Sergeant Mike Matthews at Douglas Dam.

navy blue with a campaign hat. Initially the TVA Police wore white shirts similar to the U.S. Capitol Police, but the color was soon changed to navy blue. Officers were issued Sig Sauer 9mm semiautomatic pistols as sidearms.

The commission chairman took an interest in the badge and wanted a star on it and the TVA seal. Blackinton was asked to design a custom badge. Board members were given badge numbers 1, 2 and 3. The executive officer of TVA got badge 4 and the director of the TVA Police got 5. Watson got badge number 7. Each officer was assigned three badges, a breast badge, a hat badge that was a smaller version of the breast badge and a wallet badge.

A third generation of the Smith family became a part of TVA law enforcement in 1995 when Charles Robin Smith, the son of Charles A. Smith and grandson of Ernest Smith, joined the TVA Police at the rank of lieutenant. Robin Smith served as a member of the Sevierville Police Department for 16 years. Charles Smith's other son, Chris, joined the Pigeon Forge Police Force in 1988. When Charles Smith retired as commander of the Eastern District he was replaced by his son Robin Smith who was serving as commander of the Central District at the time.

Assistant Director Steve Watson formed the Inspections Division of TVA Police in 1996 with responsibility for the review of the activities of agency. He also initiated the accreditation process for the TVA Police before he retired in December 1996. The agency was first accredited in 1998.

Forty-five-year-old TVA Police Officer Timothy Patrick Huckaby was killed near Knoxville on November 24, 1998, when a wheel broke off an oncoming car and struck his patrol Jeep. Officer Huckaby died of severe head injuries. He had served over twenty years on the force.

Following the terrorist attacks of September 11, 2001, TVA Police developed a homeland security strategy to insure the protection of the critical national resources of the TVA. Lieutenant Steve Browder was given responsibility of homeland security at TVA in January 2003.

Today the TVA Police is a federally commissioned, nationally accredited law enforcement agency that provides protection for TVA employees, properties and visitors to TVA recreation facilities. They have an 80,000-square-mile service area in seven states.

Duties of the force include routinely patrol work at dams and other projects. Policing TVA's lakes and campgrounds includes dealing with drownings, criminal incidents and disturbances. TVA Police also enforces the Archaeological Resources Protection Act, protecting relics and artifacts. Homeland security issues remain a priority concern for the TVA Police.

Other federal law enforcement agencies served proudly in Tennessee. Officers of a number of those agencies have given their lives in the line of duty.

Postal Inspector Elbert Perry Lamberth was investigating a dispute between a rural postal carrier and the post office on August 16, 1917. The postal carrier invited Inspector Lamberth into his Gibson, Tennessee, home and shot him in the head, neck and abdomen.

Federal narcotics officers began enforcement work in Tennessee following passage of the Harrison Act regulating opiates in 1914. Nashville office Director George W. Cunningham and Narcotics Officer W. R. Williams of the U.S. Treasury Department's Narcotics Division made two arrests and confiscated $20,000 of cocaine and morphine in Nashville in June 1926.

The Federal Bureau of Narcotics was created in 1929. It broke up a major drug ring in December 1934 in coordinated raids nationwide. Tennessee based agents including W. R. Williams and A. E. Myers under the command of Director George W. Cunningham made 37 arrests during raids across the state. The operation was the biggest in the history of the Bureau.

In recent years two federal officers have died in accidents. Forest Service Officer Stephen Allen Bowman was killed on June 24, 1998, in a helicopter crash while he and a National Guardsman were searching for marijuana plants. Secret Service Special Agent Scott Evan Deaton was en route to a protective assignment in Memphis on June 11, 1999, when he lost control of his vehicle on Interstate 40 during a severe thunderstorm and was killed instantly when struck by a tractor-trailer.

Certain law enforcement personnel function under federal authority even though they are not federal employees. Railroad police are given interstate jurisdiction under U.S. Code: Title 49: Section 28101. Illinois Central Railroad Special Agent Victor C. Benner was killed on December 7, 1911, in a gun battle at the Memphis Nonconnah Yard. Benner had previously served as a Shelby County deputy sheriff. Nashville, Chattanooga & St. Louis Railroad Police Officer Felix G. Presson was found mortally wounded in a railway yard at Memphis. He had been shot four times and died on August 22, 1937, before he could make a statement. Presson's killer was arrested in New York City in 1941 after shooting at a detective and confessed to the murder of Officer Presson while he was confined at Sing Sing prison.

Many members of Tennessee law enforcement agencies also served as railroad police. For example, former Deputy U.S. Marshal Charles H. King became the chief special agent of the Gulf, Mobile & Ohio Railroad in 1922. Madison County Deputy Sheriff Edgar Lee "Edd" Stansell took a position as special agent of the Gulf, Mobile & Ohio Railroad in 1942. Highway Patrolman Carlton French joined the Illinois Central Railroad as a special agent in 1945.

Airport police also function under federal authority. One Tennessee airport police officer has fallen in the line of duty. Nashville International Airport Police Officer John Michael Richardson died on April 29, 1999, from injuries he received the day before when he

Special agents of the Illinois Central Railroad assigned to Memphis. The officer on the right is Special Agent Carlton French. They wore the same style insignia as the Memphis Police Department.

lost control of his cruiser and struck a bridge on Interstate 40. The 26-year-old canine officer had been with the department for four years. Officer Richardson's canine, Tossy, received only minor injuries.

Security forces at military installations, research facilities such as those at Oak Ridge and other U.S. properties also work under federal authority. Since the creation of the Department of Homeland Security, cooperation of local and state agencies with federal law enforcement has greatly expanded.

Federal officers play a key role in Tennessee law enforcement today and face the same dangers as a part of their duty to the citizens of Tennessee as all crime fighters.

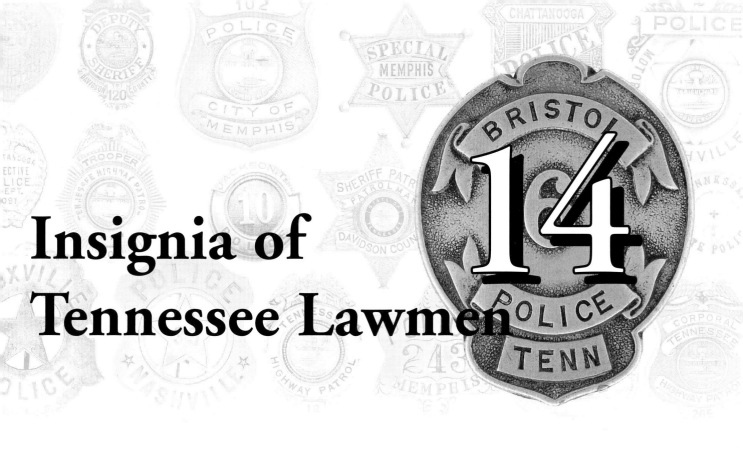

Insignia of Tennessee Lawmen

Insignia worn by law enforcement officers symbolizes the authority vested in them to protect life and property in their community. The historical development of Tennessee insignia was consistent with that in other parts of the United States.

The breast badge is the predominant insignia worn by law enforcement personnel and can be traced to the heraldic designs of feudal Europe and more generally it is linked to symbols of authority used from ancient times.

The nature and design of police insignia varied significantly from the earliest days. Early insignia was as often made of cloth as metal and was found in the form of a band around the arm or a ribbon pinned to a coat. The first night watchmen in many locales had only a nightstick or alarm rattle to denote their office. In some areas the only insignia was on the hat of the sheriff or constable. By the middle of the nineteenth century, however, a metal breast badge had become essential insignia for lawmen.

Some basic designs for the badge quickly grew to prominence. The star and the pinched-shield were the predominant badge forms. Often these forms were combined with others, such a shield with a star cut in the center, a star set in a crescent or a star with a wreath around it. The wreath around the star was most frequently represented by a plain circle of metal, forming the badge style know as a circle-star. An American

eagle as the symbol of the United States was placed at the top of many badges, especially shields. Another badge style developed using the circle with an eagle on top and accented with designs that incorporated additional panels for rank or other designations. Many variations of this style and others were created in the late nineteenth and early twentieth centuries.

The manufacture of early badges ranged from simple handmade stars to very ornate jeweler made badges. The "tin star" badge was often actually cut from a piece of thin metal as a quick and practical item for frontier lawmen. Some jewelers made fancy suspension badges or decorated badges with precious gems. Most of the time the more ornamental forms were presentation badges given to a well-respected lawman by a citizens group or by the members of the department. Most early badges were made by stamp and die companies, some of which became known as badge makers.

By the turn of the twentieth century most police departments had also incorporated a hat badge as part of the insignia. These were primarily wreaths encircling a number or rank. For this reason, hat badges were often called "wreaths." Some were cloth or felt with the wreath stitched in bullion, much as seen in military hat insignia of the period. Bullion stitched hat insignia was more frequently worn by supervisors. Most wreaths worn by patrolmen were made of metal.

Some early wreaths carried either the name or initials of the department. Sheriff's offices did not typically wear uniforms until the mid-twentieth century and wore only breast badges.

As manufacturing techniques improved, the variety of badge forms increased. Many badges were small at the turn of the twentieth century, often no more than an inch and a half tall. State and city seals grew to become central to the design of both breast and hat badges. Enamel was used to add color to badges early in the twentieth century and by the third quarter of the century enamel became extensively used.

Most major agencies changed badge styles four or five times over the last century and a quarter. Prior to that time badges were usually purchased for new officers coming on the force without much concern that the badge exactly match other being worn. The badge was frequently purchased by the officer himself. As department began to provide insignia, the larger the agency the less frequently badge styles changed. This was mostly due to the cost of replacing insignia for the entire department. Generally speaking, sheriff's offices changed badge styles more frequently than police departments. A newly elected sheriff typically wanted to distinguish himself from his predecessor, especially if he were of a different political party. In addition, a new sheriff often did not keep all deputies previously appointed, particularly special deputies, and changing badge styles was a way to cancel their authority.

Shoulder patches appeared on uniforms near the first of the twentieth century. The earliest patches were used to denote special units such as traffic or mounted and carried a motif consistent with that particular duty. Early traffic patches were in the form of a spoked wheel and later wings were added as an indication of speed. Early patches were more properly arm patches than shoulder patches because they were worn not on shoulder, but half way between shoulder and elbow.

Generally, it was not until after World War II that agency patches were designed and intended to be worn by all uniformed officers. Shoulder patches have changed through the years with designs as a rule becoming more elaborate.

Tennessee produced a number of badge makers that provided insignia for lawmen in the state in the late nineteenth and first half of the twentieth century. The most prolific was the George C. Dury Company at 420 Union Street in Nashville. The maker mark "G. C. Dury Co., Nashville" appears on Nashville police insignia from the turn of the twentieth century until about 1950. Dury also made badges for other local and state agencies. The first badges worn by the Tennessee Highway Patrol were produced by Dury.

The Dury family in America began with George Dury, a court painter of Bavaria in the reign of Ludwig I. He fled Munich to seek a life in the democracy of the United States in 1849. He subsequently settled in Nashville and continued his profession as a portrait painter. His third child George Carl Dury established the G. C. Dury Company following the Civil War and sold art and photographic supplies. The company expanded into to other lines to supply the business community. For a period Dury partnered with Finney and a few badges are maker marked "Dury & Finney." Dury's still exists as a photographic supplier, but has not produced badges for law enforcement since the mid-twentieth century.

Although Dury produced many of the shield-cut-out-stars worn by Nashville policemen, the badge they are best know for is the custom circle star used by the department between 1930 and 1952. The badge was a unique design featuring a six-point star in a circle decorated with an art nouveau design and number panel at the top. The Tennessee state seal was featured at the center of the star.

Memphis badge maker W. J. Cooley & Company, located for many years on the second floor of 80 S. Front Street, made many badges for agencies in the Memphis area. The Cooley Company was a successor to Wm. C. Ellis company, established by William C. Ellis (1835-1923). Ellis was a merchant blacksmith from Crownland, England, who moved to Memphis prior to the Civil War. Ellis was listed in the 1860 *Memphis City Directory* as a "die sinker, stencil cutter, wood and copper plate engraver" located at 40 Monroe, between Main and Second. He established a foundry on Front Street in 1862.

Wm. C. Ellis became Wm. C. Ellis & Sons around 1880. The company made metal stencils for marking cotton bales, heavy steel stamps and branding hammers for lumber. Later they made rubber stamps, numbering and dating machines, trade tags and tokens and from time to time police badges for the Memphis Police Department. Ellis made six-point stars for the MPD in the late 1870s and 1880s with the maker mark "Ellis, Maker, Memphis." Some of the badges were jeweler engraved.

Willson J. Cooley joined the Ellis firm in 1909 and became general manager four years later. In 1918 Cooley bought out the stamp and seal business and Ellis Stamp & Seal became W. J. Cooley & Company.

Maker marks of Tennessee badge makers. Wm. C. Ellis & Sons, left, made badges for the Memphis Police Department in the 1880s and 1890s. G. C. Dury Co., center, made badges for the Nashville Police Department and other local and state agencies from the 1890s through the 1930s. W. J. Cooley & Co., right, made badges for Memphis, Shelby County, and other law enforcement agencies during the first half of the twentieth century.

Wm. C. Ellis and Sons Iron Works continued in business in Memphis through the twentieth century, but no longer produced law enforcement insignia.

W. J. Cooley & Company produced various types of badges including chauffeur badges, trade badges and dog tags in addition to law enforcement insignia. The Shelby County Sheriff's Office was a principle insignia client of W. J. Cooley & Co. during the 1920s and 1930s. The maker mark "W. J. Cooley, Maker, Memphis, Tenn." appears on many of the six-point stars worn by deputy sheriffs of Shelby County. The W. J. Cooley & Company waned following World War II, but continued to produce rubber stamps into the 1950s.

Another early maker of MPD stars was V. B. Thayer, owner of the Memphis Engraving Works. The *Memphis Daily Avalanche*, March 11, 1872, identifies him as the maker of the new badge of the Memphis Police Department. Thayer appeared in the 1872 city directory as "Thayer V. B. engraver, moving car at 299 2nd, r. 215 Beale." He may have been an itinerant and no badge has been found with his maker mark.

The earliest form of the unique style Memphis police badge known as the acorn is maker marked "Bailer, Memphis" The Bailer Jewelry Manufacturing Company of Memphis likely created the insignia form in 1922. The badge was originally designed for sergeants. It later was used for all supervisory ranks.

Agencies and individual law enforcement officers have relied on many other jewelers, engravers, stamp and seal producers and others to provide insignia. Many early badges were ordered individually by officers from whatever source was available. Numerous jewelers have produced badges through the years as presentation pieces. Quarles Jewelers of Chattanooga produced many custom gold badges for command officers of the city police. Today badges are almost exclusively provided by highly specialized insignia manufacturers outside of Tennessee.

Insignia used by Tennessee law enforcement are documented in color in the Special Insignia Section. Following are miscellaneous insignia not recorded in that section. Not all the insignia used by the various agencies in the state are shown. No examples of some early badges and patches are known to exist. The variety of insignia used in some agencies is extensive and an exhaustive record has not been attempted here. Major badge styles and patches used in large state and local law enforcement agencies are presented, along with some example of unique or unusual insignia. Images in this section are approximately half the size of originals, except where noted. Images in the color section are approximately two thirds of the originals, except where noted.

Mock-up, based on photographs, of the insignia worn by the state police force from 1926 to 1929. Breast badge of was an eagle-top shield. Arm patch was a generic winged wheel under a rocker panel designating the agency.

Revenue Inspector Richard Jack Bowers "R.J.B." carried a THP badge in the 1930s.

Alcohol tax unit investigator used this badge in the 1940s.

Badge of a veterinary inspector of the Department of Agriculture.

Hat badge of the Safety Education unit created in 1937.

Badge used to promote safety by the THP circa 1937.

License revocation officers were used for a short time.

Honorary THP badge from the seventies.

Title of Internal Affairs investigators was change to special agent.

Badge used by academy personnel.

The THP shoulder patch features the state seal and has not changed since the creation of the Patrol. The designation "Highway Patrol" changed to "State Trooper" in the late sixties.

Shoulder patch worn by Capitol Police officers.

Joel Plummer's badge when TBI was part of Dept. of Safety.

Patch of TBI TIES computer information system user group established in 1985.

The first patch designating the THP Tactical Squad was a rocker panel worn over the dark green should patch.

Progression of hat patches worn by Tact Squad members. "THP" was the only designation on the first cap. An eagle and lightening bolt was worn on the second cap. The cap then carried miniatures of the shoulder patch.

Shoulder patch of the Alcohol Tax Unit of the Department of Revenue.

Nashville badges designated either rank, as in the case of the sergeant's badge, or assignment. The sergeant badge was coated with a silver alloy and maker marked Dury. The other badges indicated the duty assignment of the officers. The rightmost inspector's badge was not the inspector rank, which would have been gold tone and a different style. The officer had an unspecified inspection duty. (Sergeant badge courtesy of Clarence Gibson)

Badge presented to Chief Alex Barthell in 1915. (Nashville Banner photo)

Badge of one of the private suburban police services. (Courtesy of Paul Margulies)

Volunteer Police of the WWI era federal home guard program. (Courtesy Paul Margulies)

Auto detective badge used from 1930 to 1952.

Badge of special police used in 1930s and 1940s.

Duty assignment designations continued on the badges issued in 1930. New department functions, such as the implementation of the radio system and public transportation, resulted in new badge designations.

Jeweler made solid gold police woman's badge. (Courtesy of Monica Jett)

Badges issued after 1952 continued duty assignment designations. The hat badge also specified the assignment. Most supervisor badges included only rank.

A reserve force was established in the 1950s.

Metro Park Police badge used 1963-1973.

Metro badges did not include duty assignments for regular police officers, but different badge styles were used for separate units such as special police and the school mother's patrol.

200th Anniversary badge worn during 2006 by Metro Nashville officers.

Shoulder patches were developed for special units.

The Metro shoulder patch was created in 1963, although the badge was not available until 1964.

Memphis badge of the 1880s made by Ellis & Sons not engraved. *(Courtesy of Clarence Gibson)*

The MPD Patrol Driver drove the patrol wagon or "Black Maria" after it was acquired in 1890.

Business watchmen in the late 1800s were licensed by the MPD.

Early sanitation officer of the Dept. of Health.

Special police badge from the turn of the 20th century.

Badge 142 was issued to Oran F. Brown 2/15/12. The Chicago-made star was adopted in 1912.

Honorary badge given to talent show host Major Bowes.

Badge issued to members of the MPD youth patrol.

Warrant officer rank was used briefly following WW II.

The Memphis airport police became a separate agency in the 1960s.

Investigator badge of the 1980s before officers used badges with rank designations only.

First patch worn by communication officers.

Memphis shoulder patch worn from 1967 to 1982.

Shoulder patch adopted by the MPD in 1982, left, and one of several unit patches, right, designed in the same style.

Jeweler made badges of Knoxville police matron and charity police were the same size worn by regular officers.

Knoxville detective badge used prior to 1955.

Millennium badge worn during 2000 by Knoxville PD.

Department-wide shoulder patch was created in the late 1940s.

The current shoulder patch was adopted in the 1970s.

 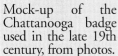    

Mock-up of the Chattanooga badge used in the late 19th century, from photos.

Version of the pinched shield with a star in center, likely for a supervisor.

Special police of the Chattanooga Electric Company rail car line.

Department-wide patch was issued in the early 1950s.

One of several unit patches used by Chattanooga PD in late 20th century.

Chattanooga SWAT patch worn by current members of the team.

Shoulder patch adopted in 1977 featured the city seal in full color.

Badge style of the Clarksville force prior to the 1960s.

Current badge of the Clarksville PD.

Early patch of Clarksville PD.

Clarksville Police patch adopted in the 1980s, designed by Helen Zachary.

Badges worn by the Jackson Police Department since 1947, when the shield, left, was adopted. The eagle-top circle, center, was adopted in 1974. The teardrop was adopted in 1989.

JPD's first shoulder patch was adopted in the mid-1960s.

Tactical Unit patch used since the 1980s was replaced with a round one in 2003.

Current shoulder patch of the Jackson PD, adopted in 1989.

Belle Meade breast and hat wreath worn in the 1940s.

A variety of badge styles were used by cities in the first half of the twentieth century.

Custom design badges, as the one created by a Germantown chief, or well accepted designs, as the Cleveland teardrop, were used after the sixties.

Art Deco design badge worn in the 1930s by Davidson County deputies.

Davidson County police in the 1950s replaced a number of private forces.

Breast and hat badge of the Davidson County Highway Patrol from 1946 to 1954.

Current badge of the Davidson County Sheriff's office.

Shelby County special deputy badge from the 1920s and 1930s.

Shelby County adopted an eagle-top circle badge, left, in 1959; and returned to a star, right, in 1970.

Badge worn by Madison County deputies from 1960 to 1978.

Knox County deputy badge worn in the 1940s.

Hamilton County badges used a hundred years apart. The small circle was used during the turn of the 20th century, and the seven-point star at the turn of the 21st century.

Badges used by county officers in the late 19th and early 20th centuries were typically simple stars, circle stars, or crescent stars.

Badges of railroad police featuring the state sear. GM&O badge was carried by Special Agent Edd Stansell.

The seven points of the TVA star represents the seven states served by the federal corporation.

Special
Insignia
Section

Lieutenant Elmer Craig, commander of the Yellow Jackets motorcycle unit of the Tennessee Highway Patrol, wore the colorful uniform designed for the special unit. The issue badge was worn by the unit. The shoulder patch worn by the Yellow Jackets was a color variation of the standard issue shoulder patch. *(Badge and patch approximately actual size. Other badges in this section shown in approximately two-thirds actual size unless noted.)*

Presentation Badges

Well respected officers were often presented with badges made of precious metal and some embellished with jewels. A few are shown below. *(Badges approximately actual size.)*

Solid gold badge with diamonds of Claude A. Armour, Memphis Commissioner of Fire and Police, 1950-67. *(Courtesy of Mary Armour)*

Solid gold badge of THP Chief Elmer V. Craig, 1965-67, with platinum seal and diamonds at points. *(Courtesy of Kenneth Lucas)*

Solid gold badge of Ivey Young, sheriff of Davidson County from 1937 to 1940.

Solid gold badge of Claude A. Armour, Memphis Chief of Police, 1949-50. *(Courtesy of Mary Armour)*

Solid gold badge of Chief John Henry "Jack" Shasteen, 1979-80. The badge was made by Quarles Jewelers.

Solid gold badge of T. C. Betterton, Chattanooga's first Commissioner of Police and Fire, 1911-19. *(Courtesy of Pat Olvey)*

Gold badge, with diamond and rubies, of Wilson County Sheriff Perry T. Burnett, 1936-40. *(Courtesy of Austelle Smartt)*

Tennessee Highway Patrol and the Department of Safety

The first breast badge worn by the Tennessee Highway Patrol was an eagle-top circle with the state seal, left. Revenue agents and other non-uniformed personnel carried a smaller badge, right. Both were made by G. C. Dury Co.

The Tennessee Highway Patrol adopted an eagle-top pinched shield, or clam shell, breast badge in 1937. The cross-baton hat badge, right, was also worn with the first breast badge. This set of badges was worn by Greg O'Rear.

The rank of corporal was created in 1941, and was discontinued late in 1955 when the basic rank title became Trooper.

The sergeant's badge adopted in 1937 was the same style as the patrolman, but gold-tone in color. Later hat badges, as the one above, were slightly larger and the seals varied.

Supervisors above sergeant began wearing eagle-top sunburst breast badges in the mid-1930s. Breast badge above was made by Federal Laboratories, Inc. The hat badge, right, used an early flourished seal and an applied rank panel.

The title of the commanding officer of the Patrol was Chief from 1929 until 1955. When Trooper became the basic rank, the chief rank became Troop Commander, but the title Chief continued to be used unofficially.

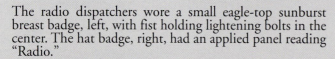

The radio dispatchers wore a small eagle-top sunburst breast badge, left, with fist holding lightening bolts in the center. The hat badge, right, had an applied panel reading "Radio."

Badges of the Troop Commander, chief officer between 1955 and 1971. This was the badge worn by Troop Commander Charles W. Danner from 1967 to 1971 when his rank became Colonel.

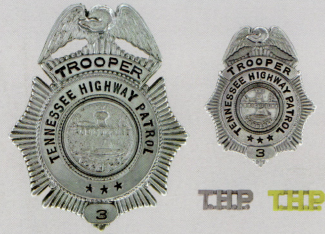

Trooper became the basic rank of the Highway Patrol in late 1955 and an eagle-top sunburst was adopted as the breast badge, left. A smaller version served as a hat badge, right. Both had an applied number panel and plain seal. "THP" collar brass, lower right, was worn by all.

The staff sergeant rank was created to assist with administration of district offices. A special hash mark system, lower right, noted five years of service with a star and two years with a bar, all in a small state shaped patch worn at the end of the sleeve. Patch represents 19 years.

Badges changed in the sixties when Braxmar of New York made breast badges. The seal with edge flourishes was restricted to use by the THP only. Numbers were stamped directly into the badge. When uniform caps were worn from 1959 to 1971, the hat badges reverted to the crossed-baton style with "Trooper" in the panel.

Sergeant badges worn after the introduction of the Montana Peak campaign hat and military motif hat badges in 1971. For a brief time in the late eighties sergeants wore the small badge on the hat, but in recent years a smaller version of the sergeants stripes has been worn. Buttons featured the state seal.

Captain badges worn after 1971 when military hat badge motif was adopted. In recent years, numbers have been reintroduced to the captain's breast badge.

Colonel became the rank of the top uniformed officer of the Patrol in 1971.

Badge of Commissioner of the Department of Safety Claude A. Armour, 1971-75.

The first badge of the Criminal Investigation Division, 1983, had a large eagle and a full color seal. Later badges were standard issue. Investigator rank became Special Agent in the 1990s.

Pilots held the rank Warrant Officer for a period in 1979, and were issued wings featuring the state seal.

Medal of Valor of the Tennessee Highway Patrol, awarded only once, to Trooper John Mann, killed in the line of duty in 2001.

The arm patch adopted by the Patrol featured the state seal. It was made of felt and worn midway between the shoulder and the elbow of the uniform jacket.

The first shoulder patch worn on shirts was ordered by individual patrolmen in 1949. Official shirt patches were issued in 1951.

The Water Safety unit that existed from 1963 to 1965 wore a special shoulder patch.

Communications officers replaced early radio men. Supervisors wore gold tone shields.

Drivers license examiners were named after the state began issuing licenses in 1937.

Badge style worn be drivers license examiners in the 1970s.

Drivers License Division returned to the badge style worn by others in the 1980s.

Breast and hat badge worn by motor vehicle enforcement officers while the unit was part of the Department of Revenue.

Motor vehicle enforcement wore THP style badges in 1983 after becoming a part of the Department of Safety

Breast and hat badge worn by enforcement officers of the Public Service Commission prior to transfer to the Department of Safety in 1996.

A nightwatch was established for the capitol building in 1899. Early officers wore a number of badge styles.

Badge worn by Capitol Police officers in the mid-twentieth century.

This custom design breast and hat badge was worn by officers of the Capitol Police when the agency became a part of the Department of Safety in 1972.

Tennessee Bureau of Investigation

TBI agents carried a simple sunburst badge from 1951 to 1975. Later versions of the badge had a black enamel ring around the state seal.

An eagle-top version of the sunburst with a full color state seal was adopted by the TBI in 1975. The Inspector rank was later replaced by Special Agent in Charge.

Patch of the Tennessee Bureau of Criminal Investigation. A smaller version was worn on caps.

Bullion patch worn by SAC Jimmie Van Leach as pocket badge in the 1970s for court and special events.

The seal of the independent TBI designed in 1980 was reproduced on the Bureau's patch.

TBI Director Arzo Carson presents the agency's new badge to Deputy Director Steve Watson. The two were instrumental in the design of the new insignia.

A new badge for the independent TBI was designed in 1980. All TBI officers wore the "Special Agent" badge except the director. Director John Carney carried these badges. Lapel pins worn by agents featured the TBI seal.

Other Tennessee Law Enforcement

Badges issued to the Tennessee State Police in 1919 when the agency was created. Badge on the left was the official issue badge, and badge on the right was made as a substitute.

Badges used by tax inspectors and agents of the Department of Revenue in the early decades of the twentieth century.

Guards at the various state correctional facilities wore different style badges in the nineteenth and most of the twentieth century. These badges were worn in the 1930s to the 1950s.

Correctional Officer insignia was unified in the 1960s and 1970s. A full-color state seal was adopted in the 1980s.

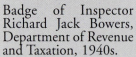

Badge of Inspector Richard Jack Bowers, Department of Revenue and Taxation, 1940s.

Inspectors of regulatory boards of the Department of Commerce carried small badges made by Dury in the 1930s.

Plain shield Game Warden badge worn in the 1920s and 1930s.

Badge style adopted by the Game and Fish Commission in the 1950s.

Metropolitan Nashville Police Department

The badge style of the Nashville Police Department from the Civil War to 1930. Around 1920 the department adopted a crossed-baton hat badge.

Custom breast and hat badges were adopted in 1930. The insignia had an Art Nouveau design and featured the state seal.

Detective badge used prior to 1930. (Courtesy of Paul Margulies)

Chief J. Hadley Clack in the 1897 supervisors uniform of the Nashville police force.

Detective and Identification Officer badges adopted in 1930. Often called the "lapel badge" because detectives wore it behind the lapel and flashed it for identification.

Badge style adopted in 1952. Breast badge was stock eagle-top sunburst with the city seal. Hat badge was a stock sunburst with open number panel.

Custom breast and hat badge of the Metropolitan Police Department worn from 1964 featured a full-color Metro seal. Insignia was designed by Ruth Strube.

The Auto Detective was created in the teens with the increased numbers of automobiles and related crimes.

Health department officers replaced sanitation police, but retained police powers.

A standing motorcycle unit existed by 1930.

Supervisor badges issued in 1952 had gold-filled fronts.

Badges from the late 1950s and early 1960s had larger number panels. The policewoman designation was used briefly, and the inspector rank was dropped in 1964.

Metro Nashville Lieutenant breast and hat badge. Badges of commanders and supervisors were gold tone badges with full-color enamel seal.

Shoulderpatch of radio patrolmen in the 1930s. Design was same as painted on doors of radio car. This patch worn by Radio Patrolman "Big Jim" Dorman.

Shoulder patch of 1950s traffic officers on three-wheeler motorcycle duty. Also two buttons styles worn in 20th century.

Shoulder patch adopted in 1958 was a simple shield with an eight-point star design. *(Courtesy of Paul Margulies)*

Memphis Police Department

Engraved example of the badge worn in the 1880s, maker marked Ellis, Maker, Memphis. A traditional wreath was worn on hats and helmets.

The Chicago-style "pie-plate" star was adopted in 1912 with the state seal and brass numbers. A custom shield and wreath hat badge was also adopted.

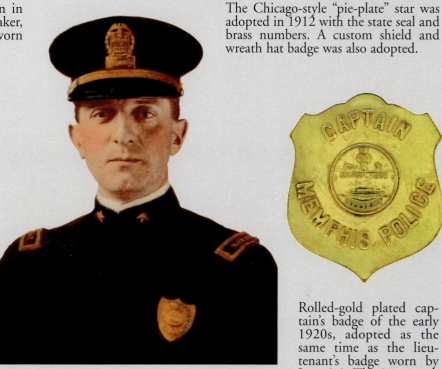

Stars used circa 1900 were hand cut from sheet metal with a spring pin attached. All ranks wore a six-point star at the turn of the century.

Rolled-gold plated captain's badge of the early 1920s, adopted as the same time as the lieutenant's badge worn by Lucarini. The inspector's badge was similar to the lieutenant's badge but larger.

Lieutenant Vincent Lucarini, killed in 1921, wore the badge and uniform of the early 1920s.

Stock shield breast badge was adopted in 1947. The hat badge remained the shield and wreath. Badges continued to feature the state seal.

Custom shield adopted in 1979. Badge design was similar to the previous style, but featured the city seal. Badges were marked Rhodium Electroplate.

The badge style referred to as the "acorn" was orginated in Memphis in 1922 as a sergeant's badge. The example on the left is maker marked Bailer, Memphis, a jeweler. The second version of the badge, center, was used from around 1967 into the 1970s primarily by sergeants, but by other supervisors as well. Note the use of the Memphis seal created in 1962. The third version of the acorn, shown on the right, was adopted as the issue badge for all supervisors in 1979.

Badge of one of the volunteer units that served as special police in the 1920's.

A special police star with engraving added to the stamped design worn circa 1900.

Stock badge style issued to special police in the early 20th century.

A full-color state seal was applied to issue badges in the 1970s.

Current acorn-style badge worn by all supervisors after 1979.

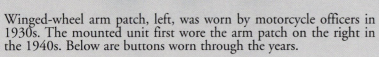

Winged-wheel arm patch, left, was worn by motorcycle officers in 1930s. The mounted unit first wore the arm patch on the right in the 1940s. Below are buttons worn through the years.

First department-wide shoulder patch was adopted in 1964. The patch was replaced in 1967 with a smaller oval version.

Knoxville policemen wore a shield-star until around 1920. Most were jeweler made. The badge on the left dates from the mid-nineteenth century. The smaller versions were worn at the turn of the century. *(Early badge courtesy of George Jackson Jr.)*

Early twentieth century detective's badge.

A pinched shield featuring the city seal was adopted circa 1920. The style was worn until the mid-1940s. The shield and wreath hat insignia was adopted and used until 1955.

Supervisor's version of the shield included an eagle at the top. The rank panel of supervisor's hat badge was hand cut.

Two breast badge styles were worn briefly from the mid-1940s until 1955. The circle and city seal on the left was worn in the late 1940s, and the shield with open number panel was worn in the early 1950s.

New insignia adopted in 1955. The teardrop breast badge and complementary hat badge were silver tone with gold tone panels for both basic and supervisory ranks.

Chattanooga Police Department

Circle-star that replaced a large shield as Chattanooga police insignia around 1892. A wreath was worn as a hat badge.

Cincinnati-style pinched shield adopted in 1909. The first hat badge was replaced shield/wreath.

Badge adopted circa 1925, known as radiator style, was called the "church door" badge in Chattanooga.

Detective badges used in the mid-twentieth century. *(Courtesy of Thomas Herring)*

Badge adopted in 1941 featured the state seal. The shield and wreath hat insignia was retained. This badge set was worn by Jack Shasteen.

Breast and hat badge adopted for supervisors in 1941. Many supervisors wore jeweler made solid gold breast badges with the issue hat badge.

Custom shield and hat insignia adopted in 1977 featured a full-color city seal. All officers wore the same badge without rank designation. Badge set #7 was issued to Jack Shasteen.

Patch worn by the Special Services division or David Squad in the seventies, and pin worn by current SWAT officers.

Patch and pin worn by the Blue Lightning motorcycle unit in the seventies.

Other Cities and Towns

Three badges that represent the designations of chief law enforcement officers in Tennessee. The constable or town constable title was used in some towns into the twentieth century. The city marshal title preceded the chief of police rank in most cities.

Chief of police badge and wreath worn in Jackson between 1974 and 1989. This example was issued to Chief Ed Alderson.

Badges used in the twentieth century prior to 1920. Circle badge #10 and hat badge #15 were worn by Jackson patrolmen from the teens and into the 1930s along with other styles. The Lebanon shield and Bristol badge #6 were worn in the same era.

Badges worn in the mid-twentieth century. Inglewood-Madison was a private force later replaced by the Davidson County Sheriff's Patrol. The small Jackson lieutenant's badge was carried as a wallet badge.

Jackson PD's only Medal of Honor was awarded posthumously to Sergeant Andy Bailey in 2005.

Sheriff's Offices and TVA

Davidson County Deputy Sheriff worn in the 1940s. Seal and eagle applied.

Davidson County Sheriff Patrol of the late 1950s and early 1960s. Engraved accents were added.

Shelby County deputy sheriffs wore stars until around 1960. Field deputies worked patrol and staff deputy worked courts or other assignments.

Badge worn by Constable and Deputy B. L. Cunningham in the 1940s.

The title High Sheriff was not frequently used on insignia.

Badge of Sheriff Joel Plummer from 1966 to 1972.

Deputy badges worn in the late nineteenth and early twentieth centuries.

Early TVA PSS officers wore a stock breast badge, left. Early badges had a center disk with the rank, but soon a federal eagle was affixed. A custom, Art Deco style, PSS hat badge, right, was worn in the 1930s.

TVA PSS officers worn custom badges in the 1980s and 1990s.

TVA Police were created in 1995 and issued custom designed insignia.

Bibliography

Published and Unpublished Manuscripts

Achord, David. Officers killed in the line of duty, *The Police Beat*. Nashville: Metropolitan Nashville Police Department, Deputy Chief Faulkner's office, 1998ff.

Allison, John. *Dropped Stitches in Tennessee History*. Johnson City: The Overmountain Press, 1991 (originally published in 1897).

Ash, Stephen V. *Messages of the Governors of Tennessee*, 1907-1921 (Volume 9), and 1921-1933 (Volume 10). Nashville: The Tennessee Historical Commission, 1990.

Ashmore, Eddie M. *A Chronicle of Law Enforcement in the South, The History of the Jackson, Tennessee, Police Department*. Frankland: Hillsboro Press, 2002.

Berg, Bruce L. *Law Enforcement: An Introduction to Police in Society*. Boston: Allyn & Bacon, Inc., 1991.

Berg, Bruce L. *Policing in Modern Society*. Boston: Butterworth-Heinemann, 1999.

Buck, Mary Fleming, author of history section. *Clarksville Police Department - Highlights 1820-1997*. Clarksville, Tennessee: Clarksville Police Department, 1997.

Byrne, J. P., editor. *Reports of Departments of the City of Nashville for the Fiscal Year Ending December 31, 1899*. Nashville: Foster & Webb, Stationers and Printers, 1900.

Cartmell, Robert. Unpublished diaries written between 1849 and 1915 (not inclusive).

Caruthers, R. L. and A. O. P. Nicholson, editors. *A Compilation of the Statutes of Tennessee of a General and Permanent Nature*. Nashville: Printed at the Steam Press of James Smith, 1836.

Chaffin, Leland D., author of history section. *Tennessee Department of Safety 75th Anniversary*. Paducah, Kentucky: Taylor Publishing Co., 2005.

Chattanooga Police Department Illustrated. Chattanooga: MacGowan & Cooke Co., 1899.

Clarksville Police Department 1820-2003. Clarksville, Tennessee: Clarksville Police Department, 2003.

Cooling, Benjamin Franklin. *Fort Donelson's Legacy: War and Society in Tennessee and Kentucky, 1862-1863*. Knoxville: The University of Tennessee Press, 1997.

Crew, H. W., ed. *History of Nashville, Tenn*. Nashville: H. W. Crew, 1890.

Cunningham, Bill. *On Bended Knees*. Nashville: McClanahan Publishing House, 1983.

Davidson County Sheriff's Office: Serving the Community Since 1783. Paducah, Kentucky: Turner Publishing Co., 2005.

Doyle, Don H. *Nashville in the New South 1880-1930*. Knoxville: University of Tennessee Press, 1985.

Doyle, Don H. *Nashville Since the 1920s*. Knoxville: University of Tennessee Press, 1985.

Dozier, Steve R. *Prohibition and the Enforcement of the Nashville Police Department (1905-1933)*. (Undergraduate Paper at Vanderbilt University), Nashville, Tennessee: N.p., 1978.

Drake, Edwin L., editor. *The Annals of the Army of Tennessee and Early Western History*. Jackson: The Guild Bindery Press, 1994.

Eilders, Lon and Skip Vaughn. Centurion, *A History of the Chattanooga Police Department, 1852-1977*. Chattanooga Inter-Collegiate Press, 1976.

Ferguson, Rick, and Ida Webb, editors. *To Protect and Serve: History of the Knoxville Police Department 1849-2001*. Paducah, KY: Turner Publishing Co., 2001.

Francis, Sandra. *Notes on Metropolitan Nashville officers killed in the line of duty*. Nashville: N. p., 2002.

Gibson, Carol H. *Narative History of the Domestic Violence Movement [Metropolitan Nashville/Davidson County Police Department]*. Nashville: N. p., 2004.

Goodspeed, publisher. *The History of Tennessee*. Nashville: The Goodspeed Publishing Co., 1887.

Goodstein, Anita Shafer. *Nashville 1780-1860: From Frontier to City*. Gainesville: University of Florida Press, 1989.

Haney, Ken. *Medals and Shoulder Patches of the Jackson Police Department*. Jackson: N. p., 2005.

Haywood, John and Robert L. Cobb, editors. *The Statute Laws of the State of Tennessee of a Public and General Nature*. Knoxville: F. S. Heiskell, 1831.

Hymers, George William Jr. *Exciting Days as an FBI Special Agent*. Jackson, Tennessee: N. p., 1985.

Ikard, Robert W. *No More Social Lynchings*. Franklin: Hillsboro Press, 1997.

Jacobs, Thomas N. Jr. and Warren B. Causey. *The Stringbean Murders*. Kennesaw, Georgia: Brenden Publishing Co., 1997.

Knoxville Fire and Police Departments (Illustrated Souvenir).

Knoxville: Crocket & Conklin, Press of Bean, Warters & Co., 1900.

Lawrence, J. Pinckney, publisher. *Tennesseans in the Civil War: Part I*. Nashville, Civil War Centennial Commission, 1964.

Lindsley, John Berrien, editor. *The Military Annals of Tennessee (Confederate)*. Spartanburg: The Reprint Company, 1974 (originally published 1886).

McAlister, William K. Jr., compiler. *Ordinances of the City of Nashville*. Nashville: Marshall & Bruce, Stationers, 1881.

McCann, Kevin D. *"Hurst's Wurst": A History of the 6th Tennessee (U.S.) Cavalry*. Ashland City, Tennessee: Liberty Publications, 1995.

McGavock, Randal W. *Pen and Sword*. Jackson, Tennessee: McGowat-Mercer Press, 1960.

Memphis Police Department Illustrated. Memphis: Police Charity Fund, The Tracy Print, Co., 1899.

Memphis Police Department 1827-1975. Marceline, Missouri: Walsworth Publishing Co., 1975.

Memphis Police Department Commemorative Album 1987-1994. Nashville: Taylor Publishing Co., 1994.

Miller, Kim. *Centurion II, 1852-1989*. Nashville: Taylor Publishing Co., 1989.

Mowrey, Robert T. *The Evolution of the Nashville Police from Early Times to 1880* (Senior Thesis at Princeton University). Princeton: N. p., 1974.

Police Department of the City of Nashville, Tennessee - Souvenir Containing History, Portraiture and Biography of the Members [etc]. Atlanta, June 12, 1896.

Rains, James E., compiler. *A Compilation of the General Laws of the City of Nashville*. Nashville: J. O. Griffith & Company, Printers, 1860.

Rules and Regulations Governing All Departments Now or That May Hereafter Be under Civil Service in the City of Nashville. Nashville: 1912.

Schott, Fred W. Jr., author of history section. *"Servants . . . not Lords," A History of the Tennessee Highway Patrol 1929-1979, Fifty Years of Heritage*. Nashville: Taylor Publishing Co., 1981.

Shelby County Sheriff's Department. Marceline, MO: Walsworth Publishing Co., 1976.

Sherrill, Charles A. and Tomye M. Sherrill. *Tennessee Convicts: Early Records of the State Penitentiary, Volume I 1831-1850*. Mt. Juliet, Tennessee: Charles A. Sherrill, 1997.

Skinner, V. A., editor. *Shelby County Sheriff's Office Yearbook 1994*. Memphis: Shelby County Sheriff's Office, 1994.

Smith, Ersa Rhea Noland. *Flyin' Bullets and The Resplendent Badge*. Sevierville, Tennessee: Nandel Publishing Company, 1989.

Smith, John Hugh and John M. Lea, compilers. *The Revised Laws of the City of Nashville*. Nashville: Harvey M. Watterson, Printers, 1850.

Smith, Jonathan K. T. *Annotated Gleanings, Circuit Court Minute, Madison County, Tennessee, 1869-85*. Jackson: N. p., 2000.

Smith, Jonathan K. T. *Antebellum Militia, Justices and Some Early Taxpayers, Madison County, Tennessee*. Jackson: N. p., 1998

Smith, Jonathan K. T. *Genealogical Asides from Several West Tennessee Supreme Court Cases, 1830s*. Jackson: N. p., 1997.

Souvenir of Company "C" First Regiment, N.G.S.T. 1893. St. Louis: Woodward & Tiernan Printing Company, 1893.

Spragins, R. F., editor. *Laws, Bylaws and Ordinances of the Municipality, Mayor and Aldermen of the City of Jackson*. Jackson: McCowat-Mercer Printing Co., 1909.

Sprogle, Howard O. *The Philadelphia Police - Past and Present*. Philadelphia: Copyrighted By Howard O. Sprogle, 1887.

Squires, James D. *The Secrets of the Hopewell Box*. New York: Random House, 1996.

Summers, Judy, editor. *Night Riders of Reelfoot Lake Scrapbook*. N. p., 1965.

Sutton, John P. *Cleveland Police Department - 1930-1940*. (Undergraduate Paper at Lee University), Cleveland, Tennessee: N.p., 1988.

Taylor, Andrew Thompson Jr. *The Taylor Family History with the Recollections of Judge Andrew T. Taylor*. Atlanta: N.p., 1994.

Taylor, Lytton, compiler. *Laws of Nashville*. Nashville: Albert A. Tavel, Law Publisher, 1888.

Tennessee Department of Safety 1974. Marceline, MO: Walsworth Publishing Co., 1975.

Tennessee Department of Safety 1986-1990. Nashville: Taylor Publishing Co., 1990.

Thomas, Jane. *Old Days In Nashville*. Nashville: Charles Elder Booksellers and Publisher (facimile reproduction), 1967.

Vanderwood, Paul J. *Night Riders of Reelfoot Lake*. Memphis: Memphis State University Press, 1969.

Walk, Joseph E. *Chronological Listings of Selected Local Officials, Government Buildings, African-American Officials, Policemen* (Over Varying Periods). Memphis: N. p., 1996.

Walk, Joseph E. *The Development of Memphis Law Enforcement, A Chronology of Organization - Procedures - Personnel*. Memphis: N. p., 1997.

Walk, Joseph E. *A History of African-Americans in Memphis Government*. Memphis: N. p., 1996.

Walk, Joseph E. *Law Enforcement Line of Duty Deaths in Memphis and Shelby County*. Memphis: N. p., 1996, revised 2000.

Walk, Joseph E., editor and author of history section. *Memphis Police Department, Memphis Police Association* (in 3 volumes). Marceline, MO: Walsworth Publishing Co., 1987.

Walk, Joseph E. *Memphis Police Department Motor Vehicles - A Chronology*. Memphis: N. p., 1996.

Walk, Joseph E. Memphis Police Department, Some *Highlights and Sidelights from the Past*. Memphis: N. p., 1987.

Walker, Samuel. *The Police in America*. New York: McGraw Hill, 1998.

Williams, Emma Inman. *Historic Madison, the Story of Jackson and Madison County Tennessee from Mound Builders to World War I*. Jackson: Madison County Historical Society, 1946.

Official Records

Acts of Congress of the United States

Acts of the General Assembly of Tennessee

Annual Reports of the City of Nashville

Annual Reports of the Nashville Police Department

Archives of the U. S. Marshals Service

Death Certificates and Funeral Records

Minutes of the Board of the Town/City of Jackson, Tennessee

Minutes of the Board of the Town/City of Nashville, Tennessee

Roster of United States Marshals

United States Census of Tennessee, 1820, 1830, 1840, 1850, 1860, 1870, and 1880

Various directories, manuals, letters, memoranda, press releases, speeches, notes, and other documents

Newspapers and Periodicals

American Historical Magazine, New York, New York

Athens Post-Athenian, Athens, Tennessee

Athens Press, Athens Tennessee

Bolivar Bulletin, Bolivar, Tennessee

Carthage Courier, Carthage, Tennessee

Chattanooga News-Free Press, Chattanooga, Tennessee

Chattanooga Times, Chattanooga, Tennessee

Clarksville Leaf-Chronicle, Clarksville, Tennessee

Columbia Herald, Columbia, Tennessee

Cookeville Dispatch, Cookeville, Tennessee

Cookeville Herald, Cookeville, Tennessee

Courier-Chronicle, Humboldt, Tennessee

Daily News-Journal, Murfreesboro, Tennessee

Daily Telegram, Jackson, Tennessee

Daily West Tennessee Plain-Dealer, Jackson, Tennessee

Dayton Herald, Dayton, Tennessee

Greeneville Sun, Greeneville, Tennessee

Harper's Weekly, New York, New York

Inside TVA, Knoxville, Tennessee

Jackson Daily Whig, Jackson, Tennessee

Jackson Pioneer, Jackson, Tennessee.

Jackson Sun. Jackson, Tennessee.

Johnson City Press-Chronicle, Johnson City, Tennessee

Kingsport News, Kingsport, Tennessee

Kingsport Times, Kingsport, Tennessee

Knoxville Journal, Knoxville, Tennessee

Knoxville News-Sentinel, Knoxville, Tennessee

Madison News, Madison, Tennessee

Memphis Appeal, Memphis, Tennessee

Memphis Commercial Appeal, Memphis, Tennessee

Memphis Daily Appeal, Memphis, Tennessee

Memphis Daily Avalanche, Memphis, Tennessee

Memphis Press-Scimitar, Memphis, Tennessee

Morristown Tribune, Morristown, Tennessee

Nashville American, Nashville, Tennessee.

Nashville Banner. Nashville, Tennessee.

Nashville Daily Press and Times, Nashville, Tennessee

Nashville Patriot, Nashville, Tennessee.

Nashville Tennessean. Nashville, Tennessee.

Nashville Tennessean and Nashville American, Nashville, Tennessee.

Nashville Whig, Nashville, Tennessee.

Newport Plain Talk, Newport, Tennessee

News Scimitar, Memphis, Tennessee.

Pulaski Citizen, Pulaski, Tennessee

Republican, Jackson, Tennessee

Shelbyville Sun, Shelbyville, Tennessee

Southern Statesman, Jackson, Tennessee

Springfield Times, Springfield, Tennessee

Tennessee Law Enforcement Journal, Nashville, Tennessee

Truth Teller and Western District, Jackson, Tennessee

Tullahoma News, Tullahoma, Tennessee

Washington Post, Washington, District of Columbia

Waynesboro News, Waynesboro, Tennessee

West Tennessee Whig, Jackson, Tennessee.

Winchester Chronicle, Winchester, Tennessee.

Whig and Tribune, Jackson, Tennessee

Internet Sites

www.ci.knoxville.tn.us/kpd/ - Knoxville Police Department

www.cityofmemphis.org/framework.aspx?page=213 - Memphis Police Services

www.chattanooga.gov/police/ - Chattanooga Police Department

www.coalcreekaml.com/Legacy.htm - Coal Creek: War and Disasters

www.columbiatn.com/pdweb/history.htm - Columbia, TN, Police Department

www.familysearch.org - Family Search

www.fbi.gov/libref/historic/history/historymain.htm - FBI History

www.geocities.com/Heartland/Plains/3661/ - Friends of Metropolitan Archives of Nashville and Davidson County, Tennessee.

www.knoxcotn.org/history/debow.html - Incidents in the Early Settlement of East Tennessee and Knoxville

www.knoxsheriff.org/about/history.php - Knox County Sheriff's Office

www.nleomf.com/ - National Law Enforcement Officers Memorial Fund

www.odmp.org - Officer Down Memorial Page

www.police.nashville.org/ - Metropolitan Nashville Police Department

www.state.tn.us/safety/ - Tennessee Department of Safety

www.state.tn.us/sos/bluebook/online/bbonline.htm - Tennessee Blue Book Online

www.tennessee.gov/correction/history.html - Tennessee Department of Corrections

www.tennesseeencyclopedia.net/ - Tennessee Encyclopedia of History and Culture

www.tnyesterday.com/yesterday_henderson/hurst/hurst.htm - Yester-day's Tennessee - Hurst! (by W. Clay Crook)

www.tva.gov/abouttva/history.htm - A Short History of the TVA

www.usmarshals.gov/history/index.html - United States Marshals Service: Historical Perspective

Various Media

The 25th Anniversary of SWAT. Compact Disc produced by the Metropolitan Nasvhille Police Department, Nashville, Tennessee, 2001.

Video tapes of news broadcasts of WSMV TV, Nashville, Tennessee.

Vaious video and audio tapes of law enforcement related materials.

Interviews

Achord, David. Detective, Metropolitan Nashville Police Department. Nashville, Tennessee, August 7, 2003.

Acuff, M. L. "Rocky." Lieutenant (retired), Jackson Police Department. Jackson, Tennessee, January 18, 2002, et al.

Acuff, Thomas. Captain (retired), Jackson Police Department. Jackson, Tennessee, June 21, 2001, et al.

Allen, John B. Jr. Sergeant (retired), Tennessee Highway Patrol. Riceville, Tennessee, January 18, 2006.

Allen, Linuel L. Captain, Tennessee Highway Patrol. Jackson, Tennessee, September 12, 2003.

Anderson, Steve. Deputy Chief of Police, Metropolitan Nashville Police Department. Nashville, Tennessee, January 18,2006 (by phone).

Azbill, Gary. Special Agent, Tennessee Bureau of Investigation. Jackson, Tennessee, November 11, 2003

Baird, Eleanor. Daughter of Perry W. Burnette, Sheriff of Wilson County, 1936-1940. Mt. Juliet, Tennessee, November 6, 1999.

Baird, Woodrow. Long-time resident of Wilson County and son-in-law of Sheriff Perry Burnette. Mt. Juliet, Tennessee, November 6, 1999.

Ball, Jim. Detective Sergeant (retired), Metropolitan Nashville Police Department. Murphresboro, Tennessee, May 29, 2003.

Bastin, Jerry. Special Agent (retired), Federal Bureau of Investigation. Medina, Tennessee, January 10, 2006.

Beal, James. Lieutenant (retired), Tennessee Highway Patrol. Nashville, Tennessee, April 30, 2005 (by phone).

Blackwell, David. Special Agent (retired), Tennessee Bureau of Investigation. Murfreesboro, Tennessee, September 20, 2005 (by phone).

Blackwell, Thomas J. "Jack." Special Agent in Charge (retired), West Tennessee district of the Tennessee Bureau of Investigation. Somerville, Tennessee, February 8, 2003; October 10, 2003. (Jack Blackwell died March 26, 2005.)

Bowers, R. Jack Jr. Son of R. Jack Bowers, former Tennessee Department of Revenue and Taxation Agent and Jackson Chief of Police, Tennessee. Jackson, Tennessee, June 2001.

Browder, Steve. Lieutenant Colonel (retired), Tennessee Highway Patrol; Tennessee Valley Authority. Jackson, Tennessee, March 6, 2004.

Cantwell, T. J. Trooper (retired), Tennessee Highway Patrol. Sevierville, Tennessee, July 28, 2004.

Carney, John Jr. Former Director, Tennessee Bureau of Investigation. Clarksville, Tennessee, September 14, 2005.

Carson, Arzo. Director (retired), Tennessee Bureau of Investigation. Huntsville, Tennessee, July 28, 2004.

Casey, Joe Dixon. Chief of Police (retired), Metropolitan Nashville Police Department. Nashville, Tennessee, September 19, 2003.

Castellaw, Ike. Former Sergeant, Jackson Police Department. Jackson, Tennessee, April 18, 2002.

Cepparulo, Edmond. Lieutenant, Jackson Police Department. Jackson, Tennessee, August, 2001.

Chaffin, Leland D. Major, Tennessee Highway Patrol. Nashville, Tennessee, May 5, 2005.

Cheatam, Roy B. Captain (retired), Tennessee Highway Patrol. Memphis, Tennessee, December 18, 2004 (by phone).

Cherry, James N. Jr. Deputy Chief (retired), Jackson Police Department. Jackson, Tennessee, September 19, 2001.

Cobb, Fred. Lieutenant (retired), Metropolitan Nashville PoliceDepartment, Nashville, Tennessee, November 20, 2003; January 20, 2004.

Cole, Eddie Stephen. Special Agent-Criminal Investigator (retired), Tennessee Bureau of Investigation; Major (retired), Tennessee Highway Patrol. Jackson, Tennessee, January 23, 2004.

Coleman, William E. Jr. Special Agent (retired), Tennessee Bureau of Identification. From video tape recorded in Nashville, Tennessee, March 2001. (Bill Coleman died February 10, 2004.)

Craig, Johnny. Sergeant (retired) and son of Chief Elmer Craig, Tennessee Highway Patrol. Nashville, Tennessee, October 20, 2004.

Crews, Barney E. Jr. Captain (retired), Jackson Police Department. Jackson, Tennessee, October 1, 2001.

Crews, Walter. Director (retired), Memphis Police Department. Memphis, Tennessee, September 1, 2004.

Cunningham, Fred. Chief Deputy Sheriff (retired), Madison County Sheriff's Department. Jackson, Tennessee, April 15, 2005.

Cunningham, Tommy, Chief Deputy Sheriff, Madison County Sheriff's Department. Jackson, Tennessee, April 15, 2005.

Curlin, R. E. "Gene." Executive Deputy Chief (retired), Jackson Police Department. Jackson, Tennessee, October 4, 2001.

Currey, George H. Major (retired), Metropolitan Nashville Police Department. Nashville, Tennessee, September 19, 2003.

Dailey, Robert Jr. Deputy Chief (retired), Jackson Police Department. Jackson, Tennessee, October 7, 1999.

Danner, Charles W. Colonel (retired), Tennessee Highway Patrol. Mt. Juliet, Tennessee, December 21, 2004.

Dollarhide, Carl "Sonny." Major (retired), Metropolitan Nashville Police Department. Nashville, Tennessee, November 20, 2003.

Dorman, Gary W. Sergeant (retired), Metropolitan Nashville Police Department. Nashville, Tennessee, February 28, 2006 (by phone)

Dover, Melton A. "Mike." Captain and Chief Pilot (retired), Tennessee Highway Patrol. Dickson, Tennessee, April 28, 2005 (by phone).

Dozier, Thomas. Major (retired), Metropolitan Nashville Police Department. Nashville, Tennessee, September 18, 2003.

Dunaway, William. Sergeant (retired), Metropolitan Nashville Polce Department. Nashville, Tennessee, December 15, 2003.

Dutton, Michael. Superintendent, Tennessee Correction Academy. Tullahoma, Tennessee, January 5, 2006 (by phone).

Eilders, Lon L. Manager of Accreditation and Planning and Lieutenant (retired), Chattanooga Police Department. Chattanooga, Tennessee, October 18, 2004.

English, Lucion. Special Agent (retired), Tennessee Bureau of Investigation. Brownsville, Tennessee, April, 15, 2004.

French, Carlton V. Former Tennessee Highway Sergeant, Memphis Police Officer, and Special Agent (retired) for the Illinois Central Railroad. Memphis, Tennessee, February 1, 2003. (Carlton French died December 1, 2005.)

Fyke, Bobby H. Trooper (retired), Tennessee Highway Patrol. Clarksville, Tennessee, September 14, 2005.

Gilleland, R. Maxey. SAC Narcotics (retired), Tennessee Bureau of Investigation. Ashland City, Tennessee, October 24, 2005 (by phone).

Gillmann, Loretta. Policewoman (retired), Jackson Police Department. Jackson, Tennessee, May 8, 2000.

Goodwin, Robert. Director (retired), Tennessee Bureau of Criminal Investigation. Lebanon, Tennessee, February 26, 2004 (by phone).

Grinalds, Richard Leigh. Former Special Agent, Tennessee Bureau of Investigation. Jackson, Tennessee, September 8, 2005.

Grubbs, Geno. Lieutenant (retired), Clarksville Police Department. Clarksville, Tennessee, September 14, 2005.

Gunter, Jack. Photographer, Editor (retired), Nashville Banner. Nashville, Tennessee, November 20, 2003.

Gwyn, Mark. Director, Tennessee Bureau of Investigation. Nashville, Tennessee, September 13, 2005.

Hall, Larry E. Special Agent-Forensic Scientists Supervisor, Tennessee Bureau of Investigation. Nashville, Tennessee, November 20, 2003.

Hamby, Tom, and Patsy Hamby Lay. Son and daughter of Chester Hamby, former Patrolman, Tennessee Highway Patrol. Harriman, Tennessee, June 25, 2003.

Hamm, Archibald B. Executive Director (retired), Tennessee Bureau of Investigation. Nashville, Tennessee, November 20, 2003.

Harmon, John W. Sergeant, Tennessee Highway Patrol. Dunlap, Tennessee, August 26, 2005 (by phone).

Herald, James Roy. Major (retired), Metropolitan Nashville Police Department. Nashville, Tennessee, September 18, 2003.

Higgins, Richard. Captain, Jackson Police Department. Jackson, Tennessee, January 10, 2002.

Hitchcock, Larry D. Captain (retired), Tennessee Highway Patrol. Nashville, Tennessee, December 7, 2004.

Holt, Bobby. Captain (retired), Jackson Police Department. Jackson, Tennessee, October 19, 2001.

Horton, John W. Lieutenant (retired), Tennessee Highway Patrol. Savannah, Tennessee, January 4, 2006 (by phone).

Huckeby, Preston. Special Agent in Charge (retired), East Tennessee district, Tennessee Bureau of Investigation. Rock Island, Tennessee, October 8, 2005 (by phone).

Jett, Marie. Widow of former Davidson County Sheriff Leslie Jett. Nashville, Tennessee, June 24, 2003.

Jett, Monica. Sergeant (retired), Metropolitan Nashville Police Department, daugher of former Davidson County Sheriff Leslie Jett, and niece of former Inspector R. Willard Jett of the Nashville Police Department. Nashville, Tennessee, June 24, 2003 and February 7, 2004.

Johnson, Claude Isaiah. Special Agent in Charge (retired), Tennessee Bureau of Investigation. Memphis, Tennessee, April 6, 2004 (by phone).

Johnson, Jerry Lee. Captain (retired), Jackson Police Department. Jackson, Tennessee, September 10, 2001.

Jones, Bill L. Commissioner (retired), Tennessee Department of Safety. Murfreesboro, Tennessee, January 11, 2006.

Keesling, James F. Assistant Director (retired), Tennessee Bureau of Investigation; and Chief of Police (retired) Kingsport, Tennessee. Kingsport, Tennessee, August 26, 2005 (by phone).

Kelton, Louise. Captain, Metropolitan Nashville Police Department. Nashville, Tennessee, November 29, 2005.

Kelly, William G. Sheriff, Fayette County Tennessee. Somerville, Tennessee, March 8, 2006 (by phone).

King Denny W. United States Marshal, Middle District of Tennessee. Former Commissioner of the Tennessee Department of Safety. Nashville, Tennessee, January 24, 2006 (by phone).

Kirchner, Robert E. Jr. Chief of Police (retired), Metropolitan Nashville Police Department. Nashville, Tennessee, November 29, 2005 (by phone).

Kornberg, Mitchell. Officer, Metropolitan Nashville Police Department. Nashville, Tennessee, November 28, 2005 (by email).

Lambert, John. Lieutenant, Jackson Police Department. Jackson,Tennessee, November 20, 2001.

Lashlee, Arthur M. Lieutenant Colonel (retired), Tennessee Highway Patrol. Nashville, Tennessee, December 6, 2004.

Leach, Jimmie Van. Former Special Agent in Charge of East Tennessee District of the Tennessee Bureau of Investigation and Director of the Criminal Investigation Division of the Department of Safety. Jackson, Tennessee, June 12, 2003 and other.

Lipford, David Randel. Special Agent (retired), Tennessee Fire Marshal's Office. Jackson, Tennessee. January 16, 2006.

Manning, John. Major (retired), Metropolitan Nashville Police Department. Nashville, Tennessee, January 18, 2006 (by phone) and April 26, 2006.

Mansfield, Curtis. Lieutenant, Tennesseee Highway Patrol. Jackson, Tennessee, March 1, 2006.

Margules, Paul. Former Patrolman, Metropolitan Nashville Police Department. Jackson, Tennessee, July 20, 2003.

Mays, Dennis. Commander, Jackson Police Department. Jackson, Tennessee, September 7, 2001.

McFadden, Robert. Special Agent-Forensic Scientists, Tennessee Bureau of Investigation. Nashville, Tennessee, November 20, 2003.

Mehr, John R. Special Agent in Charge, Tennessee Bureau of Investigation. Jackson, Tennessee, January 20, 2004.

McCord, John. Major (retired), Tennessee Highway Patrol, Spring Hill, Tennessee, May 2, 2004.

Miller, Leon W. Sergeant (retired), Tennessee Highway Patrol, and Special Agent (retired), Tennessee Bureau of Criminal Investigation. Rockwood, Tennessee, June 25, 2003. (Leon Miller died July 2, 2004.)

Miller, Leonard Michael. Assistant Chief, Metropolitan Nashville Polce Department. Nashville, Tennessee, August 7, 2003.

Miller, Michael L. Mayor of Rockwood and son of Leon Miller, THP and TBI. Rockwood, Tennessee, October 19, 2004.

Mitchel, Michael D. Captain (retired), Metropolitan Police Department of Nashville and Davidson County. Nashville, Tennessee, December 7, 2002.

Moore, Thomas D. Sergeant (retired, Tennessee Highway Patrol, and Special Agent (retired), Tennessee Bureau of Identification. Cookeville, Tennessee, February 25, 2004 (by phone) and July 27, 2004.

Moore, Charles Thomas. Deputy Commissioner (retired),

Tennessee Department of Safety. Nashville, Tennessee, July 26, 2004

Moss, Ambrose R. Inspector (retired), Tennessee Bureau of Criminal Investigation. Nashville, Tennessee, November 20, 2003; January 17, 2004 (by phone).

Mott, Hugh B. Chief of Police (retired), Metropolitan Nashville Police Department. Nashville, Tennessee, August 8, 2003. (Hugh Mott died June 24, 2005.)

Murphy, D. L. Lieutenant (retired), Jackson Police Department. Jackson,Tennessee, September 7, 2001.

O'Rear, Larry. Special Agent (retired) Tennessee Bureau of Investigation. Cookeville, Tennessee, December 22, 2004.

Paar, Daniel. Captain, Madison County Sheriff's Office. Jackson, Tennessee, April 15, 2005.

Parish, Gerald Franklin. Former Motorcycle Officer, Jackson Police Department. Jackson,Tennessee, January 18, 2002.

Patton, John. Sergeant, Metropolitan Nashville Police Department. Nashville, Tennessee, January 19,2006 (by phone).

Phillips, Hoyt Eugene. Special Agent-Forensic Scientists, Tennessee Bureau of Investigation. Nashville, Tennessee, November 20, 2003.

Pipkin, Norman. Lieutenant (retired), Jackson Police Department. Jackson, Tennessee, September 5, 2001. (Norman Pipkin died March 14, 2005.)

Plummer, Joel. Former Commissioner, Tennessee Department of Safety. Nashville, September 28, 2005.

Price, Larry. Lieutenant, Jackson Police Department. Jackson, Tennessee, July 19, 2001.

Quin, Marjorie J. Special Agent, Tennessee Bureau of Investigation. Nashville, Tennessee, January 11, 2006.

Redd, Barnard. Special Agent in Charge of Narcotics (retired). Tennessee Bureau of Investigation. Nashville, Tennessee, October 19, 2005 (by phone).

Rice, Franklin. Lieutenant (retired), Jackson Police Department. Jackson, Tennessee, July 18, 2001.

Roberts, Warren. Madison County Sheriff (retired), former Captain, Jackson Police Department. Jackson, Tennessee, July 27, 2001.

Russell, Steve. Lieutenant, Tennessee Highway Patrol. Jackson, Tennessee, April 28, 2005.

Schott, Fred Jr. Major (retired), Tennessee Highway Patrol. Springfield, Tennessee, May 28, 2003.

Siler, Mike. Lieutenant, Jackson Police Department. Jackson, Tennessee, January 17, 2002.

Singleton, Jim. Metropolitan Nashville Polce Department (retired). Nashville, Tennessee, December 15, 2003.

Smith, Charles. Assistant Chief (retired), Metropolitan Nashville Police Department. Nashville, Tennessee, November 20, 2003.

Smith, Charles A. Captain (retired), Tennessee Valley Authority Police. Sevierville, Tennessee, July 28, 2004.

Smith, Kenny. Former Detective Lieutenant, Humboldt Police Department. Jackson, Tennessee, November 20, 2005.

Sorace, John A. Assistant Chief (retired), Metropolitan Nashville Police Department. Nashville, Tennessee, September 19, 2003.

Stansell, Maurice. Son of former Madison County Chief Deputy Sheriff and Mobile and Ohio Railroad Special Agent Ed L. Stansell, Jackson, Tennessee, March 8, 2003.

Staples, Richard. Chief of Police, Jackson Police Department. Jackson, Tennessee, July 27, 2001, and January 3, 2002.

Stone, Oscar Roderick Jr. Lieutenant (retired), Metropolitan Nashville Police Department. Nashville, Tennessee, June 23, 2003. (Oscar Stone died August 31, 2003.)

Taylor, Jim. Special Agent in Charge (retired), Tennessee Bureau of Investigation. Hendersonville, Tennessee, January 30, 2004.

Thomas, Robert D. Lieutenant (retired), Tennessee Highway Patrol. Nashville, Tennessee, May 1, 2004.

Thompson, William Carothers. Special Agent in Charge (retired), Tennessee Bureau of Investigation. Nashville, Tennessee, October 13, 2005.

Tune, James Buford. Officer (retired), Metropolitan Nashville Police Department. Nashville, Tennessee, April 26, 2006.

Turner, Emmett H. Chief of Police (retired), Metropolitan Nashville Police Department. Nashville, Tennessee, November 22, 2005.

Uselton, Paul H. Deputy Chief (retired), Metropolitan Nashville Police Department. Nashville, Tennessee, September 18, 2003.

Vaughn, T. E. "Skip." Deputy Chief, Chattanooga Police Department. Chattanooga, Tennessee, October 18, 2004.

Walk, Joseph E. Patrolman (retired) and histroian, Memphis Police Department. Numerous interviews in Memphis over the period of 1998-2003, during which Mr. Walk shared many research notes, including the transcript of interviews with retired Lieutenant Grover E. McCarver.

Wallace, Larry D. Director (retired), Tennessee Bureau of Investigation and for Colonel of Tennessee Highway Patrol. Athens, Tennessee, October 19, 2004.

Watson, Steve O. Deputy Director (retired), Tennessee Bureau of Investigation. Sevierville, Tennessee, March 4, 2004 (by phone) and July 27, 2004.

Weathers, Cleve. Nephew of Lawrence County Sheriff Cleve Weathers (killed in line of duty, January 12, 1943). Nashville, Tennessee, January 22, 2005 (by phone).

Willis, Patrick. Lieutenant, Jackson Police Department. Jackson, Tennessee, November 12, 2001.

Wilson, James A. "Tony." Sergeant, Tennessee Highway Patrol. Nashville, Tennessee, December 10, 2004.

Woodlee, Douglas D. Assistant Director, Tennessee Bureau of Investigation. Nashville, Tennessee, November 20, 2003.

Woolfork, David. Sheriff, Madison County Tennessee. Jackson, Tennessee, January 28, 2005.

Index